Pillars in the History of Biblical Interpretation

McMaster Divinity College Press
Biblical Studies Series 2

# Pillars in the History of Biblical Interpretation

Volume 1: Prevailing Methods before 1980

edited by
STANLEY E. PORTER
and
SEAN A. ADAMS

PICKWICK *Publications* · Eugene, Oregon

PILLARS IN THE HISTORY OF BIBLICAL INTERPRETATION
Volume 1: Prevailing Methods before 1980

Copyright © 2016 Wipf and Stock Publishers. All rights reserved. Except for brief quotations in critical publications or reviews, no part of this book may be reproduced in any manner without prior written permission from the publisher. Write: Permissions, Wipf and Stock Publishers, 199 W. 8th Ave., Suite 3, Eugene, OR 97401.

McMaster Divinity College Press
1250 Main Street West
Hamilton, Ontario, Canada
L8S 4K1

Pickwick Publications
An Imprint of Wipf and Stock Publishers
199 W. 8th Ave., Suite 3
Eugene, OR 97401

www.wipfandstock.com

PAPERBACK ISBN: 978-1-4982-0236-7
HARDCOVER ISBN: 978-1-4982-8761-6
EBOOK ISBN: 978-1-4982-0237-4

Manufactured in the U.S.A.   08/11/16

Scripture portions marked NRSV are taken from the Revised Standard Version of the Bible, copyright © 1946, 1952, and 1971, National Council of the Churches of Christ in the United States of America. Used by permission. All rights reserved.

Contents of Volume 1

Preface / ix

Abbreviations / xiii

Contributors to Volume 1 / xix

Biblical Criticism before around 1980: An Overview of Volume One
—Stanley E. Porter / xxiii

The History of Biblical Interpretation: An Integrated Conspectus
—Stanley E. Porter / 1

1. J. J. Griesbach and Karl Lachmann—*Brandon D. Crowe* / 71

2. Friedrich Schleiermacher: His Contribution to New Testament Studies
—*Jan H. Nylund* / 91

3. Ferdinand Christian Baur's Historical Criticism and *Tendenzkritik*
—*Hughson T. Ong* / 118

4. Brooke Foss Westcott, Fenton John Anthony Hort, and Joseph Barber Lightfoot—*Ronald Dean Peters* / 139

5. Theodor Zahn, Adolf Harnack, and Adolf Schlatter
—*Andreas J. Köstenberger* / 163

6. William Wrede and Julius Wellhausen—*Dieter T. Roth* / 189

7. Albert Schweitzer: A Jewish-Apocalyptic Approach to Christian Origins
—*Andrew W. Pitts* / 211

8. G. Adolf Deissmann's Influence on New Testament Interpretation
—*Philip D. Burggraff* / 239

9. Martin Dibelius and Rudolf Bultmann—*James D. Dvorak* / 257

10 B. H. Streeter and the Synoptic Problem—*Paul Foster* / 278

11 William Ramsay and Ernst Haenchen—*Daniel So* / 302

12 Günther Bornkamm and Redaction Criticism—*Jae Hyun Lee* / 321

13 C. H. Dodd as New Testament Interpreter and Theologian
—*Beth M. Stovell* / 341

14 Walther Eichrodt: His Times and His Theology
—*William K. K. Kapahu* / 367

Index of Modern Authors / 387

Index of Ancient Sources / 397

The Following Chapters are in Volume 2: Prevailing Methods after 1980

Biblical Criticism after around 1980: An Overview of Volume Two
—Stanley E. Porter

The History of Biblical Interpretation: An Integrated Conspectus
—Stanley E. Porter

15 Dietrich Bonhoeffer's Lutheran Existentialism in Theological Interpretation—*Jonathan D. Numada*

16 Martin Heidegger, Hans-Georg Gadamer, and Paul Ricoeur—*Edward Ho*

17 Edmund Leach and Structuralism—*Lois K. Fuller Dow*

18 Martin Hengel, the New Tübingen School, and the Study of Christian Origins—*Andrew W. Pitts*

19 Peter Stuhlmacher and Biblical Theology—*Michael P. Naylor*

20 Edwin Judge, Wayne Meeks, and Social-Scientific Criticism
—*James D. Dvorak*

21 Mary Douglas: Living in Literature—*D. James Boreland*

22 Philip F. Esler and Social-Scientific Criticism—*Lois K. Fuller Dow*

Contents of Volume 1

23   Elisabeth Schüssler Fiorenza, Phyllis Trible, and Feminist Biblical Interpretation—*Sherri Guenther Trautwein*

24   Hans Dieter Betz, George A. Kennedy, and Rhetorical Criticism—*Daniel So*

25   Eugene A. Nida and Johannes P. Louw and Their Linguistic Contribution—*Stanley E. Porter and Hughson T. Ong*

26   James Barr and Theological Lexicography—*Sean A. Adams*

27   Daniel Patte: A Structural Semiotic Model for Interpreting Didactic Discourse—*Andrew W. Pitts*

28   Brevard S. Childs and the Canonical Approach—*Joel Barker*

29   James A. Sanders and Canonical Criticism—*William K. K. Kapahu*

30   Anthony C. Thiselton's Use of Speech-Act Theory—*Philip D. Burggraff*

31   Richard B. Hays and a Narrative Approach to the Pauline Letters—*Jae Hyun Lee*

32   Loveday Alexander, David Rhoads, and Literary Criticism of the New Testament—*Sean A. Adams*

33   Francis Watson and Steven E. Fowl as Theological Interpreters of Scripture—*Patrick S. Franklin*

Preface

THIS VOLUME, LIKE ITS companion in this two-volume set, attempts to make a contribution to a growing genre of literature in biblical studies concerned with the history of biblical interpretation. The volumes are divided according to those interpreters who primarily functioned before 1980 and those who primarily functioned after this date. A number of newer approaches became more popular after around 1980.

There have been a number of works in this genre of biblical interpretation through the years. Most of these are single-volume treatments that attempt to outline in broad terms the history of interpretation. There have always been and no doubt will continue to be monographs on a range of interpretive topics, sometimes focusing upon time periods and other times on individuals or on movements and approaches of various sorts. This genre of volumes on biblical interpretation has recently found its culmination in two multi-volume projects that go into more detail regarding the history of biblical interpretation, one by Henning Graf Reventlow and the other by William Baird. Reventlow's four-volume treatment goes back to the earliest times of biblical interpretation, the Bible itself, and traces this history through its various historical periods until well into the last century. This major work makes a sizable and significant contribution to the history of interpretation, in that it well illustrates that biblical studies as a discipline has a long, complex, and important history. We stand at the end of a long process of the development of biblical interpretation. Another major strength of Reventlow's approach is that he treats interpreters of the Bible, whether Old or New Testament. What becomes clear is that the differentiation of Old and New Testament interpretation is, for the most part, a recent phenomenon, with many of the most important figures in the history of interpretation having made contributions to the study of the Bible, including both testaments. If there is a major weakness to Reventlow's treatment, it is that he does not offer as many individual interpreters as some other treatments, and his account is incomplete for the twentieth century. Baird's three-volume work focuses upon New Testament interpretation, and so does not treat a number of those included by Reventlow and especially those Old

Preface

Testament interpreters who have made a contribution to nineteenth- and twentieth-century interpretation.

This volume follows in the tradition of those who have gone before within this genre, but it also has several distinctive features worth mentioning. The first is that it does not attempt to provide the kind of running history of interpretation of either or of both testaments as is found in many of the volumes mentioned above. The second feature is that this book instead provides selective instances of "pillars" in the history of biblical interpretation. There will no doubt be discussion and debate over whether each of these "pillars" is of equal height, circumference, and even strength. However, we believe that each one of those treated here deserves mention—and we acknowledge that there are many others who could have been selected and presented as well. We have, of necessity, been selective, and realize that we have missed out on the opportunity to explore the work of a number of major scholars in the history of interpretation. The third feature is that this volume focuses upon the individual scholar as well as the criticism represented, rather than simply focusing upon particular types of criticism or historical periods or the like. We acknowledge that these topics enter into the discussion, and that some of the treatments focus in various amounts of detail upon various types of criticism, but the effort throughout is to embody each of these interpretive stances in one or more biblical interpreter(s). The approach of this volume is to attempt to understand the history of biblical interpretation by recognizing that interpretive approaches are contextual in nature. They arise out of certain circumstances, in the form of the work of various scholars, and they are influenced by and have influences upon other interpreters. We have attempted to capture this contextual feature by treating individuals who have contributed to biblical interpretation. The fourth feature is that, although this volume styles itself as concerned with biblical interpretation, most of the interpreters are of recent vintage and concerned with interpretation of the New Testament. This in no way judges the relative merits of Old and New Testament interpretation, but is simply the result of the contributions that were deemed suitable for inclusion. Finally, we admit that this is far from a complete or narrative history of biblical interpretation. Its selective nature means that there are some areas that might be over-represented due to the scholars selected and that other areas might be under-represented due to that same process of selection. An attempt is made in the introduction to the volume to try to provide a narrative that links both major strands of biblical interpretation to the work of various individuals, showing how these strands are interwoven to form a complex tapestry of interpretation.

The editors wish to thank the various contributors to this volume. This volume originated in work done by a variety of graduate (mostly PhD) students in a graduate level course in the History of Interpretation at McMaster Divinity College. Many if not most of the students who have contributed to this volume have completed their graduate studies and are now involved in some way in the teaching of biblical studies. However, this volume includes the work of a number of other, senior scholars who have also contributed to this discussion. We thank all of them for their contribution and work—as well as their patience as this volume has taken longer to see print than we had anticipated. Nevertheless, we believe that the volume has a rightful contribution to make as a guide to the research and writing of a number of major figures in the history of biblical interpretation and we anticipate responses to it.

Stanley E. Porter
Sean A. Adams
Editors

Abbreviations

AB	Anchor Bible
ABD	*Anchor Bible Dictionary.* Edited by David Noel Freedman. 6 vols. New York: Doubleday, 1992.
AGJU	Arbeiten zur Geschichte des antiken Judentums und des Urchristentums
AGSU	Arbeiten zur Geschichte des Spätjudentums und Urchristentums
ANRW	*Aufstieg und Niedergang der römischen Welt: Geschichte und Kultur Roms im Spiegel der neueren Forschung.* Edited by H. Temporini and W. Haase. Berlin: de Gruyter, 1972–.
AThR	*Anglican Theological Review*
BAGL	*Biblical and Ancient Greek Linguistics*
BDAG	Walter Bauer, Frederick W. Danker, W. F. Arndt, and F. W. Gingrich. *Greek-English Lexicon of the New Testament and Other Early Christian Literature.* 3rd ed. Chicago: University of Chicago Press, 2000.
BECNT	Baker Exegetical Commentary on the New Testament
BETL	Bibliotheca Ephemeridum Theologicarum Lovaniensium
BFCT	Beiträge zur Förderung christlicher Theologie
BHT	Beiträge zur historischen Theologie
BI	Biblical Interpretation
BibInt	*Biblical Interpretation*
BJRL	*Bulletin of the John Rylands University Library of Manchester*
BLG	Biblical Languages: Greek
BRS	Biblical Resource Series
BSac	*Bibliotheca Sacra*
BT	*The Bible Translator*

Abbreviations

BZ	*Biblische Zeitschrift*
BZAW	Beihefte zur Zeitschrift für die alttestamentliche Wissenschaft
BZNW	Beihefte zur Zeitschrift für die neutestamentliche Wissenschaft und die Kunde der älteren Kirche
CBQ	*Catholic Biblical Quarterly*
CEMCT	*The Continuum Encyclopedia of Modern Criticism and Theory*
ChrCent	*Christian Century*
CTL	Cambridge Textbooks in Linguistics
CurRBS	*Currents in Research: Biblical Studies*
CurTM	*Currents in Theology and Mission*
DMBI	*Dictionary of Major Biblical Interpreters*
EBC	Expositor's Bible Commentary
EKKNT	Evangelisch-katholischer Kommentar zum Neuen Testament
ELS	English Language Series
ET	English translation
EvQ	*Evangelical Quarterly*
EvK	*Evangelische Kommentare (Zeitschrift)*
ExAud	*Ex Auditu*
ExpTim	*Expository Times*
FAT	Forschungen zum Alten Testament
FN	*Filología Neotestamentaria*
FRLANT	Forschungen zur Religion und Literatur des Alten und Neuen Testaments
GNT	Grundrisse zum Neuen Testament
HBT	*Horizons in Biblical Theology*
HTR	*Harvard Theological Review*
IBS	*Irish Biblical Studies*
ICC	International Critical Commentary
IESS	*International Encyclopedia of the Social Sciences*, edited by David L. Sills and Robert K. Merton. 17 vols. New York: Macmillan, 1968.
IKZ	*Internationale kirchliche Zeitschrift*
Int	*Interpretation*
JAAR	*Journal of the American Academy of Religion*

JBL	*Journal of Biblical Literature*
JBR	*Journal of Bible and Religion*
JETS	*Journal of the Evangelical Theological Society*
JGRChJ	*Journal of Greco-Roman Christianity and Judaism*
JLIABG	*Journal of the Linguistics Institute of Ancient and Biblical Greek*
JR	*Journal of Religion*
JRH	*Journal of Religious History*
JSJSup	Journal for the Study of Judaism in the Persian, Hellenistic, and Roman Periods Supplement Series
JSNT	*Journal for the Study of the New Testament*
JSNTSup	Journal for the Study of the New Testament Supplement Series
JSOT	*Journal for the Study of the Old Testament*
JSOTSup	Journal for the Study of the Old Testament Supplement Series
JTS	*Journal of Theological Studies*
KEK	Kritisch-exegetischer Kommentar über das Neue Testament (Meyer-Kommentar)
LBS	Linguistic Biblical Studies
LHBOTS	Library of Hebrew Bible / Old Testament Studies
LNTS	Library of New Testament Studies
LSJ	H. G. Liddell and R. Scott. *A Greek-English Lexicon*. 9th ed. rev. H. S. Jones. Oxford: Clarendon, 1961.
LXX	Septuagint
MNTC	Moffatt New Testament Commentary
MTS	Marburger Theologische Studien
Neot	Neotestamentica
NICNT	New International Commentary on the New Testament
NIGTC	New International Greek Testament Commentary
NIVAC	New International Version Application Commentary
NovT	*Novum Testamentum*
NovTSup	Supplements to Novum Testamentum
NTM	New Testament Monographs
NTS	*New Testament Studies*

Abbreviations

OTL	Old Testament Library
PAST	Pauline Studies
PNTC	Pillar New Testament Commentary
PRSt	*Perspectives in Religious Studies*
PSTJ	*Perkins (School of Theology) Journal*
RelSRev	*Religious Studies Review*
RL	*Religion in Life*
RGV	Religionsgeschichtliche Volksbücher
SBG	Studies in Biblical Greek
SBL	Society of Biblical Literature
SBLDS	Society of Biblical Literature Dissertation Series
SBLMS	Society of Biblical Literature Monograph Series
SBLRBS	Society of Biblical Literature Resources for Biblical Study
SBLTT	Society of Biblical Literature Texts and Translations
SBS	Stuttgarter Bibelstudien
SBT	Studies in Biblical Theology
SHS	Scripture and Hermeneutics Series
SJT	*Scottish Journal of Theology*
SNTSMS	Society for New Testament Studies Monograph Series
SP	Sacra Pagina
Spost-B	Studia Post Biblica—Supplements to the Study of Judaism
SR	*Studies in Religion*
SUNY	State University of New York
TDNT	*Theological Dictionary of the New Testament.* Edited by Gerhard Kittel and Gerhard Friedrich. Translated by Geoffrey W. Bromily. 10 vols. Grand Rapids: Eerdmans, 1964–76.
ThTo	*Theology Today*
TJ	*Trinity Journal*
TLZ	*Theologische Literaturzeitung*
TMSJ	*The Master's Seminary Journal*
TS	*Theological Studies*
TSAJ	Texte und Studien zum antiken Judentum

TSJTSA	Texts and Studies of the Jewish Theological Seminary of America
TU	Texte und Untersuchungen
TUGAL	Texte und Untersuchungen zur Geschichte der altchristlichen Literatur
TynBul	*Tyndale Bulletin*
TZT	*Tübingen Zeitschrift für Theologie*
UBS	United Bible Societies
UBSGNT	*United Bible Societies Greek New Testament*
VTSup	Supplements to Vetus Testamentum
WBC	Word Biblical Commentary
WTJ	*Westminster Theological Journal*
WUNT	Wissenschaftliche Untersuchungen zum Neuen Testament
ZAW	*Zeitschrift für die alttestamentliche Wissenschaft*
ZDPV	*Zeitschrift des deutschen Palästina-Vereins*
ZECNT	Zondervan Exegetical Commentary on the New Testament
ZNW	*Zeitschrift für die neutestamentliche Wissenschaft und die Kunde der älteren Kirche*
ZRGG	*Zeitschrift für Religions- und Geistesgeschichte*
ZTK	*Zeitschrift für Theologie und Kirche*
ZWT	*Zeitschrift für wissenschaftliche Theologie*

Contributors to Volume 1

Sean A. Adams is Lecturer in New Testament and Ancient Culture at the University of Glasgow, UK. He has written widely on the relationship between the New Testament and Greek literature and is the author of *The Genre of Acts and Collected Biography* and *Baruch and the Epistle of Jeremiah*.

Philip D. Burggraff is Teaching Pastor at Clearwater Community Church in Dunedin, FL, and formerly Associate Professor of Bible and Biblical Languages at Clearwater Christian College.

Brandon D. Crowe is Associate Professor of New Testament at Westminster Theological Seminary in Philadelphia, PA. He has published on a variety of topics relating to the history and theology of the New Testament and early Christianity, including *The Obedient Son: Deuteronomy and Christology in the Gospel of Matthew*.

James D. Dvorak is Associate Professor of Greek and New Testament at Oklahoma Christian University. He is co-editor of *Baptism: Historical, Theological, and Pastoral Perspectives* (with Gordon L. Heath) and *The New Testament Church: The Challenge of Developing Ecclesiologies* (with John Harrison).

Paul Foster is Professor of New Testament and Early Christianity in the School of Divinity at the University of Edinburgh, UK. He has published widely on the Gospels, including a critical edition and commentary on the *Gospel of Peter*. He has written extensively on the sayings source Q, and issues relating to the Synoptic problem.

William K. K. Kapahu is an adjunct professor and guest lecturer in Old Testament and Second Temple Judaism at New Hope Christian College, WA. He is studying for his PhD with a focus on unit delimitation within ancient biblical manuscripts.

Contributors to Volume 1

Andreas Köstenberger is Senior Research Professor of New Testament and Biblical Theology at Southeastern Baptist Theological Seminary in Wake Forest, NC. He is the founder of Biblical Foundations™, the editor of the *Journal of the Evangelical Theological Society*, and the author or editor of numerous books, including *Invitation to Biblical Interpretation*.

Jae Hyun Lee is Chaplain at Handong Global University, Pohang, Korea. He is also the author of *Paul's Gospel in Romans: A Discourse Analysis of Romans 1:16—8:39*.

Jan Nylund is a PhD student in New Testament exegesis at Lund University in Sweden. His research interests include New Testament language studies (specifically verbal aspect and discourse analysis), hermeneutics, and New Testament research history. He has been teaching and supervising since 2009 and has more than 25 publications.

Hughson T. Ong is Lecturer in New Testament and Managing Editor of McMaster Divinity College Press at McMaster Divinity College, Hamilton, ON, Canada. He has published numerous journal articles and essays on various New Testament topics, including linguistics and sociolinguistics, and is the author of *The Multilingual Jesus and the Sociolinguistic World of the New Testament*.

Ronald D. Peters is Professor of New Testament at Great Lakes Christian College, MI. His most significant publication is *The Greek Article: A Functional Grammar of ὁ-Items in the Greek New Testament with Special Emphasis on the Greek Article*.

Andrew W. Pitts is Assistant Professor of Biblical Studies at Arizona Christian University. He is the author (with Stanley E. Porter) of *Fundamentals of New Testament Textual Criticism*, and is an editor of Early Christianity in Its Hellenistic Context, an ongoing series of edited volumes focusing upon Christian Origins.

Stanley E. Porter is President, Dean, and Professor of New Testament, as well as holder of the Roy A. Hope Chair in Christian Worldview, at McMaster Divinity College, Hamilton, ON, Canada. He has written widely on most topics in New Testament studies, and has an interest in the history of interpretation. His latest books include *Constantine Tischendorf: The Life and Work of a 19th Century Bible Hunter*, *Linguistic Analysis of the Greek New Testament*, *John, His Gospel, and Jesus*, and *The Book of Romans: A Linguistic and Literary Commentary*.

Dieter T. Roth is Wissenschaftlicher Mitarbeiter (Post-Doctoral Fellow) at Johannes Gutenberg-Universität Mainz, Germany. He is the author of *The Text of Marcion's Gospel*.

Daniel So is Associate Pastor at Grace Community Church, Surrey, BC, Canada.

Beth M. Stovell is Assistant Professor of Old Testament at Ambrose University in Calgary, AB, Canada. Beth has authored *Mapping Metaphorical Discourse in the Fourth Gospel* and *Minor Prophets: Hosea-Micah* and co-edited *Biblical Hermeneutics: Five Views* (with Stanley E. Porter).

Biblical Criticism before around 1980

An Overview of Volume One

STANLEY E. PORTER

THIS FIRST VOLUME OF two volumes on major figures in biblical interpretation is concerned with biblical criticism before around 1980. The second volume focuses upon biblical criticism after that date. As a result, this volume contains essays about biblical interpreters who are associated with what might be characterized as "traditional" approaches to interpretation. Any attempt at characterizing approaches to biblical interpretation is bound to fail to be satisfactory, however, because of the complex and intertwined nature of such interpretation. The introduction to biblical interpretation in this volume attempts to chronicle in brief form how five major strands of intellectual development that were present at the beginning of the modern interpretive era have developed into most if not virtually all of the current approaches to biblical interpretation. As a result, this particular volume contains essays about major biblical interpreters who practiced approaches that came into widespread development and use during the period from the rise of historical criticism to around 1980. There is nothing special about the year 1980, however, apart from the fact that, when we examine the history of biblical interpretation, there was if not a major groundswell of change at least a shift in emphases within biblical interpretation at this time. This shift in emphases, if not simply displacement of methods, is reflected in the nature of the models of interpretation used by various biblical interpreters before and after that time, even if the traditional approaches continued to flourish long after.

As a result, this first volume encompasses both many of the historically important interpreters who are credited with establishing biblical interpretation in the modern era, and many of the traditional and standard forms of criticism that have long been associated with biblical studies. One of the traditional divisions of biblical interpretation is a distinction between supposed lower and higher criticism. Lower criticism

Biblical Criticism before around 1980

involves textual criticism, which establishes the foundation upon which all of the "higher" forms of criticism build. Higher criticism is often equated with form, source, and redaction criticism. This volume, therefore, encompasses the major biblical interpreters who established the fields of textual criticism, and pioneered form, source, and redaction criticism. As the introductory essay attempts to illustrate, it would be a serious mistake to assume that either these few types of criticism constitute the basis of the range of critical interpretation of the Bible or that they in any way continue to occupy a privileged or exclusive place within the field—even if they may have, at least in the eyes of some, at an earlier time. This simply is not the case today, and perhaps never was. However, they have maintained positions of considerable importance in the history of interpretation and still continue to play decisive roles. The stage was set for their importance by the work of a number of important predecessors, some of whom laid the very foundations of biblical studies as a modern intellectual discipline. These scholars were supported in their work by other interpreters who explored related fields of study. These are the types of interpreters and their approaches that are found in this first volume.

This volume follows roughly a chronological order of the various scholars presented. Thus, after offering an integrated historical conspectus upon the entirety of post-Enlightenment biblical interpretation, we begin with a study of two important scholars who helped to establish the textual basis of New Testament studies, J. J. Griesbach and Karl Lachmann. This is followed by an essay on the important work of Friedrich Schleiermacher, whose work in theology and biblical interpretation set the stage for much of the continuing work of biblical interpretation. In many ways, Schleiermacher defined the fields of both hermeneutics and modern critical interpretation of the Bible. The only scholar who could be said to be more important, at least in the area of New Testament interpretation, is Ferdinand Christian Baur, whose *Tendenzkritik* provided the theoretical platform for a rewriting of early Christian history. The essay on Baur is followed here by consideration of the so-called Cambridge triumvirate, B. F. Westcott, F. J. A. Hort, and J. B. Lightfoot, whose work in many different areas of New Testament studies, but in particular in historical backgrounds, not only countered the influence of Baur but helped to establish British biblical studies as a discipline in its own right. However, the center of biblical criticism continued to focus upon German criticism, as do the essays in this first volume. They include chapters on a number of German contemporaries, such as the liberal Adolf Harnack and his more conservative contemporaries, Theodor Zahn and Adolf Schlatter, whose work on the formation of early Christianity continues to be important, even if their theological positions are often questioned. More radical German criticism is seen in the work of William Wrede in the New Testament and Julius Wellhausen in the Old, whose work in both instances brought to a culmination some of the major developing trends in biblical interpretation. Albert Schweitzer is representative of those who drew upon Jewish backgrounds in support of understanding the New Testament, while Adolf

Deissmann looked to the Greco-Roman backgrounds. Among the form critics of the Gospels, Martin Dibelius and Rudolf Bultmann still loom large as two of the most important practitioners—besides their work in a variety of other areas. B. H. Streeter also contributed to Gospel studies, but in the area of source criticism with development of the four source hypothesis. Within this milieu, William Ramsay rejected the Baur hypothesis regarding the history of early Christianity, while Ernst Haenchen took a more positive stance in his traditions history approach to Acts. Günther Bornkamm is often viewed as the first of the Gospel redaction critics, although he too did work across the span of New Testament studies. Within English scholarship, C. H. Dodd, while influenced by German scholarship, took a much more moderate view in a range of fields, such as form criticism, Johannine studies, and Jesus studies. This first volume concludes with the Old Testament scholar and biblical theologian Walther Eichrodt, whose approach to Old Testament theology continues to have widespread influence.

With these essays, the first volume of our "pillars" in biblical interpretation offers an important, representative sample of major scholars who have laid the foundation for much of the continuing interpretation of the Bible.

The History of Biblical Interpretation
An Integrated Conspectus

STANLEY E. PORTER

INTRODUCTION

THE RISE OF WHAT we know today as biblical interpretation has a long and complex history.[1] One of the problems of defining this history is determination of how retrospective to be in ascertaining its beginnings. Some would argue, with good reason, that biblical interpretation, at least critical interpretation, originates with the rise of modernism and the historical-critical method, sometime in the eighteenth century. Others would argue that such critical interpretation arose in reaction to a previous generation of biblical interpretation as seen in the Reformers, and that the history of biblical interpretation begins with the Reformation and the historical-grammatical method that led to much exegetical attention to the text of the Bible itself.[2] Others would argue, like those before them, that Reformation interpretation was itself a reaction to previous periods of biblical interpretation, in particular various types of reading the Bible that developed in medieval Scholasticism, with its heavy dependence upon philosophical, and in particular Aristotelian, thought.[3] Still others would argue

---

1. This introduction addresses biblical interpretation as a whole, but places its greatest emphasis upon interpretation of the New Testament, because of the emphasis of the essays found within this volume and my expertise. I have no doubt made mistakes in my formulations. Nevertheless, I have made no effort at completeness but have tried to indicate those scholars I consider significant in the history of discussion, usually those who have instigated movements and trends, not simply those who have followed in the wake. I apologize for any oversights of those that should have been included. I do not specify particular works where that information is either reasonably well known or available in other sources cited.

2. See, e.g., Hahn and Wiker, *Politicizing the Bible*; Reventlow, *History of Biblical Interpretation*, vol. 3.

3. See, e.g., Reventlow, *History of Biblical Interpretation*, vol. 2.

that the history of New Testament interpretation goes back to the early church Fathers, who drew upon various more and less literalistic approaches to reading—some resulting in relatively stable and others highly allegorical interpretations—that attempted to bring the meaning of the text into dialogue with its then contemporary readers. There are those who might legitimately argue that the history of New Testament interpretation began with the New Testament writers themselves, perhaps in later authors who in their writings interpreted earlier traditions that they had inherited whether through oral or written sources, or who were themselves interpreters of the Jewish Scriptures that they had adopted.[4] Finally, there are those who might find the origins of biblical interpretation within the Old Testament itself, either through a process of generative canonical re-interpretation or later interpretation of earlier traditions.[5] A legitimate argument can be made for each of these, and, depending upon various chroniclers of this history, such accounts have been offered. There is much to be learned from what is probably best referred to as pre-modern interpretation (rather than pre-critical interpretation), in the sense that it was critically astute within the parameters of its time, even if it is not critical in the same sense as Enlightenment criticism and its legacy. This essay, however, like the book that follows to which it is the introduction, begins the history of biblical interpretation with the modern period. I do so not because of lack of interest in earlier periods and certainly not because of a wish to denigrate pre-modern interpretation, but because the advent of modern interpretation during the Enlightenment led to a number of developments that have the strongest direct influence on contemporary biblical interpretation. In other words, if we want to understand contemporary biblical interpretation most fully, we probably need to understand the major trends from the Enlightenment to the present.[6]

In this essay, I will offer an overview of major trends and movements as they have developed within biblical and especially New Testament interpretation, as well as attempting to chart (figuratively, at least)[7] an intricate set of interconnections among these various trends and movements. In anticipation of the result, allow me simply to say that the history and development of biblical interpretation resembles in many ways the complex root system of bamboo. There is no single point of origin but perhaps many points of origin (I identify five below). As these several originating points

---

4. See, e.g., Bray, *Biblical Interpretation*, 47–164; Reventlow, *History of Biblical Interpretation*, 1:47–200.

5. See, e.g., Reventlow, *History of Biblical Interpretation*, 1:5–45.

6. For an analysis of the Enlightenment from a philosophical standpoint, see Cassirer, *Philosophy of the Enlightenment*. One notes that there are many areas in which Enlightenment and post-Enlightenment thoughts diverge.

7. When I teach a course entitled History of Biblical Interpretation, I attempt to construct an ever-changing chart of the intricate relations among various streams within biblical interpretation. In this essay, I must do so figuratively rather than graphically. I attempt to draw such lines of connection, realizing that I no doubt overlook important interconnections (and probably could draw more of them without much effort).

develop their root systems, there are numerous interconnections as they develop further. If one is examining such a root system as I am describing from the endpoint, such as the relatively early twenty-first century, and looking back to the beginnings of this entity called biblical interpretation, then the vascular system might appear, at least in its individual strands, as a relatively simple and straightforward retrogressive path to its origins. If one examines this same system from its points of origin, one may also be able to trace the vascular system forward, but by tracing this path one sees many divides and splits, without necessarily knowing whether or if there is a reason for such a division or whether taking one path over the other provides a productive way forward. Such is the history of biblical interpretation, including that of the New Testament. The development of biblical interpretation forms a complex and interconnected set of pathways that lead from a relatively small number of initial points of origin into the complex and intertwined set of interpretive agendas that we have today. This essay is an attempt, at least by me, to chronicle this growth and development by focusing upon the major productive strands.

THE DEVELOPMENT OF MODERN BIBLICAL INTERPRETATION

Historical criticism did not one day simply take the Western world, and in particular Germany, by storm once it emerged from the head of Friedrich Schleiermacher (1768–1834), who is often credited with marking the beginning of modern critical study of the Bible (and hermeneutics).[8] In fact, the history of development of biblical research from the rise of Deism to the emergence of theological liberalism, and with it the eventual triumph of historical-critical thought, goes back to before Schleiermacher. The rise of Deism created an intellectual vacuum that demanded theological, philosophical, and scientific filling—at least for those who were contemplating such issues.[9] This intellectual movement combined with the renewal of learning brought about by the Renaissance to create an environment in which a broad range of human intellectual exploration occurred—including in the fields of biblical and theological studies. The confluence of factors included the revived interest in classical learning, the recognition of the distinction between theology as dogmatics and theology as related to ancient texts, the abundance of ancient documents that were coming into purview as the result of discovery and rediscovery, and the recognition that advances in human learning had direct bearing on questions of understanding and interpretation.

---

8. The first five paragraphs of this section are directly dependent upon Porter, *Constantine Tischendorf*, 81–89, with additions.

9. There are many helpful works on this period. For example, see W. Baird, *History of New Testament Research*, 1:3–391 passim, which provides much useful background information that I draw upon in my treatment; Kümmel, *New Testament*, 40–161; Neill and Wright, *Interpretation*, 1–35; Morgan with Barton, *Biblical Interpretation*, 44–92; O'Neill, *Bible's Authority*, 1–166; Harrisville and Sundberg, *Bible in Modern Culture*, 21–145; Sandys-Wunsch, *What Have They Done to the Bible*, 169–331; Bray, *Biblical Interpretation*, 225–69; and Grant with Tracy, *Short History*, 100–18.

This cauldron of simmering ideas encompassed all major arenas of human thought, leading to gradual distinctions being made between various types of human intellectual endeavor, and with such distinctions the necessary recognition that there were both common and distinct intellectual concepts that attended to these individual yet also related disciplines.

During this time, many of the major enduring issues in biblical studies, including New Testament interpretation, came to be identified. These include:

- the nature of interpretation, what it entails and how it is conducted
- textual criticism
- the rise of the historical-grammatical method as a prelude to development of the historical-critical method
- the recognition of the issue of canon
- introduction to the books of the Bible as a distinct discipline separate from the issue of interpretation of the texts themselves
- the Bible as literature movement as an attempt to examine the Bible as if it were just like any other piece of ancient literature
- the rise of biblical theology as distinct from systematic theology.

With the rise of critical Enlightenment thought, there came recognition that simply accepting dogmatic assertion was neither intellectually nor spiritually rewarding. As a consequence, some scholars began to develop principles of interpretation, geared to providing a way of attending to the many and varied details of the text—whether they be grammatical, historical, or theological—in order to find their underlying unity.[10] These developments were a major part of the origins of German pietism. What began as a largely commendable pietist response through scholarship to the intellectual challenges of the Enlightenment, however, soon resulted in its own reductionism that overlooked major critical issues found within the text.[11]

The seismic intellectual changes that were occurring led directly to the definition of individual scholarly areas of pursuit, as part of either the rise of historical criticism or the pietist response. Several of these areas of investigation are worth noting. The development of textual criticism resulted from the increasing recognition that a variety of manuscripts—and with this a variety of manuscript traditions—existed.[12]

---

10. See, e.g., Baird, *History of New Testament Research*, 1:62–69; Reventlow, *History of Biblical Interpretation*, 4:133–44, on August Hermann Francke (1663–1727).

11. See, e.g., Baird, *History of New Testament Research*, 1:58–62; Reventlow, *History of Biblical Interpretation*, 4:123–32, on Philip Jakob Spener (1635–1705). This pietistic bifurcation between theology and critical scholarship still seems to persist in much German scholarship, much to its detriment. The result is theology apparently unrelated to critical exegesis.

12. See, e.g., Baird, *History of New Testament Research*, 1:69–80; McKim, *DMBI*, 184–88, on Johann Albrecht Bengel (1687–1752).

The abundance of newly discovered source texts also led to textual comparison, which naturally proceeded to conceptual comparison, in which the ancient texts of various religious and philosophical groups—besides Christianity and Judaism—were examined, such as the ancient Greek and Latin writers.[13] The development of the historical-grammatical method as a necessary prelude to the historical-critical method shifted the emphasis of interpretation from the underlying unity—which was still affirmed by many—to the various localized issues regarding the text itself.[14] The new emphasis was placed upon defining principles of interpretation—in some sense providing rationally based schemata that placed theology on the same ground as other intellectual endeavors—by which one could fully appreciate and understand the text, without allegorical or metaphorical transmutation.[15]

With the rise of the historical-grammatical method, and a growing disenchantment with dogmatism, came recognition of the problems associated with the canon. This was brought to the fore by acknowledgment of a variety of historical and theological factors. The historical factors included the recognition of the mixed bag of books contained within the Old and New Testaments, and the tensions that existed around their being found within one Bible—which could not avoid the matter of the controversial place of the Apocrypha throughout church history. The theological factors addressed the question of whether there was an underlying unity to the Bible, when there appeared to be such widespread diversity among its various authors.[16]

The field of introduction as a distinctly separate discipline within theology, and in particular biblical studies, was in some ways not simply an inevitability, but a tacit admission that there were other problems that surrounded the study of the Bible than simply its content.[17] With the issue of canon having been raised, in that regard the technical field of introduction became important for its identification of the individual histories and circumstances of each biblical book, apart from their simply being found together within one canonical text. As a result, the genre of biblical introduction began to analyze these attendant circumstances of each biblical book, even if questions regarding authorship were only to emerge gradually over the next century.

---

13. See, e.g., Baird, *History of New Testament Research*, 1:101–7; Reventlow, *History of Biblical Interpretation*, 4:79–81, on Johann Jakob Wettstein (1693–1754).

14. A significant figure in North American biblical scholarship is Moses Stuart (1780–1852). See Baird, *History of New Testament Research*, 2:21–27; McKim, *DMBI*, 952–56; Harrisville, *Pandora's Box Opened*, 148–61; cf. Giltner, *Moses Stuart*.

15. See, e.g., Baird, *History of New Testament Research*, 1:108–14; McKim, *DMBI*, 418–21, on Johann Augusti Ernesti (1707–81), perhaps more infamously known as J. S. Bach's principal at the Thomasschule in Leipzig. Bach, apparently, was suspicious of some of Ernesti's ideas.

16. See, e.g., Baird, *History of New Testament Research*, 1:117–27; Reventlow, *History of Biblical Interpretation*, 4:175–90; Kümmel, *New Testament*, 62–69; O'Neill, *Bible's Authority*, 39–53; McKim, *DMBI*, 910–14; Harrisville, *Pandora's Box Opened*, 105–13, on Johann Salomo Semler (1725–91).

17. See, e.g., Baird, *History of New Testament Research*, 1:127–38; Kümmel, *New Testament*, 69–73; O'Neill, *Bible's Authority*, 28–38; McKim, *DMBI*, 736–39, on Johann David Michaelis (1717–91).

Once scholars had begun to recognize a distinction between theology and religion, or theology and the Bible, the study of the Bible as literature (*belles-lettres*, as opposed simply to written texts) was a next logical step.[18] Other ancient texts, such as those of the classical authors, had begun to be investigated for their literary and historical and other qualities, and so it seemed legitimate to read the Bible in the same light—as another set of ancient texts, not necessarily with literary pretensions but as a literary record of an ancient people or peoples.

Finally, the rise of biblical theology as separate from theology or dogmatics was a means of retaining the theological significance of the Bible, while also attempting to bring into play its critical study.[19] If one could not simply dogmatically invoke theology, one could at least examine the theological ideas of the individual writers or groups of writers within the Bible. A product of this development, in some sense a reaction against but also an affirmation of it, was not only the rise of German pietism but also evangelicalism. Both of these were movements that affirmed traditional Christian theological beliefs and that were concerned with the directions in which biblical criticism was moving, and they attempted to counter such methods by, in essence, embracing the rationalism by which they were conducted and increasingly dominated. As a consequence, some of the strongest accomplishments of pietism and evangelicalism became the foundation for further development of the historical-critical method.

This is the environment into which Schleiermacher stepped, but that he did not create—an environment already highly problematized within emerging critical biblical scholarship.[20] He rejected his pietistic upbringing, with its focus upon what he perceived as self-abnegation, and instead embraced the role of the self as the center of interpretation. The rise of romanticism, with focus upon the self and its experiences, went hand in hand with the rise of liberalism (and its human-centeredness) within theological thought. The scholar who reflected this rise of liberalism more than any other—and who in his voluminous writings reflected the founding and rise of historical criticism, including theories of Pentateuchal origins and the forms of the

---

18. See, e.g., Baird, *History of New Testament Research*, 1:165–83; Reventlow, *History of Biblical Interpretation*, 4:190–202; Kümmel, *New Testament*, 79–83; O'Neill, *Bible's Authority*, 13–27 and 66–77, on Gotthold Ephraim Lessing (1729–81) and Johann Gottfried Herder (1744–1803).

19. See, e.g., Baird, *History of New Testament Research*, 1:184–87; Reventlow, *History of Biblical Interpretation*, 4:211–29; Kümmel, *New Testament*, 98–104; McKim, *DMBI*, 452–56, on Johann Philipp Gabler (1753–1826).

20. The literature on Friedrich Schleiermacher (1768–1834) is enormous. See, e.g., Baird, *History of New Testament Research*, 1:208–20; Harrisville and Sundberg, *Bible in Modern Culture*, 62–82; Porter and Robinson, *Hermeneutics*, 23–33; Christian, *Friedrich Schleiermacher*; Clements, *Friedrich Schleiermacher*; Tice, *Schleiermacher*; McKim, *DMBI*, 885–91; Harrisville, *Pandora's Box Opened*, 113–25; cf. Zachhuber, *Theology as Science*, 12–17. An important precursor who helped to set the scene for the rise of critical biblical scholarship was Benedict Spinoza (1632–77). See Harrisville and Sundberg, *Bible in Modern Culture*, 30–45; Reventlow, *History of Biblical Interpretation*, 4:89–109; Yoon, "Life and Career." On the nineteenth century and its biblical scholarship, see Bray, *Biblical Interpretation*, 270–375, and on the twentieth century, 376–448, although with a different narrative around the developments than I relate here. Cf. also Riches, *Century*, who takes a topical approach.

Psalms, among others—was Wilhelm de Wette (1780–1849). In many ways a follower of Schleiermacher in his romanticism, de Wette, reflective of the rise of Enlightenment thought, attempted to merge rationalism and supernaturalism.[21] Into this ontological vacuum stepped German philosophical idealism. German idealism, based upon the thought of Immanuel Kant (1724–1804), was realized in the philosophy of Georg Wilhelm Friedrich Hegel (1770–1831).[22] Hegel provided a philosophy that appeared at first to fill this ontological void by its endorsement of the Absolute Spirit, which could be equated with the God of Christianity. Whereas many at first welcomed Hegel's apparently Christianly-sympathetic dialectic, his philosophical scheme also vacated Christianity of its strong biblical basis.[23] This led directly to the kind of radical questioning of biblical authority that resulted both in Schleiermacher's assertion of a general hermeneutics and in the kind of wide-open historical reconstructionism by followers of Hegel, such as the New Testament scholar David Friedrich Strauss (1808–74)[24] and his equally pessimistic or radical, yet more academically established, teacher Ferdinand Christian Baur (1792–1860),[25] and the Old Testament biblical theologian Johann Karl Wilhelm Vatke (1806–82). Strauss went much further first in his *The Life of Jesus Critically Examined* and then in his more popularly focused "Life of Jesus for the German People" than did Schleiermacher.[26] Noticeably Hegeleian in orientation, Baur defined in an enduring way the polarities of early Christianity between the Jewish and Hellenistic parties, as depicted in his *Paul the Apostle of Jesus Christ*.[27] Vatke cast his entire Old Testament theology within a Hegelian framework, which encompasses

---

21. Baird, *History of New Testament Research*, 1:221–29; Reventlow, *History of Biblical Interpretation*, 4:231–45; McKim, *DMBI*, 355–58. See also Rogerson, *Old Testament Criticism*, 28–49; and the more detailed Rogerson, *W. M. L. de Wette*.

22. Wolfreys, *CEMCT*, 9–29 (see also below).

23. On Hegel in relation to New Testament studies, see Baird, *History of New Testament Research*, 1:244–45. On Hegel in general, see Jones, *History of Western Philosophy*, 4:108–44. Cf. O'Neill, *Bible's Authority*, 54–65 on Kant.

24. On Strauss, see Harris, *David Friedrich Strauss*, as well as Baird, *History of New Testament Research*, 1:246–58; Reventlow, *History of Biblical Interpretation*, 4:245–62; Kümmel, *New Testament*, 120–26; Neill and Wright, *Interpretation*, 13–20; Harris and Sundberg, *Bible in Modern Culture*, 83–103; O'Neill, *Bible's Authority*, 108–16; Morgan with Barton, *Biblical Interpretation*, 44–52; McKim, *DMBI*, 941–45.

25. On Baur, see Harris, *Tübingen School*, esp. 11–54, 137–80, as well as Baird, *History of New Testament Research*, 1:276–85; Reventlow, *History of Biblical Interpretation*, 4:276–85; Kümmel, *New Testament*, 126–43 (who combines Strauss with Baur); Neill and Wright, *Interpretation*, 20–29; Morgan with Barton, *Biblical Interpretation*, 62–68; Harrisville and Sunderg, *Bible and Modern Culture*, 104–22; McKim, *DMBI*, 177–81; Harrisville, *Pandora's Box Opened*, 125–30; and Porter, *When Paul Met Jesus*, ch. 2.

26. Strauss, *Das Leben Jesu kritisch bearbeitet*; ET *Life of Jesus Critically Examined*; Strauss, *Das Leben Jesu für das deutsche Volk*; ET *New Life of Jesus*.

27. Most of Baur's essays remain untranslated into English, even though they were formative for the discipline of biblical studies. Many of his conclusions regarding the early centuries of Christianity are found in Baur, *Church History*.

Vatke's developmental view of Israelite religion.[28] Schleiermacher's opening up of the questions of hermeneutics released an avalanche of both pent-up anti-dogmatic critical biblical interpretation and, to some extent as a profitable result, new waves of biblical interpretation, especially of the New Testament and of early Christian history. There developed an entire Tübingen school around the thought of Baur[29] and others who followed various equally radical paths in related historical areas, such as study of Jesus.[30]

The result of this initial wave of critical thought was to set the agenda for the next nearly two hundred years of biblical scholarship. Many of the findings in these areas have had an enduring legacy in biblical research, as proposals developed during this time continue to generate interest within biblical studies. By around 1850, sufficient questions had been raised regarding the nature of interpretation that there were those who followed Baur and those that rejected his approach. The divide was more than simply over whether one was a Tübingen member or not. Baur's *Tendenzkritik* had both historical and, perhaps even more importantly, social/psychological elements to it and set the agenda for an entire area of development within New Testament studies (see below on discussion of social-scientific criticism). There were those who, however, rejected this approach and continued to work within the framework of the historical-grammatical method inherited from the Reformers or before, even as it was transformed into the historical-critical approach of the Enlightenment.[31] One of those who rejected this conservative backlash and the philosophical-historical approach of the Tübingen school, instead arguing for a rigorous form of historical criticism, was Heinrich Ewald (1803–75). Despite his relatively conservative conclusions, Ewald

---

28. Rogerson, *Old Testament Criticism*, 69–78.

29. On the Tübingen school, see Harris, *Tübingen School*, 55–123, with discussions of the major figures Eduard Zeller (1814–1908), Albert Schwegler (1819–57), Karl Christian Planck (1819–80), Karl Reinhold Köstlin (1819–94), Albrecht Ritschl (1822–89), Adolf Hilgenfeld (1823–1907), and Gustav Volkmar (1809–93), most of whom are not well known today; see Zachhuber, *Theology as Science*, 25–134; as well as Baird, *History of New Testament Research*, 1:269–78, esp. on Zeller, the most significant of Baur's followers, and Hilgenfeld, arguably the movement's most accomplished New Testament scholar. An example of the extreme ends to which thought can be taken is found in Bruno Bauer (1809–82). See O'Neill, *Bible's Authority*, 150–66.

30. See, e.g., the radical work on Jesus by Ernest Renan (1823–92) and Theodor Keim (1825–78) (Baird, *History of New Testament Research*, 1:375–90). We are still in the same pursuit of Jesus, even if some attempt to define periods within it. See Porter, *Criteria for Authenticity*, 28–62.

31. For example, Baird, *History of New Testament Research*, 1:278–93, cites Ernst Wilhelm Hengstenberg (1802–69), who rejected historical criticism and continued to use a historical-grammatical approach found in Scholasticism, and August Tholuck (1799–1877), who also retained a form of historical-grammatical exegesis inspired by German pietism. On Hengstenberg, see Reventlow, *History of Biblical Interpretation*, 4:286–98; on Hengstenberg and Tholuck, see Rogerson, *Old Testament Criticism*, 79–90; cf. McKim, *DMBI*, 517–20, 975–79. Much of later Roman Catholic New Testament scholarship, at least until the Second Vatican Council, seems to have continued along this path. There were some who utilized some of the developments of historical criticism (e.g., J. L. Hug [1765–1846]), but the gains remained modest. One of the products of this type of Roman Catholic scholarship was the *Sensus Plenior*.

demonstrates a rigorous attempt at what might have then been called a scientific method.[32] Some of the most important advances in Old Testament research occurred in the development of historical criticism in such areas as the source theories of the Pentateuch, and along with it theories of authorship of the Old Testament. This led also to the development of various alternatives to source theories with development of a situationally based form criticism.[33] Similarly, some of the most recognizable advances in New Testament research occurred in the development of historical criticism in such areas as the relations among the Synoptic Gospels. In Synoptic studies, theories regarding oral tradition, written sources, and Markan priority were all proposed during this time, and received their proponents and opponents (see below).[34] To a large extent, the subsequent history of Synoptic research has returned to the complex interrelationship of these three factors, including development of form, source, and redaction criticism. The authorship of John's Gospel, and in particular whether it was written by the Apostle (and when), also became an important question.[35] John's Gospel, which during the patristic era had been heralded for its important early theology, was now questioned both regarding date and certainly concerning authorship, and subsequently concerning its theology.[36]

In New Testament studies, the advent of knowledge of ancient languages and their manuscripts, along with various theories of Gospel origins, led to development of textual criticism along lines that had potentially destructive tendencies.[37] The growing number of manuscripts, and with this the ability to identify the numerous textual variants among manuscripts, resulted in various theories of the relationships of these manuscripts and how to evaluate them, and with them theories of the origins of the New Testament textual tradition. Whereas now we often think of an abundance of manuscripts as a sign of relatively secure textual attestation and even stability, the increase of manuscripts and the recognition of the varied environments out of which they apparently emerged—whether these environments were based on location

---

32. On Ewald, see Baird, *History of New Testament Research*, 1:287–93; Reventlow, *History of Biblical Interpretation*, 4:298–303; Rogerson, *Old Testament Criticism*, 91–103; McKim, *DMBI*, 426–29.

33. See Harrison, *Introduction to the Old Testament*, 11–38.

34. See Baird, *History of New Testament Research*, 1:295–311, including Johann Carl Ludwig Gieseler (1792–1854), who advocated for a common oral tradition behind the Gospels (somewhat reminiscent of the later work of Westcott; see below); Herbert Marsh (1758–1839) on a common written Gospel as the source; and Hajo Uden Meijboom (1842–1933), who identified the major problems with Markan priority; and others discussed below.

35. See Porter, "Date of John's Gospel."

36. Baird, *History of New Testament Research*, 1:311–19, where he treats Karl Gottlieb Bretschneider (1776–1848) and John James Tayler (1797–1869); cf. 203–4.

37. See Baird, *History of New Testament Research*, on various important early figures in textual criticism, including: John Mill (1645–1707), 1:25–28; Richard Bentley (1662–1742), 1:29; Johann Albrecht Bengel (1687–1752), 1:69–80; Wettstein, 1:101–7; Johann Jakob Griesbach, 1:138–48; Karl Lachmann (1793–1851), 1:319–22; and Constantine Tischendorf, 1:322–28. See also Kümmel, *New Testament*, 47–50, 74–75, 146–48; Porter, *Constantine Tischendorf*; Reventlow, *History of New Testament Interpretation*, 4:202–4; and McKim, *DMBI*, 184–88, 489–96 (but who excludes a good number).

or theology—led to an undermining of textual confidence. The readily perceivable and abundant variants and even alterations in the manuscripts led to development of criteria for doing textual criticism, but these were in some ways seen as means of identifying and controlling an apparently increasingly chaotic situation of textual proliferation reflected in manuscript multiplication. The efforts of Constantine Tischendorf (1815–74) were self-consciously designed to counter such tendencies that he saw resulting from the destructive rise of German philosophically-influenced historical and related criticism.[38] He was followed by a succession of scholars who capitalized upon the multitudinous finds of the nineteenth century (an area where Tischendorf himself excelled), continued to develop principles of textual criticism, and subsequently developed the modern eclectic Greek New Testament. There are a number of scholars who can be named in this category—and this section probably merits its own further discussion below. However, for the sake of brevity, allow me to summarize developments in the field of textual criticism here.

In some respects, the field of textual criticism has changed the least, when compared to other areas of biblical study. Old Testament textual criticism has continued to use a single manuscript, based upon the Leningrad and now the Aleppo codex. The single most important development in Old Testament textual criticism has been the discovery of the Dead Sea Scrolls, which are being reflected in the critical apparatus of the latest Hebrew Bible project (*Biblia Hebraica Quinta*). The existence of biblical manuscripts significantly older than the standard Masoretic text, along with some other discoveries, has resulted in much discussion of these textual traditions, as well as how they might play a role in establishing the Hebrew Bible.[39] Nevertheless, textual criticism of the Hebrew Bible has retained its use of a single manuscript tradition. Here is perhaps also the place to mention study of the Septuagint or Old Greek of the Old Testament, traditionally examined for its insights into the underlying Hebrew text.[40]

In contrast, New Testament textual criticism has continued to follow the path of using an eclectic text based upon progressive knowledge of newly discovered manuscripts. Even so, New Testament textual criticism has been slow to develop as a field, until more recent times.[41] There are four areas worth noting in development of New Testament textual criticism. The first area is the continued development of

---

38. See Porter, *Constantine Tischendorf*, 11–76, but passim, including Tischendorf's essay on the early church and its development (111–74).

39. On textual criticism of the Hebrew Bible, see Würthwein, *Text of the Old Testament*, 103–19; Weingreen, *Introduction*, 1–10, 25–37; McCarter, *Textual Criticism*; and Tov, *Textual Criticism*, esp. 287–91, but passim. On the importance of the Dead Sea Scrolls for Hebrew Bible textual criticism, see VanderKam, *Dead Sea Scrolls Today*, 121–58; Ulrich, "Scrolls and the Study of the Hebrew Bible"; and VanderKam and Flint, *Meaning*, 103–53.

40. For a history of Septuagint studies, see Jobes and Silva, *Invitation*, 265–87. The new Brill Septuagint Commentary Series, however, approaches the Greek text on its own terms, and marks a significant development in English-language Septuagint studies (see ibid., 90, 362).

41. See Baird, *History of New Testament Research*, 3:241–58; Porter, *How We Got the New Testament*, 9–75; and Porter and Pitts, *Fundamentals*, 1–6, 73–78, 88–96, 137–43.

the eclectic text tradition. This encompasses publication of a variety of eclectic texts, beginning especially with the text of Brooke Foss Westcott (1895–1901) and Fenton John Anthony Hort (1828–92) published in 1881,[42] but also includes those of Bernhard Weiss (1827–1918), Hermann von Soden (1852–1914), and especially Eberhard Nestle (1851–1913) and now the editions of Nestle-Aland (in its 28th edition) and *UBSGNT* (now in its 5th edition), among a number of others.[43] There have also been various arguments against the eclectic text, including advocates for the Byzantine or the Majority text, or, more plausibly, for single manuscript editions. The second area is exploration of means of categorizing manuscripts and describing their tendencies. There have been various localist and family theories, as well as theories attempting to create profiles for manuscripts, such as the Claremont Profile Method and responses to it.[44] Third has been the analysis of the principles of textual criticism, beginning with Johann Jakob Griesbach (1745–1812) and continuing to today. Most scholars continue to be reasoned eclectic critics following in the lines of Kurt Aland (1915–94) or Bruce Metzger (1914–2007),[45] although there are some who argue for thoroughgoing eclecticism (e.g., G. D. Kilpatrick [1910–89] and his student J. Keith Elliott). The fourth, and arguably most important, area is reconceptualization of the task of New Testament textual criticism. Whereas the traditional purpose of textual criticism has been to establish the authorial text, recent efforts have identified various tendencies in textual criticism that emphasize the socio-historical dimension, so that the goal is recounting of the process of textual transmission of the "initial text." This approach is followed in varying ways by such scholars as Eldon J. Epp, Bart Ehrman, David Parker, and those of the Coherence-Based Genealogical Method and the *Editio Critica Maior* project. I find such a development as the last, though potentially illuminating for various periods of textual history, ultimately unsatisfying and unsatisfactory as the goal of New Testament textual criticism.[46] One of the surprising results of much discussion of the text of the Old and New Testaments is how other areas of study have only recently been brought to bear in serious ways on textual criticism—such as advances in linguistics and social-scientific knowledge. These are areas that clearly await further influence and advancement.

Most of the modern forms of biblical interpretation can be seen to have their origins in some way within this intellectual climate that prevailed especially in Germany in the first half of the nineteenth century. It is impossible to offer a simple accounting of these various methods as they are related to each other. Instead, what I offer is an attempt to trace some of the diachronic lines, appreciating their associative and synchronic interconnections. I realize that I run the risk of failing to mention a number of

---

42. McKim, *DMBI*, 1038–43.
43. Baird, *History of New Testament Research*, 2:60–65, 73–82, 101–11, 398–401.
44. See ibid., 2:265–66, on B. H. Streeter (1874–1937).
45. McKim, *DMBI*, 728–33.
46. See Porter, *How We Got the New Testament*, 33–36.

scholars along the way—those that others (or even themselves) consider important to the discussion.[47] For that I apologize, but the number of scholars engaged in continuing biblical interpretation precludes mentioning everyone, including some who no doubt merit such recognition.

Historical criticism has had a number of major important developments in the last one hundred and fifty or more years. In the rest of this introductory essay, I wish to trace how some of the initial subjects of Enlightenment criticism became major developments in the history of biblical criticism. I identify five major strands for discussion, realizing that I am bound to miss some important developments, perhaps to misconstrue others, and no doubt to impose my own analytical focus upon the entire scenario. The five areas I examine are: historical criticism, literary criticism (and along with it rhetoric), philosophy, language studies, and the human sciences.

HISTORICAL CRITICISM

For many, historical criticism is the primary, if not virtually the only, development of Enlightenment thought.[48] I, however, differentiate historical criticism from other areas of intellectual endeavor of the Enlightenment, each of which has also led to important developments within critical thinking. In that sense, I suppose one could call all of the subject matter of this essay higher criticism, of which historical criticism (and the others treated below in various ways) is a subcategory. Nevertheless, the rise of theological liberalism is often (still) associated with historical criticism and its developments. One of the first and still most important figures in this rising movement was Albrecht Ritschl (1822–89), a student of Ferdinand Christian Baur (1792–1860) who departed from his teacher on particulars but essentially embedded theological liberalism in the German theological psyche.[49] Ritschl continued the developments of Schleiermacher's romanticism and its regard for religious consciousness, with Christianity being embodied in the human Jesus. Within New Testament scholarship, Ritschl did important work on the Gospels, being an important step in the further development of source criticism of the Gospels (he saw Mark as the earliest Gospel used by Luke). His most important work was in Pauline theology, where he disputed the traditional Lutheran view of justification, and adopted instead a view that emphasizes the love of God over his justice. Others, such as Eduard Reuss (1804–91) and Carl Weizsäcker (1822–99),

---

47. As an example, Baird in his third volume fails to mention a number of scholars that I would consider worthy of mention, and in fact fails to mention some areas of development within New Testament research. I also think that he includes some who should not be mentioned, because they are not the kind of significant or innovative scholars who should be mentioned in such a treatment. However, I realize that Baird wrote his book and I am writing my article, and we are bound to disagree on such matters. I am thankful for the work that he has done.

48. Cf. Krentz, *Historical-Critical Method*, for another view of its development. For a defense of it and its major practitioners, but that does not put it within its larger context, see Harrisville, *Pandora's Box Opened*.

49. Baird, *History of New Testament Research*, 2:86–92; Zachhuber, *Theology as Science*, 135–285.

both of whom further promoted the two-document hypothesis and views that called into question traditional views of Paul, combined a theological/philosophical framework.[50] The kind of liberal scholarship that dominated especially German scholarship of the time is seen in the work of Heinrich Holtzmann (1832–1910), whose two major works of New Testament introduction and theology encapsulated most of the received tradition of historical criticism and theological liberalism.[51] These traditions included views of Jesus and his religious consciousness, the importance of the kingdom of God, the development of Christianity within Jewish and Hellenistic Christianity, and the like. Holtzmann is attributed with the basic formulation of the two-document hypothesis. Liberalism reached its peak in Adolf Harnack (1851–1930), the longtime Berlin professor, though not of New Testament but of history (he proved to be too controversial as a New Testament scholar).[52] It is hard to summarize Harnack's contribution, because he was on the one hand a synthesis of much that had gone before him in the rise of liberalism, and on the other one who addressed a vast range of subjects from church dogmatics to particular issues in New Testament studies. However, what distinguished his work was his historical-critical orientation to the New Testament and early Christianity. In some ways, liberalism fell apart after Harnack, especially with the atrocities of the first World War, but he nevertheless taught a number of students who continued to influence German and American and other scholarship well into the twentieth century and even to this very day.[53]

Although theological liberalism soon came under scrutiny, this does not mean that the historical-critical method suffered as well. There no doubt were important scholars who took a more conservative approach to historical-critical matters. In Old Testament studies, these included J. C. K. von Hofmann (1810–77), who as a historian saw God's divine guidance behind the events of history (salvation history) and hence identified the limits of secular history, and Franz Delitzsch (1813–90), whose Old Testament commentaries generally conclude with views in opposition to those of such critical scholars as Wilhelm de Wette (1780–1849) and defend Mosaic involvement in the Pentateuch and a single Isaiah.[54] Similar New Testament scholars are found in Bernhard Weiss (1827–1918), who produced a series of important and traditional (perhaps better, conservative, at least by German standards) commentaries and produced a Greek text of the New Testament (already noted above), Theodor Zahn (1838–1933), who besides

---

50. Baird, *History of New Testament Research*, 2:93–101.

51. Ibid., 2:111–22; Reventlow, *History of Biblical Interpretation*, 4:303–10.

52. Baird, *History of New Testament Research*, 2:122–35; O'Neill, *Bible's Authority*, 214–29; McKim, *DMBI*, 504–7.

53. Harnack was the teacher of such scholars as Adolf Jülicher (1857–1938), Shirley Jackson Case (1872–1947), Edgar J. Goodspeed (1871–1962), and Karl Barth (1886–1968), among others. See Baird, *History of New Testament Research*, 2:123; cf. 2:156–62, 317–30; 3:64–85; Reventlow, *History of Biblical Interpretation*, 4:379–93.

54. Rogerson, *Old Testament Criticism*, 104–20; cf. McKim, *DMBI*, 606–9; and on von Hofmann, Harrisville and Sundberg, *Bible in Modern Culture*, 123–45; McKim, *DMBI*, 533–57.

writing some commentaries produced what are still arguably unsurpassed works in the formation of the New Testament canon,[55] Adolf Schlatter (1852–1938), who also wrote numerous traditional commentaries and studies of the New Testament,[56] and the Dominican scholar and founder of the École Biblique in Jerusalem Marie-Joseph Lagrange (1855–1938), whose work in textual criticism and commentaries on the Gospels (which in some ways anticipated redaction criticism—see below) represented a balance between the use of criticism and maintenance of a position of faith.[57]

As far as their enduring legacies within the development of biblical scholarship, for good or for bad, these more conservative scholars were, within their own day and certainly in many circles since then, often overlooked or overshadowed by the more radical historical-criticism practiced by others. Franz Overbeck (1837–1905), developing further the perspective of Baur, was skeptical about most of the New Testament, including John's Gospel, Acts, and the history of early Christianity.[58] William Wrede (1859–1906), though he published little due to his early death, still did enough to put into concrete form the notion that Paul was the second founder of Christianity, as he called him in his popular book on Paul, and to permanently shape the notion of there being a theological not historical "messianic secret" (better perhaps "messianic enigma") in Mark's Gospel.[59] Julius Wellhausen (1844–1918), the student of Heinrich Ewald (1803–75), when he was not radically transforming much Old Testament scholarship with his source theories (the documentary hypothesis) and views of the history of Israel, was developing source theories for the Gospels, especially regarding their Aramaic origins.[60] Wellhausen was followed in English-speaking circles by William Robertson Smith (1846–94), even if from a more conservative position.[61] Adolf Jülicher (1857–1938), the teacher of Rudolf Bultmann (1884–1976), but more than that the developer of the theory that the parables contained a single "truth," wrote an introduction to the New Testament that in many ways encapsulates the historical-critical thought of the turn of the nineteenth and twentieth centuries, with its skeptical views of New Testament reconstruction and history.[62] Alfred Loisy (1857–1940)

---

55. Baird, *History of New Testament Research*, 2:367–73; McKim, *DMBI*, 1072–76.

56. Baird, *History of New Testament Research*, 2:373–83; Harrisville and Sundberg, *Bible in Modern Culture*, 169–94; McKim, *DMBI*, 881–85. Cf. Neuer, *Adolf Schlatter*.

57. Baird, *History of New Testament Research*, 2:384–93; McKim, *DMBI*, 633–36. See also Murphy-O'Connor with Taylor, *École Biblique and the New Testament*, 6–28. Lagrange anticipated a number of important Roman Catholic scholars such as Rudolf Schnackenburg (1914–2002), Raymond E. Brown (1928–98), and Joseph A. Fitzmyer. See Baird, *History of New Testament Research*, 3:396–423; McKim, *DMBI*, 227–34 (on Brown).

58. Baird, *History of New Testament Research*, 2:138–44.

59. Ibid., 2:144–51; McKim, *DMBI*, 1056–60. See also Porter, *When Paul Met Jesus*, ch. 2.

60. Baird, *History of New Testament Research*, 2:151–56; Reventlow, *History of Biblical Interpretation*, 4:311–25; McKim, *DMBI*, 1030–34.

61. Rogerson, *Old Testament Criticism*, 275–81.

62. Baird, *History of New Testament Research*, 2:156–62; McKim, *DMBI*, 585–89.

represents the heights (or depths, depending upon one's perspective) of French skepticism regarding the New Testament. Even though he was arguably an astute historian, Loisy's struggle with Roman Catholicism led to a skepticism that plagued both him and his career.[63] Werner Georg Kümmel (1905–95), who wrote a variety of works including a standard New Testament introduction and theology, represents a more moderate but mainstream German historical criticism that is typical of the kind of continuing critical work that came to dominate German scholarship during the twentieth century,[64] and was followed by Helmut Koester (1926–2016), one of Bultmann's students, who, through the writing of an introduction to succeed that of Kümmel (and better informed in more recent archaeological research), continued the German historical-critical tradition.[65] The English-language equivalent might be the introduction of James Moffatt (1870–1944).[66] This critical tradition is seen in a number of Old Testament scholars who have written introductions, such as the German scholar Ernst Sellin (1867–1946), revised and expanded by Georg Fohrer (1915–2002), or the English scholar S. R. Driver (1846–1914).[67]

There are three successive movements that arise from these developments of historical criticism. These include source, form, and redaction criticism, canonical criticism, and the history of religion school, and their after-effects.

I begin with source, form, and redaction criticism, because source criticism is a necessary prelude to discussion of the history of religion.[68] Source criticism early-on became one of the recognized features of Enlightenment thought regarding the Bible, in both Old Testament and New Testament studies. In Old Testament research, source criticism was most clearly seen in Pentateuchal studies.[69] Theories of parts of the Old Testament resulting from the compilation of various sources appeared as early as Benedict Spinoza (1632–77) (e.g., he questioned whether Moses could have written about his death in Deuteronomy 34), but the theory that the Pentateuch was a composite document from distinct written sources began with Jean Astruc (1684–1766),[70]

---

63. Baird, *History of New Testament Research*, 2:163–72; McKim, *DMBI*, 675–79.

64. Baird, *History of New Testament Research*, 3:338–45; McKim, *DMBI*, 625–27.

65. Baird, *History of New Testament Research*, 3:345–53. A more conservative alternative is found in D. Guthrie, *New Testament Introduction*. A clear instance of critical scholarship not knowing what to do with a scholar who entirely conforms to its methods but arrives at radically different conclusions is found in the work of John A. T. Robinson (1919–83), such as his *Redating the New Testament*. See James, *Life of Bishop John A. T. Robinson*; Neill and Wright, *Interpretation*, 430–39; McKim, *DMBI*, 874–77.

66. Baird, *History of New Testament Research*, 2:293–98; McKim, *DMBI*, 745–51.

67. Sellin and Fohrer, *Introduction to the Old Testament*; Driver, *Introduction to the Literature of the Old Testament*. A more conservative alternative is found in Harrison, *Introduction to the Old Testament*. See McKim, *DMBI*, 510–14.

68. On their interrelationship (or at least another angle on it), see Morgan with Barton, *Biblical Interpretation*, 93–132.

69. Habel, *Literary Criticism*.

70. McKim, *DMBI*, 126–28.

and continued through such scholars as Johann Gottfried Eichhorn (1752–1827),[71] de Wette (who took what is sometimes called a fragmentary view), Hermann Hupfeld (1796–1866), Karl Heinrich Graf (1815–69), and then, in its definitive form, Wellhausen, who advocated for J, E, D, and P, composed in that order reflecting the evolutionary views made current by Charles Darwin (1809–82).[72] The notion of the Old Testament having been composed out of previous literary traditions—what came in many circles to be called literary criticism of the Old Testament—began to have an incredible influence upon critical study.

Despite its proponents and its proposed solutions, source criticism led to, in some ways, an inverse process of exploration (instead of parts to whole, whole to parts), especially as it failed to answer satisfactorily all of the literary questions being asked of the text.[73] What came to be called form criticism was concerned with the individual literary traditions or units that made up a given work and their original *Sitze im Leben* (situations in life).[74] This type of Old Testament literary criticism, in some ways a descendent of previous attempts to view the Bible as literature, as well as of a number of other areas (e.g., German folklore studies, classics, ancient Near Eastern studies among others), was concerned with such literary forms (*Gattungen*) as legends, novellas, sagas, and the like. Although there were predecessors to his work, especially in Martin Kähler (1835–1912), Hermann Gunkel (1862–1932) was the single most important figure in developing the notion of Old Testament form criticism.[75] Gunkel defined these individual forms—first explored in Revelation, but also in Genesis and then in the Psalms—on the basis of situationally variable (the concept of *Sitz im Leben*) uses of language, within the context of the wider scope of the history of religion (on which see below).[76] This situationally variable language was characteristic of each form. Over the course of time, Old Testament form criticism took two major developmental steps. One of these was an attempt to integrate form criticism with source criticism, as is reflected in the work of Otto Eissfeldt (1887–1973),[77] and the second was to become more concerned with the influence of the religious community

---

71. O'Neill, *Bible's Authority*, 78–94; McKim, *DMBI*, 400–404.

72. See Archer, *Survey of Old Testament Introduction*, 81–88; Harrison, *Introduction to the Old Testament*, 19–27. Cf. also Rogerson, *Old Testament Criticism*, 131–34, on Hupfeld.

73. Hammann, *Rudolf Bultmann*, 106–7; cf. Knierim, "Criticism," 128–46.

74. See Buss, *Biblical Form Criticism*, esp. 209–62, 324–406, but passim; Tucker, *Form Criticism*; Harrison, *Introduction to the Old Testament*, 35–38.

75. McKim, *DMBI*, 499–503, 594–601; O'Neill, *Bible's Authority*, 230–47, 167–78, on Gunkel and Kähler respectively. See also Campbell, "Emergence."

76. Some will recognize in this formulation a relationship with what some in linguistic circles are inclined to define as register. This is not a coincidence, as apparently Gunkel influenced the Egyptologist and linguist Alan Gardiner (1879–1963) who had an influence upon (among a number of others) the social anthropologist Branislaw Malinowski (1884–1942), who first formulated the notion of context of situation, out of which has emerged register studies. See Buss, *Changing Shape of Form Criticism*, 152–56.

77. See Archer, *Survey of Old Testament Introduction*, 88–89; Buss, *Biblical Form Criticism*, 324.

rather than the inciting situation, as in the work of Sigmund Mowinckel (1884–1965) on the Psalms.[78] In recent times there has emerged a reactive movement called the New Form Criticism. The New Form Criticism, focusing upon the work of Martin Buss, distinguishes itself as more concerned with the situation of the formal units within their literary contexts rather than within the "situation-in-life" or history of the individual formal unit.[79]

Closely related to form criticism, as well as source criticism, is what is called redaction criticism. This is the analysis of the means by which sources are compiled or edited by authors or subsequent redactors (the term redaction criticism is used in differing ways in Old Testament studies) for various, especially theological, purposes. Redaction criticism, as an extension of form and source criticism, is found throughout Old Testament study, but is especially prominent in study of the Pentateuch (e.g., Eissfeldt) and the prophets, such as Isaiah (e.g., H. G. M. Williamson).[80] One of the best known works is by Martin Noth (1902–68) on the Deuteronomic historian.[81] As a result, source and then form criticism in the form of redaction criticism has come full circle as a type of literary criticism, even though it has had relatively little influence upon subsequent developments in contemporary literary criticism of the Bible (see below).

In New Testament studies, the rise of Gospel criticism was one of the most important early developments of historical criticism.[82] In recognizably similar ways as in Old Testament studies, source criticism grew out of what appeared to be an obvious relationship among the Synoptic Gospels. A number of the scholars already mentioned above had an important role to play in Gospel source criticism. What began with the traditional view of Matthean priority, refined by Johann Jakob Griesbach (1745–1812), developed more fully into theories regarding an *Urgospel* (Gotthold Ephraim Lessing, 1729–81) and then into Markan priority (Karl Lachmann, 1793–1851, and Christian Gottlob Wilke, 1786–1854) and the two-document hypothesis (Christian Hermann Weisse, 1801–66)[83] and then its full-fledged form in the work of Heinrich Holtzmann (1832–1910), involving not only Mark and Q, but material unique to Matthew and Luke as well.[84] This theory, the two/four-document (or two-source) hypothesis (2DH), has continued to be refined as the currently most widely recognized source-theory for the Gospels (e.g., B. H. Streeter, 1874–1937, and Geoffrey Styler),[85]

---

78. Buss, *Biblical Form Criticism*, 326; Harrison, *Introduction to the Old Testament*, 46–50; McKim, *DMBI*, 757–62.

79. See Buss, *Changing Shape of Form Criticism*, passim; cf. Buss, *Concept of Form*, passim.

80. Knierim, "Criticism," esp. 150–53; Baker, "Israelite Prophets and Prophecy," 287–91.

81. Noth, *Deuteronomistic History*. See McKim, *DMBI*, 776–82.

82. See Neill and Wright, *Interpretation*, 112–46.

83. See Baird, *History of New Testament Research*, 1:143–48, 168–69, 319–22.

84. Baird, *History of New Testament Research*, 2:111–22, esp. 115–16.

85. Streeter, *Four Gospels*; Styler, "Priority of Mark"; Baird, *History of New Testament Research*, 2:265–66; Court, *Generation*, 19–34; McKim, *DMBI*, 949–52. Others who played a role in the development of the two/four-document hypothesis (2DH) include: William Sanday (1843–1920) and F. C.

including detailed examination of Q to the point of positing a situation or situations, editions, and its own theology (e.g., John Kloppenborg).[86] There have been, however, major responses to and even rejections of this source theory, including rejection of the necessity of Q by Austin Farrer (1904–68) and Michael Goulder (1927–2010),[87] theories of oral tradition such as by Brooke Foss Westcott (1825–1901)[88] and those following the Scandinavian school such as Birger Gerhardsson (1926–2013),[89] and re-assertions of forms of Matthean priority by those following the so-called Griesbach or two-Gospel hypothesis (2GH) such as William Farmer (1921–2000).[90]

Whereas source criticism was designed to account for the origins of or at least relations among Gospels, there was still the perceived need to address the early church situation that resulted in the Gospels, and hence form criticism was introduced into Gospel study. In fact, there had early on been types of form criticism in New Testament study (e.g., in the work of Eduard Norden, 1868–1941, and Paul Wendland, 1864–1915), but the major figures who are credited with development of New Testament form criticism are Karl Ludwig Schmidt (1891–1956), Martin Dibelius (1883–1947) who apparently originated the term "form criticism," Rudolf Bultmann in Gospel studies,[91] and Ernst Lohmeyer (1890–1946) in Pauline studies.[92] The three

---

Burkitt (1864–1935). See Baird, *History of New Testament Research*, 2:263–64, 267–69.

86. Baird, *History of New Testament Research*, 3:380–84.

87. Ibid., 3:372–78.

88. Porter, "Legacy of B. F. Westcott."

89. Baird, *History of New Testament Research*, 3:568–80.

90. Ibid., 3:365–72; McKim, *DMBI*, 432–38. The idea of Markan priority, once one of the "assured results" of scholarship (Neill and Wright, *Interpretation*, 116), is now far from assured. See Porter and Dyer, *Synoptic Problem*, for interactive essays on the four major theories by Craig A. Evans (2DH), Mark Goodacre (Mark without Q), David Peabody (2GH), and Rainer Riesner (oral tradition). A recent development in Gospel studies related to such theories is that of eyewitness testimony and social memory. On eyewitness testimony, see Bauckham, *Jesus and the Eyewitnesses*. On social-memory theory, there are a number of sources, but a treatment by one who has invested much effort in traditional Synoptic issues is Allison, *Constructing Jesus*.

91. On form criticism, especially of the Gospels, see McKnight, *What Is Form Criticism?* and Buss, *Biblical Form Criticism*, 263–323. On all three major form critics, see Baird, *History of New Testament Research*, 2:269–86; cf. 3:85–117, with further discussion of Bultmann; Kümmel, *New Testament*, 325–41; Neill and Wright, *Interpretation*, 252–69 (cf. 237–51); McKim, *DMBI*, 891–95, 365–71, 261–67. On Bultmann, see Hammann, *Rudolf Bultmann*, esp. 104–17; cf. Harrisville and Sundberg, *Bible in Modern Culture*, 217–48; Porter and Robinson, *Hermeneutics*, 226–39. Bultmann studied with Gunkel in Berlin, and was influenced by him (Hammann, *Rudolf Bultmann*, 29). The scholar generally responsible for introducing form criticism to the English-language world was Vincent Taylor (1887–1968); see Baird, *History of New Testament Research*, 3:8–16, esp. 10–11; Court, *Generation*, 103–18; McKim, *DMBI*, 960–63. Also included are: R. H. Lightfoot (1883–1953), see Neill and Wright, *Interpretation*, 270–71; Court, *Generation*, 47–60; McKim, *DMBI*, 665–68; C. H. Dodd (1884–1973), see Baird, *History of New Testament Research*, 3:35–53; Court, *Generation*, 61–82; Dillistone, *C. H. Dodd*; McKim, *DMBI*, 378–83; and T. W. Manson (1893–1958), see Baird, *History of New Testament Research*, 3:27–35; Court, *Generation*, 119–34; McKim, *DMBI*, 699–702.

92. See Neill and Wright, *Interpretation*, 270; McKim, *DMBI*, 671–75. Another form-critic of the Pauline letters is Ralph P. Martin (1925–2013). See Martin, *Carmen Christi*. One might also argue that

major works on form criticism of the Gospels appeared within two years of each other (Schmidt and Dibelius in 1919 and Bultmann in 1921). Even though they each had a particular take on form-critical matters and emphasized different elements—Schmidt distinguishes the Gospel framework from the individual units inserted within it, Dibelius form-critically analyzes these units working from the church backward, and Bultmann works from the form-critical units to the life of the Christian community— their accumulative effect was to transform Gospel criticism. The development of form criticism of the Gospels has had an enduring effect on Gospel criticism as a type of literary criticism concerned with the identification and description of the implied community situation of these various forms (variously labeled by the form critics, but including such things as sayings, miracles, parables, and the like) that lay behind the Gospel texts. Early on, even though form critics saw the Gospel authors as compilers and authors, there was recognition of ways in which individual forms had been shaped in their various literary contexts. The result was an appreciation of the influence of the Gospel writers, not simply as compilers but as authors with creative theological input, and soon redaction criticism was developed. Again, there were precedents (e.g., all three of the major form critics, who, even if inadvertently, recognized the formative influence of the Gospel compilers, R. H. Lightfoot on the role of location in Mark, and Henry Cadbury [1883–1974] on Luke),[93] but Günther Bornkamm (1905–90) and his work on Matthew is often credited with being the first redaction critic, although the label itself is attributed to Willi Marxsen (1919–93) who wrote on Mark, and the first major redaction-critical work is attributed to Hans Conzelmann (1915–89) on Luke.[94] Redaction criticism, based upon the work of both source and form criticism but appreciating the theological intentions of the author, continues to be widely practiced in New Testament studies, although it has been readily observed that it has major similarities to other types of literary criticism that appreciate the formative role of the author, whether for theological or other purposes.[95]

In both Old Testament and New Testament studies, there are two further movements to note in closing this first major section. Both have connections with source and form criticism. The first movement is traditions history, similar to redaction criticism though tracing the development of traditions rather than being primarily concerned with the redactors or their redaction. In Old Testament studies, this is seen in the Old Testament theology by Gerhard von Rad (1901–71),[96] and in New Testa-

---

Adolf Deissmann (1866–1937) performed a type of form criticism on the Pauline letters, although he was concerned with them as entire letters (see Doty, *Letters*). Baird (*History of New Testament Research*, 3:7) sees the between-the-war period as the "zenith" of Enlightenment criticism.

93. On Cadbury, see Baird, *History of New Testament Research*, 3:16–26; McKim, *DMBI*, 272–77.

94. See Perrin, *What Is Redaction Criticism?* On all three major redaction critics, see Baird, *History of New Testament Research*, 3:147–68, although he only mentions Bornkamm's role in redaction criticism in passing; 3:353–65; McKim, *DMBI*, 210–16, 711–16, 324–28.

95. See Moore, *Literary Criticism*, 56–68.

96. See Rast, *Tradition History*; cf. Hasel, *Old Testament Theology*, 69–75.

ment studies, in study of the book of Acts by Ernst Haenchen (1894-1975).[97] There are also recognizable similarities of traditions history and reception theory, although reception theory extends the scope of examination beyond the limits of the biblical text itself (see below).

The second movement encompasses what are variously characterized as canonical approaches. A canonical approach, especially as found in the work of Brevard Childs (1923-2007), its strongest and best known advocate, is characterized by attention to the final form of the text—in Old Testament studies the Masoretic text—and interpreting the text in that light. According to Childs, a canonical approach does not reject historical criticism, but wishes to overcome the traditional historical-critical divide between what the text meant and what it means. Childs was primarily an Old Testament scholar, but he also wrote incisively and definitively on the New Testament.[98] In New Testament studies, some interesting work from a canonical standpoint appreciates the shaping of the canonical ordering by the various manuscript traditions.[99] It might appear odd to place canonical approaches within discussion of the historical-critical method, when canonical approaches appear to have much in common with a variety of approaches to biblical study, including literary criticism, biblical theology, and what has come to be known as narrative criticism (see below for discussion). This is no doubt true. However, the way in which Childs frames his approach is in relation to historical criticism. He bases his canonical interpretation upon a foundation of historical criticism, and in that sense canonical approaches have much in common with redaction criticism in appreciation of the role of theological perspective in interpretation of the text.[100]

A second development of historical criticism is the history of religion movement. The history of religion movement, focused originally upon Göttingen University, where many of its founding members either studied or taught in the late nineteenth century, was "not concerned with the history of religions, but with the history of one religion, Christianity, within the larger frame of religious history," and hence was not concerned with theology (either biblical or dogmatic) but with the historical development of religion.[101] This development was often seen in terms of a bifurcation between Hellenism and Judaism—with the history of religion movement focusing upon Hellenism as the origin of Christianity, and upon how Christian traditions developed within such a context of religion. The history of religion movement thrived in the late nineteenth and early twentieth century, and involved both Old Testament and

---

97. Haenchen, *Acts of the Apostles*.

98. Childs, *Introduction to the Old Testament*; Childs, *New Testament as Canon*. See D. Driver, *Brevard Childs*; Harrisville and Sundberg, *Bible in Modern Culture*, 304–28; McKim, *DMBI*, 301–10.

99. This is seen especially in the work of Robert W. Wall. See Wall and Lemcio, *New Testament as Canon*, esp. 110–28, where Wall treats the placement of Acts as a theological interpretive indicator.

100. This is seen even more so in the canonical criticism of James A. Sanders. See Sanders, *Torah and Canon*.

101. Baird, *History of New Testament Research*, 2:222.

New Testament scholars. The two leading scholars were Gunkel and Wilhelm Bousset (1865–1920), but also included Johannes Weiss (1863–1914) the son of Bernhard Weiss,[102] Wrede, and Bultmann, along with Franz Cumont (1868–1947) and Richard Reitzenstein (1861–1931), among many others.[103] Although it is sometimes said that the history of religion school emphasized tradition over literary or source criticism, we have noted above that a clear differentiation between literary criticism or source criticism and form criticism is impossible to make. Nevertheless, the influence of Gunkel and his form-critical concerns with tradition came to dominate the movement, even though others still dealt with sources (such as Bultmann in his study of John's Gospel). One of the enduring findings of the history of religion school was the origin of Christology in the Hellenistic world, a view for which Bousset is particularly known. Bousset, adopting the evolutionary developmental view of the time, saw Christianity as the highest form of religion and, under the influence of Thomas Carlyle's (1795–1881) views of the hero, Jesus as the one who liberated religion from being legalistic. Paul was seen to translate Jesus into the wider Hellenistic world, where Jesus was exalted and venerated as God.[104]

There are two developments from the history of religion movement worth noting. The first is the Biblical Theology movement and the second is the New History of Religion movement. The rise of the Biblical Theology movement was a reaction to the history of religion school, especially in North America. The Biblical Theology movement was in some ways part of a larger set of developments in biblical theology that arose as a reaction to liberalism, of which the history of religion school was definitely a part. With the advent of the first World War, and recognition that the liberal agenda was bankrupt, dialectical theology arose in response, though clothed in the language of orthodoxy (hence the apt title neo-orthodoxy), in particular in the work of Karl Barth (1886–1968). He was joined by others, including Bultmann, in a movement that has been influential in Continental biblical theology to this day.[105] Although overshadowed in some ways by the dominant biblical theology, the notion of salvation history came to provide an operative metaphor for a large number of works in biblical theology that rejected liberalism and the history of religion approach, finding its grounding

---

102. Ibid., 2:223–29; McKim, *DMBI*, 1026–30.

103. See Baird, *History of New Testament Research*, 2:222–53; Kümmel, *New Testament*, 206–25, 245–80, and 342–62, but who differentiates too many periods within the school; and Porter and Robinson, *Hermeneutics*, 233–35, where others are cited, such as Wellhausen, Ernst Troeltsch (1865–1923), and Rudolf Otto (1869–1937), along with a number of classicists, such as Ulrich von Wilamowitz-Moellendorf (1848–1931) and Norden, among others.

104. Baird, *History of New Testament Research*, 2:243–51.

105. See Porter and Robinson, *Hermeneutics*, 214–44; Baird, *History of New Testament Research*, 2:63–85; Neill and Wright, *Interpretation*, 215–27. Still an excellent source on neo-orthodoxy is Hordern, *Layman's Guide*. Barth is not treated here, not least because he does not fall within the parameters of biblical interpreters being discussed within this chapter (and is not rightly regarded as much of a biblical interpreter). The major North American figures in this movement were Reinhold Niebuhr (1892–1971), H. Richard Niebuhr (1894–1962), and Paul Tillich (1886–1965).

in the work of J. C. K. von Hofmann (1810–77) and Schlatter. In the middle of the last century, major figures who reflected the salvation-historical approach in various ways in Old Testament studies were Walther Eichrodt (1890–1978) and von Rad, both of whom wrote major Old Testament theologies, and in New Testament studies Oscar Cullmann (1902–99), who wrote a New Testament theology as well as other works capturing the salvation-history movement.[106] The Biblical Theology movement, as in many ways a part of this larger development in biblical theology, consciously rejected the previous emphasis upon Hellenism and placed its emphasis upon Judaism. A number of features came to be identified with this movement, including the return to theology (rather than to religion), seeing the Bible as unified, God's active revelation in history, a distinctive mentality of the Bible, and the Bible's contrast with its environment (rather than being a product of it).[107] In Old Testament studies, the leading figure in the Biblical Theology movement, among admittedly many, was G. Ernest Wright (1909–74), who wrote a book entitled *God Who Acts*,[108] and in New Testament studies, again among others, Cullmann, who wrote a book that came to represent many of the (negative) features of the movement, *Christ and Time*.[109] The Biblical Theology movement was soundly criticized by James Barr (1924–2006) along general linguistic lines.[110] Barr's major criticisms were that the supposed linguistic grounds for the major theological distinctions were unfounded, and included positing distinctive Greek and Hebrew mindsets on the basis of mischaracterizations of their languages and various lexical fallacies (such as confusion of word and concept, illegitimate totality transfer, etc.), arguably most poignantly illustrated in Gerhard Kittel's (1888–1948)[111] *Theological Dictionary of the New Testament* (to which many of the scholars mentioned in this essay contributed).[112] Despite the trenchant critique by Barr, which has remained unrefuted (despite some claims to the contrary), the movement in admittedly altered form has persisted without sufficient address of the criti-

106. Yarbrough, *Salvation Historical Fallacy*, passim, but 134–37 on Eichrodt and 184–88 on von Rad; Baird, *History of New Testament Research*, 3:475–88; McKim, *DMBI*, 404–9, on Eichrodt; 843–48, on von Rad; and 333–38, on Cullmann.

107. These characteristics are from Childs, *Biblical Theology in Crisis*, 32–50, who also offers a critique of the movement.

108. Wright, *God Who Acts*; McKim, *DMBI*, 1060–65. Others within the area of Old Testament include H. H. Rowley (1890–1969), see McKim, *DMBI*, 877–90; James Muilenburg (1896–1974); and in some ways Childs. See Hasel, *Old Testament Theology*.

109. Others within New Testament studies include Floyd V. Filson, John Knox (1900–99), Paul Minear (1906–2007), and, from a more conservative vantage point, F. F. Bruce (1910–90). See Baird, *History of New Testament Research*, 3:488–525. On Minear, see McKim, *DMBI*, 742–45. On Bruce, see Grass, *F. F. Bruce*; McKim, *DMBI*, 234–37. See also Hasel, *New Testament Theology*.

110. McKim, *DMBI*, 150–55.

111. Ibid., 614–18.

112. See Barr, *Semantics of Biblical Language*; and Barr, *Biblical Words for Time*. Cf. also Gibson, *Biblical Semantic Logic*, for an extension of Barr's criticisms—also still unanswered (possibly because not understood sufficiently by its objects of criticism). There were those who continued to practice the approach, while recognizing its shortcomings. See Hill, *Greek Words*.

cisms leveled by Barr. The result is that there is now a revival of the Biblical Theology movement in the work of such scholars as Francis Watson, among others.[113] Although the violations of sound linguistics are not as obvious as in a previous generation, many of the same assumptions still seem to remain in place.

The second development is the New History of Religion school. This development is often tied to what is sometimes called the New Tübingen school. By this is meant that there have been a number of recent (as opposed to the times of Baur) scholars at Tübingen, led by Martin Hengel (1926–2009), who have taken the matter of Christianity within its context seriously but have seen that context as being either Judaism within Hellenism (as in the work of Hengel) or primarily Judaism.[114] In other words, they reject the bifurcation that finds Hellenism as the foundation of Christianity and attempt to restore a balance, with recognition of the importance of Judaism for the origins of Christianity. The result of the latter recognition has been a major revisiting of the question of how Jesus became God (the major issue of Bousset). Various answers have been proposed within the Judaism of the time, such as the recognition of other mediatorial figures (e.g., Charles A. Gieschen), divine identity (e.g., Richard Bauckham), attribution of worship (e.g., Larry W. Hurtado), or relational categories (e.g., Chris Tilling).[115] There are no doubt other categories that could be considered as well, but the point is made that one need not appeal to Hellenistic divinization to make sense of the divinity of Christ within the world of the first century. This is the major contribution of the New History of Religion school.

Historical criticism continues to be an important part of biblical interpretation, as is evidenced in a number of the changes and developments that have occurred within this area of study. However, it is also clear that historical criticism is closely related to various other areas of biblical interpretation, many of these studied in the strands outlined below.

LITERARY CRITICISM

Ancient rhetoric provided the basis for the analysis of literature for the medieval period, and then provided the basis for what came to be the study of literature in the Enlightenment, even though fairly early on rhetoric came to be associated with speech and the study of literature with writing and both housed within English literature

---

113. Watson, *Text and Truth*. See also Childs, *Biblical Theology of the Old and New Testaments*; Barr, *Concept of Biblical Theology*. The changing perspectives on what constitutes biblical theology are seen in Boers, *What Is New Testament Theology?* and Via, *What Is New Testament Theology?* There is some question whether the Theological Interpretation of Scripture movement will coalesce enough to constitute an enduring theology. See Fowl, *Theological Interpretation of Scripture*.

114. Baird, *History of New Testament Research*, 3:310–23. Others in this "camp" would be Otfried Hofius and Peter Stuhlmacher.

115. Gieschen, *Angelomorphic Christology*; Bauckham, *Jesus and the God of Israel*; Hurtado, *Lord Jesus Christ*; Tilling, *Paul's Divine Christology*. Others who have argued along related lines are Gordon D. Fee and Richard N. Longenecker.

departments.¹¹⁶ The development of rhetorical and literary study is one of the five strands that formed the basis of modern biblical interpretation. There are several trends within this strand to note.¹¹⁷ These include: the Bible as literature movement, the rise of formalist criticism in particular the "New Criticism," narrative criticism, reader-oriented criticism, the revival of ancient rhetoric, and the rise of the New Rhetoric, along with lines of connection of literary criticism to ideological criticism and thematic criticism. A number of ties to philosophical and language studies are evident and will be noted as well.

The Bible as literature movement has had an intriguing, but often ignored, history in which it has continued to develop within biblical studies (more in Old Testament than in New Testament studies) but has also taken on a life of its own outside of biblical studies.¹¹⁸ This literature movement, which began as early as the Old Testament scholar Robert Lowth (1710–87)¹¹⁹ and the English cultural commentator Matthew Arnold (1822–88), has extended to the present,¹²⁰ and has included such figures as Benjamin Jowett (1817–93) and Erich Auerbach (1892–1957).¹²¹ Despite what its name might imply, the movement was concerned both with the forms of literature (and in that sense foretold the work of Hermann Gunkel [1862–1932]),¹²² and with more than simply literary features, including theology. In fact, many if not most approaches to the Bible as literature took a "genre"-based approach, and helped to set the stage for the form-critical movement.

Within literary studies in particular (but hermeneutical theory more broadly), there have been three loci of interpretive authority: the author, the text, and the

---

116. See Eagleton, *Literary Theory*, 17–53. Cf. Palmer, *Rise of English Studies*.

117. For a recent guide to the critical landscape, see Castle, *Blackwell Guide to Literary Theory*. See also Porter, "Literary Approaches"; and Longman, *Literary Approaches*, for a very basic survey.

118. Buss, *Biblical Form Criticism*, 187–208; Porter, "Literary Approaches," 78–80; Morgan with Barton, *Biblical Interpretation*, 203–68.

119. McKim, *DMBI*, 679–82.

120. Contra Buss, *Biblical Form Criticism*, 205, who sees T. R. Henn (1901–74) as "the last representative of the movement." Others included in the movement are: Richard G. Moulton (1849–1924) (uncle of James Hope Moulton and brother of the translator of G. B. Winer's grammar; see below), Charles A. Briggs (1841–1913) (see Baird, *History of New Testament Research*, 2:289–93), William Rainey Harper (1856–1906), Mary Ellen Chase (1887–1973), Northrop Frye (1912–91), Leland Ryken, and, arguably, Frank Kermode and Robert Alter, among others. See Gros Louis, Ackerman, and Warshaw, *Literary Interpretations* vol. 1; Gros Louis and Ackerman, *Literary Interpretations* vol. 2; Alter and Kermode, *Literary Guide*, for collections of various types of literary essays on the Bible.

121. These two examples illustrate the diversity of the movement. Jowett's essay appeared in the highly controversial *Essays and Reviews*, which was published in 1860 and served as an introduction to German higher criticism for an English-speaking audience. Auerbach's *Mimesis* was written during the second World War when the author had limited access to secondary materials. See Rogerson, *Old Testament Criticism*, 209–19.

122. See Porter, "Literary Approaches," 78, citing Gunkel, *What Remains*; cf. Buss, *Biblical Form Criticism*, 205–6. This is the approach of Beardslee, *Literary Criticism*, and the "genre"-based approach is still widely found in biblical studies. As examples, see Coats, *Saga*; and Aune, *New Testament*. For some of the complexities involved (and perhaps unrealized), see Frow, *Genre*.

reader. The history of literary interpretation—especially in the nineteenth and twentieth centuries—is a study of the shift of authority from author to text to reader. Most types of textual readings until the early twentieth century, whether they were focused upon sources, traditions, or forms, still focused upon authorial meaning as determinative.[123] Within the twentieth century, by far the most important movement in literary criticism was the movement in formalist criticism that came to be known as the New Criticism.[124] The New Criticism marked a major shift in authoritative center to the text. In reaction to the romantic interpretive tradition, the New Criticism was an English-language and especially North American literary-critical movement that began in the 1920s, inspired by T. S. Eliot's (1888–1965) 1919 essay "Tradition and the Individual Talent,"[125] but it had formative influences upon it from Continental formalism, in particular Russian formalism, and structuralism, in particular narratology (see below), as well as reflecting the philosophical perspective of logical positivism, with its empiricism and a prioris.[126] The New Criticism, which emerged from this variety of forces, along with agrarianism in North America, concentrated upon the self-contained literary artifact, hence the title of Cleanth Brooks's (1906–94) book, *The Well Wrought Urn* (although the movement got its name from a book by John Crowe Ransom, 1888–1974). This artifact itself set the parameters for interpretive authority, and the essay by W. K. Wimsatt (1907–75) and Monroe Beardsley (1915–85) on the intentional fallacy, which must be interpreted in light of the interests of the New Criticism, came to characterize the movement (even if the essay itself has been widely misunderstood and misapplied ever since),[127] as did the book by René Wellek and Austin Warren, *Theory of Literature*. Even though the New Criticism has ostensibly passed off the interpretive scene, being replaced by more reader-oriented approaches in the 1970s, there are many remnants of it in a variety of interpretive methods, often distinguished by "close readings" of the text, such as narrative criticism.

Literary interpretation of biblical texts was given permission by the 1969 SBL presidential address of James Muilenburg (1896–1974), who advocated going beyond form criticism to what he called rhetorical criticism, characterized by attention to structure, aesthetics, and other New Critical features.[128] His use of the term rhetori-

123. A major advocate for authorial meaning is Hirsch, *Validity in Interpretation*, still followed by many biblical scholars.

124. See Castle, *Blackwell Guide to Literary Theory*, 122–29; Selden, Widdowson, and Brooker, *Reader's Guide*, 13–28; Robey, "Anglo-American New Criticism"; and the older but still valuable Scott, *Five Approaches*, 179–85. Cf. Wolfreys, *CEMCT*, 436–50.

125. Other figures of importance are I. A. Richards (1893–1979), F. R. Leavis (1895–1978), Austin Warren (1899–1986), René Wellek (1903–95), and William Empson (1906–84), and the genre-oriented Chicago School of Richard Crane (1886–1967) and Wayne Booth (1922–2005) (not to be confused with the Chicago School of socio-historical criticism; see below). Cf. Wolfreys, *CEMCT*, 665–73.

126. See Ayer, *Logical Positivism*, for a collection of essays by major contributors to the movement. Cf. Jones, *History of Western Philosophy*, 5:218–49.

127. Wimsatt and Beardsley, "Intentional Fallacy."

128. Muilenburg, "Form Criticism"; McKim, *DMBI*, 762–65. Muilenburg was anticipated by

cal criticism, although it has caused considerable confusion between Old Testament and New Testament scholars, has been widely interpreted as the invocation of the need for literary criticism that is sensitive to literary features of the text, not primarily discussing sources or forms. Old Testament and New Testament literary criticism has developed in varying ways. Nevertheless, the major feature of such work is a synchronic approach to the text, as opposed to the kinds of diachronic approaches used in historical criticism (a distinction attributable especially to modern linguistics; see below).

Within Old Testament studies, there has been ambiguity, no doubt due to Muilenburg's terminology, regarding whether to call the formalist interpretation rhetorical or literary criticism. Despite some retaining the label rhetorical criticism, a term still used in some study of English literature,[129] most call it literary criticism of one type or another.[130] There have been two major schools or influences in literary criticism of the Old Testament, as well as many other literary interpreters. The first is the Sheffield approach, led initially in the 1970s by David Clines in his *I, He, We, They* and *The Theme of the Pentateuch*, and David Gunn in *The Story of King David*.[131] Their emphases tend to be upon the kinds of features studied by the New Criticism, such as structure, character, setting, unity, and the like. The impact of their work has been significant and has led to numerous other literary readings of the Old Testament. The second school is the Israeli school, within which I include Robert Alter and his *The Art of Biblical Narrative*, along with his *The Art of Biblical Poetry*,[132] among other works. The Israeli school includes the work of Meir Sternberg and Shimon Bar-Efrat.[133] Their approach is characterized by a less aesthetic and more structuralist approach to literary reading of the Old Testament, inspired in some ways by features of narratology (see below). They too have inspired a wealth of studies. No doubt because of ambiguity over the use of the term "rhetoric," there have also been a few who have (anachronistically) attempted to use the categories of ancient rhetoric in the study of the Old Testament (see below on rhetorical criticism).

New Testament literary studies have been less focused upon particular institutions or orientations as in Old Testament studies, but have nevertheless reflected similar concerns and interests.[134] There are two major streams of New Testament literary criticism, what might be called common-sense criticism and defined formal-

---

Wilder, *Language of the Gospel*. See Crossan, *Fragile Craft*; McKim, *DMBI*, 1052–56.

129. For example, Foss, *Rhetorical Criticism*.

130. There was no need for this ambiguity, as is shown in D. Robertson, *Old Testament and the Literary Critic*.

131. See also Berlin, *Poetics and Interpretation*.

132. This was a part of a body of literature rethinking the nature of Hebrew poetry, including also Kugel, *Idea of Biblical Poetry*; and Berlin, *Dynamics*.

133. Sternberg, *Poetics of Biblical Narrative*; Bar-Efrat, *Narrative Art*.

134. See Petersen, *Literary Criticism*, especially in contrast to Beardslee above.

ism. Common-sense criticism began in the late 1970s and early 1980s and reflects the concerns of formalism, even if it is not as methodologically self-conscious (quite possibly because these literary scholars were unknowingly influenced by the New Criticism through the course of their educations). This criticism has phenomenological elements to it, in which various notions of text and reader seem to be implied and readily accepted. Charles Talbert, in his many "readings" of various New Testament books, is one of the first and most enduring of these common-sense critics.[135] Defined formalism begins with the work of David Rhoads and Alan Culpepper.[136] David Rhoads, a New Testament scholar, wrote his major literary treatment of Mark with his colleague the literary scholar Donald Michie, and Alan Culpepper's work on John was written during a sabbatical in Cambridge when he consulted with the literary scholar Frank Kermode (1919–2010). The first edition of Rhoads and Michie's book was based upon the American narratologist Seymour Chatman's approach and the kinds of concerns are similar to those of Culpepper: various types of author (real, implied, etc.), plot, character, setting, and the like, all New Critical concerns that were also reflected in some of the fundamentals of narratology.[137] Whereas most early literary interpretation was of the Gospels, there were occasional studies of other literature.[138]

What characterizes most of the work of both Old Testament and New Testament biblical literary critics, at least in the English-speaking world, is that their initial training, if not their first publications (this is truer in New Testament than Old Testament studies), were written within the areas of traditional historical criticism. However, for a variety of reasons, perhaps not least their dissatisfaction with the kinds and extent of conclusions reachable through traditional historical-critical means, these scholars endeavored to explore the literary features of the text more fully. Whereas the first generation of literary critics often tried to balance historical and literary criticism, and even theological interests, subsequent interpreters have been literarily oriented from the start and worked more exclusively in that vein, often without regard for historical interests.[139]

Once the literary-critical barrier had been broken, there were two further developments of concern for this essay.[140] The first is the identification of what has come

135. Talbert, *Reading Luke*, among many others. See also Kingsbury, *Matthew as Story*; and Tannehill, *Narrative Unity*.

136. Rhoads and Michie, *Mark*; Culpepper, *Anatomy*. Cf. Thatcher and Moore, *Anatomies*, for various perspectives on developments since Culpepper published his book.

137. Chatman, *Story and Discourse*. Chatman's book was replaced in subsequent editions of Rhoads's and Michie's book. I think that their book lost some of its distinctiveness and possibly some of its theoretical innovation by doing so.

138. See Petersen, *Rediscovering Paul*.

139. Collections of some representative work in Old Testament and New Testament literary criticism are found in Exum and Clines, *New Literary Criticism and the Hebrew Bible*; and Malbon and McKnight, *New Literary Criticism and the New Testament*.

140. For a still trenchant analysis of some of the directions after the decline of the New Criticism, see Lentricchia, *After the New Criticism*. Cf. Clines, "Contemporary Methods."

to be called "narrative criticism" and the other is the development of reader-oriented approaches. Rhoads himself devised the term "narrative criticism" to define the kind of literary criticism in which he was interested.[141] "Narrative criticism" is a label unique to biblical studies to describe the kind of defined formalism that was then being regularly applied to biblical narratives.[142] Whereas the New Criticism had initially been defined primarily in relation to characteristics of poetry, narrative criticism explicitly reflects the interests of the New Criticism, and along with it, of narratology, as applied to biblical narratives. Whereas narratology recognizes the difference between the surface text and the underlying structure, the New Criticism is more concerned with the surface structure and features of the literary text itself, and narrative criticism concentrates upon these phenomenological features. Narrative criticism reflects less a growth and development in literary criticism of the Bible than it does a codification and application of established principles of analysis, and continues to be widely used in the study of the Bible, as in effect a type of formalism reminiscent of the New Criticism.[143]

In the wider field of literary studies, because of the post-structural revolt (see below) and a variety of other factors, there has been a shift of the locus of authority from the text to the reader and the development of reader-oriented strategies.[144] These reader-oriented strategies have been numerous,[145] but there are two main types of what has come to be called reader-response criticism that have made inroads into biblical studies.[146] The first is to conceive of reader-response as the response of a particular reader, usually the original reader.[147] In this type of reader-oriented criticism, the interpreter determines how the text has influenced the original reader. This is, in effect, a form of audience criticism,[148] and hence a type of historical criticism rather than being reader oriented in the sense that the reader plays a productive role in the creation of meaning. The second kind of reader-response criticism—and one that can lay claim to being a type of literary criticism recognizable to those within literary studies—practices the restrained reader-response criticism influenced by the

---

141. Rhoads, "Narrative Criticism and the Gospel of Mark" (1982), reprinted in Rhoads, *Reading Mark*, 1–22.

142. Powell, *What Is Narrative Criticism?* Cf. also Resseguie, *Narrative Criticism*; Fokkelman, *Reading Biblical Narrative*.

143. See Stibbe, *John as Storyteller*, still one of the best examples. Compare the recent work of S. Elliott, *Reconfiguring Mark's Jesus*, who attempts to bring post-structuralism to bear on narrative criticism.

144. See Selden, Widdowson, and Brooker, *Reader's Guide*, 47–65.

145. For handy guides, see the collections of essays in Tompkins, *Reader-Response Criticism*; and Suleiman and Crosman, *Reader in the Text*. Cf. Wolfreys, *CEMCT*, 465–72.

146. See Porter, "Why?"

147. See Beavis, *Mark's Audience*.

148. See J. Baird, *Audience Criticism*.

German literary critic Wolfgang Iser (1926–2007).[149] Iser's implicit reader (similar to Booth's implied reader) is a hypothetical reader established by the text and hence is text-immanent. Iser believes that there are parameters of interpretation defined by the text, and that the reader as interpreter exercises interpretive freedom within these parameters. In New Testament studies, Robert Fowler was one of the earliest practitioners of reader-response criticism. In his scholarship, he moves from an early literary criticism that still has strong ties to historical criticism to one that is more reflective of the kinds of interests seen in Iser and in the early Stanley Fish's "affective stylistics," which is concerned with the affect of reading on the reader.[150] Clines's innovation in formalist readings soon led him to reader-oriented strategies, as indicated in his study *What Does Eve Do to Help?*[151] Reception history is also a type of reader-oriented criticism and the two reading strategies are often discussed together. Promoted by Hans Jauss (1921–97), as well as Iser, as a development of Russian formalism, Prague school linguistics, and the work of the philosopher Hans-Georg Gadamer (1900–2002),[152] reception history has more recently emerged in biblical studies in a chastened and constrained form mostly as a history of scholarship rather than as a history of effects.[153] Robert Evans has written an insightful work that explicates the theory and provides examples of reception history that may prompt further detailed expositions.[154]

This section concludes with reference to the revival of ancient rhetoric and the rise of the New Rhetoric.[155] The two forms of rhetoric are clearly related, in that the New Rhetoric is founded upon principles gleaned from the study of ancient rhetoric, and emerges to some extent from the rise of romanticism (see below). In one sense, modern literary criticism is the contemporary equivalent of the ancient rhetorical criticism practiced in the medieval period and later, before the formation of modern literature departments. However, in relatively recent interpretive times, there has been a revival of interest in ancient rhetoric. Because rhetoric was central to the curriculum of the medieval university and then became incorporated into English and then speech departments, rhetoric never completely disappeared from the modern academic curriculum, and ancient rhetoric is still used in the teaching of writing and reading. However, the use of ancient rhetoric in the study of the Bible is the result of a revival of

---

149. Iser, *Implied Reader*.

150. Fowler, *Loaves and Fishes*, which is still historical in nature (but was on the forefront of recognizing literary questions); Fowler, *Let the Reader Understand*. Cf. Fish, *Is There a Text*, 21–67, a very important book in the history of reader-response criticism, but one that laid out an overly ambitious agenda for most biblical scholars to follow. A recent effort is Phillips, *Prologue*.

151. Cf. Clines, *Bible and the Modern World*.

152. Jauss, *Toward an Aesthetic of Reception*; Holub, *Reception Theory*; Parris, *Reception Theory*. See Wolfreys, *CEMCT*, 280–87, cf. 151–58. Cf. Porter and Robinson, *Hermeneutics*, 158–61, 74–104, and below.

153. These often take the form of works that simply record the history of interpretation.

154. R. Evans, *Reception History*.

155. See J. Richards, *Rhetoric*, for a brief history.

interest in ancient rhetoric that first began in classical studies, especially in the work of the classicist George Kennedy, and then, through him and the research of Hans Dieter Betz, in New Testament and then Old Testament studies (the use of ancient Greek and Latin rhetoric for the study of the Old Testament has been relatively less important).[156] Kennedy explores the range of ancient rhetorical practice in a number of works, including devoting a book to New Testament rhetoric,[157] and a number of New Testament scholars have adopted his rhetorical approach. This involves identifying the rhetorical unit, the rhetorical situation, and its arrangement, among other factors. He applies his findings to a range of New Testament writings, as have those who have followed him. Betz[158] focuses upon the rhetoric of Paul's letters, beginning with an analysis of the rhetorical arrangement of Galatians. He identifies the letter as an instance of apologetic rhetoric, using the ancient handbooks as guides.[159] Although Kennedy and Betz have much in common in their appreciation of ancient rhetoric, they also have a number of differences regarding their relationship to the handbook tradition, the means of securing rhetorical knowledge, and their (and their followers') estimations of the rhetorical features of various New Testament books. The use of ancient rhetoric in New Testament studies has grown exponentially.[160] The use of ancient rhetoric for the study of the Old Testament has also been attempted in a few instances.[161]

As indicated above, modern literature departments have changed significantly in the last twenty-five to thirty-five years—most of these changes are not reflected by corresponding changes in the literary study of the Bible, apart from one significant development, the rise of ideological criticism, and along with it cultural studies, and reactions to it.[162] I will discuss deconstruction below, but I simply note here that literature departments, after their exploration of post-structuralism, including deconstruction, with its heavy infusion of literary theory, have had two major reactions to such theory. The first reaction is the emergence of more intensely socially conscious ideological criticism and, as a related result, the rise of and focus upon cultural studies.[163] In other words, there has been a deepening mandate of literature

---

156. See Mack, *Rhetoric and the New Testament*, for a brief history of the early days.

157. Kennedy, *New Testament Interpretation*.

158. Baird, *History of New Testament Research*, 3:659–77.

159. Betz, *Galatians*, esp. 14–25.

160. On the early rhetoricians and some of their followers, see the various essays in T. Martin, *Genealogies*. He includes discussions of Betz, Kennedy, Wilhelm Wuellner (1921–2004), Elisabeth Schüssler Fiorenza, and Vernon Robbins. An early work that captures the movement in various papers in New Testament rhetoric is Porter and Olbricht, *Rhetoric and the New Testament*. Subsequent volumes of the Pepperdine series have similar collections of essays.

161. E.g., Möller, *A Prophet in Debate*.

162. Some may question my linking ideological criticism to cultural studies, but the ideological nature of most cultural studies seems to warrant their being placed together, even if cultural studies is considered a sub-category of ideological studies. There have been some criticisms of cultural studies as a discipline and its grounding. See, e.g., Davies, *Cultural Studies*.

163. See Leitch, *Cultural Criticism*.

departments to turn from focus upon specific literary texts to an examination and questioning of the literary canon and a re-evaluation of the ideological commitments represented in formation of any canon and interpretation of any literature. As a result, these ideological commitments have resulted in the rise of various ideological interests being brought to bear, such as postmodernism,[164] feminism, gender studies, disability studies, ethnic/racial studies, post-colonialism, ecological studies, the New Historicism (the return of a chastened Marxism or cultural materialism, influenced by Michel Foucault, 1926–84), and other culture-related topics.[165] In light of so many different interpretive interests pulling texts or interpreters in various directions, there has also been a resurgence of attention to the great themes of literature. This "thematic criticism" does so in light of a postmodernist and post-structuralist context.[166]

The lines of connection between these areas and various other areas of biblical interpretation are numerous. There are philosophical, human science, and political interpretive issues at stake. Some of the biblical interpreters who have pioneered these areas related to ideology are the Postmodern Bible project,[167] Phyllis Trible and Elisabeth Schüssler Fiorenza in feminist studies,[168] Stephen Moore in gender studies,[169] Saul M. Olyan in disability studies,[170] R. S. Sugirtharajah in post-colonial studies,[171] and David Horrell and others in ecological studies,[172] among a growing number of others.[173]

The second reaction to ideological criticism has been a backlash against the increasing emphasis upon theory, with some literary critics—even some of those who have been theory's advocates—calling for a rejection of theory. The literary theorist Terry Eagleton has written a book titled *After Theory*, in which he chronicles the gains and losses of postmodernism and criticizes it for avoiding major issues, while Valentine Cunningham has argued that theory has come to dominate reading and calls for a

---

164. Postmodernism is often said to have been initiated by Jean-François Lyotard (1924–98) in his (under the influence of Ludwig Wittgenstein's notion of language games) rejection of meta-narratives. See Lyotard, *Postmodern Condition*, xxiv–xxv; Lechte, *Fifty Key Contemporary Thinkers*, 322–32; Wolfreys, *CEMCT*, 287–93.

165. See Selden, Widdowson, and Brooker, *Reader's Guide*, 88–149, 200–266; McKenzie and Kaltner, *New Meanings*; Wolfreys, *CEMCT*, 511–19, 535–67, 768–76, 784–91, among others. Cf. Hens-Piazza, *New Historicism*.

166. See Sollors, *Thematic Criticism*; Bremond, Landy, and Pavel, *Thematics*.

167. See Castelli, Moore, Phillips, and Schwartz, *Postmodern Bible*. See also Moore, *Bible in Theory*.

168. Trible, *Texts of Terror*; Schüssler Fiorenza, *In Memory of Her*; Baird, *History of New Testament Research*, 3:590–604; McKim, *DMBI*, 895–99; and the essays in Russell, *Feminist Interpretation*. Cf. Donovan, *Feminist Literary Criticism*; Ruthven, *Feminist Literary Studies*; Collins, *Feminist Perspectives*.

169. Moore, *God's Beauty Parlor*.

170. Olyan, *Disability in the Hebrew Bible*.

171. Sugirtharajah, *Asian Biblical Hermeneutics*. See Loomba, *Colonialism*.

172. Horrell, Hunt, Southgate and Stavrakopoulou, *Ecological Hermeneutics*.

173. Liberation studies would also go in this category, although it is as much a philosophical and theological movement as it is literary. See Myers, *Binding the Strong Man*.

new humanism in response.[174] However, there are also signs of a renaissance in theory, accepting its fragmented, post-structuralist situation.[175] There has always been a questioning, if not an outright rejection, of theory in many areas of biblical studies, with literary studies of the Bible being no exception. In that sense, by rejecting the notion of theory—which usually means simply endorsing either the historical-grammatical or the historical-critical approaches (themselves theory-laden)—some have claimed that they are unaffected by theory. As has been seen above, however, there is no avoidance of theory—as all approaches to interpretation have theoretical presuppositions. So far as I know, however, there has not been an equivalent informed movement in biblical studies that has rejected the notion of theory as found in literary-critical circles (or that has re-valued it).[176]

Literary studies of the Bible have emerged as a major force in interpretation. Even though not as much on the forefront as they were twenty or so years ago, literary perspectives have become integrated into the structure of much of biblical studies, and taken from the margins into the heart of the discipline.

PHILOSOPHY

The influence of philosophy on biblical interpretation has been evident from the Enlightenment to the present, especially in German scholarship (as already seen in the introduction above). German biblical scholarship has been and continues to be highly influenced by philosophy, which is often translated into theological concerns—even in works that purport to be exegetical. Hermeneutics itself, which is rightly seen as an area within philosophical thought concerned with questions of understanding, is closely related to epistemology, and emerged as a discipline of its own in the writings of Friedrich Schleiermacher (1768–1834). As a result, it is not uncommon to find German biblical scholars still debating and mulling over what appear to be philosophical questions that are brought to bear directly on texts that do not appear to raise such questions without such philosophical prompting.

This essay is not meant to be an essay in philosophy and its development, but I will mention briefly the major philosophical trends that I believe have had an influence upon the development of biblical interpretation. These are: skepticism, German idealism, romanticism, phenomenology and existentialism, and ordinary language philosophy.

---

174. Wolfreys, *CEMCT*, 731–36; Cunningham, *Reading after Theory*. The movement against theory began earlier, as indicated in a series of essays published in the 1980s: Mitchell, *Against Theory*.

175. Leitch, *Literary Criticism*. On the one hand, there are indications that we are viewing theory from too close a perspective, and so we see more differences and distinctions than we ought. On the other hand, there is a sense in which, once the theory box has been opened, it is difficult to know how we can read without raising questions of theory.

176. Some of these issues are discussed in Moore and Sherwood, *Invention of the Biblical Scholar*.

One of the basic philosophical positions that resulted from the Enlightenment was the rise of skepticism. It might appear odd to think of skepticism as a philosophy, but in definable ways it is a determining philosophical position in that it orients the interpreter to the evidence. Whereas many of the interpretive difficulties that emerged in the Enlightenment had been raised before by those commenting upon the Bible—such as the relationships of the Synoptic Gospels, questions of authorship of various biblical books, and questions regarding the text and canon, among others—for the most part these questions had been answered from a "believing" standpoint. In his classic work on skepticism, Richard Popkin shows how skepticism began much earlier than the Enlightenment (in fact, he traces it to the Renaissance, but also acknowledges that skepticism goes back to the earliest philosophical traditions of the Greeks), but that biblical skepticism took root during that time, in particular over the nature of establishing the Greek text of the New Testament in light of manuscript discoveries and the publication of various editions of the Greek New Testament (e.g., by Desidarius Erasmus, 1466–1536, and the Spanish Polyglot Bible by Cardinal Ximenes de Cisneros, 1436–1517).[177] This skepticism extended to such topics as Mosaic authorship of the Pentateuch, the biblical strength of certain theological positions, and their resulting controversies. This rising skepticism became the platform for the work of Benedict Spinoza (1632–77), who is in many ways to be considered the originator of modern biblical criticism—at least with its skeptical orientation.[178]

German idealism, part of the larger idealistic philosophical tradition, and also related to romanticism, has had a tremendous impact upon German thought to this day. In one sense, it is appropriate to say that later German thought, whether philosophical or, perhaps in particular, theological, is still a response to German idealism, especially the relationship between the world of the senses (the result of rationalist/empirical thought) and the world of ideas. Attempts to bridge this divide have persisted in German philosophical thinking. The two major figures in German idealism are Immanuel Kant (1724–1804) and Georg Wilhelm Friedrich Hegel (1770–1831).[179] Through a number of works that addressed such topics as pure reason, practical reason, judgment, religion, and ethics, Kant was attempting, in the light of the rise of empiricism (to which I will return in a moment), to reconcile acknowledgment of the empirical world of sensory data and timeless truth or the world of ideals (the phenomenal and the noumenal). As John McCumber outlines, Kant does this through a complex process that requires three stages: acknowledgment of sensory data, arrangement of these data in relation to time and space, and experience of these data as objects and their arrangement in relationships by means of the mind. The human mind, or reason, thus constitutes the world, or non-sensed things that must exist, and this is the basis of

---

177. See Porter, *How We Got the New Testament*, 37–40. Cf. McKim, *DMBI*, 412–18.

178. See Popkin, *History of Scepticism*, 219–38.

179. McCumber, *Time and Philosophy*, 15–56; Copleston, *History of Philosophy*, vol. 6; 7:159–225; Jones, *History of Western Philosophy*, 4:14–99, 108–44. Cf. O'Neill, *Bible's Authority*, 54–65, 95–107.

metaphysics.[180] As rigorous and as compelling as Kant was in his thought, he was also attacked on a number of fronts, not least that these objects that Kant posits cannot be proved to exist, apart from our use of our mind to posit them (a form of circular argument). Kant's system ends up with so much of importance outside of the world of time and experience as to call the entire construct into question.

Around the time of the death of Kant, the Germanic world was in turmoil. Not only was their leading philosophical system seen to be increasingly problematic (especially after the death of Kant in 1804), but Germany was under attack by Napoleon (in 1806). Its philosophical "salvation" came from the unlikely quarter of Hegel, who lived a dissolute life and wrote almost impenetrable prose by even German standards. Nevertheless, his fundamental ideas come through from his earliest work, his *Phenomenology of Spirit* (or *Mind*, depending upon the translation) and his lectures on history. Hegel provided a philosophy that appeared at first to fill the ontological void of contemporary German thought by its endorsement of the Absolute Spirit, which could be equated with the God of Christianity. Hegel saw the Absolute as involved in a relationship with history, and religion was an attempt to describe how the human spirit relates to the divine. As a result, Hegel appropriated much of Christian thought but redefined it in his own idealistic way, even though many came to see his view as less Christian and more universalist. I have already offered enough summary of his thought, so here emphasize two important concepts that emerge from these works. The first is the Hegelian dialectic, already described above. In his *Phenomenology of Spirit* he begins with the Absolute Spirit interacting with the world, and through this interaction various problems are resolved and progress is made. This Hegelian dialectic is, therefore, the resolution of opposites by means of which progress results. His *Phenomenology of Spirit* proceeds from the Absolute Spirit through a process of opposites to the final resolution in consciousness, and in a sense comes full circle back to itself, but without discovering ultimate truth, because all that there is and can be known is consciousness. The second concept is the matter of history. McCumber states that whereas in his *Phenomenology of Spirit* Hegel sees reason as historicized, in his work on history, he sees history as rationalized.[181] History proceeds in a similar way as does consciousness, by means of a process of trial and error that resolves difficulties by means of reason. In other words, history is not about things as they are but is driven by mind or idea. The Hegelian dialectic in many ways became the philosophical platform for the development of historical criticism, but it also became the platform for German historicism.

German romanticism was closely related to the divide mentioned above between the phenomenal and the noumenal. Whereas seventeenth- and eighteenth-century philosophical thought had emphasized the rationalism of René Descartes (1596–1650)

---

180. McCumber, *Time and Philosophy*, 17–18.
181. Ibid., 42–43.

or of Gottfried Wilhelm Leibniz (1646–1716) (as well as Spinoza)[182] or the empiricism of John Locke (1632–1704) and David Hume (1711–76),[183] romanticism emphasized neither, and in that sense had some similarities to German idealism. Schleiermacher was one of the leading figures in romanticism, with its emphasis upon humane rather than purely rationalistic interests, imagination, creativity, emotional and passionate nature, and human freedom. Although not necessarily anti-rational, romanticism does not believe that human reason or mechanistic explanations of the universe can fully describe life, especially in relation to art, religion, and nature. Schleiermacher well illustrates the attempt to move beyond the limits of rationalism through his romantic orientation that opposes propositional theology. True religion resides in one's feeling of dependence upon God.[184] Romanticism, with its emphasis upon feeling, influenced the development of the New Rhetoric, notably in the writings of Chaim Perelman (1912–84) and Lucie Olbrechts-Tyteca (1899–1987), who are concerned with all of the means by which appeal is made to effect an argument.[185] Although it also has elements of classical rhetoric within it (as does the New Rhetoric), Vernon Robbins's Social-Rhetorical Interpretation is also a form of New Rhetoric, with its emphasis upon various "textures": inner texture, intertexture, social and cultural texture, and ideological texture.[186]

Related to these philosophical developments, German historicism developed in late eighteenth-century Germany and is the product of both romantic and idealistic thought. We can see the influences of both in two central notions of historicism: that history is determinative for forming culture and the need for intuition in appreciating other cultures and peoples. Historicism has from the outset emphasized the role of language in determining a people's identity, and hence in determining national boundaries (and helped result in the rise of modern nationalism—including the notion that all German-speaking peoples ought to be united). The idea that history is determinative leaves little basis for forming moral judgments regarding the actions of peoples, who seem to become self-justifying entities on the basis of their histories, and so leaves historicism open to abuse.[187] The influence of historicism was felt in some linguistic thought, especially that of Wilhelm von Humboldt (1767–1835) and his views of language and mentality (see below).

---

182. Copleston, *History of Philosophy*, 4:74–160, 270–336, 211–69; Jones, *History of Western Philosophy*, 3:154–237; Wolfreys, *CEMCT*, 3–9.

183. Copleston, *History of Philosophy*, 5.1:76–152; 5.2:63–156. See Reventlow, *History of Biblical Interpretation*, 4:51–64. On Locke and his influence on language, see Thomas, *Fifty Key Thinkers*, 66–71; cf. McKim, *DMBI*, 668–71.

184. Porter and Robinson, *Hermeneutics*, 27–28. Cf. Copleston, *History of Philosophy*, 7:149–58.

185. Perelman and Olbrechts-Tyteca, *New Rhetoric*. Other important figures in the New Rhetoric are I. A. Richards (1893–1979) and Kenneth Burke (1897–1993).

186. Robbins, *Tapestry of Early Christian Discourse*.

187. Bebbington, *Patterns in History*, 92–116, esp. 92–93.

Phenomenology and existentialism can be treated together for the sake of discussion here. I only mention phenomenology to bring Edmund Husserl (1859–1938) into our description. Husserl was concerned, like Kant before him, to establish a scientific foundation for philosophy (Husserl had begun as a mathematician). Whereas Kant discovered that foundation in reason, Husserl found it by beginning with perception, in which there is a consciousness of perception. In his thought, he extended this from description to an increasingly transcendental phenomenology, but always with the focus upon consciousness.[188] I recount Husserl's importance because of its influence upon especially Martin Heidegger (1889–1976). Husserl and Heidegger are two of the most important philosophers of a movement that came to be known as existentialism. Although existentialism is sometimes defined narrowly with emphasis upon a few French thinkers, existentialism as a movement is much broader and more encompassing, including such figures as Søren Kierkegaard (1813–55), Friedrich Nietzsche (1844–1900), Karl Jaspers (1883–1969), and others who followed after them.[189] What unites existentialism is emphasis on two major notions: the individual, and what constitutes authentic existence in the world. As a result, existentialism is typically characterized by realization that there is no transcendental being and that the human must face this existential reality. To use Heidegger's phrase, humans are concerned with "being-in-the-world," which is the fundamental human condition. However, within this condition, humans are free to make choices regarding the authenticity of their existence, even when faced with anxiety and guilt over the human condition.[190] Whereas existentialism is not as widely recognized as it once was, its influence upon mid twentieth-century theologians and biblical thinkers has been large. Many of the so-called neo-orthodox thinkers (mentioned above), such as Dietrich Bonhoeffer (1906–45), were influenced by existentialism. Two who were arguably most influential were Karl Barth (1886–1968) and of course Rudolf Bultmann (1884–1976), who was a colleague in Marburg with Heidegger. Much of Bultmann's rejection of the biblical worldview and his endorsement of a program of demythologization is based upon an existential philosophical foundation. In other words, the human predicament is that one does not live in the three-tiered world of the Bible, but humans are nevertheless called upon to live authentic lives when faced with their own deaths—although Bultmann admits

---

188. Porter and Robinson, *Hermeneutics*, 49–57; McCumber, *Time and Philosophy*, 127–58; Jones, *History of Western Philosophy*, 5:250–84; Lechte, *Fifty Key Contemporary Thinkers*, 36–44; Wolfreys, *CEMCT*, 73–81 (cf. 82–91 on phenomenology).

189. Copleston, *History of Philosophy*, 7:335–51, 390–420; 9:340–418; Lechte, *Fifty Key Contemporary Thinkers*, 277–85; McKim, *DMBI*, 609–14 (on Kierkegaard); Wolfreys, *CEMCT*, 52–59 (on Nietzsche). Gabriel Marcel (1889–1973), Maurice Merleau-Ponty (1908–61), and Jean-Paul Sartre (1905–80), among possible others could be included here. See also Barrett, *Irrational Man*, 149–205, 239–63; Lechte, *Fifty Key Contemporary Thinkers*, 51–57.

190. Guignon, "Existentialism," esp. 252; Porter and Robinson, *Hermeneutics*, 57–71; Jones, *History of Western Philosophy*, 5:285–331; Barrett, *Irrational Man*, esp. 206–38; Lechte, *Fifty Key Contemporary Thinkers*, 26–35; Wolfreys, *CEMCT*, 127–37.

that this existence is influenced by the gospel.[191] The New Hermeneutic, with its two leading thinkers, Ernst Fuchs (1903–83) and Gerhard Ebeling (1912–2001), is clearly dependent upon Bultmann's existentialism. They were concerned to make a practical attempt to show how the familiar biblical text can speak in a new way to the modern interpreter. As a result, they asked questions about language, and developed a theory of understanding based upon empathetic common understanding and characterized the role of language as performative or creating "word-events."[192]

The ordinary language philosophy movement began in Oxford, with the work of J. L. Austin (1911–60).[193] To some extent, ordinary language philosophy was a reaction to British logical positivism and Continental analytic philosophy.[194] Logical positivism, as noted above, believed in empiricism and a priori statements, whereas analytic philosophy was concerned with the truth-conditions of language. Ordinary language philosophy was concerned with the way in which statements are used in ordinary language, especially its non-informational purposes. There is debate over whether the philosopher Ludwig Wittgenstein (1889–1951) had any direct influence upon ordinary language philosophy. Wittgenstein had once been an analytic philosopher but came to realize that language functioned not according to logic but according to its own system (what he called language games). Even if his direct influence was minimal, they both came to similar insights.[195] Wittgenstein and the ordinary language philosophers recognized that language did more than simply convey information but that it was used in other ways that were susceptible to analysis, that is, language is performative. Austin, along with his best-known follower John Searle, recognized that the use of language (a locution), could perform certain actions given the right felicitous conditions (illocutionary force), and could result in certain actions being accomplished (perlocutionary force). Each such locution is said to be a "performative utterance," and hence the development of what has come to be called speech-act theory. Since the work of Austin and Searle, there has been much refinement of the notion of speech-acts and how they function, and speech-act theory has become one of the stable parts of the linguistic field of pragmatics.[196] Speech-act theory has had an effect on contemporary theology and to some extent biblical interpretation, in the work of such a biblical scholar as Anthony Thiselton.[197]

191. MacIntyre, "Existentialism," esp. 150–51. Cf. Porter and Robinson, *Hermeneutics*, 214–44.

192. See Porter and Robinson, *Hermeneutics*, 237; Thiselton, "New Hermeneutic." Fuchs and Ebeling were also followed by Robert Funk (1926–2005) and James Robinson. See Baird, *History of New Testament Research*, 3:454–66; McKim, *DMBI*, 446–51.

193. Austin, *How to Do Things*; Thomas, *Fifty Key Thinkers*, 206–11; Wolfreys, *CEMCT*, 703–9. Cf. Searle, *Speech Acts*.

194. See the representative essays in Klemke, *Contemporary Analytic and Linguistic Philosophies*.

195. Jones, *History of Western Philosophy*, 5:200–17, 364–99; Thomas, *Fifty Key Thinkers*, 173–78; Wolfreys, *CEMCT*, 120–26.

196. See Levinson, *Pragmatics*, 226–83.

197. Thiselton, "Parables as Language-Event"; and now at length in Thiselton, *First Epistle*.

In closing this section, I make several comments regarding contemporary philosophy and biblical studies. The first is the significance of Thomas Kuhn (1922–96). Some philosophers claim that Kuhn is the most important philosopher of the later twentieth century,[198] not only for his important efforts in philosophy of science but more for his inciting a conceptual rethinking of the entire scientific endeavor, and leading the way towards anti-foundationalism even in the hard sciences. His notion of paradigms—conceptual frameworks that govern disciplines—and how they shift on the basis of a variety of factors (not just supposedly hard evidence),[199] has become widely used in a variety of disciplines, including biblical studies. However, in some instances the implications of shifting paradigms are not always clearly understood. There has also been a recent movement to bring philosophy and biblical studies into dialogue, promoted by some philosophers but also by some biblical scholars. Contemporary Continental post-Marxist philosophers such as Alain Badiou and Giorgio Agamben have had an increasing influence upon biblical studies.[200] Badiou is concerned with issues of knowledge and truth and making sense of events in the world. Influenced by a range of contemporary thinkers, he believes that belief in an event requires faith, out of which emerges the subject. Notions of faith, good, evil, and love also occupy Badiou's thought, and provide opportunity for intersection with biblical studies. Agamben is a political philosopher concerned with what it means to be human in a post-Holocaust world of horror, and how modern society threatens the sacredness of life.[201] He draws a distinction between life as a physiological creature and life lived well in community. As a result, Agamben is interested in how the Bible characterizes humans. One of his most important works in this regard is his commentary on Romans.[202] The influence of contemporary philosophy on biblical studies is seen in Herman Waetjen's commentary on Romans, which attempts to come to terms with developments in the Continental philosophical tradition.[203] There have also been several volumes that include contributions by a variety of biblical scholars and contemporary philosophers on a number of contemporary issues in philosophy.[204]

There can be little doubt that philosophy will continue to have an important place in the development of biblical studies. Even though many biblical scholars may not realize the role that philosophy has played in the development of their discipline, more recent intersections promise to bring this knowledge to the fore.

---

198. Rorty, *Philosophy and Social Hope*, 175.

199. Kuhn, *Structure of Scientific Revolutions*.

200. Lechte, *Fifty Key Contemporary Thinkers*, 233–41, 207–16. See also the neo-Marxist Slavoj Žižek, who was heavily influenced by Jacques Lacan (1901–81). See Lechte, *Fifty Key Contemporary Thinkers*, 250–59; Wolfreys, *CEMCT*, 390–98.

201. McCumber, *Time and Philosophy*, 373–80.

202. Agamben, *The Time that Remains*.

203. Waetjen, *Romans*.

204. Harink, *Paul*; Milbank, Žižek, and Davis, *Paul's New Moment*.

LANGUAGE STUDIES

From the time of the Renaissance to the Enlightenment and into the present, the study of the Hebrew and Greek languages has been central to biblical studies. However, when compared to the other areas noted above, relatively speaking, language criticism has had less development and interconnection than some other interpretive strands. Language study not only has led to developments in textual criticism—which has continued along much the same path, until recently shifting away from the emphasis on discovering the original text (see above)—but has also led to a variety of language-related studies. In this section, I note the three major periods in language study and their related developments, and then trace several noteworthy movements: Structuralism including Russian formalism and the Prague school, narratology, and post-structuralism. I then summarize some recent developments.

There are three periods of Enlightenment and post-Enlightenment thought regarding language: the rationalist period, comparative philology, and modern linguistics.[205] I will concentrate upon these developments in language study, with some mention of lexicography.

The rationalist period of language discussion, which typified the eighteenth and early nineteenth centuries, reflects the rationalist and empirical philosophy of the time, and is characterized by the work of William Jones (1746–94) on the perfect structure of Sanskrit, or Étienne Bonnot de Condillac (1714–80) on the origins of language.[206] Two major figures stand out in Hebrew and Greek study. In Hebrew study, the grammar of Wilhelm Gesenius (1786–1842) was written from the rationalist perspective.[207] The rationalist dimension is evidenced in the logical ordering seen in the language, the use of Western (no doubt Latin-inspired) language categories for description (e.g., tense, mood, and flexion to describe the verb, where Hebrew is seen to be poor, in comparison with European languages), and description of Hebrew as defective because it does not have vowels written as letters.[208] In Greek study, the grammar of Georg Winer (1789–1858) was also from within the rationalist

---

205. For a brief guide to the history of linguistics, see Robins, *Short History of Linguistics*, 148–264 (used below), although he makes clear that such firm distinctions are difficult. I also note that those working in the biblical languages tend to lag behind the work being done in general linguistics. This is seen in the history of Hebrew grammar by Waltke and O'Connor (*Biblical Hebrew Syntax*, 31–43), who note the comparative method lasting from the mid eighteenth to mid nineteenth centuries, and then the comparative-historical method from the mid nineteenth to the twentieth centuries, but the modern linguistic approach only from the 1940s (to which they devote a single paragraph). I further note that Knight and Tucker, *Hebrew Bible*, has no separate article devoted to Hebrew language studies.

206. Robins, *Short History of Linguistics*, 149, 165.

207. Kautzsch, *Hebrew Grammar*, v, n. 1, where it is noted that the first edition was published in 1813. Gesenius himself was responsible for the first thirteen editions, with the fourteenth to the twenty-first being produced by E. Rödiger, and the twenty-second to the twenty-eighth by E. Kautzsch. It was translated into English in 1898. There were other Hebrew grammars, but this seems to be the one that has endured, as opposed to the one by Ewald.

208. Kautzsch, *Hebrew Grammar*, 99–103, 117, 5 (where these examples are found).

perspective.[209] As Winer himself states, the object of his grammar is to "check the unbounded arbitrariness with which the language of the New Testament had so long been handled" and "to apply the results of the rational philology . . . to the Greek of the New Testament."[210] This is seen, for example, in his handling of the tense-forms, where he says, for example, that "It is only in appearance that the aorist [which he says is a past tense] stands for the future."[211]

The comparative philological movement is also a distinctly historical period, but characterized by the development of various sound laws based upon the comparison of languages that were newly realized to be genetically related. For example, Jacob Grimm (1785–1863), who along with his brother did work in Germanic folklore and influenced the work of Hermann Gunkel (1862–1932), identified "Grimm's law" (1822) regarding sound changes in different classes of consonants across languages.[212] Wilhelm von Humboldt (1767–1835), in anticipation of later linguistic thought, appreciated the innate language ability of humans but also recognized the individual character of languages. He focused upon usage by a language community, and hence also anticipated the theory of linguistic determinism (the so-called Sapir-Whorf hypothesis), in which there is a close relationship between language and thought.[213] The comparative philological movement culminated in the so-called New Grammarians (*Junggrammatiker*), who held to ineluctable laws of sound change.[214] One of the leaders of this group was Karl Brugmann (1849–1919), who, along with Berthold Delbrück (1842–1922), wrote one of the most important comparative philological grammars (and apparently coined the word *Aktionsart* to describe types of action represented by verbs).[215] Most of the early modern linguists were trained by the New Grammarians, including Ferdinand de Saussure (1857–1913) and Leonard Bloomfield (1887–1949), among others. In Old Testament studies, the influence of comparative and historical study is seen in the career of Julius Wellhausen (1844–1918). Because of his work on source theory, Wellhausen was forced to resign his position in Old Testament at Greifswald and then became a professor of Semitic languages at Marburg, where he turned to work on Arabic, before moving to Göttingen again in Old Testament, but where he also did research in New Testament and on the relation of the Gospels to possible Semitic sources.[216] Even with the rise of comparative Semitics, however, there

---

209. Winer, *Grammar of New Testament Greek*, was first published in 1822 and went through six editions in Winer's lifetime, and then two further editions after his death (1868 and 1894–98). There were also a number of different translations into English (1859, 1860, 1870).

210. Ibid., xxii.

211. Ibid., 345.

212. Thomas, *Fifty Key Thinkers*, 97–103.

213. Ibid., 92–97.

214. See Jankowsky, *Neogrammarians*.

215. Thomas, *Fifty Key Thinkers*, 140–45.

216. See Reventlow, *History of Biblical Interpretation*, 4:312–15. Gustav Dalman (1855–1941), among others, also worked on the languages of Jesus. See Baird, *History of New Testament Research*,

has apparently been no complete comparative Hebrew grammar written, although subsequent editors of Gesenius's grammar have added comparative material.[217] This was also the period of the rise of Hebrew lexicography, beginning with the lexicon of Gesenius, followed by Frants Buhl, and then the still-standard lexicon from this period by Francis Brown, S. R. Driver, and Charles A. Briggs (1907).[218] The rise of comparative Semitics, which became very important especially in the United States, and ancient Near Eastern studies is a direct continuation of this period and orientation, as seen in the work of such scholars as James Montgomery (1866–1949) and William Foxwell Albright (1891–1971), among a number of others.[219]

In New Testament Greek studies, there are numerous works that reflect the comparative philological approach. The first and most important, and one that compares New Testament Greek with classical Greek, is the New Testament Greek grammar by the classical philologist Friedrich Blass (1843–1907), later revised by the comparative philologist Albert Debrunner (1884–1958).[220] Those following this path include the first two volumes of James Hope Moulton's (1863–1917) and Wilbert Francis Howard's (1880–1952) grammar and the massive grammar of A. T. Robertson (1863–1934).[221] Greek lexicography goes back earlier than the comparative period (in fact, defining its beginnings is difficult), but the major advance in lexicographical study was precipitated by the discovery of the Greek documentary papyri in Egypt. Due to the work of Adolf Deissmann (1866–1937) and Moulton (including Moulton's lexicon of the Greek Bible's vocabulary), among others, there was a reconfiguration of New Testament Greek from being seen as anomalous (whether Semitic Greek or some type of divinely inspired Greek) to being seen as a dialect of the general koine.[222] The Greek lexicon tradition is represented by two examples: the lexicon written in 1841

2:195–99.

217. Waltke and O'Connor, *Biblical Hebrew Syntax*, 41.

218. Ibid. On Briggs, see McKim, *DMBI*, 219–23.

219. C. Gordon, *Pennsylvania Tradition*. Zellig Harris (1909–92) was a student of Montgomery and wrote his doctoral dissertation on Phoenician. See Barsky, *Zellig Harris*. Harris was the teacher of Noam Chomsky. On Albright, see McKim, *DMBI*, 103–6.

220. Baird, *History of New Testament Research*, 2:184–85. The first three editions were by Blass (the first edition was translated into English by Henry St. John Thackeray, 1869–1930), then the next eight by Debrunner, two by David Tabachovitz (1895–1970) (although the changes were minimal), and the subsequent editions (up to the current 18th) by Friedrich Rehkopf. Robert Funk (1926–2005) made some adjustments in his English translation. However, the grammar is in many ways fundamentally unchanged from its first edition. Cf. the work of Alexander Buttmann; see Baird, *History of New Testament Research*, 2:184.

221. Moulton, *Prolegomena*; Moulton and Howard, *Accidence*; A. T. Robertson, *Grammar*. See Baird, *History of New Testament Research*, 2:186–89, 412–14. The two subsequent volumes of Moulton's grammar by Nigel Turner had a different conception of the Greek of the New Testament. In Septuagint studies, see Thackeray, *Grammar*.

222. The history of this discussion is traced in the essays in Porter, *Language*. This is part of a larger study of sociolinguistics of New Testament Greek. See Watt, *Code-Switching*, for one of the earliest full studies.

by Christianus G. Wilke, revised in 1868 by C. L. W. Grimm,[223] and translated into English in 1886 by Joseph H. Thayer (1828–1901), who also translated Winer's grammar in 1869, and the lexicon published in 1910 by Erwin Preuschen (1867–1920), expanded in two editions (1928, 1937) by Walter Bauer (1877–1963),[224] and then in 1988 by Kurt Aland (1915–94) and Barbara Aland, and translated into English and revised to the present (1957, 1979, 2000) by William F. Arndt, F. Wilbur Gingrich (1901–93), and Frederick W. Danker (1920–2012).[225] This latter lexicon remains a standard lexicon for New Testament Greek studies.

The third and final period is the modern linguistic period. This period is often identified with the theories of Saussure, who began as a New Grammarian. In his posthumously published lectures on language, he defined a number of key distinctions, such as the difference between synchrony and diachrony, the difference between *langue* (the language system) and *parole* (instances of usage), and the systematic nature of language, among others.[226] In fact, Saussure was not the only one thinking of such issues. Some of the same insights were already being explored by others, such as the Russian formalists and members of what came to be known as the Prague circle of linguists.[227] The application of principles of modern linguistics has been less in biblical studies than one might expect, with the result that many of the older grammatical works are still being used, despite further developments in linguistic thought. As a result, there are few Hebrew grammars that can be said to be linguistic in orientation. The grammar by Christo H. J. van der Merwe, Jackie A. Naudé, and Jan H. Kroeze (1999) is a useful exception.[228] In the area of Hebrew lexicography, a major advance has been made in the lexicon by David J. A. Clines.[229] This lexicon emphasizes syntax, comprehensiveness, and inclusiveness, with a generally sound linguistic framework. In New Testament studies, a similar situation obtains, with one of the few linguistically informed grammars being that of Stanley E. Porter.[230] New Testament studies has benefited from several advances in lexicography. These include the volume by Moisés

---

223. See Baird, *History of New Testament Research*, 2:185–86. There is no known relation to the Grimm brothers, Jacob and Wilhelm, so far as I can determine. There was also a lexicon written by Hermann Cremer (1834–1903), which anticipated Kittel and Friedrich's *TDNT*; see Baird, *History of New Testament Research*, 2:185.

224. Baird, *History of New Testament Research*, 2:415–17.

225. See Lee, *History*, esp. 329–68, but passim. Cf. Porter, *Linguistic Analysis*, 61–80.

226. Robins, *Short History of Linguistics*, 219–21. Cf. Thompson, *Fifty Key Thinkers*, 145–51; Lechte, *Fifty Key Contemporary Thinkers*, 176–84; Wolfreys, *CEMCT*, 70–73.

227. Porter and Robinson, *Hermeneutics*, 155–62.

228. Van der Merwe, Naudé, and Kroeze, *Biblical Hebrew Reference Grammar*. See also Jöuon and Muraoka, *Grammar of Biblical Hebrew*, although the grammar may be accused of not being entirely satisfactory, because Muraoka brings his modern linguistic sensitivities to a grammar reflective of a previous era (see Pardee, "Review of *A Grammar of Biblical Hebrew*").

229. Clines, *Dictionary of Classical Hebrew*. See Sawyer, *Semantics in Biblical Research*.

230. Porter, *Idioms*.

Silva that introduces general principles of lexical semantics[231] and, more importantly, the semantic-domain lexicon by Johannes P. Louw (1932–2011) and Eugene A. Nida (1914–2011).[232] This lexicon of the entire Greek New Testament uses componential analysis to differentiate 93 semantic domains (or semantic fields). Whereas the lexicon is far from perfect, it represents a major advance in lexicography biblical or otherwise.

Four movements and their influence are also worth noting in relation to biblical studies.[233] The first is structuralism and along with it Russian formalism and the Prague Linguistic Circle. Despite its disparate origins, structuralism was one of the most important intellectual movements of the twentieth century. On the basis of principles developed by Saussure and others, including the arbitrary nature of the sign, the notion of difference, syntagmatic versus paradigmatic relations, and language as social entity, besides the distinction between synchrony and diachrony, *langue* and *parole*, and language as system, structuralism came to dominate Western intellectual thought and provided such a pervasive framework of analysis as to take on the character of an ontology. The founder of the Prague Linguistic Circle, which lasted from 1926 to 1948, was Vilém Mathesius (1882–1945), who began his work in phonology, and he was succeeded by Jan Mukarovsky (1891–1975), who extended the circle's interests to include aesthetics. The Prague linguists also emphasized the functional use of language.[234] As already noted, similar principles were also being developed by the linguists, literary critics, and folklorists in the Russian formalist school with its interest in developing scientific rigor for the study of literature, including determining the "morphology" of a work (such as a folktale).[235] Besides what is noted below, the enduring heritage of Russian formalism is seen in the work of Mikhail Bakhtin (1895–1975).[236] Despite being a dense and elusive thinker, Bakhtin's heritage is developed today usually in terms of heteroglossia, polyphony, dialogism, and carnival—although there is more to Bakhtin's thought than is often given him credit. His legacy is seen in several books

---

231. Silva, *Biblical Words and Their Meaning*.

232. Louw and Nida, *Greek-English Lexicon*. Cf. Nida and Louw, *Lexical Semantics*. See Lee, *History*, 155–66, for summary of debate about the project; cf. Porter, *Linguistic Analysis*, 47–60. Juan Mateos (1917–2003) and Jesús Peláez have also developed a semantic analysis lexicon, based on principles of lexical analysis that they innovated. See Mateos and Peláez, *Diccionario Griego-Español*. For a summary and critique, see Porter, *Linguistic Analysis*, 74–76.

233. On what follows, see Porter and Robinson, *Hermeneutics*, 155–67. See also Lepschy, *Survey of Structural Linguistics*; Culler, *Structuralist Poetics*; Scholes, *Structuralism in Literature*; Jameson, *Prison-House of Language*; and Robey, "Modern Linguistics."

234. See Vachek, *Prague School Reader*; and Vachek, *Linguistic School of Prague*. Another member of the circle was Karl Bühler (1879–1963), who had an influence upon both Mukarovsky and indirectly upon Michael Halliday. Cf. Porter, *Linguistic Analysis*, 307–38.

235. Selden, Widdowson, and Brooker, *Reader's Guide*, 29–46. See Lemon and Reis, *Russian Formalist Criticism*, who collect essays by Victor Shklovsky, Boris Tomashevsky, and Boris Eichanbaum, and Jefferson, "Russian Formalism", although Jefferson excludes Vladimir Propp (1895–1970) from her analysis. See Propp, *Morphology of the Folk Tale*; Milne, *Vladimir Propp*.

236. Clark and Holquist, *Mikhail Bakhtin*; Lechte, *Fifty Key Contemporary Thinkers*, 11–18; Wolfreys, *CEMCT*, 168–74.

by Barbara Green and others.[237] Several members of the Russian formalist school fled to central Europe and became associated with the Prague Linguistic Circle, including Roman Jakobson (1896–1982) and Nikolai Trubetzkoy (1890–1938).[238] Their views of form, structure, and opposition, especially in phonetics, but also their thoughts in other areas, such as general theories of communication, had a strong influence upon a number of others outside their immediate sphere. Structuralism soon encompassed a wide range of fields, the most important for our purposes being language study, anthropology, sociology, and literary studies, among others.[239] In language study, most structural linguists had some contact with either Saussure's followers in the Geneva school or, more importantly, the Prague circle, including Bloomfield, with his theory of immediate constituent analysis.[240] Jakobson had a direct influence upon the anthropologist Claude Lévi-Strauss (1908–2009) in the formulation of his structural anthropology (see below). The anthropologist Branislaw Malinowski (1884–1942), who was influenced indirectly by Gunkel through Gardiner (as noted above), developed the notion of situational context and influenced his linguistic colleague J. R. Firth (1890–1960),[241] whose notion of usage in context became fundamental for Michael A. K. Halliday,[242] whose Systemic Functional Linguistics has had a growing influence on New Testament Greek studies. Malinowski also had an influence upon his student, the anthropologist Edmund Leach (1910–89), who popularized Lévi-Strauss for an English audience, and who influenced Mary Douglas (1921–2007), with her work on cultural behavior such as taboos. Franz Boas (1858–1942), early influenced by structuralism, worked in native American languages, and his theories regarding their differences in structure from European languages[243] had an influence upon his student Edward Sapir (1884–1939) and Benjamin Lee Whorf (1897–1941), with their theory of linguistic determinism.[244] After emigrating to North America, René Wellek (1903–95), the literary critic influenced by Mathesius, became one of the leaders of the New Criticism school of thought.

This leads to the second and third topics: narratology and post-structuralism. There were two major developments of structuralism. The first was narratology.[245]

237. Green, *How Are the Mighty Fallen?*; Green, *Mikhail Bakhtin*; Vines, *Problem of Markan Genre*.

238. Thomas, *Fifty Key Thinkers*, 190–95; Lechte, *Fifty Key Contemporary Thinkers*, 94–102. Cf. Wolfreys, *CEMCT*, 114–20.

239. See Robey, *Structuralism*, with separate chapters on structuralism and linguistics (by John Lyons and Jonathan Culler), social anthropology (by Edmund Leach), semiotics (by Umberto Eco), literature (by Tzvetan Todorov), philosophy (by John Mepham), and mathematics (by Robin Gandy). See also Lane, *Introduction to Structuralism*, with essays by many of the leading figures.

240. Thomas, *Fifty Key Thinkers*, 167–73.

241. Ibid., 178–84.

242. Ibid., 238–43.

243. Boas, *Race, Language, and Culture*.

244. Thomas, *Fifty Key Thinkers*, 162–67, 195–200.

245. See Selden, Widdowson, and Brooker, *Reader's Guide*, 66–87; Porter and Robinson,

This was a particular development of French structuralism. Drawing upon the earlier work on the Russian folktale by Propp, figures such as A.-J. Greimas (1917–92) and Tzvetan Todorov attempted to develop structural theories of narrative meaning. They proceeded from a text's smallest to largest (discourse) parts, based upon fundamental structural distinctions, one of those being the difference between surface and deep structure (variously characterized in relation to narrative and event time). For Greimas this analysis consisted of six basic functions (that he called actants). These structuralists have had an influence upon many others, including Mieke Bal and Seymour Chatman, who have had direct influence upon biblical studies. Despite the influence of structuralism upon the wider intellectual world, its influence apart from language studies has been less than one might expect in biblical studies. In Old Testament studies, one of the best known structuralists was Robert Polzin and his work on Job.[246] In New Testament studies, the best known structuralist has been Daniel Patte, who came to structuralism early on in his career (after initial work in the historical-critical method). He reflects the influence of Greimas in his analysis, and has written a number of books both outlining his understanding of structuralism, and exegeting texts along structuralist lines.[247] Despite the prodigious work of Patte, however, structuralism has essentially faded from New Testament studies.

The second development of structuralism is what has come to be known as post-structuralism, and in particular deconstruction.[248] Post-structuralism is an encompassing term describing those who have moved beyond structuralism by rejecting its ontological foundations while still also embracing many of its fundamental assumptions regarding the sign and signification. Roland Barthes (1915–80) captures the movement from structuralist to post-structuralist.[249] Beginning as a social critic, he soon embraced the structuralist linguistic agenda found in such authors as Emil Benveniste (1902–76)[250] and Halliday, resulting in various structuralist taxonomies, such as can be found in his *Elements of Semiology* (1964). Then, in the late 1960s, Barthes came into contact with a number of important thinkers who were questioning the foundations of Western thought, such as Jacques Derrida (1930–2004) and

---

Hermeneutics, 166–67; Wolfreys, *CEMCT*, 265–73. See also Culler, *Structuralist Poetics*.

246. Polzin, *Biblical Structuralism*; also Calloud, *Structural Analysis*; and Detweiler, *Story*.

247. Patte, *What Is Structural Exegesis?*; Patte, *Structural Exegesis*; Patte, *Paul's Faith*; Patte, *Gospel according to Matthew*. See Porter and Robinson, *Hermeneutics*, 167–79.

248. Selden, Widdowson, and Brooker, *Reader's Guide*, 150–99; Williams, *Understanding Post-structuralism*. A number of works have responded (both positively and negatively) to deconstruction. See, in particular, Culler, *On Deconstruction*; Leitch, *Deconstructive Criticism*; Norris, *Deconstruction*; Ellis, *Against Deconstruction*; Johnson, *Wake of Deconstruction*. Cf. Wolfreys, *CEMCT*, 458–65. In biblical studies, see Moore, *Mark and Luke*; and Moore, *Poststructuralism*.

249. See Jackson, *Poverty of Structuralism*, 124–67; Lechte, *Fifty Key Contemporary Thinkers*, 146–55; Wolfreys, *CEMCT*, 257–65.

250. Lechte, *Fifty Key Contemporary Thinkers*, 59–64. Benveniste had a major influence upon a number of subsequent thinkers, including Jacques Lacan, Julia Kristeva (see Lechte, *Fifty Key Contemporary Thinkers*, 395–404), and Barthes, among others.

Jacques Lacan (1901–81), along with others such as Michel Foucault (1926–84) and Louis Althusser (1918–90).[251] Their enquiry led to the severing of the relationship between the sign and the signified. Barthes abandoned structuralism, as is indicated in his work *S/Z*, and took up the interests of other post-structuralists, whose work is characterized in literary circles by the term deconstruction. The emergence of deconstruction is usually marked by Derrida's 1966 lecture, "Structure, Sign, and Play in the Discourse of the Human Sciences," followed by such publications as *Of Grammatology* and *Writing and Difference*.[252] The movement spread, especially to North America.[253] Deconstruction is more than simply a way to approach a text, but is a reaction to the entire Western philosophical tradition. It offers a critique of Western intellectual thought by de-centering its traditional metaphysics, so that Derrida criticizes notions of referentiality of language and objectivity and is anti-foundational in orientation. Instead of there being any kind of transcendental signification, Derrida finds only endless play that connects signs with each other, in which meaning is always variable, deferred, provisional, incomplete, and unstable. The influence of deconstruction, while short-lived in its direct impact, has continued to affect a wide range of subjects, including biblical studies. In the field of Old Testament studies, Clines early not only embraced reader-oriented strategies but recognized the endless play of language in texts, as is evidenced in a number of his works.[254] In New Testament studies, Stephen Moore has followed a similar path to that of Clines by moving from reader-oriented to deconstructive readings.[255]

There have been, however, three further more sweeping movements within both Hebrew and Greek studies over the last approximately one hundred years that are worth consideration. The first is developments in verbal aspect studies. In Hebrew, these studies began with the work of Ewald, who recognized the Hebrew so-called tense-forms as not temporal but indicating *Aktionsarten* or kinds of time, and of S. R. Driver, for whom they reflected relative or subjective views of kind of time or what some have called aspect.[256] Despite a temporal-view backlash,[257] various views of the non-temporal but either aspectual or modal nature of the Hebrew verbal structure have continued to be defined.[258] A similar discussion occurred in Greek studies,

---

251. On some of these thinkers, see Lechte, *Fifty Key Contemporary Thinkers*, 129–37, 102–10, 137–46; Wolfreys, *CEMCT*, 196–205, 312–26.

252. See esp. Derrida's essay "Structure," which appeared in *Writing and Difference*, 278–93.

253. The manifesto of North American deconstruction is the work by Bloom, de Man (1919–83), Derrida, Hartman, and Miller, *Deconstruction and Criticism*. Cf. Wolfreys, *CEMCT*, 472–86.

254. This is traceable in Clines, *On the Way to the Postmodern*.

255. Moore, *Literary Criticism* to Moore, *Mark and Luke*, etc. See Porter and Robinson, *Hermeneutics*, 285–91.

256. S. R. Driver, *Treatise*; O'Neill, *Bible's Authority*, 135–49; McKim, *DMBI*, 387–94.

257. See, e.g., Blake, *Resurvey of Hebrew Tenses*.

258. Major contemporary studies are by Joosten, *Verbal System of Biblical Hebrew*; and John Cook, *Time and the Biblical Hebrew Verb*.

beginning with Georg Curtius (1820–85) and Brugmann, and is reflected in the grammars of especially Blass, Moulton, and Robertson, that Greek tense-forms are used to describe kinds of action (*Aktionsarten*). This further developed into a theory of aspect, in which tense-forms are seen to reflect the authorial choice of conception of an action. K. L. McKay (1922–2009), Porter, and Buist Fanning, among others who have followed, have taken an aspectual approach, and now aspectual studies are some of the most lively in New Testament Greek studies.[259] The second area of major development is in the field of discourse analysis. As with aspectual studies, Hebrew language study led the way. Apart from work undertaken by Bible translators in the Summer Institute of Linguistics (much of which has not made its way into formal biblical studies), in Hebrew Bible studies there have been a number of works on discourse analysis, one of the first being by the linguist and biblical scholar Robert Longacre (1922–2014) on the Joseph Story.[260] In New Testament Greek discourse analysis, there have been a variety of methods employed, with Systemic Functional Linguistic (e.g., Jeffrey T. Reed)[261] and cognitive/functional models (e.g., Stephen H. Levinsohn)[262] appearing to be on the rise. The third area of development is linguistic methods. There is significant variety in methods on display in both Hebrew and Greek studies. In Hebrew, many of the most recent works[263] approach the language with some type of transformational-generative grammar (e.g., Cynthia Miller)[264] or a cognitive approach (e.g., Ellen van Wolde),[265] along with some influences of Continental functionalism.[266] In Greek New Testament studies, by contrast, Chomskyan inspired methods have been relatively few

---

259. McKay, *New Syntax* (but whose work in this direction began in the 1960s); Porter, *Verbal Aspect*; and Fanning, *Verbal Aspect*. In Septuagint studies, see T. Evans, *Verbal Syntax*.

260. Longacre, *Joseph*. Longacre's influence has been significant in Old Testament discourse analysis. Others include Dawson, *Text-Linguistics*; Endo, *Verbal System*; and Heimerdinger, *Topic*.

261. Reed, *Discourse Analysis of Philippians*. See also G. Guthrie, *Structure of Hebrews*, for an eclectic method. A summary is in Porter and Pitts, "New Testament Greek Language," 235–41. A collection of essays by a wide range of practitioners of various types of discourse analysis is Porter and Reed, *Discourse Analysis*.

262. Levinsohn, *Discourse Features* (more explicitly cognitive in the second edition than the first); followed by Runge, *Discourse Grammar*. See Olsson, *Structure and Meaning*, for one of the earliest, following the Continental model.

263. Older works used other methods, such as tagmemics (Andersen, *Hebrew Verbless Clause*). On Kenneth Pike (1912–2000), the originator of tagmemics, see Thomas, *Fifty Key Thinkers*, 211–16.

264. Miller, *Representation of Speech*. This is not the place to comment on the work of the linguist Noam Chomsky, who has developed and inspired a wide range of models that I am lumping together under transformational-generative grammar. See, among many others, Smith, *Chomsky*; Thomas, *Fifty Key Thinkers*, 249–55; Lechte, *Fifty Key Contemporary Thinkers*, 72–80.

265. Wolde, *Reframing Biblical Studies*.

266. See, e.g., van der Merwe, Naudé, and Koetze, *Biblical Hebrew Reference Grammar*, xx, who note that the authors represent different linguistic orientations including that of Chomsky (transformational-generative grammar), Simon Dik (1940–95) (Continental functionalism) and Deirdre Wilson (relevance theory). I make no comment on how this works in practice.

of late,[267] but various types of functional theory, in particular Systemic Functional Linguistics (e.g., Stanley E. Porter, and his followers),[268] along with some types of cognitive and relevance theory (see Levinsohn above), have been more prominent.

One way of summarizing recent developments in language studies of the Bible is to recognize the slow emergence of what might generically be called linguistic criticism. Linguistic criticism offers linguistically informed though not linguistically specific analyses of the languages of the biblical texts. Such criticism appropriates various linguistic approaches and can be applied to anything from small passages to entire biblical books.[269]

THE HUMAN SCIENCES

The fifth and final strand identified here is the field of human science. The importance of the human sciences for the rise of modern critical biblical interpretation has tended to be overlooked in concentrating upon some of the more technical elements involved. However, one of the major, fundamental tenets of the Enlightenment was the importance of the individual human, and so the human sciences had a role to play in the rise and development of modern biblical criticism.

The fields of sociology and anthropology are intertwined enough to warrant their treatment together as the field of social science.[270] The origins of the social sciences are difficult to determine because a number of figures important in philosophy and related fields have had an impact on the field (e.g., August Comte, 1798–1857; John Stuart Mill, 1806–74; Karl Marx, 1818–83), but the field itself, broadly conceived, is usually attributed to such people as Herbert Spencer (1820–1903) the evolutionist,[271] Émile Durkheim (1858–1917) who formulated the major sociological question of the relation of the individual to the group,[272] Max Weber (1864–1920) who established the philosophical and methodological foundations of sociology,[273] and Bronislaw

---

267. See Schmidt, *Hellenistic Greek Grammar*, and a few (surprisingly very few) since. See also Louw, *Semantics*.

268. Porter, *Linguistic Analysis*. Some have referred to this as the "Halliday-Porter school of systemic-functional linguistics" (Jongkind, "Review of *The Greek Article*") or "Stanley Porter school of grammatical analysis" (Sim, "Review of *Verbal Aspect in Synoptic Parallels*," 141).

269. Porter, "Linguistic Criticism."

270. See Raison, *Founding Fathers*, for precedent, as he includes those that would be identified as sociologists and anthropologists. See also Westby, *Growth of Sociological Theory*; and S. Gordon, *History and Philosophy*. Cf. Morgan with Barton, *Biblical Interpretation*, 133–66; Wilson, *Sociological Approaches*. Psychology has had relatively little influence on biblical studies. See Wuellner and Leslie, *Surprising Gospel*.

271. See Goldthorpe, "Herbert Spencer."

272. Durkheim, *Elementary Forms*; see Rex, "Émile Durkheim."

273. Weber, *On Charisma and Institution Building*; Rex, "Max Weber." I note that Weber was dependent upon the lawyer Rudolph Sohm (1841–1917), who wrote on church law, for the notion of charisma, even if the two developed the concept in different ways. I wish to thank my PhD student, Jennifer Frim, for this information.

Malinowski (1884–1942) whose fieldwork helped establish social anthropology as a discipline.[274] They were followed by a number who tested their hypotheses, with the single biggest development probably being the influence of structuralism. This is evidenced in the work of Franz Boas (1858–1942) on race, language, and culture, and Claude Lévi-Strauss (1908–2009) on kinship, mythology, primitivism, and various types of classification,[275] and in their students, such as the two sociologists/anthropologists who have written more on the Bible than probably any others, Edmund Leach (1910–89) and Mary Douglas (1921–2007), to name only two of great significance.[276]

There have been many developments in sociology and anthropology that merit discussion in a wider venue but that cannot be treated here. Besides the continuing influence of structuralism (and post-structuralism in the form of postmodernism), two of these developments stand out for their continuing significance within biblical studies. These are, first, the notion of the social construction of reality, developed by the sociologists Peter Berger and Thomas Luckman. This theory in the sociology of knowledge argues that "reality is socially constructed [from both objective and subjective realia] and . . . the sociology of knowledge must analyze the processes in which this occurs," and that such factors as religion and language, rather than being extraneous to discussion, are central to this construction.[277] This theory falls within the wider field of what has been called "interpretive sociology,"[278] and this orientation characterizes most of the research by biblical social-science scholars (with a few exceptions, such as Marxist interpretation). The second development is the changing notion of ethnography within anthropology. Ethnography, or the concern for description of ethnic groups, has been a constant in cultural anthropology, as evidenced from the early work by, for example, Malinowski, to the present. This field, however, has needed to change in light of the ways race and ethnicity are viewed, the need to consider the diverse locations of various ethnographic groups, and the diverse backgrounds of anthropologists.[279]

One of the major earliest confrontations over the nature of the human can be seen in the conflict between Ferdinand Christian Baur (1792–1860) and the Tübingen school and the English scholar J. B. Lightfoot (1828–89) over the history of the early church.[280] The kind of criticism found in Baur and others of the Tübingen school,

---

274. Malinowski, "Problem of Meaning"; see A. Richards, "Bronislaw Malinowski."

275. Lechte, *Fifty Key Contemporary Thinkers*, 111–20; Wolfreys, *CEMCT*, 235–41.

276. See, e.g., Leach, *Lévi-Strauss*; and Douglas, *In the Wilderness*. See Gordon, "Mary Douglas."

277. Berger and Luckman, *Social Construction of Reality*, 1, and passim.

278. See Poloma, *Contemporary Sociological Theory*, 147–208. See also Ritzer, *Contemporary Sociological Theory*; and Mair, *Introduction*.

279. See Marcus, *Ethnography*, who discusses these changes. Note that ethnography of communication is a sociolinguistic model developed by Hymes, *Foundations in Sociolinguistics*, 3–27.

280. Baird, *History of New Testament Research*, 2:66–73; McKim, *DMBI*, 661–65. Cf. Neill and Wright, *Interpretation*, 306, who call J. B. Lightfoot one of only two "great historians" to be concerned with first-century Christianity (the other being Eduard Meyer, 1855–1930).

besides its philosophical framework, was (or at least claimed to be) heavily dependent upon historical criticism—although what that in fact tended to mean was the influence of German idealism upon conceptualization of early Christian history. Whereas Baur and his followers were skeptical of biblical history, there was a significant backlash within some historical criticism that rejected their minimalist and inevitably temporally protracted reconstructions and argued for a maximalist and compressed reconstruction. The most noteworthy of these proponents was Lightfoot and to some degree F. J. A. Hort (1828–92).[281] Lightfoot directly attacked what had come to be identified as the German perspective on the historical origins of Christianity, rigorously approaching the subject as a historian and not as a theologian (theology being a common and enduring orientation of German New Testament scholarship to this day). I think that it is fair to say that (especially) Lightfoot won the day with his reconstruction of early Christianity by showing that the Apostolic Fathers, in particular 1 Clement, Ignatius, and Polycarp, did not contain the evidence that Baur needed to establish his proposed conflict between Jewish and Pauline Christianity. The nature of Baur and Lightfoot's opposition is complex, but one way of examining it is to see it as a contest between philosophy and human science. Baur approached the problem with his philosophical categories firmly in mind, including his Hegelan dialectic, while Lightfoot approached it on the basis of the evidence regarding the nature of human life reflected in the pertinent documents. He did not believe that the contemporary writings of the second century—which should have evidenced the same features as Baur thought he found in the New Testament documents that he wished to date to the second century—displayed such features. There was no strong evidence of early Catholicism or the like.

Theological liberalism, especially in Germany, did not take serious or corrective note of the work of Lightfoot and those who followed him, although there are some social-scientific similarities in the work of a generation of German historical critics, represented most fully by Adolf Deissmann (1866–1937).[282] Deissmann was concerned with both historical and social implications of his analysis of early Christianity, and it is to him that we in large part owe the characterization of Christianity as a religion of the lower classes. He found this in the authentic Pauline letters, which he characterized as genuine letters as opposed to epistles written by those of the higher (and hence more literate) social classes. The area of Old Testament studies tended to be dominated by the study of comparative Semitics, but one outstanding contribution to the human sciences was by William Robertson Smith (1846–94) and his *Lectures on the Religion of the Semites*.[283] Taking an anthropological approach, Smith dealt with

---

281. Baird, *History of New Testament Research*, 2:60–82.

282. Baird, *History of New Testament Research*, 2:178–84.

283. Rogerson, *Bible and Criticism*, 56–162; McKim, *DMBI*, 925–29. Cf. Harrison, *Introduction to the Old Testament*, 33–34. Note also James G. Frazer (1854–1941), but who is now strongly condemned for his work.

the evolutionary development of ancient Semitic religion. He began with multiplicity and primitiveness and traced its development through sacrificial ritual. This book is thought to have had an influence upon Durkheim.[284]

A number of other biblical scholars also showed interest in human society as part of the wider question of the development of ancient Judaism or early Christianity. Several early trends within biblical studies may be characterized as either sociological or anthropological in nature, even if they are not full-fledged instances of either. Many, if not most, of these attempts follow what might be called social description, as opposed to social theory. Social description is an inductive approach that identifies and describes the social phenomena within a given society or culture, and then draws upon these data to formulate generalized categories to describe the individuals within that culture. Besides those already mentioned above, we can include the following. In historical geography, William Ramsay (1851–1939) began his career as a supporter of Baur but through his archaeological investigations came to view the New Testament accounts in Acts as accurately reflecting the cultural and historical settings of early Christianity.[285] In the area of Jewish social-historical backgrounds, Emil Schürer (1844–1910), beginning in 1874, produced a compendium of research on the history of the Jewish people that is still valuable today (especially after its revision by Geza Vermes, 1924–2013);[286] Robert Henry Charles (1855–1931), besides producing a major commentary on Revelation, edited a number of important Jewish pseudepigrapha (compiling an important early collection) to provide background into the social, cultural, and religious background of the Jewish people, especially in the area of apocalyptic;[287] George Foot Moore (1851–1931) provided descriptions of Judaism in the first century that helped to set the foundation for the New Perspective on Paul (see below);[288] and Joachim Jeremias (1900–79) studied the Jewish historical and social context of early Christianity, especially the parables.[289] In the equivalent work in Hellenistic social-historical backgrounds, Paul Wendland (1864–1915) wrote on Hellenistic and Roman culture, including the importance of Stoicism for setting the stage for early Christianity, Edwin Hatch (1835–89) traced the importance of various Greek ideas upon Christianity, Otto Pfleiderer (1839–1908) developed Baur's views further in terms of religious backgrounds,[290] and Arthur Darby Nock (1901–63) explored the notion of conversion among the ancients, an important early social-scientific study.[291] In some respects, the works mentioned previously culminated in the more recent but

---

284. See Morgan with Barton, *Biblical Interpretation*, 140.
285. Gasque, *Sir William M. Ramsay*; McKim, *DMBI*, 848–53.
286. Baird, *History of New Testament Research*, 2:199–204.
287. Ibid., 2:204–9.
288. Ibid., 2:422–28.
289. Ibid., 3:282–90; McKim, *DMBI*, 560–65.
290. Baird, *History of New Testament Research*, 2:209–20.
291. Ibid., 2:429–33.

more self-conscious attempts at social description found in the work of Edwin A. Judge and then Wayne Meeks. Their investigations were foundational in establishing modern social-scientific research into the New Testament (see below). In his short but useful study, Judge examines the social structure of early Christianity within its Roman context.[292] In his now classic study of the formation of early Christian communities, Meeks draws upon data regarding the composition of Roman society to analyze the composition of the early Pauline church.[293]

It is appropriate here to mention the development of the New Perspective on Paul, at least insofar as it is an exploration of the human sciences (it is not, in the eyes of many). The New Perspective purports to be a re-evaluation of our tradition-laden descriptions of Judaism, less on the basis of traditional Protestant (usually read as Lutheran) theology and more in terms of contemporary Jewish religious thought and culture (even if the treatments make little appeal to sociological or anthropological theory, so far as I can tell). In that sense, the New Perspective has a sociological and anthropological dimension as a rethinking of how the Jewish people of the first century thought of themselves (as various Judaisms or as part of a larger entity now called common Judaism) and how they thought of themselves in relationship to God (saved not by works but by means of a relationship grounded in covenantal nomism, in which they were bound to God by covenant and responded in obedience). Besides the work of Moore mentioned above, two other precursors of this movement are W. D. Davies (1911–2001), who offered a re-evaluation of Paul and Rabbinic Judaism in what were characterized as more authentically Jewish terms,[294] and Krister Stendahl (1921–2008), who doubted the individualistic elements of Pauline theology as reflected in Reformation and subsequent thought.[295] The major figure in development of the New Perspective, however, is E. P. Sanders.[296] He is the one who conceived of the term "covenantal nomism" and fomented the re-evaluation of the various views of how Paul conceived of and related to Judaism, and what constituted Jewish belief structure.[297] Whether Sanders and others would see this as an exploration within the human sciences, as opposed to theology, is another question.

The first group of scholars that can be seen as a cohesive school that was aware of developments in the human sciences is the Chicago School, focused upon the

---

292. Judge, *Social Pattern*.

293. Meeks, *First Urban Christians*. There have been a variety of responses to Meeks. See Still and Horrell, *After the First Urban Christians*, for a collaborative discussion and evaluation.

294. Baird, *History of New Testament Research*, 3:293–99; McKim, *DMBI*, 350–55.

295. Stendahl, "Apostle Paul."

296. Sanders, *Paul and Palestinian Judaism*.

297. Baird, *History of New Testament Research*, 3:299–310; Neill and Wright, *Interpretation*, 424–39. Others important in the development are Heikki Räisänen and James D. G. Dunn. See Baird, *History of New Testament Research*, 3:548–68. There are many who have followed this school of thought. There are also many who have responded to it. One of the most effective respondents is Westerholm, *Perspectives Old and New*.

University of Chicago Divinity School.[298] The University of Chicago was founded in 1892 with the generous help of John D. Rockefeller, and from the outset benefited from its being a Baptist institution with a theologically-oriented purpose. Its first president was William Rainey Harper (1856–1906), who set the tone for the developing "school."[299] However, there is no doubt that its interests were socio-historical in orientation, with some calling the period from 1906 to 1966 "The Era of Socio-Historical Method." There are several characteristics of the Chicago School: its socio-historical orientation to the study of religion and in particular Christianity, its attention to method, and its being distinctly American rather than European in approach (though three of its four major faculty members studied in Europe, the exception being Case). There were four major members of the school. These were: Ernest De Witt Burton (1856–1925), the founder of the school;[300] Shailer Mathews (1863–1941), the intellectual leader of the school who published on the social teaching of Jesus, taking what amounted to a functional approach to sociology; Shirley Jackson Case (1872–1947), who advocated what might be called an interpretive view of social history; and Edgar Johnson Goodspeed (1871–1962), whose socio-historical orientation emerged in his reconstructions in a number of books of the early history of the Pauline letters.[301]

Although from the early twentieth century onward there continued to be biblical research influenced by sociology and anthropology, a few significant figures in its more recent emergence as social theory merit mention. In Old Testament studies, there are two figures to note.[302] The first is the Sheffield professor John Rogerson. One of the results of the rise of the Biblical Theology movement, as already noted above, was promotion of a form of anthropology regarding Hebrew psychology. Scholars such as H. Wheeler Robinson (1872–1945) (in particular but not uniquely) argued for a primitive Hebrew psychology of corporate personality that did not differentiate or recognize the individual, what he called a "psychic unity."[303] This view contributed to the position that there was a major distinction between the Hebrew and Greek

---

298. See Baird, *History of New Testament Research*, 2:305–6; Rylaarsdam, "Introduction"; Harrisville, *Pandora's Box Opened*, 198–204 (and who describes other schools of study of the Bible at Harvard, Yale, Union, and Princeton, 204–51). This is not to be confused with the Chicago School of sociology—which arose and had its heyday about the same time as the Chicago School of biblical studies with its socio-historical orientation. The major sociological figure was George Herbert Mead (1863–1931) and his symbolic interactionism. See Ritzer, *Contemporary Sociological Theory*, 55–61, 65–67. I cannot find any direct correlations, but there may well have been some.

299. See Wind, *Bible and the University*; McKim, *DMBI*, 504–10.

300. McKim, *DMBI*, 267–71.

301. Baird, *History of New Testament Research*, 2:306–30. Cf. Rylaarsdam, "Introduction"; J. I. Cook, *Edgar Johnson Goodspeed*; McKim, *DMBI*, 469–73.

302. Others have cited the examples of Johannes Pedersen (1883–1977), *Israel*, and Roland de Vaux (1903–71), *Ancient Israel*. These are possible predecessors. However, Pedersen seems to be susceptible to some of the faults of the Biblical Theology movement, and de Vaux has not had continuing impact. See Morgan with Barton, *Biblical Interpretation*, 141.

303. H. W. Robinson, *Christian Doctrine of Man*; McKim, *DMBI*, 870–74.

mindset (which has had a tendency to be perpetuated in biblical studies). In an important article, Rogerson went beyond simply defining and then refuting this particular hypothesis of corporate personality, and presented an anthropological approach appropriate for Old Testament studies. He further warned about the use and misuse of cultural comparisons and identification of what are sometimes called primitive societies.[304] A second figure in Old Testament studies is Norman K. Gottwald on *The Tribes of Yahweh*. He characterizes this work as "A Sociology of the Religion of Liberated Israel." In light of what Gottwald identifies as a hesitation to see ancient Israel as a "social totality," he attempts to provide such a sociological analysis.[305] He draws upon a number of the leading figures in social-scientific study, such as Durkheim, Weber, and Marx, as well as a number of different models including what he calls "structural-functional" and "historical-dialectical" models (both structuralist in nature).[306] The result is a detailed, comprehensive, social-scientifically grounded study of the emergence of Israel. There have been other studies since then that have continued in this vein.[307] There are clear relationships between some of Gottwald's social theories and various ideological criticisms noted above.

In New Testament studies, there have been a number of major practitioners of various social-scientific approaches.[308] In the field of sociology, John Gager wrote one of the first full-fledged sociological treatments of the New Testament.[309] In his *Kingdom and Community* he analyzes Christianity in relation to a number of theoretical categories from the social sciences. These include the nature of Christianity as a millennial movement, its quest for legitimacy as a charismatic movement, Christianity within the Roman social order, and Christianity's various competitors as a developing religion. Gager shows that he is aware of many of the major social-scientific thinkers, including Berger, Douglas, Lévi-Strauss, and Weber. In the field of anthropology, Bruce Malina has been one of the major advocates for a cultural anthropological approach to the New Testament. Malina wrote an important introduction to cultural anthropology for New Testament study, in which he treats many of the standard topics in anthropology: honor and shame, the dyadic personality, kinship, and purity.[310] Many of the topics discussed by these two liminal works continue to appear in more recent social-scientific studies.[311]

---

304. Rogerson, "Hebrew Conception."

305. Gottwald, *Tribes of Yahweh*, 5.

306. Ibid., 21.

307. See the essays in Lang, *Anthropological Approaches*; and Chalcraft, *Social-Scientific Old Testament Criticism*, for representative examples.

308. See Holmberg, *Sociology*, esp. 1–20.

309. Gager, *Kingdom and Community*. See also Holmberg, *Paul and Power*.

310. Malina, *New Testament World*.

311. See, e.g., Theissen, *Social Setting*; Theissen, *Social Reality*; J. Elliott, *Home for the Homeless*; and Esler, *First Christians in their Social Context*; among others who have followed.

The area of social-scientific criticism of the Bible is still in its relative infancy, at least so far as method is concerned. There is plenty of scope for biblical scholars to explore various areas, especially as they relate to ideological/cultural criticism mentioned above, as those areas share some important figures in common.

CONCLUSION

Not much more needs to be said in conclusion of this essay, except to summarize some of the major issues that now confront biblical studies. I select three. The first is that the field of biblical studies is an incredibly complex one. I realize the shortcomings of my own knowledge in the attempt to tie many of the different strands together. However, any attempt to do so belies the complex nature of biblical studies, in which various schools of thought or areas of interest and research are linked in a variety of conscious and unconscious ways to other areas of biblical studies. I have attempted to chronicle some of those relations, but I acknowledge that there are many more that I have missed and that must also be recognized and taken into account. The second conclusion is that knowledge of the history of biblical criticism makes clear that the traditional historical-critical method (however that might be defined, but usually with reference to source, form, and redaction criticism) has a complex and intertwined history of its own in relation to the wider field of biblical interpretation. Historical criticism did not emerge without precedents, it did not and does not exist in isolation and without connection to other types of criticism, and it will not continue to exist without such connections. In fact, historical criticism, although it has been important in the history of biblical criticism, encompasses a variety of criticisms that cohere for a variety of historical, cultural, and related reasons at a particular point or at particular points in time. In all probability, because there was a time when historical criticism did not exist, there is also a time when it will no longer exist, at least as we have come to understand it and as some continue to practice it. The third and final conclusion to draw from this survey is that the field of biblical studies is not only a complex and intertwined one, but it deserves its place within the wider field of human interpretation, whatever kind of interpretation we are speaking of. In some instances, forms of biblical criticism are clearly derivative of other criticisms not developed for biblical studies, but in other instances there are types of biblical criticism that have acted as mediators and translators, or even as instigators, of other interpretive methods across what sometimes appear to be huge divides. This is not to say that biblical scholars have always been at the forefront of interpretive models—in many respects they have not. However, the entire field of interpretation is a complex dialogue among multiple and diverse voices, and biblical scholars have been, continue to be, and need to be full participants in this continuing discussion and interpretive development.

BIBLIOGRAPHY

Agamben, Giorgio. *The Time that Remains: A Commentary on the Letter to the Romans*. Translated by Patricia Dailey. Stanford: Stanford University Press, 2005.

Allison, Dale C., Jr. *Constructing Jesus: Memory, Imagination, and History*. Grand Rapids: Baker, 2010.

Alter, Robert. *The Art of Biblical Narrative*. London: George Allen & Unwin, 1981.

———. *The Art of Biblical Poetry*. (1985). Rev. ed. New York: Basic, 2011.

Alter Robert, and Frank Kermode, eds. *The Literary Guide to the Bible*. London: Collins, 1987.

Andersen, Francis. *The Hebrew Verbless Clause in the Pentateuch*. Nashville: Abingdon, 1970.

Archer, Gleason L., Jr. *A Survey of Old Testament Introduction*. Rev. ed. Chicago: Moody, 1974.

Auerbach, Erich. *Mimesis: The Representation of Reality in the Western Literary Tradition*. Translated by Willard R. Trask. Princeton: Princeton University Press, 1953.

Aune, David E. *The New Testament in Its Literary Environment*. Philadelphia: Westminster, 1987.

Austin, J. L. *How to Do Things with Words*, edited by J. O. Urmson and Marina Sbisà. (1962). 2nd ed. Oxford: Oxford University Press, 1975.

Ayer, A. J., ed. *Logical Positivism*. New York: Free Press, 1959.

Baird, J. Arthur. *Audience Criticism and the Historical Jesus*. Philadelphia: Westminster, 1969.

Baird, William. *History of New Testament Research*. 3 vols. Minneapolis: Fortress, 1993–2013.

Baker, David W. "Israelite Prophets and Prophecy." In *The Face of Old Testament Studies: A Survey of Contemporary Approaches*, edited by David W. Baker and Bill T. Arnold, 266–94. Grand Rapids: Baker, 1999.

Bar-Efrat, Shimon. *Narrative Art in the Bible*. Sheffield: Almond, 1989.

Barr, James. *Biblical Words for Time*. Rev. ed. London: SCM Press, 1969.

———. *The Concept of Biblical Theology: An Old Testament Perspective*. Minneapolis: Fortress, 1999.

———. *The Semantics of Biblical Language*. Oxford: Oxford University Press, 1961.

Barrett, William. *Irrational Man: A Study in Existential Philosophy*. Garden City, NY: Doubleday, 1958.

Barsky, Robert F. *Zellig Harris: From American Linguistics to Socialist Zionism*. Cambridge, MA: MIT Press, 2011.

Barthes, Roland. *Elements of Semiology*. Translated by Anette Lavers and Colin Smith. London: Jonathan Cape, 1967.

———. *S/Z*. Translated by Richard Miller. New York: Hill & Wang, 1974.

Bauckham, Richard J. *Jesus and the Eyewitnesses: The Gospels as Eyewitness Testimony*. Grand Rapids: Eerdmans, 2006.

———. *Jesus and the God of Israel*. Grand Rapids: Eerdmans, 2008.

Baur, Ferdinand Christian. *The Church History of the First Three Centuries*. Translated by Allan Menzies. 2 vols. London: Williams & Norgate, 1873–75.

———. *Paul the Apostle of Jesus Christ: His Life and Works, His Epistles and Teachings: A Contribution to a Critical History of Primitive Christianity*. Translated by Allan Menzies. 2 vols. London: Williams & Norgate, 1873–75. Reprint, Peabody, MA: Hendrickson, 2003.

Beardslee, William A. *Literary Criticism of the New Testament*. Philadelphia: Fortress, 1970.

Beavis, Mary Ann. *Mark's Audience: The Literary and Social Setting of Mark 4.11–12.* Sheffield: Sheffield Academic, 1989.

Bebbington, D. W. *Patterns in History: A Christian View.* Downers Grove, IL: InterVarsity, 1979.

Berger, Peter L., and Thomas Luckmann. *The Social Construction of Reality: A Treatise in the Sociology of Knowledge.* Garden City, NY: Doubleday, 1966.

Berlin, Adele. *The Dynamics of Biblical Parallelism.* (1985). Rev. ed. Grand Rapids: Eerdmans, 2008.

———. *Poetics and Interpretation of Biblical Narrative.* Sheffield: Almond, 1983.

Betz, Hans Dieter. *Galatians.* Hermeneia. Philadelphia: Fortress, 1979.

Blake, Frank R. *A Resurvey of Hebrew Tenses.* Rome: Pontifical Biblical Institute, 1951.

Bloom, Harold, Paul de Man, Jacques Derrida, Geoffrey Hartman, and J. Hillis Miller. *Deconstruction and Criticism.* New York: Continuum, 1979.

Boas, Franz. *Race, Language, and Culture.* Chicago: University of Chicago Press, 1940.

Boers, Hendrikus. *What Is New Testament Theology? The Rise of Criticism and the Problem of a Theology of the New Testament.* Philadelphia: Fortress, 1979.

Bray, Gerald. *Biblical Interpretation: Past and Present.* Downers Grove, IL: InterVarsity, 1996.

Bremond, Claude, Joshua Landy, and Thomas Pavel, eds. *Thematics: New Approaches.* Albany: SUNY Press, 1995.

Brooks, Cleanth. *The Well Wrought Urn: Studies in the Structure of Poetry.* San Diego: Harcourt Brace Jovanovich, 1947.

Buss, Martin J. *Biblical Form Criticism in Its Context.* Sheffield: Sheffield Academic, 1999.

———. *The Changing Shape of Form Criticism: A Relational Approach.* Sheffield: Sheffield Phoenix, 2010.

———. *The Concept of Form in the Twentieth Century.* Sheffield: Sheffield Phoenix, 2008.

Calloud, Jean. *Structural Analysis of Narrative.* Translated by Daniel Patte. Philadelphia: Fortress, 1976.

Campbell, Antony F. "The Emergence of the Form-critical and Traditio-historical Approaches." In *Hebrew Bible / Old Testament: The History of Its Interpretation.* Vol. 3, *From Modernism to Post-Modernism (The Nineteenth and Twentieth Centuries). Part 2: The Twentieth Century—From Modernism to Post-Modernism*, edited by Magne Saebø, with Peter Machinist and Jean Louis Ska, 125–49. Göttingen: Vandenhoeck & Ruprecht, 2015.

Cassirer, Ernst. *The Philosophy of the Enlightenment.* Translated by Fritz C. A. Koelln and James P. Pettegrove. Princeton: Princeton University Press, 1951.

Castle, Gregory. *The Blackwell Guide to Literary Theory.* Oxford: Blackwell, 2007.

Castelli, Elizabeth A., Stephen D. Moore, Gary A. Phillips, and Regina M. Schwartz, eds. *The Postmodern Bible.* New Haven: Yale University Press, 1995.

Chalcraft, David J., ed. *Social-Scientific Old Testament Criticism: A Sheffield Reader.* Sheffield: Sheffield Academic, 1997.

Chatman, Seymour. *Story and Discourse: Narrative Structure in Fiction and Film.* Ithaca, NY: Cornell University Press, 1978.

Childs, Brevard S. *Biblical Theology in Crisis.* Philadelphia: Westminster, 1970.

———. *Biblical Theology of the Old and New Testaments: Theological Reflections on the Christian Bible.* Minneapolis: Fortress, 1992.

———. *Introduction to the Old Testament as Scripture.* Philadelphia: Fortress, 1979.

———. *The New Testament as Canon: An Introduction.* Valley Forge, PA: Trinity International, 1994.

Christian, C. W. *Friedrich Schleiermacher.* Waco, TX: Word, 1979.

Clark, Katerina, and Michael Holquist. *Mikhail Bakhtin.* Cambridge, MA: Belknap, 1984.

Clements, Keith. *Friedrich Schleiermacher: Pioneer of Modern Theology.* London: Collins, 1987.

Clines, David J. A. *The Bible and the Modern World.* Sheffield: Sheffield Academic, 1997.

———. "Contemporary Methods in Hebrew Bible Criticism." In *Hebrew Bible / Old Testament: The History of Its Interpretation.* Vol. 3, *From Modernism to Post-Modernism (The Nineteenth and Twentieth Centuries). Part 2: The Twentieth Century—From Modernism to Post-Modernism*, edited by Magne Sæbø, with Peter Machinist and Jean Louis Ska, 148–69. Göttingen: Vandenhoeck & Ruprecht, 2015.

———. *The Dictionary of Classical Hebrew.* 9 vols. Sheffield: Sheffield Phoenix, 1993–2016.

———. *I, He, We, and They: A Literary Approach to Isaiah 53.* Sheffield: JSOT Press, 1976.

———. *On the Way to the Postmodern: Old Testament Essays, 1967–1998.* 2 vols. Sheffield: Sheffield Academic, 1998.

———. *The Theme of the Pentateuch.* Sheffield: Sheffield Academic, 1978.

———. *What Does Eve Do to Help? And Other Readerly Questions to the Old Testament.* Sheffield: Sheffield Academic, 1990.

Coats, George W., ed. *Saga, Legend, Tale, Novella, Fable: Narrative Forms in Old Testament Literature.* JSOTSup 35. Sheffield: JSOT Press, 1985.

Collins, Adela Yarbro, ed. *Feminist Perspectives on Biblical Scholarship.* Chico, CA: Scholars, 1985.

Cook, James I. *Edgar Johnson Goodspeed: Articulate Scholar.* Atlanta: Scholars, 1981.

Cook, John A. *Time and the Biblical Hebrew Verb: The Expression of Tense, Aspect, and Modality in Biblical Hebrew.* Winona Lake, IN: Eisenbrauns, 2012.

Copleston, Frederick. *A History of Philosophy.* 9 vols. Garden City, NY: Image, 1946–67. Reprint, 1985.

Court, John M. *A Generation of New Testament Scholarship: British Scholars of the 1920s and 1930s.* Blandford Forum, UK: Deo, 2012.

Crossan, John Dominic. *A Fragile Craft: The Work of Amos Niven Wilder.* Atlanta: Scholars, 1981.

Culler, Jonathan. *Structuralist Poetics: Structuralism, Linguistics and the Study of Literature.* Ithaca, NY: Cornell University Press, 1975.

———. *On Deconstruction: Theory and Criticism after Structuralism.* Ithaca, NY: Cornell University Press, 1982.

Culpepper. R. Alan. *Anatomy of the Fourth Gospel: A Study in Literary Design.* Philadelphia: Fortress, 1983.

Cunningham, Valentine. *Reading after Theory.* Oxford: Blackwell, 2002.

Davies, Ioan. *Cultural Studies and Beyond: Fragments of Empire.* London: Routledge, 1995.

Dawson, David Allan. *Text-Linguistics and Biblical Hebrew.* Sheffield: JSOT Press, 1994.

De Vaux, Roland. *Ancient Israel: Its Life and Institutions.* Translated by John McHugh. New York: McGraw-Hill, 1961.

Derrida, Jacques. *Of Grammatology.* Translated by Gayatri Chakravorty Spivak. Baltimore: Johns Hopkins University Press, 1976.

———. *Writing and Difference.* Translated by Alan Bass. Chicago: University of Chicago Press, 1978.

Detweiler, Robert. *Story, Sign, and Self: Phenomenology and Structuralism as Literary-Critical Methods*. Philadelphia: Fortress; Missoula, MT: Scholars, 1978.

Dillistone, F. W. *C. H. Dodd: Interpreter of the New Testament*. London: Hodder & Stoughton, 1977.

Donovan, Josephine, ed. *Feminist Literary Criticism: Explorations in Theory*. 2nd ed. Lexington: University Press of Kentucky, 1989.

Doty, William G. *Letters in Primitive Christianity*. Philadelphia: Fortress, 1973.

Douglas, Mary. *In the Wilderness: The Doctrine of Defilement in the Book of Numbers*. Sheffield: Sheffield Academic, 1993.

Driver, Daniel R. *Brevard Childs, Biblical Theologian: For the Church's One Bible*. Reprint, Grand Rapids: Baker, 2012.

Driver, S. R. *An Introduction to the Literature of the Old Testament*. New York: Scribner, 1910.

———. *A Treatise on the Use of the Tenses in Hebrew and Some Other Syntactical Questions*. (1874). Reprint, Grand Rapids: Eerdmans, 1998.

Durkheim, Émile. *The Elementary Forms of the Religious Life*. Translated by Joseph Ward Swain. London: George Allen & Unwin, 1915.

Eagleton, Terry. *After Theory*. London: Allen Lane, 2003.

———. *Literary Theory: An Introduction*. Minneapolis: University of Minnesota Press, 1983.

Eliot, T. S. "Tradition and the Individual Talent." (1932). In *Selected Essays*, 13–22. 3rd ed. London: Faber & Faber, 1941.

Elliott, John H. *A Home for the Homeless: A Social-Scientific Criticism of I Peter, Its Situation and Strategy*. Minneapolis: Fortress, 1981.

Elliott, Scott S. *Reconfiguring Mark's Jesus: Narrative Criticism after Poststructuralism*. Sheffield: Sheffield Phoenix, 2011.

Ellis, John M. *Against Deconstruction*. Princeton: Princeton University Press, 1989.

Endo, Yoshinobu. *The Verbal System of Classical Hebrew in the Joseph Story: An Approach from Discourse Analysis*. Assen: Van Gorcum, 1996.

Essays and Reviews. London: Longman, Green, Longman, and Roberts, 1860.

Esler, Philip F. *The First Christians in their Social Worlds: Social-Scientific Approaches to New Testament Interpretation*. London: Routledge, 1994.

Evans, Robert. *Reception History, Tradition and Biblical Interpretation: Gadamer and Jauss in Current Practice*. London: Bloomsbury, 2014.

Evans, T. V. *Verbal Syntax in the Greek Pentateuch: Natural Greek Usage and Hebrew Interference*. Oxford: Oxford University Press, 2001.

Exum, J. Cheryl, and David J. A. Clines, eds. *The New Literary Criticism and the Hebrew Bible*. Sheffield: Sheffield Academic, 1993.

Fanning, Buist. *Verbal Aspect in New Testament Greek*. Oxford: Clarendon, 1990.

Fish, Stanley. *Is There a Text in This Class? The Authority of Interpretive Communities*. Cambridge, MA: Harvard University Press, 1980.

Fokkelman, J. P. *Reading Biblical Narrative: An Introductory Guide*. Translated by Ineke Smit. Louisville, KY: Westminster John Knox, 1990.

Foss, Sonja K. *Rhetorical Criticism: Exploration and Practice*. 3rd ed. Prospect Heights, IL: Waveland, 2004.

Fowl, Stephen E. *Theological Interpretation of Scripture*. Eugene, OR: Cascade, 2009.

Fowler, Robert M. *Let the Reader Understand: Reader-Response Criticism and the Gospel of Mark*. Minneapolis: Fortress, 1991.

———. *Loaves and Fishes: The Function of the Feeding Stories in the Gospel of Mark*. Chico, CA: Scholars, 1981.
Frow, John. *Genre*. London: Routledge, 2006.
Gager, John G. *Kingdom and Community: The Social Worlds of Early Christianity*. Englewood Cliffs, NJ: Prentice-Hall, 1975.
Gasque, W. Ward. *Sir William M. Ramsay: Archaeologist and New Testament Scholar*. Grand Rapids: Baker, 1966.
Gibson, Arthur. *Biblical Semantic Logic: A Preliminary Analysis*. Oxford: Blackwell, 1981.
Gieschen, Charles A. *Angelomorphic Christology: Antecedents and Early Evidence*. Leiden: Brill, 1998.
Giltner, John H. *Moses Stuart: The Father of Biblical Science in America*. Atlanta: Scholars, 1988.
Goldthorpe, John H. "Herbert Spencer." In *The Founding Fathers of Social Science*, edited by Timothy Raison, 76–84. Harmondsworth: Penguin, 1969.
Gordon, Cyrus H. *The Pennsylvania Tradition of Semitics: A Century of Near Eastern and Biblical Studies at the University of Pennsylvania*. Atlanta: Scholars, 1986.
Gordon, J. Dorcas. "Douglas, Mary (1921–2007)." In *Handbook of Women Biblical Interpreters*, edited by Marion Ann Taylor, 171–73. Grand Rapids: Baker, 2012.
Gordon, Scott. *The History and Philosophy of Social Science*. London: Routledge, 1991.
Gottwald, Norman K. *The Tribes of Yahweh: A Sociology of the Religion of Liberated Israel, 1250–1050 B.C.E.* Maryknoll, NY: Orbis, 1979.
Grant, Robert M., with David Tracy. *A Short History of the Interpretation of the Bible*. 2nd ed. London: SCM, 1984.
Grass, Tim. *F. F. Bruce: A Life*. Grand Rapids: Eerdmans, 2011.
Green, Barbara. *How Are the Mighty Fallen? A Dialogical Study of King Saul in 1 Samuel*. London: Sheffield Academic, 2003.
———. *Mikhail Bakhtin and Biblical Scholarship: An Introduction*. Atlanta: SBL, 2000.
Gros Louis, Kenneth R. R., with James S. Ackerman and Thayer S. Warshaw, eds. *Literary Interpretations of Biblical Narratives*. Vol. 1. Nashville: Abingdon, 1974.
Gros Louis, Kenneth R. R., with James S. Ackerman, eds. *Literary Interpretations of Biblical Narratives*. Vol. 2. Nashville: Abingdon, 1982.
Guignon, Charles B. "Existentialism." In *The Shorter Routledge Encyclopedia of Philosophy*, edited by Edward Craig, 252–61. London: Routledge, 2005.
Gunkel, Hermann. *What Remains of the Old Testament and Other Essays*. London: Allen & Unwin, 1928.
Gunn, David M. *The Story of King David: Genre and Interpretation*. Sheffield: JSOT Press, 1978.
Guthrie, Donald. *New Testament Introduction*. Rev. ed. Downers Grove, IL: InterVarsity, 1990.
Guthrie, George H. *The Structure of Hebrews: A Text-Linguistic Analysis*. Leiden: Brill, 1994.
Habel, Norman C. *Literary Criticism of the Old Testament*. Philadelphia: Fortress, 1791.
Haenchen, Ernst. *The Acts of the Apostles: A Commentary*. Translated by Bernard Noble and Gerald Shinn. Philadelphia: Westminster, 1971.
Hahn, Scott W., and Benjamin Wiker. *Politicizing the Bible: The Roots of Historical Criticism and the Secularization of Scripture*. New York: Crossroad, 2013.
Hammann, Konrad. *Rudolf Bultmann: A Biography*. Translated by Philip E. Devenish. Salem, OR: Polebridge, 2013.

Harink, Douglas, ed. *Paul, Philosophy, and the Theopolitical Vision: Critical Engagements with Agamben, Badiou, Žižek, and Others.* Eugene, OR: Cascade, 2010.

Harris, Horton. *David Friedrich Strauss and His Theology.* Cambridge: Cambridge University Press, 1973.

———. *The Tübingen School: A Historical and Theological Investigation of the School of F. C. Baur.* Cambridge: Cambridge University Press. (1975). Reprint, Grand Rapids: Baker, 1990.

Harrison, Ronald Kenneth. *Introduction to the Old Testament.* Grand Rapids: Eerdmans, 1969.

Harrisville, Roy A. *Pandora's Box Opened: An Examination and Defense of Historical-Critical Method and Its Master Practitioners.* Grand Rapids: Eerdmans, 2014.

Harrisville, Roy A., and Walter Sundberg. *The Bible in Modern Culture: Baruch Spinoza to Brevard Childs.* 2nd ed. Grand Rapids: Eerdmans, 2002.

Hasel, Gerhard. *New Testament Theology: Basic Issues in the Current Debate.* Grand Rapids: Eerdmans, 1978.

———. *Old Testament Theology: Basic Issues in the Current Debate.* 3rd ed. Grand Rapids: Eerdmans, 1982.

Hegel, Georg Wilhelm Friedrich. *The Phenomenology of Mind.* Translated by J. B. Baillie. 2nd ed. New York: Macmillan, 1931.

Heimerdinger, Jean-Marc. *Topic, Focus and Foreground in Ancient Hebrew Narratives.* Sheffield: Sheffield Academic, 1999.

Hens-Piazza, Gina. *The New Historicism.* Minneapolis: Fortress, 2002.

Hill, David. *Greek Words and Hebrew Meanings: Studies in the Semantics of Soteriological Terms.* Cambridge: Cambridge University Press, 1967.

Hirsch, E. D., Jr. *Validity in Interpretation.* New Haven: Yale University Press, 1967.

Holmberg, Bengt. *Paul and Power: The Structure of Authority in the Primitive Church as Reflected in the Pauline Epistles.* Philadelphia: Fortress, 1978.

———. *Sociology and the New Testament: An Appraisal.* Minneapolis: Fortress, 1990.

Holub, Robert C. *Reception Theory: A Critical Introduction.* London: Routledge, 1984.

Hordern, William E. *A Layman's Guide to Protestant Theology.* Rev. ed. New York: Macmillan, 1968.

Horrell, David G., Cherryl Hunt, Christopher Southgate, and Francesca Stavrakopoulou, eds. *Ecological Hermeneutics: Biblical, Historical and Theological Perspectives.* London: T. & T. Clark, 2010.

Hurtado, Larry W. *Lord Jesus Christ: Devotion to Jesus in Earliest Christianity.* Grand Rapids: Eerdmans, 2003.

Hymes, Dell. *Foundations in Sociolinguistics: An Ethnographic Approach.* Philadelphia: University of Pennsylvania Press, 1974.

Iser, Wolfgang. *The Implied Reader: Patterns of Communication in Prose Fiction from Bunyan to Beckett.* Baltimore: Johns Hopkins University Press, 1974.

Jackson, Leonard. *The Poverty of Structuralism: Literature and Structuralist Theory.* London: Longman, 1991.

James, Eric. *A Life of Bishop John A. T. Robinson: Scholar, Pastor, Prophet.* Grand Rapids: Eerdmans, 1987.

Jameson, Fredric. *The Prison-House of Language: A Critical Account of Structuralism and Russian Formalism.* Princeton: Princeton University Press, 1972.

Jankowsky, Kurt R. *The Neogrammarians: A Re-evaluation of Their Place in the Development of Linguistic Science*. The Hague: Mouton, 1972.

Jauss, Hans Robert. *Toward an Aesthetic of Reception*. Translated by Timothy Bahti. Brighton: Harvester, 1982.

Jefferson, Ann. "Russian Formalism." In *Modern Literary Theory: A Comparative Introduction*, edited by Ann Jefferson and David Robey, 24–45. 2nd ed. London: Batsford, 1986.

Jobes, Karen H., and Moisés Silva. *Invitation to the Septuagint*. 2nd ed. Grand Rapids: Baker, 2015.

Johnson, Barbara. *The Wake of Deconstruction*. Oxford: Blackwell, 1994.

Jones, W. T. *A History of Western Philosophy*. 5 vols. New York: Harcourt Brace Jovanovich, 1969–75.

Jongkind, Dirk. "Review of *The Greek Article* . . ." *Journal for the Study of the New Testament Booklist* 37 no. 5 (2015) 122.

Joosten, Jan. *The Verbal System of Biblical Hebrew: A New Synthesis Elaborated on the Basis of Classical Prose*. Jerusalem: Simor, 2013.

Joüon, Paul. *A Grammar of Biblical Hebrew*. 2 vols. Translated and revised by T. Muraoka. Rome: Pontifical Biblical Institute, 1991.

Judge, Edwin A. *The Social Pattern of Early Christian Groups in the First Century: Some Prolegomena to the Study of the New Testament Ideas of Social Obligation*. London: Tyndale, 1960.

Kautzsch, E. *Gesenius' Hebrew Grammar*. 2nd ed., edited by A. E. Cowley. Oxford: Clarendon, 1910.

Kennedy, George A. *New Testament Interpretation through Rhetorical Criticism*. Chapel Hill: University of North Carolina Press, 1984.

Kingsbury, Jack Dean. *Matthew as Story*. 2nd ed. Philadelphia: Fortress, 1988.

Kittel, Gerhard, and Gerhard Friedrich, eds. *Theological Dictionary of the New Testament*. Translated by Geoffrey W. Bromiley. 10 vols. Grand Rapids: Eerdmans, 1964–76.

Klemke, E. D., ed. *Contemporary Analytic and Linguistic Philosophies*. Buffalo: Prometheus, 1983.

Knierim, Rolf. "Criticism of Literary Features, Form, Tradition, and Redaction." In *The Hebrew Bible and Its Modern Interpreters*, edited by Douglas A. Knight and Gene M. Tucker, 123–65. Philadelphia: Fortress; Chico, CA: Scholars, 1985.

Knight, Douglas A., and Gene M. Tucker, eds. *The Hebrew Bible and Its Modern Interpreters*. Philadelphia: Fortress; Chico, CA: Scholars, 1985.

Krentz, Edgar. *The Historical-Critical Method*. Philadelphia: Fortress, 1975.

Kugel, James L. *The Idea of Biblical Poetry: Parallelism and Its History*. New Haven: Yale University Press, 1981.

Kuhn, Thomas. *The Structure of Scientific Revolutions*. 2nd ed. Chicago: University of Chicago Press, 1970.

Kümmel, Werner Georg. *The New Testament: The History of the Investigation of Its Problems*. Translated by S. MacLean Gilmour and Howard Clark Kee. Nashville: Abingdon, 1970.

Lane, Michael, ed. *Introduction to Structuralism*. New York: Basic, 1970.

Lang, Bernhard, ed. *Anthropological Approaches to the Old Testament*. London: SPCK; Philadelphia: Fortress, 1985.

Leach, Edmund. *Lévi-Strauss*. London: Fontana, 1970.

Lechte, John. *Fifty Key Contemporary Thinkers: From Structuralism to Post-Humanism*. 2nd ed. London: Routledge, 2008.

Lee, John A. L. *A History of New Testament Lexicography*. New York: Peter Lang, 2003.
Leitch, Vincent B. *Cultural Criticism, Literary Theory, Poststructuralism*. New York: Columbia University Press, 1992.
———. *Deconstructive Criticism: An Advanced Introduction*. New York: Columbia University Press, 1983.
———. *Literary Criticism in the Twenty-First Century: Theory Renaissance*. London: Bloomsbury, 2014.
Lemon, Lee T., and Marion J. Reis, eds. *Russian Formalist Criticism: Four Essays*. Lincoln: University of Nebraska Press, 1965.
Lentricchia, Frank. *After the New Criticism*. Chicago: University of Chicago Press, 1980.
Lepschy, Giulio C. *A Survey of Structural Linguistics*. London: Andre Deutsch, 1982.
Levinsohn, Stephen H. *Discourse Features of New Testament Greek*. Dallas, TX: SIL, 1992; 2nd ed. 2000.
Levinson, Stephen C. *Pragmatics*. Cambridge: Cambridge University Press, 1983.
Longacre, Robert E. *Joseph: A Story of Divine Providence. A Text Theoretical and Textlinguistic Analysis of Genesis 37 and 39–48*. Winona Lake, IN: Eisenbrauns, 1989.
Longman, Tremper, III. *Literary Approaches to Biblical Interpretation*. Grand Rapids: Zondervan, 1987.
Loomba, Ania. *Colonialism/Postcolonialism*. 2nd ed. London: Routledge, 2005.
Louw, J. P. *Semantics of New Testament Greek*. Philadelphia: Fortress; Chico, CA: Scholars, 1982.
Louw, Johannes P., and Eugene A. Nida. *Greek-English Lexicon of the New Testament Based on Semantic Domains*. 2 vols. New York: United Bible Societies, 1988.
Lyotard, Jean-François. *The Postmodern Condition: A Report on Knowledge*. Translated by Geoff Bennington and Brian Massumi. Minneapolis: University of Minnesota Press, 1984.
MacIntyre, Alasdair. "Existentialism." In *The Encyclopedia of Philosophy*, edited by Paul Edwards, 3:147–54. 8 vols. New York: Macmillan/Free Press, 1967.
Mack, Burton L. *Rhetoric and the New Testament*. Minneapolis: Fortress, 1990.
Mair, Lucy. *An Introduction to Social Anthropology*. Oxford: Clarendon, 1965.
Malina, Bruce J. *The New Testament World: Insights from Cultural Anthropology*. London: SCM, 1981.
Malinowski, Bronislaw. "The Problem of Meaning in Primitive Languages." In *The Meaning of Meaning*, by C. K. Ogden and I. A. Richards, 296–336. New York: Harcourt Brace, 1923.
Malbon, Elizabeth Struthers, and Edgar V. McKnight, eds. *The New Literary Criticism and the New Testament*. Sheffield: Sheffield Academic, 1994.
Marcus, George E. *Ethnography through Thick and Thin*. Princeton: Princeton University Press, 1998.
Martin, Ralph P. *Carmen Christi: Philippians 2:5–11 in Recent Interpretation and in the Setting of Early Christian Worship*. Cambridge: Cambridge University Press, 1967. Reprint, Grand Rapids: Eerdmans, 1983.
Martin, Troy W., ed. *Genealogies of New Testament Rhetorical Criticism*. Minneapolis: Fortress, 2014.
Mateos, Juan, and Jesús Paláez. *Diccionario Griego-Español del Nuevo Testamento*. 6 vols. to date. Córdoba: Ediciones El Almendro, 2000–.

McCarter, P. Kyle, Jr. *Textual Criticism: Recovering the Text of the Hebrew Bible*. Philadelphia: Fortress, 1986.

McCumber, John. *Time and Philosophy: A History of Continental Thought*. Montreal: McGill-Queen's University Press, 2011.

McKay, K. L. *A New Syntax of the Verb in New Testament Greek: An Aspectual Approach*. New York: Peter Lang, 1994.

McKenzie, Steven L., and John Kaltner, eds. *New Meanings for Ancient Texts: Recent Approaches to Biblical Criticisms and Their Applications*. Louisville, KY: Westminster John Knox, 2013.

McKim, Donald K., ed., *Dictionary of Major Biblical Interpreters*. Downers Grove, IL: InterVarsity, 2007.

McKnight, Edgar V. *What Is Form Criticism?* Philadelphia: Fortress, 1969.

Meeks, Wayne A. *The First Urban Christians: The Social World of the Apostle Paul*. New Haven: Yale University Press, 1983.

Milbank, John, Slavoj Žižek, and Creston Davis, with Catherine Pickstock. *Paul's New Moment: Continental Philosophy and the Future of Christian Theology*. Grand Rapids: Brazos, 2010.

Miller, Cynthia L. *The Representation of Speech in Biblical Hebrew Narrative: A Linguistic Analysis*. Atlanta: Scholars, 1996.

Milne, Pamela J. *Vladimir Propp and the Study of Structure in Hebrew Biblical Narrative*. Sheffield: Almond, 1988.

Mitchell, W. J. T., ed. *Against Theory: Literary Studies and the New Pragmatism*. Chicago: University of Chicago Press, 1985.

Möller, Karl. *A Prophet in Debate*. London: Sheffield Academic, 2003.

Moore, Stephen D. *The Bible in Theory: Critical and Postcritical Essays*. Atlanta: SBL, 2010.

———. *God's Beauty Parlor: And Other Queer Spaces in and around the Bible*. Stanford: Stanford University Press, 2001.

———. *Literary Criticism and the Gospels: The Theoretical Challenge*. New Haven: Yale University Press, 1989.

———. *Mark and Luke in Poststructuralist Perspectives: Jesus Begins to Write*. New Haven: Yale University Press, 1992.

———. *Poststructuralism and the New Testament: Derrida and Foucault at the Foot of the Cross*. Minneapolis: Fortress, 1994.

Moore, Stephen D., and Yvonne Sherwood. *The Invention of the Biblical Scholar: A Critical Manifesto*. Minneapolis: Fortress, 2011.

Morgan, Robert, with John Barton. *Biblical Interpretation*. Oxford: Oxford University Press, 1988.

Moulton, James Hope. *A Grammar of New Testament Greek*. Vol. 1, *Prolegomena*. 3rd ed. Edinburgh: T. & T. Clark, 1908.

Moulton, James Hope, and Wilbert Francis Howard. *A Grammar of New Testament Greek*. Vol. 2, *Accidence and Word-Formation*. Edinburgh: T. & T. Clark, 1919–29.

Muilenburg, James. "Form Criticism and Beyond." *JBL* 88 (1969) 1–18.

Murphy-O'Connor, Jerome, with Justin Taylor. *The École Biblique and the New Testament: A Century of Scholarship (1890–1990)*. Freiburg: Universitätsverlag; Göttingen: Vandenhoeck & Ruprecht, 1990.

Myers, Ched. *Binding the Strong Man: A Political Reading of Mark's Story of Jesus*. Maryknoll, NY: Orbis, 1988.

Neill, Stephen, and Tom Wright. *The Interpretation of the New Testament 1861–1986.* 2nd ed. Oxford: Oxford University Press, 1988.

Neuer, Werner. *Adolf Schlatter: A Biography of Germany's Premier Biblical Theologian.* Translated by Robert W. Yarbrough. Grand Rapids: Baker, 1995.

Nida, Eugene A., and Johannes P. Louw. *Lexical Semantics of the Greek New Testament.* Atlanta: Scholars, 1992.

Norris, Christopher. *Deconstruction: Theory and Practice.* Rev. ed. London: Routledge, 1991.

Noth, Martin. *The Deuteronomistic History.* Sheffield: JSOT Press, 1981.

Olsson, Birger. *Structure and Meaning in the Fourth Gospel: A Text-Linguistic Analysis of John 2:1–11 and 4:1–42.* Lund: Gleerup, 1974.

Olyan, Saul M. *Disability in the Hebrew Bible: Interpreting Mental and Physical Differences.* Cambridge: Cambridge University Press, 2008.

O'Neill, J. C. *The Bible's Authority: A Portrait Gallery of Thinkers from Lessing to Bultmann.* Edinburgh: T. & T. Clark, 1991.

Palmer, D. J. *The Rise of English Studies.* London: Oxford University Press, 1965.

Pardee, Dennis. "Review of *A Grammar of Biblical Hebrew* by Paul Joüon, translated and revised by T. Muraoka." *Journal of Near Eastern Studies* 56 no. 2 (1997) 144–47.

Parris, David Paul. *Reception Theory and Biblical Hermeneutics.* Eugene, OR: Pickwick, 2009.

Patte, Daniel. *The Gospel according to Matthew: A Structural Commentary on Matthew's Faith.* Philadelphia: Fortress, 1987.

———. *Paul's Faith and the Power of the Gospel: A Structural Introduction to the Pauline Letters.* Philadelphia: Fortress, 1983.

———. *Structural Exegesis for New Testament Critics.* Minneapolis: Fortress, 1990.

———. *What Is Structural Exegesis?* Philadelphia: Fortress, 1976.

Pedersen, Johannes. *Israel: Its Life and Culture,* I–II. Oxford: Oxford University Press, 1926.

Perelman, Chaim, and L. Olbrechts-Tyteca. *The New Rhetoric: A Treatise on Argumentation.* Notre Dame, IN: University of Notre Dame Press, 1969.

Perrin, Norman. *What Is Redaction Criticism?* Philadelphia: Fortress, 1969.

Petersen, Norman R. *Literary Criticism for New Testament Critics.* Philadelphia: Fortress, 1978.

———. *Rediscovering Paul: Philemon and the Sociology of Paul's Narrative World.* Philadelphia: Fortress, 1985.

Phillips, Peter M. *The Prologue of the Fourth Gospel: A Sequential Reading.* London: T. & T. Clark, 2006.

Poloma, Margaret M. *Contemporary Sociological Theory.* New York: Macmillan, 1979.

Polzin, Robert M. *Biblical Structuralism: Method and Subjectivity in the Study of Ancient Texts.* Philadelphia: Fortress; Missoula, MT: Scholars, 1977.

Popkin, Richard. *The History of Scepticism: From Savonarola to Bayle.* Rev. ed. Oxford: Oxford University Press, 2003.

Porter, Stanley E. *Constantine Tischendorf: The Life and Work of a 19th Century Bible Hunter, Including His* When Were the Gospels Written? London: Bloomsbury, 2015.

———. *The Criteria for Authenticity in Historical-Jesus Research: Previous Discussion and New Proposals.* Sheffield: Sheffield Academic, 2000.

———. "The Date of John's Gospel and Its Origins." In *The Origins of John's Gospel,* edited by Stanley E. Porter and Hughson T. Ong, 11–29. Leiden: Brill, 2016.

———. *How We Got the New Testament: Text, Transmission, Translation.* Grand Rapids: Baker, 2013.

———. *Idioms of the Greek New Testament*. 2nd ed. Sheffield: Sheffield Academic, 1994.

———, ed. *The Language of the New Testament: Classic Essays*. Sheffield: JSOT Press, 1990.

———. "The Legacy of B. F. Westcott and Oral Gospel Tradition." In *Earliest Christianity within the Boundaries of Judaism: Essays in Honor of Bruce Chilton*, edited by Alan J. Avery-Peck, Craig A. Evans, and Jacob Neusner, 326–45. Leiden: Brill, 2016.

———. *Linguistic Analysis of the Greek New Testament: Studies in Tools, Methods, and Practice*. Grand Rapids: Baker, 2015.

———. "Linguistic Criticism." In *Dictionary of Biblical Criticism and Interpretation*, edited by Stanley E. Porter, 199–202. London: Routledge, 2007.

———. "Literary Approaches." In *Approaches to New Testament Study*, edited by Stanley E. Porter and David Tombs, 77–128. Sheffield: Sheffield Academic, 1995.

———. *Verbal Aspect in the Greek of the New Testament, with Reference to Tense and Mood*. New York: Peter Lang, 1989.

———. *When Paul Met Jesus: How an Idea Got Lost in History*. Cambridge: Cambridge University Press, 2016.

———. "Why Hasn't Reader-Response Criticism Caught on in New Testament Studies?" *Journal of Literature and Theology* 4 (1990) 278–92.

Porter, Stanley E., and Bryan R. Dyer, eds. *The Synoptic Problem: Four Views*. Grand Rapids: Baker, 2016.

Porter, Stanley E., and Thomas H. Olbricht, eds. *Rhetoric and the New Testament: Papers from the 1992 Heidelberg Conference*. Sheffield: Sheffield Academic, 1993.

Porter, Stanley E., and Andrew W. Pitts. *Fundamentals of New Testament Textual Criticism*. Grand Rapids: Eerdmans, 2015.

———. "New Testament Greek Language and Linguistics in Recent Research." *Currents in Biblical Research* 6 (2008) 214–55.

Porter, Stanley E., and Jeffrey T. Reed, eds. *Discourse Analysis and the New Testament: Approaches and Results*. Sheffield: Sheffield Academic, 1999.

Porter, Stanley E., and Jason C. Robinson. *Hermeneutics: An Introduction to Interpretive Theory*. Grand Rapids: Eerdmans 2011.

Powell, Mark Allen. *What Is Narrative Criticism? A New Approach to the Bible*. London: SPCK, 1990.

Propp, Vladimir. *Morphology of the Folktale*. Translated by L. Scott. Edited by L. A. Wagner. 2nd ed. Austin: University of Texas Press, 1968.

Raison, Timothy, ed. *The Founding Fathers of Social Science*. Harmondsworth: Penguin, 1969.

Rast, Walter E. *Tradition History and the Old Testament*. Philadelphia: Fortress, 1972.

Reed, Jeffrey T. *A Discourse Analysis of Philippians: Method and Rhetoric in the Debate over Literary Integrity*. Sheffield: Sheffield Academic, 1997.

Resseguie, James L. *Narrative Criticism of the New Testament: An Introduction*. Grand Rapids: Baker, 2005.

Reventlow, Henning Graf. *History of Biblical Interpretation*. 4 vols. Translated by Leo G. Perdue. Atlanta: SBL, 2010.

Rex, John. "Émile Durkheim." In *The Founding Fathers of Social Science*, edited by Timothy Raison, 128–35. Harmondsworth: Penguin, 1969.

———. "Max Weber." In *The Founding Fathers of Social Science*, edited by Timothy Raison, 170–77. Harmondsworth: Penguin, 1969.

Rhoads, David. *Reading Mark, Engaging the Gospel*. Minneapolis: Fortress, 2004.

Rhoads, David, and Donald Michie. *Mark as Story: An Introduction to the Narrative of a Gospel*. Philadelphia: Fortress, 1982.

Richards, Audrey. "Bronislaw Malinowski." In *The Founding Fathers of Social Science*, edited by Timothy Raison, 188–96. Harmondsworth: Penguin, 1969.

Richards, Jennifer. *Rhetoric*. London: Routledge, 2008.

Riches, John K. *A Century of New Testament Study*. Cambridge: Lutterworth, 1993.

Ritzer, George. *Contemporary Sociological Theory*. 3rd ed. New York: McGraw-Hill, 1992.

Robbins, Vernon. *The Tapestry of Early Christian Discourse: A Guide to Socio-Rhetorical Interpretation*. London: Routledge, 1996.

Robertson, A. T. *A Grammar of the Greek New Testament in the Light of Historical Research*. (1914). 4th ed. Nashville: Broadman, 1934.

Robertson, David. *The Old Testament and the Literary Critic*. Philadelphia: Fortress, 1977.

Robey, David. "Anglo-American New Criticism." In *Modern Literary Theory: A Comparative Introduction*, edited by Ann Jefferson and David Robey, 73–91. 2nd ed. London: Batsford, 1986.

———. "Modern Linguistics and the Language of Literature." In *Modern Literary Theory: A Comparative Introduction*, edited by Ann Jefferson and David Robey, 46–72. 2nd ed. London: Batsford, 1986.

———, ed. *Structuralism: An Introduction*. Oxford: Clarendon, 1973.

Robins. R. H. *A Short History of Linguistics*. 3rd ed. London: Longman, 1990.

Robinson, John A. T. *Redating the New Testament*. Philadelphia: Westminster, 1976.

Robinson, H. Wheeler. *The Christian Doctrine of Man*. 3rd ed. Edinburgh: T. & T. Clark, 1926.

Rogerson, John W. *The Bible and Criticism in Victorian Britain: Profiles of F. D. Maurice and William Robertson Smith*. Sheffield: Sheffield Academic, 1995.

———. "The Hebrew Conception of Corporate Personality: A Re-examination." *JTS* 21 (1970) 1–16.

———. *Old Testament Criticism in the Nineteenth Century: England and Germany*. Minneapolis: Fortress, 1984.

———. *W. M. L. de Wette, Founder of Modern Biblical Criticism: An Intellectual Biography*. Sheffield: Sheffield Academic, 1992.

Rorty, Richard. *Philosophy and Social Hope*. London: Penguin, 1999.

Runge, Steven E. *Discourse Grammar of the Greek New Testament: A Practical Introduction for Teaching and Exegesis*. Peabody, MA: Hendrickson, 2010.

Russell, Letty M., ed. *Feminist Interpretation of the Bible*. Philadelphia: Westminster, 1985.

Ruthven, K. K. *Feminist Literary Studies: An Introduction*. Cambridge: Cambridge University Press, 1984.

Rylaarsdam, J. Coert. "Introduction: The Chicago School—and After." In *Transitions in Biblical Scholarship*, edited by J. Coert Rylaarsdam, 1–16. Chicago: University of Chicago Press, 1968.

Sanders, E. P. *Paul and Palestinian Judaism: A Comparison of Patterns of Religion*. Philadelphia: Fortress, 1977.

Sanders, James A. *Torah and Canon*. Philadelphia: Fortress, 1972.

Sandys-Wunsch, John. *What Have They Done to the Bible? A History of Modern Biblical Interpretation*. Collegeville, MN: Liturgical, 2005.

Sawyer, John F. A. *Semantics in Biblical Research: New Methods of Defining Hebrew Words for Salvation*. London: SCM, 1972.

Schmidt, Daryl D. *Hellenistic Greek Grammar and Noam Chomsky*. Chico, CA: Scholars, 1981.

Scholes, Robert. *Structuralism in Literature: An Introduction.* New Haven: Yale University Press, 1974.

Schüssler Fiorenza, Elisabeth. *In Memory of Her: A Feminist Theological Reconstruction of Christian Origins.* New York: Crossroad, 1992.

Scott, Wilbur. *Five Approaches of Literary Criticism.* New York: Collier, 1962.

Searle, John R. *Speech Acts: An Essay in the Philosophy of Language.* Cambridge: Cambridge University Press, 1969.

Selden, Raman, Peter Widdowson, and Peter Brooker. *A Reader's Guide to Contemporary Literary Theory.* 4th ed. London: Prentice Hall/Harvester Wheatsheaf, 1997.

Sellin, Ernest, revised by Georg Fohrer. *Introduction to the Old Testament.* (1910). Translated by David E. Green. Nashville: Abingdon, 1968.

Silva, Moisés. *Biblical Words and Their Meaning: An Introduction to Lexical Semantics.* Grand Rapids: Zondervan, 1983.

Sim, Margaret. "Review of *Verbal Aspect in Synoptic Parallels . . .*" *Journal for the Study of the New Testament* Booklist 36 no. 5 (2014) 140–41.

Smith, Neil. *Chomsky: Ideas and Ideals.* Cambridge: Cambridge University Press, 1999.

Smith, W. Robertson. *Lectures on the Religion of the Semites.* Edinburgh: A. & C. Clark, 1889.

Sollors, Werner, ed. *The Return of Thematic Criticism.* Cambridge, MA: Harvard University Press, 1993.

Stendahl, Krister. "The Apostle Paul and the Introspective Conscience of the West." (1960/1961). In *Paul among Jews and Gentiles and Other Essays*, 78–96. Philadelphia: Fortress, 1976.

Sternberg, Meir. *The Poetics of Biblical Narrative: Ideological Literature and the Drama of Reading.* Bloomington: Indiana University Press, 1985.

Stibbe, Mark W. G. *John as Storyteller: Narrative Criticism and the Fourth Gospel.* Cambridge: Cambridge University Press, 1992.

Still, Todd D., and David G. Horrell, eds. *After the First Urban Christians: The Social-Scientific Study of Pauline Christianity Twenty-Five Years Later.* London: T. & T. Clark, 2009.

Strauss, David Friedrich. *Das Leben Jesu, kritisch bearbeitet.* 2 vols. Tübingen: Osiander, 1835. ET *The Life of Jesus Critically Examined.* Translated by Georg Eliot from fourth German edition. London: George Allen, 1848.

———. *Das Leben Jesu für das deutsche Volk bearbeitet.* Leipzig: Brockhaus, 1865. ET *A New Life of Jesus.* 2 vols. London: Williams and Norgate, 1879.

Streeter, Burnett Hillman. *The Four Gospels: A Study of Origins Treating of the Manuscript Tradition, Sources, Authorship, and Dates.* London: Macmillan, 1924.

Styler, G. M. "The Priority of Mark." In *The Birth of the New Testament*, by C. F. D. Moule, 285–316. 3rd ed. London: SCM, 1982.

Sugirtharajah, R. S. *Asian Biblical Hermeneutics and Postcolonialism: Contesting the Interpretations.* Sheffield: Sheffield Academic, 1999.

Suleiman, Susan R., and Inge Crosman, eds. *The Reader in the Text: Essays on Audience and Interpretation.* Princeton: Princeton University Press, 1980.

Talbert, Charles H. *Reading Luke: A Literary and Theological Commentary on the Third Gospel.* New York: Crossroad, 1982.

Tannehill, Robert C. *The Narrative Unity of Luke-Acts: A Literary Interpretation.* 2 vols. Philadelphia: Fortress, 1986–90.

Thackeray, Henry St. John. *A Grammar of the Old Testament in Greek.* Cambridge: Cambridge University Press, 1909.

Thatcher, Tom, and Stephen D. Moore, eds. *Anatomies of Narrative Criticism: The Past, Present, and Futures of the Fourth Gospel as Literature.* Atlanta: SBL, 2008.

Theissen, Gerd. *Social Reality and the Early Christians: Theology, Ethics, and the World of the New Testament.* Translated by Margaret Kohl. Minneapolis: Fortress, 1992.

———. *The Social Setting of Pauline Christianity: Essays on Corinth.* Translated by John H. Schütz. Philadelpha: Fortress, 1982.

Thiselton, Anthony C. *The First Epistle to the Corinthians.* Grand Rapids: Eerdmans, 2000.

———. "The New Hermeneutic." In *New Testament Interpretation: Essays in Principles and Methods*, edited by I. Howard Marshall, 308–33. Grand Rapids: Eerdmans, 1977.

———. "The Parables as Language-Event." *SJT* 23 (1970) 437–68.

Thomas, Margaret. *Fifty Key Thinkers on Language and Linguistics.* London: Routledge, 2011.

Tice, Terrence. *Schleiermacher.* Nashville: Abingdon 2006.

Tilling, Chris. *Paul's Divine Christology.* Reprint, Grand Rapids: Eerdmans, 2015.

Tompkins, Jane P., ed. *Reader-Response Criticism: From Formalism to Post-Structuralism.* Baltimore: Johns Hopkins University Press, 1980.

Tov, Emanuel. *Textual Criticism of the Hebrew Bible.* Minneapolis: Fortress; Assen/Maastricht: Van Gorcum, 1992.

Trible, Phyllis. *Texts of Terror: Literary-Feminist Readings of Biblical Narratives.* Philadelphia: Fortress, 1984.

Tucker, Gene M. *Form Criticism of the Old Testament.* Philadelphia: Fortress, 1971.

Ulrich, Eugene. "The Scrolls and the Study of the Hebrew Bible." In *The Dead Sea Scrolls at Fifty*, edited by Robert A. Kugler and Eileen M. Schuller, 31–42. Atlanta: SBL, 1999.

Vachek Josef. *The Linguistic School of Prague: An Introduction to Its Theory and Practice.* Bloomington: Indiana University Press, 1966.

———, ed. *A Prague School Reader in Linguistics.* Bloomington: Indiana University Press, 1964.

VanderKam, James. *The Dead Sea Scrolls Today.* Grand Rapids: Eerdmans, 1994.

VanderKam, James, and Peter Flint. *The Meaning of the Dead Sea Scrolls: Their Significance for Understanding the Bible, Judaism, Jesus, and Christianity.* San Francisco: HarperSanFrancisco, 2002.

Van der Merwe, Christo H. J., Jackie A. Naudé, and Jan H. Kroeze. *A Biblical Hebrew Reference Grammar.* Sheffield: Sheffield Academic, 1999.

Via, Dan O. *What Is New Testament Theology?* Minneapolis: Fortress, 2002.

Vines, Michael E. *The Problem of Markan Genre: The Gospel of Mark and the Jewish Novel.* Atlanta: SBL, 2002.

Waetjen, Herman C. *The Letter to the Romans: Salvation as Justice and the Deconstruction of Law.* Sheffield: Sheffield Phoenix, 2011.

Wall, Robert W., and Eugene E. Lemcio. *The New Testament as Canon: A Reader in Canonical Criticism.* Sheffield: Sheffield Academic, 1992.

Waltke, Bruce K., and M. O'Connor. *An Introduction to Biblical Hebrew Syntax.* Winona Lake, IN: Eisenbrauns, 1990.

Watson, Francis. *Text and Truth: Redefining Biblical Theology.* Edinburgh: T. & T. Clark, 1997.

Watt, Jonathan M. *Code-Switching in Luke and Acts.* New York: Peter Lang, 1997.

Weber, Max. *On Charisma and Institution Building: Selected Papers*, edited by S. N. Eisenstadt. Chicago: University of Chicago Press, 1968.

Weingreen, J. *Introduction to the Critical Study of the Text of the Hebrew Bible.* Oxford: Clarendon, 1982.

Wellek, René, and Austin Warren. *Theory of Literature.* (1942). 3rd ed. San Diego: Harcourt Brace Jovanovich, 1956.

Westby, David L. *The Growth of Sociological Theory: Human Nature, Knowledge, and Social Change.* Englewood Cliffs, NJ: Prentice-Hall, 1991.

Westerholm, Stephen. *Perspectives Old and New on Paul: The "Lutheran" Paul and His Critics.* (1988). Grand Rapids: Eerdmans, 2004.

Wilder, Amos. *The Language of the Gospel: Early Christian Rhetoric.* New York: Harper & Row, 1964.

Williams, James. *Understanding Poststructuralism.* Stocksfield, UK: Acumen, 2005.

Wilson, Robert R. *Sociological Approaches to the Old Testament.* Philadelphia: Fortress, 1984.

Wimsatt, W. K., Jr., and Monroe C. Beardsley. "The Intentional Fallacy." In *The Verbal Icon: Studies in the Meaning of Poetry,* by W. K. Wimsatt, 3–18. New York: Noonday, 1954.

Wind, James P. *The Bible and the University: The Messianic Vision of William Rainey Harper.* Atlanta: Scholars, 1987.

Winer, G. B. *A Treatise on the Grammar of New Testament Greek.* (1822). Translated by W. F. Moulton. 3rd ed. Edinburgh: T. & T. Clark, 1882.

Wolde, Ellen van. *Reframing Biblical Studies: When Language and Text Meet Culture, Cognition, and Context.* Winona Lake, IN: Eisenbrauns, 2009.

Wolfreys, Julian, ed. *The Continuum Encyclopedia of Modern Criticism and Theory.* New York: Continuum, 2002.

Wright, G. Ernest. *God Who Acts: Biblical Theology as Recital.* London: SCM, 1952.

Wuellner, Wilhelm H., and Robert C. Leslie. *The Surprising Gospel: Intriguing Psychological Insights from the New Testament.* Nashville: Abingdon, 1984.

Würthwein, Ernst. *The Text of the Old Testament: An Introduction to the Biblia Hebraica.* Translated by Erroll F. Rhodes. Grand Rapids: Eerdmans, 1979.

Yarbrough. Robert W. *The Salvation Historical Fallacy? Reassessing the History of New Testament Theology.* Leiden: Deo, 2004.

Yoon, David I. "The Life and Career of Spinoza: A Lesson in Biblical Interpretation." *McMaster Journal of Theology and Ministry* 14 (2012–14) 171–99.

Zachhuber, Johannes. *Theology as Science in Nineteenth-Century Germany: From F. C. Baur to Ernst Troeltsch.* Oxford: Oxford University Press, 2013.

1

J. J. Griesbach and Karl Lachmann

BRANDON D. CROWE

J. J. GRIESBACH

Biography

JOHANN JAKOB GRIESBACH (1745–1812) was a German theologian and exegete whose major contributions to the field of New Testament interpretation are in the areas of textual and source criticism of the Gospels. Griesbach was born January 4, 1745 in Butzbach, Germany. His father was a pastor of the pietistic strand, and his mother read both Latin and Greek.[1] He spent his childhood in Frankfurt, where he made the acquaintance of the German literary giant Johann Wolfgang von Goethe. These men, who remained friends their entire lives, were part of a culture in Frankfurt in which, according to Goethe, "everyone cherished the sure hope that they would accomplish outstanding things in State and Church."[2]

Griesbach studied in Tübingen, Halle, and Leipzig, with the most formative of these years in Halle where he studied under J. S. Semler, a pioneer of the historical-critical approach to the New Testament, who greatly influenced the course of Griesbach's life.[3] As a student (and after later travels) Griesbach lived with Semler, who encouraged his gifted student to pursue text-critical research.[4] After receiving his master's degree in philosophy at age twenty-three, Griesbach did additional research in Germany, the Netherlands, London (British Museum), Oxford (Bodleian Library), Cambridge, and Paris. The primary purpose of his tour was to avail himself of the wealth of New Testament manuscripts housed in these locations. Indeed, Griesbach's

---

1. Much of this biographical sketch comes from Walls's translation of Delling, "Griesbach."
2. Cited in ibid., 5.
3. Ibid., 7.
4. Ibid.; Baird, *History*, 1:138.

travels would pay dividends for his work in textual criticism for the rest of his life.[5] After his educational tour Griesbach returned to Halle where he wrote a treatise on the importance of the Greek Fathers for textual criticism and was appointed instructor at Halle in 1771.[6] He was promoted to Assistant Professor of Theology in Halle in 1773, and in 1775 became professor in Jena, where he taught church history, dogmatics, introduction to the New Testament, and New Testament exegesis.[7] From 1776 to 1793 Griesbach wrote a number of biblical-theological treatises, including a "mildly orthodox" dogmatics textbook.[8] It was also in Jena that Griesbach taught J. P. Gabler, widely considered to be the father of "Biblical Theology," who was his pupil from 1778 and succeeded him at Jena in 1804.[9] It should also be noted that Griesbach preferred to write primarily in Latin rather than German, which makes his work less accessible to many modern-day readers.

Personally, Griesbach was said to be kind, serious, discreet, upright, reliable, and had a large and powerful physical build.[10] H. E. G. Paulus noted that an irenic spirit also characterized Griesbach, who did not begrudge views that differed from his own. He was willing to adopt and work with opposing positions if they became accepted.[11] It has additionally been observed that Griesbach, even in his polemical writings, always remained "extraordinarily proper and courteous."[12]

Contributions to New Testament Studies

Text Criticism

J. J. Griesbach made perhaps a greater contribution than any other scholar to New Testament textual criticism from the beginning of the eighteenth century to the middle of the nineteenth century.[13] His influence is to be found, first of all, in his endeavor to print a New Testament text that did not conform entirely to the so-called Textus Receptus, or Received Text.[14] The Textus Receptus is a term that derives from a 1633 edition of the Greek New Testament that claims in its preface to contain the New Testament text as it has been received by all, free from alterations and corruptions.[15] Even though this statement asserted more than was warranted, subsequent

---

5. Delling, "Griesbach," 7.

6. Baird, *History*, 1:138.

7. Ibid.

8. Kümmel, *New Testament*, 475–76. Many of Griesbach's shorter theological writings are found in Gabler, *Griesbachii opuscula*.

9. Delling, "Griesbach," 12.

10. Baird, *History*, 1:138; Delling, "Griesbach," 13.

11. Cited in Delling, "Griesbach," 13–14.

12. Reicke, "Griesbach's Answer," 52.

13. So Neill and Wright, *Interpretation*, 71.

14. Kümmel, *New Testament*, 74.

15. Metzger and Ehrman, *Text of the New Testament*, 149–52. This 1633 edition was published by

publishers were nevertheless hesitant to introduce changes into the Textus Receptus, which became, *de facto*, the unquestioned text of the New Testament. Bruce Metzger, commenting on the difficulties of the Textus Receptus, observes: "So superstitious has been the reverence accorded to the *Textus receptus* that in some cases attempts to criticize or emend it have been regarded as akin to sacrilege. Yet, its textual basis is essentially a handful of late and haphazardly collected minuscule manuscripts, and in a dozen passages its rendering is supported by no known Greek witness."[16] It was this text that Griesbach set out to improve by incorporating the testimony of the best New Testament manuscripts, especially those he had been able to consult first-hand in his research in Britain and on the Continent. He also paid greater attention to New Testament quotations in the Greek Fathers, as well as to several versions not often studied: Gothic, Armenian, and Philoxenian Syriac.[17] The consummation of Griesbach's labors can be found in the second edition of his *Novum Testamentum Graece*, which appeared in 1796 (vol. 1) and 1806 (vol. 2).[18] However, even though Griesbach was groundbreaking in his printing of a new recension of the received text, in the end his text of the New Testament did not differ all that much from the Textus Receptus.[19]

A second contribution of Griesbach derived from his work on the text of the New Testament is his 1774 edition of the Gospels (*Synopsis Evangeliorum*). This work is remarkable for the way he organized Matthew, Mark, and Luke in the form of a *synopsis*—arranging the parallel accounts in columns for ease of reference. In fact, this is most likely the origin of the oft-used moniker "Synoptic Gospels" in biblical studies today.[20] By his synopsis Griesbach was not intending to construct a harmony of the Gospels, nor was he trying to determine the actual chronological sequence of the biblical accounts. As Griesbach himself states:

> I have serious doubts that a harmonious narrative can be put together from the books of the evangelists, one that adequately agrees with the truth in respect of the chronological arrangement of the pericopes and which stands on a solid basis. For what if none of the evangelists followed chronological order exactly everywhere and if there are not enough indications from which could be deduced which one departed from the chronological order and in what places? Well, I confess to this heresy![21]

Bonaventure and Abraham Elzevir and closely resembled earlier editions published by Theodore Beza and Robert Estienne (Stephanus), whose editions were greatly indebted to Erasmus.

16. Ibid., 152.

17. Ibid., 165.

18. Baird, *History*, 1:142. The first edition appeared from 1774 to 1777.

19. So ibid.

20. So Neill and Wright, *Interpretation*, 113.

21. Griesbach, from the preface to the second edition of *Synopsis Evangeliorum*, cited in Greeven, "Gospel Synopsis," 27.

Instead, the purpose for the parallel layout was to provide Griesbach's students with an aid for following his lectures. Griesbach's *Synopsis Evangeliorum* allowed his students to read each Gospel continuously while also having the parallel passages in front of them.[22] Griesbach's synopsis was not only a significant development in itself, but also led him to another important conclusion in the area of source criticism, which will be considered below.

Third, Griesbach advanced the understanding of text types and text-critical methodology. In the prolegomena to his *Novum Testamentum Graece* Griesbach set out fifteen canons for evaluating textual variants,[23] including some of the standard tenets of textual criticism. For example, Griesbach's first canon declares: "The shorter reading . . . is to be preferred to the more verbose, for scribes were much more prone to add than to omit. They scarcely ever deliberately omitted anything, but they added many things; certainly they omitted some things by accident, but likewise not a few things have been added to the text by scribes through errors of the eye, ear, memory, imagination, and judgment."[24] Griesbach qualifies this statement, noting that the shorter reading is not to be preferred in instances where, for example, homoeoteleuton or conflation of texts may be a factor. An additional canon included by Griesbach is the principle of *lectio difficilior*: "The more difficult and obscure reading should be preferred to that in which all things are plain and clear."[25]

Griesbach also recognized the need to classify and weigh New Testament manuscripts according to family relationships.[26] Building on the work of J. A. Bengel and J. S. Semler, Griesbach posited three text types for the New Testament: Alexandrian, Western, and Byzantine (or Constantinopolitan). Griesbach considered the Alexandrian witnesses to be the most reliable, and he included here majuscules C, L, K; minuscules 1, 13, 33, 69, 106, 118; Bohairic, Armenian, Ethiopic, and Harclean Syrian versions; and the citations of Origen, Clement of Alexandria, Eusebius, Cyril of Alexandria, and Isidore of Pelusium. Among these, Origen's testimony was considered to be the most important. Included among the Western witnesses were Codex D and the Latin versions. Griesbach considered the Byzantine text type to be a later derivation from the other two, and was represented by Codex A in the Gospels and most of the later majuscule and minuscule manuscripts, along with a large proportion of patristic quotations. The Byzantine text family was, therefore, the least important text type for Griesbach's reconstructed text.[27]

---

22. Ibid.

23. Griesbach, *Novum Testamentum Graece*, 1:lx–lxix. These fifteen are indebted to the earlier work of G. von Mästricht and J. A. Bengel (cf. Vaganay and Amphoux, *Introduction*, 79–80).

24. Cited in Metzger and Ehrman, *Text of the New Testament*, 166.

25. Griesbach, *Novum Testamentum Graece*, 1:lxi, cited in Baird, *History*, 1:142–43.

26. Neill and Wright, *Interpretation*, 71.

27. Metzger and Ehrman, *Text of the New Testament*, 165–66; Baird, *History*, 1:142.

Source Criticism

Gordon Fee has observed: "That there is an interrelationship between textual criticism and the Synoptic Problem is the presupposition of most Synoptic studies."[28] Thus, it is not surprising that Griesbach's work in New Testament textual criticism, and especially his *Synopsis Evangeliorum*, led to his foray into the relationships among the Synoptic Gospels. Indeed, for many today, Griesbach's name is primarily associated with the "Griesbach Hypothesis." This hypothesis argues that Matthew was the first Gospel written; that Luke subsequently used Matthew; and that Mark then used both Matthew (primarily) and Luke in the writing of his Gospel (see Figure 1).[29] This view was a modification of the dominant view in Griesbach's day, that of Augustine, who hundreds of years earlier had suggested that Mark was the abbreviator of Matthew, but not of Luke.[30] Griesbach thus deviated from Augustine by including Luke among the sources used by Mark.[31] Griesbach's position, which had been anticipated by Englishman Henry Owen in 1764, is argued in two major essays.

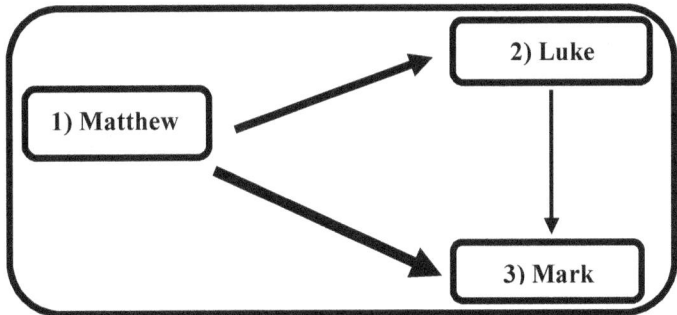

Figure 1: Griesbach Hypothesis

The first essay, "Inquiry into the sources from which the Evangelists drew their narratives of the resurrection of the Lord," was written in 1783.[32] Here Griesbach argued that Matthew served as a general model for Luke, but in the resurrection accounts Luke was the primary source for Mark.[33] However, this essay was not as persuasive or influential as his 1789 contribution, "Treatise by Which It Is Demonstrated that the Entire Gospel of Mark Was Extracted from the Records of Matthew and Luke."[34] In

---

28. Fee, "Modern Text Criticism," 154.

29. Cf. Bruce, "History of New Testament Study."

30. Other views of Griesbach's day include those of Hugo Grotius (Mark's use of Matthew, and Luke's use of Matthew and Mark), and G. C. Storr (Mark was used independently by Matthew and Luke). Cf. Baird, *History*, 1:144.

31. Bo Reicke, "Griesbach's Answer," 50.

32. Baird, *History*, 1:144–45. The essay can be found in Gabler, *Griesbachii opuscula*, 2:241–56.

33. Reicke, "Griesbach's Answer," 53. Reicke notes that when Griesbach wrote this essay he focused on the so-called "longer ending" of Mark (16:9–20), which he later considered to be spurious.

34. The original (*Commentatio qua Marci Evangelium totum e Matthaei et Lucae commentariis*

this essay Griesbach's keen mind and logic are evident as he presents a strong case that Mark used both Matthew and Luke. Given the significance of this essay, it will now be considered in some detail.

In the first section, Griesbach states his thesis: "This is a summary of the opinion we are defending: That Mark when writing his book had in front of his eyes not only Matthew but Luke as well, and that he extracted from them whatever he committed to writing of the deeds, speeches and sayings of the Saviour."[35] He then includes fifteen points that specify the ways in which Mark gleaned from Matthew and Luke. These points set forth the differences between Mark and the other two Synoptic Gospels, with particular focus on the specific aims of Mark, who, Griesbach claims, sought brevity in light of the specific purposes for which he was writing. Griesbach proposes that Matthew was the primary guide for Mark, but Mark often deviated from Matthew in order to follow Luke. Yet, where Mark "stuck closely to Matthew, he nevertheless did not lose sight of Luke but matched him together with Matthew, and *vice versa*."[36] For Griesbach, Mark's audience was a community far removed from Palestine, for whom the rules and regulations of Palestinian Jews were not known or relevant.[37] He also observes that Mark "in no wise copies [Matthew and Luke] word for word, but in *his own* way, i.e., he narrates what he has read in them, in other formulas and phrases."[38]

The second section of Griesbach's essay comprises three arguments for Mark's use of Matthew and Luke. The first is the argument from order. Griesbach argues that there is a recognizable order to Mark's use of Matthew and Luke, such that it can easily be shown where he follows one and then the other. Griesbach further states that Mark "retained the order observed by Matthew in such a way, that wherever he forsakes it he sticks to the path of Luke and follows him and the order of his narrative step by step."[39] Here Griesbach's hypothesis has the virtue of being a simpler solution than some other proposals of his day, which depended on "numerous hypotheses devised in a highly artificial manner."[40] The second argument for Mark's use of Matthew and Luke is built on the recognition that (except for 24 verses) all of Mark is contained in Matthew and Luke. For Griesbach the implication is clear: although Jesus performed a myriad of memorable works, it is quite remarkable that Mark included virtually nothing in his Gospel beyond what Matthew or Luke recorded by way of precedent or in

---

decerptum esse monstratur) can be found in Latin and in English translation by Orchard, in Griesbach, "Demonstration." The following references are taken from Orchard's translation and reflect the page numbers of the 1978 volume.

35. Ibid., 106.
36. Ibid.
37. Ibid.
38. Ibid., 107; italics original.
39. Ibid., 108.
40. Ibid., 109–10.

similar form.[41] This is further consonant with what Griesbach perceived Mark's aims to be. According to Griesbach, Mark intended to select from Matthew and Luke what was most useful for his intended readers.[42] For Griesbach it would be astonishing if Mark had not used Matthew and Luke but still came to the same conclusions and included the same materials that they did.[43] The third positive argument for Mark's use of Matthew and Luke is Mark's alternating agreement with Matthew and Luke. That is, Griesbach observed a zigzag pattern in the way Mark alternated between Matthew and Luke: "When Mark has closely adhered to either Matthew or Luke for a long stretch, he often passes with a sudden leap from one to the other, but soon returns to his former guide; and this could not have been done unless he had simultaneously seen and compared the works of each."[44]

The third section of Griesbach's essay anticipates eight objections to his position and provides his answers to these objections. Most of Griesbach's rejoinders focus on the aims of Mark, who, he maintained, generally sought brevity in his Gospel, although Mark also "amplified, with greater abundance of detail and even at times with circumlocutions, much material from the Gospel of Luke, material spaced between the narrative of Matthew, and also a good deal that he has transferred from Matthew into his own treatise."[45] Among other objections, Griesbach notes the historical objection that Mark wrote his Gospel based on Peter's testimony, and therefore would not have been dependent on Matthew and Luke. Griesbach answers by pointing out the lack of reliability among the early church Fathers, even asserting that early church tradition relies on "vague rumours and arguments with little foundation."[46] Griesbach also answers the objection that, if Mark was a combination of Matthew and Luke, there would be no real need for his Gospel since he added very little material that was not already included in Matthew and/or Luke. To this Griesbach replies that Mark was serving the needs of his community by providing a short outline of Jesus' life, and he combined Matthew and Luke because neither contained everything he thought his readers should know.[47] In answer to the objection that Matthew may have used Mark,

---

41. Ibid., 110.

42. Ibid., 110–11. It should be noted that Griesbach did believe Mark had roots in Jerusalem and was a close acquaintance of Peter and Paul (cf. Acts 12:12, 25; 13:5; Col 4:10; Phlm 24; 1 Pet 5:13), which enabled Mark to enrich his narrative with a number of special details. Nevertheless, Griesbach argued that, although Mark knew more than he included, he did not put any additional anecdotes in his Gospel because this was not in line with his purpose. However, Griesbach did not think that Mark wrote under the guidance of Peter, strictly speaking. This will be discussed in more detail below.

43. Ibid., 111.

44. Ibid., 113. By way of example, Griesbach notes how Mark 13:24–25 strictly follows Matthew. Mark 13:26 then switches from Matthew and follows Luke, while Mark 13:27–32 agrees almost word for word with Matthew.

45. Ibid., 114. Griesbach thus disagreed with Augustine who said simply that Mark was the abbreviator of Matthew.

46. Ibid., 115–18; quotation from p. 116.

47. Ibid., 118.

Griesbach thinks it is inconceivable that Matthew, whom he considered to be an apostolic eyewitness, would have chosen Mark as his guide to writing the life of Jesus, since Mark had not been present himself.[48] He also finds no satisfactory explanation as to why Matthew (and Luke) would both omit some parts of Mark if they found the rest of his Gospel to be so appealing.[49] Regarding discrepancies that might suggest Markan priority, Griesbach notes that the only disagreements are in particular details, never in the general drift of the narrative. He also suggests that some discrepancies can be attributed to the fact that Mark is following Luke instead of Matthew, and that Mark's interest is not in strict chronology.[50] This selection of Griesbach's responses to a number of objections is illustrative of the thoroughness and coherence of his overall argument.

In section four Griesbach lists thirteen conclusions that summarize his argument, several of which are worth noting.[51] First, Griesbach restates his view that Mark wrote after Matthew and Luke finished their works. He further discounts the early church's testimony regarding the claim that Mark wrote under the direct influence of Peter. He also believes that the evangelists whose names are associated with the books are the actual authors, rejects the hypothesis that the evangelists composed their books from hypothetical documents (whether Greek, Hebrew, or Aramaic), believes that the order of Matthew and Luke was established by the time of Mark's composition, suggests that Mark understood the purpose and use of his Gospel differently from those who followed him, and, lastly, asserts that "those who argue that Mark wrote under the influence of divine inspiration must surely regard it as being a pretty meagre one!"[52]

KARL LACHMANN

Biography

Karl Konrad Friedrich Wilhelm Lachmann (1793–1851), like J. J. Griesbach, is also best remembered for his work in New Testament textual criticism and his theory on the relationships among the Synoptic Gospels. Lachmann was born March 4, 1793 in the German town of Braunschweig. His father was a pastor, and his mother died tragically at age twenty-one when he was not yet two years old.[53] He first studied theology at Leipzig, then focused on classical philology in Göttingen.[54] By 1815 he

---

48. Reicke, "Griesbach's Answer," 51, considers this to be the decisive point for Griesbach.
49. Griesbach, "Demonstration," 119–21.
50. Ibid., 128–33.
51. Ibid., 133–35.
52. For more on Griesbach's view of divine inspiration, see Delling, "Griesbach," 11. Briefly, Griesbach criticized the orthodox teaching of verbal inspiration, i.e., that the text of the New Testament was directly inspired by God. Instead, he affirmed that the apostles received the Spirit at Pentecost who henceforth continued to be effective throughout their entire lives.
53. Hertz, *Lachmann*, 1.
54. Ibid., 7.

was an Instructor at Göttingen, and then in Berlin in 1816. He later became Assistant Professor of German and Classical Philology in Königsberg (1818) before moving to Berlin in 1825 where he was Assistant Professor, and then Professor from 1827. Lachmann was first of all a classical philologist, and made significant contributions as an editor of classical and middle-high German texts, with particular focus on meter and interpolations. Some of the literature studied by Lachmann includes Propertius, Catullus, Tibullus, Lucretius, Homer, and medieval epics and lyrics.[55]

Lachmann's biographer observes that he inherited from his mother nobility of disposition along with a tender, nervous constitution, and he was generally known to be cheerful, friendly, and kind.[56] Physically he was thin, with a sharp nose and full head of blond hair that naturally stretched upward, and his great learning was said to be, in part, due to his indefatigable work ethic.[57] Like Griesbach, Lachmann's first language was German, but he preferred to write in Latin.

Even though Lachmann was primarily a renowned philologist, his influence extended well into the field of New Testament studies. As the following survey will show, Lachmann set his hand to preparing important editions of the Greek New Testament that challenged the Textus Receptus, and he suggested a different way forward than Griesbach with respect to the Synoptic Problem.

Contributions to New Testament Studies

Text Criticism

In his study of classical literature, most notably Lucretius, Lachmann had demonstrated how comparing manuscripts could enable one to make judgments regarding the lost archetypes of those manuscripts, including their condition and pagination. This allowed him to make transpositions of the received text.[58] Lachmann then took a similar approach to textual criticism of the New Testament, which led him to emend the Textus Receptus in a much more thoroughgoing manner than Griesbach. Lachmann comments on the need to move beyond Griesbach and the Textus Receptus: "As soon as I surveyed the field of New Testament criticism it became clear to me that, if I wished to make a significant contribution, Griesbach could not be my guide. Not that I doubt Griesbach's independence and thoroughness, or the great and timely contribution he made. His criticism, however, is too incomplete and, because he wants to be cautious, too incautious. No one knew as well as he how accidentally the common reading, the so-called 'received text,' had come into being, and yet he made it basic."[59]

---

55. Metzger and Ehrman, *Text of the New Testament*, 170; Baird, *History*, 1:319.
56. Hertz, *Lachmann*, 1, 225.
57. Ibid., 1, 226.
58. Metzger and Ehrman, *Text of the New Testament*, 170.
59. Lachmann, "Rechenschaft," 817–20, 826, cited in Kümmel, *New Testament*, 146.

The first edition of Lachmann's *Novum Testamentum Graece* that sought to move beyond the impasse of the Textus Receptus appeared in 1831 after five years of labor. This edition does not contain a full textual apparatus, but is focused instead on the text itself. More thorough is the second edition of 1842–50, which contains Lachmann's Greek text on the top of the page, the Latin Vulgate with some notations on the bottom of the page, and an apparatus in the middle partitioning the two languages.[60] In this edition the number of variants included is extensive, even though Lachmann only had access to a relatively small collection of textual witnesses.[61]

Lachmann viewed the task of determining the text of the New Testament to be primarily a historical one, and his editions of the Greek New Testament are significant as the first text to be based exclusively on the oldest manuscripts rather than on a printed edition of the New Testament.[62] Lachmann clarifies his approach in contrast to Griesbach:

> "Is there reason to depart from the usual reading?" was [Griesbach's] question, whereas the natural one can only be, "Is there reason to depart from the best authenticated reading? . . . " Shall we not then preferably regard the reputation of the text that the Church has employed for three hundred years as unfounded, when it is possible to obtain one that is fourteen hundred years old and to approach one that is sixteen hundred years old? Is it not worthier of a critic to assume responsibility both for what he allows to stand, as for what he changes?[63]

Since Lachmann's method was to use the most ancient manuscripts then available, his goal was not to reconstruct the original text of the New Testament per se, but to reconstruct a provisional text—the text used by the Eastern church at the end of the fourth century.[64] In the words of Lachmann, "I have not established the true text . . . but only the oldest among those that can be proved to have been in circulation."[65] To this end Lachmann adopted a rather mechanical methodology that ignored later minuscule manuscripts and focused on early majuscules along with the Old Latin, Vulgate, and patristic sources, including Irenaeus, Origen, Cyprian, Hilary, and Lucifer.[66]

Although Karl Lachmann's work had its limitations (see "Evaluation" below), his more historical approach to reconstructing the text of the Greek New Testament marks an even more decided step away from what had become for many an almost slavish adherence to the Textus Receptus.

60. Lachmann, *Novum Testamentum*.
61. Baird, *History*, 1:322.
62. Kümmel, *New Testament*, 146–47.
63. Lachmann, "Rechenschaft," 817–20, cited in Kümmel, *New Testament*, 146.
64. Baird, *History*, 1:321.
65. Lachmann, "Rechenschaft," 826, cited in Kümmel, *New Testament*, 147.
66. Ibid.; Metzger and Ehrman, *Text of the New Testament*, 170–71.

Source Criticism

While Lachmann's work on a Greek text that differed from the Textus Receptus has led some scholars to the conclusion that his greatest contribution is to be found in the area of textual criticism,[67] others consider his most lasting influence to be found in the study of the Synoptic Gospels.[68] In 1835 Lachmann wrote a landmark article titled "On the Order of the Narratives in the Synoptic Gospels" that paved the way for the acceptance of Markan priority.[69] As the title of Lachmann's article indicates, he focuses primarily on one issue: the order of the accounts within the Gospels.[70] Lachmann proclaims at the beginning that: "The ordering of the gospel stories does not vary as much as most people think. The variation appears greatest if all three writers are compared together, or if Luke is compared with Matthew: it is less if Mark is compared with the others one by one."[71] Lachmann does not, however, argue that Matthew and Luke used Mark, but instead that Mark is the more original Gospel because it stands closer to a preexisting common source (whether oral or written) of all three Synoptic evangelists. Lachmann clarifies his thesis near the end of his essay:

> If my suggestions are correct and there is such precise and comprehensive agreement between both Matthew and Luke and the order of the gospel according to Mark that what little variations there are can be supposed made by them each for his own purposes, and if it is clear, in spite of this complete agreement, that they did not have before them a copy of Mark to imitate, the only remaining possibility is to say that the more or less prescribed order which all three follow was settled and established by some authority and tradition of the gospel, before they themselves wrote.[72]

Before stating this conclusion, Lachmann begins his argument by dealing with Matthew's departures from Mark, and then those of Mark from Luke. Regarding Matthew, Lachmann first observes that all the points where Mark differs from Matthew occur in one section (Mark 1:21–6:13//Matt 4:24–13:58).[73] For Lachmann these differences are not all that significant, as they concern only eight sections, and these are not "jumbled together indiscriminately."[74] He further notes that the "remaining sections can be divided into two parts in such a way that in neither did the writers

---

67. So Baird, *History*, 1:321. But see the less laudatory appraisal of Aland and Aland, *Text of the New Testament*, 11, which will be discussed in more detail in the "Evaluation" section below.

68. So Kümmel, *New Testament*, 147.

69. So Bruce, "History of New Testament Study," 39. Much of Lachmann's original article, "De ordine narrationum" is included in translation along with notations of original pagination in Palmer, "Lachmann's Argument." The following references are derived from Palmer's article.

70. Lachmann, "De ordine narrationum," 574.

71. Ibid.

72. Ibid., 582.

73. Ibid., 574.

74. Ibid., 576.

differ in their ordering."[75] Lachmann concludes that both Gospels were following the same source, the order of which they did not depart from unless they were compelled by some necessity.[76]

It is also relevant at this point to consider Lachmann's theory of Matthean composition. In contrast to Griesbach, Lachmann did not believe that the Gospel of Matthew was written by an apostle, but followed Schleiermacher's theory of a double composition of Matthew.[77] Lachmann clarifies this theory, stating: "the gospel of Matthew I regard as originally composed of discourses of the Lord Jesus Christ, collected and woven together, with other stories stuck in afterwards."[78] Lachmann thus believed that Matthew (the apostle) composed a collection of sayings of Jesus, which later interpolators then combined with narrative material to form the Gospel as we now have it.[79] In conjunction with his denial of the apostolic authorship of Matthew, Lachmann also disagrees with Griesbach's position on Matthean priority:

> Even more implausible... is the view of Mark as a bungling dilettante, unsure of his way, borne hither and thither between Matthew's and Luke's gospels by boredom, desire, carelessness, folly, or design. Adherents of this view must have been taken in by a certain discussion of Griesbach's which, though it looks clever and subtle, is really not ingenious at all, but an absolute frost.[80]

Lachmann includes some explanations for why the authors of Matthew arranged the Gospel material in a different order from Mark, including their desire to respect as much as possible the original arrangement of the apostle Matthew's sayings of Jesus.[81] Lachmann also points out how some material was rearranged to make better sense of the flow of Matthew's narrative. Two examples are the location in Matthew's Gospel of the raising of the ruler's daughter and the healing of two blind men (Matt 9:18–31), which are in a different position than Mark. Lachmann explains that these were relocated in Matthew to provide specific examples to support Jesus' response to the messengers of John the Baptist in Matt 11:5.[82]

Lachmann also addresses the correspondences between Mark and Luke, which he considers to be even less debatable than the similarities between Mark and Matthew: "But not even obstinacy and scepticism, I suppose, could drive [my dissenters] to deny that Luke hardly ever departs from Mark, once they have examined a little

75. Ibid.
76. Ibid.
77. Ibid., 577.
78. Ibid.
79. So ibid., 578.
80. Ibid., 577.
81. Ibid., 578.
82. Ibid.

more closely those places where there is some difference."[83] Lachmann divides these into two classes. The first class includes sections where the order of the pericopes change, but the words in both are "very much the same," while the second class describes some sections "in which displacement is accompanied by a remarkable difference in the facts and the words."[84] Lachmann admits that this second class of texts had led a number of writers to conclude that Luke was actually telling different stories. Lachmann, however, disagrees: "if it now seems credible that [Luke] was acquainted with the Gospel stories in the order in which Mark used them, it is surely inconceivable that he should have omitted those unless he was sure he could present them as received from other authorities in a different and indeed more reliable manner."[85] Lachmann then explains rationally how and why Luke rearranged and reworded certain stories for his own purposes, yet he insists these were not really different stories from those included in Mark. Instead, Luke reworked them for his own purposes consistent with what he considered to be more reliable sources.

Lachmann concludes his argument by warning against taking too seriously the strict historicity of the chronology of the Synoptic Gospels: "I shall be satisfied if it is understood that in determining the precise chronology of the history of Jesus, and deciding which events should be thought to have happened before or after others, no greater weight can be placed on the witness of three evangelists than if a single and indeed unknown author had testified."[86] He then stresses again that before the Gospels were written, the narrative order was settled, and he suggests that the real point worthy of inquiry is how and by what means that original order was composed and arranged.[87]

APPLICATION

In order to illustrate the approaches of Griesbach and Lachmann, we will now apply their methods to three apparently parallel passages from the Synoptic Gospels that involve both text critical issues and Synoptic Gospel relationships. The passages to be considered are Matt 8:18–22//Mark 4:35//Luke 9:57–62. The pericopes in Matthew and Luke deal with Jesus' radical call to discipleship, whereas only one comparable line of this account is included in Mark. This Markan excerpt simply recounts the movement of Jesus to a surrounding region, and is found in a slightly different context (i.e., the calming of a storm; cf. Matt 8:23–27; Luke 8:22–25). We will first consider how each scholar actually dealt with a text critical issue in these passages in relation to the Textus Receptus. Then we will consider hypothetically how each likely would

83. Ibid., 579–80.
84. Ibid., 581.
85. Ibid.
86. Ibid., 582–83.
87. Ibid., 583.

have explained the reasons for each Gospel's inclusion (or exclusion) of the pericope in light of their theories of Synoptic priority.

The first issue to be addressed is a textual variant found in Matt 8:22. One question in this verse is whether the first verb should read λέγει or εἶπεν. The Textus Receptus in this instance reads εἶπεν, supported by majuscules L, W, and Θ. The more likely reading, however, is λέγει, which is supported by the generally better witnesses for the Gospels ℵ, B, and C. Griesbach's text reads εἶπεν, in line with the Textus Receptus and the Byzantine text type. Even though λέγει has stronger support from what Griesbach himself agreed to be the better Alexandrian text type, his decision to side with the Byzantine witnesses can be explained by a number of factors. First, Codex Sinaiticus (ℵ) was still unknown in Griesbach's time.[88] Second, even though Griesbach did utilize Codex Vaticanus (B) in his apparatus, he had not studied it in person and his knowledge of this codex in all likelihood was not as thorough as his knowledge of those manuscripts that he had been able to consult first-hand in his travels.[89] This may be one reason he did not list the variant reading from Vaticanus (λέγει) in his apparatus for Matt 8:22. (In fact, Griesbach did not include any indication in his *Novum Testamentum Graece* that εἶπεν may not be the original reading.)[90] Third, even if Griesbach were aware of these better witnesses, he may still have been hesitant to disagree with the Textus Receptus, to which he often deferred in his text.

In contrast to Griesbach, Lachmann did depart from the Textus Receptus in this passage, as his text reads λέγει instead of εἶπεν. Although his 1831 edition did not include a textual apparatus, it is clear from his 1842 edition that Lachmann's basis for including λέγει was the testimony of Codex Vaticanus (B) and Codex Ephraemi Syri Rescriptus (C).

Second, we will now consider the explanation each scholar would likely have given regarding the origins of these pericopes. As one who argued for Matthean priority, Griesbach would certainly have seen the account in Matthew to be the more original. He further would have viewed Matthew's account as apostolic, eyewitness testimony. Regarding Mark's omission of this pericope, Griesbach would argue that Mark was distilling Matthew and Luke for a specific audience. Griesbach would likely be hesitant to surmise precisely *why* Mark left out this account, but he would be content to state that Mark had his own reasons that are not always evident to us. However, he might conjecture that this passage included some cultural details that were relevant

---

88. Codex Sinaiticus was discovered in 1859 by Constantin von Tischendorf in St. Catherine's monastery at Mount Sinai. Cf. Metzger and Ehrman, *Text of the New Testament*, 62–67.

89. Vaticanus has been housed at the Vatican Library since at least 1475, but access to it seems to have been restricted until photographs were made available in 1889–90 (ibid., 67–69). Griesbach apparently consulted an edition of Vaticanus edited by Birchius (Griesbach, *Novum Testamentum Graece*, 1:xcviii).

90. Thus Griesbach also did not include the reading of Codex Ephraemi Syri Rescriptus (C). However, he did acknowledge the variant reading λέγει in his *Symbolae criticae*, 1:15.

for or well-known among Palestinian Jews (such as burial customs) that would not have been as germane to Mark's audience, which was far removed from Palestine.[91]

For Lachmann, Mark's Gospel reflects the most original order among the Synoptic Gospels as it stands closest to a common source used by all three Synoptics. Thus the excerpt from Mark 4:35 would probably also reflect this supposed original source, especially since Matthew contains similar phrasing at Matt 8:18. For Lachmann, the authors of Matthew's Gospel most likely altered the order known in Mark for their own purposes, as they sought coherence in the overall narrative. In sum, Lachmann would view the arrangement of Mark's Gospel to be antecedent to Matthew, and say that the authors of Matthew adjusted Mark's order to fit with the collected sayings of Jesus. Although Luke contains a similar story to Matthew, he does not share the excerpt that appears to be common to Matt 8:18 and Mark 4:35. For Lachmann, this may have been due to Luke's dependence on other sources he felt to be more reliable.[92]

EVALUATION

Text Criticism

The influence of J. J. Griesbach on New Testament textual criticism can hardly be exaggerated, as he laid the foundation for all the work on the text of the Greek New Testament that came after him.[93] His significance in this area is found primarily in his editions of the Greek New Testament. In these editions Griesbach dared to depart (in places) from the Textus Receptus and printed readings with better support in accordance with his study of ancient manuscripts. It was his work, according to Kümmel, that marked the end of the unquestioned reign of the Textus Receptus.[94] It should also be recognized, however, that Griesbach was not as successful as he might have hoped in his aim to produce the most reliable text possible of the Greek New Testament, since in the end he relied more than he should have on the Textus Receptus.[95]

Griesbach has also had a lasting influence in his articulation of text types of New Testament manuscripts. The three text types proposed by Griesbach—Alexandrian, Western, and Byzantine (or Constantinopolitan)—are still utilized today, albeit in a slightly more nuanced form. In addition, his assessment that the Alexandrian is the most reliable text type and the Byzantine is a secondary derivation also remains widely accepted. Kurt and Barbara Aland, however, are more guarded in their approbation of Griesbach's influence, whose breakthroughs in the articulation of text types they see as

---

91. Cf. Griesbach, "Demonstration," 106–7.

92. Lachmann did not comment explicitly on the shared material between Matthew and Luke, but his theory of a double composition of Matthew that involves the combination of a narrative source with collected sayings of Jesus anticipates some elements of the later theory of Q.

93. Such is the assessment of Metzger and Ehrman, *Text of the New Testament*, 165, 167.

94. Kümmel, *New Testament*, 74.

95. So Neill and Wright, *Interpretation*, 73.

already present in the work of Bengel and Semler.[96] While Bengel and Semler, Griesbach's teacher, certainly paved the way for his insights, it is also true that Griesbach's own work has had an immense impact in the field of New Testament textual criticism.

Related to his work in textual criticism, Griesbach's introduction of his *Synopsis Evangeliorum* was also an important development. This helpful layout has been adopted and modified by a number of different scholars through the years, but these permutations generally reflect Griesbach's innovation.[97] Moreover, it has even been suggested that all scholarly discussion surrounding the relationship of the Synoptic Gospels for the past two centuries goes back to the publication of Griesbach's *Synopsis Evangeliorum*[98] which, as noted above, first led Griesbach himself to consider the relationship among the Synoptics.

Karl Lachmann's text of the New Testament also marked a positive advancement in the field of New Testament textual criticism. Lachmann went even further than Griesbach in questioning the Textus Receptus by reconstructing the most ancient text possible from known manuscripts.[99] However, Lachmann's efforts were hindered because he did not have a sufficiently deep reservoir of manuscripts to pursue his method as thoroughly as he desired.[100] In addition, because of the nature of the manuscript evidence, Lachmann's highly mechanical approach led him to accept some passages he knew were spurious (such as Mark 16:9–20).[101] Kümmel further observes that Lachmann's primary error was his belief that it was possible to reconstruct a text "without interpretation."[102]

Despite the limitations and shortcomings of the critical texts of Griesbach and Lachmann, both men were significant for seeking to improve the widely accepted but sometimes ill-attested text of the New Testament by an appeal to earlier and better manuscripts. Moreover, their methodologies in the production of these texts have been highly influential beyond the limits of their own editions of the New Testament. For example, their approaches were later refined by Westcott and Hort as explained in their introduction to the Greek New Testament,[103] itself a watershed work that remains one of the most significant treatments of New Testament textual criticism available today.

---

96. Aland and Aland, *Text of the New Testament*, 9.
97. A standard modern edition is Aland, *Synopsis quattuor Evangeliorum*.
98. Reicke, "Introduction."
99. So Westcott and Hort, *New Testament*, 13.
100. So ibid.
101. So ibid.; Kümmel, *New Testament*, 147.
102. Ibid.
103. So Metzger and Ehrman, *Text of the New Testament*, 175.

Source Criticism

Griesbach's theory of Matthean priority has proved to be a lasting one, as a number of scholars still find the "Griesbach Hypothesis" to be highly plausible.[104] Some of the strongest arguments for this theory are the minor agreements of Matthew and Luke against Mark, which may point to Luke's use of Matthew.[105] However, the majority of scholars still remain unconvinced by the "Griesbach Hypothesis." In contrast to Griesbach's theory, many of his dissenters consider it to be more likely that Luke did not know Matthew. It is observed that Matthew and Mark frequently agree, and Mark and Luke frequently agree, but Matthew and Luke agree much less often. This suggests, as Lachmann's article indicates, that Mark (rather than Matthew) is a shared source among the Synoptics. A related objection to Griesbach's view is, despite Griesbach's appeals to Mark's unique purposes, Mark's complete omission of such material as the Sermon on the Mount (or Sermon on the Plain), the birth narratives of Jesus, and an account of the resurrected Jesus, all of which are significant aspects of Matthew and Luke. Those who argue for Markan priority suggest that it makes more sense for Mark not to include these portions of Matthew and Luke if he wrote first, but it is more difficult to comprehend if Matthew and Luke were known to him.[106] In addition, both Matthew and Luke appear to smooth out Mark's sometimes less eloquent style, which mitigates against Griesbach's view. Finally, Griesbach's contention that Mark simply worked from written copies of Matthew and Luke open in front of him does not seem to account for the more complex interplay between written and oral sources in the composition of the Gospels that many scholars posit today.[107]

A majority (though by no means all) of scholars today opt for some form of the Two-Source Hypothesis to explain the Synoptic Problem. The Two-Source Hypothesis states that Matthew and Luke used Mark and another source(s) of Jesus' sayings, known as Q. Although this theory was not articulated by Lachmann, his work was influential in paving the way for the acceptance of Markan priority. Kümmel summarizes Lachmann's influence: "Lachmann thus advanced an irrefutable argument for the priority of Mark vis-à-vis the other two Synoptics and at the same time drew attention to the need of assuming still another source for the other synoptic matter."[108] Kümmel's assessment of Lachmann's argument as "irrefutable," however, is too bold; Lachmann's argument is not without its faults. For example, his view of the double composition of Matthew, following Schleiermacher, is not espoused by many today.[109]

---

104. So, e.g., Farmer, *Synoptic Problem*; Cf. Tuckett, *Revival*.
105. For a concise introduction to the theories of interdependence among the Synoptic Gospels (which is utilized in this section), see Carson and Moo, *Introduction*, 88–103.
106. So, e.g., France, *Matthew*, 40.
107. See, for example, Dunn, *Jesus Remembered*, 222–23.
108. Kümmel, *New Testament*, 148.
109. So Palmer, "Lachmann's Argument," 377.

In addition, Lachmann assumes too much, especially in relation to the supposed common source underlying all three Synoptic Gospels.

The term "the Lachmann Fallacy," which does not actually apply to Lachmann himself, should also be noted. This is a term that is sometimes used in reference to the unproven assumptions of Lachmann's followers, specifically in relation to arguments for Markan priority on the basis of order.[110] Arguments for Markan priority on the basis of Mark's order are not the best way to determine which Gospel came first, although the order of the narratives likely does indicate Mark is a middle term for Matthew and Luke. But to determine which order is more original, one must decide if it is more likely that Matthew and Luke reworked Mark's order, or if Mark reworked Matthew's and Luke's orders.[111] Most scholars today, in accordance with Lachmann, opt for the former.

In spite of the widespread adoption of Markan priority and the Two-Source Hypothesis to explain the Synoptic Problem, the question remains open; scholars continue to debate which Synoptic Gospel was written first. The complexity of the data is not conducive to conclusive answers, and it seems as though the only real consensus that has been reached is that there is no consensus. Therefore, since the issue of the literary relationships among the Synoptic Gospels remains a conundrum with no definitive resolution on the horizon, the works of Griesbach and Lachmann in this area continue to be important components of an ongoing conversation.

BIBLIOGRAPHY

Aland, Kurt, ed. *Synopsis quattuor Evangeliorum: Locis parallelis Evangeliorum apocryphorum et patrum adhibitis.* 15th ed. Stuttgart: Deutsche Bibelgesellschaft, 1996.

Aland, Kurt, and Barbara Aland. *The Text of the New Testament: An Introduction to the Critical Editions and to the Theory and Practices of Modern Textual Criticism.* Translated by Erroll F. Rhodes. 2nd ed. Grand Rapids: Eerdmans, 1989.

Baird, William. *History of New Testament Research.* 2 vols. Minneapolis: Fortress, 1992.

Bruce, F. F. "The History of New Testament Study." In *New Testament Interpretation: Essays on Principles and Method*, edited by I. Howard Marshall, 21–59. Carlisle: Paternoster, 1977.

Butler, B. C. *The Originality of St Matthew: A Critique of the Two-Document Hypothesis.* Cambridge: Cambridge University Press, 1951.

Carson, D. A., and Douglas J. Moo. *An Introduction to the New Testament.* 2nd ed. Grand Rapids: Zondervan, 2005.

Davies, W. D., and Dale C. Allison, Jr. *A Critical and Exegetical Commentary on the Gospel according to Saint Matthew.* 3 vols. ICC. Edinburgh: T. & T. Clark, 1988–97.

Delling, Gerhard. "Johann Jakob Griesbach: His Life, Work and Times." In *J. J. Griesbach: Synoptic and Text-Critical Studies 1776-1976*, edited by Bernard Orchard and Thomas R. W. Longstaff, 5–21. Translated by Ronald Walls. SNTSMS 34. Cambridge: Cambridge University Press, 1978.

---

110. Cf. Butler, *Originality*, 62–71; Farmer, "Lachmann Fallacy."

111. So Davies and Allison, *Matthew*, 1:100.

Dunn, James D. G. *Jesus Remembered*. Christianity in the Making 1. Grand Rapids: Eerdmans, 2003.

Farmer, William R. "The Lachmann Fallacy." *NTS* 14 (1968) 441–43.

———. *The Synoptic Problem: A Critical Analysis.* Dillsboro, NC: Western North Carolina Press, 1976.

Fee, Gordon D. "Modern Text Criticism and the Synoptic Problem." In *J. J. Griesbach: Synoptic and Text-Critical Studies 1776–1976*, edited by Bernard Orchard and Thomas R. W. Longstaff, 154–69. SNTSMS 34. Cambridge: Cambridge University Press, 1978.

France, R. T. *Matthew: Evangelist and Teacher.* Downers Grove, IL: InterVarsity, 1989.

Gabler, J. P., ed. *Io. Iacobi Griesbachii opuscula academica.* 2 vols. Jena: n.p., 1824–25.

Greeven, Heinrich. "The Gospel Synopsis from 1776 to the Present Day." In *J. J. Griesbach: Synoptic and Text-Critical Studies 1776–1976*, edited by Bernard Orchard and Thomas R. W. Longstaff, 22–49. Translated by Robert Althann. SNTSMS 34. Cambridge: Cambridge University Press, 1978.

Griesbach, J. J. "A Demonstration that Mark Was Written after Matthew and Luke." In *J. J. Griesbach: Synoptic and Text-Critical Studies 1776–1976*, edited by Bernard Orchard and Thomas R. W. Longstaff, 103–35. Translated by Bernard Orchard. SNTSMS 34. Cambridge: Cambridge University Press, 1978.

———, ed. *Novum Testamentum Graece. Textum ad fidem codicum, versionum et patrum recensuit et lectionis varietatem adjecit D. Jo. Ja. Griesbach.* 2nd ed. 2 vols. London: Elmsly, 1796–1806.

———. *Symbolae criticae ad supplendas et corrigendas variarum N. T. lectionum collectiones. Accedit multorum N. T. codicum Graecarum descriptio et examen.* 2 vols. Halle: Impensis Io. Iac. curtii viduae, 1785–93.

———. *Synopsis Evangeliorum Matthaei Marci et Lucae una cum iis Joannis pericopis quae omnino cum caeterorum evangelistarum narrationibus conferendae sunt. Textum recensuit et selectam lectionis varietatem adjecit D. Jo. Jac. Griesbach.* 4th ed. Halle: Curtian, 1822.

Hertz, Martin. *Karl Lachmann: Eine Biographie.* Berlin: Wilhelm Hertz, 1851.

Kümmel, Werner Georg. *The New Testament: The History of the Investigation of Its Problems.* Translated by S. McLean Gilmore and Howard C. Kee. NTL. London: SCM, 1973.

Lachmann, Karl. "De ordine narrationum in Evangeliis synopticis." *Theologische Studien und Kritiken* 8 (1835) 570–90.

———, ed. *Novum Testamentum Graece et Latinae, Carolus Lachmannus rescensuit, Philippus Buttmannus, Ph. F. Graecae lectionis auctoritates apposuit.* 2 vols. Berlin: G. Reimer, 1842–50.

———. "Rechenschaft über seine Ausgabe des Neuen Testaments von Professor Lachmann in Berlin." *Theologische Studien und Kritiken* 3 (1830) 817–45.

Metzger, Bruce M., and Bart D. Ehrman. *The Text of the New Testament: Its Transmission, Corruption, and Restoration.* 4th ed. Oxford: Oxford University Press, 2005.

Neill, Stephen, and Tom Wright. *The Interpretation of the New Testament 1861–1986.* 2nd ed. Oxford: Oxford University Press, 1988.

Palmer, N. H. "Lachmann's Argument." *NTS* 13 (1967) 368–78.

Reicke, Bo. "Griesbach's Answer to the Synoptic Question." In *J. J. Griesbach: Synoptic and Text-Critical Studies*, edited by Bernard Orchard and Thomas R. W. Longstaff, 50–67. Translated by Ronald Walls. SNTSMS 34. Cambridge: Cambridge University Press, 1978.

———. "Introduction" [to Griesbach's *Commentatio qua Marci Evangelium totum e Matthaei et Lucae commentariis decerptum esse monstratur*]. In *J. J. Griesbach: Synoptic and Text-Critical Studies 1776–1976*, edited by Bernard Orchard and Thomas R. W. Longstaff, 68–73. SNTSMS 34. Cambridge: Cambridge University Press, 1978.

Tuckett, Christopher M. *The Revival of the Griesbach Hypothesis: Analysis and Appraisal.* SNTSMS 44. Cambridge: Cambridge University Press, 1979.

Vaganay, Léon, and Christian-Bernard Amphoux. *An Introduction to New Testament Textual Criticism.* Translated by Jenny Heimerdinger. 2nd ed. Cambridge: Cambridge University Press, 1991.

Westcott, B. F., and F. J. A. Hort. *The New Testament in the Original Greek: Introduction, Appendix.* Cambridge: Macmillan, 1882.

2

Friedrich Schleiermacher

His Contribution to New Testament Studies

Jan H. Nylund

INTRODUCTION

FRIEDRICH DANIEL ERNST SCHLEIERMACHER (1768–1834) is often referred to as the father of modern theology and thus not only the originator of new theology, but of a new era.[1] Mariña ranks him with Calvin, Aquinas, and Augustine.[2] The claim that he is the father of modern liberalism is certainly justified, but too simplistic. Unlike Luther, Schleiermacher consciously endeavored to revolutionize the area of theology. He had a total reconstruction of Christian theology in mind.[3]

Schleiermacher's importance within the field of New Testament research is, however, often overlooked.[4] This topic will be the main focus in our treatment of Schleiermacher, accounting for and discussing his *Introduction to the New Testament*, *The Life of Jesus*, and his *Critical Essay on the Gospel of St. Luke*, Schleiermacher's primary exegetical work on that Gospel. Below, an initial overview of Schleiermacher's life is given; a short section introduces some principal characteristics of his theological outlook; then, as mentioned, the bulk of the article focuses on Schleiermacher's New Testament research. In my concluding remarks an evaluation of Friedrich Schleiermacher's contributions is attempted.

---

1. Karl Barth uses the same words that Schleiermacher himself used about Frederick the Great to define Schleiermacher's contribution: "He did not found a school, but an era" (Barth, *Protestant Theology*, 425).

2. Mariña, "Introduction," 1.

3. Christian, *Friedrich Schleiermacher*, 12–13.

4. Baird, *History of New Testament Research*, 208–9; Helmer, "Schleiermacher's Exegetical Theology," 229.

THE LIFE AND CONTRIBUTIONS OF FRIEDRICH SCHLEIERMACHER

In the case of Schleiermacher, it may be argued that to an unusual degree his own life and personal experiences made up the context for everything he wrote, and conditioned it. Therefore, a fairly detailed overview of Schleiermacher's life will be provided. Terrence Tice lists and accounts for as many as thirteen crucial events in Schleiermacher's life that he argues had a formative influence on his thought.

Friedrich Schleiermacher was born in 1768 into a family where he became the third in a line of Reformed preachers. Friedrich's father, Gottlieb Schleiermacher, was a Reformed army chaplain and his mother, Katharina-Maria Stubenrauch, was an unusually devout Christian.[5] Because of the Bayer Succession war in 1778, the Schleiermacher family had to move from Breslau to Pless. It was in the Herrnhuter Brethren[6] colony Gnadenfrei near his new home that the eleven-year-old Friedrich came to the understanding that eternal life was granted to humanity by grace and not as reward for a virtuous life. A few years later, in April 1783, when the family spent two weeks in Gnadenfrei, Friedrich experienced what he later would refer to as the birth of his "higher life":

> Here my consciousness of the relation of human beings to a higher world first arose . . . Here there first developed that mystical disposition which is so essential to me and has saved and preserved me under all assaults of skepticism.[7]

In his autobiography, there is a letter from Schleiermacher where he writes to his sister about his experience among the Herrnhut brethren:

> There is not throughout Christendom, in our day, a form of public worship which expresses more worthily, and awakens more thoroughly the spirit of true Christian piety, than does that of the Herrnhut brotherhood![8]

The pietistic element of Herrnhut came to be a decisive element of Schleiermacher's thought, even though he broke with the biblical literalism and orthodoxy of the Herrnhut Brethren. In the Brethren school in Niesky, Schleiermacher received an excellent education and developed a strong self-discipline. After two years in Niesky, Schleiermacher and his close friend Johann Baptist von Albertini were promoted to the Brethren school in Barby that educated pastors and teachers. In the months

---

5. Tice, *Schleiermacher*, 1.

6. The Herrnhuter Brethren had earlier been located in Moravia, but had been expelled by the Hapsburgs during the Thirty Years' War. The Brethren settled in Herrnhut, a small village built on the lands of Count Zinzendorf, who later became the bishop of the Brethren. The Herrnhut Brethren became known for educational excellence, their international work in missions, and their enthusiastic and warm piety. The Herrnhut community still exists and continues its international work. Herrnhut had also certainly contributed to what came to be Methodism when John Wesley visited Herrnhut fifty years before Schleiermacher (Tice, *Schleiermacher*, 2–3).

7. Ibid., 2.

8. Schleiermacher, *Life of Schleiermacher*, 2:23.

following from September 1786, Schleiermacher was experiencing a spiritual crisis regarding his orthodox beliefs.[9] In December and January he renounced his "supernatural feelings" and belief in the two natures of Christ, eternal punishment, and total corruption.[10] Schleiermacher was eighteen at the time.[11] Despite his spiritual change, his experience of communal pietism in Niesky would stay with him for all of his life.[12]

Schleiermacher felt compelled to leave Barby. He left to attend the University of Halle, where pietism had had a formative influence on the university and on leading German Enlightenment figures, such as Gottfried Wilhem Leibniz (1648–1716) and Christian Wolf (1679–1754). During his time in Halle, Schleiermacher did what came to be a life pattern: he formed a close and permanent friendship. The Swedish diplomat Carl Gustav von Brinckmann introduced Schleiermacher to cultured circles and to the world of women. The experiential and practically-minded orientation of the professors of the university would fundamentally influence Schleiermacher, who would pair it with a strong theoretical interest. Even though as many as 70 percent of all students at the university were theology students, Schleiermacher chose to focus on classical studies, philosophy, philology, ethics, epistemology, French, and English.

In 1789, Schleiermacher moved to Drossen. Here he began to focus on the reading of ancient writers and Immanuel Kant, whose *Critiques* had recently been published (1781, 1785, 1788). Kant became a source of inspiration for Schleiermacher and it was in his response to and reflection over Kant that he developed his critical, nonrationalist, nonbiblicist, non-Enlightenment, and nonsupernaturalist theological perspective.[13] In the summer of 1789 Schleiermacher developed his first close friendship with a woman, Frau Beneke, whose marriage he saved. Throughout his life Schleiermacher would entertain close friendships with a number of cultured women.[14] Schleiermacher wrote:

> Only through knowledge of the inner spirit of women have I gained knowledge of the true worth of a human being . . . It lies very deep in my nature that

---

9. This was partly due to his involvement in a secret philosophical club, which he himself started, where he came in contact with literature by authors such as Kant, Goethe, Wieland, and Rousseau. Such material was forbidden at the seminary (Gerrish, *A Prince of the Church*, 39; Tice, *Schleiermacher*, 4; Mariña, "Introduction," 2).

10. Schleiermacher informed his father that he could not believe in doctrines that lacked support "on critical, exegetical and philosophical grounds" (Schleiermacher, *Soliloquies*, 40).

11. Tice, *Schleiermacher*, 3–4.

12. The connection between feeling and religion became part and parcel of his theology. He also inherited from the Moravians the insight that religious feeling and religious awareness are experienced on the basis of God's grace. Schleiermacher defines religion as a feeling of absolute dependence on God. The personal and deep devotion to Jesus as the source from which faith arises and the centrality of the redemptive work of Christ are yet other elements of the Moravian heritage (Christian, *Friedrich Schleiermacher*, 36–37).

13. Tice, *Schleiermacher*, 5.

14. Ibid., 6.

I should always attach myself more closely to women than to men, for there is
so much in my spirit that men rarely understand.

In 1790 Schleiermacher found a position as tutor for the six children of Count von Dohna at the beautiful estate of Schlobitten in Eastern Prussia.[15] From the Schlobitten experience he extracted the value of human community in family and marriage.[16] He wrote about this period in *Über den Wert des Lebens* (*On What Gives Value to Life*) (1792–93).[17] At Schlobitten he experienced a Christianity that was both intelligent and conservative.[18] In *Monologen: Eine Neujahrsgabe* (*Soliloquies: An English Translation of the Monologen*) (1800), Schleiermacher writes: "in a stranger's home my sense for the beauty of human friendship was first awakened."[19] During his time in Landsberg an der Warthe (1794–96) as assistant to Pastor Schumann, he reflected upon the debate regarding Baruch Spinoza's pantheism and deterministic view of God, human life, and so on. Schleiermacher's perspective is monotheistic and envisions God as the provider of a world where human freedom is allowed to thrive.[20] With regard to his attitude to the supernatural, Schleiermacher follows Spinoza believing that God is at work in creation, but since God works through rather than against nature, the concept of a miracle would be unnatural.[21] In *Christian Faith* Schleiermacher writes:

> Now some have represented miracles in this sense as essential to the perfect manifestation of the divine omnipotence. But it is difficult to conceive, on the one side, how omnipotence is shown to be greater in the suspension of the interdependence of nature than in its original immutable course which was no less divinely ordered.[22]

During the six years of Schleiermacher's second pastorate at Charity Hospital in Berlin, he was part of the German Romantic movement that was in its heyday from 1796 to 1802. The romantic movement was a reaction against the cold rationality of the Enlightenment. Romanticism opened up supplementary roads to understanding by means of intuition and imagination. This appealed to Schleiermacher's experiential orientation and convictions that originated from his Moravian experience.[23] What

---

15. From this experience Schleiermacher developed the educational theory regarding the process of learning for which he would become famous in German educational circles.

16. Tice, *Schleiermacher*, 6–7.

17. The focus of his value theory is the pursuit of what is good, *viz.* what is important for a human to grow, and that the sharing of human life is where life is at its best (Tice, *Schleiermacher*, 7).

18. Christian, *Friedrich Schleiermacher*, 34.

19. Schleiermacher, *Soliloquies*, 74.

20. Tice, *Schleiermacher*, 8.

21. Baird, *History of New Testament Research*, 211.

22. Schleiermacher, *Christian Faith*, 179.

23. Among these was his conviction that individuality is formed in the context of family—a notion that found its confirmation in romanticism's emphasis on humanity's place in an organic totality. Other elements of Moravian origin that made romanticism appealing were his aversion to rationalistic

might be the strongest Romantic trait in Schleiermacher is the creative and identity-forming tension between diversity and unity, the paradigm through which the pairs of *individual-community*, *inorganic-organic*, and *particular-universal* are understood.[24]

While in Berlin, Schleiermacher socialized with the intellectuals of his day, among them his poet friend Friedrich Schlegel. Schlegel encouraged Schleiermacher to write his famous *Über die Religion: Reden an die Gebildeten unter ihren Verächtern* (*On Religion: Speeches to Its Cultured Despisers*) in which he asserts that misunderstanding is the basis for modern intellectuals' rejection of religion, the experience of which is, in fact, essential to human existence.[25] The following year, in 1800, he published his well-known *Soliloquies*. Around 1800 Schleiermacher fell in love with another pastor's wife and waited for six years to propose to her, but the woman finally turned him down. In 1804 the Prussian king engaged in moral reforms, and as part of this reform he encouraged more worship and decreed that services be held at the University of Halle led by a university preacher—Schleiermacher was appointed as the first university preacher.[26] In 1806 Napoleon invaded Halle and closed down the university. Schleiermacher moved back to Berlin in 1807 where he remained the rest of his life. From this time onwards, Schleiermacher was always writing something. In 1807 he published his critical works on *First Timothy* and *Heraclitus*.[27] The so-called later Berlin years (1808–34) were intense years.[28] From 1808 Schleiermacher was teaching at what was to become the University of Berlin.[29] The same year he was called by a decree from the Prussian king to pastor the Reformed congregation of Dreifaltigkeitskirche. Schleiermacher conducted the worship and preached[30] almost every Sunday.[31] He also taught the young in confirmation classes, among them Otto von Bismarck, who would become Prussia's chancellor.[32] In 1809, at the age of forty, Schleiermacher married Henriette Sophie Elizabeth von Muehlenfels, who was a widow with two children.[33]

---

religion and his appreciation of "flawed but concrete communities of worship" (Christian, *Friedrich Schleiermacher*, 39).

24. Christian, *Friedrich Schleiermacher*, 39–40.

25. Baird, *History of New Testament Research*, 209.

26. As a Reformed lecturer at the Lutheran University of Halle, he was met with suspicion and, initially, few students wanted to attend his lecturers.

27. Tice, *Schleiermacher*, 9–11.

28. Schleiermacher normally got by with four or five hours of sleep and usually spent late evenings and part of the night writing and then met his students between 6:00 and 9:00 o'clock in the morning (Tice, *Schleiermacher*, 12).

29. At the time, Berlin had the only theological institution in all of Prussia.

30. Around 600 sermons have been published from the period 1787–1834. Yet another 150 sermons are to be found in archives.

31. Tice, *Schleiermacher*, 14.

32. Baird, *History of New Testament Research*, 210.

33. Together they had four children. The Schleiermacher home was warm and busy and students were often visiting, but certain principles, found in *The Christian Household* (1820), were followed

Schleiermacher co-founded the University of Berlin with Wilhelm von Humboldt, serving as dean of the theological department for many years and as the headmaster of the entire university in 1815–16. During the Napoleonic era he served as a spy in Berlin. From 1808 and onwards Schleiermacher also became the foremost proponent of progressive education in the German lands. He was consistently opposed on almost all issues by his conservative colleague Georg Wilhelm Friedrich Hegel (1770–1831), whom he had brought to the university in 1818.[34] By 1821 there were 200 theology students at the university and a decade later 600. During his 26 years at the university, half of the courses he taught were on New Testament exegesis. Schleiermacher was also a member of the Berlin Academy of Sciences. Throughout his time in Berlin he published some of his most important works.[35] Schleiermacher died in 1834 and his casket was followed by about 20,000 people through the streets of Berlin. The queen's carriage was in the entourage.[36]

Tice divides the reception of Schleiermacher's work in the English-speaking world into five periods. (i) *Ignorance and rejection* (1799–1899): In the early 1800s knowledge of German was not widespread among English-speaking theologians. One theologian who did know German, Connop Thirlwall, issued Schleiermacher's 1817 exegetical work on Luke in translation in 1825. The work was not well received since it was considered diabolical. Several other works of Schleiermacher were also translated into English during this period, such as *Brief Outline* (1850) and *Christmas Eve* (1890). Schleiermacher's general reputation during the period was "that of being a heretically 'liberal' interpreter of the Bible and of having sacrificed Christian faith to secular trends."[37] (ii) *Awakening awareness and limited respect* (1900–1939): The second-hand knowledge of Schleiermacher's achievements spread slowly through the works of scholars, such as Harnack, Dilthey, Troeltsch, Barth, Brunner, and many other German scholars. *Soliloquies* (1926) and *Christian Faith* (1928) were also translated. (iii) *Neo-Orthodox enmity and new reappraisals* (1949–59): In 1941, Richard

---

(Tice, *Schleiermacher*, 12–14).

34. Schleiermacher and Hegel were colleagues at the University of Berlin for thirteen years (1818–31). Even though generally they both kept to their respective essential perspectives and views, neither of them could express a view within philosophy or theology without indirectly opposing the perspective of the other. Nevertheless, they shared a few basic views: (i) The university should not only be an educational place but also one of shaping; (ii) there should be an accommodation between Christian faith and teaching, and modern thought, including natural science and humanistic research; (iii) Kant's efforts to "reconcile us to the world by defining the limits of pure reason" were not enough, but a new synthesis was needed (Crouter, *Friedrich Schleiermacher*, 71–73).

35. *Brief Outline* (1811, 1830), a critical study of *Luke* (1817), *Election* (1819), *The Christian Household* (1820), *Christian Faith* (1821–22, 1830–31), *Trinity* (1822), *Christian Festival Sermons* (1826, 1833), *On the Glaubenslehre* (1828), the *Berliner Gesangbuch* (1830–31). Most of Schleiermacher's works are collected in the 42-volume *Gesamtausgabe*, which is still to be completed. However, his works on New Testament criticism are for some reason not included in the *Gesamtausgabe*.

36. Tice, *Schleiermacher*, 15–16.

37. Tice, "Schleiermacher Yesterday, Today, and Tomorrow," 309–10.

Brandt published the first comprehensive work on Schleiermacher's contributions within philosophy, *Schleiermacher's Philosophy*. After World War II, the Neo-Orthodox perspective was increasingly acknowledged and Schleiermacher was occasionally, but usually scathingly, referred to.[38] (iv) *The "Schleiermacher Renaissance" begins in the Americas* (1960–84): A new period of Schleiermacher studies began with the publication of Richard R. Niebuhr's work *Schleiermacher on Christ and Religion* in 1964. Terrence Tice began writing on Schleiermacher, putting forth a thesis on *Schleiermacher's Theological Method* in 1961 (unpublished). A new and increased attention to Schleiermacher could be noted in German and English but also in French and Italian works. A gathering of scholars with interest in Schleiermacher was held at Vanderbilt in 1967. In the early 1980s, interest in Schleiermacher arose in the nineteenth-century theology group of the American Academy of Religion, resulting in the forming of a Schleiermacher seminar and group. (v) *The Americans take a significant part in international dialogue and research* (1986–the present): Schleiermacher scholarship has seen rapid growth in the last 30 years. A Berlin congress—The International Congress—was held in celebration of the 150th anniversary of the death of Schleiermacher. This event resulted in increased activities within Schleiermacher research, such as more than twenty published volumes of translations of Schleiermacher's works, monographs, conference volumes, and festschrifts (Edwin Mellen Press). A new series, *New Athenaeum/Neues Athenaeum*, in which a number of volumes have since been published, was also started. The International Schleiermacher Society was founded in the middle of the 1980s and has since then organized a number of international conferences in England, the United States, Italy, and Germany. Several new publishing houses have started publishing Schleiermacher research. A growing number of scholars from a broader variety of countries, such as France, Italy, the Netherlands, Japan, Korea, India, Scandinavia, and Turkey, are getting involved. Translations of most of the remaining untranslated works of Schleiermacher into English have been undertaken.[39] In summation, it is not an overstatement to conclude that Schleiermacher now makes his own voice heard in English in the English-speaking world.

THE THEOLOGY OF SCHLEIERMACHER

Except for the particular influence of certain events and experiences of Schleiermacher on his thought, the influence of the ideas and values current in society in his time should not be underestimated. In his time, Christian faith was challenged by a new, largely secular, worldview that was optimistic regarding humanity's ability to master the world by means of reason, and nothing was allowed to pass as "true" unless it could be verified by the human mind. The empirical method of the practical

---

38. Ibid., 310–11.
39. Ibid., 311–12.

sciences increasingly became the basis for all accepted knowledge.[40] This posed a real challenge to the church, which based its authority on special revelation in a distant past as contained in the Scriptures. A confident humanism, based on humanity as rational, self-sufficient, and good, began to take shape.[41] The structural science that had co-existed with biblical history was now replaced by a historically-based science that sought to explain the origins of the present order. In the wake of the Enlightenment, the 1800s was a time when all disciplines and sciences became historical. Schleiermacher was the man of the hour, creating and forming the discipline of historical theology. This historical consciousness stimulated an interest in the history of Christianity, in both a positive and negative sense.[42] When the biblical account was subjected to the historical-critical method, the result was a questioning of the historical inerrancy of Scripture and a general skepticism about elements, such as miracles and the divine nature of Jesus, that did not comply with naturalistic presuppositions. The crux of affirming Christian orthodoxy in the face of historical criticism was addressed by Schleiermacher in *Die Weihnachtsfeier: Ein Gespräch*. The irreconcilability of the notions of absolute truth and the relativism of empirical rationalism—described as "the end of all certainty"—is another critical issue that was raised and has, since then, remained a challenge in the history of Christian thought.[43]

The significance of Schleiermacher's contribution lies in the clarity with which he analyzed these new challenges. He conceived of the dawning empiricism as superficial in its incapacity to penetrate anything beyond the obvious. Schleiermacher was an empiricist in the broad sense of including religious experience[44]—from which theological thought is then derived. To Schleiermacher, theology is *experiential*. Pure and simple appeal to authority (Scripture) is no longer enough for the validation of theology. The experiential as a foundation for faith permeates Schleiermacher's theology and serves as the justification of Christian faith from the viewpoint of the modern mind.[45] Adams notes that Schleiermacher has been charged with substituting human conscience for God and concludes that there is a certain truth in this accusation even though the claim that "religious faith and theology, in Schleiermacher's view, are not about God, but only about human states of mind, is to adopt a badly one-sided reading."[46] On the basis of evidence from his theological writings, there are indications that Schleiermacher's concept of religious consciousness makes reference to "a being much greater than ourselves."[47] On the basis of an experiential foundation,

---

40. Christian, *Friedrich Schleiermacher*, 19–21.
41. Ibid., 22–23.
42. Ibid., 25–26.
43. Ibid., 26–27.
44. This pertains especially to religious experience as experienced in the worship of the church.
45. Christian, *Friedrich Schleiermacher*, 28.
46. Adams, "Faith and Religious Knowledge," 35.
47. Ibid.

Schleiermacher endeavors to reverse the correlation between Christ and Scripture by separating the two in order to safeguard the integrity of faith as well as allowing scientific inquiry of the Bible.[48] However, as we shall see, this is where Schleiermacher takes a wrong turn; one cannot be separated from the other without detriment to both. Schleiermacher is also thoroughly *historical* in his approach and absorbed by the question of nineteenth-century Christianity's comprehension of its past and how to relate it to the present. Schleiermacher understands the necessity of redefining theological thought in historical terms.[49] Another trait of Schleiermacher's theology is its *communal* character. Schleiermacher argues that theology should always be seen as something that is formed within the church[50] and not by religious genius. Theology is something that is created by the church and given a new shape with every generation.[51] To the extent that theology is formed for the expression of faith it is *confessional* in character.[52] The purpose of theology is not primarily to be a scientific discipline, but to meet the needs of the worshipping community, that is, it is *pastoral*[53] in its orientation.[54] Even though Schleiermacher does not suggest that all pastors should be theologians and vice versa, he advocates "thinking pastors."[55] In his view, theological theory is worthless without being put into practice.[56] To Schleiermacher, theology has to be *systematic* as well, in the sense that there is clarity of thought as to the internal coherence of church dogma. By this he means that dogma should be understandable and that the doctrine of the church should be relatable to all knowledge. The combination of inner coherence and this external relationship is referred to as "the scientific value" of theology. To Schleiermacher, theology is also *ontological*. He was aware of the dilemma for anyone searching for the truth and he realized that, ultimately, the confessor would ask himself whether or not his confession is true.[57]

Having provided an overview of Schleiermacher's life and accounted for those experiences that came to form his scholarship as well as his interaction with the thoughts and intellectual challenges current in the society of his time, we now turn to Schleiermacher's contribution to New Testament criticism.

---

48. Helmer, "Schleiermacher's Exegetical Theology," 231.

49. Christian, *Friedrich Schleiermacher*, 29.

50. Ibid., 30.

51. In this context the theologian should always remain a servant of the church.

52. Christian, *Friedrich Schleiermacher*, 30.

53. Schleiermacher is opposed to the theologian/minister separation (Schleiermacher, "Kurze Darstellung," §10).

54. Ibid., §11.

55. He refers to the ideal leader who is able to do theology competently within the context of the church as a "Prince of the Church" (ibid., §9).

56. Christian, *Friedrich Schleiermacher*, 30.

57. Ibid., 31–32.

SCHLEIERMACHER AND NEW TESTAMENT CRITICISM

Friedrich Schleiermacher's exegetical work has received fairly little attention for several reasons. First, his contributions in other areas have been so monumental that his exegetical contributions have tended to end up in the shadow. Second, very few of Schleiermacher's exegetical works have been published.[58] In 1809, when Schleiermacher was asked to participate in the organization of the University of Berlin, his task was to produce a curriculum for the theological department. This was later published as *Kurze Darstellung des theologischen Studiums* (*Brief Outline*).[59] In this work, Schleiermacher describes the art of criticism:

> ... the art of Criticism which has not been worked out as a separate discipline, and concerning which but few rules can be given in the way of teaching; so that its attainment depends almost exclusively upon the possession of a certain natural capacity, and upon practice.[60]

Here Schleiermacher puts emphasis on "natural capacity" and "practice." Regarding the criticism of texts, Schleiermacher argues that a sharp line cannot be drawn between higher and lower criticism.[61] As to the function of higher and lower criticism he argues as follows:

> It is necessary that the Protestant Church should vindicate its claim to be still occupied continually in the more precise determination of the Canon; and it is this which constitutes the highest exegetico-theological problem for Higher Criticism . . . [which] solves its problem, for the most part, only by approximation.[62]

> The definite problem of lower Criticism [is] that of discovering the original reading, throughout, as accurately as possible . . .[63]

Regarding the rules for performing exegesis, Schleiermacher contends:

> Therefore the New Testament Critic, also, is both bound to follow the same rules, and entitled to make use of the same means, as are applicable elsewhere. Hence it cannot be forbidden, in case of necessity to hazard conjectures; nor can any special rules have existence, which are not necessarily capable of being deduced from such as are common.[64]

---

58. Helmer, "Schleiermacher's Exegetical Theology," 229.
59. This work is an excellent introduction to everything that Schleiermacher would later publish.
60. Schleiermacher, *Brief Outline*, §18.
61. Tice, "Editor's Introduction," 7.
62. Schleiermacher, *Brief Outline*, §110, 113.
63. Ibid., §118.
64. Ibid., §119.

Schleiermacher's *Einleitung ins Neue Testament* (Introduction to the New Testament)

In *Einleitung ins Neue Testament*, Schleiermacher accounts for his critical position. In the first section Schleiermacher provides a general introduction to the New Testament and then deals with canon history and the relation between today's New Testament text and the original one. In the second section he deals with all the different types of New Testament books. The third section covers the literary context of the New Testament. In his *Einleitung*, Schleiermacher argues that "Later readers must put themselves in the place of those whom the author had in mind; to the extent that they can do this, the subject matter will be accessible and understandable to them."[65] Schleiermacher notes that this procedure is complicated by the fact that we have to make a choice whether to put ourselves into the position of the original reader/s with regard to the entire collection of New Testament books or each book separately. He concludes that we should limit ourselves to each book separately, since the author of each book must have had certain persons or a group of readers in mind.[66] As to the actual order of the inquiry, Schleiermacher suggests that one should start with the general, that is, the canon and its formation, and then move on to the specific, the history of the New Testament texts. Regarding the term *canon*, Schleiermacher contends that it does not communicate per se what the basis was for the collection of certain books into a canon. He points to the necessity of finding the specific witnesses that carry weight in this issue. By going back in history, earlier witnesses should be found that in their turn may lead to even earlier material.[67]

With regard to the language of the original New Testament, Schleiermacher argues that Greek was used in the society surrounding Christ and the first Christians, and that they might have come into direct contact with the Greek language: "Therefore it may by no means straight out be maintained that Christ and his disciples did not know Greek."[68] Schleiermacher puts forward the question of whether the Greek of our Greek New Testament is the same as that of the original canonical collection. Regardless of whether the texts were originally in Greek or Aramaic (though Schleiermacher argues that Greek was predominant), they were, among themselves, very different in terms of character and style. Influence from Syrian and Hebrew seems likely. Schleiermacher concludes: "Therefore, according to the nature of the matter one has to assume a κοινή in the New Testament that is not purified by the means of literary competence,

---

65. Schleiermacher, *Einleitung*, 7.
66. Ibid., 9–10.
67. Ibid., 32.
68. Ibid., 77.

but rather one that is mixed with Hebraisms and Syriasms."[69] Schleiermacher also discusses Eichhorn's hypothesis of an *Ur-evangelium*.[70] Schleiermacher comments: "Strictly speaking, the entire historical set of facts at hand also speaks against this hypothesis."[71] Schleiermacher also rejects the idea that the authors of the Gospels used each other's accounts to inform their own. In terms of significance, Schleiermacher values the Synoptic Gospels less than the Gospel of John, which he considers to be the most authoritative.[72] The reason for Schleiermacher's high regard for the Gospel of John is his observation that it was composed by an eyewitness,[73] thus foreshadowing the view recently argued by Richard Bauckham in *Jesus and the Eyewitnesses*.[74] To Schleiermacher, Matthew is the earliest Gospel, but not written by an eyewitness. In the critical work on the Gospels, Schleiermacher underlines that in the use of "divinatory criticism" one should exercise the criticism with caution and in a very limited fashion since it is not possible to decide with certainty where clear-cut reports and authentic sayings might be. In Schleiermacher's view, each Gospel writer had his own perspective and unique context and—in extension—his own theology.[75] Tice notes, in his introduction to Schleiermacher's *Luke*, that this is the beginnings of *redaction criticism*.[76] Schleiermacher's analysis of the intricacies of the material, which he refers to as "shapes," corresponds to what later was termed *form criticism*. The *Quest for the historical Jesus* also had its beginning with Schleiermacher.[77]

Schleiermacher's *Das Leben Jesu* (*The Life of Jesus*)

Schleiermacher's New Testament research peaks in *Das Leben Jesu* (*The Life of Jesus*),[78] in which theological and exegetical thought are synthesized. The series of lectures on the life of Jesus, starting in 1820, was repeated four times but was not published until 1864. Schleiermacher argues that even though Jesus should be understood in a historical context, "the meaning," in Baird's words, "of his inner life transcends historical limitations."[79] Albert Schweitzer, who wrote the monumental work on the so-called

---

69. Ibid., 75–79.
70. Ibid., 224–28.
71. Ibid., 226.
72. Baird, *History of New Testament Research*, 214.
73. Schleiermacher, *Einleitung*, 283.
74. Bauckham, *Jesus and the Eyewitnesses*, 358–83.
75. Tice, "Editor's Introduction," 9.
76. Ibid.
77. DeVries, "Schleiermacher," 353.
78. From now on I will occasionally quote both from the original German editions and their translations into English.
79. Baird, *History of New Testament Research*, 217.

First Quest of the historical Jesus, acknowledges that Schleiermacher was the first[80] to lecture about the life of Jesus, but his appraisal of Schleiermacher's *Life* is not very flattering: "Schleiermacher is not in search of the historical Jesus, but of the Jesus Christ of his own system of theology; that is to say, of the historic figure which seems to him appropriate to the self-consciousness of the Redeemer as he represents it. For him the empirical has simply no existence."[81]

Schleiermacher bases his historical reconstruction on the Synoptic Gospels, on the one hand, and on the Gospel of John, on the other. In the choice between the two, John's account is given priority, even though Schleiermacher claims that a correct and complete biography cannot be produced: "it is undeniable that we cannot achieve a connected presentation of the life of Jesus."[82] In his *Einleitung*, he notes that speech and dialogue are predominant characteristics of the Gospel of John.[83] In his *Leben Jesu*, Schleiermacher divides Jesus' life into three *Zeiträume*, or periods: "Das Leben Jesu vor seinem öffentlichen Auftreten," "Das öffentliche Leben Jesu bis zu seiner Gefangennehmung," and "Von der Gefangennehmung bis zu seinem Tode." With regard to the first period, "The life of Jesus before his public appearance," Schleiermacher asserts that Matthew's account is more historical, whereas Luke's birth story is more poetic.[84] Concerning Jesus' childhood, Schleiermacher argues, "so must it then come forth as unlikely to everyone that the disciples would have asked about such things, and just as unlikely that he on his own initiative would have communicated to them such narratives."[85] Even though Mary, the mother of Jesus, would be a possible source, the fact that John, who was closer to Mary than the other disciples, does not account for the early years of Jesus indicates to Schleiermacher that she was not a source. However, John was likely familiar with the Gospels of Mark and Matthew and perhaps saw no need to repeat this information in his Gospel. Schleiermacher also asks himself whether any information about the early life of Christ would have been of any interest to the disciples. Answering in the negative, he argues that the later public life of Christ would have been more interesting,[86] a position that indicates Schleiermacher's indifference regarding the christologically significant issue of Christ's origin. Concerning the birth of Christ, Schleiermacher states that "a report of the birth of Christ does essentially not belong in the writing of Gospel history; otherwise it would not be missing in the gospel of John or Mark."[87] As for the two natures of Christ, Schleiermacher

---

80. He was followed by a number of writers who published lives of Jesus, e.g., Strauss (1825, 1864), Paulus (1828), and Renan (1863).

81. Schweitzer, *The Quest of the Historical Jesus*, 62.

82. Schleiermacher, *Life of Jesus*, 43.

83. Schleiermacher, *Einleitung*, 209.

84. Baird, *History of New Testament Research*, 217.

85. Schleiermacher, *Leben Jesu*, 47.

86. Ibid., 48.

87. Ibid., 58.

argues that the two cannot be combined in the person of Christ.[88] Regarding the notion of Jesus' supernatural conception, it is based on the idea of hereditary sin, which, in Schleiermacher's mind, is not relevant for the Christian faith. A major concern in this section is to demonstrate Jesus' gradual development of God-consciousness and dependence on God. The temptation account right before Jesus is launched into his public ministry is, in Schleiermachian Christology, not historical; the temptation to throw himself down from the pinnacle of the temple was no real temptation to Jesus since it "would have been wholly unworthy of Christ."[89]

The second period of Jesus' career, "The public life of Jesus until his incarceration," is divided into two categories: external events and internal events. Miracles are placed in the category of external events.[90] Schleiermacher argues that these were not likely as many as suggested by the Gospels since they are frequently attributed to supernatural causation.[91] To external events belong also outward circumstances and locality, whereas internal events concern doctrine and the forming of a society (*Gesellschaftsstiftung*).[92] Dealing with internal events, Schleiermacher concentrates on Jesus' self-description in the Gospel of John, where Jesus portrays himself as the one sent from God "to reveal a unique God-consciousness."[93] To Schleiermacher, the return of Christ is not to be taken literally in the sense that he will return in person.[94]

The third and last period of Jesus' life, "From the incarceration to his ascension," includes a description of Jesus' death that Schleiermacher denotes as spiritual death,[95] though after the resurrection Jesus returns to the same body he had before his death.[96] Schleiermacher states: "So then, after the resurrection Christ returned to a truly human life."[97] With regard to the resurrection and ascension, Baird notes that Schleiermacher vacillates between supernatural and natural understandings.[98] On Jesus' life post-resurrection, Schleiermacher comments:

> I regard this whole second life appearance [the life after the resurrection] of Christ just as I do every individual miracle. There is something in it that is wholly factual, but the genesis of it is incomprehensible to us . . . because it is connected with something that in its way is unique and for which there is no

---

88. Ibid., 85–86.
89. Schleiermacher, *Life of Jesus*, 148.
90. Schleiermacher, *Leben Jesu*, 165.
91. Baird, *History of New Testament Research*, 218.
92. Schleiermacher, *Leben Jesu*, 165.
93. Baird, *History of New Testament Research*, 218.
94. Ibid.
95. Schleiermacher, *Life of Jesus*, 219.
96. Baird, *History of New Testament Research*, 219.
97. Schleiermacher, *Life of Jesus*, 469.
98. Baird, *History of New Testament Research*, 219.

analogy... The facts are genuine facts, but how that second life began and how it ended are matters which we cannot conceive factually.[99]

Schleiermacher's *A Critical Essay on the Gospel of St. Luke* (*Ueber die Schriften des Lukas: Ein kritischer Versuch*)

Schleiermacher's *Ueber die Schriften des Lukas: Ein kritischer Versuch* (also published as *A Critical Essay*[100] *on the Gospel of St. Luke* and *Luke: A Critical Study*[101]) is one of the few witnesses[102] to the adoption of Schleiermacher's historical-critical method. Tice comments that Schleiermacher's 190 year-old *Critique* of Luke is remarkably up-to-date. In a comparison with the two major commentaries on the Gospel of Luke (Joseph A. Fitzmyer and Hans Conzelmann), the critical conclusions of Schleiermacher correspond well, particularly with those of Fitzmyer.[103] I will give an account of his study,[104] and discuss and comment on points of particular interest.

Preface by the Author

Schleiermacher makes some conspicuous comments in his preface. After having excused himself for writing a book that could only be read side-by-side with a copy of the Gospel of Luke, he states:

> And I am the better pleased that it was out of my power to do so [to make his book readable without constant reference to a copy of the Gospel of Luke], as this is the best mode of keeping off improper readers, who, unacquainted with the original language and theological matters in general, still think that it concerns their piety to go hunting in works of this nature, to try if they can catch some scent of heresy in them. For this class of persons begins, particularly too with us, to multiply exceedingly, among high and low, learned and unlearned, and, without profit to others or themselves, to create a great deal of scandal, and perplex their neighbours' consciences. To bar their intrusion is indeed

---

99. Schleiermacher, *Life of Jesus*, 479–80.

100. Here we should note that the word *essay* in the title is very misleading, for Schleiermacher's *Essay* is a 320-page volume. Schleiermacher excuses himself in his preface, stating: "But my reason for calling this only an Essay is the inartificial connexion of the parts, and the negligence in the diction" (Schleiermacher, *Critical Essay*, ii–iii).

101. Three editions of Schleiermacher's *Luke* are referenced here: the original German edition: *Ueber die Schriften des Lukas: Ein kritischer Versuch*, 1817, reproduced in *Kritische Gesamtausgabe*; a reprint of the 1825 English translation: *A Critical Essay on the Gospel of St. Luke*; and a critical edition in English translation from 1993, *Luke: A Critical Study* in the series Schleiermacher Studies and Translation 13.

102. Schleiermacher, who lectured on the exegesis of many of the books of the New Testament, was planning to publish studies of Acts and the other Gospels, but passed away before he was able to realize his plans (Tice, "Editor's Introduction," 1, 3).

103. Tice, "Editor's Introduction," 15, 17–25.

104. Including his own preface and introduction.

> impossible; but it is at all events wholesome thoroughly to force upon them the consciousness, that they do not understand what they are talking of.[105]

In this elitist statement, Schleiermacher seems, more or less directly, to ward off criticism from those who do not agree with him, since they are "improper readers" that are "unacquainted with the original language and theological matters in general," though he admits that "this class of persons" can be found "among high and low, learned and unlearned." These people, out of concern for the Christian faith, are out to "catch some scent of heresy." Schleiermacher regrets that "to bar their intrusion is indeed impossible." He argues that "it is at all events wholesome thoroughly to force upon them the consciousness, that they do not understand what they are talking of." These words seem to indicate that Schleiermacher was aware that there were elements in his *Essay* that would not be well received by Christians in general.

Schleiermacher considers the Gospels to contain eyewitness material that is reliable to a fairly high degree. In regard to the authorship of Luke, he states that "it is at all events safer that he should appear as the compiler and arranger only, not as the author"[106] and that "the authority of our writer appears to me at least to gain, instead of losing, when his work is referred to earlier works of original and inspired witnesses of the facts."[107] In connection to this, Schleiermacher brings up the question regarding the agency of the Holy Spirit in the composition of Scriptures—he contends that the operation is divided. First, the agency of the Spirit is in those who were witnesses and reporters of the events and speeches of Christ: "by this they were enabled to apprehend every thing from the right point of view, and to report it in such a manner as to render the truth of the matter obvious."[108] And, second, in the collector:

> [T]here is the agency of the Spirit in the person who collected and digested. For, in ascribing the result to human investigation and selection, I do not mean a technically critical process, which was foreign to those times and men, or that the governing principle could be any other than the spirit of Christianity recognizing its own work.[109]

However, one should note that from Schleiermacher's point of view the inspiration of the Holy Spirit does not make any difference when it comes to the actual interpretation of the text. To Schleiermacher, the text is still, in Thiselton's words, "a text written in language addressed to human situations and human persons."[110] Baird comments regarding Schleiermacher's view of Scripture, "Since the Bible is supported by no

---

105. Schleiermacher, *Critical Essay*, iii–iv.
106. Schleiermacher, *Luke: A Critical Study*, v.
107. Ibid., vi.
108. Ibid., v.
109. Ibid.
110. Thiselton, *New Horizons in Hermeneutics*, 208–9.

external doctrine of inspiration, it is fully open to historical investigation."[111] Helmer summarizes Schleiermacher's position in *Second Letter to Friedrich Lücke*: "Schleiermacher wrote that the supernaturalism of orthodox Christology and a pneumatologically inspired Bible could no longer be supported by historical research on the Bible."[112]

Introduction by the Author

In his introduction, Schleiermacher refutes Eichhorn's idea that the Synoptic evangelists independently of each other made use of a common source.[113] Schleiermacher argues that if that had been the case, the first Christians would have been more anxious to preserve this first authorized version of the Gospel "without either addition or curtailment."[114] It also seems unlikely that the original Gospel would be lost so early; even if this original Gospel was not an authorized version, but rather a private initiative, Schleiermacher argues that it is hard to see why this particular version would be so dominant, since it must have been the case that the idea to tell the story of the life of Jesus must have come to the mind of quite a few people at about the same time.[115] Schleiermacher finds the choice between positing one common source and borrowing from each other to be a false dichotomy; instead he prefers a combination of sources, some shared and others not.[116] Schleiermacher's own theory, the *fragmentary hypothesis*, has not stood the test of time because of its inability to explain the high degree of agreement of order between the Synoptic Gospels.[117] However, Schleiermacher can be credited for introducing the symbol Q (from German *Quelle*, that is, "source") to represent the hypothetical document behind the material that the Gospels of Matthew and Luke have in common.[118]

Schleiermacher divides his *Essay* into four parts, the first including the time before Jesus' public ministry (Luke 1–2), the second consisting of some of Jesus' actions and discourses (Luke 3:1—9:49), the third containing similar accounts that are centered around Christ's journey to Jerusalem and that are unique to Luke (Luke 9:50—18:14) and the fourth dealing with Jesus' last days on earth (Luke 18:15—24:53).[119] Even though Schleiermacher himself considers the beginning and end of Jesus' ministry

---

111. Baird, *History of New Testament Research*, 211.

112. Helmer, "Schleiermacher's Exegetical Theology," 231. Helmer further comments that with Schleiermacher, there is a relocation of the center "from the written letter to religion's 'inner power'" which is to be equalled with "faith's certainty" (ibid.).

113. Schleiermacher, *Critical Essay*, 1–2.

114. Ibid., 4.

115. Ibid., 5.

116. Ibid., 7.

117. Stein, *Studying the Synoptic Gospels*, 49.

118. Blomberg, *Jesus and the Gospels*, 102.

119. Schleiermacher, *Critical Essay*, 19–20.

to be less interesting than the parts in between, we will limit ourselves to a look at Schleiermacher's critical analysis of the first two (the first division) and the last five chapters (the fourth division) of Luke's Gospel, since these theologically speaking are the most significant chapters of Luke's account and are therefore also the most telling ones with regard to Schleiermacher's perspective.

First Division—Before Jesus' Public Ministry

Schleiermacher comments on the style of the language in Luke 1 and discusses several theories, but concludes that there is no conclusive evidence in any direction.[120] He views the first chapter as a poetical composition rather than a historical narrative. He argues that from a historical supposition: "no one will adopt, or contend that the angel Gabriel announced the advent of the Messiah in figures so purely Jewish and in expressions taken mostly from the Old Testament . . . or that Zacharias at the instant of recovering his speech made use of it to utter the hymn, without being disturbed by the joy and surprise of the company."[121] Here Schleiermacher's arguments come forth as strikingly weak. What would be more natural than an angel expressing himself in terms typically Jewish and in the style of Old Testament utterances, considering the fact that God's chosen people were Jewish and that the girl whom the angel was addressing was Jewish? Here Schleiermacher's anti-Judaistic perspective is hinted at. Furthermore, it is not unlikely that the Spirit of God came upon Zechariah to utter these words at this special occasion. Taking Schleiermacher's advice of reading Luke's Gospel together with his *Essay*, we note that the first thing that happened when Zechariah recovered his speech was that "he began to speak, praising God" (Luke 1:64).[122] A few verses later, that is, a few moments after the first reactions and joyful expressions, "Zechariah was filled with the Holy Spirit and spoke this prophecy . . ." (Luke 1:67). There is nothing in particular in this context suggesting that this would have been unnatural. Schleiermacher's interpretation appears to be influenced by his view that to God, any utterance of the supernatural is unnatural. With regard to the formulation of the prophecy, Schleiermacher remarks that Luke "enriched the historical narrative by the lyrical effusions of his own genius."[123] The alternative would be that Luke did his best to find out what Zechariah actually prophesied; after all, there were a number of persons present who heard these words spoken.

Schleiermacher also considers the historical narrative to be fraught with difficulties, such as chronology, circumstances, Zechariah's dumbness, the identification of apocryphal poetical writings with a style similar to Luke's first chapter and so on, and concludes that he "cannot see here a literal historical narrative . . . yet neither would

---

120. Ibid., 21–22.
121. Ibid., 25.
122. NRSV is used here and onwards.
123. Schleiermacher, *Critical Essay*, 25.

I treat the whole as fictitious."[124] Schleiermacher's exegetical analysis comes forth as skewed and marked by general skepticism, where he prefers speculation to investigating what case could be made for the historical reliability of the text. His starting point is not the text, but rather preconceived ideas that are forced on the text. In his analysis of Luke 2, Schleiermacher performs what could be described as a redaction-critical analysis of the interaction between the first compiler and the material that he compiled on the one hand, and Luke's interaction with and redaction of the material on the other.[125] Schleiermacher asserts that Luke 2:1–20, which includes Jesus' birth and the visit of the shepherds, does not have the same author as the previous chapter since no lyrical passage is introduced. The shepherds, rather than Joseph and Mary, are the source of this narrative. Schleiermacher argues that it is most likely that no one recorded any of these events in writing, nor is it probable that any rumor about the events spread very far. Instead the affair was brought back from oblivion—and confirmed by Mary—many years later when Jesus became famous.[126] Concerning Luke 2:22–40, Schleiermacher finds it hard to understand Mary's astonishment at Simeon's prophetic words over Jesus, insisting that they imply "that she herself did not know yet who her son was."[127] Here Schleiermacher's analysis strikes one as unreflective; any woman who has been told by an angel from God that she will give birth to the Son of God will probably remain amazed for the rest of her life. Even though she was technically given this information earlier, she most probably was not able to digest the implications of this message, but was rather taken aback by these words about her son.

Schleiermacher completes the first division by a comparison with Matthew's Gospel, concluding that Luke's first two chapters do not have any single point in common with the corresponding section in Matthew, and that they are not even supplemental, or, in other words, that they are almost entirely mutually exclusive. Schleiermacher says: "Hence then if in any one point the narrative of the one evangelist is correct, that of the other, so far as it relates to the same epoch, cannot be so."[128] Schleiermacher is clearly begging the question, however. First, he discusses the annunciation, claiming that it is unlikely that Mary set off to visit Elizabeth without telling Joseph about the angelic visit and that he later found out about her pregnancy from a third person.[129] Schleiermacher aims to make it impossible to accept both Matthew's and Luke's accounts at the same time and he has a clear tendency of seeking to invalidate Luke's account in favor of Matthew's. However, Schleiermacher's argumentation, mixing skepticism with psychological speculation, leads him to unsolid ground.[130]

124. Ibid., 25–27.
125. Ibid., 28–31.
126. Ibid., 31–35.
127. Ibid., 39.
128. Ibid., 44–45.
129. Ibid., 45.
130. Ibid., 45–46.

Information about *how* and *when* Mary told Joseph about the angelic visit and the conception by the Holy Spirit is not given in Luke's account, but it is implied from the context that she at some point did. According to Matthew's version (Matt 1:20–21) Joseph also had an angelic visit (in a dream) confirming the annunciation. Whether this event took place before or after Mary left to visit Elizabeth cannot be established with any certainty from the texts of either Luke or Matthew, but the most likely time is perhaps directly after the annunciation and before Mary went on her journey. The meaning of εὑρέθη 'she was found' [to be pregnant] in εὑρέθη ἐν γαστρὶ ἔχουσα ἐκ πνεύματος ἁγίου in Matt 1:18 is a key point on the time line. If εὑρέθη refers to Mary simply noting that she was pregnant and telling Joseph about the angelic visit and the pregnancy by the Holy Spirit, and Joseph then having the angelic visit in his dream, the pregnancy issue was probably settled before Mary left for the visit to Elizabeth, which in this case was a convenient escape for Mary in this tumultuous and difficult situation. Using this reasoning, Luke's and Matthew's accounts work nicely together. It is evident that Schleiermacher does not make much of an effort to explore the compatibility of the accounts of the two evangelists, a deficiency that is symptomatic of his redaction-critical approach.

Second, Schleiermacher argues that Luke's two accounts of the shepherds and the presentation in the temple do not agree with the two in Matthew, the visit of the magi and the Bethlehem massacre.[131] Schleiermacher points out that the magi must have come to pay homage to the infant Jesus in Bethlehem just before the presentation of the child in the temple since "Luke make[s] the parents return immediately after that ceremony to Nazareth."[132] Also, Schleiermacher questions that Joseph and Mary went to Jerusalem with Jesus for the presentation in the temple (as described in Luke), arguing that the magi (as described in Matthew) probably told Joseph and Mary about the dream, warning them not to return to Jerusalem. From this viewpoint, Schleiermacher finds it logical that Joseph and Mary, according to Matthew's account, instead fled to Egypt to protect the child.[133]

Against Schleiermacher's analysis two things could be argued. First, on the basis of Matthew's account it is not likely that the time of the magi's arrival was before the presentation of Jesus in the temple in Luke 2:22–38. A crucial point is the understanding of the genitive absolute in Matt 2:1, Τοῦ δὲ Ἰησοῦ γεννηθέντος, which can be translated "and after Jesus was born," without qualification as to how much time had passed after the birth before the magi arrived in Jerusalem. Important for the establishment of the timeline of these events is Matt 2:7 which describes Herod's action directly after the arrival of the magi: "Then Herod secretly called for the wise men and learned from them *the exact time when the star had appeared.*"[134] If we assume that

---

131. Ibid., 46.
132. Ibid.
133. Ibid., 47.
134. Italics are my own.

the appearance of the star was at the time of Jesus' birth and read Matt 2:16b, which states: "He [Herod] sent men to kill all the children in Bethlehem and throughout the surrounding region *from the age of two and under, according to the time he had learned from the wise men* [my italics]," we can conclude that the magi came to Eretz Israel one or two years after the birth of Jesus. Jesus must thus have been somewhere between one and two years of age, according to the precise information about the time that Herod had received from the magi. Second, regarding the location of Jesus when the magi came to Jerusalem, we read in Matt 2:4–6 how Herod found out from the chief priests about *the place of Jesus' birth* (that is, not his whereabouts at the time) and therefore, in Matt 2:8, sent the magi to Bethlehem, believing that Jesus was there. However, after leaving Herod, the magi once again saw the ἀστήρ, the light in the sky, and following it they were led to the place (probably Nazareth) where Jesus was at that time, that is, one or two years after his birth. This is probably the time when Joseph and Mary fled with Jesus to Egypt. When Herod realized that he had been deceived by the magi (whom he seems to have made promise that they would come back to him and tell him about the whereabouts of Jesus [vv. 8–9]) he reacted by sending soldiers to Bethlehem, where he believed Jesus was. From this perspective, the problem of the alleged conflicts between Luke's and Matthew's accounts, pointed to by Schleiermacher, could have a natural set of explanations.

Finally, Schleiermacher comments on Matthew's report (2:23). This verse might indicate that Joseph and Mary settled in Nazareth for the first time, after first having been intent on going to Judea, whereas Luke reports (2:39) that after the presentation of Jesus in the temple, they returned "to their own city, Nazareth."[135] If we follow the scheme laid out above, we conclude that these two reports do not refer to the same point in time. We note that Matthew reports about Joseph (and his family) that after the Egypt stay "he made his home in a town called Nazareth" (Matt 2:23). Matthew does not indicate whether Joseph and Mary had lived there before. Matthew might not bother to give this information or he might simply not know that Nazareth was the place where Joseph and Mary lived before their escape to Egypt. But even if Matthew knew that Joseph and Mary lived in Nazareth before, he might merely be interested in giving the location of their residence since his point of focus here is to underline fulfillment of prophecy, for in the second half of the verse (23b) he states: "Then what had been spoken by the prophets was fulfilled, that Jesus would be called a Nazarene." In conclusion, the accounts of Luke and Matthew seem rather to be much more complementary than they are radically contradictory as Schleiermacher suggested.

Summing up, Schleiermacher concludes that Luke 1–2 has "a portion which . . . [is] presented in a poetical rather than an historical shape" and "another, which bears in itself evident marks of artless and unadulterated tradition."[136] As for Matthew, Schleiermacher argues that the account of the magi merely has "a completely symboli-

---

135. Ibid., 48.
136. Ibid., 49.

cal character," whereas the massacre "can scarcely be a mere fiction."[137] Schleiermacher finds the alleged mix of facts and fiction in the Gospels of Luke and Matthew excusable, first, because this is *only* "a prelude to the proper subject of the history, which was the public life of Jesus"; second, because the evangelists stood in a tradition "where poetry and history are nowhere kept quite distinct, and [. . .] they therefore neither could have, nor needed that discriminating sense"; and third, because "their purity of feeling has kept them from the extravagance and romance [. . . of those that] were possessed with the confused spirit of rabbinical Judaism."[138]

As well as what has already been commented on above, several other points could be argued against these assertions, but here it will suffice to note, first, that the theological significance of Luke 1–2 is far greater than Schleiermacher maintains and, second, that Schleiermacher's view that the evangelists were not able to make a difference between fact and fiction does not hold in the face of the most recent research.

Fourth Division—From Judas's Decision to Betray Jesus to Jesus' Departure

The fourth division covers Luke 20:1 to 24:53. Schleiermacher argues that even though there is a striking similarity between Luke 21, Matthew 24, and Mark 13, where we find the prediction of the destruction of the temple, the signs of the parousia, the beginnings of the troubles, the desolating sacrilege, the parousia of the Son of Man, the parable of the fig tree, and the time of the parousia, this fact "cannot be explained from their being founded on a common original Gospel, but only from the fact that none of the three had here the benefit of supplemental and auxiliary pieces."[139] When discussing Luke 22:1—23:49, Schleiermacher praises what he considers to be a virtue in Luke's manner of operation: "the compiler of the whole has remained perfectly true to his praiseworthy rule, of altering nothing in his original documents for the sake of a better connexion."[140]

As for the account of the Lord's Supper (Luke 22:7–24) and the elements preceding and following it, Schleiermacher asserts that the relatively detailed description of the preparations of the Eucharist may indicate either that the possibly unpracticed narrator started out writing in more detail than he could or wanted to continue with, or because he found them "marvellous, or at least very striking and remarkable, which," Schleiermacher comments, "certainly does not in fact belong to it [the institution of the Lord's Supper]."[141] However, Schleiermacher interprets this (in his opinion) uneven section as genuine and original. This is supported by the fact that it is Peter and John whom Jesus sends to prepare for the paschal supper, information

137. Ibid., 50.
138. Ibid., 51.
139. Ibid., 269.
140. Ibid., 286.
141. Ibid., 292.

that is lacking in Matthew's otherwise much more detailed version, which may signify that this information probably would have been lost if it had been processed through several hands. Also, Schleiermacher argues, it is unlikely that this information could have been added later. Schleiermacher also maintains that the account does not give the impression of having been reworked by a later hand.[142] The sparse rendition of Jesus' words at the supper also indicates the recollection of an oral source. However, Schleiermacher questions whether Jesus uttered the words "But see, the one who betrays me is with me, and his hand is on the table" in v. 21, so directly after the institution words. Instead he thinks that the original account ended with verse 20.[143] However, there is no pressing need to question whether Jesus uttered these words directly after the institution of the Eucharist; the betrayal by the hand of Judas and the new covenant in the blood of Jesus are closely and naturally linked elements in the atonement drama, both relating to Jesus' redeeming death on the cross in their own way. Continuing, Schleiermacher also asks if it is really possible that, as in vv. 23–24, there could be two arguments on apparently opposite topics—who would betray Jesus and who among them was the greatest—going on at the same time. He argues that "we cannot but believe that such a dispute did not take place at all on this evening."[144] However, the distance between the two topics is not necessarily that great, but is rather a case of "two sides of the same coin." It is not difficult to imagine how the argument about who could be the betrayer could lead to assertions regarding who was the most loyal to Jesus and therefore also the greatest.

Regarding Peter's denial in Luke 22:55–62, Schleiermacher asserts that it "is related circumstantially indeed, but not with the liveliness of reality." He bases his argument on Luke 22:61: "The Lord turned and looked at Peter. Then Peter remembered the word of the Lord, how he had said to him, 'Before the cock crows today, you will deny me three times,'" asserting that this verse proves that "we have not here the account of an eye-witness." Schleiermacher maintains that Jesus could not have looked at Peter from where he stood and if he looked at him when he was led away, an account by an eyewitness would have described the circumstances in more detail.[145] Schleiermacher's argumentation appears to be purely speculative.

Concerning the crucifixion account, Schleiermacher asserts that "the author speaks as an eye-witness," though he questions that the rending of the temple veil actually took place because those who saw it would surely have done their utmost to conceal it. On the other hand, one could argue that news of such a spectacular event would almost surely spread rapidly before any thought of concealing it could have been contrived. Schleiermacher also asks himself why there is no reference to this event in Acts or Hebrews. There might be, however, an allusion to this event in

142. Ibid., 292–93.
143. Ibid., 294.
144. Ibid., 295.
145. Ibid., 301–3.

Heb 10:19–20. With regard to the crucifixion itself, it is striking that Schleiermacher hardly writes a word about it; instead he is busy with the rending of the veil, the unreliability of Matthew's account, and the denouncing of Eichhorn's original Gospel hypothesis.[146] Neither does he write anything about the resurrection. Discussing the walk to Emmaus, the ascension, and the so-called appendix (from v. 44 onwards) in the last chapter, Schleiermacher argues against the notion that oral tradition preserves Gospel material unabridged; instead the material is compressed "[f]or it is impossible that an original narrative of Christ's parting can have been so short as this."[147]

Schleiermacher finishes up his *Essay* on Luke with an evaluative statement regarding Luke or "the compiler": "He is from beginning to end no more than the compiler and arranger of documents which he found in existence, which he allows to pass unadulterated through his hands." To Schleiermacher, Luke's merit is "that of the arrangement . . . [b]ut the far greater merit is this, that he has admitted scarcely any pieces but what are peculiarly genuine and good; for this was certainly not the effect of accident, but the fruit of a judiciously instituted investigation, and a well weighed choice."[148]

CONCLUDING REMARKS

Schleiermacher pioneered a number of new concepts and approaches with great inventiveness and genius, not only within New Testament exegesis, but also within theology and hermeneutics. The holistic perspective of Schleiermacher puts each element within the theological disciplines in their proper place in the greater context of the church. Schleiermacher rightly notes that the task of the theologian is to serve the church, and that the ultimate concern in all research within theology should be its practical application.

Schleiermacher's broad understanding of empiricism is helpful. Schleiermacher notes that the empiricism of his day was too superficial in not being able to penetrate anything more than the obvious. In Schleiermacher's view, true empiricism includes not only what can be perceived by our physical senses, but also what we can perceive and experience spiritually. In this way he keeps the scope broad enough—at least in a theoretical sense—for the interpreter to contain in his interpretation a strictly scholarly approach that includes a genuine spiritual perspective. Schleiermacher himself claims that the experiential, pietistic element that he inherited from the Herrnhut Brethren preserved him from skepticism. However, Schleiermacher's experiential spirituality combined with a low view of Scripture opens up to subjectivism and speculation. Schleiermacher's type of Christianity becomes doctrinally weak. In Schleiermacher's scheme, faith in Christ tends to become more separated from history and its

---

146. Ibid., 304–11.
147. Ibid., 312.
148. Ibid., 313–14.

foundation in Scripture tends to be replaced by subjective experientialism as the new foundation of faith and is therefore more vaguely defined, resulting in a transcendent and supra-historical Christ whose soteriological universality is in stark contrast with the historical Jesus of Scripture. The experiential element of Schleiermacher is thus a two-edged sword. On the one hand it is an acknowledgment of the individual experience of God by the believer, but on the other hand the experiential element alone becomes a poor and shaky substitute for Scripture as the foundation of faith. Moreover, even though Schleiermacher acknowledges spiritual experientialism as a component compatible with a scholarly approach, he largely rejects the same, highly frequent, spiritual component of supernaturalism in the Gospels.

Schleiermacher's historical-critical method, in its constructive format, brings to our attention fresh perspectives that make the text come alive and step into three-dimensionality. In Schleiermacher we see the beginnings of redaction criticism and form criticism, approaches that can be helpful tools for the understanding of the interaction between the handling of source material and theological intent in the process of composition, particularly with regard to the Gospels. The historical-critical method makes us ask questions that we otherwise would never ask and to consider options that otherwise would not be part of the interpretive inquiry. Schleiermacher also contributes to the discussion of the Synoptic problem with his *fragmentary hypothesis* even though his approach never won any acclaim because of its inability to account for the great extent of agreement in the order of the Synoptic material. Schleiermacher's initiative to form the discipline of historical theology also stimulated a positive interest in the history of Christianity. However, his separation between faith in Christ and scientific inquiry has far-reaching fatal consequences. In scientific inquiry, Scripture, as a consequence of its separation from the world of faith, tends to become the object of a dry, skeptical investigation where a narrow-minded, naturalistic empiricism is enforced upon its supernatural world, resulting in Schleiermacher's aggressive, psychologizing, and speculative cut-and-paste analysis; the choice of methods for the evaluation and analysis of supernatural events—with their inherent anti-supernatural presuppositions—turns out to be methodologically inept. Schleiermacher's historical approach has a minimalistic tendency where the point of departure implicitly suggests that only what is provable from a naturalistic historical-empirical point of view can be held to be true. This means that historical events of great significance for the Christian faith that do not agree with a naturalistic agenda are rejected. It is symptomatic of Schleiermacher's thought that his interest in the life of Jesus excludes the significance of those elements that carry the most weight for Christianity. This perspective is the basis for Schleiermacher's anti-supernaturalism. He subjects the supernatural to a naturalistic minimum and concludes that supernatural events—even by the agency of God—are unnatural and that they would not be conducive to the glorification of God. His version of the historical-critical method also brings with it a sizable dose of unhealthy skepticism. Though Schleiermacher's intention was to safeguard the integrity of both worlds—faith *and* science—the separation of the two has resulted in failure on both sides.

No matter how we view his contributions it remains a fact that Friedrich Schleiermacher is a significant figure in the history of New Testament interpretation and that his influence has made and still makes itself felt.

BIBLIOGRAPHY

Adams, Robert Merrihew. "Faith and Religious Knowledge." In *The Cambridge Companion to Friedrich Schleiermacher*, edited by Jacqueline Mariña, 35–52. Cambridge: Cambridge University Press, 2005.

Baird, William. *History of New Testament Research*. Vol. 1, *From Deism to Tübingen*. Minneapolis: Fortress, 1992.

Barth, Karl. *Protestant Theology in the Nineteenth Century: Its Background and History*. London: SCM, 1972.

Bauckham, Richard. *Jesus and the Eyewitnesses: The Gospels as Eyewitness Testimony*. Grand Rapids: Eerdmans, 2006.

Blomberg, Craig. *Jesus and the Gospels: An Introduction and Survey*. 2nd ed. Nashville, TN: B & H Academic, 2009.

Christian, C. W. *Friedrich Schleiermacher*. (1919). Waco, TX: Word, 1979.

Crouter, Richard E. *Friedrich Schleiermacher: Between Enlightenment and Romanticism*. Cambridge: Cambridge University Press, 2005.

DeVries, D. "Schleiermacher, Friedrich Daniel Ernst (1768–1834)." In *Historical Handbook of Major Biblical Interpreters*, edited by Donald K. McKim, 350–55. Downers Grove, IL: InterVarsity, 1998.

Gerrish, B. A. *A Prince of the Church: Schleiermacher and the Beginnings of Modern Theology*. Philadelphia: Fortress, 1984.

Helmer, Christine. "Schleiermacher's Exegetical Theology and the New Testament." In *The Cambridge Companion to Friedrich Schleiermacher*, edited by Jacqueline Mariña, 229–48. Cambridge: Cambridge University Press, 2005.

Mariña, Jacqueline. "Introduction." In *The Cambridge Companion to Friedrich Schleiermacher*, edited by Jacqueline Mariña, 1–12. Cambridge: Cambridge University Press, 2005.

Schleiermacher, Friedrich. *Aus Schleiermacher's Leben: In Briefen*. Vol. 1. Berlin: Reimer, 1860. Reprint, Berlin: Walter de Gruyter, 1974.

———. *Brief Outline of the Study of Theology*. Edinburgh: T. & T. Clark, 1963.

———. *Christian Faith*. 1830–31. Reprint, Louisville, KY: Westminster John Knox, 1994.

———. *A Critical Essay on the Gospel of St. Luke*. London: John Taylor, 1825. Reprint, Whitefish, MT: Kessinger, 2007.

———. *Das Leben Jesu*. Vol. 6 of Part 1, *Zur Theologie* of *Friedrich Schleiermachers Sämmtliche Werke*. Berlin: Reimer, 1864.

———. "Die Weihnactsfeier: Ein Gespräch." (1806). In *Schriften aus der Hallenser Zeit, 1804–1807*, Vol. 5 of Part 1, *Schriften und Entwürfe*, of *Friedrich Daniel Ernst Schleiermacher Kritische Gesamtausgabe*, 39–98. Berlin: Walter de Gruyter, 1995.

———. "Monologen: Eine Neujahrsgabe." (1800). In *Schriften aus der Berliner Zeit, 1800–1802*. Vol. 3 of Part 1. *Schriften und Entwürfe*, of *Friedrich Daniel Ernst Schleiermacher Kritische Gesamtausgabe*, 1–62. Berlin: Walter de Gruyter, 1988.

———. *Einleitung ins Neue Testament.* Vol. 8 of Part 1, *Zur Theologie,* of *Friedrich Schleiermachers Sämmtliche Werke.* Berlin: Reimer, 1864.

———. *Kurze Darstellung des theologischen Studiums.* In *Universitätsschriften. Herakleitos, Kurze Darstellung des theologischen Studiums,* Vol. 6 of Part 1, *Schriften und Enwürfe,* of *Friedrich Daniel Ernst Schleiermacher Kritische Gesamtausgabe,* 243–446. Berlin: Walter de Gruyter, 1998.

———. *The Life of Jesus,* edited by J. C. Verheyden. Translated by S. M. Gilmour. Lives of Jesus. Philadelphia: Fortress, 1975.

———. *The Life of Schleiermacher, as Unfolded in His Autobiography and Letters.* Translated by Frederica Rowan. 2 vols. London: Smith, Elder, 1860.

———. *Luke: A Critical Study.* 1817. Schleiermacher: Studies and Translations 13. Lewiston, NY: Edwin Mellen, 1993.

———. *On What Gives Value to Life.* Lewiston, NY: Edwin Mellen, 1995.

———. *Soliloquies: An English Translation of the Monologen.* Chicago: Open Court, 1926.

———. "Über die Religion: Reden an die Gebildeten unter ihren Verächtern." In *Schriften aus der Berliner Zeit 1796–99,* Vol. 2 of Part 1, *Schriften und Entwürfe,* of *Friedrich Daniel Ernst Schleiermacher Kritische Gesamtausgabe,* 185–326. Berlin: Walter de Gruyter, 1984.

———. "Ueber die Schriften des Lukas: Ein kritischer Versuch." (1817). In *Exegetische Schriften.* Vol. 8 of Part 1, *Schriften und Entwürfe,* of *Friedrich Daniel Ernst Schleiermacher Kritische Gesamtausgabe,* 1–180. Berlin: Walter de Gruyter, 2001.

Schweitzer, Albert. *The Quest of the Historical Jesus.* Translated by W. Montgomery. (1906). Reprint, New York: Macmillan, 1961.

Stein, Robert H. *Studying the Synoptic Gospels. Origin and Interpretation.* 2nd ed. Grand Rapids: Baker Academic, 2001.

Thiselton, Anthony C. *New Horizons in Hermeneutics.* Grand Rapids: Zondervan, 1992.

Tice, Terrence. "Editor's Introduction." In *Luke: A Critical Study,* edited by Terrence N. Tice, 1–25. Schleiermacher Studies and Translations 13. Lewiston, NY: Edwin Mellen, 1993.

———. *Schleiermacher.* Nashville: Abingdon, 2006.

——— "Schleiermacher Yesterday, Today, and Tomorrow." In *The Cambridge Companion to Friedrich Schleiermacher,* edited by Jacqueline Mariña, 307–18. Cambridge: Cambridge University Press, 2005.

3

Ferdinand Christian Baur's Historical Criticism and *Tendenzkritik*

HUGHSON T. ONG

NEW TESTAMENT SCHOLARSHIP has certainly recognized F. C. Baur's *Tendenzkritik* (Tendency Criticism) as a type of historical criticism in the history of New Testament interpretation.[1] But little critical work that evaluates this theoretical framework has been done in New Testament studies. The majority of secondary sources on Baur have only sought to present his life and works in a summative way,[2] and few have actually examined the application and the applicability of Baur's *Tendenzkritik* to the interpretation of the New Testament.[3] In fact, it is accurate to say that Harris's unreflective comment that Baur does not seem to have a systematic account of his historical-theological views may be the typical view held by most New Testament scholars today.[4] But this study will show that this typical view might not necessarily be an accurate assessment of Baur's historical-critical methodology in the light of the evidence we would discover if we would carefully examine the theoretical foundation and formulation of *Tendenzkritik* and its application to the study of the New

---

1. Andrews, "*Tendenz* versus Interpretation," 264, points out the identical meaning of the term "*tendenz*" in Baur's terms and the contemporary use of the term "interpretation." The term is used predominantly in Baur's work on Luke–Acts.

2. A few notable works deserve special mention here. Harris, *Tübingen School*; Hodgson, *Formation*; Hodgson, *Baur on the Writing of Church History*; and Kümmel, *New Testament* (120–84) are full-volume works that deal extensively with the primary sources on Baur. Three main bibliographical sources for the Baur corpus can be found in Harris, *Tübingen School*, 263–84; Hodgson, *Formation*, 285–94; and Smart, *Nineteenth Century Religious Thought*, 287–89.

3. See Andrews, "*Tendenz* versus Interpretation"; Andrews, "Super-Historical Gospel." These works survey Baur's criticisms of the Gospels of Luke and John respectively, but they lack a critical analysis of Baur's *Tendenzkritik* and its integrative framework with his historical-critical theories, from which the New Testament is studied.

4. Harris, *Tübingen School*, 160.

Testament.⁵ The three main sections in the remainder of this essay will attempt to examine and discuss these key elements in understanding Baur's *Tendenzkritik*.

The first main section briefly presents Baur's life and works, and the historical-theological context of the eighteenth and nineteenth centuries that served as the contextual background of Baur's thoughts and ideas. I discuss in this section three formative periods in his life that most historians have considered to be "pivotal" in the publication of his key works. The next section discusses the historical-theological context of the time that would have shaped the development of Baur's historical-critical method. This section provides a perspective for understanding various possible scenarios behind the conceptualization of Baur's historical-critical method. In the second major section, I articulate three critical components that constitute the epistemological framework of Baur's historical method, as well as his *Tendenzkritik*. In the third and final section, I present Baur's application of his historical-critical method and *Tendenzkritik* to the New Testament. Thereafter, I give a summative critique in the conclusion.

BAUR'S LIFE, MAJOR WORKS, AND HISTORICAL-THEOLOGICAL CONTEXT

Few people in the history of biblical interpretation have reached the level of prominence Baur achieved.⁶ Such a notable reputation, however, has also come with serious criticisms from other scholars who have not shared Baur's theory. That his historical framework is an "ingenious blunder," that his Hegelian theory is a "fantasy imposed on Christian history," and that his account of Christianity's origin is a "gross caricature" are some of the kinds of criticisms scholars have leveled against Baur.⁷ These criticisms, however, I believe, need to be clarified, and if necessary, they even need to be corrected. The failure of taking into account the theologian's historical-theological context can easily result in an inaccurate assessment of a person's belief or theology. I therefore wish to say a few things about Baur's life and works as well as his historical-theological context that merits reflection in working with his theology.

---

5. Baur's well-known Hegelian thesis–antithesis framework is still utilized by some scholars with varying degrees of emphases. See Fisk, "Paul," 321; Scott, "Parties in the Church of Jerusalem," 217. Various proponents of a two-stage (Jewish and Hellenistic) and a three-stage (Jewish, Hellenistic, Gentile) Christianity in the early Church are some examples of such a thesis–antithesis framework. See Marshall, "Palestinian and Hellenistic Christianity," 271-72.

6. Honored as the greatest church historian and scholar of his time, Baur is typically known as the scholar who attempted to attach the New Testament to its true historical background and the most reputable pioneer and practitioner of historical theology. See Baird, *History*, 258; Dilthey, "Ferdinand Christian Baur," 431; Bacon, *Mark*, 17; Morgan, "Biblical Classics," 4.

7. Reist, "F. C. Baur," 140. See also Bruce, "Ferdinand Christian Baur," 33. The Tübingen School has been caricatured as the "bogey of English clergymen," and because Baur's work appears to begin with philosophy (largely because of his Hegelian framework) he has been charged with a "false start" in his work. See Morgan, "Lectures," 202.

Baur's Life and Works

There are three formative periods in Baur's life that can help us paint a more accurate portrait of his life and theology.[8] The first period (1792-1826) encompasses the time from his birth to shortly before he was appointed professor at Tübingen in 1826. Born to Christian Jakob, an orthodox evangelical pastor, on June 21, 1792, Baur received his childhood education from his father who taught him Greek, Hebrew, and Latin. In 1805 he entered Blaubeuren Seminary, where he studied New Testament exegesis, rhetoric, history, and philosophy. Four years later, Baur went to the Tübingen School and stayed there for five years (1809-14) for his advanced theological training. His most influential teacher was Ernst Gottlieb Bengel, who was one of the most liberal supernaturalists and students of Kantian philosophy and rational criticism. Baur's time with Bengel ignited his interest in historical theology. It was also at this time that he came across Friedrich Schleiermacher's *The Christian Faith*, of which he admired the author's dialectical skill and the relevance of his work for the Christian faith, although he also criticized it for acknowledging miracles and supernaturalism.[9] After his study at Tübingen, Baur was hired as professor at Blaubeuren Seminary in 1825. Within his ten-year professorship tenure at Blaubeuren, Baur published his first monograph *Symbolik und Mythologie* (1824), a significant piece of work that showed traces of Schleiermacher's ideas and that provided a comparative study between "nature" religions and "history" religions.[10]

The second formative period in Baur's life (1826-45) began when he was appointed as a professor at Tübingen. One key event during this period was the publication of his inaugural dissertation on Schleiermacher's Christology in 1827, where he arrived at the conclusion that Schleiermacher's Christology fails to bring one to Christ.[11] Against what his former student David Strauss argued in his famous *The Life of Jesus Critically Examined*,[12] Baur argued that the union between God and humans is in the person of the historical Jesus.[13] The second significant event was his encounter with Hegelian philosophy. Although the degree of his Hegelian influence

---

8. My discussion in this section draws from Hodgson, *Formation*, 8-36; Harris, *Tübingen School*, 11-54; Baird, *History*, 258-69.

9. Schleiermacher's influence in New Testament hermeneutics cannot be overestimated. At the peak of the rationalistic period of the eighteenth century, Schleiermacher, a philosopher, philologist, pastor, and theologian, sought for inward religious experience as the basis of his theological concern, which, in turn, was influenced by romanticism, pietism, and Kant's notion of self-consciousness. For summaries of Schleiermacher's works and influence on New Testament studies, see Porter and Robinson, *Hermeneutics*, 7-8, 24-33; Baird, *History*, 208-20; and the previous chapter in this volume.

10. See Hodgson, *Formation*, 15, 98-99. Cf. Reist, "F. C. Baur," 142.

11. A concise summary of the content of this doctoral dissertation can be found in Hodgson, *Formation*, 43-47, 50.

12. Strauss rejected the historical Jesus as the realization of God; he only recognized the Christ of faith as a symbol of the union between God and humans. For a concise summary of Strauss's life and thought, see Baird, *History*, 246-58, esp. 249; Harris, *Strauss*.

13. Baird, *History*, 260.

at this time is indeterminable, many thought that Baur had become a pantheist and mystic when they read *Symbolik und Mythologie*. This situation aroused controversy over his coming to Tübingen. In Baur's work, however, the evidence for his use of the Hegelian framework only came after the publication of his seminal essay "The Christ Party in the Corinthian Church" (1831).[14] Many scholars would in fact acknowledge that this essay contains the programmatic principle that underlies his understanding and interpretation of New Testament history, where he contends for the ideas regarding the conflict between a Petrine Jewish Christianity (thesis) and a Pauline Gentile Christianity (anti-thesis) that eventually merged and evolved into second-century Catholicism (synthesis).[15]

The third event to note is Baur's development of his "tendency" theory in analyzing both the sources and content of the New Testament. By "tendency" Baur was referring to the intentions and perspective of the New Testament writers.[16] To be sure, Baur applied his *Tendenzkritik* to the book of Acts and found a certain "tendency" in the writer of Acts to harmonize the theological differences between Peter and Paul. For this reason, Baur claimed that Acts is not a purely historical work.[17]

In the thirty-four year period of his professorship at Tübingen, Baur was also offered professorships in Berlin (1834) and Halle (1836).[18]

The final years of Baur's life (1845-60) were actively devoted to his most important publications that left an indelible mark on the history of New Testament studies. He wrote four of his greatest works during this period. The first was *Paul the Apostle of Jesus Christ: His Life and Work, His Epistles and His Doctrine* published in 1845, where he argued that only Romans, Galatians, and the two Corinthian letters are genuinely Pauline and that Acts is not apostolic in origin. As the title suggests, the book is divided into three parts and indicates that the theology of the New Testament should be based on historical and literary investigation.[19] The second important book was *The Epochs of Church Historiography* (1852), in which he investigated the doctrine of reconciliation and the doctrine of the Trinity from the history of the beginnings of the early church to the nineteenth century. His third significant work during this period was *The Church History of the First Three Centuries* (1855), a historical reconstruction

---

14. Still in German, the essay's full title is "Die Christuspartei in der korinthischen Gemeinde, der Gegensatz des petrinischen und paulinischen Christenthums in der ältesten Kirche, der Apostel Petrus in Rom."

15. Cf. Reist, "F. C. Baur," 142–43, who suggests that the opposing Petrine legalism and Pauline freedom eventually synthesized into late-second-century Catholicism; see also Baird, *History*, 264, who points out that the council meeting in Acts resulted in "two spheres of mission, and a continuing battle between Jewish particularity and Pauline universalism."

16. Reist, "F. C. Baur," 143.

17. Baur, *Paul*, 1:241.

18. For a detailed discussion of Baur's invitation to teach at the Universities of Berlin and Halle, see Harris, *Tübingen School*, 29–39.

19. Morgan, "Biblical Classics," 4.

of Christianity in the early church with Jesus as its founder.[20] This was his first full attempt at providing the historical sequence of the New Testament books.

Nearing his last days, Baur suffered two heart attacks and died on 2 December 1860.[21] His fourth and final work was published posthumously (1865-67) under the title *Introduction to Lectures on the History of the Christian Doctrine*. Taken from his lectures beginning in the 1840s, this work shows how Baur's theological judgment gradually turned from Hegelian metaphysics that carries with it the "divine Idea" to a Kantian Christianity[22] with its emphasis on moral examples, commands, and teachings.[23] Hodgson describes Baur's life as "the integration of pietism and criticism."[24] This was true from the time he "carried his heavy schedule of research, writing, lecturing, preaching, and administration . . . until the end."[25]

The Historical-Theological Context of the Eighteenth and Nineteenth Centuries

The rationale behind this section is best framed by the words of Hodgson:

> To do theology in Baur's spirit (as he himself would insist), we must not return to the past but venture into an unknown future. But the venture into the future can be charted, to some extent, by learning from those whose work placed them at the cutting edge of theology in their own time.[26]

In what follows I survey the period shortly before the Enlightenment to the period of philosophical idealism based on William Baird's chronology.[27]

It is said that biblical criticism began with the Enlightenment in the eighteenth century, a period characterized by the fading away of the old orthodox authoritarian investigation of the New Testament and the dawning of the new methods of empiricism and rationalism called science. During this time the books of the New Testament

---

20. Baur, *Church History*, 1:23.

21. Harris, *Tübingen School*, 53.

22. Immanuel Kant (1724-1804) argued that a person can only know what can be known by their own mind or self. Thus, the life of Jesus is reduced to being an ethical example, since Kant's metaphysics does not allow the mind to comprehend the supernatural, such as that Jesus is God. See Hill and Rauser, *Christian Philosophy*, 99-101; Thiselton, *Encyclopedia*, 155-57.

23. Baur, *Writing*, 5, esp. n. 8. Cf. Reist, "F. C. Baur," 144-45.

24. Hodgson, *Formation*, 8, 33-36.

25. Ibid., 33. Zeller wrote: "Summer and winter he arose at 4:00 a.m., and in winter he customarily worked for several hours in an unheated room out of consideration for the servants, although on especially cold nights the ink froze; and thereafter the regular midday or evening walk was invariably the single long interruption in this scholarly day of work" (Zeller, "Ferdinand Christian Baur," 363).

26. Hodgson, *Baur on the Writing of Church History*, 7-8.

27. See Baird, *History*, 3-294. Cf. Hodgson, *Formation*, 37-38, who identifies three formative periods: (1) The period of revolution (1750-1815), when rationalism and historical-critical study of the biblical documents began; (2) the period of reaction, synthesis, and mediation (1815-30), when there was a search for a synthesizing theology; and (3) the period of disintegration (1830-50), when the attempted synthesis mediating faith and criticism fell apart.

began to be viewed as historical documents. In theological matters, however, the scenario remained fairly orthodox, until the English deists took New Testament research to the extreme left by rejecting orthodox faith and ecclesial authority.[28]

The deists advocated a natural and universal religion. With them, Christianity was nearing its dead end. In central Europe, however, an opposition to the deist movement emerged in the hands of the pietists, who regarded the Bible as authoritative in all areas of thought and practice.[29] But pietism was too weak for the European mind, and as a result, the Enlightenment phenomenon moved from England across the English Channel. At this time, logic and mathematics ruled the world, so that there was then a distinction between "truths of fact" (perceived by the senses) and "truths of reason" (perceived by analysis and comparison). This period set the stage for the development of the historical criticism of the New Testament through the works of three scholars, Turretin, Wettstein, and Ernesti, whose methodological approaches to the Bible shifted away from the study of doctrines to the study of its texts.[30]

Tensions became stronger as new discoveries in science, literature, and history continued to be refined in the eighteenth century. A group of progressive thinkers called neologians, like Semler and Michaelis, attempted to integrate divine revelation, reason, and theology. This period saw the rise of higher criticism, which would continue to dominate biblical studies for the next two centuries.[31] But the kinds of historical criticism that these scholars advanced did not attract the pulpit and the pew. Consequently, a cultural tide called romanticism, which claimed that truth is to be found in nature and is best expressed by feelings, flowed in during the time of the French Revolution.[32] Meanwhile, a variety of interpretive methods, in search of bridging the gap between history and its meaning, continued to emerge. This provided the impetus at the turn of the nineteenth century for the historical investigation of the sources of the Gospels and the development of the life and faith of the early church.[33]

This then led to the period called Liberalism, where a mixture of diverse ideas was added to the shared dominion of rationalism (with its concomitant historicism) and romanticism. It is fair to say that during this time the force of the Enlightenment from the previous century had been in some ways neutralized. And this impasse paved the way for a new method of inquiry to emerge, which was undertaken by one of the greatest philosophical thinkers in the nineteenth century, Georg Wilhelm Friedrich Hegel (1770-1831).[34]

---

28. See Baird, *History*, 3-30. Cf. McGrath, *Christian Theology*, 85-95.
29. See Baird, *History*, 31-90. Cf. McGrath, *Christian Theology*, 73-81.
30. See Baird, *History*, 91-115.
31. See ibid., 116-54.
32. For a good overview of romanticism, see McGrath, *Christian Theology*, 95-98.
33. See Baird, *History*, 155-95.
34. See ibid., 244-94. The Liberalism period is critical in the history of biblical interpretation with its distinctive requirement of allowing a "significant degree of flexibility in relation to traditional

THE HISTORICAL-THEOLOGICAL DEVELOPMENT OF BAUR'S METHODOLOGY

Accepted knowledge tells us that Baur's historical-critical method is simply Hegelian in orientation. Though this may be the case, there are two immediate reasons that suggest a qualification of this assessment is necessary. First, as noted earlier, Baur's Hegelian framework only became evident in the publication of his seminal essay "The Christ Party in the Corinthian Church" in 1831. Second, it is apparent in the preceding section that Baur's epistemological framework is an amalgamation of the diverse vestiges from each of these critical periods in the history of New Testament research. The treatment of the New Testament as historical documents by the precursors of the Enlightenment, the rational method of investigation by the English deists, the emphasis on religious experience by the pietists and romanticists, the "defining" of historical research by the pre-critical scholars and its "refining" by the neologians, and eventually, the influence of Hegel, all contributed in varying degrees to Baur's theological presuppositions and conceptualization of history.[35] They were his intellectual and theological teachers. While space does not permit me to discuss how each exerted its influence on Baur, the point is that this is the kind of historical-theological situation Baur was dealing with during his time. In terms of his professional-theological context, Baur actually sought to bridge Lessing's "ugly ditch,"[36] which apparently was popularized by David Strauss in the publication of his *The Life of Jesus Critically Examined*.[37] As such, it is perhaps best to view Baur's work from the perspective of the quest for mediating between philosophy/history and religion/faith, which is my main subject in the next section.

Schleiermacher and Hegel: Baur's Epistemological Framework

As noted above, Baur's inaugural dissertation in 1827 was on Schleiermacher's Christology. But his very first encounter with him began when he read Schleiermacher's *Glaubenslehre* in 1821-22. Baur was drawn to Schleiermacher's concept of religious

---

Christian theology" and its emphasis on the reconstruction of faith as an essential component of Christianity. The fruit of Liberalism can be seen in the various theological movements that have emerged since its inception until the present. See McGrath, *Christian Theology*, 101-30.

35. Cf. Hodgson, *Baur on the Writing of Church History*, 6-8, who has a similar argument and observation when he points out the various similar hermeneutical problems and issues that confronted theologians in the period following Schleiermacher and Hegel.

36. Lessing, "On the Origin of Revealed Religion."

37. Strauss says that Jesus "is to be regarded as a person, as a great—and as far as I am concerned, the greatest—personality in the series of religious geniuses, but still only a man like others, and the Gospels are to be regarded as the oldest collections of the myths [i.e., supernatural, therefore, unhistorical, since they are legendary creations] which were attached around the core of this personality" (Strauss, *Christ of Faith*, 161). For a summary of Strauss's theological position, see Kümmel, *New Testament*, 120-26. For a summary of Strauss's life and his works, see Baird, *History*, 246-58.

consciousness that frees the individual from the authority of inspired biblical text.[38] This was the very thing Baur had been searching for—the true mediation between faith and reason. In other words, he was concerned with how to link the ecclesiastical content of Christianity with concrete historical facts. In rationalism, Baur argues, the relationship between faith and history is only explained artificially and externally, since it is unable to account for the reality of history and supernatural revelation.[39] For instance, the occurrence of a "miracle," such as "Jesus turned water into wine" (John 2), cannot be explained on the basis of pure reason, since a miraculous event is in contradiction to the normal order of nature and history.[40] Hence, a miracle is a supernatural event. Even though Baur did not deny God's existence, he did believe that God's revelation and action in nature and history could not be understood as happening supernaturally.

In Schleiermacher's "ideal rationalism," however, there is no violation of the order of nature and history, since the mediating agent is found within the person *themselves*—the consciousness of the self,[41] world, and God in chronological order.[42] In simplistic terms, humans by nature know that both God and the supernatural merely exist. In christological terms, the historical Jesus and his works are treated as functions of religious consciousness (self), and he is known in conjunction with the historical church (world). But the "ideal Christ" is prior to the historical Jesus, since he is the religious experience of redemption. This subsequently implies that, in Schleiermacher's terms, there becomes no distinction between the natural and the supernatural, since the mediating agent (or better, the supreme agent) is the self.[43] The natural "self" precedes the supernatural "God." I have provided a schematic illustration of Schleiermacher's "ideal rationalism" in Figure 1.

---

38. Cf. Porter and Robinson, *Hermeneutics*, 29. In a letter to his brother, Baur gives great appreciation to Schleiermacher not only for the richness of the content of the book, but also especially for its significance for true Christian faith (Hodgson, *Formation*, 13).

39. For an extended discussion on rationalism and supernaturalism, see Hodgson, *Baur on the Writing of Church History*, 12–17.

40. Baur defines miracle as "an interruption of the natural continuity, dependent on an immanent law, of cause and effect, which is not further explicable by natural causes and which results from an external, intermittently operating causality" (Baur, *Paul*, 1:97).

41. "An immediacy of awareness" in a quasi-ontological sense (Thiselton, *Encyclopedia*, 277); or cognitive revelation (Hill and Rauser, *Christian Philosophy*, 167).

42. Porter and Robinson, *Hermeneutics*, 29–30, describe Schleiermacher's theological program as "a theology of experience"; thus, his hermeneutics is more "subjective, individualistic, and psychologizing (having to do with the human mind and mental processes) than traditional methodologies that attempt to provide objective-historical accounts of the Bible on its own terms."

43. See Hodgson, *Formation*, 5 n. 13, 43–47, 190–96.

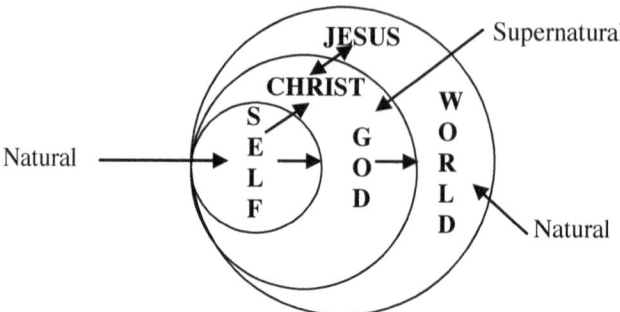

Figure 1: A Schematic Representation of Schleiermacher's "Ideal Rationalism"

Despite this attraction, the obvious flaw in Schleiermacher's theory did not escape Baur's critical eye. Baur pointed out that the basic problem in Schleiermacher's *Glaubenslehre* was its false starting point. Because he did not begin with the historical Jesus, Baur thinks that Schleiermacher did not really succeed in getting to him, that is, the dichotomy between the historical Jesus and the ideal Christ that Schleiermacher sought to establish is, for Baur, the root of the problem. If the "ideal Christ" is (non-historically) instantiated in the historical Jesus, then it follows that the historical appearance and person of Jesus is a supernatural and miraculous event, since they are at once identical. And Baur wanted to reject this supernatural explanation (as we will see shortly), since it disconnects the historical Jesus from other historical events.[44] For this reason, Baur asserted that Schleiermacher's theory was highly speculative and his argument was still predominantly dogmatic, since it was simply "an assertion of faith, namely, that God-consciousness is completely actualized in one historical figure."[45] This being the case, there is no need of the historical Jesus.[46] This made Baur turn to Hegel's philosophy.

Baur saw in Hegel's doctrine of the Trinity a clearer explanation for the relationship between history and faith, or the Christ of faith and the historical Jesus. Hill and Rauser summarize Hegel's theory well:

> [Hegel argues] that humanity can be thought of as a collective subject, which he called *Geist* (Spirit). This collective subject is coming to self-consciousness through the myriad individual conflicts of history, each of which is incorporated into the final resolution. Hegel termed the conclusion to this process of self-knowledge "Absolute Spirit." This process is explicated through the doctrine of the Trinity by seeing God's beginning as pure consciousness. But consciousness requires an object, and so God created the world, which is the object of divine consciousness. The relationship of God to the world

---

44. Baur, *Vorlesungen*, 3:531–32.
45. Hodgson, *Formation*, 48.
46. Ibid., 50.

is symbolized in the person of Jesus Christ. Then, when the world returns to God, the process is completed in Spirit and God becomes self-conscious.[47]

Baur adopted from this Hegelian framework the idea of thesis (God),[48] antithesis (world), and synthesis (Christ). Hegel's doctrine or idea of reconciliation (synthesis) attracted Baur's attention, even though he also found a major problem with it. Baur noted that, since God and the world will be consummated together, it is still unclear whether it will be God who will be absorbed by the world or vice versa in the end. For Hegel, however, these matters, including who or what the mediating agent is, were irrelevant. The important issue is that reconciliation is mediated historically. It is at this point, Baur argued, that Hegel's theory becomes a speculative theory of the mind. Although Baur did not object to a speculative theory in probing the meaning of redemption, he did object to this Hegelian concept of a final consummation, if the consummation is in the form of some abstract dialectic thought. Baur pointed out that this violates Hegel's own philosophy of religion that respects the historicity of the divine life.[49] In other words, for Baur, in the final consummation of things, the last "being" standing must be God.[50] Thus, rejecting Hegel's Christology, Baur only adopted the Hegelian philosophical framework as "an objective basis for interpreting Christianity as an historical process and for understanding speculatively the meaning of reconciliation."[51] I have illustrated this Hegelian framework in Figure 2 below.

Religion (or Theology) as Reconciliation: Baur's Presupposition for Historical-Critical Study

Baur brought this Hegelian epistemological framework into his discussion of religion (or theology) as the mediating agent between history and faith. Religious dogma (or doctrine) was Baur's fundamental presupposition for his historical-critical study of the theology of the New Testament:

> The historian of dogma can take his position only from the standpoint of the most recent dogmatic consciousness . . . Where else can he obtain the clear conception of the object whose historical movement is the problem with

---

47. Hill and Rauser, *Christian Philosophy*, 81.

48. In Hegelian terms, "thesis" is the first-level proposition formed in the dialectical reasoning process.

49. See Strauss, *Streitschriften*, 3:61, 197.

50. See Hodgson, *Formation*, 54–66.

51. Ibid., 64. Baur denied being a disciple of Hegel: "I am not a disciple of any philosophical system, because I well know how deceptive it is to make oneself dependent on human authority; but likewise I have the conviction that there is a great deal for theology to learn from Hegel" (Baur, "Abgenöthigte Erklärung," 225). Yet in another work, Baur claims to be Hegelian: "It is in general the Hegelian method which the author of this article employs in order to provide a solution to the task he has set himself" (Baur, "Gegensatz," 421).

which he ought to concern himself, other than from the consciousness of the present? The historian can move back into the past only from the present.[52]

For him, religious doctrine, with its source and center in the person of Christ, served as the basic manifestation of the self-revelation of God in history. "It is the conceptual articulation of a fundamentally conceptual reality."[53] Religious doctrines are also the first and most important "forms" (a "form" is a tangible thing) that express the "content" of the Christian faith. This means that the only way to proceed with a historical investigation of the early Christian church is through the study of its doctrines in the present. By the same token, these doctrines can only be gleaned and understood from their systematic formulation in history, which includes creeds, church symbols, confessions, and theology in all its forms.[54] In this articulation, Baur sounds circular in his understanding. On the one hand, history (goal) can only be studied through doctrines (forms). On the other hand, doctrines can only be found in their systematic formulation in history. In my view, Baur appears to take the historical "past" (with all its events in the form of doctrines) as the "internal records" to work with for the reconstruction of history in the present.

There are two obvious differences to note between Baur's and Hegel's framework.[55] One is that Hegel's *Geist* (Absolute Spirit) seems to disappear in Baur's model; nevertheless, it is plausible to think that Baur might have regarded it as the entirety of history from its inception to its consummation, since the repetitive cycle of historical reconstruction in the present entails the assimilation of all its "past" historical events. A second less obvious difference concerns the function for which the model is being used. Baur's model appears to be less "organic" than Hegel's in that doctrine (in the New Testament text) is used to reconstruct the historical situation of the early church and not faith in the abstract. We turn now to look at his theories for this historical reconstruction of the early church.

---

52. Baur, *Vorlesungen*, 1:12. See Hodgson, *Formation*, 90.

53. Hodgson, *Baur on the Writing of Church History*, 27–28.

54. Ibid., 29; Hodgson, *Formation*, 90. Cf. Reist, "F. C. Baur," 152–53.

55. Figure 3 below shows how Baur adopts and fits Hegel's theory into his own historical-critical framework.

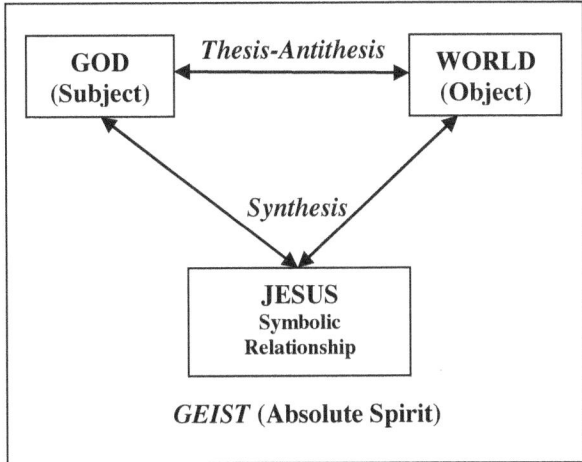

Figure 2: A Representation of Hegel's Trinitarian Thesis-Antithesis-Synthesis Framework

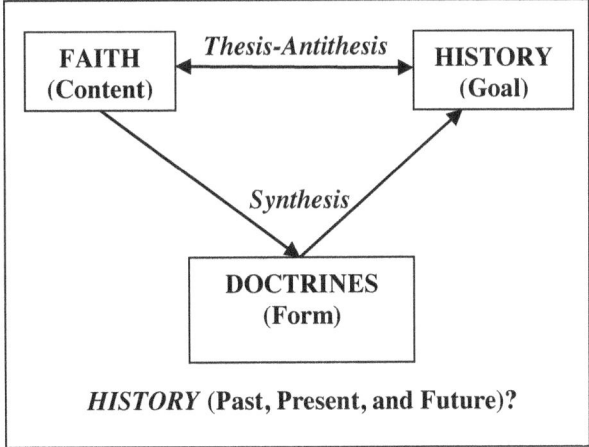

Figure 3: A Schematic Representation of Baur's Framework for Historical-Critical Study

Historical Event and Historical Knowledge: Baur's Foundation for Historical-Critical Study

Baur claimed that the notion of "history" elicits two connotations; it is the objective event, and at the same time, the critical knowledge of that objective event. Therefore, a historical event is one that is known by historical means. Events that are known by faith or other non-historical means in principle are not historical events, for a historical event is known by a historical-critical investigation. The problem of such historical-critical investigation, however, is the temporal distance between the historical event and the investigator, which naturally leads to the issue of historical presentation.[56]

The subject matter of historical presentation involves in the first instance an understanding of the meaning of a historical process. It is fair to argue that Baur's notion of a historical process consists of stages one and two of his theory of religion as reconciliation, as discussed above. So if historical process is simultaneously the divine revelation and divine self-manifestation, history exists out of the inward self-manifestation of God who reveals himself outwardly. In this case,

> God "lives" in history; he mediates himself historically; therefore history exists. The ontological foundation of history is God. Since history is part of the very life of God, it cannot cease to exist unless or until God should cease to mediate himself outwardly; but the Christian Gospel declares that it is the nature and purpose of God thus to live. This is a dogmatic affirmation that undergirds Baur's historical-critical theology.[57]

This brings us to Baur's use of "idea" as a category for historical interpretation and presentation. An "idea" is a form or an instantiation of thought, where God mediates himself to become a free, thinking, and conscious Spirit.[58] Whereas the thought of God shapes reality, the thought of humans only contributes to it. The historical process takes place when there is congruence between ideas and manifestations, the mark of a true historical event. This relationship can otherwise be expressed as that between concept and fact, content and form, or divine Spirit and human consciousness. Because congruence of ideas and manifestations exists, this accounts for the *necessity* of a historical event.[59] And this historical event then allows for a continuity and rationality of a series of historical events (a connected whole and not a random collection) that can be historically-critically investigated. An example of a historical event is the historical Jesus.

Tendency Criticism

According to S. Neill, *Tendenzkritik*, a theory that seeks to determine a "tendency" in theology, is the strength of Baur's methodology.[60] He first used this method in his seminal essay "Die Christuspartei in der korinthischen Gemeinde" in 1831, although the preparation of the article began as early as 1826. As mentioned above, this may

---

56. Hodgson, *Formation*, 144-45.
57. Ibid., 146-47.
58. Ibid., 147.
59. Ibid., 148-50; cf. Hodgson, *Baur on the Writing of Church History*, 32-36.
60. Neill, *Interpretation*, 19. *Tendenzkritik* is also known as literary-historical criticism or scientific historiography.

indicate that his views in this article were not yet Hegelian.[61] The essay presents the argument that primitive Christianity consists of the opposition between a Petrine (Jewish) Christianity and Pauline (Gentile) Christianity. Another major work where Baur applied his *Tendenzkritik* was *Paul the Apostle of Jesus Christ*. Baur stated the underlying principle behind *Tendenzkritik* in *Die kanonischen Evangelien*:

> Why ought not this [procedure], with which in general no one can quarrel, also find its application with respect to our canonical Gospels? That they offer themselves as historical presentations of the life of Jesus in no way excludes the supposition that their authors were guided in their presentations by definite motives and interests. Indeed, it cannot be otherwise thought than that they are literary products of the time in which the authors lived. The first question that every criticism of these Gospels needs to ask must be concerned with the will and intention of each of the authors. With this question we first come to the firm ground of concrete historical truth.[62]

In saying this Baur was positing that a literary-historical study of the New Testament must include an investigation of its sources, statements, date, and occasions through the intentions and perspectives of its authors.[63]

There are two fundamental rules in the application of *Tendenzkritik* to a biblical text. The first rule is the placement of the biblical text in its original historical context. This procedure requires an identification of historical "tendencies" or "directions" that are associated with a particular theological point of view, in which an understanding of a particular saying or story unfolds. In other words, a biblical text exhibits the theological perspective of the author. The second procedure requires that any purported *facts* contained in the biblical text must be assessed based on the theological and historical perspectives of the text. Specifically, the theological intention of the author dictates the authenticity of the factual elements in a biblical story or text. In this case, *Tendenzkritik* can be said to be a criticism that engages itself in the theological and historical interpretation of the biblical text, since theology and history are so interdependent in its procedural analysis.[64]

While Baur's *Tendenzkritik* has received serious criticisms from various scholars, it is important to note that his approach is in the interest of rigorous historical research to determine the intentions and perspectives of the New Testament writers. His procedure cannot be regarded as *a priori* or speculative on this ground. As we will see in the next section, his application of his historical methodology, particularly

---

61. Baur, "Christuspartei," 75, 114. Cf. Hodgson, *Formation*, 22 n. 85. Hodgson, however, points out that the term is used as a polemic by Baur's opponents to ridicule his method of inquiry (Hodgson, *Formation*, 200).

62. Baur, *Kritische Untersuchungen*, 74, cited in Hodgson, *Formation*, 197.

63. Reist, "F. C. Baur," 143.

64. Hodgson, *Formation*, 197-98. Klaus Scholder thinks, however, that Baur makes a distinction between these two methods of interpretation. See Scholder, "Ferdinand Christian Baur," 453-58.

Tendenzkritik, can be seen as a major advancement in New Testament studies and thus deserves careful consideration.

BAUR'S APPLICATION OF HISTORICAL CRITICISM AND *TENDENZKRITIK* TO THE NEW TESTAMENT

Baur's literary output was substantial. Even if one devoted an entire section to one of his books to survey how he applied his historical methods to the New Testament, the task would still be formidable. In what follows, therefore, I will attempt to both discuss and critique in a summative way Baur's most important work that exemplifies his *Tendenzkritik*, as well as his historical-critical approach to the New Testament. In a number of ways, his *Paul the Apostle of Jesus Christ* is the most significant book to examine.[65]

From what we have seen in the development of Baur's theological foundation in his historical-critical approach, it is very likely that he was primarily concerned with the meaning of Christianity, in which its central figure is the historical Jesus. This is most evident in his adoption of the Hegelian philosophical framework to explain the inter-relationship between faith, doctrines, and history, as well as his search for the authorial intention of the New Testament writers, in order to distinguish the historical from the non-historical elements in the biblical text. From these epistemological frameworks, Baur assimilated and analyzed the history and theology of the first two centuries of primitive Christianity on the basis of the internal evidence found in the Gospels, Acts, and the Pauline letters. What Baur found in this preliminary stage of investigation was that a new religion, Christianity, with all its tensions with Judaism in the first century, was able to break away and was freed from Jewish particularities through the apostle Paul.[66] This particular event, Baur claimed, is an "undeniable historical fact."[67] This became his "monolithic singular principle"[68] that Baur used as a lens to interpret primitive Christianity. This principle states:

> there were really but two parties, one that of Paul and Apollos, and the other ... that of Peter and Christ. Taking into consideration the acknowledged relation in which Paul and Peter, one as the Apostle to the Gentiles, the other to the Jews, really stood towards each other, or at least the relation in which they

---

65. According to Hodgson, this book, *Paul the Apostle of Jesus Christ*, was Baur's entry point to the study of the "mysteries" of the New Testament, which he also considered to be the "foundation and firm support" for his later writings (Hodgson, *Formation*, 202–3). Similarly, Morgan claims that the book was "[Baur's] own favourite of all his writings, and occupies both chronologically and materially a central position from which his entire life's work can be understood ... [it] is in fact the backbone of Baur's whole reconstruction of early Christian history" (Morgan, "Biblical Classics," 4).

66. Baur, *Paul*, 1:5.

67. Ibid. Baur asserts that Paul "was the receptive soil in which the principle of Christian consciousness, which through him for the first time obtained its living features, developed into a concrete consciousness" (ibid., 2:277).

68. Reist, "F. C. Baur," 149.

were thought to stand towards each other by the chief parties of the oldest Christian church, there can be no doubt that the chief difference lay between the two sects which called themselves after Paul and Cephas.[69]

Through this interpretive lens, Baur arrived at a conclusion that there are only four indisputably authentic Pauline epistles, and these are the ones we can use as the reliable historical sources for the life of Paul. The Epistles to the Romans, Galatians, and 1 and 2 Corinthians all affirm the new gospel of Jesus Christ against the old Jewish legalism and particularities.[70] For instance, on the one hand, the opposition between Paul and his Judaizing opponents with their legal strictures is evident in Galatians.[71] On the other hand, the gospel that extends to all nations, the gospel that is accepted by the Gentiles but rejected by the Jews, is the central theme of Romans.[72] In the two Corinthian letters, Baur claimed, although the opponents appear to be different from those in Galatians, they still represent a unified opposition against Paul's apostleship, since Paul reproves them sharply with his authority as the repentant persecutor-turned-apostle of Christianity.[73] According to Baur, there were only two factions in Corinth (not four): the Jews (the parties of Christ and Peter) and the Pauline group (Paul and Apollos). Whether this is the actual case, there is also evidence that Paul's opponents in the Corinthian letters could have been charismatics who claimed to have special gifts, or proto-Gnostics who claimed to possess special knowledge.

By contrast, Baur found Acts plagued with miracle stories and displaying theological modifications by the author. According to Morgan, Baur highlighted the apologetic character of Acts, which compromises with a negative attitude towards the law and finds parallels between Paul and Peter. Baur further pointed out that Paul's speech in Acts 13 is clearly intended to harmonize the theologies of the two apostles. The most obvious authorial "tendency" in Acts, however, is found in the exaltation of the apostles in its opening chapters, shortly before the dissension that arises in Acts 6.[74] On the basis of this, Baur questioned the reliability of Acts as a historical source for the life of Paul and its early date and authorship, even though he was convinced that Acts still remained an important secondary historical source.[75] With respect to Ephesians and Colossians, the Christian "universalism," such as the idea of cosmic reconciliation, as well as the peculiarly Pauline conception of faith with Gnostic influence, led Baur to treat these letters as post-Pauline.[76] A clear case in point is Baur's

69. Baur, *Paul*, 1:274.
70. Hodgson, *Formation*, 205.
71. Baur, *Paul*, 1:261–63.
72. Ibid., 1:322.
73. Ibid., 1:271.
74. For a detailed summary and assessment of Baur's arguments concerning Acts, see Morgan, "Biblical Classics," 5–6.
75. Baur, *Paul*, 1:5–6, 8, 13, 32–33.
76. Ibid., 2:18–21, 35–42.

understanding of ἐν ὁμοιώματι ἀνθρώπων γενόμενος (being in the likeness of humans; Phil 2:7) and ἐν ὁμοιώματι σαρκὸς ἁμαρτίας (in the likeness of those who have a sinful nature; Rom 8:3), in which he claims that only the latter is authentically Pauline. The former, he argued, shows Gnostic influences.[77] With reference to the remaining Pauline letters (Philippians, 1 Thessalonians, Philemon, and the Pastorals), Baur claimed that they either lacked originality or did not display distinctively Pauline elements; hence, they are probably inauthentic.[78]

Using his two basic procedures of *Tendenzkritik*, Baur also applied his approach to the Gospel of Matthew. One immediately recognizes the necessity of analyzing a body of literature describing certain events to find its particular theological tendency. Baur considered the Gospel of Matthew to be the earliest and most historically reliable Gospel because of its "very Jewish" character. This conclusion was derived from an exclusive examination of the one Gospel, a method in contrast to a comparative synchronic analysis of similar stories or texts from more than one Gospel. In Baur's literary-historical criticism, the latter method indicates a disregard for the historical nature and aspects of the writings, that is, that the Gospels were written at different times and occasions. Nevertheless, Baur still found it extremely difficult to sort out, for example, the actual sayings of Jesus from Matthew's peripheral literary stories. And so in his investigation of Matthew's Gospel, Baur formulated the criterion that any text that transcends Judaism radically, and shows a break with Jewish messianic expectations, represents the authentic teachings of Jesus.[79] In short, those texts that do not conform to the Jewish elements of early Christianity are the ones that show the least possibility of authorial tendencies.[80]

So far we have only tackled how Baur used this thesis-antithesis criterion as a lens to study the New Testament. We turn now to explore how he reconciled these two opposing groups in primitive Christianity based on his Hegelian framework.[81] There are two characteristic features of the antithesis between Jewish and Pauline Christianity in Baur's historical reconstruction that he believed could explain this reconciliation. First, these two opposing forces in primitive Christianity were seen as originating from the person of the historical Christ, the perfect union of the divine and the human, the universal and the particular, who is both Jewish and "Gentile" at the same time. Moreover, these opposing forces are related in terms of form and content (or idea and reality); Jewish Christianity puts emphasis on "form," whereas Gentile Christianity places its emphasis on "content." Nonetheless, both are indispensable

---

77. Ibid., 2:52.

78. See ibid., 1:246-47; 2:45-46, 81, 85, 99-100.

79. In contemporary historical Jesus studies, this is somewhat similar to what is otherwise known as the "Criterion of Dissimilarity." See Porter, *Criteria*, 70-76.

80. Hodgson, *Formation*, 199.

81. Figure 4 below shows a diagram of Baur's application of his Hegelian framework and *Tendenzkritik* to the New Testament.

because the existence of one element presupposes the other. These forces, however, are neutralized in the person of Christ. This necessity of mutual complementation is the second characteristic feature. Baur saw Pauline Christianity as the horizontal propagation of the gospel to all nations through its Gentile mission, and Jewish Christianity as the erected hierarchical structure upon which primitive Christianity is founded. To put it differently, Jewish Christianity with its doctrines (form) serves as the presupposition of the forward movement of Pauline Christianity throughout history (see the section "Religion as Reconciliation" above).[82]

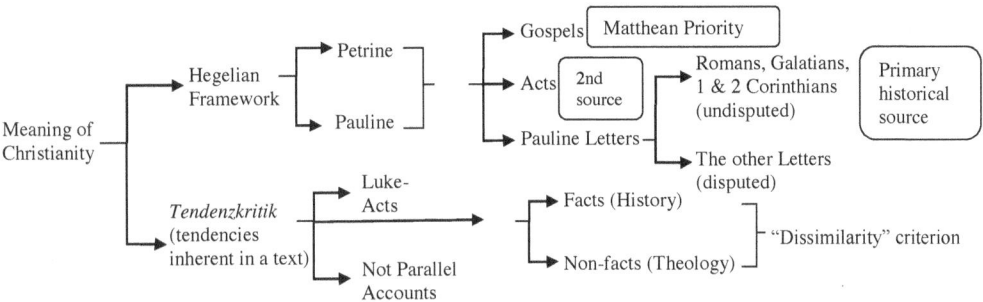

Figure 4: A Schematic Diagram of Baur's Application of a Hegelian Framework and *Tendenzkritik* to the New Testament

CONCLUSION

As I have noted above, serious criticisms have been lodged against Baur, and his historical-critical method and *Tendenzkritik* have been represented by many as purely speculative.[83] However, I have shown in this study that, despite Harris's uncritical comment, Baur did have a clear methodological approach to his historical-theological inquiry of the New Testament, even though previous studies of his life and works may not have articulated it in a succinct way.[84] Nevertheless, because a theoretical framework is clear does not mean that it does not have its pronounced flaws and weaknesses. This is first evident in the many voices raised against *Tendenzkritik* in the mid-nineteenth century by some of Baur's contemporaries (e.g., H. A. W. Meyer, M. Schneckenburger, J. A. W. Neander, G. V. Lechler, M. Baumgarten, C. E. Leckbusch), as well as his own students (e.g., A. Ritschl).[85] In fact, Ritschl, who criticized Baur's "value judgments" and was unconvinced of his identification of the two opposing par-

---

82. Hodgson, *Formation*, 209–11.

83. Cf. Rollman, "Historical Methodology," 115.

84. But cf. Hodgson, "Alienation," esp. 42–48, who argues that "Whereas Hegel describes the Christian religion only in a speculatively transfigured form, Baur translates this philosophical language back into more specifically theological and doctrinal concepts and is attentive to historical-critical details in a way foreign to Hegel himself," although Gasque, "Historical Value," 74 n. 26, has pointed out that Hodgson's *Formation* appears to have defended Baur almost entirely.

85. See Gasque, "Historical Value," 80 nn. 55–61, for the works of these scholars.

ties in early Christianity, as well as his dating of the New Testament writings, was Baur's staunchest detractor.[86] These detractors, however, were unsuccessful in their attempts to hone Baur's theory, as they were writing at a time when "Hegel was king."[87] It was a group of more radical heirs of the Tübingen School, Bruno Bauer, Franz Overbeck, and Paul Wilhelm Schmiedel, who merely rejected the notion that Acts was a conciliatory writing and argued that Jewish and Gentile reconciliation was already a reality in Acts, who toppled Baur's popular view at Tübingen. To them, Acts is to be considered an expression of Catholicism.[88] Because of the influential work of these scholars, radical German criticism began to wane.

Finally, I close by identifying two critical points where Baur's methodology seems to lack clarity and coherence. On the one hand, it is not altogether clear in Baur's writings whether he sees a correlation or continuity between the Jewish Old Testament (which Jesus said he came to fulfill) and the Jewish world in which Jesus lived. Though it can be assumed that he followed Schleiermacher who disregarded the Old Testament, this assumption cannot be confirmed, since Baur's goal from the very start was to look for a way to explain "religion as reconciliation," a position that suggests "continuity" in his Hegelian framework. On the other hand, with reference to his complementing a Hegelian framework with *Tendenzkritik*, it appears that they were both used as presuppositions (i.e., his prior understanding based on an initial reading of the New Testament, notably 1 Corinthians) and as a lens to interpret the New Testament writings. Therefore, his interpretation of early Christianity as composed of two opposing parties precedes the application of his Hegelian concept; the latter was imposed on the former. In any event, Baur's *Tendenzkritik*, which argues that the message of the New Testament writings is tainted with the theological bias of their authors, can be seen as an early form of redaction criticism, and his contribution to New Testament studies, not only in the mid-nineteenth century but also until today, should not be understated.

BIBLIOGRAPHY

Andrews, Mary E. "*Tendenz* versus Interpretation." *JBL* 58 (1939) 263–76.

———. "The Super-Historical Gospel: F. C. Baur's Criticism of the Gospel of John." *AThR* 26 (1944) 212–24.

Bacon, Benjamin W. *The Gospel of Mark: Its Composition and Date*. New Haven: Yale University Press, 1925.

Baird, William. *History of New Testament Research*. Vol. 1, *From Deism to Tübingen*. Minneapolis: Fortress, 1992.

Baur, F. C. "Abgenöthigte Erklärung gegen einen Artikel der *Evangelischen Kirchenzeitung*, herausgegeben von D. E. W. Hengstenberg, Prof. der Theol. an der Universität zu Berlin. Mai 1836." *TZT* 9 (1836) 179–232.

---

86. See Strimple, "Modern Search," 49–50; Gasque, "Historical Value," 80.
87. Gasque, "Historical Value," 80.
88. Ibid., 81–82.

———. *The Church History of the First Three Centuries.* Translated by Allan Menzies. 2 vols. 3rd ed. London: Williams & Norgate, 1878.

———. *Das Christenthum und die christliche Kirche der drei ersten Jahrhunderte.* 3 vols. Tübingen: L. F. Hues, 1853–61.

———. "Der Gegensatz des Katholicismus und Protestantismus nach den Principien und Hauptdogmen der beiden Lehrbegriffe. Mit besonderer Rüchsicht auf Hernn Dr. Möhler's Symbolik." *TZT* 3, 4 (1833) 1-438.

———. "Die Christuspartei in der korinthischen Gemeinde, der Gegensatz des petrinischen und paulinischen Christenthums in der ältesten Kirche, der Apostel Petrus in Rom." *TZT* 5 (1831) 61-206.

———. *Kritische Untersuchungen über die kanonischen Evangelien, ihr Verhältniss zu einander, ihren Charackter und Ursprung.* Tübingen: L. F. Fues, 1847.

———. *Paul the Apostle of Jesus Christ: His Life and Work, His Epistles and His Doctrine; A Contribution to a Critical History of Primitive Christianity.* Translated by Allan Menzies. 2 vols. London: Williams & Norgate, 1875. Reprint, Peabody: Hendrickson, 2003.

———. *Vorlesungen über die Christliche Dogmengeschichte.* 3 vols. Leipzig: Fues's Verlag, 1865, 1866, 1867.

———. *On the Writing of Church History.* Edited and translated by Peter C. Hodgson. New York: Oxford University Press, 1968.

Bruce, A. B. "Ferdinand Christian Baur and His Theory of the Origin of Christianity and the New Testament." In *Living Papers Concerning Christian Evidences, Doctrine, and Morals*, vol. 7, 3-58. Cincinnati: Cranston & Stowe, 1886.

Dilthey, Wilhelm. "Ferdinand Christian Baur." In *Gesammelte Schriften*, 403-32. Vol. 4, *Die Jugendgeschichte Hegels und andere Abhandlungen zur Geschichte des deutschen Idealismus.* 2nd ed. Leipzig: B. G. Teubner, 1925.

Fisk, Bruce. "Paul: Life and Letters." In *The Face of New Testament Studies*, edited by Grant Osborne and Scot McKnight, 76-103. Grand Rapids: Baker, 2004.

Gasque, W. Ward. "The Historical Value of the Book of Acts." *EvQ* 41 (1969) 68-88.

Harris, Horton. *David Friedrich Strauss and His Theology.* Cambridge: Cambridge University Press, 1973.

———. *The Tübingen School.* Oxford: Clarendon, 1975.

Hill, Daniel J., and Randal D. Rauser. *Christian Philosophy A-Z.* Edinburgh: Edinburgh University Press, 2006.

Hodgson, Peter C. "Alienation and Reconciliation in Hegelian and Post-Hegelian Perspective." *Modern Theology* 2 (1985) 42-63.

———, ed. *Ferdinand Christian Baur on the Writing of Church History.* Translated by Peter C. Hodgson. New York: Oxford University Press, 1968.

———. *The Formation of Historical Theology: A Study of Ferdinand Christian Baur.* New York: Harper & Row, 1966.

Kümmel, George W. *The New Testament: The History of the Investigation of Its Problems.* Nashville: Broadman & Holman, 1970.

Lessing, Gotthold E. "On the Origin of Revealed Religion." In his *Philosophical and Theological Writings*, edited and translated by H. B. Nisbet, 35-36. Cambridge: Cambridge University Press, 2005.

Marshall, I. Howard. "Palestinian and Hellenistic Christianity: Some Critical Comments." *NTS* 19 (1973) 271-87.

McGrath, Alister E. *Christian Theology: An Introduction.* 2nd ed. Oxford: Blackwell, 1997.

Morgan, Robert. "Biblical Classics: II. F. C. Baur: Paul." *ExpTim* 90 (1978) 4-10.

———. "F. C. Baur's Lectures on New Testament Theology." *ExpTim* 88 (1977) 202-6.

Neill, Stephen. *The Interpretation of the New Testament 1861-1961*. London: Oxford University Press, 1964.

Porter, Stanley E. *The Criteria for Authenticity in Historical-Jesus Research: Previous Discussion and New Proposals*. Sheffield: Sheffield Academic, 2000.

Porter, Stanley E., and Jason C. Robinson. *Hermeneutics: An Introduction to Interpretive Theory*. Grand Rapids: Eerdmans, 2011.

Reist, John S., Jr. "F. C. Baur." In *Historians of the Christian Tradition: Their Methodology and Influence on Western Thought*, edited by Michael Bauman and Martin I. Klauber, 139-65. Nashville: Broadman & Holman, 1995.

Rollman, Hans Josef. "The Historical Methodology of William Wrede." Unpublished MA thesis, McMaster University, 1979.

Scholder, Klaus. "Ferdinand Christian Baur als Historiker." *Evangelische Theologie* 21 (1961) 435-58.

Scott, Julius J. "Parties in the Church of Jerusalem as Seen in the Book of Acts." *JETS* 18 (1975) 217-27.

Smart, Ninian. *Nineteenth Century Religious Thought in the West*. Cambridge: Cambridge University Press, 1985.

Strauss, David F. *The Christ of Faith and the Jesus of History: A Critique of Schleiermacher's Life of Jesus*. Edited and translated by Leander E. Keck. Philadelphia: Fortress, 1977.

———. *Streitschriften zur Vertheidigung meiner Schrift über das Leben Jesu und zur Charakteristik der gegenwärtigen Theologie*. Tübingen: C. F. Osiander, 1841.

Strimple, Robert B. *The Modern Search for the Real Jesus: An Introductory Survey of the Historical Roots of Gospels Criticism*. Phillipsburg, NJ: P & R, 1995.

Thiselton, Anthony C. *A Concise Encyclopedia of the Philosophy of Religion*. Grand Rapids: Baker, 2002.

Zeller, Eduard. "Ferdinand Christian Baur." In *Vorträge und Abhandlungen geschichtlichen Inhalts*, 354-434. Leipzig: Fues's Verlag, 1865.

4

Brooke Foss Westcott, Fenton John Anthony Hort, and Joseph Barber Lightfoot

RONALD DEAN PETERS

INTRODUCTION

WHEN DISCUSSING NINETEENTH-CENTURY BIBLICAL scholarship in England, three names inevitably come to the fore: B. F. Westcott, F. J. A. Hort, and J. B. Lightfoot. These distinguished scholars are often identified collectively as the Cambridge Triumvirate, or words to that effect, a fact that by itself testifies to their lasting and profound influence. The three worked individually in private labor and together in cooperation, as both colleagues and close friends. On the one hand, we may consider them as a composite: Westcott, Hort, and Lightfoot. On the other hand, each deserves to be treated as an individual scholar, whose personal contribution stands on its own.

With regard to their collaborative efforts, the three planned to write a complete commentary series on the New Testament. Westcott was to take the Johannine corpus, Lightfoot the Pauline Epistles and Hebrews, and Hort the Synoptic Gospels, the non-Pauline Epistles and Revelation. It is noteworthy that Westcott and Lightfoot had certain reservations about Hort taking on the Synoptic Gospels. This was due to their perception of him as holding unorthodox views regarding Synoptic origins. Hort responded to these concerns in a letter to Lightfoot dated May 1, 1860, in which he graciously offered to remove himself from the project, while at the same time contending that his views were little different from those of Westcott.[1] In the end, their confidence in his abilities as a scholar overrode any concerns. Unfortunately, Hort never wrote his volumes, though after his death, abbreviated commentaries based on his notes on a few New Testament books were published. Westcott completed his commentar-

---

1. Hort, *Life and Letters*, 1:418–21.

ies on the Johannine corpus; Lightfoot completed several of his commentaries, but sadly not all. The most famous of their cooperative efforts was Westcott and Hort's revision and publication of an updated text of the New Testament, supplanting the mighty Textus Receptus.[2] Other combined efforts were also proposed. For example, at one point Westcott suggested that the three contribute essays in response to the controversial *Essays and Reviews*. However, Hort demurred and the suggested work was never produced.

Individually, Westcott and Lightfoot were the more prolific writers, publishing many books in addition to their New Testament commentaries. Hort published sparingly during his lifetime, but his tendency towards perfectionism, combined with maintaining a crushing workload, prevented him from accomplishing more. After his death, however, as already mentioned, several books were published in his name, based on his notes.

Though fast in friendship, Westcott, Hort, and Lightfoot were quite different in temperament, as well as theological orientation. Stephen Neill provides the following comparison and contrast of the three:

> At certain points the three men closely resembled one another. There was little difference in age . . . All three were scholars, and later Fellows, of Trinity College, Cambridge. All had made an intensive study of the Latin and Greek classics, and were masters of both languages in their classical form . . . The differences, however, were also many and interesting; it was because of these differences that each of the trio was able to make his own special contribution, and at certain special points to compensate for the weaknesses of the others . . . Though all shared many gifts in common, Lightfoot was primarily the historian, Hort the philosopher, and Westcott the exegete.[3]

Regarding their theological orientations, Westcott and Lightfoot were more conservative. Hort, conversely, was sympathetic to many of the new ideas emerging in their time. Despite such differences, all three were committed to studying the Bible based on the best available historical, critical, and linguistic methods of their time. Additionally, all three were believing, practicing Christians, a fact that is evident in their writings. Individually they were giants. Together they presented a formidable triumvirate of scholarship.

B. F. WESTCOTT

Mention the name Westcott and almost inevitably the name Hort follows. Indeed, if one surveys collections of influential biblical interpreters, Westcott and Hort typically compromise a single, joint entry. This is no wonder, since it was for their combined efforts in assembling a new, critical edition of the Greek text of the New Testament that

---

2. Westcott and Hort, *The New Testament in the Original Greek*.
3. Neill, *Interpretation of the New Testament*, 33–34.

they are primarily remembered. This text challenged and ultimately supplanted the Textus Receptus as the accepted Greek text of the New Testament upon which study and translation would be based. It is not unjust that Westcott and Hort should be thus remembered, for this accomplishment is arguably their *magnum opus*. However, this point having been conceded, it should be remembered that Westcott produced much that bears his name alone. Working independently of his close associate, he published many books, including an introduction to the Gospels, a history of the canon of Scripture, and commentaries on several New Testament books. Therefore, while we may remember him primarily as the first half of "Westcott and Hort," he also deserves to be remembered as simply "B. F. Westcott." While the influence of Westcott and Hort is felt to this day, the echo of Westcott's voice speaking singularly may also still be heard.

Brooke Foss Westcott (1825–1901) graduated from Trinity College, Cambridge in 1848. From 1849 to 1852 he was a Fellow at Cambridge, and was ordained in 1851. He was Assistant Master and Housemaster at Harrow from 1852 to 1869, during which time he published several books.[4] He became Regius Professor of Divinity at Cambridge in 1870 and served until 1890, during which time he was consecrated Bishop of Durham. It was during his time as Regius Professor that he and F. J. A. Hort prepared their critical edition of the Greek New Testament, which was published in 1881. In 1892 he was made an honorary Fellow of King's College, Cambridge.

On the one hand, Westcott, like his friends Lightfoot and Hort, was clearly a man of his time, fully acceptant of and immersed in the application of the historical-critical and linguistic methodology. Westcott's own words provide ample illustration of this point:

> The historical foundation rightly precedes and underlies the theological interpretation . . . The truest and most faithful historical criticism alone can bring out into full light that doctrine of a Divine Providence separating (as it were) and preserving special books for the perpetual instruction of the church.[5]

> All intelligent interpretation of scripture must then be based upon a strict analysis of its idioms and words. To suppose that words and cases are convertible, that tenses have no absolute meaning, that forms of expression are accidental, is to betray the fundamental principles on which all intercourse between men is based. A disbelief in the exactness of language is a prelude to all philosophical skepticism.[6]

> Carelessness, we allow, has given currency to false readings in the text of Scripture; but the number and variety of the authorities which may be used to correct them is not only unequalled but unapproached in the range of ancient

---

4. Westcott, *History of the Canon of the New Testament* (1855); Westcott, *Introduction to the Study of the Gospels* (1860); Westcott, *General View of the History of the English Bible* (1868).

5. Westcott, *Bible in the Church*, viii.

6. Westcott, *Introduction to the Study of the Gospels*, 62–63.

literature. The laws of criticism are absolute, and the Christian may confide with implicit reverence in their issues.[7]

These quotations provide the material with which one may begin to construct a picture of Westcott the interpreter. He clearly shared the optimism of nineteenth-century biblical scholarship, an optimism no doubt also held by Hort and Lightfoot. It was widely believed among biblical scholars of this time that they, more than any previous generation, held in their possession the necessary tools to interpret Scripture accurately and correctly. In their estimation, by the critical application of historical and linguistic analysis, one would be able to determine the precise meaning of Scripture.

We also encounter what appears (at least on the surface) to be a paradoxical view of Scripture. On the one hand, Westcott clearly views the Bible as a human production:

> If I am not wholly wrong in interpreting the sure facts which I have recorded, they teach us that the formation of the collection of Holy Scriptures was—to use a term which ought never to be supposed even to veil the action of a Present God—according to natural laws . . . They teach us that a corrupted Bible is a sign of a corrupted Church, a Bible mutilated or imperfect, a sign of a Church not yet raised to the complete perception of Truth. It is possible that we might have wished much of this or all this otherwise: we might have thought that a Bible of which every part should bear a visible and unquestioned authentication of its divine origin, separated by a solemn act from the first from the sum and fate of all other literature, would have best answered our conceptions of what the written records of revelation should be. But it is not thus that God works among us. In the Church and in the Bible alike He works through men. As we follow the progress of their formation, each step seems to be truly human; and when we contemplate the whole, we joyfully recognize that every part is also divine.[8]

Upon first reading one might question Westcott's confidence in Scripture as God's revelation to humankind. One might even be tempted (hastily) to lump him with the skeptics of Liberal Protestantism. Yet statements like "to use a term which ought never to be supposed even to veil the action of a Present God" and "every part is also divine" clearly indicate his belief in God's immanent work in the creation and collection of the writings that were to become the Bible. Westcott clearly wrestled with the difficulty of reconciling what he saw as undeniable evidence that Scripture bears the marks of both a human hand and the hand of God. However, he never suggested that the Bible was solely a product of human effort or that God did not communicate through it. Whatever difficulties he encountered he maintained, in spite of these, a high view of Scripture.

---

7. Ibid., 65.
8. Westcott, *Bible in the Church*, xi–xii.

This leads to the "other hand" foreshadowed above. While committed to the historical-critical method, Westcott was also a man of deep faith. In particular, he was keenly aware of and committed to the influence of God's Spirit in the work of the interpreter: "The task [of interpretation] is something more than a merely mechanical or intellectual process. Whoever has watched attentively the working of his own mind, will feel that in criticism and philology there is still room for the operation of that Spirit of God which is promised to the Christian scholar."[9] Westcott was a scholar, but he was not "just a scholar." He was a Christian who truly believed in the immanent presence of the Holy Spirit guiding him and others in their work. He was not a deist, believing in a remote and removed God; he was a devout believer who anticipated and enjoyed the presence of God in his life. In fact, it may be argued that Westcott fully recognized the potential danger that an over-emphasis on scholarship presented: "The mind shrinks from analysis, lest criticism should take the place of devotion."[10] In this short sentence, we are able to catch a glimpse of the heart of the interpreter Westcott. What emerges is at once simple, yet multi-faceted and dynamic. As his own writing clearly illustrates, Westcott was committed to the scholarly study of Scripture. Such study inevitably raises issues that challenge the simple, one might even say naive (but if it is naivety it is the state one would expect of those who have not been confronted by or wrestled with critical issues), faith of the ordinary believer. It is not to be wondered at that scholars are highly susceptible to skepticism and that many, as a result, abandon their faith. Westcott himself must have been all too aware of this potential, but he did not see it as the necessary result of critical study. He wrote:

> It cannot be denied that the real origin of many, perhaps most of the objections to the Gospels, lies deeper than textual criticism. The objections to the record rest on a fundamental objection to the implied fact. An unexpressed denial of the possibility of miracles is the foundation of detailed assaults upon a miraculous narrative. Critical difficulties are too often, in the first instance, the excuse for a foregone conclusion, or at least fall in with a definite bias. A charge of prejudice is alleged against the defenders of the Gospels, and it lies more truly against those who attack them.[11]

In Westcott, the reader encounters a man who believes the biblical exegete must be at once both a scholar and a person who lives a life of simple devotion to his or her God and Savior. Faith and scholarship need not be opposing forces; instead, they work hand in hand, each reinforcing the other. Faith compels one to study; study raises and asks questions dealing with critical issues; the answers to those issues may result in the modification of faith and its expression, but they may also serve to make faith stronger, just as resistance, when it is met and overcome, strengthens a muscle.

---

9. Westcott, *Introduction to the Study of the Gospels*, 44.
10. Ibid., 297.
11. Ibid., 390.

In Westcott, we meet a man who embraced the methods of scientific study while at the same time rejecting the skepticism that was all too often its close companion. As a result, he set an example for the blending of scholarship and faith.

F. J. A. HORT

Fenton John Anthony Hort (1828–92) was born in Dublin, Ireland. In 1846 he took up study at Trinity College, Cambridge, where he read for the Classics and Mathematics tripos and graduated four years later. In 1852, he was elected to a Fellowship at Trinity, the same time as J. B. Lightfoot. From 1857–1872 he served as a parish priest in the village of St. Ippolyts in Hertfordshire. Unfortunately, as time went on, Hort found less and less joy in his work. However, there can be no doubt that he held parish ministry in the highest regard. If there was any criticism of his person, it was a charge Hort leveled against himself; others did not bring it. He spent nearly the entire time struggling with his own sense of inadequacy for the task: "The fact remains . . . that in the course of years the conviction grew on him that this was not his true sphere. His extreme sensitiveness and shyness were real hindrances, and he was well aware of the fact."[12]

In addition to this, he was never able to separate himself from his true passion: scholarship. When he was not engaged in parish duties he immersed himself in scholarly pursuits. It was during this time that he joined the plan with Westcott and Lightfoot to publish their comprehensive commentary series on the New Testament. Hort worked long hours and rested little. As a result, he suffered frequent health problems and was forced to take extended leaves from his parish duties. In 1872, he finally left parish work when he was elected to a Fellowship and Lectureship in Theology at Emmanuel College, Cambridge. In 1878 he was elected to the Hulsean Professorship of Divinity.

It was during his time as a fellow at Trinity that his interest in New Testament interpretation began to grow. It was also during this period that he and Westcott finally completed their work on the revised text of the Greek New Testament (published in 1881), arguably the single work for which he will always be remembered. Hort had become critical of the current Greek text of the New Testament, the so-called Textus Receptus,[13] and determined with the help of Westcott to produce a fresh edition based on the latest manuscript evidence. At an early age, Hort expressed a disdain for the Textus Receptus combined with an appreciation of the value of recently discovered

---

12. Hort, *Life and Letters*, 1:359.

13. First published in 1624 by the Elzevir publishing house, the version that came to be known as the Textus Receptus was based on the previous editions of Erasmus, Stephanus, and Beza. The preface to the second edition (1633) made the claim that it was now the text "received by all." This claim eventually was universally accepted and the Textus Receptus (from the Latin wording of the claim) reigned supreme as the authoritative Greek text until the publication of the Westcott-Hort text. For a survey of the history of the Textus Receptus, see Metzger and Ehrman, *Text of the New Testament*, 152; Porter, *How We Got the New Testament*, 40–41.

manuscripts and the light they cast on the New Testament. This is clearly demonstrated in a letter written to the Reverend John Ellerton, dated Dec. 29 and 30, 1851:

> I had no idea till the last few weeks of the importance of texts, having read so little Greek Testament, and dragged on with the villainous *Textus Receptus* ... Tischendorf I find a great acquisition, above all, because he gives the various readings at the bottom of his page ... Think of that vile *Textus Receptus* leaning entirely on late MSS; it is a blessing there are such early ones.[14]

Here the reader may clearly observe the beginning of the sentiment that will later motivate him, along with Westcott, to take up the task of revising the Greek New Testament. Less than a year and a half later, he again writes to Ellerton declaring that he and Westcott "are going to edit a Greek text of the N.T. some two or three years hence, if possible."[15] His time line proved overly optimistic, as the proposed text took nearly thirty years to complete.

Unlike Westcott and Lightfoot, Hort was sympathetic to many of the new ideas emerging during his time. It should not, however, be assumed that Hort uncritically accepted all the new ideas, as evidenced by his reference to "the deadly poison of socialism."[16] The same orientation that led him to be receptive to new ideas produced a willingness to question long-standing dogmas and traditions of the church. Though his mother was a strong supporter of the contemporary evangelical movement, Hort became increasing critical of evangelicalism. He also wrestled with many traditional Christian doctrines, while at the same time feeling a strong internal resistance to rejecting them outright. For example, the notion of eternal punishment for the unrighteous was particularly problematic for him. This struggle is evidenced in a letter written to the Reverend F. D. Maurice, dated November 16, 1849, in which he appeals to the reverend for assistance in resolving this matter: "I have therefore resolved to ask you to guide me, if you can, to a satisfactory solution of a question which has been long tormenting me ... the question whether any man will be hereafter punished with never-ending torments, spiritual or physical."[17] On the one hand, Hort expresses reluctance to abandon this doctrine: "I dare not rashly and hastily discard a conviction entertained by nearly all Christians, and sanctioned, as it appears to me, by such plain language in the Gospels and Apocalypse, as well as in our Liturgy and the Athanasian Creed."[18] On the other hand, he also observes that this expectation is conspicuously absent from the epistles. The question so plagues him that he feels the need to seek assistance in order to come to some sort of resolution.

---

14. Hort, *Life and Letters*, 1:211.
15. Ibid., 1:250.
16. Ibid., 1:139.
17. Ibid., 1:116.
18. Ibid.

Though Hort was willing to question traditional views, and did so aggressively, he was wary of promoting wholesale revolution. As demonstrated above, he was divided in his own mind, feeling both a draw to the new and a reluctance to abandon the old. This probably explains why he declined an invitation to contribute to the influential and controversial publication *Essays and Reviews*. Though sympathetic to the positions espoused therein, he believed it was too controversial for its time. He voiced these concerns in a letter written to Dr. Rowland Williams declining an invitation to participate in the project:

> It is surely likely to bring on a crisis; and that I cannot think desirable on any account. The errors and prejudices, which we agree in wishing to remove, can surely be more wholesomely and also more effectively reached by individual efforts of an indirect kind than by combined open assault. At present very many orthodox but rational men are being unawares acted on by influences which will assuredly bear good fruit in due time, if the process is allowed to go on quietly; but I cannot help fearing that a premature crisis would frighten back many into the merest traditionalism.[19]

In Hort's opinion, the newly emerging ideas should be allowed to slowly grow and work their way into the mainstream. His concern was that *Essays and Reviews* was too much, too soon. He believed that the initial response to the publication would be so strongly reactionary that the good it hoped to accomplish would be overwhelmed and lost. The resulting backlash against this publication would appear to have confirmed his fears. At one point, he was invited by Westcott to join in writing a response to *Essays and Reviews*. He respectfully declined to participate:

> I could not consent to join in any volume of essays which could be plausibly regarded as simply an orthodox protest against the *Essays and Reviews*. Probably I would agree with you in all essential points as to their shortcomings and positive errors, and perhaps also as to the amount of truth which they contain; but I do not know whether you feel as strongly as I do as to the extreme importance of that side of truth which they exhibit.[20]

Clearly, Hort felt as though his own position left him caught between two opposing forces, with both of which he had certain sympathies. Since he could not unreservedly align himself with either side of the debate, he chose to remain neutral.

Darwin's *Origin of Species* also impressed Hort. While he did not abandon a theistic worldview, he was clearly impressed by and sympathetic to Darwin's presentation, which he expressed in a letter to Westcott: "Have you read Darwin? How I should like a talk with you about it! In spite of difficulties, I am inclined to think it unanswerable. In any case it is a treat to read such a book."[21] Regarding this book,

---

19. Ibid., 1:401.
20. Ibid., 1:428.
21. Ibid., 1:414.

Hort immediately recognized its potential. In fact, his sense of its significance was almost prophetic: "*The* book which has most engaged me is Darwin. Whatever may be thought of it, it is a book that one is proud to be contemporary with. I must work out and examine the argument in detail, but at present my feeling is strong that the theory is unanswerable. If so, it opens up a new period in—I know not what."[22] Like most of his contemporaries, and in contrast to modern views, Hort did not view Darwin's theories as a challenge to a theistic worldview. He believed that both could operate side by side. This position was made tenable by the belief that science and theology were two separate realms of study. Thus, neither should be used to attack the other.

Hort maintained a high view of the authority of Scripture, even if he questioned its historicity. On the one hand, he confirmed a belief in divine inspiration. On the other, he appears to have been more willing to admit the possibility of errors than his two friends and colleagues. He expressed this sentiment in a letter to Westcott written in response to concerns voiced by Lightfoot regarding the assigning of commentaries on the Synoptic Gospels to Hort:

> I do most fully recognize the special "providence" which controuled [sic] the formation of the canonical books . . . But I am not able to go as far as you in asserting the absolute infallibility of a canonical writing. I may see a certain fitness and probability in such a view, but I cannot set up an *a priori* assumption against the (supposed) results of criticism . . . If I am ultimately driven to admit occasional errors, I shall be sorry; but it will not shake my conviction of the providential ordering of human elements in the Bible.[23]

Once again, one observes Hort attempting to navigate a mediating position between two contrasting views with which he shares certain sympathies. As with previous issues, he does not seem to have arrived at a resolution.

It is reasonable to suggest that the various and frequent instances of tension that Hort so often felt were why he produced little published work outside of the Greek New Testament edition. Such tension would have had little impact on his contribution to an updated Greek text. However, unresolved theological questions and divided positional sympathies may have resulted in intellectual paralysis. If this analysis is correct, these issues prevented him from producing any kind of definitive work that would have been representative of his own unique contribution to the field.

J. B. LIGHTFOOT

Joseph Barber Lightfoot (1828–89) was born on April 13, 1828, in Liverpool. His family moved to Birmingham in 1843 after the death of his father. Like his friend B. F. Westcott, he studied at King Edward's School, though the two were never classmates, as Lightfoot took up attendance shortly after Westcott's departure. In 1847, again

---

22. Ibid., 1:416.
23. Ibid., 1:422.

following in the footsteps of Westcott, he became a student at Trinity College, Cambridge where he studied the classics tripos. Lightfoot performed his studies with distinction. His vast knowledge of classical literature, history, and language would later provide him with the resources necessary to become a distinguished historical/critical scholar. Lightfoot was convinced that the Bible must be understood in the context of its historical situation and based on the meaning of the original language in which it was written. His education guaranteed he would be able to apply this principle with all diligence. Over the course of his career, he held several distinguished posts. In 1852 he was elected to a Fellowship at Trinity College. In 1861 he was made Hulsean Professor of Divinity and in 1875, Lady Margaret's Professor. In 1879 he accepted the appointment of Bishop of Durham, which he held until his death on Dec. 21, 1889.

That Lightfoot was a critical scholar *par excellence* is well known. In this, he serves as a worthy example for those of later generations to follow. However, like Westcott (as demonstrated above), he is also an example of a *believing* critical scholar. For example, after presenting a critical argument for the authenticity and genuineness of John's Gospel, Lightfoot makes the following declaration:

> One word more, and I conclude. I have treated this as a purely critical question, carefully eschewing any appeal to Christian instincts. As a critical question I wish to take a verdict upon it. But as I could not have you think that I am blind to the theological issue directly or indirectly connected with it, I will close with this brief confession of faith. I believe from my heart that the truth which this Gospel more especially enshrines—the truth that Jesus Christ is the very Word Incarnate, the manifestation of the Father to mankind—is the one lesson which, duly apprehended, will do more than all our feeble efforts to purify and elevate human life here by imparting to it hope and light and strength, the one study which alone can fitly prepare us for a joyful immortality hereafter.[24]

For Lightfoot, criticism had a rightful place in biblical scholarship; it serves a legitimate function. However, it is not of necessity that this should supplant, or even be used to challenge, faith. Lightfoot studied the Bible critically, but he also believed it faithfully.

In contrast to Hort, Lightfoot was convinced of the veracity of the scriptural witness. As noted above, he expressed concerns regarding Hort's views in this area, which led Lightfoot initially to question Hort's suitability for the writing of commentaries on the Synoptic Gospels. Consider the following: "The genuineness of St John's Gospel is the centre of the position of those who uphold the historical truth of the record of our Lord Jesus Christ given us in the New Testament. Hence the attacks of the opponents of revealed religion are concentrated upon it."[25] This illustrates how much

---

24. Lightfoot, *Biblical Essays*, 44.
25. Ibid., 47.

Lightfoot believed was at stake with regard to issues pertaining to the genuineness of the Gospels. This also explains why he would have reservations regarding the choice of Hort. His conviction that the theological truths of John's Gospel were grounded on its genuineness led him to write an exhaustive defense based on an examination of both internal and external evidence. So thorough was his research and so compelling were his conclusions that many of his arguments are used to this day. It cannot be said, however, that Lightfoot was merely an apologist for the New Testament. He was eminently qualified to render critical judgments on matters of historicity, thanks to his education in classics. His thoroughness of research is evidenced in his many detailed studies. For example, his treatment of Paul's life before his conversion is based on an examination of Jewish, Greek, and Roman cultural considerations and how they may have shaped the apostle.[26] His commentaries include introductions that provide a detailed presentation of the historical setting, which serves as a necessary backdrop for a correct understanding of the text. With regard to the text, Lightfoot was committed to using the principles of textual criticism in order to establish his working text: "It is no longer necessary, I trust, to offer any apology for laying aside the received text. When so much conscientious labour has been expended on textual criticism, it would be unpardonable in an editor to acquiesce in readings which for the most part are recommended neither by intrinsic fitness nor by the sanction of antiquity."[27]

While Lightfoot's vast historical and linguistic knowledge provided him with the tools to defend the genuineness of the Gospels, they were also the means by which he was able to demonstrate that other works were most certainly spurious. This is exemplified in his critical analysis of the supposed correspondence between the apostle Paul and the Roman philosopher Seneca.[28] By examining both the language and the historical references, Lightfoot demonstrates the high degree of improbability that the letters are genuine.

Lightfoot's historical research led him to write on a wide variety of topics addressing historical matters related to the early church. These included studies on the development of the episcopacy, the exact relationship of Jesus and his brothers, and the question of whether the Galatians were Celts or Teutons, just to name a few. One of his best-known works, one that continues to exert influence through updated editions, is his collection and translation of the writings of the Apostolic Fathers. The current work was originally published posthumously by J. R. Harmer, based on Lightfoot's notes and his larger, two-volume edition. It has been most recently updated by Michael W. Holmes.

---

26. Ibid., 201–11.
27. Lightfoot, *St. Paul's Epistle to the Galatians*, vii.
28. Ibid., 270–333.

SUMMARY

As individuals, when we study our own ancestry, we often learn much about ourselves. Knowing about our parents, grandparents, and more distant relations provides insight into why we are who we are. As scholars, understanding where we stand in relationship to our predecessors helps us to understand ourselves and how were have arrived where we are. We owe a great debt to scholars like Westcott, Hort, and Lightfoot. Our understanding of the Bible, and the methods we use to achieve that understanding, would be greatly impoverished were it not for their work. In addition, they serve as enduring examples of faith and scholarship.

WESTCOTT AND SOURCE CRITICISM

As previously stated, Westcott will be primarily remembered for his contribution to the establishment of a new critical edition of the Greek New Testament. As a result, he is viewed as a leading and influential figure in the field of textual criticism. However, he had much to say regarding the formation of the New Testament writings, in particular the Gospels. In his *Introduction to the Study of the Gospels*, he writes at length on the subject of the formation of the Gospels, dealing with sources used by the Gospel writers. Specifically, he addresses the issues of how the details of Jesus' life (teachings, miracles, passion) were preserved, circulated, and put into a set form by the earliest Christians before the production of the written Gospels.

One of the first things one notices when reading Westcott's presentation of the pre-written Gospel period is what is missing. Words and concepts such as "Q," "Markan Priority," and "two-source theory" are notably absent. However, as will be seen, there is evidence of ideas that will eventually develop into these hypotheses.

According to Westcott, during the years preceding the production of the written Gospels, the specifics of Jesus' life and teaching were preserved and transmitted in a primarily, if not exclusively, oral form:

> The men who were enabled to penetrate most deeply into the mysteries of the new revelation, and to apprehend with the most vigorous energy the change which it was destined to make in the world, seem to have placed little value upon the written witness to words and acts which still, as it were, lived among them.[29]

At this early stage, Jesus' followers saw little or no need to commit their remembrances to writing. On the one hand, this may be the result of an expectation of the imminent return of Jesus; there may simply have been no impetus for preserving his teachings in writing if the dominant belief was that he would return shortly. On the other hand, there may have been additional reasons for the reluctance, or perhaps lack of interest, in creating written records:

---

29. Westcott, *Introduction to the Study of the Gospels*, 174–75.

> It was most unlikely that men who had been accustomed to a system of training generally, if not exclusively oral, should have formed any design to commit to writing a complete account of the history or of the doctrines of the Gospel. The whole influence of Palestinian habits was most adverse to such an undertaking.[30]

Thus, according to Westcott, the primary method of preservation and transmission for the time period in general, and the early church specifically, was oral tradition. To argue for an early written text contradicts the facts, as he understood them. Jesus' followers, in all likelihood, did not simply choose not to put his words into writing, as if they considered the option but rejected it. Instead, they preserved his life in the manner in which they were accustomed, indeed in which they were trained through a lifetime of exposure: through the development of oral traditions. While it is true that they had in their possession Scripture in written form (i.e., the Hebrew Scriptures), the words of the Jewish teachers, the Rabbis, were passed on from one generation to the next in oral form. It was not until long after Jesus' lifetime that these, too, were committed to writing. Thus, it can be argued that the method of preservation and transmission chosen by Jesus' followers was that which was most natural to them.

As further argument for adopting the theory of a predominantly oral presentation, Westcott cites Jesus' command to "preach the Gospel" as one of the driving forces behind the disciples' choice of medium.[31] The apostles were preachers, following the example of their now-departed Master. At no point were they commanded to write down the words Jesus spoke. This does not suggest they took this as a negative command to avoid committing his words to writing. It is simply that, especially in their day and age, preaching and writing were not mutually inclusive. Preaching was their priority. Therefore, the life and teaching of Jesus would be preserved and communicated via this medium. It was through preaching that new believers would become acquainted with their Savior and learn to live lives consistent with his commands. As Westcott observes, "This, then, was the first great stage in the Apostles' work—the first step in the composition of the Gospels—to adapt the lessons which they learned with Christ to the requirements of the growing Church."[32] Thus, he concludes, it was in the act of preaching that the apostles fulfilled their mission.

Moving on to the generation immediately following that of the apostles, Westcott sees further evidence, even after the Gospels had been written, for the dominance of oral tradition as the primary witness to Jesus' life and teaching:

> Till the end of the first century, and probably till the time of Justin Martyr, the "Gospel" uniformly signifies the substance and not the records of the Life

---

30. Ibid., 175–76.
31. Ibid., 177.
32. Ibid., 179.

of Christ.[33] Even in the sub-apostolic age the same general feeling survived, though it was modified by the growing organization of the Christian Church. The knowledge of the teaching of Christ and the details of His life were generally derived from tradition, and not from writings.[34]

Westcott appeals to the testimony of Irenaeus who wrote: "the foundation and pillar of our faith" is the "tradition manifested in the whole world" and "kept in the several churches through the succession of presbyters." In this he sees evidence that oral tradition continued to have primacy over the written word.

Next, Westcott appeals to the testimony of the Book of Acts as to the oral nature of the early Gospel tradition. When Peter goes to the house of Cornelius, he relates the details of Jesus' life and ministry. While Luke, in all likelihood, records an abbreviated version of the speech, he does include certain specific details. Peter tells them about Jesus' baptism, his preaching tours in Galilee and Judea, his healing ministry, and his death and resurrection. In like manner, Paul relates the story of Jesus in the synagogue of Antioch. In his proclamation, as recorded by Luke, Paul refers specifically to the work of John the Baptist and Jesus' crucifixion and resurrection. Both serve as examples of how the traditions of Jesus' life and teaching were proclaimed through the apostolic period.

From the apostolic period, Westcott moves directly to the second generation of believers. The testimony of Papias influences his understanding of the development of the Jesus traditions, and he is less critical of his witness than those who will follow him. For example, he accepts at face value Papias's testimony that there was a Hebrew archetype of Matthew's Gospel. He also accepts that Mark based his Gospel on the testimony of Peter, though there is enough variety and outright contradiction in the witness of the early Fathers to prevent us from reaching a definitive conclusion regarding the circumstances leading up to and surrounding the actual writing of Mark's Gospel. This view can be seen in his conclusion:

> All the evidence which can be gathered from the circumstances of the early Church, and the traditions of the origin of the Gospels, has tended to establish the existence of an original oral Gospel, definite in general outline and even in language, which was committed to writing in the lapse of time in various special shapes, according to the typical forms which it assumed in the preaching of different Apostles.[35]

Turning to the internal evidence of the Gospels, he begins by providing some basic statistics that serve to illustrate the strong similarities between the Synoptics. This demonstrates the concord between them at the general level of common stories and the specifics of verbal or near verbal agreement. However, any theory of origins

33. Ibid., 180.
34. Ibid., 181.
35. Ibid., 198.

must address not only the phenomenon of agreement but that of difference as well. Westcott recognizes two basic solutions: "One class of solutions rests upon the assumption that the later Evangelists made use of the writings of their predecessors; another supposes that the similarity is to be traced to the use of common sources, either written or oral."[36]

Neither solution is satisfactory to Westcott. Regarding the first, there have been too many proponents arguing for the priority of each of the Gospels making the others dependent upon it:

> This variety of opinion is in itself an objection to the hypothesis, for it is a case where it might seem reasonable to expect a clear and unquestionable proof of dependence. But it is further evident that the assumption of a mutual dependence, while it may explain the general coincidences between the Gospels, offers no explanation of the peculiar distribution of the coincidences, or of the differences between the several narratives.[37]

Regarding the second solution, though it has also found a variety of expressions, they are not without weaknesses. The first he addresses is the belief that there must have been earlier Greek documents that provided the foundation of the Synoptic Gospels but have since passed out of existence. Once again, he finds this solution wanting and rejects it because it can only explain similarities between the Synoptics, but cannot adequately address the problem of the differences. Another solution argued for an Aramaic original:

> Though the loss of an Aramaic text is in itself not unlikely, yet the absence of all mentions of the existence of such a document is a serious objection to its reality; and the translation of a common original would not explain the peculiar distribution of the verbal coincidences of the Gospels which has been pointed out. In addition to this, the existence of any single written source would leave the phenomena of the differences of the Gospels still unaccounted for.[38]

This theory became the basis for another, expanded theory, in which it was argued that the Synoptic writers used the original Aramaic Gospel "after it had been variously increased by new additions."[39] Thus, the differences between these three Gospels were the result of each using different redactions of the original. In response to this theory Westcott writes:

> This hypothesis is certainly capable of being so adapted as to explain all the coincidences and differences of the Gospels . . . but the extreme artificiality by which it is characterized renders it wholly improbable as a true solution of the

---

36. Ibid., 206.
37. Ibid.
38. Ibid., 208–9.
39. Ibid., 209.

problem. Such a combination of research and mechanical skill in composition as it involves is wholly alien from the circumstances of the apostolic age, and at variance with the prevailing power of a wide-spread tradition.

Having assessed the various proposals, he provides his conclusion on the matter:

> It has been shown already that the hypothesis of an oral Gospel is most consistent with the general habit of the Jews and the peculiar position of the Apostles: that it is supported by the earliest direct testimony, and in some degree implied in the Apostolic writings . . . The general form of the Gospels points to an oral source.[40]

> The successive remoulding of the oral Gospel according to the peculiar requirements of different classes of hearers, furnishes a natural explanation of the general similarity in form and substance between the several Gospels, combined with peculiarities and differences in arrangement and contents.[41]

In Westcott's opinion, the model of an orally preserved tradition is the only model that is consistent with the actual cultural practices of the time. In addition, it is the only model that adequately resolves the issues regarding both the similarities and differences between the Synoptic Gospels.

Having made his argument for oral tradition as the primary source for the Gospels, Westcott addresses one last difficulty that arises from this conclusion. Some would suggest that "to admit a traditional [oral] source for the Gospels is to sacrifice their historical value."[42] This concern is unwarranted for several reasons. First, oral-tradition education was the norm of the time, as the Jews preserved the teachings of the rabbis with strict accuracy. Thus, there is no reason to conclude the Jesus traditions could not be so preserved. In addition, these traditions existed only during the lifetime of their authors: "No period was left for any mythic embellishment . . . when they passed away, it was already fixed in writing."[43] In the end, as far as Westcott is concerned, there is no reason to argue against oral tradition as the source for the written editions, which we now possess as the canonical Gospels.

SOURCE CRITICAL INTERPRETATION OF MATT 13:53–58//MARK 6:1–6//LUKE 4:16–30

Westcott did not write a commentary on any of the Synoptic Gospels, focusing rather on the Johannine corpus. Thus, modern interpreters are without an example of how he might approach an account from the triple tradition. However, knowing what we do about his emphasis on the priority of oral tradition, we may be able to formulate an

---

40. Ibid., 212.
41. Ibid., 214.
42. Ibid., 215.
43. Ibid.

interpretation in a "Westcottian mode." Jesus' teaching in the synagogue in Nazareth, as recorded in all three Synoptic Gospels, will be employed as a test case for such an analysis.

All three Synoptic Gospels record Jesus' confrontation with the people of Nazareth in the synagogue of that town. A cursory reading of the three clearly reveals that they relate the same story, yet there are notable differences between them. The question that will be addressed below is whether the details reveal anything about the sources employed by the authors.

The dominant view of Markan priority argues that both Matthew and Luke used Mark as a primary source. There is no question that, in a side-by-side comparison of Matthew's and Mark's versions, they are strikingly similar. Luke's version, however, diverges significantly from the others both verbally and in content. His version is longer and contains many details the others leave out. Luke alone records the content of Jesus' teaching that day, whereas Matthew and Mark record only the bare fact that he taught. We will begin our examination by first focusing on the common elements of all three accounts. This should allow us to draw specific conclusions regarding what the key elements of the original underlying tradition were. Next, we will examine the distinctive features that set each apart from the others and hypothesize regarding what this may indicate regarding the use of source material.[44]

There are several elements common to all three accounts. The most obvious is the climactic saying toward which all build. While there is verbal disagreement, it is conceptually the chief point of unity. When faced with the rejection of the people of his hometown, Jesus responds by saying "a prophet is not honorless except in his hometown" (Matthew and Mark), or "no prophet is welcome in his hometown" (Luke). We will address the differences between the versions of this saying below. For now, it is sufficient to draw attention to this saying as the conceptual center and unifying factor of all three accounts, since this saying embodies the theme of the story in each passage. Everything else is built around it and for it, for the story is the substructure that supports this saying. It provides the context for the saying, gives it significance, and answers the question: "Why did Jesus say this?" The saying, in turn, provides the interpretation of the event. It explains why the people responded the way they did.

There are several details shared by the three accounts. The first is the use of the word πατρίς, "hometown." Both Matthew and Mark introduce the account by indicating Jesus came εἰς τὴν πατρίδα αὐτοῦ, "into his hometown." Luke is more explicit by identifying the town by name, *Nazareth*. However, the word does appear later in one of the elements unique to Luke. He records the people urging Jesus to do the miracles he performed in Capernaum ὧδε ἐν τῇ πατρίδι σου, "here in your hometown." With

---

44. It should be noted that the analysis undertaken herein is meant to be representative of the approach Westcott may have taken and the conclusions he would have drawn. No attempt is made to engage modern research in the field of oral tradition or memory research, or the fields of Greek grammar and linguistics, such as verbal aspect theory.

regard to the central statement of the episode, Luke disagrees with Matthew and Mark using the word δεκτός, "welcome," versus their ἄτιμος, "honorless." Yet all agree that this assessment of a prophet is characteristic ἐν τῇ πατρίδι αὐτοῦ, "in his hometown." Thus, it may be argued that this word was considered a key element in the tradition, both for the climactic saying and for the setup leading to it. Regarding the climactic saying, all three preserve it, indicating that, while the exact word used to communicate the nature of the rejection may be open to variation, the fact that it comes from the people of his hometown is what makes it tragic. Its presence in the saying probably explains why all versions incorporated it into the setup. By emphasizing the aspect of *hometown* early, the irony and tragedy of the saying is made explicit. From this, we may conclude that, from the beginning, the significance attached to the tradition was not one of mere rejection, but that of hometown rejection.

The second element common to all is the location of and circumstances leading up to the saying. All three agree it took place in the synagogue at Nazareth and that it came after Jesus had taught the people in the synagogue. Mark and Luke both record that this took place on the Sabbath, while Matthew leaves this detail out. Once again, we may draw a conclusion: those who were initially responsible for preserving the tradition saw a direct relationship between Jesus' teaching and the rejection of the people of his hometown.

The third element common to all three is the reference to Jesus' miracles. In Matthew's and Mark's versions, it is the people who, in amazement, call attention to his δυνάμεις, "miracles." In Luke, Jesus calls attention to them, but he does so by anticipating what the people will say to him, "That which we heard came to pass in Capernaum, do also here in your hometown." The implication is that, as in Matthew and Mark, the people are aware of his miraculous works and are astonished. This, too, ultimately leads to their rejection.

From these common elements, we may draw general conclusions regarding the significance attached to this episode at its earliest stage and why it was preserved by Jesus' followers. First, Jesus' statement about rejection by one's hometown was considered the focal point. All that preceded and followed this statement was placed there to explain it or be explained by it (as will be further demonstrated below). Both the irony and tragedy are highlighted by the word πατρίς. The people of Jesus' hometown would have been those who knew him best. They should have been the most sympathetic and open since he was one of their own. Yet they rejected him. This rejection was probably the result of their familiarity with him, as the saying goes, "familiarity breeds contempt." It is the underlying fact that these people have known Jesus all his life that explains their surprise. For thirty years he lived among them and was just another builder/hired laborer. He was a nobody. Now he comes back with miracles and wise teaching. It is too much for their minds to accept. Whatever he may say or do, in their minds he is just Jesus, the builder, and the builder's and Mary's son. They know him and his family too well to think of him as anything else, no matter what his words and deeds might suggest.

Jesus' disciples would probably have used this episode to encourage and comfort the fledgling church as it, too, experienced rejection, particularly the rejection of the Jews. This particular incident foreshadows the wholesale rejection of God's Son by his own people. In the same way, if Jesus was rejected by his own people, his followers should not be surprised when they experience the same kind of rejection. One might imagine the disciples emphasizing the word *hometown* to make their point, "Even his *hometown* rejected him."

From here, the tradition seems to have developed along two divergent lines: the long version found in Luke and the shorter version of Matthew and Mark. We will first explore the relationship between Matthew and Mark. Later, we will compare and contrast them with Luke.

What is striking about Matthew and Mark is how they use the same words differently. What appears on the surface as verbal agreement is actually a significant difference. First, as stated above, Matthew and Mark begin their accounts by stating that Jesus came εἰς τὴν πατρίδα αὐτοῦ, "into his hometown." Yet consider how differently each says it:

Matt 13:54 καὶ ἐλθὼν εἰς τὴν πατρίδα αὐτοῦ . . .

Mark 6:1 καὶ ἔρχεται εἰς τὴν πατρίδα αὐτοῦ . . .

Matthew uses an aorist participle whereas Mark uses a present indicative verb. Each author's choice reveals his narrative agenda. Matthew's use of a participial phrase indicates that his reference to Jesus' arrival in his hometown is a historical and narrative detail that sets the scene. The aorist participle provides background information that helps the reader better understand the narrative as it unfolds.[45] Such background information is thus useful, though it may not necessarily represent the most salient element of the narrative with regard to author's main point. Mark, conversely, seems to be more interested in foregrounding Jesus' arrival in his hometown, drawing greater attention to this detail.[46] We may conclude that this narrative element is more salient for Mark than for Matthew.

From this point, Matthew quickly sets the scene:

Matt 13:54 καὶ ἐλθὼν εἰς τὴν πατρίδα αὐτοῦ ἐδίδασκεν αὐτοὺς ἐν τῇ συναγωγῇ αὐτῶν

Contrast this with Mark's presentation:

---

45. Porter, "Prominence: An Overview," 54, says, "In narrative, supporting information for the background can be provided through the use of infinitive, participle and secondary constructions."

46. Porter, *Idioms*, 31. See also Porter, "Prominence: An Overview," 58–61.

Mark 6:1–2 Καὶ ἐξῆλθεν ἐκεῖθεν καὶ ἔρχεται εἰς τὴν πατρίδα αὐτοῦ, καὶ ἀκολουθοῦσιν αὐτῷ οἱ μαθηταὶ αὐτοῦ. καὶ γενομένου σαββάτου ἤρξατο διδάσκειν ἐν τῇ συναγωγῇ

Matthew leaves out the reference to Jesus' disciples and the fact that it is the Sabbath. Matthew refers to the place as "their synagogue" whereas Mark says simply "the synagogue." These variations could be explained as Matthew's attempt to clean up and tighten Mark's presentation. If Matthew had a copy of Mark in front of him, this would make sense. However, this does not explain all the changes, especially one-word changes like the addition of "their." A more probable explanation would be that both drew upon a well-known oral tradition. The flexibility of an oral version would allow the author to choose which details he wished to incorporate. As long as certain key words and elements were maintained, the exact wording could remain fluid.

Nothing illustrates this fluidity more than the appeal to Jesus' familial relations:

Matt 13:55 οὐχ οὗτός ἐστιν ὁ τοῦ τέκτονος υἱός;

Mark 6:3 οὐχ οὗτός ἐστιν ὁ τέκτων

Matthew identifies Jesus as "the son of the builder," while in Mark he is simply "the builder."

Matt 13:55 οὐχ ἡ μήτηρ αὐτοῦ λέγεται Μαριάμ

Mark 6:3 ὁ υἱὸς τῆς Μαρίας

According to Matthew, Jesus' mother "is called Mary"; by contrast, in Mark, he is "Mary's son."

Matt 13:55 καὶ οἱ ἀδελφοὶ αὐτοῦ Ἰάκωβος καὶ Ἰωσὴφ καὶ Σίμων καὶ Ἰούδας

Mark 6:3 καὶ ἀδελφὸς Ἰακώβου καὶ Ἰωσῆτος καὶ Ἰούδα καὶ Σίμωνος

Matthew writes, "his brothers are James and Joseph and Simon and Judas"; whereas according to Mark he is "the brother of James and Joses (i.e. Joseph) and Judas and Simon."

Matt 13:56 καὶ αἱ ἀδελφαὶ αὐτοῦ οὐχὶ πᾶσαι πρὸς ἡμᾶς εἰσιν;

Mark 6:3 καὶ οὐκ εἰσὶν αἱ ἀδελφαὶ αὐτοῦ ὧδε πρὸς ἡμᾶς;

Both refer to Jesus' sisters, but arrange the wording differently. The chief variation is Matthew's "all with us" versus Mark's "here with us." While these variations may seem trivial, they nevertheless require an explanation. Variation of style is possible, but it is difficult to justify since neither commends itself as stylistically superior to the other. Variation in oral retelling is far more likely. Copying from a printed page is frequently a word-for-word process, but oral retelling is more often shaped by the speaker's preferences. Both accounts incorporate the same information; they simply word it differently. The references to Jesus' mother, brothers, and sisters all bear the marks of oral retelling rather than literary copying.

Another example of the same information worded differently is the initial reaction of the people to Jesus' teaching:

Matt 13:54 ὥστε ἐκπλήσσεσθαι αὐτοὺς καὶ λέγειν

Mark 6:2 καὶ πολλοὶ ἀκούοντες ἐξεπλήσσοντο λέγοντες

Matthew introduces their reaction with ὥστε followed by two present infinitives: "[with the result] they are amazed and say . . ." Mark's wording is obviously different: "and many, hearing, were amazed, saying . . ."

Matt 13:54 πόθεν τούτῳ ἡ σοφία αὕτη καὶ αἱ δυνάμεις

Mark 6:2 πόθεν τούτῳ ταῦτα, καὶ τίς ἡ σοφία ἡ δοθεῖσα τούτῳ, καὶ αἱ δυνάμεις τοιαῦται διὰ τῶν χειρῶν αὐτοῦ γινόμεναι

Both authors record the same reactionary question. For both, Jesus' wisdom and power leave the onlookers stumped, prompting them to question where he acquired them. Though both authors employ the same words, Matthew's economy of expression stands in marked contrast to Mark's expanded representation of their reaction. Identifying the source tradition is problematic, in that it is equally possible that either Matthew contracted a longer source or Mark expanded a more concise source. As noted above, the flexibility of an oral tradition that preserves certain key elements while allowing each author to shape the details to fit the needs of his narrative lends itself as a plausible explanation for either scenario.

Both Matthew and Mark agree word for word when they present the climax of the people's reaction, καὶ ἐσκανδαλίζοντο ἐν αὐτῷ "and they were offended by him" (Matt 13:57/Mark 6:3). However, though they record the same result, they once again do so differently:

Matt 13:58 καὶ οὐκ ἐποίησεν ἐκεῖ δυνάμεις πολλὰς διὰ τὴν ἀπιστίαν αὐτῶν

Mark 6:5–6 καὶ οὐκ ἐδύνατο ἐκεῖ ποιῆσαι οὐδεμίαν δύναμιν, εἰ μὴ ὀλίγοις ἀρρώστοις ἐπιθεὶς τὰς χεῖρας ἐθεράπευσεν. καὶ ἐθαύμαζεν διὰ τὴν ἀπιστίαν αὐτῶν

Both record that Jesus only performed a few miracles. Matthew does so very succinctly and ascribes this directly to the unbelief of the people. Characteristically, Mark's version is more vivid as he writes that Jesus was unable to do any miracles except for healing a few sick people when he laid his hands on them. In his version, Jesus is amazed by their unbelief, in contrast to Matthew's version where unbelief is the cause of his inability to perform any miracles.

Matthew and Mark record the climactic saying nearly verbatim:

Matt 13:57a ὁ δὲ Ἰησοῦς εἶπεν αὐτοῖς

Mark 6:4a καὶ ἔλεγεν αὐτοῖς ὁ Ἰησοῦς ὅτι

Matt 6:57b οὐκ ἔστιν προφήτης ἄτιμος εἰ μὴ ἐν τῇ πατρίδι

Mark 6:4b οὐκ ἔστιν προφήτης ἄτιμος εἰ μὴ ἐν τῇ πατρίδι αὐτοῦ

Matt 13:57c καὶ ἐν τῇ οἰκίᾳ αὐτοῦ

Mark 6:4c καὶ ἐν τοῖς συγγενεῦσιν αὐτοῦ καὶ ἐν τῇ οἰκίᾳ αὐτοῦ

Once again, Mark's introduction suggests a closer relationship to the oral version of the tradition. His use of the imperfect tense (along with the present tense earlier) creates the sense of action in process, which creates the effect of positioning the listener within the story. Matthew again demonstrates sensitivity to the conventions of written communication by avoiding such process verbs.

The precision with which this saying is preserved suggests its place of priority within the overall tradition. This may be for two reasons. The first may be that these are the words of Jesus himself. Since they came directly from the mouth of the Master there was, in all likelihood, a strong sense of responsibility to preserve them as accurately as possible. The second reason is that this saying is the climax of the tradition. Up to this point, the priority seems to have been on certain key details but not on wording. Now, precision of wording is central. The addition/omission of ἐν τοῖς συγγενεῦσιν αὐτοῦ could be explained two ways: either Matthew considered it redundant and omitted it, or Mark added it to make the saying more tragic by emphasizing rejection by Jesus' relatives. Markan priority must argue that Matthew omitted the saying. Oral tradition leaves either possibility open. It is perhaps a bit more likely that Matthew would leave out a portion of the saying if he felt that what was left was sufficient, than that Mark added to the words of the Master. However, it must be admitted that this is in no way conclusive and at best can only influence the decision slightly in one direction.

What we see, then, in Matthew and Mark, is a strong emphasis on certain specific details coupled with a general flexibility in wording. As stated above, when copying from a written page, the tendency is to reproduce exactly or nearly so. This is what one would expect to see if Matthew had made use of Mark as his source. Certain variations may be explained as stylistic preferences (Matthew does seem to have condensed the story somewhat). Overall, though, the two versions strongly suggest independent use of an established oral tradition. This would better account for both the similarities and the differences.

The version found in Luke is conceptually similar to that in Matthew and Mark. Though there is a significant difference in detail, it is clear that his version is based upon the same incident. Rather than contradict one another, the two versions complement one another. Luke's version provides many of the specific details that the version used by Matthew and Mark glosses over. However, the differences are so vast that one must conclude that Luke used a different source. If he was acquainted with Mark's

Gospel or with the version of the tradition used by Matthew and Mark, he rejected it in favor of the one he incorporated into his Gospel. Thus, we may conclude that both versions spring from one source. However, two distinct traditions developed relating the same incident. Luke clearly did not use either Matthew or Mark as a source for his version. Many would argue for Matthew's dependence upon Mark for his version, but the verbal evidence, in my opinion, more strongly reflects independent use of an oral source.

EVALUATION OF SOURCE CRITICISM

As a method of interpretation, source criticism used by itself provides little insight into the meaning of a text. Its primary value is historical: it is a process by which we may begin to answer questions about the origins and development of Jesus traditions. When dealing with the sources used by the writers of the Gospels, Westcott is addressing historical issues, not interpretive issues. Thus, source criticism is foundational, but it is only valuable if something further is built upon it. It is the beginning of the process, not the end; it is not an end unto itself. For the purposes of interpretation, source criticism will ultimately lead to some sort of form and/or redaction criticism. Once we are able to draw reasonable conclusions regarding the nature of the source of a tradition we must then ask questions about the writer's use of the tradition. Examples of such questions are: "What reason(s) did the writer have for rewording or modifying the tradition?" and "What significance did the writer attach to the tradition and how did it contribute to their overall agenda for writing?"

In recent decades, source criticism has been used to challenge traditional views of Jesus' life, teaching, and ministry. Theories arguing for the existence of earlier documents that present a Jesus vastly different from the one encountered in the canonical Gospels lie at the center of these challenges. Source criticism still has value for answering these challenges. In this way, the exercise may have a more direct influence on interpretation. Rather than breaking the Gospels apart in search of the "authentic" words of Jesus, source criticism has the potential to allow us to argue effectively and decidedly for the authenticity of the traditions as they are preserved within the canonical Gospels.

BIBLIOGRAPHY

Hort, A. F. *Life and Letters of Fenton John Anthony Hort.* 2 vols. London: Macmillan, 1896.
Lightfoot, J. B. *Biblical Essays.* Reprint, Grand Rapids: Eerdmans, 1979.
———. *St. Paul's Epistle to the Galatians.* Reprint, Lynn, MA: Hendrickson, 1981.
———. *The Apostolic Fathers.* 2 vols. London: Macmillan, 1890.
Metzger, Bruce M., and Bart D. Ehrman. *The Text of the New Testament: Its Transmission, Corruption, and Restoration.* 4th ed. New York: Oxford University Press, 1992.
Neill, Stephen. *The Interpretation of the New Testament 1861–1961.* London: Oxford University Press, 1964.

Porter, Stanley E. *How We Got the New Testament: Text, Transmission, Translation*. Acadia Studies in Bible and Theology. Grand Rapids: Baker, 2013.

———. *Idioms of the Greek New Testament*. BLG 2. 2nd ed. Sheffield: Sheffield Academic, 1994.

———. "Prominence: An Overview." In *The Linguist as Pedagogue*, edited by Stanley E. Porter and Matthew Brook O'Donnell, 45–74. Sheffield: Sheffield Phoenix, 2009.

Westcott, B. F. *The Bible in the Church: A Popular Account of the Collection and Reception of the Holy Scriptures in the Christian Churches*. New York: Macmillan, 1864.

———. *A General View of the History of the English Bible*. New York: Macmillan, 1905.

———. *A General Survey of the History of the Canon of the New Testament during the First Four Centuries*. Cambridge: Macmillan, 1855.

———. *Introduction to the Study of the Gospels with Historical and Explanatory Notes*. Boston: Gould & Lincoln, 1862.

Westcott, B. F., and F. J. A. Hort. *The New Testament in the Original Greek*. London: Macmillan, 1881.

5

Theodor Zahn, Adolf Harnack, and Adolf Schlatter

ANDREAS J. KÖSTENBERGER

THEODOR RITTER VON ZAHN, Karl Gustav Adolf von Harnack, and Adolf Schlatter lived in the engulfing shadows of the Enlightenment. This movement, with its quest for scientific objectivity and its confidence in human reason, affected every scholarly discipline, including biblical studies. One of the products of the Enlightenment was the historical-critical method pioneered by Johann Salomo Semler (1725-91) and Johann David Michaelis (1717-91). This approach reached a peak in Harnack,[1] with Zahn and Schlatter representing a conservative counterpoint to the prevailing scholarly climate.

These three scholars not only lived in the heyday of historical criticism, they also did their work at the onset of a new movement, the return to a theological interpretation of the Bible. Stephen Neill and Tom Wright call this the "Re-entry of Theology,"[2] with the best-known representative of this movement being Karl Barth (1886-1968). Harnack, Zahn, and Schlatter, then, lived at a time when historical criticism was a formidable dam concealing increasing cracks that were gradually to give way to the "new" theological methods.

THEODOR RITTER VON ZAHN (1838-1933)

Biographical Information

Theodor Zahn was the ninth child born to Franz L. Zahn (1798-1890) and Anna Schlatter (1800-53; note the family relation to Adolf Schlatter, see below) in Mörs, Rhenish Prussia (now Germany) on October 10, 1838. Although his great-grandfather, Johann Michael Zahn, was a Christian and initially taught philosophy and later studied theology and served as a pastor in Wassertallebel (1711), his grandfather, Gottlieb

---

1. Baird, *History of New Testament Research*, 2:122.
2. Neill and Wright, *Interpretation of the New Testament*, 205.

Zahn (1762–1845), was a rationalistic non-Christian who begrudged the conversion of his children and grandchildren. Ironically, Gottlieb reared two pastors and one missionary. Franz, Gottlieb's third son and Theodor's father, was one of these two pastors. Although raised beneath his father's rationalistic umbrella, Franz became a Christian at the University of Jena where he was studying jurisprudence (1817) before switching to theological studies (1822). After practicing law and training elementary teachers, Franz became pastor of a church in Mörs, his hometown.

With such a father, Theodor Zahn was no stranger to academics, theology, or rationalism, as he was exposed to each from an early age. His erudition and academic promise were evident already in his translation of the eight books of Caesar's *Gallic Wars* from Latin into German at the age of ten (1847–48). Zahn was educated at the Universities of Basel, Erlangen, and Berlin. Encouraged by his father to attend the University of Basel, Zahn studied theology and was influenced by the church historian Karl Rudolf Hagenbach. While studying at Erlangen for three semesters (1856–57), Zahn was greatly impacted by his professor and mentor, Johann Christian K. von Hofmann (central figure of the so-called "Erlangen school"). Zahn completed his studies in Berlin, seeking to fill gaps in his knowledge, which he thought to be dogmatics, history of theology, and the study of Martin Luther and Friedrich Schleiermacher. These formative years shaped Zahn into an orthodox Lutheran as well as a New Testament and patristics scholar practicing a conservative form of historical criticism.

Zahn described the three years subsequent to his graduation (1858–61) as full of trials. During this time, while teaching at his father's school, he suffered from a major eye disease that hindered his reading and writing for an entire year. Once recovered, Zahn taught religion, world history, and German literature at the Gymnasium (middle and high school) of Neustrelitz (1861–65) before becoming a student lecturer at the University of Göttingen (1865–68). While at Göttingen, he advanced to *Privatdozent* (lecturer) in 1868 and then to Associate Professor in 1871, publishing works on Marcellus of Ancyra (1867), the *Shepherd of Hermas* (1868), Ignatius of Antioch (1873), and a critical edition of the Epistles of Ignatius and Polycarp (1876). In addition, he earned his doctorate and served as university preacher. Unable to secure a permanent position in Göttingen, he left in 1877 to become professor at Kiel, where he formed a lifelong friendship with Friedrich Blass, known especially for his work in New Testament Greek grammar. Zahn remained in Kiel for only eleven months before moving to Erlangen where he was called to replace Hofmann, his former mentor. Ten years later, in 1888, he moved to Leipzig, where he remained until 1892, to serve as Dean of the theological faculty. He then returned to Erlangen, where he spent the rest of his career (1892–1909) teaching pedagogy and New Testament exegesis.

Zahn's contemporaries knew him as a scholar and a practitioner. Throughout his academic life, he frequently preached in surrounding churches, addressing many of life's practical concerns. Although he retired from Erlangen in 1909, he continued to study, write, and preach until his death on March 15, 1933, at the age of ninety-five.

Major Views and Methodology

Zahn's scholarly goal throughout his life was to present a historical understanding of early Christianity through an independent investigation of the historical sources from the biblical and patristic records (including the *Shepherd of Hermas* and Ignatius's letters) up to 450 CE.[3] Although Zahn preferred to characterize his method as "historical-philological,"[4] it bore a resemblance to the historical-critical method widely practiced in his day. Unlike most of his scholarly peers, however, Zahn believed that the Bible was historically and theologically accurate, including its record of supernatural events.

According to Zahn himself, the question that remained close to his heart was, "How is a sanctifying faith in Jesus related to the facts by which God revealed Himself to us in Jesus, through Jesus, and by Jesus?"[5] Since Zahn believed that the New Testament accurately recorded history, he was convinced that through an ardent study of the New Testament data one could accurately reconstruct the historical events surrounding the life of Christ. Thus Jesus' virgin birth, his sacrificial and atoning death, and his literal bodily resurrection were not fabrications or misrepresentations by the New Testament and early Christian writers but were in keeping with actual historical events. Zahn confidently stated: "The Christian faith is indeed based on facts and is tied to facts, regarding its origin as well as its continued existence, to such an extent that it stands or falls with these facts."[6] Likewise, Zahn regarded the Old Testament as an accurate record of the history prior to Christ's coming.

Methodologically, Zahn reached the conclusion that the New Testament was accurate by *tracing canonical history backward* from the third century CE.[7] His argument was as follows. A new Christian sect, the Montanists, arose in the mid-third century that laid claim to new inspiration. This claim forced the early church in 170–220 CE to state that authority was confined to the apostolic writings. Zahn suggested that during this time of the formation of the Christian canon the church accepted the four Gospels, Paul's thirteen Epistles, Acts, and Revelation as authoritatively inspired.[8] Continuing his retrospective argument, Zahn examined the era 140–170 CE. He concluded that rather than creating the first canon, Marcion simply responded to an already-fixed orthodox recognition of canonical works. This he found confirmed by the use of canonical books by other heretics.

Given the depth, consistency, and distribution of this tradition by the mid-second century CE, Zahn concluded that the canon (the four Gospels, Acts, and Paul's

---

3. Zahn, "Theodor Zahn: Mein Werdegang," 233.
4. Merk, "Zahn," 479.
5. Zahn, *Apostles' Creed*, 5.
6. Zahn, *Altes und Neues*, 16.
7. Zahn, *Forschungen*.
8. Others recognized Hebrews, 1 Peter, and 1 John, while fewer included the *Shepherd of Hermas* and the *Didache*.

Epistles) was solidified as early as 80–110 CE.[9] The New Testament tradition, then, prompted by the Apostles and maintained accurately by the early church Fathers, reliably portrays history and represents an orthodoxy that was faithfully perpetuated in successive generations. Unlike many of his conservative contemporaries, however, Zahn arrived at this conclusion not through dogmatic presuppositions but by way of a historical-critical study of the data.

Similarly, Zahn argued for the reliability of the Apostles' Creed utilizing historical rather than dogmatic means. For Zahn, the Apostles' Creed was the hallmark of orthodoxy and historically and theologically accurate. In *Apostles' Creed*, Zahn argued that the "contents of the Creed ... give no ground for supposing it to have come into existence later than 120 [CE], but rather allow of its being referred back to the 1st century, even to the lifetime of St. Peter and St. Paul."[10] For Zahn, the "assertion that the Apostles' Creed was a production of the 5th or 6th century" is historically dubious.[11] His affirmation of the Creed is a natural corollary of his belief in the historical and theological accuracy of the New Testament documents. Since the latter are correct and since the Creed represents them accurately, the Creed is to be trusted. Zahn concluded: "History, not legend, gives us a right to the ennobling thought that in and with our Creed we confess that which since the days of the Apostles has been the faith of united Christendom."[12]

Since the New Testament and later Christian writings, including the Apostles' Creed, were historically and theologically accurate, Zahn's goal as an exegete was simply to expound upon, reconstruct, and harmonize the data found in these documents. According to Zahn, the exegete's task was to determine what the original author said and meant (i.e., to ascertain "authorial intent"). The historian's task was to address the question of historical validity.[13] Thus Zahn distinguished the role of the interpreter from that of the historian, maintaining that it was not the former's task to question the historicity of events recorded in the biblical texts (following Gottlob Keil [1788–1810]).[14]

Zahn's diligence as an exegete and interpreter is evident in his voluminous biblical commentaries. His commentary on Galatians (1905) serves as an example of his efforts to harmonize biblical data. A demonstration of exegetical detail is found in his commentary on John's Gospel (1908). Zahn's belief that exegetical detail forms the foundation for theological conclusions is apparent in his Romans commentary

---

9. Baird, *History of New Testament Research*, 2:368.
10. Zahn, *Apostles' Creed*, 78.
11. Ibid., 101.
12. Ibid., 222.
13. Zahn, *Evangelium des Matthäus*, 1.
14. Swarat, *Alte Kirche und Neues Testament*, 422.

(1910). His concern for factual history can be seen clearly in his commentary on Luke (1913).[15]

Although Zahn's conclusions were conservative, he rejected the notion of inerrancy, which he called a "dogmatic theory" not found in any Lutheran confession. Instead, Zahn claimed to be interested only in "a historical investigation regardless of the desired results."[16] However, he never claimed to be without presuppositions but approached the Bible as a believer, contending that faith does not make one uncritical but gives one "greater freedom in the literary-historical and material criticism of the Gospels" than naturalistic philosophy.[17]

In summary, Zahn's methodology and interpretive theory were similar to those of his liberal peers in at least two respects. First, he desired to uncover actual history by way of critical methods. Second, he tirelessly engaged the primary sources, seeking to be true to the historical background of the biblical and extrabiblical data. At the same time, he differed from his contemporaries. Most importantly, he consistently came to conservative conclusions, affirming the historical accuracy of Scripture and other early Christian sources. Also, rather than upholding the ideals of scientific neutrality and complete objectivity, Zahn believed that a scholar's faith could aid rather than hinder his historical investigation.

Contribution

Zahn contributed to the ongoing debate prompted by the historical-critical method used by his predecessors and contemporaries. Adherents to this approach, epitomized by Harnack (see below), were typically diminishing the New Testament's value as a historical source in their pursuit of objective history. Zahn represented a self-consciously conservative voice practicing a version of this method, a scholar of faith who was nonetheless committed to serious engagement with the historical data. For Zahn, unlike most of his contemporaries, faith and scholarship were two sides of the same coin.

Zahn's most important contribution to biblical scholarship is his massive *Einleitung in das Neue Testament* (*Introduction to the New Testament*) where he utilized historical criticism yet came to consistently conservative conclusions. Thus Zahn argued that Paul wrote all the letters attributed to him at the dates traditionally assigned to him. Although he was uncertain regarding the author of Hebrews, Zahn nonetheless affirmed the book's canonicity. Zahn also made a case for the Petrine authorship of both 1 and 2 Peter.

The Gospels, according to Zahn, were written by the authors whose names they bear, with Matthew, originally written in Aramaic, preceding Mark, who literarily

---

15. Baird, *History of New Testament Research*, 2:372–73.
16. Swarat, *Alte Kirche und Neues Testament*, 478.
17. Ibid., 479.

depended on Matthew. Luke, also the author of Acts, used Mark but not Matthew's Aramaic version. John probably used the Synoptics while composing his Gospel. In addition, Zahn believed, there were other sources, both written and oral.[18] Many of these conclusions challenged F. C. Baur's thesis that, out of the thirteen letters traditionally attributed to Paul, only four were authentically Pauline (the so-called *Hauptbriefe* ["Major Epistles"], Romans, 1–2 Corinthians, and Galatians).[19]

KARL GUSTAV ADOLF VON HARNACK (1851–1930)
Biographical Information

Adolf Harnack was born May 7, 1851, in Dorpat (now Tartu), Estonia. He enjoyed a long, fruitful academic career and died on June 10, 1930. From an early age, Harnack was at home in the academic world, since his father Theodosius (1817–89), a theologically orthodox Lutheran, was Professor of Pastoral Theology, and his maternal grandfather served as professor at the University of Dorpat. Harnack's mother, née Evers, a highly intellectual woman, died at the age of 49, leaving behind five children.

Harnack's academic journey began with studies at the universities of Dorpat and Leipzig. In 1874, he was appointed *Privatdozent* (lecturer) at Leipzig and subsequently became professor in 1876. Three years later, in 1879, Harnack was appointed Professor of Church History at the University of Giessen, where he taught until 1886. After teaching for three years at Marburg (1886–88), the faculty at Berlin called him amidst objections from conservative Lutheran leaders, beginning a 38-year tenure there as professor.

During his years of teaching at Berlin, Harnack's accomplishments were as diverse as they were impressive. Besides writing voluminously, Harnack co-founded and edited the *Theologische Literaturzeitung* (1876), became an active member of the Prussian Academy of Sciences (1890), and served as President of the Evangelical Congress (1902–12) and as Director of the Royal Library in Berlin (1905–21). In addition, Harnack guided his students in editing the weekly *Christliche Welt*, a paper that targeted educated members of Protestant churches.

Many of Harnack's peers classified him as a liberal because he was a student and follower of Albrecht Ritschl.[20] The Prussian Church, for example, forbade him to serve as an academic examiner for prospective pastors and barred him from any official role in the Church or on its councils. Nevertheless, Harnack is widely considered to have been a leading figure in nineteenth- and early twentieth-century German Protestantism. He often receives the title "Prince of Church Historians" owing to his work in

---

18. Baird's assessment of Zahn's *Einleitung* in *History of New Testament Research*, 2:369–71.

19. Baur, *Paul the Apostle of Jesus Christ*, 1–111.

20. Baird, *History of New Testament Research*, 2:122, discusses Harnack under the heading "The Zenith of Liberalism."

patristics. Moreover, because of his extraordinary teaching acumen, "thousands of students who later became ministers gave him an enthusiastic hearing."[21]

Major Views and Methodology

Harnack's complexity and depth, demonstrated in his over 1,600 (!) publications, make reducing his historical, theological, and biblical positions to a few simple propositions a virtual impossibility. Harnack was an ardent practitioner of the historical-critical method and approached his task with scientific fervor and generally anti-supernatural presuppositions. At the risk of oversimplification, the following discussion attempts to describe some of the numerous ways in which Harnack applied critical methods to his research.

The effort to understand Harnack's theories involves an examination of at least two facets of his life and method. To begin with, Harnack viewed himself foremost as a historian. It is therefore fitting to start with his historical theories and methodologies. In addition, Harnack made a contribution to theology and biblical interpretation as he applied his historical method to the study of specific passages of Scripture. Thus these two aspects of Harnack's work each require examination in their own right.

Harnack the Historian

Before calling himself a theologian or an exegete, Harnack would have called himself a church historian. Historical study was Harnack's driving passion, because he thought that, when rightly pursued, this avenue of research would result in a positive impact with regard to both the present and the future. Thus Harnack was essentially a church historian for whom historical study was not just about discovering "what happened." Rather, he saw historical study as the opportunity to intervene in the course of history in a proper way. One does this by rejecting the past when it negatively affects the present and by acting responsibly in the here and now while anticipating the future in a circumspect manner. The historian, then, acts as a judge over past events in deciding what should be allowed to continue and what should be altered. In this way, the past should serve as a guide to what the historian judges to be the most desirable present and future.[22]

In terms of his overall vantage point, Harnack studied history from the perspective of *ideas*, believing that these served as impetus for the development and power of institutions, which in turn governed and perpetuated those ideas. While an idea may have called an institution into being, the institution's influence may continue long after the seminal idea has faded.[23] Applied to the history of Christianity, Harnack argued that the idea of the gospel summoned the early ecclesiastical institutions into

---

21. Pauck, *Harnack and Troeltsch*, 6, 14–18.
22. Harnack, *Reden und Aufsätze*, 7.
23. Pauck, *Harnack and Troeltsch*, 21.

existence. These institutions soon departed from the original ideas that had prompted their existence. Through the Roman Catholic Church, however, their power continued for many subsequent centuries.

The lynchpins of history, for Harnack, were not the mundane events of everyday life. Rather, they were "epoch-making" events, the memorials that they produced, and history's grand institutions that served as the cruxes of history.[24] Thus, "the way that Harnack wrote history was to [establish] that basic idea which a particular person (or movement, or epoch) manifested, and then to identify its power, chart its direction, and describe its result."[25] On this basis he would judge the wisdom of continuing or discontinuing these effects in the present and into the future.

In order to discover and to assess accurately the ideas in human history that prompted the emergence of institutions, movements, and epochs, and thus become an effective historian, Harnack believed that one must possess (1) a "practical wisdom" that can detect and understand the relationships between facts; (2) philological and critical competence in the use of the primary sources; (3) an ability to understand all the factors that go into historical memorials, events, and institutions; (4) the ability to understand the *Geist* (spirit or mind) of an era, which is possible, Harnack believed, because the mind that is at work in the present is the same that worked throughout history; and (5) the ability to represent the facts well.[26]

Of these five qualities, competence in the primary sources is paramount: "From the beginning to the end of his work, critical, grammatical, philological competence is held to be the *sine qua non* for the historian."[27] The historian should follow these principles with complete objectivity and without any dogmatic or theological presuppositions. Harnack, therefore, suggested that, since all other scholarly disciplines operate in this way, the study of the Bible should receive the same kind of treatment.[28] Thus one should study the writings of Scripture in keeping with this overall historical methodology.

Harnack the Theologian

According to Harnack, it was history, not dogma, that was the only proper means of studying Jesus and the Bible. Dogma was the theological layers that were added to Christianity by Jesus' early followers and by early ecclesiastical structures, creeds, and doctrinal institutions "in [their] effort . . . to render the gospel comprehensible in the . . . Hellenistic world view."[29] These layers obscure the true Christian faith by adding unnecessary accretions to it. The early church became dependent upon metaphysics

---

24. Harnack, *Reden und Aufsätze*, 15.
25. Glick, *Reality of Christianity*, 117.
26. Ibid., 111.
27. Ibid., 106.
28. Kümmel, *New Testament*, 369.
29. Pauck, *Harnack and Troeltsch*, 23.

instead of relying on true history, resulting in a "fancied Christ" who replaced the real one.[30]

The theologian's task, then, is to study ecclesiastical history, including the New Testament documents, in order to remove these dogmatic layers that the church added to the essential gospel. This was Harnack's central theoretical task around which his entire scholastic life revolved. This task of stripping the dogmatic layers off the gospel lies at the center of his work *Das Wesen des Christentums* (*The Essence of Christianity*), his most widely read publication. In this book, he sought to provide a scholarly, scientific foundation for Christianity, one that was grounded in the historical-critical method and that resulted from the rigorous study of history.

Harnack thought that the Reformers took the initial step of recovering the essence of the gospel by peeling away some of these dogmatic presuppositions. They did this through their maxim of *sola scriptura*, which, for the first time, allowed biblical interpreters to see the Bible through spectacles (partially) freed from dogma. Until this time, interpreters were shackled to the Roman Catholic Church's traditional interpretations. *Sola scriptura* wrested biblical interpretation from the ecclesiastical hierarchy and placed it squarely into the hands of individual interpreters.

Harnack believed, however, that this was only one step in the right direction, since dogmatic layers (such as the belief in Christ's deity or in biblical inspiration) continued to play a large role in post-Reformation theology. He perceived a need to remove these additional layers in order to isolate Jesus' essential teachings and deeds. Harnack held that, owing to these added dogmatic accretions, the true gospel had little in common with modern ecclesiastical positions. In order for the gospel to retain its power in our day, not unlike Bultmann after him, Harnack sought to liberate it from any associated dogmatic elements.[31]

Only when approaching the Bible historically, Harnack believed, is one capable of discerning true *revelation*. Revelation—an unscientific notion—is not found in texts to which some attribute inspiration. Rather, revelation is discovered by peeling away every dogmatic accretion, added by the ecclesiastical hierarchy, that obscures the true gospel. This true gospel, in turn, is found in the teachings of Jesus on the kingdom of God that point to God, but reveal no unique relationship between Jesus and God.[32] The Bible, for Harnack, was itself overgrown by layers of tradition and perhaps fabrications that later communities and individuals had added to the actual events of history.

These historical husks, in turn, shrouded true history and its proper interpretation and the apprehension of its significance. Ultimately, "Harnack held that the Bible is literature and therefore subject to every rule of critical literary and historical

---

30. Harnack, *Das Wesen des Christentums*, 140.
31. Harnack, *Outlines of the History of Dogma*, 1–37.
32. Glick, *Reality of Christianity*, 233.

study."³³ In fact, the sacredness of Scripture can be explained historically. Writings become sacred simply when venerable people write them, when the content is noble, and/or when they evoke holy thoughts in those who read them.³⁴

Although revelation, as Harnack defined it, could be ascertained, he rejected the notion of biblical *canonicity*. The Old Testament, while historically helpful and beneficial to read, is in no way canonical. It provided the church with a crucial aid at a particular time in history but is no longer necessary. The New Testament serves as a vehicle to retrieve accurate history but does not constitute an objective rule of faith. Such a canonical view would require the historian to lift certain documents from their historical contexts in an unscientific manner and attribute qualities to them that are not found in the documents themselves. The way Harnack saw it, this would require the interpreter to view history through the lenses of dogma.

Flowing logically from his view of canon was Harnack's view that the question of *biblical authority* is irrelevant. As mentioned, for Harnack, the historian is, or should be, the objective judge of past events. If he is the judge, then how can a historically distant document have authority over the judge? The document(s) can only contain objective authority to the extent to which the historian assigns such to it. Moreover, belief in scriptural authority requires a dogmatic presupposition that all true historians should eschew.

In summary, Harnack's theory is the epitome of the historical-critical method. The essence of the gospel is found in the life and teachings of Jesus, which have very little in common with the later dogmas of the Roman Catholic Church. All later additions to this gospel are dogmatic accretions supplied by the New Testament writers and their successors. The goal of the biblical interpreter is to remove these layers by way of objective, historical research in order to ascertain the true gospel, which is centered on Jesus, who, historically speaking, "is exemplar and beyond that—mystery."³⁵

Contribution

Harnack's illustrious career produced an astonishing amount of scholarly publication. His most significant contribution to biblical studies is his perpetuation of the historical-critical method introduced by Semler and others a century earlier. Historical criticism reaches its zenith in Harnack through his relentless pursuit of the historical method and his staunch resistance to dogmatic presuppositions. Nevertheless, within the scope of his rigorous application of the historical method, Harnack continued to believe that Jesus' teachings have an important influence on the present. Harnack also contributed significantly to scholarship as a historian by integrating the study of church history and New Testament research. Subsequent generations of scholars

---

33. Rumscheidt, "Harnack," 492.
34. Glick, *Reality of Christianity*, 220.
35. Ibid., 198.

could no longer seek to uncover the earliest forms of Christianity without reckoning with Harnack's critical and historical methods.

A giant in both historical and biblical studies, Harnack was no stranger to a variety of areas of New Testament study. Surprisingly, many of his contributions resulted in conservative conclusions, though they "largely serve[d] his liberal agenda."[36] Apart from the larger contributions noted above, Harnack contributed to a variety of specific areas of New Testament research.[37] With regard to *textual criticism*, Harnack concluded from a detailed argument that the Eastern text of Acts 15:29, which includes πνικτῶν ("that which is strangled"), is preferable to the Western text which omits it.

In his contributions to *Gospels research*, Harnack argued that Luke was the author of the Third Gospel and of Acts, reaching this conclusion by suggesting that Luke's prologue originally included the author's name. In addition, he suggested that Luke created a new genre by writing Acts. Harnack contended that Matthew's notion of the virgin birth did not derive from Hellenistic mythology but from a popular, messianic interpretation of Isa 7:14, which was already present in Judaism. Harnack also contributed to *form criticism* through his studies of the hypothetical document called "Q" (from German *Quelle*, "source") by suggesting that Matthew followed Q more closely than did Luke.

Harnack contributed to *the study of the Christian canon* by questioning the reason why the New Testament books were initially canonized. The early Christians pronounced the New Testament authoritative alongside the Old Testament in order to elevate Jesus' teachings and life, to make authoritative a certain segment of early Christian writings, to counter Marcion's canon and the Gnostic writings, and to combat the Montanists' claims. The early Christians, Harnack contended, canonized four Gospels as a compromise among various churches, each of whom preferred a different Gospel. In addition, Harnack wrote an important monograph on Marcion.[38]

Harnack also contributed to *Pauline studies*, especially with regard to the collection and canonization of Paul's letters. He suggested that thirteen of Paul's letters had been collected by the end of the first century. Another contribution was Harnack's argument that the early tradition of Christ's resurrection (1 Cor 15:3–8) was a developing rather than completed tradition. Harnack also famously suggested that Priscilla wrote Hebrews, which is rendered unlikely by the masculine participle διηγούμενον ("tell") with reference to the author in Heb 11:32.[39]

Last but not least, Harnack is known for his *missiological* contribution, in particular his monumental *The Mission and Expansion of Christianity in the First Three Centuries*.[40] Harnack held that the missionary activity of Judaism paved the way for

---

36. Ibid., 135.
37. See Baird, *History of New Testament Research*, 2:129–35, for a fuller treatment.
38. Harnack, *Marcion*.
39. Baird, *History of New Testament Research*, 2:133–34.
40. Harnack, *Die Mission und Ausbreitung*.

the early Christian mission but that it was Jesus who provided the decisive impetus. According to Harnack, the appeal of Christianity lay in its universal, all-embracing scope, its sublime ethic, its future hope, and its pervasive message of love. Only recently has Harnack's missiological work been superseded.[41]

ADOLF SCHLATTER (1852–1938)
Biographical Information

Adolf Schlatter was born on August 16, 1852 in St. Gallen, Switzerland, into the devout Christian home of Stephan (1805–80) and Wilhelmine (1819–94) Schlatter. Stephan was a Baptist, and Wilhelmine a Lutheran. Adolf Schlatter, the seventh of nine children, and, interestingly, Theodor Zahn's cousin on his mother's side of the family (see above), began his studies in Basel, Switzerland at the young age of nineteen, where he remained for two years (1871–73). This was followed by a year of study in Tübingen, Germany (1873–74). After passing his exams in Basel in 1875, Schlatter pastored churches in Kilchberg, Neumünster, and Kesswil, Switzerland. In Kesswil, he met Susanna Schoop, the 21-year old daughter of a businessman. They married on January 15, 1878. Susanna loyally supported her husband in the German world of academia, which was uncharted territory for her. They had five children: Paul, Dora, Hedwig, Theodor, and Ruth.

Soon after getting married, Schlatter began his formal scholarly career by agreeing to teach in Bern, Switzerland, where he spent the first eight years of his long teaching career (1880–88). This is also where he published his first and prizewinning monograph, *Der Glaube im Neuen Testament* (*Faith in the New Testament* [1885]). In 1888 Schlatter left Bern to teach New Testament in Greifswald, Germany, before relocating to Berlin in 1893, where he lectured in Systematic Theology until 1898. During his stay in Berlin, Schlatter encountered Harnack's liberal theology. In fact, "Schlatter's chair in Berlin was established by the king of Prussia to counterbalance Harnack's influence following a controversy when Harnack told students he wished the church would give up using the Apostles' Creed."[42] Also during his time in Berlin, Schlatter became editor of the important series Beiträge zur Förderung christlicher Theologie. In 1898, Schlatter moved to Tübingen, where he taught New Testament for twenty-four years and spent the bulk of his productive and enduring academic career.

Difficult years followed Schlatter's move to Tübingen. His wife died on July 9, 1907, and his son Paul passed away on October 14, 1914 as the result of a war wound. Schlatter remained a widower the rest of his life and continued his scholarly endeavors, focusing intensely on consolidating his prior theological work into four volumes: a two-volume *Die Theologie des Neuen Testaments* (New Testament Theology)—*Das*

---

41. See Schnabel, *Early Christian Mission*.
42. Köstenberger, "Translator's Preface," 12 n. 11; cf. Morgan, *Nature of New Testament Theology*, 172 n. 43.

Wort Jesu (1909) on Jesus and the Gospels and *Die Lehre der Apostel* (1910) on the early church and the other New Testament documents[43]—as well as *Das christliche Dogma* (1911; a Systematic Theology) and *Die christliche Ethik* (1914; a treatment of Christian Ethics). During this period, he also wrote his major New Testament commentaries: Matthew (1929), John (1930), Luke (1931), James (1932), 1–2 Corinthians (1934), Mark (1935), Romans (1935), the Pastorals (1936), and 1 Peter (1937). Shortly before his death on May 19, 1938, Schlatter penned his final publication, *Kennen wir Jesus?*, a biblical theology presented in the form of daily devotional thoughts.[44]

Schlatter's autobiography was published posthumously by his son Theodor (who added material on Schlatter's last 15 years) at the occasion of Schlatter's one-hundredth birthday in 1952.[45]

Major Views and Methodology

Schlatter's methodology is characterized by what Stuhlmacher calls "*a third way*,"[46] that is, a mediating position between a dogmatic, isolationist fundamentalism on the one hand and an anti-supernaturalist, "scientific" criticism on the other. Schlatter was comfortable utilizing the historical-critical method of his day, since "the abuse of method does not nullify its rightful use."[47] However, he would also hasten to add that "no critical method should prevent one from seeing God at work in history."[48] Schlatter addressed these theological tensions when commenting that "the desired goal [of scholarly methodology] remains for both historical and dogmatic activity that we work our way up out of the two extremes of either specialization [i.e., critical and faith-based scholarship], with its immersion in amassing of tiny details [criticism], or the abstract trafficking in accepted ideas [fundamentalism] that characterize our 'disciplines.'"[49] Schlatter's "third way" characterized and pervaded his entire methodological approach.

The majority of biblical interpreters in the tradition that grew out of the Enlightenment believed that true scientific exegesis required the setting aside of one's faith; anything less was mere fundamentalism. Decades ahead of his time, Schlatter vehemently disagreed. In his article "The Significance of Method for Theological Work,"

---

43. The scholarly responses to Schlatter's *Die Theologie des Neuen Testaments* are chronicled in Köstenberger, "Reception."

44. Translated into English as Schlatter, *Do We Know Jesus?* For additional biographical information on Schlatter, see Köstenberger, "Translator's Preface," 9–15; Neuer, *Adolf Schlatter: Ein Leben für Theologie und Kirche*; and Neuer, *Adolf Schlatter: A Biography*.

45. T. Schlatter, *Adolf Schlatters Rückblick*. Also, Schlatter's lectures for his course "Introduction to Theology" when last taught in the summer semester of 1924 were published in 2013 on the occasion of the 75th anniversary of his death as *Einführung in die Theologie*.

46. Stuhlmacher, "Schlatter's Interpretation of Scripture," 444.

47. See Yarbrough, "Schlatter's 'The Significance of Method,'" 69.

48. Ibid.

49. Ibid., 66.

Schlatter, under the subheading, "Historical and Dogmatic Work," noted that historians are not completely objective and that they need not shed their "dogmatics" (or faith) entirely. Instead of adopting a stance of utter objectivity (a virtual impossibility), interpreters ought to engage in both "historical" *and* "dogmatic" work.[50] What is more, Schlatter reminded the historical critics of his day that "behind every historical method there lurks a dogmatics."[51]

Many Enlightenment scholars also presupposed the inaccessibility of the "historical Jesus." In any case, any hypothesis regarding the historical Jesus was ultimately irrelevant, since one's personal, existential faith overrode uncertain historical events. Schlatter, by contrast, suggested that the historical Jesus was "prior to all faith"[52] and that "Jesus' person, teaching, and work could be gleaned and distinguished from what the New Testament writers proclaimed."[53] Like Zahn (see above), Schlatter stood boldly and confidently against the academic current of his day by espousing his own method for engaging in historical Jesus research. According to Schlatter, this meant "that Jesus already in his earthly life was Son of God and Christ, and that he was not only described and known as such at a later date [but was known] on the basis of the Easter event [i.e., his resurrection and appearances]."[54]

Another methodological feature of Schlatter's approach was his *emphasis on the Jewish background of Jesus and the New Testament*. In this Schlatter stood against the prevailing scholarship of his time (the history-of-religions school, including Bultmann, who came into prominence late in Schlatter's career), which held the Hellenistic and/or Gnostic background of the New Testament to be preeminent. If Jesus was the Jewish Messiah, Schlatter argued, his Jewish background must be given its full due. For this reason also, in contrast to many of his academic peers, Schlatter advocated the primacy of Jesus' Jewish background in John's Gospel.[55] It is only in recent years that Schlatter's views on the Johannine background have been fully vindicated, especially since the discovery of the Dead Sea Scrolls and in view of the affinities they display with John's Gospel.

For Schlatter, therefore, Jesus as the messianic Son of God constituted the foundational building block in his exegesis.[56] In his foreword to *Die Geschichte des Christus* (*The History of the Christ*) in 1923 Schlatter wrote, "The knowledge of Jesus is the *foremost, indispensable centerpiece* of New Testament theology."[57] This stands in marked contrast to Rudolf Bultmann, who opened his famous two-volume *New Testa-*

---

50. Ibid., 73–74.
51. Stuhlmacher, "Schlatter's Interpretation of Scripture," 440.
52. Ibid., 442.
53. Köstenberger, "Translator's Preface," 14.
54. Stuhlmacher, "Schlatter's Interpretation of Scripture," 441.
55. See esp. Schlatter, *Der Evangelist Johannes*.
56. Yarbrough, "Schlatter, Adolf," 520.
57. Schlatter, *History of the Christ*, 21.

ment Theology by declaring: "The message of Jesus is *a presupposition* for the theology of the New Testament *rather than a part of that theology itself*."[58]

The *pursuit of holistic biblical interpretation* was another of Schlatter's major methodological distinctives. While form critics in his day sought to reconstruct the oral prehistory of various textual units of Scripture, Schlatter sought to make sense of the final text of Scripture as a whole. As mentioned, Schlatter did not completely eschew the methods of his day, but rather advocated their discerning use. While employing critical methods, however, he never lost sight of the forest for the trees, utilizing these methods as a means to the end of arriving at a synthetic grasp of the entire message of Scripture, holistically conceived.

A case in point is Schlatter's *Einleitung in die Bibel* (*Introduction to the Bible*) where he sought to interpret the Old and the New Testaments in conjunction with one another.[59] Although many of his peers disparaged his work, considering it elementary and lacking scholarly rigor, some recent scholars have commended Schlatter for his holistic approach to biblical interpretation. Thus Stuhlmacher has stated, "[T]o my knowledge he [Schlatter] was the only one of the great exegetes of the later nineteenth and early twentieth centuries to do so."[60]

Another feature of Schlatter's approach is that of *methodological integration*. Instead of relying only on one specialized area of research (such as historical study), Schlatter believed that full-fledged biblical interpretation required the use of all the available tools in the scholar's exegetical toolbox, including historical and linguistic study, theological and philosophical investigation, and other forms of inquiry. This is evident in the sheer diversity of his writings (over 400 publications), which include works on history, exegesis, theology, philosophy, ethics, and devotional literature. Schlatter's prolific output in his pursuit of the integration of various scholarly disciplines stood in marked contrast to the highly specialized academic culture of his day.

Schlatter's distinction between historical and doctrinal investigation represents another vital aspect of his methodology.[61] Schlatter believed that the interpreter's first task was that of engaging in rigorous historical research, insisting, "It is the historical objective that should govern our conceptual work exclusively and completely, stretching our perceptive faculties to the limit. We turn away decisively from ourselves and our time to what was found in the men through whom the church came into being. Our main interest should be the thought as it was conceived *by them* and the truth that was valid *for them*."[62]

---

58. Bultmann, *Theology of the New Testament*, 3. In the original, Bultmann italicized "*The message of Jesus*" but here I have emphasized other words as pertinent to my discussion.

59. Schlatter, *Einleitung in die Bibel*; see also his *Erläuterungen*; cf. Stuhlmacher, "Schlatter's Interpretation of Scripture," 438.

60. Stuhlmacher, "Schlatter's Interpretation of Scripture," 438.

61. Köstenberger, "Translator's Preface," 13.

62. Schlatter, *History of the Christ*, 18.

Only *after* this, Schlatter contended, should the interpreter turn to the second, "the doctrinal task, through which we align ourselves with the teachings of the New Testament and clarify whether or not and how and why we accept those teachings into our own spiritual lives, so that they are not only truth for the New Testament community, but also for us personally."[63] Thus Schlatter was never content with uncovering merely the meaning of the ancient text in its first-century context, since to stop there would have fallen short of the proper end of biblical interpretation, that is, the application of biblical truth to the interpreter's own life and to that of his community. Schlatter thus assumed that the Bible had an enduring message that must be lived out by every generation.

Finally, Schlatter advocated and practiced a *"scholarship of humility."*[64] In an era where historical avenues of research reigned supreme, Schlatter exhorted his fellow scholars to recognize the limitations of historical research, cautioning them not to make assertions that went beyond the evidence (something Schlatter labeled "fantasy"). To be sure, scholars are called upon to venture educated guesses that stretch the limits of the available sources, but they should do so humbly, not claiming to have more knowledge than they actually possess. As Schlatter noted, there is no need to know the causes of everything that was said and done in the New Testament. Etiological pursuits are important, but they are not preeminent.[65]

In these methodological distinctives, as mentioned, Schlatter stood against the prevailing scholarly currents of his day. The impetus for his resolute stand was his faith in Jesus as God's Son and Savior, the one who, Schlatter believed, literally and physically rose from the dead and who historically understood himself to be the Messiah. While Schlatter engaged in continual dialogue with the academy, he simultaneously conversed with the church. His ardent search for historical facts never diminished his reliance on his supernatural God. These bedrock convictions provided the unshakable foundation for the application of his methods that were scorned by many of the more critically-oriented (i.e., historically skeptical) scholars of his day.

In summary, Schlatter's methodology represented the conservative minority position in his period. His entire approach stood beneath the umbrella of his "third way" by which he sought to navigate the tension between historical research and faith in the supernatural God. Schlatter applied this approach to the Bible holistically, resisting the destructive disintegrating effects of much of contemporary scholarship. He urged a careful distinction between historical and doctrinal work, maintaining that both were important in their own right, yet insisting that historical and exegetical work precede theological work and application to the interpreter's own life. Schlatter carried out his program with characteristic humility. Scholarship and faith were never at odds for Schlatter; to the contrary, they were inextricably related.

63. Ibid.
64. Köstenberger, "Translator's Preface," 14.
65. Yarbrough, "Schlatter's 'The Significance of Method,'" 74.

Contribution

Like Zahn, Schlatter contributed to the ongoing debate of his day between historical and faith-based critical methods. Succinctly put, his primary contribution to biblical scholarship "is his highly sophisticated and multifaceted defense of Scripture as primary source and arbiter for redemptive relatedness to the God who took on flesh in Jesus."[66] In an age when liberal scholarship carried the day, Schlatter stood firm in his advocacy of a conservative approach to biblical interpretation and theology. Schlatter tirelessly showed that a conservative scholar could use historical-critical methods, a contribution that continues to affect scholarly research to this day.

In this, Schlatter also contributed to Karl Barth's legacy. "Schlatter's conviction that biblical exegesis was the only proper foundation for systematic theology anticipated Barth," who thought that "historical-critical commentaries were only a 'prelude' to a commentary."[67] By contrast, historical critics, such as Harnack, thought that when one completed one's critical work, correct interpretation was achieved. Schlatter, and later, Barth, looked beyond this to suggest that exegesis is the handmaiden of theology, and biblical interpretation a necessary prerequisite to Systematics.

Another contribution made by Schlatter was his distinction between the two "'horizons' of the biblical text, the ancient and the contemporary one, and his affirmation of the preeminence of the first horizon [which] are as timely today as they were then."[68] This distinction remains prevalent among many evangelical scholars today.

Schlatter also contributed to the historical Jesus debate. "In an age when scholars had grown skeptical of the very possibility of finding the historical Jesus in and through the Gospel documents, Schlatter expressed his confidence that Jesus' person, teaching, and work could be gleaned and distinguished from what the New Testament writers proclaimed."[69] Thus he "rejected an arid scholasticism, an approach to scholarship that was primarily concerned with current critical fashions, statistics, and 'purely historical' reconstruction, urging instead a holistic understanding of the time in which Jesus lived and an effort to understand his theology comprehensively."[70]

Finally, a major contribution that largely went unrecognized at the time was Schlatter's emphasis on the Jewishness of Jesus and of the New Testament writings. In this, Schlatter stood against the towering stature of Bultmann and the history-of-religions school that gave primacy to the Hellenistic background of the New Testament. Schlatter's sustained defense of Jesus' essential Jewishness has been abundantly vindicated in the successive decades. If scholars had listened to Schlatter rather than

---

66. Yarbrough, "Schlatter, Adolf" 521.

67. Köstenberger, "Translator's Preface," 12–13; Johnson, "Barth," 437.

68. Köstenberger, "Translator's Preface," 13.

69. Ibid., 14. For a thorough analysis of Schlatter's treatment of the historical Jesus, see esp. Schmid, *Erkenntnis des geschichtlichen Christus*, 240–431.

70. Köstenberger, "Translator's Preface," 14.

Bultmann, biblical interpreters in the second half of the twentieth century might have been spared numerous scholarly dead ends.[71]

COMPARISON OF ZAHN, HARNACK, AND SCHLATTER

Of the three scholars discussed, Harnack represents theological liberalism and a full-fledged historical-critical approach to the study of Scripture as prevalent in the late nineteenth and early twentieth century, while Zahn and Schlatter pose a conservative alternative. All three men, born within fourteen years of each other, grew up during the heyday of the historical-critical method, and each had their respective followers. The following comparisons are offered.

First, Zahn and Schlatter are compared and contrasted with one another. Since both of these scholars advocated a conservative approach, more parallels than contrasts emerge. Second, Zahn and Schlatter are jointly compared to Harnack. Since Zahn and Schlatter were theologically and methodologically similar and disagreed substantially with Harnack, they are compared to Harnack jointly. Finally, Zahn and Harnack are compared at length because of sustained personal correspondence between them.

Zahn and Schlatter

Zahn and Schlatter shared more commonalities than differences. The work of both held the following presuppositions and distinctives in common. (1) Both believed that God exists. He is not the figment of an overzealous imagination. Rather, God is the Creator and Sustainer of the universe who is actively involved in his creation. (2) Both agreed that Jesus is God's Son, who was God incarnate and came to earth to redeem humanity from its sin. (3) Both adhered to a belief in the supernatural. They held that the miraculous claims of the Bible are historically accurate and consistent with the existence of a supernatural God. Both, therefore, accepted the major tenets of historic Christianity, including the virgin birth, Jesus' deity, and his bodily resurrection. (4) Both believed that the Bible was inspired by God and thus theologically and spiritually authoritative. They viewed the Bible as a book that is special in relation to other documents in history, including those written concurrently with the Bible. Yet neither of them affirmed the doctrine of biblical inerrancy. Both affirmed the Bible was true and authoritative, but neither argued there could be no errors, however minor, in any biblical claim, statement, or representation. (5) Both considered the historical-critical method to be a useful tool in biblical interpretation. However, they agreed that this method alone was inadequate for a full and proper hermeneutic, believing that faith was an important part of the interpretive process.

---

71. Ibid. Concerning the continuing relevance of Schlatter's contribution, see also Bockmühl, *Die Aktualität*; and Yarbrough, "Schlatter on the Pastorals."

Aside from these larger agreements, Zahn and Schlatter also agreed on many detailed historical and biblical points of interpretation. (1) Both held that the thirteen letters traditionally attributed to Paul were authentically Pauline (contra F. C. Baur). (2) Both adhered to Matthean priority and believed that the Gospels were written early (prior to 90 CE). (3) Both believed that Luke wrote both the Gospel and Acts. (4) Both held that the apostle John wrote the Gospel attributed to him around 80 CE. (5) Both affirmed the authenticity of the Catholic Epistles (except that Schlatter did not hold to the Petrine authorship of 2 Peter).

The differences between Zahn and Schlatter are minor in comparison and are due primarily to specific scholarly interests and emphases rather than to underlying methodological disagreements. Zahn was a patristics scholar who was relentlessly concerned about historical detail. By comparison, Schlatter was more philosophically and hermeneutically oriented, often focusing on larger theological issues. He rivaled Zahn in philological rigor, as his monographs on faith and Josephus, as well as his extensive rabbinic researches, indicate. Zahn devoted much of his effort to detailed exegesis, which he thought would produce an accurate reconstruction of history. Schlatter, for his part, tended to view history holistically, since he thought it resulted from a complex of cause-and-effects events.[72] Zahn was unswervingly committed to the historical-critical method. Schlatter utilized this method while simultaneously warning against an "atheistic" view of history, that is, one that neglects God in the interpretive process.[73]

Zahn/Schlatter and Harnack

Harnack parted company with Zahn and Schlatter on many core issues while, surprisingly, coming to similar conclusions on some peripheral matters. The agreements between Harnack and Zahn/Schlatter are as follows. (1) All three agreed that God existed, though Zahn and Schlatter differed from Harnack concerning God's interaction with creation. (2) All three believed that Paul penned the thirteen letters traditionally attributed to him. (3) All concurred that Luke wrote both the Gospel and Acts as a sequel. (4) All adhered to the early dating of the Gospels, a conclusion perhaps surprising in Harnack's case. (5) All believed that Isa 7:14, not Hellenistic mythology, was the major impetus for the biblical teaching on Jesus' virgin birth. (6) All three adhered to the historical-critical method, though each to varying degrees. For example, Harnack and Zahn placed more emphasis on and trust in the historical-critical method than did Schlatter.

The points of disagreement between Zahn/Schlatter and Harnack centered on broader philosophical and theological issues and are as follows. (1) Zahn and Schlatter disagreed with Harnack concerning the existence of the supernatural. In contrast

---

72. See Baird, *History of New Testament Research*, 2:374.
73. Schlatter, *History of the Christ*, 18–19; Neuer, *Adolf Schlatter: A Biography*, 211–25.

to Zahn and Schlatter, Harnack presupposed the non-authenticity of (Jesus') miracles. Thus, for Harnack, the virgin birth, Jesus' resurrection, and other beliefs propagated by historic Christianity were later, inauthentic, and erroneous additions to the Gospel accounts. From Harnack's point of view, Christianity was strictly a historical phenomenon that had no miraculous impetus, whether by Jesus or Paul. Zahn and Schlatter, conversely, thought that Christianity had a supernatural origin while agreeing that the biblical writings should be studied historically. (2) Zahn and Schlatter disagreed with Harnack about the nature of Christ, holding that Jesus was divine, while Harnack concluded that he was merely human. Closely related to this was Harnack's emphasis on Jesus' teachings and ethics and Zahn and Schlatter's emphasis on Jesus' divinity, although not to the exclusion of Jesus' teachings. (3) Zahn and Schlatter disagreed with Harnack on the nature of the Bible, believing it to be inspired and authoritative. Harnack, on the other hand, thought that the Bible was simply a collection of ancient writings no different from any other documents in antiquity. (4) Zahn and Schlatter disagreed with Harnack regarding the nature of early Christianity. Harnack maintained that Christianity was syncretistic, reflecting a fusion of earlier religions and cultures, while Zahn and Schlatter believed that Jesus founded Christianity by supernatural means (albeit not divorced from history and culture), that Paul perpetuated it, and that later sects corrupted its earlier, pure version.

Zahn and Harnack

Zahn and Harnack deserve a lengthier and more thorough comparison since they corresponded personally for over 55 years (1873–1929), although not always amicably.[74] Harnack's dissertation, "Source Criticism of the History of Gnosticism," appeared in 1873 when Harnack was only 22 years old. The 35 year-old Zahn responded very positively and sent Harnack his new book on Ignatius of Antioch. Harnack responded to Zahn in a letter on July 6, 1873, expressing appreciation for the gift but also offering a critical review of the book.

Harnack and Zahn, along with Oskar von Gebhardt, collaborated in 1875 to produce a reliable edition of the Apostolic Fathers. Letters between them during this time expressed deep trust and cordiality, evident in Harnack addressing Zahn no longer as "Mr. Zahn" but as "Dear Zahn." Amidst this cordiality, however, Harnack frequently faulted Zahn for brushing aside critical concerns in favor of church tradition.[75]

Harnack and Zahn had a sharp falling out beginning in 1883 or 1884.[76] When Zahn, in 1888, published the first volume of his *Geschichte des neutestamentlichen*

---

74. Schlatter and Harnack, who taught simultaneously in Berlin, also corresponded, becoming good friends amidst their theological differences. They did not exchange letters, however, to the extent that Zahn and Harnack did. See Neuer, *Adolf Schlatter: A Biography*, 95–97.

75. Hauck, "Briefe Adolf Harnacks," 497–98.

76. Documented in an interchange in the *Theologische Literaturzeitung* (1883) 487–88 and (1884) 321–22. See Hauck, "Briefe Adolf Harnacks," 497–98.

Kanons, Harnack countered with *Das Neue Testament um das Jahr 200* (*The New Testament around 200 CE*). In 1900, Zahn called passages in Harnack's work "trivial," "frivolous," "examples of evil exegesis," and "nonsense."[77] Some specific disagreements are as follows. Zahn and Harnack disagreed about the canon. Zahn thought that the early church canonized the Bible before 100 CE, while Harnack believed that the canon was codified after 150 CE.

Moreover, Zahn accentuated the *continuity* between Jesus' disciples and the early church while Harnack strongly maintained that the two stood in marked *discontinuity*. Zahn saw Irenaeus as a faithful witness of apostolic tradition while Harnack saw him as a major representative of the new early Catholicism, that is, the ecclesiastical hierarchy forming in the second century. Zahn criticized Harnack for his inadequate knowledge of Syriac and Greek, his lack of thoroughness in exegesis, his overconfidence in his dating of primary sources, and his inability to connect historical data chronologically.[78]

Harnack felt similarly about Zahn, warning him not to be overconfident in establishing dependencies and interconnections.[79] In reviewing Zahn's *Geschichte des neutestamentlichen Kanons*, Harnack charged Zahn with biased research (*Tendenzkritik*) that did not qualify as scientific.[80] Most crucially, each had different faith commitments over the role and meaning of the Apostles' Creed. Zahn thought it accurately represented Christianity, while Harnack thought it obscured the true gospel.[81]

After decades of bitter dispute, a string of amiable letters from 1914 to 1928 culminated in two final letters from 1929 that signaled reconciliation.[82] Harnack sent Zahn a letter wishing him a happy ninety-first birthday, calling him "the senior of theological studies" and thanking him for "rich stimulation, instruction, and correction." In return, Zahn sent Harnack a new publication, and Harnack responded with a heartfelt appreciative note of thanks.[83]

Methodological Application

Based on the characterization of the respective approaches by Zahn, Harnack, and Schlatter, the following case study will seek to apply these insights to a specific text of Scripture, John 14:6, where Jesus is quoted as saying, "I am the way and the truth and the life. No one comes to the Father except through me." It appears that none of these

---

77. Swarat, *Alte Kirche und Neues Testament*, 459.

78. For recent confirmation of Zahn's point with reference to Harnack's hasty dating and erroneous attribution of authorship of another important ancient text, see Tzamalikos, *Ancient Commentary*, 8 n. 34, 37 n. 309, 57 n. 493, 86–88.

79. Swarat, *Alte Kirche und Neues Testament*, 461–66.

80. Merk, "Zahn," 479, with reference to Zahn, *Geschichte des neutestamentlichen Kanons*.

81. Bandstra, "Zahn," 399.

82. Kantzenbach, "Adolf Harnack und Theodor Zahn," 242–44.

83. Hauck, "Briefe Adolf Harnacks," 498, 502.

scholars commented extensively on John 14:6.[84] In light of their presuppositions and methodologies, how would they likely have understood this passage?

Theodor Zahn held to a high view of both Scripture and Jesus, affirming his divinity. As mentioned, Zahn believed it was not the role of the exegete to question statements such as John 14:6 in Scripture but rather to interpret them in such a way as to encourage others in the faith. At the same time, he believed in the historical investigation of biblical texts. In the case of John 14:6, he would therefore have pursued the question of the historicity of Jesus' saying.[85] In light of the Gospels' witness elsewhere, did Jesus likely claim that he was "the way, the truth, and the life" and that he alone provided access to God?

To answer this question, Zahn might have looked at later texts reflecting the beliefs of the early church, such as Acts 4:12, where Luke cites Peter as saying, "Salvation is found in no one else, for there is no other name given under heaven by which we must be saved." Contextual study reveals that the name spoken of here is unambiguously that of Jesus, as a look at Acts 4:10–11 indicates: "It is *by the name of Jesus Christ of Nazareth . . . that this man stands before you healed. Jesus* is 'the stone you builders rejected, which has become the cornerstone'" (Ps 118:22). This makes the same claim that access to God and salvation are found only in Jesus. The willingness of many in the early church to suffer martyrdom rather than renounce their faith likewise is most plausibly accounted for on the assumption of the historicity of Jesus' statement.

Adolf Harnack, for his part, approached Scripture with an unbounded belief in the validity of the historical-critical method and a bias against Jesus' deity and the supernatural. He also believed that the Gospel texts in their present form were overgrown by layers of accretions that must be removed by painstaking historical research on the basis of modern research methodologies. At the same time, he believed that Jesus' example and teachings, once uncovered, were important in providing us with the essence of Christianity—its underlying "ideas"—especially as far as its ethical and moral standards are concerned.

Applying this perspective to John 14:6 indicates that Harnack might have questioned the historical basis for the statement attributed to Jesus there.[86] He might have argued that Jesus never claimed to provide exclusive access to God and that this teach-

---

84. It is hard to identify a passage that none of these three scholars engaged in his scholarly work, but John 14:6 is a good choice in that the passage does not feature centrally in any of these scholars' writings. For references to John 14:6 in the writings of these three scholars see further below.

85. As in Schlatter's case (see below), John 14:6 only receives one passing reference in Zahn's three-volume *Introduction to the New Testament* (3:315). His commentary on John's Gospel, *Das Evangelium des Johannes*, 557–58, does include an exegetical treatment of the passage, though Zahn does not specifically address Jesus' claim that no one comes to the Father except through him.

86. Harnack does not comment on John 14:6 in any of his major works, which is in part explained by the fact that Harnack wrote primarily as a historian rather than as a biblical exegete. He does provide a very interesting general treatment under the heading "The Gospel of Jesus Christ according to His Own Testimony concerning Himself" in *Outlines of the History of Dogma*, 58–76, which can serve as an overall framework for the present discussion.

ing was imposed on the Gospel record by John (whom Harnack held to be the author of the Gospel) at a later time. This would be in keeping with the *discontinuity* asserted by Harnack between Jesus and the early church. Harnack might have concluded that Jesus may never have uttered the saying and instead was a good moral teacher of high ethical ideals (such as those found in the Matthean Sermon on the Mount).[87] These ideals, for their part, are present in Christianity to a high degree, but they are also held by the proponents of other major world religions. In fact, Harnack believed, Christianity itself developed in many ways in dialogue with, and imitation of, other religious movements and ideas. In this view, it is these *ideas*, not any *exclusive claim of salvation through faith in Jesus*, that are the driving force of history, and it is these ideas that must form our ultimate point of reference as serious scholars and historians. In our quest to apprehend the true essence of Christianity, faith must not get in the way, lest our objectivity be clouded by religious sentimentality and scholarly dogmatism.

Adolf Schlatter, finally, would have approached John 14:6 decidedly as a believer, yet open to investigate the passage historically, especially in relation to other New Testament texts.[88] He would have looked for evidence elsewhere in the Gospel of John and the other canonical Gospels suggesting that Jesus claimed to possess a unique relationship to God and most likely would have concluded that Jesus did indeed assert such a claim. Thus he would have judged that the statement in John 14:6 was historically plausible and should be believed by Christians everywhere.

Schlatter would have maintained that there was no dichotomy between scholarship and faith and that, to the contrary, faith aided the Christian scholar in understanding the spiritual nature of biblical texts, including John 14:6. The interpreter of Scripture must submit to Scripture and be prepared to act in obedience to the claims made in the text. In the present case, this involved the proclamation of Jesus as the Messiah and Son of God and the assertion that salvation was found only in Jesus, calling people everywhere to repent and believe in Jesus and the gospel.

CONCLUSION

Theodor Zahn, Adolf Harnack, and Adolf Schlatter sustained a fascinating relationship. Zahn and Schlatter were not only related in a familial sense, they also shared in common their approach to Scripture as believers and yet as rigorous historians. Both also saw as their overall goal that of establishing others more firmly in the faith. Harnack, while sharing their concern for historical research, viewed Christian faith on the part of the scholar as unhelpful and sought to rely solely on the historical-critical

---

87. See, however, Harnack's apparently positive assessment in ibid., 65 n. 2: "See the farewell discourses in John, the fundamental ideas of which are, in my opinion, genuine, that is, proceed from Jesus" (but note that he speaks of "the fundamental *ideas*" here; see also ibid., 64 n. 3).

88. John 14:6 receives only one passing reference in Schlatter's two-volume *New Testament Theology*. His John commentary includes a brief exposition (*Der Evangelist Johannes*, 293–94), and his popular commentary (*Erläuterungen*, 236) includes a short pious treatment. See also his devotional treatment of John 14:5–6 in *Andachten*, 85.

method. The theological liberalism he espoused soon gave way to a more realistic view of the world. Yet Harnack remains a towering figure in exemplifying rigorous historical research. Zahn and Schlatter, for their part, have bequeathed to conservative evangelical interpreters a rich legacy of faith-based Christian scholarship that nonetheless believes in the serious historical, literary, and theological investigation of the writings of Scripture.

BIBLIOGRAPHY

Baird, William. *History of New Testament Research*. Vol. 2, *From Jonathan Edwards to Rudolf Bultmann*. Minneapolis: Fortress, 2003.

Bandstra, A. J. "Zahn, Theodor (1838–1933)." In *Historical Handbook of Major Biblical Interpreters*, edited by Donald K. McKim, 398–402. Downers Grove, IL: InterVarsity, 1998.

Baur, F. C. *Paul the Apostle of Jesus Christ: His Life and Work, His Epistles and His Doctrine*. Translated by A. Menzies. London: Williams & Norgate, 1875.

Bockmühl, Klaus, ed. *Die Aktualität der Theologie Adolf Schlatters*. Brunnen: Giessen, 1988.

Bultmann, Rudolf. *Theology of the New Testament. Complete in One Volume*. Translated by Kendrick Grobel. Upper Saddle River, NJ: Prentice Hall, 2007. Reprint of 2 vol., New York: Charles Scribner's Sons, 1951 and 1955.

Glick, G. Wayne. *The Reality of Christianity: A Study of Adolf von Harnack as Historian and Theologian*. New York: Harper & Row, 1967.

Harnack, Adolf von. *Das Neue Testament um das Jahr 200*. Freiburg: Mohr, 1889.

———. *Das Wesen des Christentums*. Leipzig: J. C. Hinrichs, 1902.

———. *Die Mission und Ausbreitung des Christentums in den ersten drei Jahrhunderten*. 2nd ed. 2 vols. Leipzig: J. C. Hinrichs, 1907. ET: *The Mission and Expansion of Christianity in the First Three Centuries*. Translated by James Moffatt. Harper Torchbooks Cloister Library. New York: Harper & Brothers, 1961.

———. *Marcion: Das Evangelium vom fremden Gott: Eine Monographie zur Geschichte der Grundlegung der katholischen Kirche*. 2nd ed. TU 45. Leipzig: J. C. Hinrichs, 1924. ET: *Marcion: The Gospel of the Alien God*. Translated by John E. Steely and Lyle D. Bierma. Durham, NC: Labyrinth, 1990.

———. *Outlines of the History of Dogma*. Translated by Edwin Knox Mitchell. Boston: Beacon, 1957.

———. *Reden und Aufsätze*. Vol. 4. Giessen: Ricker, 1917.

Hauck, Friedrich. "Briefe Adolf Harnacks an Theodor Zahn." *TLZ* 77 (1952) 497–502.

Johnson, W. S. "Barth, Karl (1886–1968)." In *Historical Handbook of Major Biblical Interpreters*, edited by Donald K. McKim, 433–38. Downers Grove, IL: InterVarsity, 1998.

Kantzenbach, Friedrich Wilhelm. "Adolf Harnack und Theodor Zahn." *Zeitschrift für Kirchengeschichte* 83 no. 2 (1972) 226–44.

Köstenberger, Andreas J. "The Reception of Schlatter's New Testament Theology 1909–23." In *The Theology of the Apostles*, by Adolf Schlatter, 9–22. Translated by Andreas J. Köstenberger. Grand Rapids: Baker, 1999. Reprint of "Schlatter Reception Then: His New Testament Theology." *Southern Baptist Journal of Theology* 3 no. 1 (1999) 40–51.

———. "Translator's Preface." In *The History of the Christ*, by Adolf Schlatter, 9–15. Translated by Andreas J. Köstenberger. Grand Rapids: Baker, 1997.

Kümmel, Werner Georg. *The New Testament: The History of the Investigation of Its Problems.* Translated by S. McLean Gilmour and Howard C. Kee. Nashville: Abingdon, 1972.

Merk, Otto. "Zahn, Theodor von (1838–1933)." In *Theologische Realenzyklopädie* 36:478–82. New York: Walter de Gruyter, 2004.

Morgan, Robert. *The Nature of New Testament Theology: The Contribution of William Wrede and Adolf Schlatter.* SBT 25. Naperville, IL: Alec R. Allenson, 1973.

Neill, Stephen, and Tom Wright. *The Interpretation of the New Testament 1861–1986.* 2nd ed. Oxford: Oxford University Press, 1988.

Neuer, Werner. *Adolf Schlatter: A Biography of Germany's Premier Biblical Theologian.* Translated by Robert W. Yarbrough. Grand Rapids: Baker, 1995.

———. *Adolf Schlatter: Ein Leben für Theologie und Kirche.* Stuttgart: Calwer, 1995.

Pauck, Wilhelm. *Harnack and Troeltsch: Two Historical Theologians.* New York: Oxford University Press, 1968.

Rumscheidt, H. M. "Harnack, Adolf von (1851–1930)." In *Historical Handbook of Major Biblical Interpreters*, edited by Donald K. McKim, 491–94. Downers Grove, IL: InterVarsity, 1998.

Schlatter, Adolf. *Andachten.* Stuttgart: Calwer Vereinsbuchhandlung, n.d.

———. *Das christliche Dogma.* Calw/Stuttgart: Verlag der Vereinsbuchhandlung, 1911.

———. *Der Evangelist Johannes. Wie er spricht, denkt und glaubt: Ein Kommentar zum vierten Evangelium.* 2nd ed. Stuttgart: Calwer, 1948.

———. *Der Glaube im Neuen Testament.* Leiden: E. J. Brill, 1885.

———. *Die christliche Ethik.* Stuttgart: Calwer, 1914.

———. *Die Theologie des Neuen Testaments.* Vol. 1, *Das Wort Jesu.* Stuttgart: Calwer, 1909.

———. *Die Theologie des Neuen Testaments.* Vol. 2, *Die Lehre der Apostel.* Calw/Stuttgart: Verlag der Vereinsbuchhandlung, 1910.

———. *Do We Know Jesus? Daily Insights for the Mind and Soul.* Translated by Andreas J. Köstenberger and Robert W. Yarbrough. Grand Rapids: Kregel, 2005. Translation of *Kennen wir Jesus? Ein Gang durch das Jahr im Gespräch mit Ihm.* Stuttgart: Calwer, 1937.

———. *Einführung in die Theologie*, edited by Werner Neuer. Stuttgart: Calwer, 2013.

———. *Einleitung in die Bibel.* Stuttgart: Calwer, 1889.

———. *Erläuterungen zum Neuen Testament.* 10 vols. Stuttgart: Calwer, 1961–65.

———. *The History of the Christ.* Translated by Andreas J. Köstenberger. Grand Rapids: Baker, 1997. Translation of *Die Geschichte des Christus.* 2nd ed. Stuttgart: Calwer Vereinsbuchhandlung, 1923.

Schlatter, Theodor, ed. *Adolf Schlatters Rückblick auf seine Lebensarbeit.* Gütersloh: C. Bertelsmann, 1952.

Schmid, Johann Heinrich. *Erkenntnis des geschichtlichen Christus bei Martin Kähler und bei Adolf Schlatter.* Basel: Friedrich Reinhardt, 1978.

Schnabel, Eckhard J. *Early Christian Mission.* 2 vols. Downers Grove, IL: InterVarsity, 2004.

Stuhlmacher, Peter. "Adolf Schlatter's Interpretation of Scripture." *NTS* 24 (1978) 433–46.

Swarat, Uwe. *Alte Kirche und Neues Testament: Theodor Zahn als Patristiker.* Wuppertal/Zürich: R. Brockhaus, 1991.

Tzamalikos, P[anayiotis]. *An Ancient Commentary on the Book of Revelation: A Critical Edition of the* Scholia in Apocalypsin. Cambridge: Cambridge University Press, 2013.

Yarbrough, Robert W. "Adolf Schlatter's 'The Significance of Method for Theological Work': Translation and Commentary." *Southern Baptist Journal of Theology* 1/2 (1997) 64–76.

———. "Schlatter, Adolf (1852–1938)." In *Dictionary of Major Biblical Interpreters*, edited by Donald K. McKim, 881–85. Downers Grove, IL: IVP Academic, 2007.

———. "Schlatter on the Pastorals: Mission in the Academy." In *New Testament Theology in Light of the Church's Mission*, edited by Jon C. Laansma et al., 295–316. Eugene, OR: Cascade, 2011.

Zahn, Theodor. *Altes und Neues in Vorträgen und kleineren Aufsätzen für weitere Kreise*. Leipzig: A. Deichert, 1928.

———. *The Apostles' Creed: A Sketch of Its History and an Examination of Its Contents*. Translated by C. S. Burn and A. E. Burn. London: Hodder & Stoughton, 1899.

———. *Das Evangelium des Johannes*. 5th and 6th ed. Leipzig/Erlangen: A. Deichert, 1921.

———. *Das Evangelium des Matthäus*. Wuppertal: R. Brockhaus, 1922.

———. *Einleitung in das Neue Testament*. 2 vols. Leipzig: A. Deichert, 1897, 1899. ET: *Introduction to the New Testament*. 3 vols. Edinburgh: T. & T. Clark, 1909.

———. *Forschungen zur Geschichte des neutestamentlichen Kanons und der altkirchlichen Literatur*. 9 vols. Leipzig: A. Deichert, 1881–1916.

———. *Geschichte des neutestamentlichen Kanons*. 4 vols. Erlangen/Leipzig: A. Deichert, 1888–1892.

———. "Theodor Zahn: Mein Werdegang und meine Lebensarbeit." In *Die Religionswissenschaft der Gegenwart in Selbstdarstellungen*, edited by Erich Stange, 220–48. Leipzig: Felix Meiner, 1925.

6

William Wrede and Julius Wellhausen

DIETER T. ROTH

INTRODUCTION

IN HIS IMPORTANT WORK, *The New Testament: The History of the Investigation of Its Problems*, Werner Georg Kümmel discusses Julius Wellhausen and William Wrede in a chapter titled "The Radical Historical Criticism."[1] There certainly are compelling reasons for presenting the contributions of Wellhausen and Wrede to New Testament interpretation together, though in doing so it is important to recognize both the points of contact and the significant differences in their approaches. In this chapter, after providing biographical sketches and individual discussions of Wellhausen's and Wrede's interpretive approaches, the hermeneutical methods of these two scholars are highlighted in a brief discussion of their approaches to interpreting Revelation 12. A final section on the influence of Wellhausen and Wrede concludes the discussion. The bibliography includes works cited as well as a few additional selected works on the New Testament by these men. Though Wellhausen was fifteen years Wrede's senior, Wellhausen's contributions to New Testament studies came at the conclusion of his scholarly career, and largely post-dated the work of Wrede.[2] For this reason, attention will first be given to Wrede.

WILLIAM WREDE
Biography

The son of a Lutheran pastor, Friedrich Georg Eduard William Wrede was born on May 10, 1859, at Bücken in Hannover, Germany. After his early training in humanities

---

1. Kümmel, *New Testament*, 281–88, 295–99, 301–2, 304–5.
2. In addition, because Wrede died in 1906, several of Wellhausen's New Testament works, or second editions of works, appeared after the death of Wrede.

at the Gymnasium Ernestinum in Celle, Wrede, despite "the competing proclivity for classical philology," decided to pursue theological studies.[3] He first studied in Leipzig (1877–79) under K. F. A. Kahnis, C. E. Luthardt, and F. Delitzsch, with whom he quickly became disappointed and even disillusioned to the point of considering changing his course of study.[4] He ultimately continued his theological education, and it was only because of the young Adolf Harnack and his circle of students that Wrede felt himself to have left Leipzig more firmly established in his studies.[5] From 1879 to 1880 Wrede studied in Göttingen, where Albrecht Ritschl and Hermann Schultz received specific mention of gratitude for the four semesters that Wrede considered "the most profitable and memorable of [his] studies."[6] After teaching in a private school in Lewe-Liebenburg in 1881, Wrede became a seminarian in the elite Lutheran theological institution at Locum (1882–84).[7]

In 1884 Wrede gained a tutor's post back in Göttingen where he spent the next two years.[8] It was during this time that he formed a close friendship with Albert Eichhorn, whose strict historical-critical method as opposed to Ritschl's more church-focused liberal theology would strongly influence Wrede's later academic writing.[9] After spending 1887–89 in a pastorate in Langenholzen and Hörsum, he prepared for his *Habilitation* in 1891, which he received with the thesis "Untersuchungen zum ersten Klemensbrief." During this period in Göttingen, Wrede was part of a group of young scholars who, along with the above-mentioned Albert Eichhorn, formed the core of the *religionsgeschichtliche Schule* (history-of-religions school).[10] Other

---

3. For Wrede's life up to September 3, 1884, we have Wrede's own description, which can be found in the *Vitae Hospitum Luccensium*. Wrede's entry into this register can be found in Lüdemann and Schröder, *Die religionsgeschichtliche Schule*, 106–8. The citation above is found on p. 106. Translations of German here and throughout are my own. A timeline of Wrede's life is found in ibid., 91. For additional biographical details see Strecker, "William Wrede," 67–68. Also helpful are two dictionary entries by Rollmann ("Wrede, William [1859–1906]," and "Wrede, Friedrich Georg Eduard William [1859–1906]"), though both articles contain slight errors regarding dates.

4. Wrede wrote, "Erkannte ich diese Fakultät später als eine falsch berühmte, so war ich doch zuerst ganz von ihr angethan" (Lüdemann and Schröder, *Die religionsgeschichtliche Schule*, 106).

5. Ibid., 107.

6. Ibid. The other men under whom Wrede studied during this time were Duhm, Lotze, Reuter, Schoeberlein, Wendt, and Wiesinger (see Rollmann, "*Paulus alienus*," 38).

7. Wrede passed his first theological examination in 1881.

8. Wrede passed his second theological examination at the end of this time in 1886.

9. Eichhorn, who received his *Habilitation* in Halle in 1886, was in Göttingen preparing for his *Lizentiatenexamen* due to its library (see Lüdemann, "Die religionsgeschichtliche Schule," 328). His influence on Wrede is clearly seen in the prefatory comments to *Über Aufgabe und Methode*: "In this work I have often thought with special gratitude of my friend A. Eichhorn in Halle. Though the occasion may seem to some too trivial to say it, I am still obliged to indicate that with regard to historical method I have learned most from discussion with him." The English translation is from Morgan, *Nature of New Testament Theology*, 182 n. 1. See also Rollmann, "William Wrede, Albert Eichhorn," 79–88.

10. The movement, though vitally important, cannot be discussed further here. For general discussion, in addition to Lüdemann and Schröder, *Die religionsgeschichtliche Schule*, and Lüdemann,

prominent members of this "school" included Wilhelm Bousset, Hermann Gunkel, Ernst Troeltsch, and Johannes Weiß.[11]

In 1893 Wrede accepted an appointment as *Professor extraordinarius* (associate professor) in the University of Breslau and in 1895 became *Professor ordinarius* (professor) at the same institution. It was during his time at Breslau that Wrede offered significant contributions to New Testament studies, including his three most influential works: *Über Aufgabe und Methode der sogenannten neutestamentlichen Theologie* (1897), *Das Messiasgeheimnis in den Evangelien: Zugleich ein Beitrag zum Verständnis des Markusevangeliums* (1901), and *Paulus* (1904).[12] Wrede died only eleven years after his appointment as full professor, on November 23, 1906, at the age of 47.[13]

Hermeneutical Method

As regards Wrede's contribution to New Testament interpretation, nearly all of his works contain methodological considerations; nevertheless, four works are especially important for the insights they provide into Wrede's hermeneutical method.[14] These works are here considered in chronological order.

First, though Wrede's *Habilitationsschrift* already set the stage for his later and more developed discussions of methodology,[15] his comments in the final pages of an 1896 review of Gunkel's *Schöpfung und Chaos in Urzeit und Endzeit* reveal the foun-

---

"Religionsgeschichtliche Schule," see Greßmann, *Albert Eichhorn*, 25–51; Graf, "Der 'Systematiker' der 'Kleinen Göttinger Fakultät'"; Holmström, *Das eschatologische Denken der Gegenwart*, 30–41; Klatt, *Hermann Gunkel*; Lüdemann, *Die "Religionsgeschichtliche Methode"*; Verheule, *Wilhelm Bousset*; and Weiß, *Die Aufgaben*, 48–55.

11. I have placed "school" in quotation marks not to question its existence, but rather to draw attention to the challenges involved in clearly defining it. Gunkel himself stated, "Eine seltsame 'Schule' freilich war es, die so entstand. Eine Schule ohne Lehrer und zunächst auch ohne Schüler! Es war ein durch wechselseitige Freundschaft eng verbundener Kreis junger Gelehrter, die sich in Göttingen unter Ritschls Katheder zusammengefunden hatten, deren *primus inter pares* lange Zeit der geniale Eichhorn war" ("Gedächtnisrede," 158). Rollmann observes "This school had no unified approach but shared methodological procedures and foci. Notably they were imbued with the nineteenth-century ethos for 'presuppositionless' historical-critical research and sought to exclude from theology any philosophical and theological guiding interests not directly found within the sources . . . Their major methodological contribution consisted of understanding the Bible as the product of living faith communities, which they studied with categories of a psychological or sociological kind" ("Wrede, William [1859–1906]," 396). For discussion of the differences and commonalities found within the movement, see Ittel, "Die Hauptgedanken der 'Religionsgeschichtle Schule.'" On the movement as a whole, its later developments, and its application towards the end of the twentieth century, see Müller, "Die religionsgeschichtliche Methode."

12. English translations can be found in Wrede, "Task and Methods"; Wrede, *Messianic Secret*; and Wrede, *Paul*.

13. Nearly all the leading scholars of the *Religionsgeschichtliche Schule* died at a young age: Bousset at 55, Troeltsch at 57, Heitmüller at 56, Gressmann at 50, with only Eichhorn and Gunkel living to be 70 (see Klatt, *Hermann Gunkel*, 21 n. 15).

14. For extended discussion of Wrede's critical method, see Rollmann, "Historical Methodology of William Wrede."

15. On this point see especially Rollmann, "From Baur to Wrede," 450–54.

dation upon which Wrede would construct his major discussion of hermeneutical method in the following year.[16] Here Wrede stated that the most important element of Gunkel's book, particularly for "us theologians," is the methodological component.[17] Gunkel's basic insight was that "nearly every religious notion, with which we are confronted in a particular author, has a long or short prehistory [*Vorgeschichte*]."[18] For this reason every author is only relatively free in his literary creation as there are significant restraints due to what has been passed on to him. Therefore, the task that presents itself is the pursuit of the transmission history (*Ueberlieferungsgeschichte*) of every such notion in order, ideally, to recognize its origin and the stages of its development up to the point from which one started. Only then has the religious notion become historically understandable.[19] Wrede contended that the basic problem with the literary approach current in his day was that one contented oneself prematurely and superficially with a final "literary" date of the composition, as if in this way the origin of a religious conception were explained. An immersion into Gunkel's method would reveal many overlooked problems as "our New Testament studies, at least, despite some fresh impulses, suffer from a paucity of problems."[20]

In 1897, Wrede's most important and extensive discussion of method appeared in the already-mentioned *Über Aufgabe und Methode der sogenannten neutestamentlichen Theologie*.[21] Because of its significance, I give considerable space here to describing it.[22] In the opening section Wrede indicated, "My comments presuppose the strictly historical character of New Testament theology" and as such it "has its goal in itself, and is totally indifferent to all dogma and systematic theology."[23] Vitally important for Wrede is his contention that, since the old doctrine of inspiration has been recognized to be untenable by academic theology, the necessary consequence is that "[w]here the doctrine of inspiration has been discarded, it is impossible to maintain the dogmatic conception of the canon."[24] Therefore, New Testament theology as a historical discipline insists on examining, not simply the New Testament, but the entirety of early Christian literature that historically belongs together. For Wrede, the provisional answer to the question of how much literature beyond the New Testament

---

16. Wrede, Review of *Schöpfung und Chaos*.

17. Ibid., 628.

18. Ibid.

19. See ibid.

20. Ibid., 629.

21. This work is a slightly edited version of a lecture delivered during a vacation course for clergy, April 21–23, 1897, organized by the theological faculty in Breslau (Morgan, *Nature of New Testament Theology*, 182 n. 1).

22. Strecker appropriately called the work "grundlegend" for understanding Wrede ("William Wrede," 68). Räisänen comments that it "can be regarded as the declaration of the programme of the history-of-religions school, which was just beginning" (*Beyond New Testament Theology*, 21).

23. Wrede, "Task and Methods," 69.

24. Ibid., 70.

"historically belongs together" is that it includes the Apostolic Fathers, but ends before the Apologists.[25]

In the second section of his essay, Wrede criticized the dominant method of New Testament theology, which he labeled "the method of doctrinal concepts."[26] This method is guilty of four errors in particular. First, it does considerable violence to the New Testament writers and documents in that it assumes that an author's ideas are essentially completely present in his work; however, writings like 1 and 2 Peter, Jude, or James are simply too brief to allow for the extraction of doctrinal positions. Even Hebrews and the Pauline letters contain only extracts from their world of thought. Thus, the method "continually falls prey to the danger of regarding as characteristic what in fact is not."[27] Second, the term "doctrinal concept" reveals the assumption that the New Testament contains doctrine, which is true in a certain sense but inappropriate on closer inspection. Doctrine only really exists "when thoughts and ideas are developed for the sake of teaching"; yet, "that happens only rarely in the New Testament."[28] For this reason, a doctrinal approach forces material "into a mould which does not fit the historical reality and robs it of its living colours."[29] Third, it is not every single concept that is important, but "only the historically important and typical aspects which are relevant."[30] The minute hair-splitting of a source criticism "which finds connections of thought and expression between the documents at every point and tries to establish literary influence and dependence in matters great and small" was attacked by Wrede as "an undifferentiated attention to detail which is unable to recognize, as it should, the difference between what is historically important and what is not."[31] The final error is that New Testament theology is seen as a series of individual doctrinal concepts, or of clear, little biblical theologies. The attempt is then made "to place them in chronological succession, make a few comparisons and glance at what has gone before," a procedure that Wrede viewed as completely inadequate for a truly historical presentation.[32]

---

25. See ibid., 71–73. The provisional nature of the answer was highlighted later in the work when Wrede returned to the question of the limits of the discipline of New Testament theology and stated that the answer "'The Apostolic Fathers belong to the material of the discipline, but the Apologists do not' is insufficient" and that "a *fixed literary boundary* cannot be given" (ibid., 102; here and throughout, italics are original). Wrede therefore concluded, "It can only be said that the border is where new movements in the church begin, new ideas gain momentum and the old has run its course. This moment coincides in the literature *approximately* with the transition from the Apostolic Fathers to the Apologists" (ibid., 103).

26. Ibid., 73.

27. Ibid., 74.

28. Ibid., 75.

29. Ibid., 76.

30. Ibid., 77. Wrede discusses examples from Paul and James in the following pages.

31. Ibid., 79, 81. In a note to the term "literary [i.e., source] criticism" on p. 79, Wrede makes reference to his discussion of this approach in the review of Gunkel's work (see n. 16 above).

32. Ibid., 81–82. To illustrate his point Wrede provided a scenario in which two thousand years

In section three, Wrede, against Heinrich Holtzmann's conception of New Testament theology as the task of a scientific setting forth of the religious and ethical content of the canonical writings of the New Testament, argued that the discipline "has to lay out the history of early Christian religion and theology."[33] Though the approaches may sound identical, "one approach looks closely at the content of *writings* whereas the other simply considers the *subject-matter*."[34] Thus, Wrede argued that New Testament theology should not seek for what certain writings say about certain concepts such as faith or hope; rather "we at least want to know *what was believed, thought, hoped, required and striven for* in the earliest period of Christianity."[35] In the fourth section Wrede expanded this thought in presenting his proposed method as both genetic and comparative. He stated:

> How something emerges is always to be understood as a psychological-historical question, not merely a literary one . . . Equally, we try to argue not simply from individual passages, but also on a basis of the development . . . In a sense our procedure is always constructive; i.e., we draw conclusions which extend as well as connect what the documents say . . . We can no longer pose questions simply in the light of the literary material. We must pose them as far as possible in view of the subject-matter, the historical situation.[36]

Worth noting is that, in this section, Wrede illustrated one way in which he saw external history strongly conditioning the early Christian world of ideas, with the comment, "Paul would never have formed his characteristic doctrine of justification by faith had he not taken in hand the task of converting Gentiles."[37] Thus, almost a decade before his book on Paul appeared, Wrede had already set forth the basic tenet underlying one of the most famous statements from his later work: "It [justification by faith] is the *polemical doctrine* of Paul, is only made intelligible by the struggle of his life, his controversy with Judaism and Jewish Christianity, and is only intended for this."[38]

In the fifth and final section Wrede offered some insight into aspects of how he envisioned the application of his methodology. He began this section with the

---

from his time of writing someone wanted to study the social democratic movement in the nineteenth century. By presenting the hypothetical literary remains and mentioning certain ideas found therein Wrede attempted to reveal how the method of doctrinal concepts provokes caricature.

33. Ibid., 84. For Holtzmann's view see his *Lehrbuch der neutestamentlichen Theologie*.

34. Wrede, "Task and Methods," 84.

35. Ibid.

36. Ibid., 96–98.

37. Ibid., 100. Wrede continued the thought, "The doctrine had a practical origin and practical purpose. It was not the other way round, as though the praxis were developed from a doctrine which had been created by religious thought and experience."

38. Wrede, *Paul*, 123. Wrede's discussion of Paul's doctrine of justification by faith is found on pp. 122–47. A helpful and brief summary can be found in Westerholm, *Perspectives Old and New on Paul*, 105–6.

statement, "The first main theme of New Testament theology is *Jesus' preaching*."[39] At the same time Wrede quickly pointed out, "We do not possess *ipsissima verba* of Jesus. We only know about Jesus from later accounts. In these accounts, which are all directed towards the Christ of faith, the picture of Jesus' personality and his preaching is overlaid and obscured by numerous later conceptions and interpretations."[40] Therefore, at every decisive point, that which is original and that which has come later must be distinguished. Wrede himself tackled this task in his work on the messianic secret in Mark, in which he concluded that features such as the incomprehension of the disciples and certain teachings of Jesus were not historical events in the life of Jesus, but rather reflected "a theological construct used by Mark to reconcile the primitive view of Jesus as human with the messianic view of Jesus' life and person after the resurrection."[41] This view led to the conclusion that the Gospel of Mark "belongs to the history of dogma" and "is already very far removed from the actual life of Jesus and is dominated by views of a dogmatic kind."[42]

Turning his attention from Jesus to the church, Wrede noted that there are significant difficulties in being able to present an adequate historical account of its faith and doctrine in the earliest period. He pointed out that there is considerable obscurity concerning chronology, geography, external events, and personalities.[43] At the same time, one fact, according to Wrede, is clear and immovable: "Paul is *the* epoch-making figure in the history of primitive Christianity" and, by virtue of his missionary activity making Christianity independent over against Judaism and naturalizing it on Gentile soil, is "the creator of a Christian theology."[44] This "fact" led Wrede to contend, "Paul signifies a very wide distance from Jesus, and simply cannot adequately be understood on a basis of Jesus' preaching. Nobody can write a New Testament theology as the development and continuation of Jesus' teaching. Everything in Jesus revolves around an ethical imperative born of the most exalted religious individualism. Paul's center is faith in a system of redemptive facts that took place simultaneously in heaven and on earth (incarnation, death and resurrection of Christ)."[45] Once again, Wrede adumbrates the statement in his book on Paul: "It follows then conclusively . . . that Paul is to be regarded as *the second founder of Christianity*,"[46] a sentiment that elicited strong

---

39. Wrede, "Task and Methods," 103.

40. Ibid., 104.

41. Rollmann, "Wrede, Friedrich Georg Eduard William (1859–1906)," 660.

42. Wrede, *Messianic Secret*, 131, 145. Wrede's own summary of the work can be found in his announcement of the book in Wrede, "Selbstanzeige." For further discussion of Wrede's work, reactions to it, and expansions of its theory, see especially Blevins, *Messianic Secret in Markan Research*, and Räisänen, '*Messianic Secret' in Mark*.

43. Wrede, "Task and Methods," 105.

44. Ibid., 106.

45. Ibid., 108.

46. Wrede, *Paul*, 179. Wedderburn rightly observes, "the suggestion that this man [Paul] was the 'second founder' of Christianity, as William Wrede claimed (thus, as in so many other matters, setting

reaction in the firestorm of controversy concerning Jesus and Paul that erupted in the first two decades of the twentieth century.

Although as he neared the conclusion of his presentation Wrede indicated, "This is not the place to give a programmatic sketch," he offered a series of intimations to illustrate further the type of work needed to come to a historical understanding. Included here are comments concerning the church, Judaism, and the Old Testament. Wrede stated that neither Jesus nor Paul is intelligible apart from "late Jewish theology."[47] In fact, "Judaism, not the Old Testament, is the basis of Christianity in the history of religion."[48] At the same time, however, it is important that Greco-Roman paganism not be ignored in biblical theology even if "when we are considering the mother-soil of Christianity, paganism is in a different position from Judaism."[49] Also worth mentioning is the issue of Gnosticism, which Wrede presupposed was older than Christianity and far from growing out of it was actually amalgamated into it.[50] Finally, in the light of his entire discussion, Wrede concluded, "the name New Testament theology is wrong in both of its terms."[51] The New Testament is not concerned merely with theology, but far more with religion, and the restriction to the New Testament is entirely inappropriate.[52] Wrede, therefore, suggested that the appropriate name is "early Christian history of religion, or rather: the history of early Christian

---

the agenda for the theological discussion of this century), would have far-reaching implications" (*Paul and Jesus*, 11). Of course, Wrede was not the first to problematize the relationship between Jesus and Paul (see the excellent study by Furnish, "The Jesus–Paul Debate"). A more recent bibliography can be found in Rollmann, "*Paulus alienus*," 24 n. 3. It is noteworthy that Schweitzer, though critical of numerous elements in the work, said of Wrede's *Paulus*, "Of the value and the remarkable literary beauty of the book it is impossible to say too much. It belongs, not to theology, but to the literature of the world" (*Paul and His Interpreters*, 168). Also worth consulting is Wiefel, "Zur Würdigung William Wredes," though Rollmann, "*Paulus alienus*," 33–38 is important as a corrective to Wiefel's attempt to link Wrede and Paul de Lagarde.

47. Wrede, "Task and Methods," 114. With many German scholars of his day, Wrede referred to what is more appropriately called Second Temple Judaism as late Judaism.

48. Ibid.

49. Ibid., 115.

50. Ibid., 111. Note Wrede's comment here: "I believe that the Gospel of John is to be understood in this way," which is yet another sentiment that he developed further in a later work, namely *Charakter und Tendenz des Johannesevangeliums*.

51. Wrede, "Task and Methods," 116.

52. Räisänen helpfully summarizes Wrede's view concerning the first observation: "The New Testament, and other early Christian literature, consists only to a very small degree of 'doctrine,' let alone of 'theology.' Most authors do not attempt to 'teach' their readers; their aims are of a practical nature. The New Testament is a document, not of theology, but of religion" (*Beyond New Testament Theology*, 22).

religion and theology."[53] Wrede's parting comment is that this discipline "is not yet in the true and strict sense a historical discipline at all. May it become one!"[54]

The final two essays discussed here were both originally delivered at the university in Breslau. In 1898 Wrede spoke on biblical criticism in theological studies.[55] Not surprisingly, he indicated that by "biblical criticism" he did not mean simply criticism of biblical books or traditions concerning those books, but the historical evaluation of all that the Bible contains including texts, accounts, and beliefs. It is this historical impetus, according to Wrede, that had transformed biblical studies since the Enlightenment and even in the past fifty years.[56] The beliefs of the New Testament were now considered with a view towards their development and how they were related to other beliefs current in the first century, which had served to distance the discipline from dogmatics.[57] Once again, Wrede reiterated his view that the fall of the belief in authoritative and inspired Scripture likewise meant the "fall of the boundaries, which specifically set these texts apart from others of its time."[58]

Several years later, in 1903, Wrede delivered a lecture on a related topic, namely theological studies and the history of religions.[59] Given the variety of scholars employing the term *Religionsgeschichte*, and the various ways in which the term was utilized, Wrede began by enumerating five motifs among the slightly differing approaches.[60] He stated, however, that he would consider only the first two motifs, namely a "purely historical interest in the history of religions generally" and "the derivation of early Christian thoughts and beliefs from non-Christian religions."[61] Concerning these points Wrede again emphasized the importance of Second Temple Judaism and Hellenistic backgrounds to the New Testament, though he also highlighted the way in which Gunkel, in particular, had shed light on how Eastern thought, via Second Temple Judaism, impacted early Christianity.[62] Wrede clearly considered this final element

---

53. Wrede, "Task and Methods," 116. A literal translation of Wrede's German title is "On the Task and Method of the So-called New Testament Theology." The reason for the "so-called" here becomes clear.

54. Ibid.

55. See Wrede, "Biblische Kritik."

56. Ibid., 41–42.

57. Ibid., 43–44. A few pages later Wrede argued that Dogmatics must engage historical arguments and that historical views can only be met with better historical arguments. Without such arguments, Dogmatics must accept the historical viewpoints and come to grips with them (ibid., 51). Autobiographically, Wrede mentioned that he, as a professor, was keenly aware "that, for example, in every important element of the Gospel accounts that one declares unhistorical, a piece of the soul of students, or of many, is attacked, [a piece] which looses itself only through pain and wounds" (ibid., 59–60).

58. Ibid., 48.

59. See Wrede, "Das theologische Studium."

60. Ibid., 65–67.

61. Ibid., 67.

62. Ibid., 68–69. Wrede also mentioned the contributions of Bousset, Heitmüller, Eichhorn,

significant and important, though he also recognized the challenges of positing direct derivation from one particular Eastern religion, and cautioned that one should only do so with the greatest caution.[63] Nevertheless, "in certain contexts actually existing parallels suggest themselves."[64] Not surprisingly, in Wrede's estimation such parallels (Wrede lists examples from Revelation, John, the infancy narratives, and Christology) provide important insight into New Testament texts and teaching, and indeed are vital for understanding early Christianity.[65]

JULIUS WELLHAUSEN

Biography

Julius Wellhausen was born May 17, 1844 in Hameln, Germany and, as was the case with Wrede, was the son of a Lutheran pastor.[66] He attended the Volkschule and Progymnasium in his hometown, and in 1859 went to Hannover to attend the Gymnasium there. In 1862 he began his theological studies in Göttingen, where it was not the theology of Ritschl, but rather the historical analysis of Heinrich Ewald that captured his attention.[67] Ewald taught Wellhausen to study Scripture with the same standards and methods applied to other literature, and not to become distracted in details that would hinder the ability to see history as development and thwart attempts to pursue comprehension of the whole (a *Ganzheitserfassung*).[68] Unfortunately, differing political opinions after the conquest of Hannover and Göttingen by Prussia under Bismarck in 1866 eventually led to a bitter rejection of the young Wellhausen by

---

Zimmern, and Pfleiderer (ibid., 69–70).

63. Ibid., 71. See also the comments on pp. 73–74.

64. Ibid., 71.

65. See ibid., 73–74, and the concluding comments on pp. 80–82. The second half of Wrede's address focused primarily on the issue of whether theological departments should be changed into history-of-religions departments. He interacted and disagreed with Harnack's 1901 address, in which Harnack had answered the question in the negative. On this topic see Rollmann, "Theologie und Religionsgeschichte," especially the letter from Wrede to Harnack, 79–80.

66. In a memorial address for Wellhausen by Eduard Schwartz, reprinted as "Julius Wellhausen (1918)," Schwartz recounted Wellhausen's own description of his father and childhood (329–30). On Wellhausen's life, in addition to literature cited below, see especially the contributions by Smend: "Julius Wellhausen"; *From Astruc to Zimmerli*, 91–102; "Wellhausen, Julius (1844–1918)"; and *Julius Wellhausen*. Also worth consulting are *Semeia* 25 (1982), an entire issue dedicated to Wellhausen, edited by Douglas A. Knight and titled *Julius Wellhausen and His Prolegomena to the History of Israel*; Banks, *Writing the History of Israel*, 50–75; the foreword by Knight to Wellhausen, *Prolegomena to the History of Israel*; Schwartz, "Julius Wellhausen (1918)"; and Timmer, "Julius Wellhausen," 11–21.

67. Schwartz reported Wellhausen's account that Ritschl "blieb ohne Einfluß; ich verstand seine Dogmatik nicht" and "Die theologischen Probleme verstand ich nicht. Mich interessierte Ewald und darum die Bibel" ("Julius Wellhausen [1918]" 333). On Wellhausen's time in Göttingen as a student see Smend, "Wellhausen in Göttingen," 308–15.

68. See Barnikol, "Wellhausens Briefe," 29; Schwartz, "Julius Wellhausen (1918)," 333–34; and Timmer, "Julius Wellhausen," 12–13.

his most important teacher.[69] In 1870 Wellhausen received his licentiate degree from Göttingen, where he worked as *Privatdozent* (adjunct professor) until the university in Greifswald offered him a professorship in 1872.[70]

Wellhausen was in Greifswald for ten years,[71] and it was during this time that he made the majority of his contributions to the study of the Hebrew Bible, including his most famous and controversial work that would come to be known as *Prolegomena zur Geschichte Israels*.[72] In 1882, with the controversy still raging, Wellhausen left the theological faculty, although not, as was and is often stated, directly because of the controversy. Despite the significant challenges in precisely understanding the details surrounding his resignation, it appears that Wellhausen was no longer willing or able to fulfill his responsibilities towards the church and its ministerial candidates as a theology professor.[73] After leaving Greifswald, Wellhausen became *Privatdozent* in Semitic languages at Halle, a position in the philosophy rather than the theology department. He remained within this discipline when he accepted a professorship in Marburg in 1885 and then returned to Göttingen in 1892.[74] Wellhausen completed his focus on Old Testament studies about the time he took the professorship in Marburg, where he turned his attention to Arabic and Islamic studies.[75] In 1902 Wellhausen embarked on the final stage of his scholarly career as he immersed himself in New Testament studies. He wrote "commentaries" on all four Gospels along with an introduction to

---

69. For the account see Schwartz, "Julius Wellhausen (1918)," 337, and Smend, "Wellhausen in Göttingen," 314. Smend elsewhere ("Wellhausen, Julius [1844–1918]," 630) notes that Ewald also "did not approve of the academic direction W. [Wellhausen] chose: Pentateuchal Criticism" (cf. Klatt, *Hermann Gunkel*, 47 n. 6).

70. Wellhausen's licentiate dissertation was titled *De gentibus et familiis Judaeis quae 1. Chr. 2.4. enumerantur*.

71. On this period, see especially Jepsen, "Wellhausen in Greifswald," and Smend, "Wellhausen in Greifswald."

72. The English translation of the work is titled *Prolegomena to the History of Israel* (1885). The work was written as volume 1 of a planned two-volume work to be titled *Geschichte Israels*. Though technically not published as volume two, Wellhausen's 1894 volume *Israelitische und jüdische Geschichte* completed the work. Smend notes that prior to the publication of "volume two" only Wellhausen's sketch of the history of Israel in the 9th edition (1881) of the *Encyclopaedia Britannica* and a slightly edited German version of the article in 1884 had appeared (see Smend, "Wellhausen in Göttingen," 318; see also Smend, "Wellhausen in Greifswald," 175–76). The *Encyclopaedia Britannica* article was reprinted as an appendix to the English translation of the *Prolegomena* (Knight, "Prolegomena") and also appeared as a stand-alone work titled *Sketch of the History of Israel and Judah*.

73. See the nuanced discussions in Smend, "Wellhausen in Greifswald," 167–72, and Timmer, "Julius Wellhausen," 16–17. Already in January 1873, in a letter to Lagarde, Wellhausen stated that often theological *Wissenschaft* is quite distantly related to pastoral praxis, "perhaps even in apparently hostile opposition" (cited in Smend, "Wellhausen in Greifswald," 145–46).

74. On Wellhausen's time in Göttingen as a professor, see Smend, "Wellhausen in Göttingen," 316–24.

75. A list of representative writings is most easily accessible in Knight, "Foreword." For Wellhausen's contributions to this field, see Rudolph, "Wellhausen as an Arabist."

the Synoptic Gospels, as well as analyses of Revelation and Acts.[76] Throughout the time of his work on the New Testament, Wellhausen's health was deteriorating, as since the turn of the century he had been losing his hearing and arteriosclerosis led to increasing difficulties.[77] He delivered his final lectures in the summer of 1913 and died January 7, 1918, in Göttingen.

Hermeneutical Method

The opening words to John Timmer's *Julius Wellhausen and the Synoptic Gospels: A Study in Tradition Growth* undoubtedly are correct: "The name Julius Wellhausen usually is associated with Old Testament and Arabic scholarship."[78] As the present volume focuses mostly on New Testament interpretation, the works for which Wellhausen is best known will not figure prominently in the following discussion. Also important to note is that, unlike Wrede, Wellhausen, in the words of Smend, "did not bother himself or his readers with methodological considerations."[79] Therefore, the most significant points concerning Wellhausen's hermeneutical method must be read out of the studies he provided.

Again, Timmer sets a helpful trajectory with his statement "Wellhausen must first of all be considered an historian."[80] In Wellhausen's work on the Gospels, this interest manifested itself initially in his interest in the text and language of the documents.[81]

---

76. Smend notes that Wellhausen studied the letters of Paul in the final years of his life but was never in a position to bring a work on Paul's epistles to literary completion ("Wellhausen, Julius [1844–1918]," 630). I have placed "commentaries" in quotation marks, for, as Wikgren noted, "the works on the Gospels usually referred to as 'commentaries' are hardly comprehensive enough, except perhaps in the case of Mark, to deserve that title as it is ordinarily used. Wellhausen gives place and emphasis mainly to points of particular interest to himself" ("Wellhausen on the Synoptic Gospels," 174 n. 4). Smend provides two citations from letters by Wellhausen in 1902 and 1906 where he lamented the existence of so many exegetes of the New Testament, making reference to the Arabic, saying, "Die Kamele verekeln einem die Quellen" where the German allows the word-play of camels making a spring/source revolting. Smend notes that Wellhausen helped himself in this regard in that he "largely simply ignored the commentaries" ("Wellhausen in Göttingen," 321).

77. See Smend, "Wellhausen in Göttingen," 323.

78. Timmer, "Julius Wellhausen," 11. In the *Festschrift* for Wellhausen titled *Studien zur semitischen Philologie und Religionsgeschichte*, none of the twenty-one articles deals with New Testament studies. Several decades later, an article by Irwin, "Significance of Julius Wellhausen," made no mention of Wellhausen's New Testament work. This led Wikgren to write: "The following observations are offered as a complement to this [Irwin's] treatment in the conviction that a centennial memorialization should also give adequate recognition to Wellhausen's achievements in the area of New Testament studies" ("Wellhausen on the Synoptic Gospels," 174).

79. Smend, *Julius Wellhausen*, 48. Smend here makes reference to Wellhausen's maxim: "It doesn't depend only on the glasses, but also on the eyes."

80. Timmer, "Julius Wellhausen," 13. This description of Wellhausen as a historian also appears repeatedly, in Dahl, "Wellhausen on the New Testament"; Hengel, "Einleitung," iv; and Smend, *Julius Wellhausen*. On Wellhausen's historical method in Old Testament studies, see Perlitt, *Vatke und Wellhausen*, 153–243.

81. The first two chapters of Wellhausen, *Einleitung*, are titled "Die handschriftliche Überlieferung" and "Die Sprache der Evangelien."

In this regard Dahl called him "one of the pioneers for the study of the Aramaic background of the Gospels."[82] Concerning the text of the Synoptic Gospels, Wellhausen did not use a critical edition, but compared the readings of א, A, D, and the Old Latin and Syriac versions. Worth noting is that in adjudicating between readings, Wellhausen relied strongly on internal criteria related to the exegesis or style of the individual authors. In addition one should give preference to readings with "unliterary" Greek and "especially Semitisms."[83] Further, on the issue of language, Wellhausen provided an extended philological discussion supporting his view that Mark was originally written in Aramaic.[84] In addition, he contended that some variants between Matthew and Luke in the triple tradition are best explained as misunderstandings of an Aramaic original.[85] At the same time, Wellhausen observed that Matthew and Luke improved Mark's Greek, thus apparently assuming that they had Mark's Gospel in both Aramaic and Greek.[86] Finally, Wellhausen fully embraced the Two-Source hypothesis; however, he argued that Mark not only contained the primary narrative material, but also the primary version of Jesus' sayings. Thus he controversially concluded that just as "Mark has priority for the narratives, so Mark also has it for the sayings."[87] In other words, Q is secondary.[88]

Second, Wellhausen offered his basic principle for Gospel research, particularly for his work on the fourth Gospel (though it was not unrelated to his use of the Two-Source theory in his Synoptic studies) in the opening pages of his work on John.[89] In response to F. C. Baur and the Tübingen school, which Wellhausen believed still exerted the strongest influence in Johannine studies,[90] Wellhausen argued that one

82. Dahl, "Wellhausen on the New Testament," 92.

83. Wellhausen wrote, "Die Wahl zwischen den Lesarten des Vaticanus und des Sinaiticus auf der einen, des Cantabrigiensis Bezae und der ältesten Versionen auf der anderen Seite hat sich zum Teil nach der Exegese der einzelnen Stelle zu richten oder nach der Art des einzelnen Schriftstellers . . . Nichtliterarische griechische Ausdrücke haben das Vorurteil für sich. Und namentlich Semitismen haben das Vorurteil für sich" (*Einleitung*, 6–7). See the discussion in Dahl, "Wellhausen on the New Testament," 92–93, and Wikgren, "Wellhausen on the Synoptic Gospels," 175–76.

84. See Wellhausen, *Einleitung*, 10–26. On p. 26 Wellhausen stated, "das Wahrscheinliche ist doch, daß das Evangelium, welches von Haus aus aramäisch war, zuerst auch aramäisch niedergeschrieben wurde."

85. Ibid., 26–27. Wellhausen provides several examples of this phenomenon on p. 27.

86. See ibid., 37.

87. Wellhausen, *Einleitung*, 78. Wellhausen's views were strongly criticized by Bousset, Jülicher, and Harnack. For discussion see Dahl, "Wellhausen on the New Testament," 97; Timmer, "Julius Wellhausen," 43–48, 121–24; and Wikgren, "Wellhausen on the Synoptic Gospels," 177.

88. As was the case for Mark, Wellhausen believed that Q was originally written in Aramaic. He went on to state, however, that one should not assume that Matthew and Luke had Q in both Aramaic and Greek. Rather, Greek Q existed in several recensions, in many places due to corrections based on the original Aramaic, and that differences between Q material in Matthew and Luke are due to their having different recensions of Q (*Einleitung*, 60).

89. Timmer also recognized this point (*Julius Wellhausen*, 42).

90. See Wellhausen, *Evangelium Johannis*, 3.

"may not ask what is valuable and authentic, or what is worthless and inauthentic. One may in no way at the outset construct a comprehensive viewpoint; with that one must conclude, not begin. One must rather set out from individual challenges that are revealed through exegesis and which appear in both didactic and historical sections."[91] Wellhausen concluded, "The task is not to remove inauthentic elements from the authentic whole, but to distinguish between two or more literary layers."[92] Important to recognize is the way in which Wellhausen begins with *source analysis* before engaging in *source criticism*. In other words, distinguishing between various layers in the text precedes the attempt to discern the historical value of that text.[93] Only at the end of the exegetical work and analysis may a comprehensive picture be presented.[94]

A third important methodological point was already attested early in Wellhausen's scholarly career. Jepsen recounted that in the winter semester of 1876–77, Wellhausen held a seminar on Josephus, "since it seemed important to point out that the Old Testament does not flow directly into the New Testament, but rather that a period of Judaism lies in between, the knowledge of which is of no little significance for the Old as well as the New Testament."[95] Thus, for example, when Wellhausen began working on the New Testament he argued that the developments in Jewish eschatology in post-exilic Israel were important for understanding New Testament eschatology,[96] and that basic elements in the New Testament concept of the "kingdom of God" arose out of the Old Testament and Second Temple Judaism.[97] In addition, in his *Analyse der Offenbarung Johannis*, Wellhausen argued that a John, but not the apostle John, wrote Revelation using Zealotic, Pharisaic, and Old Testament sources.[98] Interestingly, Smend points out that in the 1870s Wellhausen was one of the few theologians to see the importance of Second Temple Judaism for New Testament studies, but that it was through the *Religionsgeschichtliche Schule* that the view became common.[99]

As a final methodological consideration it remains only to mention Wellhausen's interactions with the *Religionsgeschichtliche Schule*. His often-discussed criticisms of

---

91. Ibid., 4.

92. Ibid., 5.

93. For further discussion see Dahl, "Wellhausen on the New Testament," 93.

94. True to this principle, Wellhausen's *Einleitung* appeared only after he had completed his studies on Matthew, Mark, and Luke.

95. Cited in Jepsen, "Wellhausen in Greifswald," 49, and Smend, "Wellhausen in Greifswald," 154. Wellhausen had relied heavily on the data in Josephus for his monograph *Die Pharisäer und die Sadducäer*.

96. See Wellhausen, *Einleitung*, 86–90.

97. See the discussion in Timmer, "Julius Wellhausen," 76–79.

98. See Wellhausen, *Analyse der Offenbarung Johannis*.

99. See Smend, "Wellhausen in Greifswald," 154. Lüdemann makes reference to the influence of Wellhausen's "Abriss der Geschichte Israels und Juda's" on the movement ("Die religionsgeschichtliche Schule," 343).

Gunkel's *Schöpfung und Chaos in Urzeit und Endzeit* reveal the fundamental methodological difference between Wellhausen and the movement and stand in marked contrast to Wrede's review of the work discussed above.[100] Klatt recounts an apparently oral tradition that Wellhausen referred to the work as "more chaos than creation."[101] In his written discussion of the work, despite seeing some value and helpful insights in it, his basic complaint was set forth as follows:

> The *proton pseudos* is that he [Gunkel] places significant value on the question of origins at all. It is of methodological importance to know that material is actually present in apocalypses that is not thoroughly permeated by the conceptions of the author, not always quite incorporated fully into his work,[102] and more often leaving an "obscure remainder" in our explanations; *from where*, however, that material originally derives, is methodologically irrelevant.[103]

As Klatt points out, Wellhausen's concern is the understanding of the author, not that of the materials he used.[104] The undertaking of Gunkel might have "antiquarian interest, but it is not the task of theologians and exegetes."[105] Wellhausen remained staunch in this view, even after Gunkel's response to his criticism,[106] and the aversion to the approach of the *Religionsgeschichtliche Schule* remained with Wellhausen to the end of his life.[107]

WREDE AND WELLHAUSEN ON REVELATION 12

Having considered the lives and methodological approaches of Wrede and Wellhausen, it remains to illustrate distinctive elements in their contributions to New Testament

---

100. On the dispute, see especially Klatt, *Hermann Gunkel*, 70–74, and Lüdemann and Schröder, *Die religionsgeschichtliche Schule*, 33.

101. See Klatt, *Hermann Gunkel*, 70, and his discussion of the dictum in n. 2 on the same page.

102. I have here given only the sense of the imagery used by Wellhausen of material that "in seinem [the author's] Guß nicht ganz aufgegangen ist."

103. Wellhausen, *Skizzen und Vorarbeiten*, 6:233.

104. See Klatt, *Hermann Gunkel*, 71. Wellhausen contended that the author(s) did not inquire about the original meaning, but imported, to the best of their ability, their own meaning. It is that meaning that "we must try to identify" (*Skizzen und Vorarbeiten*, 6:233).

105. Wellhausen, *Skizzen und Vorarbeiten*, 6:233.

106. See Gunkel, "Aus Wellhausens neuesten apokalyptischen Forschungen."

107. Smend, "Wellhausen in Göttingen," 324, cites a letter to Hermann in 1913 in which Wellhausen lists two theologians with whom he meets regularly, Titius and Mirbt. He found them "pleasant" and "amicable," respectively, "even though [they] compare religions." Smend notes "da haben wir Wellhausens Gegensatz zur Religionsgeschitlichen Schule." Also worth noting in Lüdemann and Schröder, *Die religionsgeschichtliche Schule*, 33, is the quotation of a section of a letter to Enno Littmann in 1915, in which a whole series of scholars in the movement are mentioned and Wellhausen states, "One must let them run riot [*austoben lassen*], the bubble will at some point burst." Schreiber, "Wellhausen und Wrede," 25, also makes reference to the dispute. This entire article is worth consulting; however, the caution by Smend not to exaggerate highly nuanced distinctions into alternatives is important to bear in mind (Smend, *Julius Wellhausen*, 47).

interpretation through an example. Since Wrede and Wellhausen are best known for their work on Mark and the way in which that work destroyed the liberal "life of Jesus" approach that largely assumed the historical reliability of Mark,[108] I will here discuss briefly a text less often mentioned in the literature, namely Revelation 12.[109] This text is particularly well suited to highlight the different historical approaches of these two scholars to the biblical text.

Wellhausen began his analysis of Revelation 12 by stating that Rev 12:7–14 describes the same vision already presented in Rev 12:1–6 and therefore is parallel to it.[110] This view is confirmed by the fact that Rev 12:15 connects equally well with Rev 12:6 and Rev 12:14 and marks the transition to the conclusion to both sections.[111] In the passage, Wellhausen viewed the dragon as the Roman Empire, the woman as Zion, and the child as the Messiah, understanding the latter two to be reflecting the Christian and not the Jewish conceptions of the terms.[112] Significantly, however, Wellhausen did not believe that the passages were originally Christian reflections on Jesus or the church; rather, the child is the fantastic (*phantastische*) Messiah of the Jews and "the vision contains Jewish prophecy throughout."[113] There are certainly Christian redactional elements in the passage,[114] and consonant with his bias towards Aramaic backgrounds, he contended that the best indicator for distinguishing the Jewish and Christian elements is the language, as the Jewish sections originally would have been written in Hebrew or Aramaic.[115] The most significant points here are that Wellhausen

---

108. Rollmann summarizes: "Wrede opposed in particular the prevailing historicization of literary data and motifs and the uncontrolled psychologizing of realia without severe controls imposed upon historical conjecture by the facts" ("William Wrede, Albert Eichhorn," 88). See also the comments by Schweitzer who, despite ultimately disagreeing with many of Wrede's conclusions, agreed with many of Wrede's objections to the liberal "Life of Jesus" models (Schweitzer, *Quest of the Historical Jesus: A Critical Study*, 328–38, and Schweitzer, *Quest of the Historical Jesus: First Complete Edition*, 303–14). Similar to Wrede's view, Wellhausen stated that "dem Evangelium Marci im Ganzen die Merkmale der eigentlichen Historie abgehn" (*Einleitung*, 43). Timmer, "Julius Wellhausen," 54–67 provides discussion of passages where Wellhausen saw a secondary tradition in Mark. Despite effecting similar results, even here, there are differences in Wrede's and Wellhausen's interpretive approaches to numerous passages (see Schreiber, "Wellhausen und Wrede," 25–36). The magnitude of some of these differences is perhaps best illustrated by the fact that Wellhausen wrote "ridiculous" (*lächerlich*) in the margin of Wrede's discussion of Mark's conception of the Messiah/Son of God in Mark 14:61 (the marginal comment can be seen in Lüdemann and Schröder, *Die religionsgeschichtliche Schule*, 32).

109. Of course, this example only serves to highlight methodological issues, for a discussion adequately representing the full extent of these two scholars' contribution to New Testament studies would extend considerably beyond the confines of this chapter.

110. Wellhausen, *Skizzen und Vorarbeiten*, 6:216.

111. Ibid., 6:217.

112. Ibid., 6:218.

113. Ibid., 6:220. Wellhausen went on to assert that it is specifically out of the circle of the Pharisees that the material in this chapter originated (ibid., 6:223).

114. Wellhausen specifically mentioned the καὶ ἐχόντων τὴν μαρτυρίαν Ἰησοῦ in v. 17 and the entirety of v. 11 (ibid., 6:224).

115. Wellhausen recognized that the opposite view, that the Christian elements consistently were

argued that the entire chapter can be understood within a Jewish framework, and that he explicitly stated that the exegete "can be content if he is able to ascertain in what sense the author himself has used his material; to go beyond that is unnecessary."[116]

Wrede, on the other hand, is much more sympathetic to the interpretive path taken by Gunkel. Though beginning with the view held by Wellhausen that Revelation 12 was a Jewish text worked into Revelation by the author of that book, Wrede continued, "but even on Jewish soil this scene is incomprehensible."[117] The vision is mythological and must originally have been an Eastern story of the gods, in which case the woman, a heavenly goddess, clothed with the sun and in birth pains is understandable. In fact, Wrede contended that parallels confirming this view exist in the Babylonian myth of Marduk, the Egyptian myth about Hathor and her son Horus, and the Greek myth about Leto and the birth of Apollos.[118] Of significant interest is that Wrede interacted with Wellhausen's comments on Revelation 12, agreeing that it is important to recognize that one is encountering these myths in Jewish or Christian contexts and that they are therefore developed beyond their original context.[119] Concerning the rest of what Wellhausen has to say, however, "His [Wellhausen's] verdict is difficult to comprehend."[120] Of course it is vital for the exegete to elucidate the meaning of the Christian author, but at the same time Wrede insisted that the exegete must also seek to explain that which is foreign and therefore not comprehensible as a creation of that author. In fact, "To explain means to place in the context of a historical development."[121] Therefore, to properly interpret Revelation 12 means much more than simply exegeting the text of a Christian author, but includes understanding it in its development out of a Jewish and ultimately Eastern mythical background.

INFLUENCE

Although the example above has highlighted similarities and differences in Wellhausen's and Wrede's hermeneutical approach to the New Testament by focusing on Revelation 12, as already mentioned, it was their work on Mark that most strongly impacted subsequent New Testament research.[122] It is often noted how their studies paved the way for form criticism in particular, but also for redaction criticism.[123] In

---

written in Greek, does not hold, and so ultimately no conclusive distinction can be made (ibid., 6:224).

116. Ibid., 6:234.

117. Wrede, "Das theologische Studium," 72.

118. Ibid.

119. Ibid., 74. This statement is marked by a typical, early-twentieth-century German view that the use of myth in other religions is simply a recasting, but its use in a "higher religion" (i.e., Judaism and then Christianity) is a further development and ennobling of the myth.

120. Ibid.

121. Ibid., 75.

122. See n. 108 above.

123. See Dahl, "Wellhausen on the New Testament," 98; Neill and Wright, *Interpretation of the New Testament*, 267–68; Schreiber, "Wellhausen and Wrede," 24; and Wikgren, "Wellhausen on the

fact, Smend points out that Wellhausen, quite in passing, supplied the term "form" for later utilizers of the method.[124] Though the impact of their work was felt in many circles, one really must go no further than the influence of these two scholars on one of the giants of early twentieth-century New Testament studies, Rudolf Bultmann, to understand the importance of Wrede and Wellhausen in New Testament interpretation.[125] Regardless of the degree to which one agrees or disagrees with the views and works of these two men, at the very least, their significance for the study of the New Testament should inspire a re-visiting and, in some ways, a rediscovery of their works.

BIBLIOGRAPHY[126]

Banks, Diane. *Writing the History of Israel*. LHBOTS. London: T. & T. Clark, 2006.

Barnikol, Ernst. "Wellhausens Briefe aus seiner Greifswalder Zeit (1872–1879) an den anderen Heinrich Ewald-Schüler Dillman." In *Gottes ist der Orient: Festschrift für Prof. D. Dr. Otto Eissfeldt DD zu seinem 70. Geburtstag am 1. September 1957*, 28–39. Berlin: Evangelische Verlagsanstalt, 1959.

Blevins, James L. *The Messianic Secret in Markan Research, 1901–1976*. Washington, DC: University Press of America, 1981.

Creed, John Martin. *The Gospel according to St Luke*. London: Macmillan, 1930.

Dahl, Nils A. "Wellhausen on the New Testament." *Semeia* 25 (1982) 89–110.

Evang, Martin. *Rudolf Bultmann in seiner Frühzeit*. BHT 74. Tübingen: Mohr Siebeck, 1988.

Furnish, Victor Paul. "The Jesus–Paul Debate: From Baur to Bultmann." *BJRL* 47 (1965) 342–81. Reprint in *Paul and Jesus: Collected Essays*, edited by A. J. M. Wedderburn, 17–50. JSNTSup 37. Sheffield: JSOT, 1989.

Graf, Friedrich Wilhelm. "Der 'Systematiker' der 'Kleinen Göttinger Fakultät': Ernst Troeltschs Promotionsthesen und ihr Göttinger Kontext." In *Troeltsch-Studien: Untersuchungen zur Biographie und Werkgeschichte*, edited by Horst Renz and Friedrich Wilhelm Graf, 235–90. Gütersloh: Gerd Mohn, 1982.

Greßmann, Hugo. *Albert Eichhorn und die religionsgeschichtliche Schule*. Göttingen: Vandenhoeck & Ruprecht, 1914.

Gunkel, Hermann. "Aus Wellhausens neuesten apokalyptischen Forschungen: Einige principielle Erörterungen." *ZWT* 7 (1899) 581–611.

———. "Gedächtnisrede auf Wilhem Bousset." *Evangelische Freiheit* n. F. 20 (1920) 141–62.

Hengel, Martin. "Einleitung." In *Evangelienkommentare: Nachdruck von "Einleitung in die ersten drei Evangelien" 2. Aufl. 1911, "Das Evangelium Matthaei" 2. Aufl. 1914, "Das Evangelium Marci" 2. Aufl. 1909, "Das Evangelium Lucae" 1 Aufl. 1904, "Das Evangelium Johannis" 1 Aufl. 1908*, v–xii. Berlin: de Gruyter, 1987.

Synoptic Gospels," 179. There certainly is some truth to the statement by Creed that in Wellhausen's work on the Gospels "are to be found the seeds of most of the more important developments of recent years" (*Gospel according to St Luke*, vii).

124. Smend, *Julius Wellhausen*, 39–40. The term appears in the first edition of Wellhausen's *Einleitung* in a note on p. 53.

125. See, for example, Evang, *Rudolf Bultmann in seiner Frühzeit*, 53, 212, and 298–99.

126. For a more extensive bibliography for Wrede, see Strecker, "William Wrede," 89–91. For Wellhausen's bibliography, including his works on the Old Testament and Arabic and Islamic Studies, see Martin, *Studien zur semitischen Philologie und Religionsgeschichte*, 353–68.

Holmström, Folke. *Das eschatologische Denken der Gegenwart: Drei Etappen der theologischen Entwicklung des zwanzigsten Jahrhunderts*. Translated by Harald Kruska. Gütersloh: C. Bertelsmann, 1936.

Holtzmann, Heinrich. *Lehrbuch der neutestamentlichen Theologie*. 2 vols. Leipzig: Mohr, 1897.

Irwin, William A. "The Significance of Julius Wellhausen." *JBR* 12 (1944) 160–73.

Ittel, Gerhard Wolfgang. "Die Hauptgedanken der 'Religionsgeschichtliche Schule.'" *ZRGG* 10 (1958) 61–78.

Jepsen, Alfred. "Wellhausen in Greifswald: Ein Beitrag zur Biographie Julius Wellhausens." In *Festschrift zur 500-Jahrfeier der Universität Greifswald, 17.10.1956*, 2:47–56. 2 vols. Greifswald: Ernst-Moritz-Arndt Universität Greifswald, 1956. (Reprinted in Alfred Jepsen, *Der Herr Ist Gott: Aufsätze zur Wissenschaft vom Alten Testament*, 254–70. Berlin: Evangelische Verlaganstalt, 1978.)

Klatt, Werner. *Hermann Gunkel: Zu seiner Theologie der Religionsgeschichte und zur Entstehung der formgeschichtlichen Methode*. FRLANT 100. Göttingen: Vandenhoeck & Ruprecht, 1969.

Knight, Douglas A., ed. "Julius Wellhausen and His Prolegomena to the History of Israel." Special issue, *Semeia* 25 (1982).

———. "Foreword." In *Prolegomena to the History of Israel: With a Reprint of the Article "Israel" from the* Encyclopaedia Britannica, by Julius Wellhausen, v–xvi. Preface by W. Robertson Smith. Atlanta: Scholars, 1994.

Kümmel, Werner Georg. *The New Testament: The History of the Investigation of Its Problems*. Translated by S. McLean Gilmour and Howard C. Kee. Nashville: Abingdon, 1972.

Lüdemann, Gerd, ed. *Die "Religionsgeschichtliche Methode": Facetten eines theologischen Umbruchs*. Studien und Texte zur religionsgeschichtliche Schule 1. Frankfurt: Peter Lang, 1996.

———. "Die religionsgeschichtliche Schule." In *Theologie in Göttingen: Eine Vorlesungsreihe*, edited by Bernd Moeller, 325–61. Göttinger Universitätsschriften 1. Göttingen: Vandenhoeck & Ruprecht, 1987.

Lüdemann, Gerd, and Martin Schröder. *Die religionsgeschichtliche Schule in Göttingen: Eine Dokumentation*. Göttingen: Vandenhoeck & Ruprecht, 1987.

Martin, Karl, ed. *Studien zur semitischen Philologie und Religionsgeschichte: Julius Wellhausen zum siebzigsten Geburtstag am 17. Mai 1914 gewidmet von Freunden und Schülern*. BZAW 27. Giessen: Alfred Töppelmann, 1914.

Morgan, Robert. *The Nature of New Testament Theology: The Contribution of William Wrede and Adolf Schlatter*. SBT 25. London: SCM, 1973.

Müller, Karlheinz. "Die religionsgeschichtliche Methode: Erwägungen zu ihrem Verständnis und zur Praxis ihrer Vollzüge an neutestamentlichen Texten." *BZ* 29 (1985) 161–92.

Neill, Stephen, and Tom Wright. *The Interpretation of the New Testament 1861–1986*. 2nd ed. Oxford: Oxford University Press, 1988.

Perlitt, Lothar. *Vatke und Wellhausen: Geschichtsphilosophische Voraussetzungen und historiographische Motive für die Darstellung der Religion und Geschichte Israels durch Wilhelm Vatke und Julius Wellhausen*. BZAW 94. Berlin: Alfred Töpelmann, 1965.

Räisänen, Heikki. *Beyond New Testament Theology: A Story and a Programme*. 2nd ed. London: SCM, 2000.

———. *The "Messianic Secret" in Mark*. Translated by Christopher Tuckett. Studies of the New Testament and Its World. Edinburgh: T. & T. Clark, 1990.

Rollmann, Hans. "From Baur to Wrede: The Quest for a Historical Method." *SR* 17 (1988) 443–54.

———. "The Historical Methodology of William Wrede." Unpublished PhD diss., McMaster University, 1980.

———. "*Paulus alienus*: William Wrede on Comparing Jesus and Paul." In *From Jesus to Paul: Studies in Honour of Francis Wright Beare*, edited by Peter Richardson and John C. Hurd, 23–45. Waterloo, ON: Wilfrid Laurier University Press, 1984.

———. "Theologie und Religionsgeschichte: Zeitgenössische Stimmen zur Diskussion um die religionsgeschichtliche Methode und die Einführung religionsgeschichtlicher Lehrstühle in den theologischen Fakultäten um die Jahrhundertwende." *ZTK* 80 (1983) 69–84.

———. "William Wrede, Albert Eichhorn, and the 'Old Quest' of the Historical Jesus." In *Self-Definition and Self-Discovery in Early Christianity: A Study in Changing Horizons: Essays in Appreciation of Ben F. Meyer from Former Students*, edited by David J. Hawkin and Tom Robinson, 79–99. Studies in the Bible and Early Christianity 26. Lewiston, NY: Edwin Mellen, 1990.

———. "Wrede, Friedrich Georg Eduard William (1859–1906)." In *Dictionary of Biblical Interpretation*, edited by John H. Hayes, 2:659–60. 2 vols. Nashville: Abingdon, 1999.

———. "Wrede, William (1859–1906)." In *Historical Handbook of Major Biblical Interpreters*, edited by Donald K. McKim, 394–98. Downers Grove, IL: InterVarsity, 1998.

Rudolph, Kurt. "Wellhausen as an Arabist." *Semeia* 25 (1982) 111–55.

Schreiber, Johannes. "Wellhausen und Wrede: Eine methodische Differenz." *ZNW* 80 (1989) 24–41.

Schwartz, Eduard. "Julius Wellhausen (1918)." In *Gesammelte Schriften*. Vol. 1, *Vergangene Gegenwärtigkeiten*, 326–61. 2nd ed. Berlin: de Gruyter, 1963.

Schweitzer, Albert. *Paul and His Interpreters: A Critical History*. Translated by W. Montgomery. London: Adam & Charles Black, 1912.

———. *The Quest of the Historical Jesus: A Critical Study of Its Progress from Reimarus to Wrede*. Translated by W. Montgomery with a preface by F. C. Burkitt. London: Adam & Charles Black, 1926.

———. *The Quest of the Historical Jesus: First Complete Edition*, edited by John Bowden with a preface by Dennis Nineham. London: SCM, 2000.

Smend, Rudolf. *From Astruc to Zimmerli: Old Testament Scholarship in Three Centuries*. Translated by Margaret Kohl. Tübingen: Mohr Siebeck, 2007.

———. "Julius Wellhausen." In *Theologen des Protestantismus im 19. und 20. Jahrhundert*, edited by Martin Greschat, 1:166–80. 2 vols. Urban Taschenbücher 284, 285. Stuttgart: Kohlhammer, 1978. Reprint in Rudolf Smend, *Deutsche Alttestamentler in drei Jahrhunderten*, 99–113. Göttingen: Vandenhoeck & Ruprecht, 1989.

———. *Julius Wellhausen: Ein Bahnbrecher in drei Disziplinen*. Themen 84. Munich: Carl Friedrich von Siemens Stiftung, 2006.

———. "Wellhausen in Göttingen." In *Theologie in Göttingen: Eine Vorlesungsreihe*, edited by Bernd Moeller, 306–24. Göttinger Universitätsschriften 1. Göttingen: Vandenhoeck & Ruprecht, 1987.

———. "Wellhausen in Greifswald." *ZTK* 78 (1981) 141–76.

———. "Wellhausen, Julius (1844–1918)." In *Dictionary of Biblical Interpretation*, edited by John H. Hayes, 2:629–31. 2 vols. Nashville: Abingdon, 1999.

Strecker, Georg. "William Wrede: Zur hundertsten Wiederkehr seines Geburtstags." *ZTK* 57 (1960) 67–91.

Timmer, John. "Julius Wellhausen and the Synoptic Gospels: A Study in Tradition Growth." Unpublished PhD diss., Free University of Amsterdam, 1970.

Verheule, Anthonie F. *Wilhelm Bousset: Leben und Werk: Ein theologischer Versuch.* Amsterdam: Ton Bolland, 1973.

Wedderburn, A. J. M. ed. *Paul and Jesus: Collected Essays.* JSNTSup 37. Sheffield: JSOT, 1989.

Weiß, Johannes. *Die Aufgaben der neutestamentlichen Wissenschaft in der Gegenwart.* Göttingen: Vandenhoeck & Ruprecht, 1908.

Wellhausen, Julius. "Abriss der Geschichte Israels und Juda's." In *Skizzen und Vorarbeiten*, 1:3–102. 6 vols. Berlin: Georg Reimer, 1884–99.

———. *Analyse der Offenbarung Johannis.* Abhandlungen der königlichen Gesellschaft der Wissenschaften zu Göttingen 9. Berlin: Weidmann, 1907.

———. *Das Evangelium Johannis.* Berlin: Georg Reimer, 1908.

———. *Das Evangelium Lucae.* Berlin: Georg Reimer, 1904.

———. *Das Evangelium Marci.* 2nd ed. Berlin: Georg Reimer, 1909.

———. *Das Evangelium Matthaei.* Berlin: Georg Reimer, 1904.

———. *De gentibus et familiis Judaeis quae 1. Chr. 2.4. enumerantur.* Licentiate diss., Göttingen, 1870.

———. *Die Pharisäer und die Sadducäer: Eine Untersuchung zur inneren jüdischen Geschichte.* Greifswald: Bamberg, 1874.

———. *Einleitung in die drei ersten Evangelien.* 2nd ed. Berlin: Georg Reimer, 1911.

———. *Erweiterungen und Änderungen im vierten Evangelium.* Berlin: Georg Reimer, 1907.

———. *Evangelienkommentare: Nachdruck von "Einleitung in die ersten drei Evangelien" 2. Aufl. 1911, "Das Evangelium Matthaei" 2. Aufl. 1914, "Das Evangelium Marci" 2. Aufl. 1909, "Das Evangelium Lucae" 1 Aufl. 1904, "Das Evangelium Johannis" 1 Aufl. 1908.* With an introduction by Martin Hengel. Berlin: de Gruyter, 1987.

———. *Israelitische und jüdische Geschichte.* Berlin: Georg Reimer, 1894.

———. *Kritische Analyse der Apostelgeschichte.* Berlin: Weidmann, 1914.

———. *Prolegomena to the History of Israel.* Translated by J. Sutherland Black and Allan Menzies with a preface by W. Robertson Smith. London: Adam & Charles Black, 1885.

———. *Prolegomena zur Geschichte Israels.* Berlin: Georg Reimer, 1878.

———. *Sketch of the History of Israel and Judah.* London: Adam & Charles Black, 1891. Reprint from "Israel." In *Encyclopaedia Britannica*, 13:396–431. 9th ed., 1881.

———. *Skizzen und Vorarbeiten.* 6 vols. Berlin: Georg Reimer, 1884–99.

Westerholm, Stephen. *Perspectives Old and New on Paul: The "Lutheran" Paul and His Critics.* Grand Rapids: Eerdmans, 2004.

Wiefel, Wolfgang. "Zur Würdigung William Wredes." *ZRGG* 23 (1971) 60–83.

Wikgren, Allen. "Wellhausen on the Synoptic Gospels: A Centenary Appraisal." *JBR* 12 (1944) 174–80.

Wrede, William. "Biblische Kritik." In *Vorträge und Studien*, by William Wrede, 40–63. Tübingen: Mohr Siebeck, 1907.

———. *Charakter und Tendenz des Johannesevangeliums.* Sammlung gemeinverständlicher Vorträge und Schriften aus dem Gebiet der Theologie und Religionsgeschichte 37. Tübingen: Mohr Siebeck, 1903. Reprinted in *Vorträge und Studien*, 179–231. Tübingen: Mohr Siebeck, 1907.

———. *Das literarische Rätsel des Hebräerbriefes: Mit einem Anhang über den literarischen Charakter des Barnabasbriefes*. FRLANT 8. Göttingen: Vandenhoeck & Ruprecht, 1906.

———. *Das Messiasgeheimnis in den Evangelien: Zugleich ein Beitrag zum Verständnis des Markusevangeliums*. Göttingen: Vandenhoeck & Ruprecht, 1901.

———. "Das theologische Studium und die Religionsgeschichte." In *Vorträge und Studien*, 64–83. Tübingen: Mohr Siebeck, 1907.

———. *Die Echtheit des zweiten Thessalonicherbriefes*. TUGAL 24. Leipzig: J. C. Hinrichs, 1903.

———. *Die Entstehung der Schriften des Neuen Testaments: Vorträge*. Tübingen: Mohr Siebeck, 1907.

———. *The Messianic Secret*. Translated by J. C. G. Greig. Cambridge: James Clarke, 1971.

———. *The Origin of the New Testament*. Translated by J. S. Hill. Harper's Library of Living Thought. London: Harper & Brothers, 1909

———. *Paul*. Translated by Edward Lummis with a preface by J. Estlin Carpenter. London: Philip Green, 1907.

———. *Paulus*. RGV Religionsgeschichtliche Volksbücher für die deutsche christliche Gegenwart. Halle: Gebauer-Schwetske, 1904. 2nd ed. Tübingen: Mohr Siebeck, 1907.

———. Review of *Schöpfung und Chaos in Urzeit und Endzeit*, by Hermann Gunkel. *TLZ* 24 (1896) 623–31.

———. "Selbstanzeige: Das Messiasgeheimnis in den Evangelien." *Die Christliche Welt* 15 (1901) 805–6.

———. "The Task and Methods of 'New Testament Theology.'" In *The Nature of New Testament Theology: The Contribution of William Wrede and Adolf Schlatter*, edited and translated by Robert Morgan, 68–116. SBT 25. London: SCM, 1973.

———. *Über Aufgabe und Methode der sogenannten neutestamentlichen Theologie*. Göttingen: Vandenhoeck & Ruprecht, 1897.

———. *Untersuchungen zum ersten Klemensbrief*. Göttingen: Vandenhoeck & Ruprecht, 1891.

7

Albert Schweitzer

A Jewish-Apocalyptic Approach to Christian Origins

ANDREW W. PITTS

ALBERT SCHWEITZER WAS THE prototypical renaissance man. Born on January 14, 1875, into an Alsatian family, Schweitzer had a strong religious heritage, with his father and grandfather both serving as Lutheran pastors. Reumann describes the context for his upbringing as that of "rural Evangelical piety and Protestant liberalism."[1] His family was also quite musical, and Schweitzer began his career as an accomplished concert pianist and organist from an early age, eventually writing significant works on musical theory and exhibiting a special fascination with Bach.[2] He earned his first doctorate in philosophy in 1899 from the University of Strassburg, at the age of 24, and began a preaching ministry at St. Nicholas Church in Strassburg during the same year. In 1900, he received his licentiate in theology, and in 1901 published his dissertation on Immanuel Kant and his first two major pieces of New Testament research, two volumes of a proposed three-volume set on the Lord's Supper—the third volume was never completed.[3] He served in a number of administrative positions in the Theological College of Saint Thomas at the University of Strassburg from 1901 to 1912, having decided to pursue a theological rather than a philosophical teaching career. During this time, he published the first edition of his famous *Quest*, under the title *From Reimarus to Wrede* (*Von Reimarus zu Wrede*).[4] In 1911, he extended his project to the Apostle Paul, assessing the history of Pauline research from the

---

1. Reumann, "Introduction," 4.
2. On Schweitzer's musical accomplishments, see Joy, *Music*.
3. Schweitzer, *Kritische Darstellung*; Schweitzer, *Problem*; Schweitzer, *Das Messianitäts- und Leidensgeheimnis*, 195–340 (ET: Schweitzer, *Mystery*).
4. The translation of *Quest* used in this chapter is the one in the bibliography.

Reformation to his own time.[5] Research on Paul was resumed later, in 1930, with a full scale analysis of the role of eschatology in Paul's thinking.[6] Although Schweitzer had said in 1911 that he would have the manuscript on this topic ready for the press "within a few weeks," his departure for Africa caused the project to be delayed.[7]

Schweitzer had decided to become a medical missionary to Africa, so he attained an MD in 1913 from the University of Strassburg, writing as his dissertation for that degree *The Psychiatric Study of Jesus*, a book arguing for the sanity of Jesus.[8] He and his wife moved to French Equatorial Africa to start his famous hospital at Lambaréné, in what is now Gabon. However, in 1917 they were sent to a French internment camp as prisoners of war for a year. After traveling Europe, lecturing and writing on music, medicine, philosophy, ethics, and theology, Schweitzer returned to Lambaréné in 1924. He spent the remainder of his life there, managing and working in his hospital while pastoring a congregation, but did occasionally travel to Europe and the United States after the end of the Second World War. In 1953 he was awarded the Nobel Peace Prize and with his $33,000 prize money he started a leprosarium at Lambaréné. After his death, in 1965, Schweitzer's daughter found a manuscript tucked away in a white linen bag. The book that this bag contained was the last of Schweitzer's works to be published. Although not in the final form that Schweitzer had in mind, it was a fitting posthumous summary of his work, geared toward a more popular audience, under the title *The Kingdom of God and Primitive Christianity*.[9]

There have been numerous studies of Schweitzer's impact upon Jesus research, for the most part portraying him as the leading figure in what has come to be considered a significant paradigm shift in the study of the historical Jesus—whether his work genuinely represents such a shift is another question, which will be addressed below.[10] Although significantly fewer scholars have sought to assess Schweitzer's contribution to Pauline studies—his research on Paul usually fading into the shadows cast by his

---

5. Schweitzer, *Geschichte* (ET: Schweitzer, *Paul*).
6. Schweitzer, *Die Mystik* (ET: Schweitzer, *Mysticism*).
7. Schweitzer, *Out of My Life*, 141–50.
8. Schweitzer, *Die psychiatrische Beurteilung Jesu* (ET: Schweitzer, *Psychiatric Study of Jesus*).
9. Schweitzer, *Reich Gottes*, 511–731 (ET: Schweitzer, *Kingdom of God*).
10. Studies on Schweitzer's contribution to the study of the historical Jesus include, for example, Bowman, "From Schweitzer to Bultmann"; Wilder, "Albert Schweitzer"; Kümmel, "Die 'Konsequente Eschatologie'"; J. M. Robinson, "Introduction"; Nicol, "Schweitzer's Jesus"; Barrett, "Albert Schweitzer"; Davies, "From Schweitzer to Scholem"; Dungan, "Albert Schweitzer's Disillusionment"; Glasson, "Schweitzer's Influence"; Nineham, "Schweitzer Revisited"; Reumann, "Problem"; Willis, "Discovery"; Pleitner, *Das Ende*; Morgan, "From Reimarus to Sanders"; Allison, "Plea"; Schmidt, "Sane Eschatology"; Weaver, *Historical Jesus*, 25–34, 62–69, 79–81; Gathercole, "Critical and Dogmatic Agenda." Standard introductions that focus more on Schweitzer's Jesus research include Neill and Wright, *Interpretation*, 205–15, and Kümmel, *New Testament*, 235–44.

massive tome on Jesus[11]—this area has not been entirely neglected.[12] Only rarely, however, does one find article- or chapter-length attempts to understand Schweitzer's project as a whole, at least in English-language scholarship.[13]

For Schweitzer, Jewish eschatology provided the key to many of the mysteries of the New Testament and should be understood as the central phenomenon that explains the emergence of primitive Christianity, a "clue" he discovered very early (in 1894) while on assigned army maneuvers.[14] This discovery, which Schweitzer happened upon in the oddest of places, would set the trajectory for the rest of his academic career. Therefore, the central role of eschatology (or what we might call today apocalyptic)[15] in the thinking and writing of Christianity's two key founders—Jesus

---

11. Indicative of this fact is Fulton's excellent well-balanced treatment of Schweitzer, indeed, one of the very best within Schweitzer's time, that devoted great energies to expounding Schweitzer's understanding of Paul (Fulton, "Life"). At first, Fulton was tempted to focus exclusively upon Paul. He says: "When I was honoured with the invitation to give the Opening Address, my first idea was to offer an account and estimate of Dr. Albert Schweitzer's book on the Mysticism of Paul the Apostle. It was published in Germany in 1930, and has recently appeared in an English translation. But I decided, on second thoughts, not to venture upon so vexed a problem as the sources of St. Paul's religious creed. There was the danger of finding myself vainly struggling in the pitfalls of the Jewish Eschatology or blindly wrestling with the obscurities of the Greek Mystery Religions. So I said, Why not speak on Schweitzer's life and work as a whole, appending an account of his book on the Pauline mysticism? For has he not captured the imagination of Christendom as no other New Testament scholar has done?" (ibid., 354). Had he done as he originally intended, it would have been one of the few abiding studies of Schweitzer's Pauline theology. Fulton had the advantage of writing on Schweitzer in the period before his work on Jesus had been given time to have its full impact. It was not yet casting great shadows over his thinking on Paul.

12. Studies on Schweitzer's contribution to Pauline studies include, especially, Matlock, *Unveiling*, 23–71; Wilckens, "Die Bekehrung"; Kümmel, "Albert Schweitzer als Paulusforscher"; Groos, *Albert Schweitzer*, 313–73; Thiselton, "Biblical Classics: VI"; Grässer, *Albert Schweitzer*, 155–205; Neill and Wright, *Interpretation*, 403–10. Significant engagement with Schweitzer's interpretation of Paul is also found in Sanders, *Paul*, and Westerholm, *Israel's Law*; cf. also Pitts, "Unity and Diversity." But as Thiselton notes, Schweitzer's work on Paul has been largely (if not entirely) neglected, especially when compared to his work on the Gospels. Concerning his book on Paul's mysticism, he says: "this book is all too often overshadowed by the impact of Schweitzer's earlier volume *The Quest of the Historical Jesus*. Thus in his survey of the history of New Testament studies W. G. Kümmel devotes over six pages and numerous scattered references to Schweitzer's work on the gospels, two pages to *Paul and his Interpreters*, but only a few lines to *The Mysticism of Paul the Apostle*. Stephen Neill includes a special section on Schweitzer in his own survey, but both this section and his other allusions to Schweitzer concern only Schweitzer's work on the gospels. In a whole book devoted entirely to Schweitzer's theology E. N. Mozley includes only six pages of his work on Paul. Yet Seaver insists, and with some justice, '*The Mysticism of Paul the Apostle* is a greater work than *The Quest of the Historical Jesus*—greater in scope, greater in depth, greater in erudition, and much greater in originality'" (Thiselton, "Biblical Classics: VI," 132). Thiselton attempts to provide a much needed corrective to this, but his article is quite brief, only quickly outlining the contents of Schweitzer's two volumes on Paul.

13. But cf. Fulton, "Life," and Baird, *History*, who both provide well-balanced treatments. In German language scholarship such a treatment is provided in Kümmel, "Albert Schweitzer als Jesus-Paulusforscher," and Grässer, *Albert Schweitzer*.

14. Schweitzer, *Out of My Life*, 17–20.

15. Since Bultmann, there has been a tendency to distinguish between eschatological and apocalyptic literature. On terminology, including relevant bibliography, see Gager, "Functional Diversity."

and Paul—is explored below. Since Schweitzer intended to assess the development of the later New Testament literature from the standpoint of his eschatological scheme, but died before he got a chance to seriously pursue it, I then make some tentative suggestions toward what this kind of analysis might have looked like in an attempt to provide a more holistic perspective on Schweitzer's eschatological project in relation to the study of Christian origins.[16]

SCHWEITZER'S APOCALYPTIC JESUS

Schweitzer's apocalyptic approach to understanding the historical Jesus was initially laid out in the first volume of his study on the Lord's Supper, and thoroughly developed in the second volume *The Mystery of the Kingdom of God* (hereafter, *Mystery*), but his ideas in these two works were hardly noticed by his contemporaries—even his *The Quest of the Historical Jesus* (hereafter, *Quest*) was received with negative or, at best, indifferent response in Germany.[17] He faulted earlier approaches for their

---

Gager proposes that such distinctions are unhelpful for assessing function, in any case, when assessing the relevant imagery and terminology as opposed to content. He prefers instead the more general notion of "end-time language" as a suitable category for analyzing the function of Paul's end-time statements. Neill notes: "It is unfortunate that Schweitzer chose the word 'eschatology' in this new and unfamiliar sense. 'Eschatology' is that which has to do with the last things; and traditionally the last things are death, resurrection, judgment, and eternal life. For the sudden intervention of God in the affairs of the world to put all things right and to bring history to an end, there is the appropriate word 'apocalyptic,' and it is this word that Schweitzer should have used" (Neill, in Neill and Wright, *Interpretation*, 210).

16. An interesting attempt to examine the first several centuries according to Schweitzer's apocalyptic thesis is Werner, *Formation*.

17. Weaver provides a helpful summary of the immediate response to Schweitzer's early work, especially the relevant book reviews. He summarizes the general mood of the scholarly response to Schweitzer: "It was a polemical rather than analytical response, something like a wounded cat striking back . . . The lukewarm, even hostile reception accorded Schweitzer is understandable. He had trampled all over the fondest flowers of the liberals, quite deliberately at that, and they would not return his deed with thanks" (Weaver, *Historical Jesus*, 33–34). Lowrie, in the introduction to his translation of Schweitzer's *Mystery*, makes similar observations. He notes that Schweitzer's German colleagues appreciated his critical analysis of eighteenth- and nineteenth-century Jesus scholarship. "Schweitzer's own view, however, though it was presented clearly in this volume, was still not taken due account of in Germany . . . The translator knows of no prominent scholar in Germany who has cordially welcomed Schweitzer's view, nor of any that has thoroughly and ably opposed it. They have been occupied there rather with Wrede's acute criticism of the messianic element in the Gospels and with the denial by Drews and others of the historical existence of Jesus" (Lowrie, "Introduction," 19–20). Both authors, however, note a much warmer reception later in England, primarily due to the frontal assault on liberalism that Schweitzer issued within the volume. English scholars saw in Schweitzer's work a platform for defending traditional orthodoxy and for attacking liberal scholarship. Koch attributes the general neglect of Schweitzer's work in Germany to a preoccupation there with history-of-religion methodologies (Koch, *Rediscovery*, 57–59). However, while this was certainly part of the picture, Schweitzer's German colleagues were undoubtedly in no hurry to jump on board with his criticism of virtually their entire heritage, at least in terms of Gospel research. For a convenient survey of the role of apocalyptic in New Testament research, evidencing Schweitzer's influence in many ways, see Rollins, "New Testament." Frequent use of apocalyptic categories in New Testament studies later led to detailed considerations of the genre of apocalyptic, as we see in *Semeia* 14.

tendencies to dismiss eschatology or to explain it through recourse to Jesus' psychological development.[18] He suggested in their place an eschatologically driven messiah whose ethics were framed by the approaching kingdom.

After sending out the disciples and receiving them back with testimonies of great power, Jesus "expects the dawn of the Kingdom in the most immediate future," although he clearly expected the eschatological kingdom to be ushered in while his disciples were away.[19] But the "Kingdom which Jesus expected so very soon failed to make its appearance."[20] Confused by this, Jesus reconsidered the Scriptures, especially Isaiah, and discovered that the Elect One must suffer and be condemned in order for the eschaton to be brought in. So Jesus attempted to force God's hand by going to Jerusalem, where he died and his hopes of initiating the eschaton did not materialize.

In the first edition of *Quest*, Schweitzer, on the one hand, sought to substantiate these conclusions by demonstrating that scholarship's rejection of previous eschatological pictures of Jesus was to its detriment, often forcing critics to deny (in his view, unnecessarily) the historicity of the Gospels, and on the other hand, he wished to clear the ground for future historical Jesus research. Although the first edition is more polemic, its agenda is not entirely negative. Schweitzer states his intentions for the book in the preface to the first edition: "I hope that it will be a stimulus which will not cause offense, but lead to new and independent thought and research."[21] Therefore, we should not accept the common assumption that Schweitzer intended to show the impossibility of Jesus research or that he sought to bring it to a stop—he clearly saw the legitimacy of the enterprise, having already entered the discussion himself in *Mystery* and having contrasted his *Mystery* with Wrede's work in *Quest*.

Schweitzer's intention to present a positive portrait of Jesus is reinforced in the second edition of *Quest*, which is masterfully structured and argued. The more constructive nature of the project of the new volume is reflected in the title change (from *From Reimarus to Wrede* to *The Quest of the Historical Jesus*) so as to reflect an investigation of the historical Jesus himself rather than a mere assessment of previous research—part of this was apparently motivated by criticisms that the first edition had an agenda of its own that escaped the strict purviews of modernist history.[22] In this book, Schweitzer carefully and critically weaves his way through the landscape of

---

18. Schweitzer, *Mystery*, 85.
19. Ibid., 261.
20. Ibid., 264.
21. Schweitzer, *Quest*, xxxiv.
22. In the preface to the second edition, Schweitzer responds with remarks that seem a bit beyond his time: "This work has been criticized in some quarters for being more than a history of research into Jesus and offering a particular view. Against this it may be observed that no one can write the history of a problem and the attempts made so far to resolve it who does not himself adopt a particular attitude to the questions. It is also argued that this book also goes beyond its title in bringing questions about the philosophy of religion connected with the historical problem into its sphere of interest and here too putting forward views of its own" (ibid., xxxiv).

nineteenth-century Jesus scholarship, highlighting key places where an eschatological framework would have helped, until he finally approaches Wrede, who provides the platform and dialogue partner for the introduction of Schweitzer's thoroughgoing eschatology. The major criticism that Schweitzer has of earlier interpreters is that their philosophically based methods have caused them to read their own worldview into that of Jesus. He states, "Whatever the definitive solution may be, the historical Jesus whom research will depict, on the basis of the problems which have been recognized and admitted, can never render modern theology the services which it claimed from its own semi-historical, semi-modern Jesus."[23] What he said about Schleiermacher is representative of his assessment of nineteenth-century interpreters of the life of Jesus: "Schleiermacher is not in search of the Jesus of history, but of the Jesus Christ of his own system of theology; that is to say, of the historical figure which seems to him appropriate to the self-awareness of the Redeemer as he represents it."[24] The problem was that the methods being used were not designed to situate Jesus within his own Jewish-eschatological context, but reflected the various romantic, liberal, rationalistic methodologies out of which they were conceived. Schweitzer probably would have perceived it as unfair, therefore, as it is common to do, to accuse him of falling into the same trap.[25] For Schweitzer, one major reason that the various lives of Jesus that he examined reflected the lives of their authors more than the life of the historical Jesus was that their methods were not tailored to Jesus' Jewish eschatology, and no one can accuse Schweitzer of not having an eschatologically driven method. The new edition added chapters on the nonhistorical Jesus, harshly criticizing advocates of a fictitious Jesus, and suggesting that an eschatological Jesus makes nonhistorical proposals obsolete.

A number of key German influences and interpreters helped Schweitzer in the development of his thinking, particularly H. S. Reimarus.[26] Schweitzer traced Weiss's influence back to Reimarus, stating: "Every sentence of Johannes Weiss's *Jesus' Proclamation of the Kingdom of God* (1892) is a vindication, a rehabilitation, of Reimarus as a historical thinker."[27] He regarded Reimarus as truly revolutionary and ahead of his time, insisting that:

> Reimarus was the first, after eighteen centuries of misconception, again to have an inkling of what eschatology really was. Then theology lost sight of it

---

23. Ibid., 478.

24. Ibid., 60.

25. E.g. Weaver, *Historical Jesus*, 38. Dunn's remarks to this effect are typical, when he says: "Schweitzer's critique of his predecessors at times was devastating, but his own attempts at reconstruction were highly vulnerable to an equivalent critique" (Dunn, "Introduction [to Part I]," 4). Again, Schweitzer's psychological critique often referred to methods that were more connected with modern philosophy and theology than with first-century Jewish apocalyptic.

26. Reimarus, *Von dem Zwecke Jesu*.

27. Schweitzer, *Quest*, 23.

again, and it was not until after the lapse of more than a hundred years that it came in view of eschatology once more, now in its true form, so far as that can be historically determined.[28]

Three entire chapters of the *Quest* are devoted to Strauss, in whose first life of Jesus (1835) Schweitzer saw remarkable value, although he was clearly not impressed with Strauss's second attempt (1865).[29] His word of commendation for the first volume must have been at least a slightly exaggerated expression of Schweitzer's opinion of the book for the purpose of the strong contrast that he desired to create with the later work: "Considered as a literary work, Strauss's first Life of Jesus is one of the most perfect things in the whole range of learned literature."[30] Strauss's impact was estimated by Schweitzer with his typical wit: in addition to its mythological explanations

> we find also in it a positive historical aspect, inasmuch as the historical personality which emerges from the mist of myth is a Jew claimant to the messiahship whose world of thought is purely eschatological. Strauss is no mere destroyer of untenable solutions, but also the prophet of a coming advance in knowledge.[31]

Schweitzer apparently understood Strauss's view to be a true "advance in knowledge." But immediately after commending Strauss for his prophetic function, he sharply criticized him for reverting back to the Jesus of liberal theology in his later 1865 publication on the issue, moving away from his earlier eschatological emphases. Therefore, according to Schweitzer, it was Strauss's "own fault that his success and merit was not recognized in the nineteenth century."[32] As he continued to plow his way through the psychologizing efforts of nineteenth-century Jesus scholars, evaluations like what he said of Christian Weisse are typical: "Weisse's psychology requires only one correction—the insertion into it of the eschatological premise."[33]

When Schweitzer finally arrived at Weiss, one of his most significant influences, he exclaimed: "In passing from Weiffenbach and Baldensperger to Johannes Weiss the reader feels like an explorer who after weary wanderings through billowy seas of reed-grass at length reaches a wooded tract, and instead of swamp feels firm ground

28. Ibid.
29. Strauss, *Das Leben Jesu* (ET: Strauss, *Life of Jesus, Critically Examined*).
30. Schweitzer, *Quest*, 74.
31. Ibid., 95.
32. Ibid., 90.
33. Ibid., 118. Another of numerous examples of this kind of polemic is found in Schweitzer's assessment of Weiffenbach, of whom he says: "From a technical perspective, the mistake on which Weiffenbach's investigation made shipwreck was the failure to bring the Jewish apocalyptic material into relation with the Synoptic data. Had he done this, it would have been impossible for him to extract an unreal and unhistorical conception of the second coming out of the discourse of Jesus" (ibid., 197). Similarly, "Weiffenbach had failed to solve the problem of the second coming, Baldensperger that of the messianic consciousness of Jesus, because both of them allowed a fake conception of the kingdom of God to keep its place among the data" (ibid., 199).

beneath his feet."[34] According to Schweitzer, while Strauss set up the first either/or (either purely historical or purely supernatural), and Holtzmann and the Tübingen school laid down the second (either Synoptic or Johannine), it was Weiss's *The Proclamation of the Kingdom of God* that presented the third: "either eschatological or non-eschatological!"[35] The response to Weiss, represented mainly by Bousset,[36] involved the claim that the eschatology inherited by Jesus from first-century Judaism was a "spiritualized" eschatology, not a real expectation of the coming kingdom, which should be understood as being presently fulfilled in Jesus.[37] After summarizing the state of play at the end of the nineteenth century, characterized by and faulted for its neglect of the eschatological (i.e., historical) Jesus, Schweitzer introduced Wrede's work on the messianic secret[38] in contrast with his own work on Jesus' messianic consciousness, *Mystery*. He believed that Weiss and his followers were to blame for Wrede's total disregard for the role of eschatology in his assessment of Jesus in the Synoptic tradition.[39] They went wrong in limiting their application of eschatology to the teaching of Jesus. It should have been applied monolithically, in a more methodologically rigorous way "to throw light upon his whole public work, the connection and lack of connection between the events."[40]

Schweitzer preferred a *konsequente* (thoroughgoing) eschatological approach to the life of Jesus: an apocalyptic framework that enlightened every dimension of Jesus' message and ministry. This approach was to be preferred over that of Wrede and earlier interpreters of Jesus' career, since it avoided assuming an introduction of significant error into the Gospel tradition. Since Wrede's Jesus had no messianic consciousness, tradition that reflected such an awareness must have been inserted later, often smuggled in using the secrecy motif. For Schweitzer, however, Mark's

---

34. Ibid., 198.

35. Ibid. A number of scholars after Schweitzer recognized the fundamental importance of this work as well. Bultmann describes it in the following way: "This epoch-making book refuted the interpretation which was hitherto generally accepted. Weiss showed that the Kingdom of God is not imminent in the world and does not grow as part of the world's history, but is rather eschatological; i.e., the Kingdom of God transcends the historical order. It will come into being not through the moral endeavour of man, but solely through the supernatural action of God. God will suddenly put an end to the world and to history, and He will bring in a new world, the world of eternal blessedness" (Bultmann, *Jesus Christ*, 12). Koester describes its impact similarly: "This book, as well as those of his other Göttingen friends, advertised the discovery that the rationalistic and moralistic categories of their time were not capable of comprehending the early Christian concept of the kingdom of God. Whereas these categories had their roots, as Johannes Weiss states, in Kant's philosophy and in the theology of enlightenment, Jesus' concept of the kingdom of God was informed by the apocalyptic mythology of ancient Judaism and was thoroughly eschatological, messianic, and supernatural" (Koester, "Jesus the Victim," 4).

36. Bousset, *Jesu Predigt*.

37. Cf. Schweitzer, *Quest*, 203.

38. Wrede, *Das Messiageheimnis* (ET: *Messianic Secret*).

39. Cf. Schweitzer, *Quest*, 315.

40. Ibid.

concealment of Jesus' identity was part of a gradual disclosure of his messianic awareness first to his disciples (those predestined to believe), starting with the most inner circles, and later to the multitudes.[41] As the end got nearer and nearer, Jesus made his messiahship more fully known. For Schweitzer, this view allowed the historical record to remain, for the most part, intact.[42] There were now two options:

> There is either the eschatological solution, which at a stroke elevates to genuine history the Markan account as it stands, with all its disconnectedness and inconsistencies; and there is, on the other hand, the literary solution, which regards the incongruous dogmatic element as interpolated by the earliest evangelist into the tradition and therefore deletes the messianic claim from the historical life of Jesus altogether.[43]

Therefore, Nineham apparently misunderstands Schweitzer when he criticizes him for the "implicit and detailed trust in the contents of both Mark and Matthew which Schweitzer's position requires."[44] Schweitzer's contention is that eschatology makes sense of the Gospel accounts and, therefore, supports their historicity. This is not a naive assumed historicity. Nineham also faults Schweitzer for these "misjudgments" that "cost Schweitzer dear," stating, "They have meant that in an important area of New Testament study—and one which has proved the chief focus of interest in the period since he wrote—his views have run directly counter to the almost universal current of opinion."[45] I am not convinced that such skepticism is "the almost universal current of opinion," but I think it is clear that Schweitzer would not have cared much either way. His views ran directly counter to the universal current of opinion in his own day too.

The impact of Schweitzer has been debated. Clearly his thoroughgoing eschatology was not the "advance in knowledge" that he hoped it would be,[46] since it only treated

---

41. Cf. ibid., 322–23.

42. Schweitzer is, however, inconsistent at this point since he is forced to deny the historicity of all non-future referring "son of man" titles. Referring to instances where Jesus uses the title as a simple, non-futuristic designation for himself (in the sense of "I," e.g., Matt 8:20; 11:19; 12:32), Schweitzer says, "But 'Son of Man' is a messianic title of futuristic character, since it always suggests a coming upon the clouds, according to Daniel 7:13, 14. Furthermore, in all of these passages the Disciples are as yet ignorant of Jesus' secret. For them the Son of Man is still an entirely distinct person. The unity of the subject is still completely unknown to them. Therefore they were not in a position to understand that by this term he refers to himself, but they must refer everything to that Son of Man of whose coming he also spoke elsewhere. Therewith, however, the passages would be meaningless, for they imply that Jesus is thus speaking of himself. Historically and philologically it is therefore impossible that Jesus could have employed the expression as a purposeless and matter of course self-designation" (Schweitzer, *Mystery*, 195). Schweitzer falls into his own criticism here, deleting the tradition that does not support his theory, instead of attempting to integrate it.

43. Schweitzer, *Quest*, 302.

44. Nineham, "Schweitzer Revisited," 128.

45. Ibid.

46. But cf. Kümmel, *Promise and Fulfillment*, esp. 54–64; Allison, "Plea," esp. 658; Allison, *End*.

futuristic elements of Jesus' eschatology.[47] The common perception of Schweitzer's two most abiding impressions upon historical Jesus scholarship can be sensed in Dunn's appraisal: "Schweitzer's history of the 'quest' still provides an unsurpassed overview of the first phase (or two phases) of the 'quest' and serves as the obvious leader of our little procession below."[48] In my view, Dunn is right in his evaluation of Schweitzer's history as an unequaled overview and analysis of (mostly) nineteenth-century German Jesus research. Schweitzer's *Quest* is a devastating critique of the modernizing, de-historicizing liberal Lives of Jesus of his day. I disagree, however, with the more implicit claim that the quests can be divided into a number of differing phases,[49] with Schweitzer bringing an end to the "old quest" and marking the beginning of a no-quest phase. As I have already noted, it is a misinterpretation of Schweitzer to understand this to be his intention, but it is also an incorrect historical assessment.[50] The view that Schweitzer stopped the quest for the historical Jesus until it was resumed in the 1950s by Käsemann (among others) is substantially undermined by Weaver's thorough analysis of Jesus research from 1900 to 1950. He concludes regarding the Old Quest—No Quest—New Quest—Third Quest schema that the "impression that remains with me after completing this research is that our usual views of the 'Quests' of the historical Jesus do not do justice to the actual history."[51] So while Schweitzer remains an excellent theologian (among his many other professions), his most lasting influence in Jesus studies has been his critique of the rationalistic, romantic, liberal, and non-historical lives of Jesus that preceded him. He did not, however, temporarily put an end to the study of Jesus.

SCHWEITZER'S APOCALYPTIC PAUL

We start to see a bit of Schweitzer's methodology emerge as we turn to his greatly underappreciated[52] work on Paul. As in his study of the historical Jesus, Schweitzer began by assessing eighteenth-, nineteenth-, and early twentieth-century works on Paul in order to pave the way for his own analysis. However, what started as a single book on Paul, comparable to *Quest* in its structure—beginning with detailed investigation of previous research before summarizing the view he espoused—turned into two books,

---

47. For similar reasons, Dodd's radical, somewhat responsive, realized eschatology did not meet with a warm reception, neglecting futuristic features. E.g., Dodd, *Parables*.

48. Dunn, "Introduction [to Part I]," 4.

49. He makes this claim explicit in Dunn, "Introduction [to Part II]," 87–89. Denton has recently laid out the dominant view quite clearly: "The standard grand narrative of the history of Jesus studies divides it into phases, traditionally named the Old Quest, the New Quest and the Third Quest. The first phase is the most widely recognized by name and by contour. The Old Quest was first identified, and presumably brought to an end, by Albert Schweitzer" (Denton, *Historiography*, 3).

50. Weaver, *Historical Jesus*. See also Allison, "Secularizing"; S. E. Porter, *Criteria*, 31–62.

51. Weaver, *Historical Jesus*, xi.

52. See notes 11 and 12 above.

one exploring Paul's interpreters and another devoted to unpacking the apocalyptic mysticism of Paul.

Paul and His Interpreters (hereafter *Paul*) originally served as the introductory chapter for *The Mysticism of Paul the Apostle* (hereafter *Mysticism*), but grew into its own independent evaluation of Pauline research.[53] *Paul* is similar to *Quest* in that it is clearly pursuing an agenda. The agenda in *Paul*, however, is not as much to show that previous interpreters have failed to understand Paul eschatologically—though that is clearly a dominant element[54]—but is more focused upon demonstrating that Paul's thinking was not significantly derived from Greco-Roman or Greco-Oriental categories, especially those drawn from Hellenistic philosophy, Egyptian mythology, and Greco-Roman mystery religions. He even rules out the possibility of a confluence of Jewish and Greek ideas within Paul's thinking, insisting that scholars who proposed such models "are in a still worse case than those which more or less neglect the former [Jewish] element. Encumbered with all the difficulties of the Hellenising theory they become involved in the jungle of antinomies which they discover or imagine, and there perish miserably."[55] According to Schweitzer, "The solution must, therefore, consist in leaving out every form and in every combination, and venturing on the 'one-sidedness' of endeavoring to understand the doctrine of the Apostle of the Gentiles entirely on the basis of Jewish primitive Christianity."[56] His most significant dialogue partners, therefore, comprise a number of scholars from the comparative religions school like Herman Usener, Gustav Anrich, Albert Eichhorn, Adolf von Harnack, Hermann Gunkel, Paul Wendland, Martin Brückner, Carl Clemen, Arthur Drews, William B. Smith, and Paul Wernle, including also those propagating significant parallels in Paul with contemporary Greek and Jewish Hellenistic literature like Heinrich J. Holtzmann, and even those more characterized by a social description

---

53. Schweitzer, *Mysticism*, vii.

54. Schweitzer criticizes a number of authors for their treatments of Paul's thought in terms of the traditional *loci* of theology for neglecting eschatology, giving themes from other *loci* equal prominence, or treating these themes independently of eschatology. For example, in his general assessment of scholars after the period of Baur, he remarks: "The authors regard with a certain amount of self-satisfaction the way that they have emphasised the importance given to the eschatology by Paul. In the chapter devoted to it they have certainly emphasised again and again, 'with the utmost energy,' the fact that he really 'shared' the eschatological expectations of his time and admitted them to an important place in his creed. The chapter in question, however, only gets its turn after the whole 'system of doctrine' has been safely housed in the earlier chapters without seeking any aid from the eschatology or even saying a word about it" (Schweitzer, *Paul*, 53). This criticism is made specifically, to cite a particular example, of Holtzmann when he says: "True to the Baur and post-Baur tradition, Holtzmann postpones the chapter on eschatology to the end" (ibid., 109). Sanders sees this as one of Schweitzer's most important insights when he says: "It was Albert Schweitzer who, with his usual critical acumen, put his finger on this question as decisive for understanding Paul. As long as one studies Paul under the loci of systematic theology, relegating eschatology to the last place in one's discussion, understanding of Paul is hindered if not completely obscured" (Sanders, *Paul*, 434).

55. Schweitzer, *Paul*, 239–40.

56. Ibid., 240.

approach drawing upon non-literary materials, such as Adolf Deissmann.[57] Numerous other Pauline interpreters are mentioned and criticized, but Schweitzer was most concerned with dismantling the predominant notion that Paul's thinking was in some way influenced by his Hellenistic surroundings.

Schweitzer's sequel volume, *Mysticism*, proceeds from the ground-clearing work of *Paul*, but because of the significant lapse of time between the two publications, there is some attempt to engage with Pauline scholars within the roughly twenty-year gap between the two volumes. In some ways, *Mysticism* states the case against a Hellenistic Pauline theology more positively. Schweitzer's summary of Paul's mysticism brings this out forcefully:

> Pauline mysticism has shown that it is closely connected with the eschatological worldview; that it finds no place for the conceptions of rebirth or deification; that it has a kind of realism which is foreign to the Hellenistic mysticism; that its conception of the Sacraments is quite different from the Hellenistic; and that the symbolism which plays so essential a part in the sacramental side of Hellenistic mysticism here plays no part at all. Thus, when any attempt is made to explain the Pauline doctrine as Hellenistic, it finds itself confronted with the greatest difficulties.[58]

Such is characteristic of Pauline eschatology. According to Schweitzer, for Paul's theology to be eschatological was for it to be (late) Jewish: "we must now consider either a purely eschatological or a purely Hellenistic explanation of his teaching."[59] Therefore, "in a most natural way the evolution from Jesus by way of Paul to Ignatius is explained. Paul was not the Hellenizer of Christianity. But in his eschatological mysticism of Being-in-Christ he gave it a form in which it could be Hellenized."[60] In *Mysticism*, Schweitzer is basically laying a foundation for this argument through developing Paul's Jewish-apocalyptic notion of Christ-mysticism and how this concept relates to other significant dimensions of Paul's theology.

The structure of the book and its argument can be understood as having essentially four elements:[61] (1) description of and issues for a mystical Pauline eschatology (chs.

---

57. Usener, *Religionsgeschichtliche Untersuchungen*; Anrich, *Das antike Mysterienwesen*; Eichhorn, *Das Abendmahl*; Wernle, *Die Anfänge*; Harnack, *Die Mission* (ET: Harnack, *Mission*); Gunkel, *Zum religionsgeschichtlichen Verständnis*; Wendland, *Die hellenistisch-römische Kultur*; Brückner, *Der sterbende und auferstehende Gottheiland*; Clemen, *Religionsgeschichtliche Erklärung*; Drews and Smith, *Die Christusmythe 1*; Holtzmann, *Lehrbuch*; Deissmann, *Licht vom Osten* (ET: Deissmann, *Light from the Ancient East*).

58. Schweitzer, *Mysticism*, 26.

59. Ibid., vii.

60. Ibid., ix.

61. Thiselton, therefore, seems to oversimplify the argument when he suggests, "The argument of *The Mysticism of Paul the Apostle* can perhaps most readily be understood if it is viewed in two parts. Over the first 140 pages Schweitzer describes Pauline Christ-mysticism and sets it within its proper eschatological frame. In the rest of the book he then shows how this fundamental perspective

1–5); (2) mystical union with Christ (chs. 6–8); (3) the relation of Pauline eschatology to other significant theological motifs in Paul (chs. 9–12); and (4) the Hellenization of Pauline Christianity and the enduring Pauline elements within it (chs. 13–14).

In the first major part of the book, Schweitzer provides a basic outline of his views and seeks to make his assumptions explicit, while attempting to answer key questions pertaining to his project, such as the extent of Greek influence upon Paul's thinking, the boundaries of the Pauline canon, and so on. Chapter 5, an especially significant chapter, argues that Paul developed his eschatology from late Jewish materials. Paul drew his eschatology not from Hellenistic sources or from the earlier futuristic Daniel/Enoch eschatological tradition, which Jesus implemented, but from the "late Jewish eschatology" found especially in the Apocalypses of Baruch and Ezra, which synthesized Danielic traditions by postulating a two-fold eschatological schema with a messiah and an eternal state of blessedness.[62] Paul develops these notions in a mystic-christological context so that Christ's physical (external) resurrection initiates a realized participatory (internal) resurrection life for the elect community who are undergoing initial physical transformation or resurrection while waiting for a final physical transformation.[63] The second section unpacks Paul's understanding of the mystical union of the believer in Christ's death and resurrection, from the perspective of both suffering and pneumatology. Paul's mystical apocalypticism is related to his view of the law, righteousness by faith, the sacraments, and ethics in the third section. John's theology is the major focus of Schweitzer's analysis of the later New Testament literature and Ignatius represents the central post-apostolic figure involved in the further Hellenization of early Christianity. This is not to say, however, that Hellenized thinking entirely overcame Paul's eschatological perspective. Numerous elements that endured through the process of the Hellenization of Christianity are mentioned in the final chapter of the book, including belief in the kingdom of God and an enduring sense of Christ-mysticism.

---

shapes Paul's thought on such subjects as the Spirit, the law, justification, and ethics" (Thiselton, "Biblical Classics: VI," 132). This description is inadequate at least on account of the fact that it separates Schweitzer's analysis of "The Mystical Doctrine of the Dying and Rising Again with Christ" (ch. 6) and "Suffering as a Mode of Manifestation of the Dying with Christ" (ch. 7) from ch. 8 "Possession of the Spirit as a Mode of Manifestation of the Being-Risen-With-Christ." These three chapters function together in the development of Paul's conception of the mystical union with Christ in his death and resurrection. Another problem with this dual structure is that it does not clearly account for the function of ch. 2, "Hellenistic or Judaic," which takes the opportunity to critique a number of Hellenistically-inspired Pauline theologies that had cropped up since his initial publication on Paul's interpreters. The third chapter, "The Pauline Epistles," which assesses introductory issues, is also out of place on this schema. The first few chapters really function more as general description and ground-clearing, dealing with Schweitzer's major assumptions and any attendant problems associated with them. Nor does Thiselton's proposed structure deal in any serious way with the treatment of the recession of eschatology and enduring Pauline elements within it, in the last two chapters of the book.

62. Schweitzer, *Mysticism*, 76, 84–90.

63. Ibid., 100. Some of these notions are more thoroughly developed in ch. 6, but the foundation is laid in ch. 5 through correlating Paul's eschatology with that of late Judaism.

The essential thesis of his book is developed in section (2), as outlined above, where Schweitzer develops the notion of mystical participation in Christ's death and resurrection—being-in-Christ is the essence of Pauline mysticism. Paul's eschatological expectations, then, involve a present mystical experience of a realized dimension of this participation while looking forward to a future ultimate fulfillment of the union when those predestined to the Messianic Kingdom are revealed—it is a participatory eschatology in this sense.[64] The element of predestination is critical to Schweitzer's apocalyptic Paul. Paul's eschatology "is that of the preordained union of those who are elect to the Messianic Kingdom with one another and with the Messiah which is called 'the community of the Saints.'"[65] Paul's understanding of redemption also has a "juridical" dimension: the "righteousness through faith [that] rests in the idea of the atoning death of Jesus."[66] And these focuses of Paul's theology work in tandem: "Paul lives at the same time in the simple ideas of the eschatological doctrine of salvation, in the complicated Rabbinical and juridical conceptions, and in the profundities of the mysticism of being-in-Christ, passing freely from the one circle of ideas to the other." Nevertheless, "Pauline personal religion is in its fundamental character mystical. It can no doubt find expression for its thought in the eschatological and juridical doctrines of salvation, but its own essential life lies in the mystical."[67]

Schweitzer's work on Paul has been quite influential in setting the trajectory for Pauline theology since he wrote, especially in a number of developmental approaches to Paul's thought initiated by the work of C. H. Dodd and John Knox.[68] While many

---

64. Matlock assesses the situation similarly: "That Paul's 'mysticism,' with its realized/anticipatory nature, is Paul's own innovation is noted in [*Paul and His*] *Interpreters* (for example, pp. 54–55, 214) and repeatedly stressed in *Mysticism*. Indeed, this 'mysticism' is Paulinism, and discovering how this present/future configuration is to be explained is for Schweitzer, once again, the central problem" (Matlock, *Unveiling*, 39). On participatory eschatology, cf. also Matlock, *Unveiling*, 40.

65. Schweitzer, *Mystery*, 101. Sanders is among those who perceive the emphasis on predestination in Schweitzer to be a distortion of the evidence: "Many aspects of Schweitzer's presentation of Paul's thought have rightly proved unacceptable to New Testament scholars. One may mention, for example, his over-emphasis of the importance of predestination in Paul's thought" (Sanders, *Paul*, 434).

66. Schweitzer, *Mystery*, 25.

67. Ibid.

68. Dodd, "Mind of Paul: II." The role of Knox in developmental schemes for Pauline thought is more foundational and indirect, as later scholars depended upon his work in Pauline chronology as the basis for positing evolutionary stages in Paul's thinking. Knox made two related contributions to the discussion. He was one of the first to emphasize the distinction between Paul's letters as primary sources and Luke–Acts as a secondary, less authoritative source for ascertaining details concerning Paul's life. See J. Knox, *Chapters*, 47–60; J. Knox, "'Fourteen Years Later'"; J. Knox, "Pauline Chronology." See also Minear, "Jerusalem Fund"; Suggs, "Date." This perspective seems to have been significantly set in motion in contemporary New Testament scholarship by Jewett, *Chronology*. Second, his chronology for Paul's life and letters functioned as a significant basis for subsequent work on the development of Pauline thought since it allows for an even longer period of time to transpire than Dodd's chronology, which attempted to reconcile the material from Paul's letters with Acts. Hurd carries over this emphasis. In his work on the development of Paul's thought, Hurd shows the importance of a chronology that allows for a fair amount of time to pass between Paul's major literary achievements—as we see especially in Knox's chronology. See Hurd, *Origin*, 3–52; Hurd, "Pauline

subsequent scholars have not subscribed to every point of chronology or development suggested by Dodd and Knox, their work, in conjunction with Schweitzer's "eschatological Paul," has served as a catalyst for a number of developmental-apocalyptic approaches to Pauline eschatology from the 1940s to the present, as well as a few non-developmental apocalyptic proposals that follow the track of Schweitzer exclusively. These include those of W. L. Knox, Oscar Cullmann, W. D. Davies, John A. T. Robinson, C. E. Faw, Donald Selby, Archibald Hunter, Hans-Joachim Schoeps, W. G. Kümmel, Stephen Smalley, Ernst Käsemann, Perrier Benoit, Victor Furnish, and now more recently, Paul Achtemeier, Jürgen Becker, John Reumann, and Udo Schnelle.[69]

Although Schweitzer opposed the trends toward developmental schemes put forward by Pauline interpreters during his day,[70] his "eschatological Paul" provides the point of departure for Dodd. Dodd lays the foundations for his study of development in Pauline thought in his analysis of Paul's psychological state.[71] Dodd applies his theory of the evolution of Pauline psychology directly to issues of theological development, and we see Schweitzer's influence in the way that Paul's early eschatology is framed. Dodd spends a substantial portion of his article "The Mind of Paul" attempting to discredit the Ephesian hypothesis (which places the writing of the prison letters, Romans, 1 and 2 Corinthians, and probably Galatians within three to four years of one another by suggesting an Ephesian imprisonment for the prison letters),[72] and instead locates the time of writing for all four letters in Paul's imprisonment at Rome recorded

---

Chronology." C. H. Buck makes similar connections. In his article ("Collection"), he builds upon the work of Knox and other chronologies of Paul that give priority to Paul's letters over Acts in his construction of a Pauline chronology based upon events surrounding Paul's collection for the saints. This chronology then serves as a fundamental basis for Buck's later developmental construction of Pauline theology with Taylor (Buck and Taylor, *Saint Paul*). The foundations for this work were already laid in the work of Lightfoot, "Chronology" (based upon his lecture notes of 1863); Gilbert, "Development"; Matheson, *Spiritual Development*; Charles, *Critical History*; Thackeray, *Relation*; Hayes, "Study"; Wood, "Paul's Eschatology"; Wood, "Paul's Eschatology. II"; F. C. Porter, "Place." However, by the time C. H. Dodd wrote, scholars had already begun to see that the tendency to locate evolutionary stages in Paul's thinking "overpressed the evidence in the interests of a neat scheme of development" so that the modern tendency was to "deny that Paul underwent any substantial development" (Dodd, "Mind of Paul: II," 83).

69. W. L. Knox, *St Paul*; Cullmann, *Christ and Time*; Davies, *Paul and Rabbinic Judaism*, 285–320; J. A. T. Robinson, *Jesus and His Coming*, 160; Selby, "Changing Views," esp. 34–35; Faw, "Death and Resurrection"; Hunter, *Paul*, 98; Schoeps, *Paul*; Smalley, "Delay"; Käsemann, *New Testament Questions*, 124–37; Kümmel, "Futuristic and Realized Eschatology"; Benoit, "Resurrection"; Furnish, "Development"; Achtemeier, "Apocalyptic Shift"; Becker, *Paul*, esp. 371–449; Reumann, *Variety and Unity*, 71–128; Schnelle, *Apostle Paul*, 248–51, 577–97.

70. Schweitzer, *Paul*, 32.

71. Dodd, "The Mind of Paul: II."

72. According to this theory, Paul wrote Philippians in the first Ephesian imprisonment and Colossians, Ephesians, and Philemon in the second. This theory is associated with Duncan, *St Paul's Ephesian Ministry*, against the prevailing Roman hypothesis. On this chronology, cf. Dodd, *Helps*, 195–97. A second alternative to the Roman hypothesis has been proposed as well, the Caesarean hypothesis. On this theory, see Johnson, "Pauline Letters," 24–26.

at the end of Acts.[73] This chronology allows Dodd to put some distance between the time of writing of these and Paul's other letters so that development in Pauline theology is a bit more plausible. The tendency for Dodd is to see eschatological elements in 1 and 2 Thessalonians, the earliest Pauline letters, reflecting a Jewish apocalyptic framework as Schweitzer insisted, with Paul expecting the Advent within his own lifetime as well as that of the majority of his converts.[74] The gradual movement away from a futuristic Jewish eschatology to a realized Hellenistic eschatology can be detected in Paul's later letters, consummating finally in the prison letters where not even a "remnant of Paul's earlier impatient expectation" can be found.[75] While Dodd has provided a platform for the incorporation of Schweitzer's ideas in Pauline eschatology, E. P. Sanders notices a number of dimensions of Schweitzer's apocalyptic presentation of Paul that have not been well received including "his over emphasis on the importance of predestination in Paul's thought, his view of baptism as *ex opere operato* and his theory of two resurrections."[76]

Some of the foundations of the so-called "new perspective on Paul" can be traced back to Schweitzer as well, although this influence is seldom recognized.[77] His work touches specifically upon questions related to the center of Pauline theology.[78] Sanders, when he first proposed his nontraditional understanding of Paul, was surprised at how few scholars had taken notice of Schweitzer's protest against treating eschatology at the end of a Pauline theology, in accord with the traditional *loci*, and understanding "righteousness by faith alone" as the central theme in Paul's thinking.[79] Sanders's considerably brief (considering its impact) exposition of Paul proceeds from the assumption that "Schweitzer's arguments against considering the terminology of righteousness by faith to be the central theme of Paul's theology, and consequently the key to his thought, are, considered cumulatively, convincing; and they have

73. Dodd, "The Mind of Paul: II."

74. Ibid., 109–10. This belief can also be detected within 1 Corinthians; however, in this letter a subtle second stage in Paul's thinking should be noticed because there seems to be less certainty regarding the number of Christians that will die before the Advent (ibid., 110). Second Corinthians paints a different picture entirely and represents a third shift in the structure of Paul's eschatology. By this point, Paul is ready to depart to be with the Lord (2 Cor 5:1–10). Statements regarding the time of the Advent in Romans are equally cautious (ibid., 111). While Paul's death prior to the Advent seems to be a very real possibility in Romans, it is still "nearer now than it was when we became Christians" (Rom 13:11–14). But cf. Longenecker, "Nature." Longenecker argues that while the form of Paul's early eschatology, as represented in 1 and 2 Thessalonians, is clearly apocalyptic, the content draws from a "functional Christology" rather than a Jewish apocalyptic framework.

75. Dodd, "Mind of Paul: II," 112.

76. Sanders, *Paul*, 438.

77. Thiselton notices the significance of Schweitzer's work for justification and even his influence upon Sanders, but he is not writing in the prime of the new Pauline perspective so points of correlation are not drawn ("Biblical Classics: VI," 135–36). Cf. also Baird, *History*, 236.

78. For a survey of various proposals for a center to Paul's theology and related issues in Pauline theology, see S. E. Porter, "Is There a Center."

79. Sanders, *Paul*, 434.

never been effectively countered."⁸⁰ Although Sanders and Schweitzer part ways at numerous points, Sanders's participationist eschatology is essentially a development of Schweitzer's being-in-Christ mysticism: "the main theme of Paul's gospel was . . . the saving action of God in Jesus Christ and how his hearers could participate in that action."⁸¹ Sanders's conception of Pauline justification is in some ways a rigorous, developed application of Schweitzer's participationist eschatology to the righteousness language in Paul. He is in complete agreement with Schweitzer when he says that Paul "is not primarily concerned with the juristic categories, although he works with them. The real bite of his theology lies in the participatory categories, even though he himself did not distinguish them this way."⁸² Sanders, then, adds to this the notion of covenantal nomism, and comes up with a covenantal community notion, which has significant points of contact with Schweitzer's "Community of the Saints," where entrance into the community is secured and maintained by good works, all the while insisting on a very Jewish eschatological Paul, again, in the spirit of Schweitzer.

Matlock also notices Schweitzer's impact upon the biblical theology movement in the work of Käsemann and Becker, the history-of-religions school in the work of Davies, Schoeps, and Sanders, and the salvation-history approach in the work of O. Cullmann, J. Munck, and Herman Ridderbos.⁸³ It is indicative of Schweitzer's significance for Pauline studies that we find in many of the most significant discussions of Pauline theology roots that go directly back to his work.

THE RECESSION OF ESCHATOLOGY IN LATER NEW TESTAMENT LITERATURE

We may now see a bit of Schweitzer's project and methodology emerging. He (1) crystallized crucial problems in New Testament research through detailed analysis of previous interpretation, especially noting certain pervasive (false) tendencies, in order to (2) clear the path for a proposed solution. His approach rarely attempted a detailed exegesis of a particular passage, but instead combined theological analysis with a history-of-religion type of model, grounded firmly in Jewish sources in order to produce a holistic account of Christian origins. His proposal essentially runs as follows: Jesus' eschatology, based upon early Jewish sources, is entirely futuristic and was ultimately frustrated by his own death. Paul turns to later Judaism, adapting the eschatologies of (especially) the Apocalypses of Baruch and Ezra, postulating realized and futuristic features within his eschatological framework. So in the shift from Jesus to Paul, we already see a recension to a more realized eschatology. After Paul, in the writings of the later New Testament, there is a push to Hellenize Christianity, initiated by John whose teaching was carried on by Polycarp and developed by Ignatius.

80. Ibid., 440.
81. Ibid., 447.
82. Ibid., 502.
83. Matlock, *Unveiling*, 52.

Part of Schweitzer's argument for the centrality of Pauline mysticism is that it packaged primitive Christian tradition eschatologically in a way that was easily resituated within the framework of contemporary Hellenistic thought—Paul's thinking provides a key transitional link between the Jewish futuristic eschatology of Jesus and the Hellenized Christianity of the early Apostolic Fathers. The incentive for this reworking of Paul's theology was brought on by "the fading of the eschatological Hope [that] quite naturally brought them to comprehend their faith afresh in terms of current Hellenistic concepts."[84] Nonetheless, "up to near the middle of the second century, at least in the Church of Asia Minor, of which we know something from Ignatius, Polycarp, and Papias, the eschatological hope still formed a living element in Christian belief."[85]

Aside from his investigation of the Johannine tendency to Hellenize Pauline Christianity through the Logos-concept,[86] we do not have much written by Schweitzer concerning later New Testament writings. These writings come at a period in the development of early Christianity in which the Christian community was beginning to have doubts regarding the parousia—doubts that would eventually call for the incorporation of a Hellenistic conceptual framework in order to bring coherence to primitive Christian beliefs. Concerning Hebrews, 2 Peter, Jude, and Justin, he says: "That the delay of the return of the Lord awakened doubts as to the certainty of the Coming of the Messianic Kingdom we know from some of the New Testament Epistles."[87] Within Schweitzer's argument, then, these writings appear to illustrate doubts that had begun to emerge within primitive Christianity that would ultimately bring about the pressures leading to the Hellenization of Pauline Christianity. Unfortunately, Schweitzer did not make many explicit statements about that material, so in order to round out his picture of Christian origins it may be helpful to consider how Schweitzer might have treated this material as it is believed that he planned to. The editor of the posthumously published *The Kingdom of God in Primitive Christianity* (hereafter *Kingdom*) notes that we have a sketch of "a further chapter dealing with the recession of eschatology, using the later New Testament as material."[88]

The most consistent application of Schweitzer's methodology would undoubtedly involve a detailed analysis of previous research on the later New Testament writings, which is clearly outside of the scope of this survey. Apparently Schweitzer did not even have this project in his purview. So instead, here I will simply plot out a few suggestions as to how that additional chapter of *Kingdom* that Schweitzer planned to write might have looked. Based upon his comments above, he probably would have

---

84. Schweitzer, *Mysticism*, ix.

85. Ibid., 337.

86. Schweitzer states: "Justin and the Gospel of John carry forward the work of Ignatius by inserting the Hellenistic union-with-Christ mysticism into the doctrine of Jesus Christ as the organ of the Logos" (ibid., 348).

87. Ibid., 337.

88. Neuenschwander, "Introduction," v.

sought to detect strands of the eschatological doubt that he believed were prevalent within the communities out of which this literature emerged. He perhaps, then, would have turned to the authors themselves to assess the eschatological framework they employed to deal with this doubt, asking how it fit in relation to Paul and the work of John and his successors in Asia Minor, noting hints of eschatological recession based upon the delayed parousia. His view was that while early Christians well after Paul continued to expect the parousia, it became much more difficult to accept Paul's understanding of the resurrection as having already begun with Christ's resurrection: "The question is therefore not how long the eschatological expectation still continued to retain some significance, but how long it continued to retain so much significance that the logical formulation of the belief in the resurrection, consequent on union with Christ, continued to be conditioned by it."[89] After Paul, the believer can no longer feel confident that he is actually "in the process of being changed into the resurrection state of existence."[90]

Schweitzer also made very little use of Luke in his portrait of Jesus, and he only accepted the authenticity of seven Pauline letters, so much of this material could be considered "late" too. But I shall focus specifically on the de-eschatologizing tendencies of the late letters that do not emerge from within the Pauline school. Again, this will involve broad strokes, seeking to detect eschatological development, tying a number of themes together as Schweitzer often did.[91]

There is uncertainty regarding the date of Jude, depending upon issues of authorship and the age of the author, if he was Jesus' brother, in relation to Jesus. It is usually dated somewhere between 60 and 80 CE. Schweitzer's thesis would probably be best served by an earlier date, perhaps seeing it even as the earliest of the post-Pauline letters. Bauckham notices the tendency in scholarship is to situate Jude later in the development of early Christianity as an instance of early Catholicism or earlier as an example of apocalyptic Judaism and argues persuasively for the latter position.[92] It is likely that Schweitzer would have concurred with an earlier date for similar reasons to those given by Bauckham. In fact, Jude might be understood as the first stage of development from Pauline thought within early Christianity because it clearly employs a late Jewish apocalyptic framework, with allusions to *1 Enoch* and *Testament of Moses*, but has not retained the connection of the mystical union to eschatological expectation, which is also markedly present (Jude 14–15). There is not yet any clear evidence of Hellenistic influence.

---

89. Schweitzer, *Mysticism*, 338–39.

90. Ibid., 339.

91. By late writings, I mean John's writings, Hebrews, the Petrine letters, Jude, and James, which are all later than Paul's writings. There could be some dispute over this, depending upon how Acts and 2 Timothy are judged and dated. Also, estimates of the date of Hebrews will vary depending upon who its author is thought to be.

92. Bauckham, *Jude*, 8–9.

Persecution contexts have led Petrine scholars to date 1 Peter as early as 60–64 CE, during Nero's reign, and as late as 111 CE (during Trajan's reign). I imagine that Schweitzer would have wanted to argue for an earlier date for 1 Peter because of its incorporation of so many Jewish conceptions and its frequent use of Scripture. Certain dimensions of Pauline Jewish eschatology are still in force. A notion similar to Paul's elect community of the saints is seen in Peter's emphasis upon associating his audience with God's chosen people (2:8–10). Paul's being-in-Christ mysticism lingers on in Peter's portrayal of Christian suffering in terms of union with Christ (4:13), but the connection between resurrection union and the future hope is altogether absent. The parousia is still very much in view (e.g., "the day of visitation," 2:12; "the end is at hand," 4:7), but as in the other late New Testament writings, it is becoming less of an emphasis and all confidence has been lost that believers are undergoing a transformation into the resurrection state. One may even still detect traces of Jewish apocalyptic in 1 Peter, especially 1 Pet 3:18–22 where allusions to traditions about Enoch may be present.[93] At this stage, Jewish apocalyptic emphases are fading, but Hellenistic conceptions have not yet been incorporated.

It is also difficult to see Hebrews as a Hellenization of Paul's theology, but at one point in *Mysticism* Schweitzer does cite references to Heb 6:11–12; 10:2, 35; and 12:12–14 in support of his view that believers were beginning to give up hope in the parousia due to extended delay.[94] The passages have in common a theme of hope and perseverance. We could add to his list Heb 3:6, 14; 6:18–19 and 12:1–2. Perhaps Schweitzer, as many scholars, would date Hebrews sometime before the fall of Jerusalem in 70 CE. On this dating, Hebrews would come just after some of the later Pauline writings so that the delayed parousia would be an issue, but at this point early Christian writers were not yet ready to turn to Hellenism, but were still employing mystical categories to deal with this tension. A late Jewish framework is still clearly operative, although it is giving way and will soon break. Evidence for such a view could be marshaled along several lines. We see some of the same participatory language in Hebrews, for example. The author speaks of "sharing in Christ" (3:14), believers have entered Christ's rest (4:1–11), being partakers of the Holy Spirit (6:4), and having the communal sharing of a heavenly calling (3:1). But the expectation of the parousia is still put forward as the basis for hope and sanctification: "And just as it is appointed for man to die once, and after that comes judgment, so Christ, having been offered once to bear the sins of many, will appear a second time, not to deal with sin but to save those who are eagerly waiting for him" (9:27–28). Hebrews, then, can probably be understood as somewhat of an extension of Paul's eschatological thinking, but the exclusion of the Pauline connection between the resurrection and the expectation of the parousia is clearly in force. Although participatory language can be found, it is no longer possible to believe in a mysticism that portrays the believer undergoing

---

93. Cf. Achtemeier, *1 Peter*, 242.
94. Schweitzer, *Mysticism*, 337.

the process of receiving their resurrection bodies. The parousia has been delayed too long to support this conception. There is also a shift away from the strong apocalyptic language that Schweitzer noticed in Paul, also present in Jude, to a greater emphasis upon cultic imagery.

James can probably be dated around a similar time as Hebrews. Although some scholars have dated James quite early, Schweitzer places the letter at least after Romans and/or Galatians.[95] James may in some ways be representative of a trend toward de-eschatologizing in that the communication of colloquial wisdom in the context of Jesus traditions seems to be more of the focus than the development of any clear eschatological understanding—although a number of implicit eschatological notions may be detected (e.g., themes of mercy and judgment, cf. Jas 2:12). The overall tenor of the letter is very Jewish in conception, drawing upon Old Testament wisdom tradition instead of late Jewish apocalyptic. As in Hebrews, this is what we would expect in the period directly after Paul where Christian thought was still framed in essentially Jewish categories, but where a shift away from apocalyptic can nevertheless be detected. Although direct eschatological statements in James are minimal, he does take up the topic toward the end of the letter in 5:7–11 where believers are exhorted to look to the parousia as a motivation for enduring suffering. In 5:7 James commands his readers to "be patient," which Schweitzer probably would have taken as evidence of a crisis within the community resulting from the now long delayed parousia. The lessened focus upon eschatology in James and Hebrews could be understood, then, as part of a gradual shift away from the apocalyptic emphasis of Jesus and Paul. The relationship between mystical resurrection existence and the parousia is also clearly lacking.

Among the Johannine letters, 1 John is the only one worthy of serious consideration within Schweitzer's scheme. John's writings are among the latest of the New Testament documents according to Schweitzer—perhaps only second to 2 Peter—and provide important evidence for the Hellenization of Pauline Christianity. Like the Gospel, 1 John evidences a developed Logos-Christology in its prologue, reflecting strong Hellenizing tendencies. Schweitzer does note that "in the First Epistle of John 'love' has at once an ethical and a metaphysical significance" and that being "in love" in the Johannine sense has to do with continuing in the fellowship of the elect.[96] The motif of "light" in 1 John, another significant dualistic conception in Hellenistic thought, could be said to have similar connotations. Light also could be argued to have realized eschatological dimensions. John speaks of being "in the light" or "abiding in the light" (1:7; 2:9, 10) in a participatory sense like Paul, and speaks of the present age as one where "darkness is passing away and the true light is already shining" (2:8). The element of participation within the elect community, as John sees it, has to do with being "in the light" or "in the darkness," "in life" or "in death" (3:14). It also has to do with the corporate eschatological notion of "abiding in him" (2:6, 28; 3:6, 9, 24;

95. Cf. ibid., 38.
96. Ibid., 352.

4:15–16). God (3:28; 4:16) and his seed (3:9) are said to abide in the believer as well. The notion of abiding is clearly an eschatological one for John (2:28), just as it was for Paul. Overcoming the evil one (2:13, 14) in John's thinking could certainly be read as a realized eschatological notion as well. A number of futuristic statements within the letter, some using a Johannine assurance formula, could be taken as a sign of pressures within the community created by the continued delay of the parousia. Especially relevant are the comments in 1 John 2:18: "Children, it is the last hour, and as you have heard that antichrist is coming, so now many antichrists have come. Therefore we know that it is the last hour." The subsequent verse talks about those who have gone out from the community because they were not elect. John points to the false teachers and their proselytes within the community as a further confirmation "that it is the last hour." People were apparently getting restless and were in need of assurance. First John 2:28 is similar: "And now, little children, abide in him, so that when he appears we may have confidence and not shrink from him in shame at his coming." So there is still an expectation in 1 John, but the connection of the expectation to the mystical union is entirely absent. Further realized notions have crept in and by this time the Hellenization of Pauline Christianity is fully underway.

Second Peter would likely have been viewed by Schweitzer as inauthentic and quite late, probably from the second century. He mentions the letter twice in *Mysticism* and only one of these references is in the context of the theological development of early Christianity. Here he uses the letter to support the notion that early Christians were having some serious doubts about an imminent parousia. He may have followed the prevailing critical notion—although we must confess it was rarely Schweitzer's tendency to do so!—that the letter represents early Catholicism. His assessment would probably, then, be similar to that of Käsemann, who notes that the letter "lacks any Christological orientation" and reflects a "relapse into Hellenistic dualism."[97] Such a conception would allow for both of the planks of Schweitzer's theory regarding the development of primitive Christian belief to be supported. The mystical Christology is lacking in the eschatology of post-Pauline Christianity, and Hellenization of Christian belief is in effect. These two points can be established, regardless of whether it is maintained that by the time 2 Peter was written there was a complete recession of belief in an imminent parousia.

Based upon this construal of the evidence, we might talk about three stages of theological development (i.e., eschatological recession) within post-Pauline Christianity as represented by the later New Testament documents: (1) Jewish Apocalyptic Christianity minus the Pauline doctrine of the resurrection, (2) non-Apocalyptic Jewish Christianity and (3) Hellenized Christianity. Jude is the primary representation of the first stage and 1 Peter is primarily in the second, but strands of Jewish apocalypticism can still be detected. Hebrews and James are firmly situated in the second category with James having even less of an emphasis upon eschatology than Hebrews.

97. Käsemann, "Apologia," 179–80.

First John and 2 Peter fall comfortably within the final category. These key stages provide the undeveloped link in Schweitzer between later New Testament literature and early Hellenized Christianity.

CONCLUDING OBSERVATIONS

What may be clearly observed from the above analysis is that important issues in both Jesus and Pauline studies have their roots in Schweitzer, witnessing to his significance within the discipline of New Testament study. Most attempts to treat Schweitzer as an interpreter have paid undue or at least imbalanced attention to Schweitzer's vision of Jesus, failing to understand his eschatological Jesus as part of a larger apocalyptic project for describing the emergence of early Christianity. This chapter has sought to provide a corrective to this situation by considering and expanding upon Schweitzer's historical religious method by attempting to understand it for what it is: an approach to Christian origins that sees them based firmly in apocalyptic Judaism.

BIBLIOGRAPHY

Achtemeier, P. J. "An Apocalyptic Shift in Early Christian Tradition: Reflections on Some Canonical Evidence." *CBQ* 45 (1983) 231–48.

———. *1 Peter*. Hermeneia. Philadelphia: Fortress, 1996.

Allison, Dale C. *The End of the Ages Has Come: An Early Interpretation of the Passion and Resurrection of Jesus*. Philadelphia: Fortress, 1985.

———. "A Plea for Thoroughgoing Eschatology." *JBL* (1994) 651–58.

———. "The Secularizing of the Historical Jesus." *PRSt* 27 (2000) 135–51.

Anrich, Gustav. *Das antike Mysterienwesen in seinem Einfluß auf das Christentum*. Göttingen: Vandenhoeck & Ruprecht, 1894.

Baird, William. *History of New Testament Research*. Vol. 2, *From Jonathan Edwards to Rudolf Bultmann*. Minneapolis: Fortress, 2003.

Barrett, C. K. "Albert Schweitzer and the New Testament: A Lecture Given in Atlanta on 10th April 1975 as Part of the Albert Schweitzer Centenary Celebration." *ExpTim* 87 (1975) 4–10.

Bauckham, Richard J. *Jude, 2 Peter*. WBC 50. Dallas: Word, 1983.

Becker, Jürgen. *Paul: Apostle to the Gentiles*. Louisville, KY: Westminster/John Knox Press, 1993.

Benoit, P. "Resurrection: At the End of Time or Immediately after Death?" *Concilium* 10 (1970) 103–14.

Bousset, Wilhelm. *Jesu Predigt in ihrem Gegensatz zum Judentum: Ein religionsgeschichtlicher Vergleich*. Göttingen: Vandenhoeck & Ruprecht, 1892.

Bowman, John Wick. "From Schweitzer to Bultmann." *ThTo* 11 (1954) 160–78.

Brückner, Martin. *Der sterbende und auferstehende Gottheiland in den orientalischen Religionen und ihr Verhältnis zum Christentum*. RVG 1.16. Tübingen: Mohr Siebeck, 1908.

Buck, C. H. "The Collection for the Saints." *HTR* 34 (1950) 1–29.

Buck, C. H., and G. Taylor. *Saint Paul: A Study in the Development of His Thought*. New York: Scribner, 1969.

Bultmann, Rudolf. *Jesus Christ and Mythology*. New York: Scribner, 1958.

Charles, R. H. *The Critical History of the Doctrine of a Future Life*. (1899). London: Adam & Charles Black, 1912.

Clemen, Carl. *Religionsgeschichtliche Erklärung des Neuen Testaments: Die Abhängigkeit des ältesten Christentums von nichtjüdischen Religionen und philosophischen Systemen*. Giessen: A. Töpelmann, 1909.

Collins, John J., ed. *Semeia 14: Apocalypse: The Morphology of a Genre*. Missoula: SBL, 1979.

Cullmann, Oscar. *Christ and Time: The Primitive Christian Conception of Time and History*. 3rd ed. Translated by F. V. Filson. London: SCM, 1962.

Davies, W. D. "From Schweitzer to Scholem: Reflections on Sabbatai SVI." *JBL* (1976) 529–58.

———. *Paul and Rabbinic Judaism: Some Rabbinic Elements in Pauline Theology*. 4th ed. Philadelphia: Fortress, 1980.

Deissmann, Adolf. *Licht vom Osten: Das Neue Testament und die neuentdeckten Texte der hellenistisch-römischen Welt*. Tübingen: Mohr Siebeck, 1908.

———. *Light from the Ancient East: The New Testament Illustrated by Recently Discovered Texts of the Graeco-Roman World*. Translated by Lionel Richard Mortimer Strachan. New York: Harper & Brothers, 1922.

Denton, Donald L. *Historiography and Hermeneutics in Jesus Studies: An Examination of the Work of John Dominic Crossan and Ben F. Meyer*. JSHJS. JSNTSup 262. Sheffield: Sheffield Academic, 2004.

Dodd, C. H. *Helps to the Study of the Bible*. London: Oxford, 1932.

———. "The Mind of Paul: II." In *New Testament Studies*, by C. H. Dodd, 83–128. Manchester: Manchester University Press, 1953. Reprint of "The Mind of St Paul: Change and Development." *BJRL* 18 (1934) 3–44.

———. *Parables of the Kingdom*. New York: Scribner, 1961.

Drews, Arthur, and William B. Smith. *Die Christusmythe 1*. Jena: Diederichs, 1909.

Duncan, George Simpson. *St Paul's Ephesian Ministry*. London: Hodder & Stoughton, 1929.

Dungan, David. "Albert Schweitzer's Disillusionment with the Historical Reconstruction of the Life of Jesus." *PSTJ* 29 (1976) 27–48.

Dunn, James D. G. "Introduction [to Part I: Classical Voices]." In *The Historical Jesus in Recent Research*, edited by J. D. G. Dunn and Scot McKnight, 3–5. SBS. Winona Lake, IN: Eisenbrauns, 2003.

———. "Introduction [to Part II: Methodology]." In *The Historical Jesus in Recent Research*, edited by J. D. G. Dunn and Scot McKnight, 87–89. SBS. Winona Lake, IN: Eisenbrauns, 2003.

Eichhorn, Albert. *Das Abendmahl im Neuen Testament*. Leipzig: Mohr Siebeck, 1898.

Faw, C. E. "Death and Resurrection in Paul's Letters." *JBL* 27 (1959) 291–98.

Fulton, William. "The Life and Work of Albert Schweitzer." *ExpTim* 43 (1932) 354–58.

Furnish, V. P. "Development in Paul's Thought." *JAAR* 38 (1970) 289–303.

Gager, J. G. "Functional Diversity in Paul's Use of End-Time Language." *JBL* 89 (1970) 325–37.

Gathercole, Simon J. "The Critical and Dogmatic Agenda of Albert Schweitzer's *The Quest of the Historical Jesus*." *TynBul* 51 (2000) 261–83.

Gilbert, G. H. "The Development of Paul's Beliefs." *JR* 14 (1892) 266–70.

Glasson, T. F. "Schweitzer's Influence: Blessing or Bane?" *JTS* 28 (1977) 289–302. Reprinted in *The Kingdom of God*, edited by B. Chilton, 107–20. London: SPCK, 1984.

Grässer, E. *Albert Schweitzer als Theologe*. BHT 60. Tübingen: Mohr Siebeck, 1979.

Groos, H. *Albert Schweitzer: Größe und Grenzen.* Munich: E. Reinhardt Verlag, 1974.

Gunkel, Hermann. *Zum religionsgeschichtlichen Verständnis des Neuen Testaments.* FRLANT 1. Göttingen: Vandenhoeck & Ruprecht, 1903.

Harnack, Adolf von. *Die Mission und Ausbreitung des Christentums in den ersten drei Jahrhunderten.* Leipzig: J. C. Hinrichs, 1902.

———. *The Mission and Expansion of Christianity in the First Three Centuries.* Translated by James Moffatt. London: Williams & Norgate, 1908.

Hayes, D. A. "A Study of a Pauline Apocalypse: 1 Thess. 4:13–14." *JR* 34 (1911) 163–75.

Holtzmann, Heinrich J. *Lehrbuch der neutestamentlichen Theologie 1.* Leipzig: Mohr Siebeck, 1897.

Hunter, A. M. *Paul and His Predecessors.* London: SCM, 1961.

Hurd, J. C. *The Origin of 1 Corinthians.* New York: Seabury, 1965.

———. "Pauline Chronology and Pauline Theology." In *Christian History and Interpretation: Studies Presented to John Knox*, edited by W. R. Farmer et al., 225–48. Cambridge: Cambridge University Press, 1967.

Jewett, Robert. *A Chronology of Paul's Life.* Philadelphia: Fortress, 1979.

Johnson, L. T. "The Pauline Letters from Caesarea." *ExpTim* 68 (1956–57) 24–26.

Joy, Charles R. *Music in the Life of Albert Schweitzer.* London: A. & C. Black, 1953.

Käsemann, Ernst. "An Apologia for Primitive Christian Eschatology." In *Essays on New Testament Themes*, by Ernst Käsemann, 169–95. Translated by W. J. Montague. SBT 41. London: SCM, 1964.

———. *New Testament Questions of Today.* Translated by W. J. Montague. London: SCM, 1967.

Knox, John. *Chapters in a Life of Paul.* New York: Abingdon, 1950.

———. "'Fourteen Years Later': A Note on Pauline Chronology." *JR* 16 (1936) 341–49.

———. "The Pauline Chronology." *JBL* 58 (1939) 15–29.

Knox, Wilfred L. *St. Paul.* New York: D. Appleton, 1932.

Koch, Klaus. *The Rediscovery of Apocalyptic.* London: SCM, 1972.

Koester, Helmut. "Jesus the Victim." *JBL* 111 (1992) 3–15.

Kümmel, Werner Georg. "Albert Schweitzer als Jesus-Paulusforscher." In *Heilsgeschehen und Geschichte.* Vol. 2, *Gesammelte Aufsätze 1965–1977*, edited by Erich Gässer and Otto Merk, 1–11. MTS 16. Marburg: N. G. Elwert, 1978.

———. "Albert Schweitzer als Paulusforscher." In *Rechtfertigung: Festschrift für Ernst Käsemann zum 70. Geburtstag*, edited by Johannes Friedrich et al., 269–89. Tübingen: Mohr Siebeck, 1976.

———. "Die 'Konsequente Eschatologie' Albert Schweitzers im Urteil der Zeitgenossen." In *Heilsgeschehen und Geschichte: Gesammelte Aufsätze 1933–1964*, edited by Erich Gässer et al., 328–39. MTS 3. Marburg: N. G. Elwert, 1965.

———. "Futuristic and Realized Eschatology in the Earliest Stages of Christianity." *JR* 43 (1963) 303–14.

———. *The New Testament: The History of the Investigation of Its Problems.* Translated by S. M. Gilmour and H. C. Kee. London: SCM, 1973.

———. *Promise and Fulfillment: The Eschatological Message of Jesus.* Translated by D. M. Barton. London: SCM, 1957.

Lightfoot, J. B. "The Chronology of St Paul's Life and Letters." In *Biblical Essays*, by J. B. Lightfoot, 215–33. London: Macmillan, 1893.

Longenecker, Richard N. "The Nature of Paul's Early Eschatology." *NTS* 31 (1985) 859-95. Reprint in Longenecker, *Studies in Paul, Exegetical and Theological*, 179-93. NTM 2. Sheffield: Sheffield Phoenix, 2004.

Lowrie, Walter. "Introduction." In *The Mystery of the Kingdom of God: The Secret of Jesus' Messiahship and Passion*, by Albert Schweitzer, 17-58. London: A. & C. Black, 1914.

Matheson, G. *The Spiritual Development of St Paul*. London: Blackwood & Sons, 1891.

Matlock, R. Barry. *Unveiling the Apocalyptic Paul: Paul's Interpreters and the Rhetoric of Criticism*. JSNTSup 127. Sheffield: Sheffield Academic, 1996.

Minear, P. S. "The Jerusalem Fund and Pauline Chronology." *AThR* 25 (1943) 389-96.

Morgan, Robert. "From Reimarus to Sanders: The Kingdom of God, Jesus and the Judaisms of His Day." In *The Kingdom of God and Human Society: Essays by Members of the Scripture, Theology and Society Group*, edited by Robin Barbour, 80-139. Edinburgh: T. & T. Clark, 1993.

Neill, Stephen, and Tom Wright. *The Interpretation of the New Testament 1861-1986*. 2nd ed. Oxford: Oxford University Press, 1988.

Neuenschwander, Ulrich. "Introduction." In *The Kingdom of God and Primitive Christianity*, by Albert Schweitzer, i-xiv. London: A. & C. Black, 1968.

Nicol, Iain G. "Schweitzer's Jesus: A Psychology of Heroic Will." *ExpTim* 86 (1974) 52-55.

Nineham, D. E. "Schweitzer Revisited." In *Explorations in Theology 1*, by D. E. Nineham, 112-33. London: SCM, 1977.

Pitts, Andrew W. "Unity and Diversity in Pauline Eschatology." In *Paul: Jew, Greek and Roman*, edited by Stanley E. Porter, 65-91. PAST 5. Leiden: Brill, 2009.

Pleitner, Henning. *Das Ende der liberalen Hermeneutik am Beispiel Albert Schweitzers*. Texte und Arbeiten zum neutestamentlichen Zeitalter. Tübingen: A. Francke, 1992.

Porter, F. C. "The Place of Apocalyptic Conceptions in the Thought of Paul." *JBL* 41 (1922) 183-204.

Porter, Stanley E. *The Criteria for Authenticity in Historical-Jesus Research: Previous Discussions and New Proposals*. JSNTSup 191. Sheffield: Sheffield Academic, 2000.

———. "Is There a Center to Paul's Thought? An Introduction to the Study of Paul and His Theology." In *Paul and His Theology*, edited by Stanley E. Porter, 1-19. PAST 3. Leiden: Brill, 2006.

Reimarus, H. S. *'Von dem Zwecke Jesu und seiner Jünger.' Noch ein Fragment des wolfenbüttelschen Ungenannten*, edited by Gotthold Ephraim Lessing. Brunswick: [n.p.], 1778.

Reumann, John. "Introduction." In *The Problem of the Lord's Supper according to the Scholarly Research of the Nineteenth Century and the Historical Accounts*. Vol. 1, *The Lord's Supper in Relationship to the Life of Jesus and the History of the Early Church*, by Albert Schweitzer, 1-42. Macon, GA: Mercer University Press, 1982.

———. "The Problem of the Lord's Supper as Matrix for Albert Schweitzer's 'Quest of the Historical Jesus.'" *NTS* 27 (1981) 475-85.

———. *Variety and Unity in New Testament Thought*. Oxford: Oxford University Press, 1991.

Robinson, J. A. T. *Jesus and His Coming: The Emergence of a Doctrine*. London: SCM, 1957.

Robinson, James M. "Introduction." In *The Quest of the Historical Jesus*, by Albert Schweitzer, xi-xxxii. London: A. & C. Black, 1968.

Rollins, W. G. "The New Testament and Apocalyptic." *NTS* 17 (1971) 454-76.

Sanders, E. P. *Paul and Palestinian Judaism*. Philadelphia: Fortress, 1977.

Schmidt, Daryl D. "Sane Eschatology: Albert Schweitzer's Profile of Jesus." *Forum* n.s. 1/2 (1998) 241–60.

Schnelle, U. *Apostle Paul: His Life and Theology.* Translated by M. E. Boring. Grand Rapids: Baker, 2005.

Schoeps, H. J. *Paul: The Theology of the Apostle in Light of Jewish Religious History.* Translated by H. Knight. London: Lutterworth, 1961.

Schweitzer, Albert. *Das Messianitäts- und Leidensgeheimnis: Eine Skizze des Lebens Jesu.* Tübingen: Mohr Siebeck, 1901.

———. *Die Mystik des Apostels Paulus.* Tübingen: Mohr Siebeck, 1930.

———. *Die psychiatrische Beurteilung Jesu: Darstellung und Kritik.* Tübingen: Mohr Siebeck, 1913.

———. *Geschichte der paulinischen Forschung von der Reformation bis auf die Gegenwart.* Tübingen: Mohr Siebeck, 1911.

———. *The Kingdom of God and Primitive Christianity*, edited by Ulrich Neuenschwander. Translated by L. A. Garrard. London: A. & C. Black, 1968.

———. *Kritische Darstellung unterschiedlicher neuerer historischer Abendmahlsauffassungen.* Freiburg in Breisgau: C. A. Wagners, 1901.

———. *The Mystery of the Kingdom of God: The Secret of Jesus' Messiahship and Passion.* Translated by Walter Lowrie. London: A. & C. Black, 1914.

———. *The Mysticism of Paul the Apostle.* Translated by W. Montgomery. London: A. & C. Black, 1931.

———. *Out of My Life and Thought: An Autobiography.* Translated by C. T. Campion. London: George Allen and Unwin, 1933.

———. *Paul and His Interpreters: A Critical History.* Translated by W. Montgomery. London: A. & C. Black, 1912.

———. *The Problem of the Lord's Supper according to the Scholarly Research of the Nineteenth Century and the Historical Accounts.* Vol. 1, *The Lord's Supper in Relationship to the Life of Jesus and the History of the Early Church.* Macon, GA: Mercer University Press, 1982.

———. *The Psychiatric Study of Jesus: Exposition and Criticism.* Translated by Charles R. Joy. Boston: Beacon, 1948.

———. *The Quest of the Historical Jesus.* Translated by W. Montgomery et al. Minneapolis: Fortress, 2001.

———. *Reich Gottes und Christentum*, edited by Ulrich Neuenschwander. Tübingen: Mohr Siebeck, 1967.

———. *Von Reimarus zu Wrede: Eine Geschichte der Leben-Jesu-Forschung.* Tübingen: Mohr Siebeck, 1906.

Selby, D. J. "Changing Views in New Testament Eschatology." *HTR* 50 (1957) 21–36.

Smalley, S. S. "The Delay of the Parousia." *JBL* 83 (1964) 41–54.

Strauss, David Friedrich. *Das Leben Jesu.* Tübingen: C. F. Osiander, 1835–1836.

———. *Das Leben Jesu für das deutsche Volk.* Leipzig: F. A. Brockhaus, 1864.

———. *The Life of Jesus, Critically Examined.* Translated by George Eliot. Reprint, Philadelphia: Fortress, 1973.

———. *A New Life of Jesus.* London: Williams & Norgate, 1865.

Suggs, M. J. "The Date of Paul's Macedonian Ministry." *NovT* 4 (1960) 60–68.

Thackeray, H. J. *The Relation of St Paul to Contemporary Jewish Thought.* London: Macmillan, 1900.

Thiselton, Anthony. "Biblical Classics: VI. Schweitzer's Interpretation of Paul." *ExpTim* 86 (1979) 132–37.

Usener, H. *Religionsgeschichtliche Untersuchungen*. Bonn: Cohen, 1889.

Weaver, Walter P. *The Historical Jesus in the Twentieth Century 1900–1950*. Harrisburg, PA: Trinity International, 1999.

Wendland, Paul. *Die hellenistisch-römische Kultur in ihren Beziehungen zu Judentum und Christentum*. Tübingen: Mohr Siebeck, 1907.

Werner, Martin. *The Formation of Christian Dogma: An Historical Study of Its Problem*. Translated by S. G. F. Brandon. London: A. & C. Black, 1957.

Wernle, Paul. *Die Anfänge unserer Religion*. Tübingen: Mohr Siebeck, 1901.

Westerholm, Stephen. *Israel's Law and the Church's Faith: Paul's Recent Interpreters*. Grand Rapids: Eerdmans, 1988.

Wilckens, U. "Die Bekehrung des Paulus als religionsgeschichtliches Problem." *ZTK* 56 (1959) 273–93.

Wilder, Amos. "Albert Schweitzer and the New Testament in the Perspective of Today." In *In Albert Schweitzer's Realms: A Symposium*, edited by A. A. Roback, 348–62. Cambridge, MA: Sci-Art, 1962.

Willis, Wendell. "The Discovery of the Eschatological Kingdom: Johannes Weiss and Albert Schweitzer." In *Kingdom of God in 20th-Century Interpretation*, edited by Wendell Willis, 1–14. Peabody, MA: Hendrickson, 1987.

Wood, I. F. "Paul's Eschatology." *JR* 38 (1911) 79–91.

———. "Paul's Eschatology. II." *JR* 38 (1911) 159–70.

Wrede, William. *Das Messiageheimnis in den Evangelien: Zugleich ein Beitrag zum Verständnis des Markusevangeliums*. Göttingen: Vandenhoeck & Ruprecht, 1901.

———. *The Messianic Secret*. Translated by J. C. C. Greig. Cambridge: J. Clark, 1971.

8

G. Adolf Deissmann's Influence on New Testament Interpretation

Philip D. Burggraff

INTRODUCTION

Trying to imagine things as other than they are can be a difficult task. It is easy for Greek students today to take for granted the fact that the language of the New Testament was the language of the general populace—*koine* Greek. The term *koine* is used so much in seminary Greek classes that the fact that it was the language of the New Testament is just assumed. Yet, this was not the case a hundred years ago, when students had a very different concept of the language of the New Testament. The shift to where the modern student stands was largely the result of a handful of scholars of the Greek language, one of whom was Adolf Deissmann.

The focus of this paper is to discuss the importance of Adolf Deissmann in relation to New Testament interpretation. It will begin with a brief historical sketch of his life, followed by discussions of his influence on New Testament interpretation and his understanding of history and theology. The paper will conclude with a brief evaluation of Deissmann's impact on New Testament interpretation and an application of his classification of letters and epistles to two New Testament texts.

BIOGRAPHY

Gustav Adolf Deissmann was born in Langenscheid, Germany in 1866. Growing up in a pastor's home, he began his studies at the Wiesbaden gymnasium in 1879, continued with theological studies at Tübingen from 1885 to 1889, and completed his seminary years at Herborn and Marburg.[1] In 1892, he was conferred the status *Privatdozent* at Marburg in the field of New Testament. While initially planning to go into pastoral

---

1. Gerber, *Deissmann*, 1.

ministry, he changed his course by writing a philological *Habilitationsschrift*, dealing with the preposition ἐν in postclassical Greek.[2] He began his career in Herborn as both a pastor and a teacher, since his pastoral position included a teaching position at the local seminary. In 1897, he took the post of professor of New Testament at Heidelberg, and in 1908, he moved into the professorship of New Testament at the University of Berlin, where he served until his death in 1937.[3]

It is evident from how he was received that Deissmann was a very influential figure in his day.[4] He is most remembered for his early work on postclassical Greek and the placement of New Testament Greek within its proper context. Yet, he was the foremost catalyst for recommencing the archaeological study of Ephesus after the First World War.[5] He was also instrumental in reconciliation efforts among Christians during the war years.[6] At the same time, the war and its aftermath caused a significant shift in Deissmann's work and area of specialization—a move away from primarily philological interests in postclassical Greek to more involvement in societal and humanitarian interests surrounding Germany and the war.[7] During his career, he received eight honorary doctorates from six countries, as well as two nominations for the Nobel Peace Prize.[8] His demanding commitments to his profession as a teacher and his involvement in these other interests served as key reasons why he failed to complete what he considered would be his most important contribution to the study of Greek in the time of the New Testament, his own lexicon.[9]

---

2. Ibid.

3. Brief sketches of Deissmann's life and career can be found in Bullard, "Deissmann," and Horsley, "Deissmann." Gerber, *Deissmann*, 1–3, provides a similar brief account at the beginning of his work, but treats each aspect of Deissmann's career, especially his contributions to philology, archaeology at Ephesus, and ecumenical work during the war years in Germany, in greater detail throughout the rest of the book.

4. Gerber, *Deissmann*, xvii, maintains that Deissmann was the most influential German New Testament scholar of his day at the time of his death in 1937. His influence waned shortly after his death to the place where he was almost forgotten, except for his work on postclassical Greek. Gerber (373), attributes this fall to two factors: (1) he had no students left after the wars to disseminate his philological achievements to the next generation; and (2) the effects of events leading up to and following the Second World War within Germany and the rest of the world.

5. Ibid., xvii. Gerber devotes an entire section (127–206) to the contributions that Deissmann made to the archaeological study of Ephesus.

6. Ibid., xvii–xviii. Gerber covers this in much greater detail in his section on Deissmann in his contemporary context (ibid., 209–370).

7. Ibid., 2.

8. Ibid.

9. Ibid., 94. Gerber extensively chronicles the development and near completion of Deissmann's lexicon, as well as the factors that led to its demise (ibid., 61–103). He shows from familial testimony that the notes (*Zettel*) were housed in about a dozen cases (*Zettel-Kasten*), measuring 350 x 200 x 150 mm. He estimates that these probably housed somewhere around 8000 *Zettel* (ibid., 95). This massive amount of lexicography based on years of notes and archaeological study was most likely destroyed by Russian soldiers, who may have used the paper as kindling, during their occupation of the Deissmann home in 1945 (ibid., 101–2).

Although some of his work never reached completion, his impact on New Testament studies is still clearly evident in the major works he produced on the study of Greek in the New Testament era. Since he was a German scholar, his important works were first published in German, but quickly made their way into English. For instance, the two German works that make up *Bible Studies*, *Bibelstudien* and *Neue Bibelstudien*, were published in 1895 and 1897, and were translated into English in 1901. His *Licht vom Osten* was first published in German in 1908 and translated into English in 1910; his work on the apostle Paul (*Paulus: Eine kultur- und religionsgeschichtliche Skizze*) was published in German in 1911 and in English translation in 1912. He was also influential in bringing German and English scholarship together.[10] In April 1927, Deissmann organized the First British–German Theological Conference at Canterbury.[11] Out of this group came the publication of *Mysterium Christi*, to which a number of prominent British and German scholars contributed essays, including Deissmann himself, Gerhard Kittel, C. H. Dodd, and Edwyn Hoskyns. From how quickly his influence spread, it is evident that Deissmann was considered one of the true scholars of his day.

DEISSMANN'S INFLUENCE ON NEW TESTAMENT INTERPRETATION

The Greek Language of Scripture

Deissmann's main goal was to make sure that the modern reader of the New Testament understood the nature of the language found there. Through his work with the archaeological finds of the late nineteenth century, he demonstrated the faulty understanding of the Greek language of the New Testament era held by scholars. While the opinion that the New Testament represented Attic Greek had passed, most New Testament scholars in Deissmann's day believed that the language of the New Testament was a distinct entity. He wrote, "It is thought that the canonical writings should form a subject of linguistic investigation by themselves, and that it is possible within such a sphere to trace out the laws of a special 'genius of language.'"[12] Thus, the New Testament was a "philological department" unto itself, which, when combined with the notion of canon, resulted in a "sacred Greek."[13] Yet, against this backdrop Deissmann was able to make his most significant contribution. Making use of papyri discovered in Egypt during the late nineteenth century, he showed that the language of Scripture was the same language found in the writings of the common person; it was *koine* Greek.[14] Beginning with the Septuagint, Deissmann argued that

---

10. Throughout his book on Deissmann, Gerber chronicles the correspondence that Deissmann had with his good friend, James Moulton.

11. Bell and Deissmann, *Mysterium Christi*, v.

12. Deissmann, *Bible Studies*, 64.

13. Ibid., 65.

14. Deissmann, *New Testament in Modern Research*, 78.

the seventy interpreters responsible for translating the Old Testament into Greek were not using "Hebraisms" that already were in existence or creating new ones in their translation; rather, these individuals were using language that was spoken and written in the Greek language popular in Egypt.[15]

The same principle applied to the New Testament. The witness of inscriptions and papyri findings throughout the ancient Near East revealed that much of the vocabulary thought to be unique to the New Testament was in fact found throughout the Greco-Roman world. Speaking of the impact of inscriptions, Deissmann wrote, "They afford us wholly trustworthy glimpses into certain sections of the sphere of ideas and of the store of words which belonged to certain definite regions, at a time when Christian churches were taking their rise, and Christian books being written."[16] Even the religious vocabulary and concepts thought to be unique to the New Testament were found to be already in existence in the locales where Christianity was emerging.[17]

Deissmann worked from the understanding that the literary remains (Atticized Greek) from the Greco-Roman world were mainly the product of an upper, cultivated class, speaking about itself.[18] Christianity stood in "natural opposition" to this class, not because it was a religion but rather because of its place in the lower classes of society.[19] Thus, the non-Christian non-literary papyri texts of the lower classes possess immense importance for the study of the New Testament and primitive Christianity. In relation to their significance, Deissmann stated the following propositions:

1. They teach us to put a right estimate philologically upon the New Testament and, with it, Primitive Christianity.

2. They point to the right literary appreciation of the New Testament.

---

15. Deissmann, *Bible Studies*, 65–74. See also Deissmann, *New Testament in Modern Research*, 88–89, where, commenting on the notion of "Hebraisms," he wrote, "Because the New Testament has been written, for the most part, by native Jews, and, what is more important, because it is influenced in many passages by the Greek translation of the Old Testament through the Septuagint, and, finally, because the sayings of Jesus had been translated from an Aramaic original, it contains, naturally, a number of Semitisms. I have never denied that. What I do deny is this: that the number of these Semitisms is enough to disprove the general view that the New Testament Greek is the colloquial Greek of the period, and to revive the view that it is Jewish Greek and to call Greek—Yiddish. The Semitisms only are the birthmarks which show us where primitive Christianity came into existence."

16. Deissmann, *Bible Studies*, 82.

17. Ibid., 84.

18. Deissmann, *Light from the Ancient East*, 6.

19. Ibid., 7, 240. For Deissmann, Jesus was not connected to the literary class, but rather he was "in company with the small peasants and townsmen of a rural civilisation—the people of the great city have rejected Him" (ibid., 240). While Paul may have ministered more within the metropolitan centers, he was able to adapt to the problems and difficulties faced by the average person.

3. They give us important information on points in the history of religion and culture, helping us to understand both the contact and the contrast between Primitive Christianity and the ancient world.[20]

Thus, Deissmann was devoted to displaying the connections between the language of Scripture and that found in the inscriptions and documents of the Greco-Roman world.

Letter versus Epistle

This contrast between the literary and non-literary language of the Greco-Roman world led Deissmann to some interesting conclusions concerning the relationship between the "letter" and "literature." Deissmann began by defining a letter as basically a private conversation in written form. A letter is a personal and intimate communication, and the closer it resembles a private conversation, the better a letter it is.[21] Because it resembles a private conversation, a letter is "destined only for the receiver," and even if it is written for an audience larger than one individual, it by no means has anything to do with the public.[22] The form of the letter and its external appearance have no real effect on determining whether or not the writing is a letter; rather, the purpose that the writing serves points to its being a letter: a true letter is a "confidential personal conversation between persons separated by distance."[23] A person writing a letter is not engaged in producing literature; therefore, such documents are non-literary.[24] To think of the ancient letters written by the average person as literary is simply wrong and perverse.[25]

In contrast to the letter, literature is writing that is designed for the public, and the writer composes it with the intention that the public will take notice of his work.[26] While the letter is similar to the conversation, literature parallels a public speech. It necessarily lacks the intimacy involved with a conversation or a letter because it intends to have more universal appeal. Again, the contents or form of the work do not affect whether or not a piece of writing is considered a book; rather a book or work of literature is labeled as such because it is designed for the public.[27]

Yet, one may ask about those letters that have persisted to the present in collections. Are these not in some sense a work of literature because they have had public/universal appeal? Deissmann answered that the original intention of a letter was still

20. Ibid., 9.
21. Deissmann, *Bible Studies*, 3; Deissmann, *New Testament in Modern Research*, 35.
22. Deissmann, *Bible Studies*, 4. See also, Deissmann, *Light from the Ancient East*, 218.
23. Deissmann, *Bible Studies*, 4.
24. Deissmann, *Light from the Ancient East*, 145.
25. Ibid., 146–47.
26. Ibid., 145, where he stated, "Literature is something written for the public (or at least for *a* public) and cast in a definite artistic form."
27. Deissmann, *Bible Studies*, 7.

private, and the author wrote a letter for a specific audience with no intention that his or her letters be collected or multiplied. At some time after the passing of great teachers or beloved friends, their students and friends would collect and disperse their writings.[28] The collection of manuscripts from an eminent person commonly occurred, and a number of these have made their way down through history to the present.[29] Yet, it is the responsibility of the modern reader to recognize the original writings as they were intended—as private letters.[30]

Deissmann maintained that literature manifests itself in a form similar to the letter—the epistle. In the evolution of communication, the letter preceded the epistle, and the main difference for Deissmann between the two was in the intended purpose: the letter is private; the epistle is public.[31] Examples of epistles include literary treatises and essays that were written in a form similar to a public speech. The only thing that makes the epistle resemble the letter is the opening and closing formulas that are basically the same for both writings. While the letter and the epistle share these features, letter-type features are only ornamental and illusory in the epistle.[32] In Deissmann's estimation, the writer of epistles had not accomplished any great feat. In fact, he wrote, "The zenith of epistolography may always be looked upon as assuredly indicating the decline of literature; literature becomes decadent—Alexandrian, so to speak—and although epistles may have been composed and published by great creative spirits, still the derivative character of the movement cannot be questioned: even the great will want to gossip, to lounge, to take it easy for once. *Their* epistles may be good, but the epistle in general, as a literary phenomenon, is light ware indeed."[33] In the end, Deissmann saw the letter as a piece of life, but the epistle as a product of literary art.[34]

---

28. Ibid., 8 where Deissmann wrote, "When the friend has forever parted from his comrades, the master from his disciples, then the bereaved bethink themselves, with sorrowful reverence, of all that the departed one was to them. The old pages, which the beloved one delivered to them in some blessed hour, speak to them with a more than persuasive force; they are read and reread, they are exchanged one for another, copies are taken of letters in the possession of friends, the precious fragments are collected: perhaps it is decided that the collection be multiplied—among the great unknown public there may be some unknown one who is longing for the same stimulus which the bereaved themselves have received. And thus it happens now and then that, from motives of reverent love, the letters of the great are divested of their confidential character: they are *formed* into literature, the *letters* subsequently become a *book*"; italics his.

29. Deissmann, *Light from the Ancient East*, 221–22.

30. Deissmann, *Bible Studies*, 9. Sarcastically, Deissmann added, "What the editor, in publishing such letters, takes from them, the readers, if they can do anything more than spell, must restore by recognising, in true historical perspective, their simple and unaffected beauty."

31. Deissmann, *Light from the Ancient East*, 220, wrote, "An epistle is an artistic literary form, a species of literature, just like the dialogue, the oration, or the drama. It has nothing in common with the letter except its form; apart from that one might venture the paradox that the epistle is the opposite of a real letter. The contents of an epistle are intended for publicity—they aim at interesting 'the public.'"

32. Ibid., 220.

33. Deissmann, *Bible Studies*, 12.

34. Deissmann, *Light from the Ancient East*, 221.

According to Deissmann, a correct understanding of the bifurcation between the letter and the epistle produces significant ramifications for understanding the writings of the New Testament. It is wrong to assume that the New Testament is literature from cover to cover.[35] The New Testament contains writings that are both literature (epistles) and letters.[36] While it would seem that Scripture was written for the public because of its wide circulation, it must be kept in mind that this was not the original purpose of the authors. The literary character of the New Testament writings must be determined on the basis of their "*pre*literary" character.[37] One can differentiate between New Testament letters and epistles just as easily as one can with ancient literature in general.[38]

In addressing the specific cases found in the New Testament, Deissmann classified the various "letters" as either letters (non-literary) or epistles (literary). To begin with, he placed all of Paul's writings, with the exception of the Pastoral writings (1 Timothy, 2 Timothy, and Titus) in the category of true letters.[39] For Deissmann, Paul's writings displayed a vested interest on Paul's part towards the specific audience to which he wrote. By their personal tone, they resembled well the same kind of letters found in the papyri of Egypt.[40] Even the sections in Paul's writings that appear to be more "doctrinal" do not require that these writings be classified as treatises, but rather they are examples of confessions and attestations on Paul's part, which are subservient to the purpose of the letter.[41] While Paul's letters form a literary collection, they were elevated to the level of literature only after he had died. The church collected them, copied them, and thus made his writings accessible to all of Christianity.[42] Besides Paul's writings, Deissmann also considered 2 and 3 John to be true letters.[43]

In contrast to the letters in the New Testament, Deissmann saw the general "letters" as representatives of the epistle, i.e., as works of literature.[44] While they contain addresses and conclusions similar to Paul's letters, the "catholicity" of their address marks them as being written to a larger Christian audience and not to a specific situation. To Deissmann, "catholic" equals literary, and literary leads to epistle.[45] James

---

35. Ibid., 145.
36. Ibid., 225.
37. Deissmann, *Bible Studies*, 36.
38. Ibid., 38.
39. Ibid., 42; Deissmann, *Light from the Ancient East*, 225–34.
40. Deissmann, *Bible Studies*, 44. See also Deissmann, *Light from the Ancient East*, 233, where he noted that Paul's urgency and tone in his letters ("absolute abandon") verifies the non-literary character of his letters as well as "their reliability, their positively documentary value for the history of the apostolic period of our religion, particularly the history of St. Paul himself and his great mission."
41. Deissmann, *Bible Studies*, 45, 47.
42. Deissmann, *Light from the Ancient East*, 232–33.
43. Ibid., 234.
44. Ibid., 234–38.
45. Deissmann, *Bible Studies*, 50–51.

serves as a good example of an epistle because it is addressed to a wide audience, "is pervaded by the expressions and topics of the aphoristic 'wisdom,'" and concerns a great subject (Christianity) rather than a great man (Christian personality exemplified by Paul).[46]

Deissmann realized that his interpretive method contained a number of inferences. In describing these methodological inferences by which he interpreted the New Testament "letters," Deissmann outlined his approach as follows:[47]

1. Critics of early Christian writings must resist the temptation to view the New Testament as a collection of homogeneous compositions. They must give due weight to the pre-literary character of certain parts of it. Since the literary portions of the New Testament possess formal similarity to Greco-Roman and Jewish literature, they should be investigated according to similar standards.[48]

2. The letters of Paul provide a fixed starting-point for the history of the origin of the early Christian "letters."[49]

3. The collection and publication of the letters of Paul was indirectly influenced by similar collections of letters made in ancient times.[50]

4. The sources, the *testimonia* and especially the *testimonia e silentio*, which allow modern readers to grasp the understanding of the New Testament letters by Christians of the post-apostolic period, possess a different historical value as they relate to letters or epistles.[51]

5. The criticism of Paul's letters must always leave room for the probability that alleged contradictions and impossibilities, which call into question their authenticity and integrity, are really evidences to the contrary. These discrepancies are common occurrences in actual letter writing.[52]

6. In order to properly exegete Paul's letters, one must recognize the nature of what Paul is writing, a personal letter. The exegete needs to interpret Paul's writings with the awareness that what he wrote was occasioned by a strong religious psychology. In order to rightly interpret such personable writings, the exegete will use his/her own insights and intuition, which will unavoidably result in subjective interpretation. In order to properly understand the early Christian epistles, one must appreciate their literary character. In contrast to the interpretation of Paul's letters, which require one to delve into his creative personality,

---

46. Ibid., 53.
47. This list is a restatement and summation of the list as found in ibid., 55–58.
48. Ibid., 55–56.
49. Ibid., 56.
50. Ibid.
51. Ibid., 56–57.
52. Ibid., 57.

the exegete of the Christian epistles interprets them as great texts. Since these texts do not possess personality, the exegete's procedure is much more objective than subjective.[53]

7. The value of the New Testament "letters," as sources for the investigation of the apostolic age, varies according to their individual character. The value of the epistles for understanding early Christianity, especially regarding its make-up and external circumstances, is not very high.[54]

8. In particular, the New Testament letters and epistles possess differing value as sources for the history of the early Christian religion. The letters of Paul provide the reader with pictures of Paul's own personal religion and his character, more so than they serve as sources of theology or doctrine. In contrast, the New Testament epistles represent a religion that was beginning to accommodate itself to external conditions. Established liturgy and doctrine were becoming a reality.[55]

This understanding of the letters as non-literary and the epistles as the literary writings of the New Testament permeated other aspects of Deissmann's understanding of early Christianity, such as an understanding of Jesus' relation to Paul and Christianity.

Deissmann's Explanation of Early Christianity

For Deissmann the foundation of Christianity is Jesus. He is the gospel, and because the gospel is summed up in a person, the gospel is non-literary. The epistles of Jesus are the saints (2 Cor 3:3), not some set of writings. As Jesus' apostle, Paul did not write in the forms of literature either. Yet, as Christianity began writing literature, the religion started to move towards a secularization of the gospel, and this movement, which possessed universal appeal, needed the medium of literature to propagate itself; hence, the New Testament.[56] The history and origin of the development of the New Testament can be summed up in the following three periods:

1. The pre-literary period of the gospel of Jesus and of his apostle, Paul.

2. The literary period of the Gospels and other apostolic books.

3. The period of the formation of the canon, which brought together the non-literary and the literary remains of the apostolic period into the canon of the New Testament.[57]

---

53. Ibid.
54. Ibid., 57–58.
55. Ibid., 58.
56. Ibid., 59. For further discussion on the non-literary nature of both Jesus and Paul, see Deissmann, *Light from the Ancient East*, 238–39.
57. Deissmann, *New Testament in Modern Research*, 38.

When describing the formation of the canon of Scripture, Deissmann had to explain how he understood the relationship between the actual history of Christianity and the traditions of the early church. This explanation manifests itself in how Deissmann did theology.

ISSUES IN HISTORICITY AND THEOLOGY

History and Jesus

Deissmann spoke to the issue of the relationship between history and Jesus. For Deissmann, the great tragedy of historical theology is that it can never fully get back to Jesus. Discussing the science of theology, he wrote, "It can never arrive at its last and greatest object by its own merits. It is true that, in the historical investigation of any great personality of the past, the investigator is bound to come to the limits of his knowledge."[58] Ultimately the historical theologian never can open the "last chamber" in order to enter into a full picture of the historical Christ.[59]

Yet, there is a way in which a full understanding of Jesus is possible. While such understanding cannot be attained through the science of history, it is reached in one's own personal experiences with him, by coming in contact with the one who is now manifested as "living energy."[60] When he lived here on earth, Jesus ministered to and dwelt with the poor, the hungry, and the sick; today, he can be found in the midst of these same groups.[61] To the question of whether or not one can truly know Jesus, Deissmann exuded optimism when he answered, "Jesus is known as much as He is loved."[62] Thus, not through historical investigation, but through actions such as love, one can truly know Jesus.

Deissmann believed that one should not overestimate the value of historical investigation for establishing the religious value of the New Testament because history is not "the basis of the holy"; the holy possesses its own primacy and autonomy.[63] Deissmann pointed out that the Gospel records are much closer to the actual time of the events they portray than almost all other ancient histories.[64] He believed that the Gospels contained both historical records and traditional material from the early church, and he held that in many cases the two could be separated to demarcate history from tradition.[65] For the most part, he believed that the miracle stories were non-

---

58. Deissmann, *Religion of Jesus*, 18.
59. Ibid., 20.
60. Ibid.
61. Ibid., 21–22.
62. Ibid., 23.
63. Deissmann, *New Testament in Modern Research*, 140.
64. Ibid., 145–46.

65. Ibid., 152, where on the historical content of the Gospels, he wrote, "The Synoptic Gospels are great treasure houses with a rich abundance of genuine reminiscences of Jesus. Side by side with the genuine there are others whose genuineness is doubtful or denied. But even those pictures of Christ

historical, but much of the "sayings" material was historical.[66] Yet, the importance of the Synoptics is that they reveal the character and "inner life" of Jesus. Deissmann believed that "it is far more important for us to know the soul of Jesus than to know the succession of the external facts of his life."[67] He concluded, "The new method of working which considers the New Testament in the clearest light of its period, of its Eastern home, and its social class, has altered the judgments on the historical value of the New Testament in many details, but on the whole confirmed its historical value, because it clamped the Holy Book to its contemporary world."[68] For Deissmann, the inclusion of non-historical elements in the Gospel records in no way caused him to question his faith because these records still brought him into contact with Christianity's founder and his on-going work in believers' lives.

Deissmann's Exegesis and Theology at Work

Deissmann's Discussion of "Faith"

In his actual exegesis and theologizing, Deissmann's work is similar to that practiced today. To cite one example, in a chapter from his book on Paul, Deissmann laid out his understanding of Paul's concept of "faith."[69] In many respects the discussion looks like a present day exegetical study of the concept within Paul. The study covers a good majority of the passages in which Paul spoke of faith and details the various subcategories of salvation involved with the concept of faith. Aside from Deissmann's references to psychological and mystical elements, what emerges is an exegetical and theological understanding of faith that many present-day scholars would be proud to produce. At times, his explanation even sounds Calvinistic. He writes:

> Faith . . . is not action, but reaction, not human achievement before God, but divine influence upon man in Christ, and justification "out of" faith or "through" faith is really justification "in" faith, justification "in Christ," justification "in the name of Jesus Christ," justification "in the blood of Christ." Faith is not the pre-condition of justification, it is the experience of justification.[70]

He even goes as far as criticizing infant baptism because a person baptized as an adult better understands the picture of death, burial, and resurrection with Christ.[71] Many Baptist evangelicals would feel comfortable with this type of exegesis.

---

which were created by the sincere art of His disciples have their value as memorials of the Apostolic Christ-cult and are therefore evidence for the powerful influence of the personality of Christ on His followers."

66. Ibid., 154–55.
67. Ibid., 155.
68. Ibid., 160–61.
69. Deissmann, *Paul*, 161–83.
70. Ibid., 169–70.
71. Ibid., 183.

Deissmann's Christ-Mysticism

One of the more unique emphases that Deissmann made in his interpretation of Paul pertained to his understanding of Paul as first and foremost a "Christ-mystic."[72] What Deissmann meant by this is that Paul was "above all and in everything" a "Christ-bearer."[73] While the tendency in theology over the last centuries has centered Paul's Christianity on a theological core, Deissmann found Paul's center in his possessing and being possessed by Christ. This possession by Christ is equated with possession by the Spirit, but Paul most often refers to this with his common expression "in Christ."[74] Describing what this meant for Paul, Deissmann wrote, "Christ is Spirit; therefore He can live in Paul and Paul in Him. Just as the air of life, which we breathe, is 'in' us and fills us, and yet we at the same time live in this air and breathe it, so it is also with the Christ-intimacy of the Apostle Paul: Christ in him, he in Christ."[75] Deissmann viewed "in Christ" as the "characteristic expression" of Paul's Christianity.[76] Ultimately, this being "in Christ" transforms the historical events of Christ's life in the past, which culminated in the cross, "into a present reality."[77] This communion with Christ is not initiated by the sacraments of baptism or the Lord's Supper, but rather this communion is brought about by God through grace.[78] Thus, through a special work of God, Paul was one "whom Christ possessed" and "a Christ-bearer."[79]

While some present-day Pauline scholars may balk at locating the heart of Paul's thought in the experiential dimension, Deissmann's "Christ-mysticism" should not simply be dismissed. He rightly recognized that Paul's spiritual experience of Christ impacted his theology. Paul's writings do not display a cold orthodoxy, but rather they bear testimony to a theology that was alive and vibrant, due to the work of Christ in his life. Further, Deissmann's "Christ-mysticism" at least serves as a precursor to much of the "participatory" emphasis found in Pauline studies over the last few decades.[80] For Deissmann, Paul's life-changing experience with Jesus Christ manifested itself in

---

72. Deissmann is careful to differentiate his understanding of *mystik* from the narrower idea of a "mystical oneness with the deity" (ibid., 148). Rather, he uses the term to describe any and every "religious tendency that discovers the way to God direct through inner experience without the mediation of reasoning" (ibid., 149). For Paul, this inner experience was Christ, thus Deissmann's term "Christ-mysticism."

73. Ibid., 136–37.
74. Ibid., 138–39.
75. Ibid., 140.
76. Ibid.
77. Ibid., 143.
78. Ibid., 144–45.
79. Ibid., 153.

80. For a recent discussion of this theme that interacts with Deissmann, see Dunn, *Theology of Paul*, 390–412; for a critical analysis of the "participation" theme that interacts with Deissmann's work, see Brondos, *Paul on the Cross*, 151–90.

APPLICATION OF DEISSMANN'S APPROACH TO THE NEW TESTAMENT

While this paper touches on a number of topics concerning Deissmann's work, the concentration has been on his approach to the non-literary versus literary dichotomy that he found in Scripture, especially in the letters/epistles of the New Testament. The conclusions he reached in regards to this dimension had ramifications for his theology and exegesis of the rest of the New Testament. The plan here will be to apply his approach to letters and epistles by looking at two examples from the New Testament: Hebrews and Galatians. The discussion will focus on the main background issues of author and audience as they are presented in each document and the overall message and content of the works. The goal will be to explain these two New Testament works in a manner consistent with Deissmann's distinction between letter and epistle.

The book of Galatians represents one of the clearest examples of a true letter from an apostle to a congregation. In this letter Paul clearly states that he is the author responsible for the writing, and he remains prominent as the speaker throughout the letter. This is evidenced by the numerous references that he makes to himself through personal pronouns and first person singular verbs (1:1—2:21; 4:1, 11, 12; 5:2; and numerous other places). In the letter he relays his own feelings and thoughts about the situation in which the audience finds itself. Throughout the letter one gets the sense that Paul is personally involved in the communication and has a close attachment to the audience. In a way, he feels responsible for this group of believers, and he does not want them to go down the false road that lies before them. Within the first two chapters of the letter, Paul tells of his past experiences in Judaism through testimonial of his background before salvation (1:1–14) and his encounters with Judaizing tendencies within Christianity (2:1–21). At the conclusion of the letter, Paul mentions the fact that he either signed or wrote some of this letter with his own hand (6:11), which again highlights the personal touch of Paul in the composition of this letter.

Similar to the emphasis on Paul's involvement in the letter is the presence of the audience. Paul addresses the recipients as the churches in Galatia (1:2). While some might infer from this that the letter is not personal because of the plurality of churches that could have read this letter, the tone of the letter suggests that Paul wrote it with a specific audience in mind who were facing a particular problem. He in no way meant this letter for an audience (a public audience) wider than these churches. He kept this audience in focus throughout the letter by using second-person pronouns, as well as a reference to them again as Galatians in 3:1.

The content of the letter also points out that this writing is a true non-literary letter. Throughout the letter, the communication between author and audience is conversational, with the author personally and authoritatively imploring his readers to refrain from falling in line with the requirements of the Judaizers. Paul provides personal examples and heartfelt pleas toward his readers. At times he engages the audience with personal questions (3:1–5) and expresses his own wishes and desires (4:20). He mentions numerous individuals, including Peter (1:18; 2:8, 9, 11, 14), Titus (2:3), James (2:9, 12), John (2:9), and Barnabas (2:13), who provide concrete, specific examples from real-life situations from Paul's past and present. The piece contains both a letter beginning and a letter conclusion similar to that found in typical personal letters of Paul's day. While Paul may have adjusted the standard forms for his own purposes, this letter still contains them. Of interest is the fact that Galatians is missing the typical thanksgiving section found in many of Paul's writings, and this fact may further reveal the personal concern and urgency with which Paul was constructing the letter. He may have been in such a hurry to get at the message of the letter that he decided to leave this section out—further evidence of Paul's personal concern coming forward in this letter. Finally, while this letter to the Galatians may contain doctrinal content and exposition of Old Testament figures and texts, these serve to bolster Paul's urgent request and demands that these Galatians not follow the Judaizers who were seducing them.

Thus, from the evidence of the author's involvement, the situation of the audience, and the content of the writing, the book of Galatians serves as an example of a non-literary letter in which Paul personally pleads with the Galatians to resist the temptations of Judaism and remain faithful to Jesus Christ.

In stark contrast to the personal letter of Galatians is the New Testament book of Hebrews. To begin with, the author provides no personal information other than the possible inference from 2:3 that he or she was a second-generation Christian who had not personally been a witness to the events of the life of Jesus. While the author at times includes him/herself with the audience through first person plural verbs and pronouns, he/she only refers to him/herself by first person singular reference in 11:32 and the concluding remarks of 13:19, 22, and 23. Thus, in much of the letter a distance or detachment is felt between the author and the audience. In speaking of past endurance during times of persecution, the author mentions the audience's perseverance, but he/she does not include him/herself as going through this trial with the audience (see 10:32–34), further highlighting the distance between the author and the audience.

As with the author, the identification of the audience is lacking. The letter provides no concrete evidence on which a non-speculative identity can be attached to the group the author is addressing. While the author addresses their need for endurance in the face of persecution and possible abandonment of the faith, their specific situation is dealt with in abstract terminology and reference with little personal and individual attention shown by the author.

The content of the letter also substantiates the claim that this writing is impersonal and represents an epistle. The author begins with no formal address whatsoever but rather immediately begins with doctrinal issues concerning God's communication to humanity through His Son Jesus Christ. While the writing does end with a more conventional letter ending, the conclusion contains little personal information about the situation of the author or specific needs or concerns of the audience. Much of the body of this writing focuses on doctrinal issues surrounding the person and work of Christ (1:1–14; 2:5—3:11; 5:1–14; 7:1—10:18), as well as commands, warnings, and encouragements by the author concerning the need for the audience to persevere and not apostatize (2:1–4; 3:12—4:16; 6:1–20; 10:19–39; 12:1–29). Thus, much of Hebrews resembles a treatise by which the author is informing the audience about a certain issue and persuading them to follow a certain course of action. The discussion of Jesus in the writing represents a high Christology with a focus on both the deity and humanity of Jesus. The vocabulary and syntax of the writing typifies a more educated Greek than much of the New Testament; as well, the systematic and stylized argument of the writing evokes recognition of rhetorical strategies prevalent in the first-century Greco-Roman world. All of this provides evidence that Hebrews was written for a wider public audience than just a single local church, which was typical of a later, more doctrinal, stage of Christianity.

In looking at these two writings, Galatians and Hebrews, it is apparent that the former represents the personal and intimate genre of "letter," while the latter is typical of the more stylized and doctrinal genre of "epistle." Galatians exemplifies the early stages of Christianity in which Paul in a personal straightforward manner addressed the needs of a specific believing community. On the other hand, Hebrews portrays a later more developed Christianity in which doctrinal issues were being formulated and attempts made to appeal to a wider public audience.

CONCLUSION AND EVALUATION

A number of points can be made in regard to Deissmann's approach to the language of the New Testament and theology. He can be seen both as a product of his generation, and as one who stood above it. Deissmann was very much a historical critic and strongly believed in the idea of getting behind the text of the New Testament to the actual history presented in it. He remained optimistic concerning the historicity of much of the sayings material, but could not see that real miracles were a historical part of Jesus' works.[81] For Deissmann, faith in Christ does not require a completely historical record of who he was and what he did here on earth. The important dimension of faith lies in the fact that God is presently working and Christ can still be a present reality in the life of the believer.[82]

81. For example, see Deissmann, *New Testament in Modern Research*, 153–55.

82. Ibid., 173–75. Deissmann wrote, "Religion, and especially Christian religion, does not consist for me in the first place in acknowledging certain facts of the past. Christian religion is to me a living and moving in the present living God, a fellowship with the living Christ, which is a fellowship of submission and of following Him. . . . The facts of the past are not the basis of faith. The only basis of our faith is the present living God, and Jesus Christ when He has become for us in some way or other a present and effective Reality. . . . It is of the greatest importance for all of us, for theologians

His approach to letter writing was a necessary correction to how letters were understood, but it has faced a number of criticisms. By using the papyri findings to illuminate his understanding of the New Testament, Deissmann was able to show that the New Testament letters, especially Paul's, contained much in common with personal correspondence. This led scholars away from comparing the New Testament letters to the highly stylized literary letters of the Greco-Roman world towards interpreting them more in the light of the more common everyday correspondence found in the papyri.[83] His distinction between the non-literary letter (reflecting real history) and the literary epistle (reflecting ideas more than history) has remained a standard distinction even into contemporary discussions of ancient letters. In his early twentieth-century work on the form of the ancient Greek letter, Francis X. J. Exler modified but essentially maintained the distinction between the "real" letter and the "unreal" epistle in the same way Deissmann understood the distinction.[84] In his work *Paul the Letter-Writer*, Jerome Murphy-O'Connor also found some validity in the distinction, but he believes the distinction has already served its purpose of bringing the common correspondence of the non-literary papyri into the discussion and, thus, is no longer necessary.[85] To this day, many still approach the ancient Greco-Roman letters with the distinction between "real" and "non-real" letters in mind because this distinction has been hard to dismiss.[86]

While aspects of Deissmann's theories on letter writing have been perpetuated,[87] his approach has faced a number of criticisms. First, Deissmann provided an important corrective through his reliance on the non-literary papyri, but at the same time he over-emphasized their importance for the letter-writing process. It is doubtful that the letter correspondence found in provincial Egyptian towns is necessarily representative of all Greco-Roman letter writing, especially that done in the Hellenistic cultural centers such as Corinth and Ephesus.[88] Second, Deissmann's distinction between the

---

and for the churches, to know that we have in the New Testament an excellent historical tradition of Jesus and His Apostles. But to know the past is not the unconditional basis for our present-day living in the higher world" (174–75).

83. Murphy-O'Connor, *Paul the Letter-Writer*, 44, further adds, "The point of the distinction, as far as Deissmann was concerned, was to force those among his contemporaries, who thought of the New Testament writings as something apart and therefore timeless and rootless, to recognize that what Paul wrote were letters, a medium of genuine communication and part of real life in the mid-first century A.D."

84. Exler, *Form of the Ancient Greek Letter*, 15–20.

85. Murphy-O'Connor, *Paul the Letter-Writer*, 43–44.

86. Ibid., 44; Stowers, *Letter Writing*, 18.

87. Stowers, *Letter Writing*, 18. Besides the distinction between the "real" letter and "non-real" epistle, Stowers mentions that Deissmann's "vividly illustrated portrait" of Christian letter writing, especially the emphasis on the spontaneity with which letter writing took place, has lasted with some modification. Stowers believes this is due to the fact that much of the twentieth-century comparative work on New Testament letters was done with the non-literary papyri.

88. Ibid., 18–19.

private letter and public epistle for either Greco-Roman society or New Testament literature is highly problematic. Paul's letters seem to represent both private and public correspondence.[89] Third, as Stowers points out, Deissmann's distinction between the "warm, personal, spontaneous, artless common-private-friendly letters and impersonal, conventional, artificial literary letters" is "misleading" because of its reliance on the romanticized ideas typical of the nineteenth and early twentieth century.[90] Commenting on the reason for the distinction between "literary" and "unliterary" writing in Deissmann's work, Pearson and Porter write,

> Of course, this delineation really had more to do with the perceived social make-up of society at the time of the New Testament writings, reflecting contemporary German Romantic ideas of natural religion and the stagnancy of the church at the time, against which the idealized New Testament Church was held up as an example. Had Paul been shown to be "literary" (meaning "upper class," "conventional" or "hierarchical"), then the whole contention that there was an ideal pattern of an early Church which could be emulated in modern times would have disappeared.[91]

Most scholars today disagree with Deissmann's notions that the letter and the epistle represent two distinct types of literature. Rather, the literary and non-literary aspects of letters should be seen as two poles on a continuum that can be used to describe the classification of individual letters.[92]

Yet, Deissmann was a pioneer in moving the understanding of ancient Greek forward. His explanations of vocabulary throughout his works are still cited today by scholars and lexicons. He was able to show that the language found in the New Testament does not represent a unique Greek, but rather was the Greek of the masses.[93] He is still the most dominant figure in the interpretation of early Christian letters,[94] and most studies of New Testament letters are responses to Deissmann's work.[95] While scholars do criticize him for some of his notions, Deissmann will always be remembered for his contributions to a better understanding of *koine* Greek and his introduction of personality into the understanding of the Pauline letters.

---

89. Ibid., 19.
90. Ibid.
91. Pearson and Porter, "Genres," 150.
92. This is the approach espoused in ibid., 151.
93. For a brief discussion on the history of the movement away from belief in a unique "Holy Ghost" Greek to the present day understanding of New Testament language as Koine Greek, see Porter, "Greek Language," 105–10.
94. Stowers, *Letter Writing*, 17.
95. Porter, "Exegesis of the Pauline Letters," 541. An example of this is White, *Form and Function*, 1–3.

BIBLIOGRAPHY

Bell, G. K. A., and Adolf Deissmann, eds. *Mysterium Christi: Christological Studies*. London: Longmans, 1930.

Brondos, David A. *Paul on the Cross: Reconstructing the Apostle's Story of Redemption*. Minneapolis: Fortress, 2006.

Bullard, John M. "Deissmann, Adolf." In *Dictionary of Biblical Interpretation*, edited by John H. Hayes, 264–65. Nashville: Abingdon, 1999.

Deissmann, G. Adolf. *Bibelstudien*. Marburg: Elwert, 1895.

———. *Bible Studies: Contributions, Chiefly from Papyri and Inscriptions, to the History of the Language, the Literature, and the Religion of Hellenistic Judaism and Primitive Christianity*. Translated by Alexander Grieve. Edinburgh: T. & T. Clark, 1901.

———. *Licht vom Osten: Das Neue Testament und die neuentdeckten Texte der hellenistisch-römischen Welt*. 2nd ed. Tübingen: Mohr, 1909.

———. *Light from the Ancient East: The New Testament Illustrated by Recently Discovered Texts of the Graeco-Roman World*. Translated by Lionel R. M. Strachan. London: Hodder & Stoughton, 1910.

———. *Neue Bibelstudien*. Marburg: Elwert, 1897.

———. *The New Testament in the Light of Modern Research: The Haskell Lectures, 1929*. Garden City, NY: Doubleday, 1929.

———. *Paul: A Study in Social and Religious History*. Translated by William E. Wilson. 2nd ed. London: Hodder & Stoughton, 1926.

———. *Paulus: Eine kultur- und religionsgeschichtliche Skizze*. 2nd ed. Tübingen: Mohr, 1925.

———. *The Religion of Jesus and the Faith of Paul: The Selly Oak Lectures, 1923, on the Communion of Jesus with God and the Communion of Paul with Christ*. Translated by William E. Wilson. London: Hodder & Stoughton, 1923.

Dunn, James D. G. *The Theology of Paul the Apostle*. Grand Rapids: Eerdmans, 1998.

Exler, Francis X. J. *The Form of the Ancient Greek Letter: A Study in Greek Epistolography*. Washington, DC: Catholic University of America Press, 1922.

Gerber, Albrecht. *Deissmann the Philologist*. BZNW 171. Berlin: de Gruyter, 2010.

Horsley, G. H. R. "Deissmann, Gustav Adolf (1866–1937)." In *Dictionary of Biblical Criticism*, edited by Stanley E. Porter, 72–73. New York: Routledge, 2007.

Murphy-O'Connor, Jerome. *Paul the Letter-Writer: His World, His Options, His Skills*. Good News Studies 41. Collegeville, MN: Liturgical, 1995.

Pearson, Brook W. R., and Stanley E. Porter. "The Genres of the New Testament." In *A Handbook to the Exegesis of the New Testament*, edited by Stanley E. Porter, 131–65. Leiden: Brill, 2002.

Porter, Stanley E. "Exegesis of the Pauline Letters, Including the Deutero-Pauline Letters." In *A Handbook to the Exegesis of the New Testament*, edited by Stanley E. Porter, 503–54. Leiden: Brill, 2002.

———. "The Greek Language of the New Testament." In *A Handbook to the Exegesis of the New Testament*, edited by Stanley E. Porter, 99–130. Leiden: Brill, 2002.

Stowers, Stanley K. *Letter Writing in Greco-Roman Antiquity*. Library of Early Christianity 5. Philadelphia: Westminster, 1986.

White, John L. *The Form and Function of the Body of the Greek Letter: A Study of the Letter-Body in the Non-Literary Papyri and in Paul the Apostle*. SBLDS 2. Missoula, MT: University of Montana Press, 1972.

9

Martin Dibelius and Rudolf Bultmann

James D. Dvorak

Discussions of form criticism immediately bring to mind the names Martin Dibelius and Rudolf Bultmann.[1] Although the two scholars agreed on the basic goal of this methodology, their starting points were very different. It is, thus, worthwhile to compare their approaches, not only to gain a better understanding of their methodology, but also to gain a more complete understanding of each scholar's contribution to the history of interpretation. After a short biographical sketch of each scholar, I will briefly describe the rise of form criticism and its basic underpinnings, followed by a description of how each scholar developed his method. I will conclude the chapter with a sample application as a means of exemplifying their approaches.

BIOGRAPHICAL SKETCHES

Martin Dibelius was born in Dresden, Germany, on September 14, 1883.[2] He studied theology and philosophy in Neuchâtel, Leipzig, Tübingen, and Berlin, eventually publishing two doctoral dissertations, earning a DPh with one and a DTh with the other.[3] In 1915, he began a thirty-two year stint as Professor of New Testament Exegesis and Criticism at the University of Heidelberg, a position he held until his death in 1947.[4]

---

1. A third important form critic was K. L. Schmidt, who argued in his main contribution, *Der Rahmen der Geschichte Jesu* (which, as of the writing of this chapter, has not been translated into English), that the author of Mark wove together various traditions into a coherent storyline by creating a narrative "framework" in which to place them. See Neill and Wright, *Interpretation*, 253–54; McKnight, *Form Criticism*, 14–15. Cf. McGinley, "Form-Criticism I," 454.

2. Dibelius, *Acts*, vii.

3. Ibid. See also Dibelius, *From Tradition to Gospel*, vii.

4. Dibelius and Conzelmann, *Pastoral Epistles*, ii. Dibelius was one of several people who led the university through the process of reopening following the Second World War in 1945. Peabody ("Dibelius, Martin Franz," 367) notes that the Allies "solicited Dibelius's counsel and aid in reconstructing

Rudolf Karl Bultmann was born in Wiefelstede, Germany, on August 20, 1884.[5] He studied three semesters at Tübingen, two semesters at Berlin, and two semesters at Marburg. He was granted a Licentiate from Marburg in 1910, and after completing qualification research, achieved *Habilitation* in 1912. He then taught at the Instructor rank until 1916. After four years as an Assistant Professor at Breslau (1916–20) and a one-year stint as a full Professor at Giessen, Bultmann returned to Marburg until his retirement in 1951.[6] He died July 30, 1976.

THE DEVELOPMENT OF FORM CRITICISM

Early twentieth-century biblical criticism is known for having bound together the eighteenth century's impulses for sans-dogmatic, historically-oriented interpretation[7] and the nineteenth century's penchant for scientific methodology.[8] The result of this combination was the creation of many new interpretative methods, one of which was form criticism (*Formgeschichte*)[9]—a critical methodology that, in its New Testament application, seeks to discover the most primitive Christian tradition by tracing its development through the careful study of its literary forms.[10] A brief review of the history of interpretation prior to Dibelius and Bultmann reveals a key factor that fertilized the soil from which *Formgeschichte* sprouted, namely the work of William Wrede.[11]

Until the nineteenth century, most mainline scholars accepted Mark's Gospel as a historical account of Jesus' life and ministry.[12] However, Wrede challenged this notion

---

the arts, schools and universities, including the academic program at Heidelberg." See also Graf, *Martin Dibelius*, 69.

5. Bultmann, "Autobiographical Reflections," 283.

6. Ibid., 284–85. See also the Evangelischer Presse-Dienst article "Rudolf Bultmann: Spagat zwischen Glauben und Verstehen."

7. See Brown, "Enlightenment Period"; Thiselton, "New Testament Interpretation."

8. See Loader and Wischmeyer, "Twentieth Century Interpretation," 377. Kümmel is exemplary: "The ancient text in itself is mute and can be revived to speak to a lesser or greater extent only by scientific operation" (quoted by Loader and Wischmeyer, 377).

9. See Sparks, "Form Criticism"; Loader and Wischmeyer, "Twentieth Century Interpretation," 378.

10. See Dibelius, *From Tradition to Gospel*, 4. See also Sparks, "Form Criticism," 111. It is important to understand that although form criticism is essentially *literary* analysis, it is at home in the historical-critical paradigm because it was developed to answer questions pertaining to *history*.

11. McGinley, "Form-Criticism I," 453–54. See Bultmann, *History of the Synoptic Tradition*, 1–2; Bultmann, "New Approach," 38–39; Neill and Wright, *Interpretation*, 266–68; McKnight, *Form Criticism*, 7–10. Also influential was the work of Wellhausen (*Matthaei*; *Marci*; *Lucae*), about which Bultmann wrote: "Especially important is Wellhausen's demonstration that the Sayings-document, like Mark, has been influenced by the theology of the primitive church: it grew out of the primitive community, and therefore gives us no infallible reflection of the preaching of Jesus" (Bultmann, "Study," 22).

12. Martin, *Mark*, 92; Bultmann, *History of the Synoptic Tradition*, 1; Neill and Wright, *Interpretation*, 254.

in his book *The Messianic Secret*.[13] Wrede argued that Jesus' messianic identity was a secret until the resurrection, at which time it was disclosed.[14] The author of Mark, writing some thirty years after the events portrayed in the Gospel,[15] interpreted the tradition(s) about Jesus that had been handed down to him in a way that retrojected messianic claims into the account of Jesus' life.[16] In other words, any historical materials the author of Mark may have had at his disposal were interpreted and arranged in the Gospel according to his own and his community's theological (dogmatic) ideas.[17] Therefore—and this is key for the development of form criticism—correctly interpreting Mark's Gospel would require that a distinction be made between history and theology (dogmatics), and the primary exegetical task must be to describe the nature, origin, and development of the earliest tradition(s) of Christianity.[18]

Although source criticism brought scholars to the conclusion that Mark and Q were likely sources for Matthew and Luke, and that Mark, Q, Matthew, and Luke were all most likely influenced by the dogmatic views of the early church, it could not bring scholars to the "pure" historical sources that would allow them to arrive at an "unbiased primitive view of the earthly Jesus."[19] As Dibelius puts it, "We are able to say now how our Gospels arose from their sources, but we cannot yet say how this whole literature arose. We have some conception how the order, increase, and variation of the materials took place, *but not how they came to be handed down and collected*."[20]

---

13. Wrede, *Messianic Secret*. Cf. Neill and Wright, *Interpretation*, 266 n. 2. For a concise overview and critique of Wrede's work, see Martin, *Mark*, 91–97. See also Dunn, "Messianic Secret."

14. Wrede, *Messianic Secret*, 67–68. Wrede goes on to say that although Jesus revealed himself to his disciples (as opposed to "the people"), he still remained "incomprehensible" until the resurrection (ibid., 113).

15. Ibid., 9.

16. Ibid., 4–5, 68; McGinley, "Form-Criticism I," 453; Bultmann, *History of the Synoptic Tradition*, 1; Bultmann, "New Approach," 37. Martin writes, "Wrede brought Mark's gospel within the orbit of theologizing and saw it as a specimen of reflective thought, not straightforward reportage" (*Mark*, 92).

17. McGinley, "Form-Criticism I," 453. Bultmann states, "W. Wrede had already demonstrated . . . that although Mark is indeed the oldest gospel, its narrative cannot be accepted as an exact account of the history of Jesus; that Mark is really dominated by the theology of the Church and by a dogmatic conception of Christ; and that he arranged and revised the old traditional material out of which his gospel is composed in accordance with his own ideas, so that one cannot make out from his narrative either the development of the Messianic consciousness and claim of Jesus or the course of his activity, nor the reasons for his failure and death" ("Study," 22). Wrede's impact on Dibelius may be clearly seen in Dibelius's *From Tradition to Gospel*, 287–301.

18. Wrede, *Messianic Secret*, 4. Cf. Telford, "Wrede," 389. See esp. Bultmann, *History of the Synoptic Tradition*, 1; Bultmann, "New Approach," 37–39; McGinley, "Form-Criticism I," 453. In a similar vein, Wellhausen (see his *Matthaei*, *Marci*, and *Lucae*) argued that the Gospels do not present a historical portrait of Jesus, but the prevailing perception of Jesus present in the early Christian community. He wrote: "The spirit of Jesus undoubtedly breathes in the utterances derived from the community at Jerusalem; but we do not derive a historical picture of Jesus himself from the conception of Jesus which prevailed in the community" (quoted in Bultmann, "New Approach," 38).

19. McKnight, *Form Criticism*, 10.

20. Dibelius, *From Tradition to Gospel*, 9; italics added.

Thus, a method was needed that was both able to distinguish between tradition and redaction and to describe how tradition was collected and handed down to the evangelists. *Formgeschichte* was developed to meet this need.

Form criticism has a number of fundamental presuppositions that were assumed to a greater or lesser extent by all its practitioners, including both Dibelius and Bultmann.[21] First, under Wrede's influence, it was thought that the Gospel accounts as we have them, though based on a relatively fixed form of tradition,[22] contain accretions from the dogmatic beliefs of the authors and their communities.[23] Thus, scholars must excavate the layers of redactional sediment added by the evangelists in order to expose the earliest, purest tradition.[24] Second, the tradition preserved by the evangelists consists of small independent units (sayings and short narratives) that they artificially stitched together.[25] The basic supposition here is there were no continuous narratives of the life of Jesus in the earliest period.[26] Third, the independent units of tradition may be classified as to their literary form.[27] These forms are categorized not by aesthetic standards but according to the purpose or function they fulfilled in various *Sitze im Leben* or typical situations in the life of the early church.[28] Finally, it is supposed that exposing the literary forms enables critics to account for the history and development of the tradition, and therefore to determine its relative age.[29]

Dibelius and Bultmann differed methodologically in several ways. First, Dibelius employed a "constructive method"—a sort of "top down" approach—with which he attempted to describe the fundamental *Sitz im Leben* from which the tradition emerged, extrapolating from there a list of forms that fit that situation.[30] Bultmann, on the

21. See McGinley, "Form-Criticism I," 456–74; McKnight, *Form Criticism*, 17–20.

22. See Dibelius, *From Tradition to Gospel*, 11.

23. Ibid., 1–4; Bultmann, *History of the Synoptic Tradition*, 1–3. Dibelius asserts that the tradition acquired its form in the pre-Pauline Hellenistic churches that were closely associated with Judaism, an early Christianity that was interested in the tradition, not for historical or literary purposes, but for the purpose of preaching (see below). Bultmann, however, was satisfied to divide early Christianity into two phases, viz. Palestinian Christianity and Hellenistic Christianity, which suited his approach well enough. See Dibelius, *From Tradition to Gospel*, 29–33; Bultmann, *History of the Synoptic Tradition*, 5; McKnight, *Form Criticism*, 18–20.

24. The epithets "earliest" and "purest" betray the epistemology of developmentalism common in the late nineteenth and early twentieth centuries.

25. Dibelius, *From Tradition to Gospel*, 3–4 (cf. 218–19, 287–88); Bultmann, "New Approach," 39; Bultmann, *History of the Synoptic Tradition*, 2. This point is based on the results of the work done by Schmidt in *Der Rahmen der Geschichte Jesu* (esp. 317).

26. Dibelius, *From Tradition to Gospel*, 178; Bultmann, "New Approach," 39. One possible exception to this is the Passion narrative.

27. Dibelius, *From Tradition to Gospel*, 4–7; Bultmann, *History of the Synoptic Tradition*, 3–4.

28. Dibelius, *From Tradition to Gospel*, 7; Bultmann, *History of the Synoptic Tradition*, 4. Cf. McKnight, *Form Criticism*, 20; McGinley, "Form-Criticism I," 471.

29. Dibelius, *From Tradition to Gospel*, 7–8; Bultmann, *History of the Synoptic Tradition*, 4.

30. Dibelius, *From Tradition to Gospel*, 10–11 (cf. 41). Dibelius's approach did use analytical methods to identify literary forms, but they were used in the service of the reconstructed *Sitz im Leben*.

other hand, employed an analytic method—a sort of "bottom up" approach—with which he first attempted to identify the forms and after having done so to extrapolate the *Sitz im Leben* on the basis of those forms.[31] Second, Dibelius confined his study to the narrative material, but Bultmann applied the method to both narrative and sayings materials. Finally, Bultmann clearly distinguished himself from Dibelius by claiming that form criticism "not only presupposes judgments of facts alongside judgments of literary criticism,[32] but [it] must also lead to judgments about [the historicity of] facts" (e.g., the historicity of reports or genuineness of sayings, etc.).[33] These differences in approach account for the variation in the kinds of forms each scholar identified, as well as how they analyzed and categorized the Synoptic material.

MARTIN DIBELIUS: FORM CRITICISM FROM THE "TOP DOWN"

Constructive Approach

Dibelius proposed that the earliest accounts of Jesus' life and teaching were formulated within the Aramaic-speaking, Palestinian circle of Jesus[34] between 30 CE and the writing of Mark's Gospel around 70 CE.[35] He believed these stories were initially propagated orally[36] (though not outside the circle of early disciples)[37] based on the assumption that the earliest Christians believed in an imminent parousia and thus saw no need to compile the teachings of Jesus.[38] On this basis, he concluded that the earliest believers were not responsible for fixing the tradition.[39]

However, sometime after the passing of the early group, but before the conversion of Paul, a relatively fixed form of tradition developed.[40] Here, Dibelius postulates that

---

31. Bultmann, *History of the Synoptic Tradition*, 11.

32. See this discussion with regard to the paradigm form in Dibelius, *From Tradition to Gospel*, 59–67.

33. Bultmann, *History of the Synoptic Tradition*, 5.

34. Dibelius, *From Tradition to Gospel*, 28.

35. Dibelius, *Fresh Approach*, 9–10, 27–46.

36. Dibelius believed that this oral tradition, in its earliest form, was passed on in the framework of "Christian Halakha," which was patterned after Jewish Halakhic tradition. See Dibelius, *From Tradition to Gospel*, 28; see also, Neill and Wright, *Interpretation*, 260.

37. Since they held to an imminent return of Jesus, there was no reason they "should spread abroad so zealously their recollections of the immediate past" (Dibelius, *From Tradition to Gospel*, 10).

38. Ibid., 9. Köhler, "Meaning," 613, envisions this as follows: "If a member of the group wished to know how he as a Christian should conduct himself on the Sabbath or in relation to the fast he betook himself to an apostle or to someone else who had been with Jesus and who said: 'I recollect that the Lord once said or did so and so.' In this way the fading recollections of the eyewitnesses became the common possession of the Christian church. Thus arose the traditions out of which our Gospels were composed."

39. Dibelius, *From Tradition to Gospel*, 28–29; McKnight, *Form Criticism*, 19.

40. Dibelius, *From Tradition to Gospel*, 29; McKnight, *Form Criticism*, 19. In Dibelius's mind, this development had to occur pre-Paul, since the traditions Paul adduces in 1 Corinthians 11 and 15 are

a number of Hellenistic Jewish Christian churches, which had grown out of Jewish churches but had not made a "logical breach with Judaism,"[41] became interested in integrating the stories about the life and teachings of Jesus into their worship, preaching, and teaching.[42] Additionally, as the idea of an imminent return of Christ was gradually replaced by that of a future parousia, motivation for heralding these stories arose.[43] This "missionary purpose," as Dibelius called it,[44] was the primary driver in transforming the mere recollections and reminiscences about Jesus into a more or less fixed tradition and the creation of primitive literary forms that could be incorporated into *evangelistic sermons*.[45] As people were subsequently converted to Christ the need arose for further instruction with regard to living as Christians in various contexts, thus giving rise to the *catechetical sermon* and more literary forms.[46] Fragments of tradition were fashioned to support the purposes of the preaching.[47] Therefore, Dibelius concludes that the laws of and motivations for sermons governed the development and fixing of the tradition.[48] He writes, "[T]he dependence of the formation of tradition upon the preaching is to be conceived somewhat in this fashion: the material of tradition gave objectivity to the preaching of salvation; it explained, expanded, and, in accordance therewith, was either introduced into the preaching, or related at its close. The oldest passages of the tradition must have corresponded, in the form they assumed, to this connection with the sermon."[49]

With regard to the Synoptic Gospels as they now exist, Dibelius argued that the writers had access to the relatively fixed tradition and were compelled to compile its pieces into something more systematic. Dibelius calls upon the introduction to Luke's Gospel as proof of this:[50] "Since many have undertaken to set down an orderly account of the events that have been fulfilled among us, *just as they were handed on to us by those who from the beginning were eyewitnesses and servants of the word*, I too

---

too well developed to be primitive forms.

41. Dibelius, *From Tradition to Gospel*, 29.
42. Ibid., 30–31.
43. Ibid., 288–89. Cf. Law, *Historical-Critical Method*, 151.
44. Ibid., 13.
45. Ibid., 14. Cf. McKnight, *Form Criticism*, 19.
46. Dibelius, *From Tradition to Gospel*, 15. Dibelius believes that other types of preaching also developed, including mission preaching, preaching during worship, and catechetical instruction. See also Dibelius, *Sermon*, 34.
47. This comes out clearly in such claims as: "The primitive Christian missionaries did not relate the life of Jesus, but proclaimed the salvation which had come about in Jesus Christ. What they narrated was secondary to this proclamation, and was intended to confirm it and to found it" (Dibelius, *From Tradition to Gospel*, 15).
48. Ibid., 11.
49. Ibid., 15. Based on the speeches and sermons recorded in Acts, Dibelius concluded that these early sermons followed a basic pattern: kerygma (i.e., the message about Jesus), scriptural proof, and exhortation to repentance (17).
50. See ibid., 11.

decided, after investigating everything carefully . . . to write an orderly account for you, most excellent Theophilus."[51] To be sure, the evangelists did not act as "literary"[52] authors in this process; rather, they were "principally collectors, vehicles of tradition, editors."[53] Their influence, though present, was constrained to "the choice, limitation, and the final shaping of the material, but not with the original moulding."[54] Thus, forms of the earliest tradition could still be found in the Synoptic accounts, though with redactional accretions linking them together.[55] Dibelius employed form criticism to identify those forms and accretions as a means of determining the "purest" tradition. He was able to identify five such forms.[56]

Form Types

Paradigms

Paradigms, which Dibelius believed to be the earliest and most trustworthy of the formal constructions,[57] are short narratives that were initially used in the early sermons as supporting material or examples (hence, "paradigm" [παράδειγμα, "example"]).[58] Stylistically, paradigms exhibit five characteristics. First, they exist in isolation,[59] that is, they exist outside a context of their own, so they could be used in just about any context. They are set off by an "external rounding-off" where the Gospel writer adds a bit of text to the beginning and ending so as to make it fit into the context of the

---

51. Luke 1:1–3 NRSV; italics added for emphasis.

52. According to Dibelius, there are three different types of "literature," and the impression of the author's personality upon the work varies according to type. The most polished type of literature, "literature proper," is that which was written with "true 'literary' intent" where the author created content and was guided by the artistic devices and tendencies of the polished literary standards of the day (*From Tradition to Gospel*, 1). On the other end of the spectrum is "unliterary" writing, the type that was neither meant to be distributed, nor made any attempt to employ the literary devices or standards of the day (ibid., 1, 6). Between these poles was a range of literature types that "passed through all the stages between private notes and the borders of literature proper" (ibid., 2). Christian writings from this segment, to which belong the Synoptic Gospels, are referred to as "primitive Christian literature" or *Kleinliteratur* (ibid., 2). These writings had ceased being private unliterary writings, and, although they exhibit some level of literary artistry, they are on the whole devoid of elegant prose and sophisticated rhetoric (*Fresh Approach*, 17; *From Tradition to Gospel*, 2).

53. Dibelius, *From Tradition to Gospel*, 3.

54. Ibid.

55. See Schmidt, *Der Rahmen der Geschichte Jesu*, 317.

56. Some (e.g., Nolland, "Form Criticism," 232) count the Passion narrative among the forms, but Dibelius treats it separately, not as a form per se, but as a series of legends (personal legends [Peter's denial] and etiological legend [crucifixion and resurrection]) with a few tales interspersed (e.g., cock crowing after Peter's denial of Jesus). See Dibelius, *From Tradition to Gospel*, 178–217.

57. Ibid., 288–89.

58. Travis, "Form Criticism," 155.

59. Dibelius, *From Tradition to Gospel*, 44.

larger narrative.[60] Second, paradigms are characteristically short and simple.[61] This must be the case, argues Dibelius, because "only short passages could be introduced into a sermon."[62] They are devoid of details of character development, setting description, and the like. In this way they can function to give emphasis to another part of the story without any artistic detail vying for the attention of the reader or hearer. In short, "they deal only with that which is essential."[63] Third, paradigms are recognizable by "the colouring of the narrative in a thoroughly religious, i.e., realistic unworldly manner."[64] Paradigms typically contain "technical" religious language such as "preached the word," "hardness of heart," or "placed hands upon them and blessed them."[65] Fourth, paradigms make the words or deeds of Jesus stand out by reaching their climax in and closing with a word or deed of Jesus.[66] This makes sense to Dibelius, because the general message of the preaching concerns Jesus and salvation found in him.[67] Finally, paradigms typically end with thoughts that are "useful for preaching purposes."[68] A closing word or deed of Jesus, or even an exclamation from the crowd, provides a meaningful way for the preacher to bridge the context between the paradigm story and the life of the hearer. In this way the preacher may use the paradigm to validate calls to repentance. Examples of texts that Dibelius classified as "pure" and "less pure"[69] paradigms include: Pure: Mark 2:1–12; 2:18–22; 2:23–28; 3:1–6; Less pure: Mark 1:23–27; 2:13–20; 6:1–6; 10:17–31.

Tales

Tales are narrative forms that typically describe Jesus' miracles.[70] Unlike paradigms, tales exhibit "that descriptiveness . . . missed in the Paradigms."[71] Further, tales exhibit "lack of devotional motives and the gradual retreat of any words of Jesus of general

---

60. Ibid.; Dibelius, *Fresh Approach*, 35.
61. Dibelius, *From Tradition to Gospel*, 48; Dibelius, *Fresh Approach*, 37.
62. Dibelius, *From Tradition to Gospel*, 48.
63. Dibelius, *Fresh Approach*, 37.
64. Dibelius, *From Tradition to Gospel*, 56.
65. Ibid.
66. Ibid.
67. Ibid. See also Dibelius, *Fresh Approach*, 38.
68. Dibelius, *From Tradition to Gospel*, 58.
69. "Less pure" paradigms are those "intermediate forms" (*Mischformen*) that exhibit traits common to two or more categories (cf. ibid., 57–59, where the fifth criterion of a paradigm is described as being in common with Tales).
70. Bultmann calls these "miracle stories," and further subdivides them into "miracles of healing" and "nature miracles" (Bultmann, *History of the Synoptic Tradition*, 209–18). Further, Dibelius postulated a class of storytellers telling these miracle stories. Bultmann dismisses such an idea (ibid., 370).
71. Dibelius, *From Tradition to Gospel*, 70.

value,"⁷² with the result that "didactic applications altogether fail."⁷³ The purpose of tales was to dress Jesus in an appropriate "disguise"⁷⁴—as the great thaumaturge (i.e., miracle worker)⁷⁵—so that he might be viewed conceptually in a manner similar to prophets, magi, and wonder workers—that is, with a nature similar to the divine.⁷⁶ Formally, tales follow a basic pattern: (1) a description of the disease or situation to be remedied; (2) a statement of the cure or solution worked by Jesus; (3) a statement of the effects of the cure or solution on the person healed or the reaction of the onlookers.⁷⁷ Dibelius believed tales came about in one of three ways: (1) by the embellishment of paradigm stories; (2) by the injection of bits of non-Christian miracle tradition into paradigmatic forms; or (3) by the adoption and transformation of non-Christian stories as a whole.⁷⁸ Examples of texts classified as tales include: Mark 1:40–45; 4:35–41; 5:1–20; 6:35–44.⁷⁹

Legends

According to Dibelius, legends are "religious narratives of a saintly [person] in whose works and fate interest is taken."⁸⁰ The main interest of legends lies in foregrounding the virtue and religiousness of the saint.⁸¹ Thus, they serve two purposes: "(1) the wish to know something of the holy men and women in Jesus' surroundings, their virtues and also their lot; (2) the desire which gradually came in, to know Jesus Himself in this way."⁸² Legends differ from tales in that tales primarily emphasize Christ and his miraculous deeds; legends are "interested in secondary things and persons."⁸³ Thus legend material exists not only about the Christ (e.g., Luke's birth narrative), but also about other important figures such as Peter. It is important to note, however, that these other characters "are not simply foils for some word of Jesus" (or Jesus himself), but "they become real people and are presented as examples to follow."⁸⁴ Examples of

---

72. Ibid., 79.

73. Ibid.

74. Ibid., 292.

75. Ibid., 80.

76. Ibid., 291.

77. Ibid., 70. See Travis, "Form Criticism," 156; Dibelius, *Fresh Approach*, 40–41.

78. Dibelius, *From Tradition to Gospel*, 99–100.

79. Ibid., 71–72.

80. Ibid., 104. See Dibelius, *Fresh Approach*, 43: "By this term is meant a narrative written in an edifying style and telling of extraordinary things about a holy man or holy place." Bultmann defines legend as "those parts of the tradition which are not miracle stories in the proper sense, but instead of being historical in character are religious and edifying" (Bultmann, *History of the Synoptic Tradition*, 244).

81. Dibelius, *Fresh Approach*, 43.

82. Dibelius, *From Tradition to Gospel*, 115.

83. Ibid., 132.

84. Travis, "Form Criticism," 157. By "real people," Travis does not necessarily mean "historical,"

texts Dibelius classified as legends include: Matt 1:18–24 and Luke 2:8–20; Matt 17:27; Luke 2:41–42; and 4:29–30.

Myths

Taking a cue from Greek mythology, Dibelius defined myths as stories "which in some fashion tell of many-sided doings of the gods."[85] These are stories that describe the actions of the divine breaking into the natural world or such things as the origin of the cosmos or human fate after death.[86] Christian myths, then, are those stories about Jesus where his divine nature as the Son of God is emphasized in some miraculous way. The key purpose of a myth is to give meaning and value regarding its subject to the community for whom it was written.[87] This process of "mythologization" occurs over time as stories are told and re-told from generation to generation. A mythological character was beginning to creep into the Gospel accounts, claimed Dibelius, but only in the stories of the baptism of Jesus (Mark 1:9–11 par.), the temptation of Jesus (Matt 4:1–11 par.), and the transfiguration (Mark 9:2–8 par.).[88] Further examples of "mythologization" may be found in the apocryphal *Gospel of Peter* 35–44, where the resurrection is painted with a mythological brush: the stone rolls from the tomb entrance on its own (v. 37); two men, presumably angels, help a third man, presumably Jesus, out of the tomb, followed by a cross (v. 39); and the head of the one being led out by the hand reaches higher than the sky.[89]

Exhortations (Paraenesis)

In the theory regarding sermons, it was noted that those who had been converted would need further instruction, which prompted the rise of the catechetical sermon. The exhortation forms were used in this kind of sermon. Exhortations are the sayings of Jesus that were capable of being directed toward everyday life.[90] There are examples of this in the Pauline and General Epistles. For example, in Rom 12:14 Paul writes,

---

but rather that they present tangible examples that people can pattern their lives after. Dibelius writes, "The term 'Legend' does not exclude historical traits, but only says that the main interest of the narrator lies elsewhere than in the historicity; it is directed to the religiousness and sanctity of the hero" (*Fresh Approach*, 43).

85. Dibelius, *From Tradition to Gospel*, 266. By the mid-nineteenth century, the term "myth"—in the sense of fictitious stories designed to glorify and exalt Jesus and promote his divinity (cf. Klein et al., *Introduction*, 340)—was applied to the miracle stories. This idea is in line with Bultmann, who maintained that the miracle stories were "hardly biographical," and they were "not proofs of his character but of his messianic authority or his divine power" (Bultmann, *History of the Synoptic Tradition*, 219).

86. Dibelius, *From Tradition to Gospel*, 266.

87. See ibid.

88. Ibid., 271.

89. Cf. Dibelius, *From Tradition to Gospel*, 270–71.

90. Ibid., 240.

"Bless those who persecute you," an echo of Jesus' words recorded in Matt 5:44//Luke 6:28. James writes, "Do not swear by heaven or earth" (Jas 5:12), which parallels Jesus' words recorded in Matt 5:34–37.[91] Formally, the exhortations included maxims (proverbs and short sayings), metaphors, parables, prophetic calls (beatitudes, woes, eschatological preaching), short commands, and extended commands where the motive for the command is given.[92] Examples of exhortation texts include: Matt 5:3–12; 5:39; 6:24; and Mark 4:30–32.

Summary

A brief sketch of Dibelius's view of the Synoptic materials is in order. Dibelius maintained that in the earliest Christian community, short stories consisting of the apostles' reminiscences of Jesus, his teachings, and his life were told among the community for very practical purposes.[93] Paradigms are the earliest, simplest, most straightforward constructions of these stories. As these stories were embellished in both content and style[94] to suit preaching in different contexts, they took on the form of tales (event-focused) or legends (person-focused). Eventually, under the pressure of individual and community theological (dogmatic) beliefs about Jesus' divinity, certain parts of the tradition (i.e., accounts of Jesus' baptism, temptation, and transfiguration) assumed the form of myth.

RUDOLF BULTMANN: FORM CRITICISM FROM THE "BOTTOM UP"

Analytic Approach

As mentioned above, Bultmann's preference was to approach form criticism analytically, first identifying literary forms in the text, then drawing conclusions regarding their *Sitz im Leben*. He thought it "wrong to proceed one-sidedly and simply deduce the forms of the tradition from the presupposed needs of the community, even if [those needs] were rightly recognized."[95] Nevertheless, he could not "dispense with a provisional picture of the primitive community and its history, which has to be turned into a clear and articulated picture in the course of my inquiries."[96] Yet, because of its analytic nature, Bultmann's method did not demand the same kind of detailed portrait of the ancient church as did Dibelius's reconstructive approach; thus, he was content

---

91. Both of these texts, as well as other New Testament and extra-canonical texts, are listed in Dibelius, *James*, 248, following a lengthy description of paraenesis (which is how Dibelius classified James).

92. Dibelius, *From Tradition to Gospel*, 247; also Travis, "Form Criticism," 157.

93. Dibelius, *From Tradition to Gospel*, 287.

94. E.g., addition of elements of setting (times, places, etc.), formulas for transitioning from one story to another (what Dibelius calls "rounding off"), characters, and/or more detail into the story itself or character(s) in the story via a narrator.

95. Bultmann, *History of the Synoptic Tradition*, 11.

96. Ibid., 5; McKnight, *Form Criticism*, 19.

to see two general phases of early Christianity during which tradition was developed: an early Palestinian Christianity and a later Hellenistic Christianity.[97]

In Bultmann's approach, identifying and classifying forms involves the examination of two things: "first, the stylistic pattern which prevails in a particular kind of utterance, such as folk-tales or riddles; and secondly, the laws conditioning the transmission of the literary fragment in either oral or written tradition."[98] Three "tools" may be used to work within this framework: (1) observing any modifications of the material of Mark and Q as it has been reworked by Matthew and Luke; (2) eliminating any secondary developments in the material and arriving at an, albeit provisional, reconstructed form that is older than what appears in the text; and (3) using analogies both for the form and the history of the tradition found in rabbinic and Hellenistic stories, as well as other sources of proverbs, anecdotes, and folk stories.[99] Bultmann put these analytical tools to work on both the sayings and narrative materials of the Synoptic Gospels, the result of which was the identification of two classifications under each: (1) apothegms and dominical sayings and (2) miracle stories and historical stories. Each of the classes has subclasses.

Form Types

Sayings Material

Apothegms

Stylistically, apothegms consist of sayings of Jesus that are set in a concise context, in which, according to the tradition, they were originally spoken.[100] Comparing these sayings with rabbinic and Hellenistic sources[101] led Bultmann to identify three distinct types of apothegm: controversy dialogues, scholastic or teaching dialogues, and biographical apothegms.[102]

Controversy dialogues arise from "some action or attitude which is seized on by the opponent and used in an attack by accusation or by question."[103] The typical

---

97. Bultmann, *History of the Synoptic Tradition*, 5; Bultmann, "Study," 17–20. Cf. also McKnight, *Form Criticism*, 20; McGinley, "Form-Criticism I," 467–68.

98. Bultmann, "New Approach," 343.

99. Bultmann, *History of the Synoptic Tradition*, 6; Bultmann, "New Approach," 345; Bultmann, "Study," 28–30. Cf. McGinley, "Form-Criticism I," 466–67; McGinley, "Form–Criticism II," 54–57.

100. Bultmann, *History of the Synoptic Tradition*, 62–63; Bultmann, "Study," 39–40; McKnight, *Form Criticism*, 25–26; McGinley, "Form-Criticism II," 57. Although these forms roughly correspond to Dibelius's paradigms, Bultmann prefers to use the term "apothegm" because their structure is similar to the apothegms of Greek literature, and *pace* Dibelius, he does not think they served as illustrations in sermons, rendering the descriptor "paradigm" misleading (see esp. *History of the Synoptic Tradition*, 11, 41).

101. See esp. Bultmann, *History of the Synoptic Tradition*, 41–42.

102. Ibid., 39, 54–55; McKnight, *Form Criticism*, 26; McGinley, "Form-Criticism II," 57.

103. Bultmann, *History of the Synoptic Tradition*, 39.

response to these challenges is a counter question or Scripture quotation.[104] Scholastic dialogues are similar in construction to controversy dialogues in that they both may begin with a question put to the Master.[105] The key difference between the two is that in controversy dialogues that begin with a question, the question serves the purpose of entrapment, but in scholastic dialogues the question serves the purpose of gaining more knowledge.[106] Because of their affinity with rabbinic disputes, Bultmann determined the *Sitz im Leben* of these dialogues to be the "discussions the [Palestinian] Church had with its opponents, and as certainly within itself, on questions of law."[107] Examples of controversy dialogues include texts such as Mark 2:1–12 and Luke 14:1–6. Scholastic dialogues include texts such as Mark 10:17–31 and 12:28–34.

Biographical apothegms are those that characterize the person of Jesus. They vary more in their construction than the controversy and scholastic dialogues, but generally, according to Bultmann, the form consists of a saying of Jesus placed in an "imaginary" context.[108] Usually, the saying, which is the point of the apothegm, appears near the end of the form.[109] As for their *Sitz im Leben*, they appear to have been developed for use as "edifying paradigms for sermons."[110] The following are examples of texts that Bultmann classified as biographical apothegms: Matt 8:19–22; Mark 1:16–20; 2:14; Luke 9:57–62.

Dominical Sayings

Based primarily on *content*, "though formal differences are involved as well," Bultmann subdivides the dominical sayings into three subcategories: (1) wisdom sayings (i.e., *logia* or proverbs); (2) prophetic and apocalyptic sayings; and (3) sayings about law and community regulations.[111] When analyzed on the basis of *form*, the "I-sayings" and parables (i.e., similitudes) are identified.[112]

---

104. Ibid., 42, 45; Bultmann, "Study," 39–45. Cf. McGinley, "Form-Criticism II," 58–59.

105. Bultmann says he regards the controversy and scholastic types as "a unitary conception" (*History of the Synoptic Tradition*, 47). See also Bultmann, "Study," 39–46, where he discusses only "controversy" and "biographical" apothegms. Cf. McGinley, "Form-Criticism II," 60–61.

106. Bultmann, *History of the Synoptic Tradition*, 54; McKnight, *Form Criticism*, 26.

107. Bultmann, *History of the Synoptic Tradition*, 41, 48; McKnight, *Form Criticism*, 26.

108. Bultmann, *History of the Synoptic Tradition*, 28 (on Luke 9:57–62), 57.

109. Though with a few exceptions. See Bultmann, *History of the Synoptic Tradition*, 55–56; cf. McGinley, "Form-Criticism II," 61.

110. Bultmann, *History of the Synoptic Tradition*, 60–61; McKnight, *Form Criticism*, 26.

111. Bultmann, *History of the Synoptic Tradition*, 69; Bultmann, "Study," 52–60; cf. McKnight, *Form Criticism*, 27; Travis, "Form Criticism," 157.

112. Bultmann, *History of the Synoptic Tradition*, 69, 150–51, 166–67; cf. Travis, "Form Criticism," 157.

Wisdom sayings are those that portray Jesus as following in the long line of great teachers of wisdom in Israel, Judaism, and throughout the Orient generally.[113] These sayings take on one of three basic forms. Declarative forms are used to present principles concerning material things (where the material thing is the subject) or people (including blessings); imperative forms are used to present exhortations or calls to action (positive or negative); and questions are used largely as a rhetorical means for leading people to certain attitudes or actions.[114] With regard to the genuineness of the wisdom sayings, Bultmann entertains several possibilities.[115] First, Jesus himself could have coined some of the proverbial sayings that the Gospel writers attribute to him. Second, Jesus could have occasionally made use of a proverb that was popular at the time, perhaps with some alteration. Third, the primitive church placed on the lips of Jesus many wisdom sayings derived from Jewish proverbial lore. In the end, Bultmann's verdict is that the wisdom sayings are "the least guaranteed to be authentic words of Jesus; and they are likewise the least characteristic and significant for historical interpretation."[116] The following texts exemplify each type of wisdom saying:

1. Declarative: Matt 6:34b (material): Each day has enough trouble of its own; Mark 10:9 par. (personal): Therefore, whatever God has joined together, a person must not separate.

2. Imperative: Luke 4:23: Physician, heal yourself; Matt 10:16b: Therefore, be shrewd as snakes, but as harmless as doves.

3. Questions: Matt 6:27 par.: Now who among you by being worried is able to add a single hour to his life? Mark 2:19 par.: The attendants of the bridegroom cannot fast while they are with him, can they?

Prophetic and apocalyptic sayings are those "in which Jesus proclaimed the arrival of the Reign of God and preached the call to repentance, promising salvation for those who were prepared and threatening woes upon the unrepentant."[117] Stylistically, these sayings are distinguished by their "brevity and vigor" and, like the *logia*, are often set off by the addition of formal introductory or transitional statements.[118] Numerous analogies with Jewish literature and the apocryphal tradition led Bultmann to claim that the prophetic and apocalyptic sayings developed by and large as the Christian tradition took over Jewish material and ascribed it to Jesus.[119] As "proof," he offers the "little apocalypse" of Mark 13:5–27, which he claimed was "Jewish apocalypse with

---

113. Bultmann, "Study," 52; cf. McKnight, *Form Criticism*, 27.
114. Bultmann, *History of the Synoptic Tradition*, 70; McKnight, *Form Criticism*, 27.
115. See Bultmann, *History of the Synoptic Tradition*, 101–2; McKnight, *Form Criticism*, 28.
116. Bultmann, "Study," 55.
117. Ibid., 56; McKnight, *Form Criticism*, 28.
118. Bultmann, "Study," 56; Bultmann, *History of the Synoptic Tradition*, 130.
119. Bultmann, *History of the Synoptic Tradition*, 125–30; Bultmann, "Study" 56–58.

Christian editing."[120] Those sayings which are judged unlikely to have originated from Jewish sources are said to be the work of later Christian prophets whose sayings were eventually attributed to Jesus.[121] The following are a few texts that Bultmann classified in this category:

1. Preaching of Salvation: Matt 11:5-6; Luke 7:22-23; Mark 10:29-30 par.

2. Minatory Sayings: Luke 6:24-26; Matt 11:21-24; Luke 10:13-15

3. Admonitions: Luke 12:35-58; Luke 21:34-36

The third group of sayings, legal sayings and church rules, are statements about the law and Jewish piety, as well as regulations of the early church community. Generally, these sayings express opposition to external, legalistic piety, and thus have their parallel in the preaching of the prophets.[122] According to Bultmann, the early church possessed a stock of sayings that went back to the preaching of Jesus,[123] a stock to which was added a number of other similar sayings from Jewish tradition.[124] These sayings were edited, expanded,[125] and adapted (e.g., scriptural citations were added) "for reception into the treasury of Christian instruction," becoming a sort of "catechism."[126] A few examples of these sayings may be found at the following references: Mark 7:15; Matt 5:17-19; 16:18-19; 18:15-17, 21-22; Luke 17:3-4.

"I Sayings" and Parables

The "I sayings" are those attributed to Jesus in which he speaks about himself, his work, or his destiny.[127] Examples include:

1. Matt 5:17: "Do not presume that I came to abolish the law or the prophets; I did not come to abolish but to fulfill [them]."

2. Matt 17:22-23: Jesus said to them, "The Son of Man is about to be handed over into the hands of men, and they will kill him, and on the third day he will be raised."

3. Mark 10:45: "For the Son of Man did not come to be served, but to serve and to give his life as a ransom for many."

---

120. Bultmann, *History of the Synoptic Tradition*, 125.
121. Bultmann, "Study," 57; McKnight, *Form Criticism*, 29.
122. Bultmann, "Study," 58.
123. Especially important are the brief conflict sayings in which Jesus expresses his attitude toward Jewish piety (Mark 3:4; 7:15; Matt 23:16-19, 23-24, 25-26). Cf. McKnight, *Form Criticism*, 29.
124. Bultmann, *History of the Synoptic Tradition*, 147; McKnight, *Form Criticism*, 29.
125. Bultmann, *History of the Synoptic Tradition*, 148-49.
126. Ibid., 145-46, 149.
127. McKnight, *Form Criticism*, 30.

Although Bultmann admits there are no grounds for denying that Jesus himself could have uttered these sayings,[128] he goes on to raise a number of what he believes to be "serious considerations" against the sayings, with the result that "one can have but little confidence even in regard to those [sayings] which do not come under positive suspicion."[129] In the end, Bultmann argues that while at least some of these sayings may have a connection back to the preaching of Jesus and subsequently to the early Palestinian church, most of them are formulations of the later Hellenistic church.[130] This is signaled by the increase of mention of Jesus' death and resurrection, as well as the fact that Jesus is portrayed, not only as the prophet sent by God, but also as Messiah and judge of the world.[131]

Influenced by Jülicher,[132] Bultmann discussed the parables of Jesus under the heading "similitudes and similar forms."[133] These are simple and fairly concise stories, which, like popular stories, used concrete imagery, hyperbole, simile, metaphor, and other "artistic devices" to cause a hearer to pass judgment on the story and then upon the real life issue(s) to which the story corresponds.[134] Formally, parables may begin with a question or a statement introduced by a comparative particle (e.g., ὡς or ὅμοιός ἐστιν) as a means of drawing the hearer into the story.[135] The point of the similitude—but not its application—is marked out by ἀμὴν λέγω ὑμῖν.[136] The ending of the parable is varied, sometimes occurring with an application (often appended by οὕτως or οὕτω + imperative), sometimes without.[137] Because of what he saw as "radical alterations"—placement of the parable into new contexts, development of "double-similitudes," allegorical expansions, and various other kinds of alterations and combinations—Bultmann claimed that the parables as they stand in the Synoptic Gospels are clearly formulations of the later church community.[138] Examples of parables abound in the Synoptic Gospels (cf. Matt 13; Mark 4; Luke 8).

---

128. Bultmann, *History of the Synoptic Tradition*, 153.

129. Ibid., 155. Cf. McKnight, *Form Criticism*, 30.

130. Bultmann, *History of the Synoptic Tradition*, 152, 163. There are, however, a number of "I sayings" that Bultmann thinks came from the Palestinian church (e.g., Matt 5:17; 15:24).

131. Bultmann, *History of the Synoptic Tradition*, 151.

132. Cf. Jülicher, *Die Gleichnisreden Jesu*. For a critique of his approach, see Blomberg, "Interpreting the Parables of Jesus."

133. Bultmann, *History of the Synoptic Tradition*, 166–67.

134. Ibid., 166–67; McKnight, *Form Criticism*, 30–31.

135. Bultmann, *History of the Synoptic Tradition*, 180–81.

136. Ibid., 182.

137. Ibid., 182–84. Often in cases when no application is appended, the parable ends with a question directed to the hearer (e.g., Luke 7:41–43; Matt 21:28–31).

138. See Bultmann, *History of the Synoptic Tradition*, 192–205.

Narrative Material

Bultmann divided the narrative material into miracle stories and historical narratives and legends. He further divided the miracle stories into miracles of healing and nature miracles.

MIRACLE STORIES

Bultmann's miracle stories roughly correspond to Dibelius's tales, where the miracle is described with careful detail since it is the main theme of the story.[139] There are two kinds of miracle stories in Bultmann's scheme, healing miracles and miracles of nature. Examples include: Mark 2:1-12 par. (healing); Mark 4:37-41 (nature); and Mark 8:22-27a (healing). In terms of both form and history, Bultmann compared the Synoptic miracle stories with those of Jewish and Hellenistic origin and demonstrated that the Gospel stories have the same style as the Hellenistic stories.[140] Each story typically has three parts: (1) a description of the condition of the patient; (2) the story of the healing itself; and (3) a report of the impression of the miracle on the crowd and/or a clear demonstration of the healing by the one healed.[141] Based on these analogies, the miracle stories—except for Mark 1:40-45; 4:35-41; 6:34-44; 8:1-9; Luke 17:14—are judged to have a later Hellenistic origin.[142]

LEGENDS AND HISTORICAL STORIES

Legends, according to Bultmann, are "those parts of tradition which are not miracle stories in the proper sense, but instead of being historical in character are religious and edifying."[143] Indeed, they may include a miraculous element, but not necessarily so—and if they do, they are still not classified as miracle stories because the point of the story is not bound up with the miracle.[144] Historical stories are those that are based on historical happenings, but are so dominated by legends that they cannot be separated from one another.[145] Bultmann comments that the origins of the legends and historical stories are diverse; some betray an influence from the Old Testament and Judaism, while others show evidence of Hellenistic influence.[146] Key texts Bultmann

---

139. McKnight, *Form Criticism*, 32.
140. Bultmann, "Study," 36-37; McKnight, *Form Criticism*, 32.
141. Bultmann, "Study," 37-39; cf. Bultmann, *History of the Synoptic Tradition*, 209-15.
142. Bultmann, *History of the Synoptic Tradition*, 215, 240-41.
143. Ibid., 244.
144. Ibid., 245.
145. Ibid.
146. Ibid., 302-7; cf. McKnight, *Form Criticism*, 33.

has categorized here include the Passion narrative, the Easter narratives, and the infancy narratives—none of which he sees as organic unities.[147]

Summary

A brief sketch of Bultmann's view of the history of development of the Synoptic material is in order.[148] He taught that in the primitive Palestinian church, apologetic and polemic motives led to the collection and production of the apothegm materials. The demands of edification and of the "prophetic spirit in the Church" led to the collection, production, and handing down of the prophetic and apocalyptic sayings of Jesus. The collection and production of other dominical sayings was driven by the need for exhortation and church discipline. This Palestinian tradition was then taken over and further developed by the Hellenistic church. It was during this part of the development that Jesus was "made" διδάσκαλος and κύριος. Legends and historical stories dominated by legends—especially the transfiguration, passion, and resurrection accounts—arose as the tradition became more about the "Christ of the faith and the cult" and less about the Jesus of history. Bultmann sums it up this way: "The tradition had to be presented as an [sic] unity from the point of view that in it he who spoke and was spoken of was he who had lived on earth as Son of God, had suffered, died, risen and been exalted to heavenly glory."[149] Like Dibelius, then, Bultmann perceived from his researches a development over time of a "Christ myth," and Mark's Gospel was informed by the tradition at this stage: "the Christ myth gives his book, the book of secret epiphanies, not indeed a biographical unity, but an [sic] unity based upon the myth of the kerygma."[150]

APPLICATION: THE TRANSFIGURATION (MARK 9:2–8 PAR.)

For Dibelius, the Transfiguration story[151] cannot be classified as a paradigm story, for the amount of detail in the story (e.g., Jesus' clothing becoming "dazzling white, such as no fuller on earth could bleach them") puts the story beyond the stylistic scope of the paradigm. Although the story records a miracle, it is of a kind different than what is typically found among the tales, which portray Jesus as the great healer and find their point in the reaction to the healing, either by the one healed, the crowd, or the opponents that may have been present. The story is closer in form to the legend, a story intended to communicate something of the holiness and virtue of Jesus. But this classification falls short as well, because the text is not merely about the holiness or virtue of Jesus, it is about his identity as the beloved Son of God. This is one of three

---

147. See Bultmann, *History of the Synoptic Tradition*, 262–301.
148. This paragraph is dependent on ibid., 368–69.
149. Ibid., 371.
150. Ibid.
151. See Dibelius, *From Tradition to Gospel*, 275–78.

texts that Dibelius classified as mythological (see above), for "the heavenly origin of the Master comes to decisive expression."[152] The epiphany described here, with emphasis on the voice from the cloud (i.e., God himself) announcing that Jesus is his beloved Son and that the disciples who were present (at least) should "listen to him" (Mark 9:27 par.), clearly communicates Jesus' divine identity. This story was used in the preaching of the later Hellenistic church as a means of supporting ascriptions of divinity to Jesus.

Bultmann's approach leads him down a slightly different path that ultimately ends up at the same location. Following Wellhausen,[153] Bultmann maintained the Transfiguration legend was originally a resurrection story, but was "antedated" back into the ministry of Jesus by Mark as a means of ratifying Peter's confession and as a prophecy of the resurrection.[154] Further, the two figures talking with Jesus were probably originally perceived as unidentified angelic beings, only later changed in the tradition to Moses and Elijah, intended perhaps as a foil against which Jesus' messiahship would be confirmed.[155] Luke further adds in his account that the Moses and Elijah figures were talking to Jesus about his impending "departure, which he was to accomplish in Jerusalem" (9:31, NRSV). In Bultmann's view, all of these features, like the Easter stories, indicate that dogmatic and apologetic purposes have impacted and caused a change in the primitive tradition. These changes occurred in the later Hellenistic period for religious and edificatory purposes, hence Bultmann classified this text as legend.

CONCLUSION

The purpose of this chapter has been to compare and contrast the form critical approaches of the method's primary developers and exponents. Martin Dibelius employed a "top-down" approach, whereby he attempted to reconstruct the *Sitz im Leben* that motivated and controlled the development of the Christian tradition. He postulated that a "*missionary purpose was the cause* and *preaching was the means of spreading abroad that which the disciples of Jesus possessed as recollections.*"[156] The albeit primitive literary forms to be found in the Gospel accounts, then, are those related to the purpose(s) of the evangelistic and catechetical sermons. The earliest form representing the most primitive tradition is the paradigm; the latest form representing the most dogmatically enhanced tradition is the myth.

Alternatively, Bultmann employed a "bottom-up" analytical approach. Based primarily on observed modifications by Matthew and Luke of Markan and Q material, as well as any similarities with analogous sources (especially rabbinic and Hellenistic

---

152. Ibid., 269.
153. Cf. Bultmann, *History of the Synoptic Tradition*, 259 n. 2.
154. Ibid., 260.
155. Ibid.
156. Dibelius, *From Tradition to Gospel*, 13; italics his.

literature), Bultmann not only categorized traditional material as to form (literary type), but also with regard to relative age and origin. While the use of literary forms cut across the ages, Bultmann postulated that the most primitive form of the tradition was that which arose in the Palestinian church; the later theologically-motivated form of the tradition was that which arose in the Hellenistic church.

BIBLIOGRAPHY

Blomberg, Craig L. "Interpreting the Parables of Jesus: Where Do We Go from Here?" *CBQ* 53 (1991) 50–78.

Brown, Colin. "Enlightenment Period." In *Dictionary of Biblical Criticism and Interpretation*, edited by Stanley E. Porter, 91–101. New York: Routledge, 2007.

Bultmann, Rudolf. "Autobiographical Reflections." In *Existence and Faith: Shorter Writings of Rudolf Bultmann*, edited by Schubert M. Ogden, 283–88. Living Age Books. New York: Meridian, 1960.

———. *The History of the Synoptic Tradition*. Translated by John Marsh. Oxford: Basil Blackwell, 1968.

———. "The New Approach to the Synoptic Problem." In *Existence and Faith: Shorter Writings of Rudolf Bultmann*, edited by Schubert M. Ogden, 35–54. Cleveland, OH: World, 1960.

———. "The Study of the Synoptic Gospels." In *Form Criticism: Two Essays on New Testament Research*, 11–76. Translated by Frederick C. Grant. New York: Harper & Brothers, 1962.

Dibelius, M. *The Book of Acts*, edited by K. C. Hanson. Minneapolis: Fortress, 2004.

———. *A Fresh Approach to the New Testament and Early Christian Literature*. The International Library of Christian Knowledge. New York: Scribner, 1936.

———. *From Tradition to Gospel*. Translated by Bertram L. Woolf. 2nd ed. London: Ivor Nicholson & Watson, 1934.

———. *James*. Hermeneia. Philadelphia: Fortress, 1976.

———. *The Sermon on the Mount*. Translated by Carl H. Kraeling. New York: Scribner, 1940.

Dibelius, Martin, and Hans Conzelmann. *The Pastoral Epistles*. Hermeneia. Philadelphia: Fortress, 1972.

Dunn, James D. G. "The Messianic Secret in Mark." *TynBul* 21 (1970) 92–117.

Graf, Friedrich Wilhelm. *Martin Dibelius: Selbstbesinnung des Deutschen*. Tübingen: Mohr Siebeck, 1997.

Jülicher, Adolf. *Die Gliechnisreden Jesu*. 2nd ed. Tübingen: J. C. B. Mohr, 1910.

Klein, William W., et al. *Introduction to Biblical Interpretation*. Dallas: Word, 1993.

Köhler, Ludwig. "The Meaning and Possibilities of *Formgeschichte*." *JR* 8 (1928) 603–15.

Law, David R. *The Historical-Critical Method: A Guide for the Perplexed*. London: T. & T. Clark, 2012.

Loader, James A., and Oda Wischmeyer. "Twentieth Century Interpretation." In *Dictionary of Biblical Criticism and Interpretation*, edited by Stanley E. Porter, 371–83. New York: Routledge, 2007.

Martin, Ralph P. *Mark: Evangelist and Theologian*. Exeter: Paternoster, 1972.

McGinley, Laurence J. "Form Criticism of the Synoptic Healing Narratives I: The Principles of Form Criticism." *TS* 2 (1941) 451–80.

———. "Form Criticism of the Synoptic Healing Narratives II: Paradigm and Apothegm." *TS* 3 (1942) 47–68.

McKnight, Edgar V. *What Is Form Criticism?* Guides to Biblical Scholarship New Testament Series. Philadelphia: Fortress, 1969.

Neill, Stephen, and Tom Wright. *The Interpretation of the New Testament 1861–1986.* 2nd ed. Oxford: Oxford University Press, 1988.

Nolland, John. "Form Criticism in the NT." In *Dictionary for Theological Interpretation of the Bible*, edited by Kevin J. Vanhoozer et al., 232–33. Grand Rapids: Baker Academic, 2005.

Peabody, D. B. "Dibelius, Martin Franz." In *Dictionary of Major Biblical Interpreters*, edited by Donald K. McKim, 365–71. Downers Grove, IL: InterVarsity, 2007.

"Rudolf Bultmann: Spagat zwischen Glauben und Verstehen." *Marburger UniJournal* 10 (October 2001). No pages. Online: http://www.uni-marburg.de/aktuelles/unijournal/10/News5.

Schmidt, Karl L. *Der Rahmen der Geschichte Jesu: Literarkritische Untersuchungen zur ältesten Jesusüberlieferung.* Berlin: Trowitzsch, 1919.

Sparks, Kenton L. "Form Criticism." In *Dictionary of Biblical Criticism and Interpretation*, edited by Stanley E. Porter, 111–14. New York: Routledge, 2007.

Telford, W. R. "Wrede, William." In *Dictionary of Biblical Criticism and Interpretation*, edited by Stanley E. Porter, 388–89. New York: Routledge, 2007.

Thiselton, Anthony C. "New Testament Interpretation in Historical Perspective." In *Hearing the New Testament: Strategies for Interpretation*, edited by Joel B. Green, 10–36. Grand Rapids: Eerdmans, 1995.

Travis, Stephen H. "Form Criticism." In *New Testament Interpretation: Essays on Principles and Methods*, edited by I. Howard Marshall, 153–64. Grand Rapids: Eerdmans, 1977.

Wellhausen, Julius. *Das Evangelium Lucae.* Berlin: G. Reimer, 1904.

———. *Das Evangelium Marci.* 2nd ed. Berlin: G. Reimer, 1909.

———. *Das Evangelium Matthaei.* Berlin: G. Reimer, 1904.

Wrede, William. *The Messianic Secret.* Translated by J. C. G. Grieg. Library of Theological Translations. Cambridge: J. Clarke, 1971.

10

B. H. Streeter and the Synoptic Problem

PAUL FOSTER

INTRODUCTION

ARGUABLY, B. H. STREETER was the most influential New Testament scholar in the English-speaking world during the twentieth century. If influence is to be measured in terms of dissemination of ideas, both through book circulation and the repetition of theories in the classroom setting, few New Testament scholars of the twentieth century would be able to rival Streeter in impact. Although Streeter wrote many books, undoubtedly his *The Four Gospels* (1924) was, and still remains, hugely influential. There are few works in modern biblical scholarship that have enjoyed such longevity.

The primary reason for this success is that the book, although not totally original in its ideas, provides the classic articulation of the Two-Document Hypothesis. Its clarity of expression and the cumulative logic of argument served both to make this the primary textbook dealing with the Synoptic problem, and to simultaneously and uncompromisingly sweep aside rival theories. What is overlooked, however, is the fact that Streeter was not himself a proponent of the basic Two-Document Hypothesis. Rather, he advocated a more detailed Four-Document Hypothesis coupled with the detection of an intermediate stage in the process of the formation of Luke. Moreover, much of Streeter's theory was predicated on the development of his text-critical theory of local text-types that went into the formation of the Gospels, with source documents originating in the great centers of Christianity in the first century.

In addition to the fame that Streeter accrued from this landmark volume on the Synoptic problem, he was also a widely-published author in the areas of spirituality[1]

---

1. Some of Streeter's works that address the broad concerns of spirituality and pastoral theology include: *Doubts and Difficulties* (1911); "God and the World's Pain" (1916); *God and the Struggle for Existence* (1919); and *The God Who Speaks* (1936).

and the interface between science and religion. B. H. Streeter was a polymath, who, while at home in the rarefied Oxford University environment, was never constrained by donnish ways or affected graces. Rather, he had a rigorous and warm intellect, willing to pursue truth wherever he thought it might lead.

BIOGRAPHY

Burnett Hillman Streeter (1874–1937) was born into the ebullient and self-confident mid-Victorian period, in the first year of Disraeli's second ministry. Unlike the first phase of Victoria's reign, this was more a period of consolidation and structured social order than an age of rapid territorial expansion and intellectual development. Many of the great intellects of the nineteenth century had died during the years immediately prior to Streeter's birth. As the historian of the period, Sir Robert Ensor, noted, "Dickens died in June 1870; Grote in 1871; John Stuart Mill in 1873. No one familiar with the main currents of Victorian thought can miss the break which these three deaths mark."[2] Thus Streeter was born into a society that was settled and well ordered, reaping the benefits of its rapid expansion and its economic security, and therefore enjoying greater freedom and time to pursue intellectual questions. His family life was no less stable than the fabric of wider society. His father, John Soper Streeter, was an unremarkable solicitor, who enjoyed the benefits of his profession and the privileges of life among the Victorian upper-middle class.

As was fitting for a family of this social station, their only son was educated at King's College School in London, which catered to the children of the emerging professional classes. The school had been established in 1829 as the junior department of the newly established King's College of the University of London, and was located on the Strand (prior to moving to Wimbledon in 1897). Here Streeter was given a strong classical education, which was to form the basis of his university studies. In 1893, Streeter went up to Oxford, having gained a classical scholarship at Queen's College. Queen's was to be Streeter's intellectual home (and for long periods also his domestic abode) for the next forty-four years, apart from a six-year appointment (1899–1905) at the nearby Pembroke College.[3]

Streeter's career at Queen's was marked, both as a student and then as an academic, by a series of distinctions. He was awarded first class results in classics moderation (1895), *literae humaniores* (1897), and theology (1898). After an initial academic appointment at Pembroke, Streeter returned to Queen's, where he was initially appointed as Fellow, Dean, and Praelector (1905). Roughly coinciding with Streeter's arrival in Oxford was the formation of what William Sanday described as a "Seminar," the subject of which was the Synoptic problem (1894). Although it is unclear when Streeter joined this group, unlike scholars such as Hawkins, Bartlett, Allen, and Sanday

---

2. Ensor, *England*, 136.
3. Grensted, "Streeter."

himself, Streeter was not a foundation member but, according to Sanday, became "a very regular and active member since he joined us."[4] The group published a volume, *Oxford Studies in the Synoptic Problem*, and Streeter's contribution to it outstripped that of his fellow authors, with him writing five of the thirteen chapters along with the only appendix in the book.[5] Three of those chapters addressed issues relating to Q, and another investigated the literary evolution of the Gospels.[6] These discussions were influential in their own right, but were also highly formative and developmental in Streeter's own thinking in relation to the Synoptic problem.

Yet during this time Streeter developed eclectic ecclesial interests, of which Gospel origins were a single, albeit major, part. In 1912, with a former Fellow of Queen's and future Archbishop of Canterbury, William Temple, and along with five other collaborators (four of whom were to become bishops), Streeter published the volume of essays titled *Foundations*. As is noted in a history of Queen's College, "[w]hen *Foundations*, edited by Streeter, appeared in 1912, the Church was stirred as it had been half a century earlier by the publication of *Essays and Reviews*."[7] Thus the impact of the scholarship of Streeter was perhaps better known through his contribution in that volume, titled "The Historic Christ," where he argued in line with the influence of Schweitzer that what is enduring in the message of Jesus cannot be divorced from the eschatological aspect of the message, but is inextricably bound to such a worldview. Thus Streeter stated, "Much of the unique moral grasp of the New Testament is in one way directly a result of the eschatological back-ground of the period."[8] Yet even here, ideas of contemporary impact and debate stemmed from Streeter's close work on the text of the New Testament.

Another aspect of Streeter's own rich spirituality that is often overlooked is the mystical dimension. The visit to Oxford of the Indian Christian mystic Sadhu Sundar Singh left an impression on Streeter that resulted in a co-authored book describing the life, teaching, and visit of Singh.[9] Apart from the mystical qualities of the individual, Streeter was also attracted to the eclectic approach to spirituality exemplified in Sundar Singh whereby insights from Hinduism could be integrated into an authentic Indian expression of Christianity. Thus Streeter observed,

> It is the genius of Christianity not to crush out natural aptitudes, whether in nations or men, but to inspire each to higher achievement along the lines of his own individual gifts . . . The Christian sadhu movement has for India the

---

4. Sanday, *Oxford Studies*, vii.

5. The Appendix was titled "Synoptic Criticism and the Eschatological Problem."

6. The other chapter was "The Trial of Our Lord before Herod." In this brief study Streeter argues for the historicity of the Lukan account of the trial before Herod Antipas (Luke 23:8–12).

7. Hodgkin, *Six Centuries*, 205.

8. Streeter, "Historic Christ," 119.

9. Streeter and Appasamy, *The Sadhu*.

> immense promise that it is truly Indian. As interpreted by Sundar Singh, it is no less truly Christian.[10]

Although he did not express it in such terms, Streeter envisioned the possibility of an enculturated form of Indian Christianity that was free from colonial controls. Such a post-colonial aspiration was in many ways a politically controversial position to adopt amidst the heightened debate over the "Indian Home Rule" movement.[11]

However, alongside these wide-ranging interests and the diversity of his writings, it is apparent from the scale of his work that Streeter must have been simultaneously developing his thinking on the Synoptic problem and writing his *magnum opus*, which was published in 1924. The rapidity with which reprints and fresh editions appeared is testimony to the impact of *The Four Gospels* on biblical scholarship. Yet, even after the publication of this landmark volume, which further established his credentials as a leading New Testament scholar, Streeter's research interests remained breathtakingly varied. His collected essays in *Reality: A New Correlation of Science and Religion*, dealing with philosophical questions surrounding the relationship between science and religion, circulated widely.[12] Thereafter, Streeter published another volume dealing with early ecclesiology, *The Primitive Church*, but even here his aim was to inform contemporary Christian discussions on reunion through a consideration of the origins of Christian ministry.[13] Another volume, *The Chained Library*, is hailed by Grensted as "one of his most interesting and learned books," who adds that it "revealed his astonishing power of assimilating large masses of detail about a subject remote from those which had made him famous."[14] This ability to comprehend a mass of detailed primary evidence and to assemble an encompassing theory to account for it all was the hallmark of Streeter's work, regardless of which subject area he was engaged in. Yet another hugely influential volume in its day was *The Buddha and the Christ*, which Streeter explicitly stated was not an exercise in comparative religion. Rather, his goal was loftier. Such a comparison was explored to answer the underlying fundamental metaphysical question:

> whether—and, if so, to what extent and in what way—materials afforded by such comparative study throw light on the character of the Unseen Power behind the Universe and so can provide the basis of a working philosophy for everyday life. For that purpose the thing that matters is, not what religion teaches, but how much of it is true.[15]

---

10. Ibid., 255–56.

11. For a wider discussion of the Indian Home Rule movement, see Owens, *British Left*.

12. Further interest in this general area is found in Streeter, *Immortality*, *The Spirit*, and *Adventure*.

13. See also Streeter, *Restatement and Reunion*.

14. Grensted, "Streeter."

15. Streeter, *Buddha and the Christ*, ix.

Streeter was, however, no mere theoretician in treating the subject of Buddhism; rather his analysis was based on empirical analysis and direct observation. As he states in his preface, he first visited India and (the then) Ceylon for five months in 1913, when he began to become acquainted with the localized practice of Buddhism. However, his deeper appreciation of Buddhism stemmed from a visit to China and Japan in 1929, during which he attended various meetings and conferences that provided insight into the religion and culture of those societies. Upon his appointment as Bampton lecturer in Oxford, Streeter prepared for his series of lectures by spending the autumn term of 1931 in Japan. The aim of this visit, in Streeter's own words, was, "the hope that (by observing the worship in temples and by discussions and contact with persons brought up in Buddhist traditions) I might attain to a more sympathetic understanding than I could derive from books alone of the living meaning of Buddhism for those who actually profess it, or to whom it is an ancestral inheritance."[16]

This study further established Streeter's reputation as a theological writer of significant impact, but at the same time in the eyes of certain critics he was viewed as being an "alarming modernist." While his work circulated widely, and he received academic recognition by being appointed Dean Ireland's Professor of the Exegesis of Holy Scripture in 1932 (a post he relinquished upon further promotion to Provost of Queen's College in 1933), his advancement within the Church of England was far more limited. This is striking when it is remembered that all except one of his fellow contributors to the *Foundations* collection of essays had been installed in episcopal office. Streeter had been ordained in 1899, and made a canon of Hereford Cathedral in 1915 (a post he held until 1934); he also served on the Archbishops' Commission on Christian Doctrine (1922–37). Despite these roles, high office in the Church of England eluded Streeter. Whether this was due to his personal desire to remain in academia, or as a result of what was perceived to be his controversial views, is debatable. The latter is perhaps more likely to be the case, since the publication of his own essay in *Foundations* "cost Streeter a couple of examining chaplaincies."[17]

During the 1930s Streeter and his wife Irene became more involved with Christian social action, especially in the form of adherence to the Oxford Group.[18] Scholars such as Streeter brought an intellectual gravitas to the movement that its founder Frank Buchman did not naturally possess. Involvement in this group was one of Streeter's many ongoing interests. However, in 1937 he and his wife made a trip to Switzerland to enjoy a period of convalescence with fellow group members. On Friday the 10th of September, 1937, the couple embarked on their return trip by air. The conditions were unusually bad. Alan Thornhill, employing the present tense (perhaps inadvertently echoing the style of the Gospel of Mark), states that the pilot

---

16. Ibid., x–xi.
17. Hardwick, "Streeter," 250.
18. The group was known as *Moral Re-Armament* from 1938 until 2001, and has been called *Initiatives of Change* since then.

leans over to the radio operator at his side. "Tell them at Basle that we are going to drop a thousand feet through this fog to see where we are."

Behind in the eight-seater plane a couple sit alone. They are the only passengers.

Suddenly the tail of the plane catches some saplings near the mountain top. In an instant the plane spins violently to the ground . . . At once the end comes to the two sitting in the cabin and to the pilot. The radio operator survives. By a merciful anaesthetic of oblivion even he is unconscious for four hours until the rescue party finds them.

The plane fell without burning. It made a clearing in the trees on the meadow crest . . . It is a spot fitted for a wayside place of prayer and encounter with the Christ Who there took two of His friends to live with Him together.

There they are laid to rest in the quiet village cemetery close by. After the service Frank Buchman and others of their friends met to thank God for all they had done. The friend of the Atlantic voyage read to them the story of how Mr. Valiant-for-truth crossed the river.[19]

B. H. Streeter is undoubtedly best known today for his contribution in the field of Gospel source criticism, but this brief biographical sketch has attempted to illustrate the multiple foci of spiritual interests that engaged the energies of this scholar, who was motivated by social activism, interested in spiritualities from Asia, concerned for the questions of the relationship between science and religion, and above all sought the value of humanity collectively and also as exemplified in each individual.

STREETER AND THE SYNOPTIC PROBLEM

When Streeter first went up to Oxford in 1893, discussions concerning matters of source criticism pertaining to the Gospels were the preserve primarily of a small group of New Testament scholars who were able to engage with the latest ideas issuing forth from their German counterparts. However, a few years after Streeter published *The Four Gospels* the topic of source criticism was a basic part of the curriculum for all theological students studying the New Testament. Moreover, the dominant solution to the Synoptic problem was that which Streeter himself had articulated in his landmark work. While not all the ideas in that volume stem originally from Streeter, his ability to synthesize, refine, and communicate such theories with clarity meant that he was seen as the chief propagator of the theory of Markan priority and the existence of a second major source of Jesus tradition (no-longer extant) that both Matthew and Luke used independently of each other—the so-called Q source. This theory established itself as the dominant paradigm in the study of the Synoptic Gospels, and although there have been a few challenges issued to its hegemony, it is accurate to say that this remains the dominant position in New Testament scholarship today.

---

19. Thornhill, *One Fight More*, 63–64.

The Original Order of Q

Streeter's first published work dealing with source criticism of the Gospels is found in the volume edited by William Sanday, *Oxford Studies in the Synoptic Problem*.[20] Streeter's primary arguments in this volume fall into a number of distinct chapters. In his first contribution, chapter 4, "On the Original Order of Q," Streeter commences by rebutting three possible objections to the notion that the double tradition material originates from a single written source. The first putative objection is the fact that some double tradition passages show large variation. In response, however, Streeter notes that "these passages are few in number" and by comparison there are "passages where if Mark had been lost Matthew and Luke might seem to be following independent traditions."[21] Consequently, it is argued that the handling of Q by Matthew and Luke is consonant with their handling of Mark. The second objection that he notes is that of the difficulty of accounting for the purpose and aim of a document that has the shape and genre of Q. He postpones discussion of this issue until a later chapter.[22] The third potential objection is the different ordering of the double tradition material in Matthew and Luke, which may be seen as suggesting that "what the two writers had in common was a number of short disconnected pieces—whether written or floating in oral tradition—which, assuming they worked independently, they could not but arrange in a different order."[23] This last objection forms the central discussion in chapter 4, and Streeter responds to it in two ways. First, again by comparison with the Matthean and Lukan handling of Mark, he argues that Markan traditions became displaced from the sequential order by the later evangelists. However, his second argument is the one he considers more important. Namely, that, "on closer examination we can detect behind the great variety of order a certain original unity of arrangement, and can usually account satisfactorily for the dislocation it has undergone at the hands of the compilers of our First and Third gospels."[24]

This statement not only reveals Streeter's confidence in reconstructing the original order of Q and explaining the later evangelists' deviation from that sequence, but it shows that he viewed the evangelists as thoughtful compilers of the traditions that they inherited. A careful study of the order and transposition in the first and third Gospels of double tradition material leads Streeter to formulate "the general rule that it is Luke rather than Matthew who preserves the original order of his authorities,

---

20. Streeter's contribution is found on pages 141–231, 425–36.

21. Streeter, "Original Order of Q," 141–42.

22. Streeter notes that some raise the objection, "Considered as a Gospel [Q] is a mere torso" (ibid., 142). For the full discussion of the genre and purpose of Q, see Streeter, "Literary Evolution," 210–15.

23. Streeter, "Original Order of Q," 142.

24. Ibid., 143.

and that his order is to be presumed as Q's order unless for some special reason the contrary appears in some particular instance."[25]

This general rule is one that remains dominant among contemporary Q scholars. The reason for its widespread acceptance is obviously because it best explains the data, but Streeter's contribution was not only formulating this principle, but also presenting explanations of how Matthew and Luke handle Markan source material as a heuristic means of assessing the use of other source material. Next, he extracted the double tradition material from the two Gospels that preserve it and illustrated the large agreements in order. Finally, he then convincingly offered explanations for a number of the transpositions that appear to have taken place from the proposed original order. The strength of his analysis lies in the clarity of his theorizing about the original order of the material in Q, combined with the deployment and discussion of the actual double tradition material to demonstrate that the raw data strongly supports the hypothesis that he advocates.

Mark's Knowledge of Q

The next chapter Streeter wrote in *Oxford Studies in the Synoptic Problem* put forward a proposal that has commanded less widespread assent and still remains highly debated. Streeter's basic proposition in this chapter is "[t]hat Mark knew Q and quoted therefrom occasionally, but probably only from memory."[26] In recent scholarship this position has been rigorously upheld by H. T. Fleddermann[27] and supported by Catchpole,[28] while the majority of scholars who have written on this topic argue with differing levels of force for the independence of Mark and Q.[29] Instead, the so-called Mark–Q overlaps are usually explained by those who hold to the Two Document Hypothesis (hereafter 2DH)[30] by the idea that Mark shares some of those traditions that were independently taken into Q.[31] By contrast, Streeter argued (at this stage of his thinking) for a much more direct relationship. This was based on his evaluation of Markan parallels in sixteen passages that showed overlap with Matthew and Luke. He stated that the text-forms of Matthew and Luke "are so striking that it is clear they must have derived their versions in part, if not wholly from some other source than Mark's."[32] For Streeter that source was obviously Q. However, the fact that the Markan

25. Ibid., 164.
26. Streeter, "St Mark's Knowledge," 165.
27. Fleddermann, "Mark's Use of Q."
28. See Catchpole, *Quest for Q*, 70.
29. Sato, *Q und Prophetie*, 383; Tuckett, "Mark and Q"; Neirynck, "Assessment."
30. The choice of 2DH = Two Document Hypothesis, rather than the other frequent abbreviation for this theory 2ST = Two Source Theory, is made here because the term "Two Document Hypothesis" was employed by Streeter, since he saw the two entities in question, Mark and Q, as coherent documents.
31. Kloppenborg, *Excavating Q*, 80.
32. Streeter, "St Mark's Knowledge," 166.

form of the tradition was invariably shorter, yet according to his assessment *not* more primitive (since the Markan narrative lacked essential narrative elements), showed that Mark's form was "a mutilation of the Q version"[33] and not an independent form of the tradition.

The striking thing to note concerning Streeter's thinking on the Markan use of Q is that by the time he came to write *The Four Gospels* some thirteen years later, his position on this question had reversed. Backing away from his earlier view he states categorically that "the evidence is decidedly against the view that Mark used Q."[34] To explain his change in thinking, Streeter notes that the principal difficulty in advocating Mark's knowledge of Q is the minimal impact it made on his composition, "not more than 50 verses."[35] Therefore, the small volume of material that Mark would have borrowed from Q led him to believe that his earlier position was untenable. Moreover, Streeter qualifies his earlier position by noting the hesitancy with which he held it, drawing attention to the fact that in the 1911 study he noted that it was unlikely "that Q lay before Mark in a *written* form."[36] While it is certainly the case that Streeter suggested that Mark drew upon Q from memory rather than from direct literary consultation, it may be left to readers to judge how hesitant Streeter was in this position as expressed initially!

The Original Extent of Q

In chapter 6 of *Oxford Studies in the Synoptic Problem*, "The Original Extent of Q," Streeter opened up a problem that remains fundamental to Q studies. That problem is how to extract all the Q material from Matthew and Luke. In the case of the double tradition passages this is a relatively mechanical process. However, what interested Streeter was "to ascertain whether any passages peculiar to Matthew or Luke can be referred to Q."[37] Streeter's approach was to consider the hypothetically similar problem of reconstructing Mark from Matthew and Luke, if Mark had been lost and Q had survived. He notes that under this scenario extracting only the passages reproduced by Matthew and Luke but not paralleled by a hypothetically existent Q would result in recovering only approximately two-thirds of Mark. As a corollary he states, "We infer therefore that the passages we can identify as Q by the fact that both Matthew and Luke reproduce them may possibly only represent about two-thirds of the original total matter in Q."[38] On strictly numerical grounds, noting that Luke fails to reproduce nearly one-quarter of Mark and Matthew one-twelfth, Streeter initially speculates that perhaps only one-half of Q is preserved as double tradition material, the other half

---

33. Ibid.
34. Streeter, *Four Gospels*, 191.
35. Ibid., 187.
36. Ibid., 191.
37. Streeter, "Original Extent of Q," 184.
38. Ibid., 185.

being classified as material peculiar to either the first or third evangelist. However, he immediately qualifies this figure by suggesting that Luke was more circumspect in his handling of Q than in his reproduction of Markan traditions. Thus he states:

> [I]f Q was, as we think likely, the work of an original eyewitness and Luke knew this, Luke may have been more chary in discarding from Q than from Mark. . . . Matthew on the other hand, who is interested in making our Lord's sayings into a sort of Christian Law Book (cf. p. 221f.), may have discarded more of what he deemed irrelevant, so that the proportion of omissions from Q by Matthew and Luke respectively may be more equal than those from Mark.[39]

Such thinking may be described either as inconsistent by Streeter's detractors, or nuanced by his supporters. This is because he uses the theory of similar editorial techniques by Matthew and Luke in handling both Mark and the double tradition to reconstruct the original order of Q, but for determining the extent of Q he argues that Matthew and Luke deviated somewhat from the way in which they handled Mark. Admittedly, he does provide a reason for supporting this difference, namely Luke's knowledge of the eyewitness character of Q and Matthew's desire to organize material thematically, but this, as Streeter clearly acknowledges, results in theorizing that Luke preserved Q with greater fidelity than was the case with his handling of the Markan source.

However, again, by the publication of *The Four Gospels*, Streeter had modified his view on the extent of Q. Commenting on the earlier arguments for Matthean omission of specific Q passages, Streeter states, "I now feel less confidence in their validity."[40] Thus Streeter declares that an additional factor needs to be considered before one can attribute Lukan or Matthean *Sondergut* to the Q source, namely, why the saying in question would have been disliked by the other evangelist. Streeter offers two passages as examples, Luke 9:51–56 and 17:20–21. The former involves an unpalatable rebuke of the apostles, the latter a view of the kingdom that Streeter suggests is discordant with Matthean theology. Thus the extent of single tradition material that may have belonged to Q had shrunk in Streeter's thinking by the time of the publication of *The Four Gospels*. He is left with a list of passages that he considers as reasonably certainly belonging to Q that amount to some 272 verses, with other passages where there is a possibility but considerable doubt being listed in brackets.[41]

---

39. Ibid., 185–86.

40. Streeter, *Four Gospels*, 290.

41. Streeter's reconstruction of Q contains the following passages listed by Lukan reference as "Lk. iii.2a–9, (10–14), 16–17, 21–22; iv.1–16a; vi.20—vii.10; vii.18–35; ix.(51–56), 57–60, (61–62); x.2–16, (17–20), 21–24; xi.9–52; xii.1b–12, 22–59; xiii.18–35; xiv.11, 26–27, 34–35; xvi.13, 16–18; xvii.1–6, 20–37; xix.11–27. Unbracketed verses = 272" (ibid., 291).

The Literary Evolution of the Gospels

Streeter's fourth and final major chapter in *Oxford Studies in the Synoptic Problem* was less focused on Q than the preceding three chapters. In chapter 7, "The Literary Evolution of the Gospels," he argued that it was possible to detect three distinct stages in the evolution of Gospel writings: the initial stage represented by the reconstructed Q, the second stage characterized by Mark, and the final stage of which both Matthew and Luke were representative. In this chapter Streeter discusses both the geographical location and temporal strata on the one hand, and the literary intention of the evangelists on the other. In relation to the former he states that "Q implies a Palestinian background in the Apostolic age, Mark is Roman and transitional, Matthew and Luke are distinctly sub-Apostolic."[42] Furthermore, the intention of each document is described without any of the qualms that modern writers have about the accessibility of authorial intent. Thus he states, "Q was intended not to supersede but to supplement an oral tradition which would have included an account of the Passion—which Q therefore omits. Mark, written later, was intended to supplement Q. Matthew and Luke, on the other hand, aim at completeness, and intend to supersede rather than supplement earlier writings or traditions."[43]

The boldness of this description should be seen for what it is, namely a confident belief that it was possible to theorize about linear developments in earliest Christianity and that the Synoptic Gospels themselves contained the materials necessary for such a reconstruction. As has been noted, Streeter reversed his thinking on Mark's knowledge of Q, which necessitated a different formulation of the purpose behind the writing of Mark, but not its geographical origin. By the time of the publication of *The Four Gospels* Streeter had developed his thinking on the evolution of the Gospels into a theory of localized texts with strong links to the prominent sees of early Christianity.

The Four Gospels is divided into four major sections. "Part I. The Manuscript Tradition," may at first appear unrelated to the subject matter of the remainder of the book. However, for Streeter, the aim of this section, which is "to broaden the basis of early evidence for the recovery of an authentic text," served a fundamental stage in his overall argument.[44] This was because, as Streeter states in his own words, "when dealing with the Synoptic Problem, where the settlement of a question of great import may depend on the minutest verbal resemblances or differences between the Gospels, it is vital to realise that in our search for the original reading we must, on occasion, go behind the printed texts."[45]

Admittedly, much of what Streeter offered in this part of the book has not been upheld by critical scholarship. However, in his realization that textual criticism was

---

42. Streeter, "Literary Evolution," 209.
43. Ibid.
44. Streeter, *Four Gospels*, xxviii.
45. Ibid., 148.

fundamentally intertwined with attempts to solve the Synoptic problem and that it provided evidence that could illustrate certain aspects of early church history, he was certainly ahead of his time.

Solving the Synoptic Problem: The Fundamental Solution

It is perhaps on first view surprising that Streeter is given credit for being the classic proponent of the dominant theory concerning Synoptic Gospel relationships—the so-called Two Document Hypothesis—when in fact he did not hold this position, but rather advocated a Four Document Hypothesis. However, when it is recognized that the Two Document Hypothesis is in fact the core of Streeter's expanded theory of four source documents, this seems far less incongruous. In fact, Streeter described the notion of Markan priority and the independent use of a second source Q (in addition to Mark) as "the fundamental solution" to the Synoptic problem. In terms of restating what was by his day accepted as a fundamental tenet of Gospel scholarship, the notion of Markan priority, Streeter stated more clearly and succinctly than his predecessors what he saw as the fundamental reason for accepting this position. He presented five main reasons for adopting it. These are worth presenting here in summary form. It should be remembered that it was the cumulative weight of these arguments that was seen as being compelling and not any individual point (which may demonstrate only the medial placement of Mark rather than the basic hypothesis of Markan priority). Therefore, these five points can be summarized as:

1. Of the material contained in Mark, Matthew produces parallels to 90 percent of this material in language largely identical; Luke does the same for more than half.

2. In the triple tradition, Mark's wording is reproduced by Matthew and Luke either alternatively or both together.

3. The Markan ordering of events is usually supported by both Matthew and Luke. If one deviates, the other generally maintains the Markan order.

4. The primitivity of Mark is shown by potentially offensive phrases that are omitted or toned down by other evangelists and by the roughness of style including preservation of Aramaic words.

5. The distribution of Markan material in the other Synoptic Gospels looks as though such material was present in a single document and Matthew and Luke were faced with the problem of combining it with other source material.[46]

A number of criticisms could potentially be raised against these points. First, point five may well be circular—but it needs to be remembered that it is framed in light of the previous four points. The first three points may only demonstrate the

---

46. Ibid., 151–52.

medial position of Mark. The fourth point may only reflect the limited skill of the Markan evangelist. While it is possible to attempt to deconstruct the argument in this way, the combined force of these points is strong. More recent formulations of Markan priority tend to be primarily restatements of Streeter's basic observations that Mark is medial and more primitive, coupled with responses to challenges made against the 2DH by proponents of other theories that do not hold to Markan priority.[47]

In his *Oxford Studies* chapters in 1911, Streeter saw the second major source of Matthew and Luke as Q. The necessity of postulating Q was seen as being in some regards a negative consequence of the implausibility of the alternatives "(a) that Luke copied Matthew (or vice versa), or (b) that the common source was oral tradition."[48] The latter was seen as being unlikely due to the high level of verbatim agreement in the Greek of the double tradition passages—a phenomenon not readily explicable on theories of oral tradition, whereas the former could not explain what would be either Matthew's or Luke's decision to remove double tradition material from the contexts in which it had been placed by the other evangelist and to place such material in a different context. This observation led to one of the most famous rhetorical flourishes in Streeter's work, which still rankles with proponents of the Farrer-Goulder (or Markan Priority without Q position), but nonetheless seems inescapable for those who uphold the 2DH:

> It then appeared that, subsequent to the Temptation story, there is not a single case in which Matthew and Luke agree in inserting the same saying at the same point in the Marcan outline. If then Luke derived this material from Matthew, he must have gone through both Matthew and Mark so as to discriminate with meticulous precision between Marcan and non-Marcan material; he must then have preceded with the utmost care to tear every little piece of non-Marcan material he desired to use from the context of Mark in which it appeared in Matthew—in spite of the fact that the contexts in Matthew are always exceedingly appropriate—in order to reinsert it into a different context in Mark having no special appropriateness. A theory which would make an author capable of such a proceeding would only be tenable if, on other grounds, we had reason to believe he was a crank.[49]

The logic and the *tour de force* of this dismissive rhetoric effectively swept aside even the most adventurous of Gospel scholars from suggesting Luke's dependence upon Matthew for more than three decades after Streeter composed it.[50] Streeter's

---

47. See Kloppenborg, *Excavating Q*, 18–28; Stein, *Studying the Synoptic Gospels*, 49–96; Goodacre, *Case against Q*, 18–45.

48. Streeter, *Four Gospels*, 153.

49. Ibid., 183.

50. In the period after the publication of *The Four Gospels* the first sustained attempt to promote the theory of Markan priority without Q, but in terms of Luke's direct use of Matthew, is found in the article by Farrer, "On Dispensing with Q."

argument was not, therefore, only a constructive defense of the 2DH as a fundamental solution, but it was also a destructive attack on other possible solutions.

Proto-Luke

Although supporting the essential assumption of the 2DH, namely that Matthew and Luke independently made use of two source documents, Mark and Q, it is Streeter's key idea in *The Four Gospels* that this is not the complete solution to the Synoptic problem. Alongside these two sources, Streeter proposed the existence of two further early sources of Jesus tradition. The first of these, the L source, represented source material unique to Luke's Gospel, which, according to Streeter, came to the third evangelist already in a combined form with Q material. In Streeter's own words, "Our hypothesis implies that the editor of the Gospel found Q, not in its original form, but embodied in a much larger document (Q+L), which was in fact a complete Gospel, somewhat longer than Mark."[51] To use Streeter's algebraic terms, Proto-Luke = Q+L, and this composite document represents an intermediate step via which both Q and L traditions were utilized by Luke at that point when he chose to incorporate Mark to form the third Gospel. Although held more hypothetically, Streeter conjectured that the author of Proto-Luke was identical with the person responsible for the composition of both Luke and Acts and "was none other than St Luke, the companion of St Paul, and that he compiled it [Proto-Luke] during the two years he spent in Cæsarea while the Apostle was in prison."[52]

It is curious that Streeter does not reference or demonstrate any dependence on the work of P. Feine, who had suggested that Luke had incorporated a source that spanned both part of his Gospel and Acts.[53] Thus it may well be the case that Streeter was unaware of Feine's work, or saw his own theory as being sufficiently distinct so as not to warrant reference to this related suggestion. Whether or not Streeter may be seen as an independent originator of the Proto-Luke theory is perhaps irresolvable. However, his presentation became the classic articulation of the Proto-Luke hypothesis and the basis of subsequent work that adopted this theory.[54] Streeter's reason for characterizing Proto-Luke as a "Gospel" was based mainly on the observation concerning what he characterized as "the centre and core of the Third Gospel," Luke 9:51—18:14.[55] He says that in this section "Luke makes no use, or practically no use, of Mark."[56] The presence of nine doublet sayings in this section where the Lukan version

---

51. Streeter, *Four Gospels*, 199.
52. Streeter, "Fresh Light on the Synoptic Problem," 110.
53. Feine, *Eine vorkanonische Überlieferung*, esp. 236–52.
54. Verheyden, contrasting Streeter's formulation with that of Feine, describes it as "the 'classic' presentation of the hypothesis . . . in which the source is limited to the Gospel" (Verheyden, "Unity of Luke–Acts," 49 n. 230).
55. Streeter, *Four Gospels*, 203.
56. Ibid., 204.

tends to agree with Matthew against Mark suggests to Streeter that Luke was following a Q version and that the lack of Markan elements suggests that this section was composed prior to an awareness of Mark. Furthermore, Streeter finds other blocks of Lukan material that he sees as corroborating his theory. For instance, in Luke 3:1—4:30 "there are indeed a few points of contact with Mark; but closer examination makes it evident that the majority of these passages are not likely to have been actually derived from Mark."[57] In particular, the picturesque description of John the Baptist's attire and diet is seen by Streeter as clear evidence of Luke's "disuse" of Mark in this section. This led Streeter to his supposition that "Q+L lay before the author of the Third Gospel as a single document and that he regarded this as his principal source."[58] Streeter concludes his discussion of Proto-Luke with a tentative listing of its contents: "Appended is a list of the passages most probably to be assigned to Proto-Luke: Lk. iii.1—iv.30; v.1–11; vi.14–16; vi.20—viii.3; ix.51—xviii.14; xix.1–27; xix.37–44; xxi.18, 34–36; xxii.14 to end of the Gospel, except for the verses derived from Mark, the identification of which is very problematical."[59]

Streeter's ideas concerning Proto-Luke did not receive the widespread acceptance that was attained by his statement of the 2DH. Perhaps what remains still the fullest presentation and development of the Proto-Luke theory is to be found in the work of Vincent Taylor, published only two years after *The Four Gospels* but in many ways the development of Streeter's ideas as they appeared in his article in *The Hibbert Journal* of 1921.[60] In many ways Taylor offers little more than Streeter in terms of the basis for postulating Proto-Luke. He concurs that the evangelist was also the author of this document,[61] and that the place of composition was Caesarea.[62] Taylor's contribution comes from more fully discussing the overall theory, exploring the theology of the document, and discussing how it differs from Mark. However, by 1937, T. W. Manson was uncommitted as to whether a Proto-Luke stage could be identified; rather he focused attention on the body of unique Lukan traditions identified as the L source.[63] Fitzmyer provided a brief summary of later scholars who adopted this hypothesis up until 1981, and he raised seven important objections to the theory including the principal idea mentioned by Manson. Fitzmyer noted that it may be more plausible to think of Luke expanding Markan tradition with Q and L, rather than supplementing Proto-Luke with Mark. Discussing the deployment of Mark's third Passion prediction

57. Ibid., 205.
58. Ibid., 212.
59. Ibid., 222.
60. Taylor, *Behind the Third Gospel*.
61. Ibid., 210.
62. Ibid., 213.

63. Manson may favor what he describes as the alternative to the Proto-Luke theory, namely "to suppose that Mk. or some more primitive document, from which Mk. is derived, is the foundational document into which the Q and L material has been inserted" (Manson, *Sayings of Jesus*, 26).

in Luke, Fitzmyer states, "[I]t is hard to understand why, if Luke were inserting this into Proto-Luke, he would not have somehow introduced it earlier into his own story of Jesus' journey to Jerusalem. Rather, the delay produced in Luke is owing to the insertion of 'Q' and 'L' material into the Marcan order."[64] For this and similar reasons, the vast majority of New Testament scholars no longer hold to any form of a Proto-Luke theory, although the notion of unique Lukan source material, L, is often still held regardless of whether this material is seen as being a unified written source or constituted of isolated units of either written or oral traditions.

The M Source

The final major component of Streeter's four document hypothesis was the so-called M source.[65] This was seen as being a unified written set of traditions utilized by the author of the first Gospel, and, according to Streeter, this source could be characterized as being "Judaistic" in outlook. In his writing on the Synoptic problem published in *Oxford Studies*, he appears not yet to have formulated a hypothesis about the M source; in fact his thinking about this source appears for the first time in *The Four Gospels*. However, Streeter was not the first scholar to postulate the existence of such a source. As early as 1904, Ernest de Witt Burton identified a collection of sayings comprising about 230 verses of unique Matthew material that he saw as forming a unified source, and designated it using the siglum M.[66] The curious thing about Streeter's formulation is that although Streeter refers to Burton's book containing the reference to a document that is designated by Burton himself using the symbol M,[67] Streeter never explicitly acknowledges Burton's previous work in the area of the M source.[68]

Streeter's formulation of the M source also carried significant historical and theological implications, which he recognized and stated forthrightly. His advocacy on behalf of what he described as other early sources of sayings is also an exercise in reclaiming more of the Synoptic material as authentic Jesus traditions. Consequently, Streeter boldly claimed: "Thus the final result of the critical analysis which has led to our formulating the Four Document Hypothesis is very materially to broaden the basis for evidence for the authentic teaching of Christ."[69]

This statement does stand in some tension with Streeter's more detailed description of the M source. He saw it as Judaistic in character, originating in Jerusalem,

---

64. Fitzmyer, *Luke I–IX*, 91.
65. For a complete discussion of the M Source see, Foster, "M Source."
66. Burton, *Some Principles*.
67. Ibid., 41.
68. It is notable that Streeter does make numerous references to this very volume by Burton (see Streeter, *Four Gospels*, 186, 186 n. 1, 297 n. 2, 301, 303, 309, 328) and even to the specific page on which the comments about M are found, but not to that part of the discussion itself.
69. Ibid., 226, 270.

and composed or compiled around 60 CE.[70] Moreover, it is significant to note that according to Streeter, M does not represent a primitive Jewish Christian strand of tradition, but rather "a later Judaistic reaction against the Petro-Pauline liberalism in the matter of the Gentile mission and the observance of the Law."[71] Therefore, it appears that Streeter believed that M contained many authentic Jesus traditions but these had either been preserved because they contained authentic sayings that promoted Torah obedience, or been re-cast to promote allegiance to the Law. It is notable that at this stage Streeter did not possess the terminology or the conceptual framework to describe the "redactional" tendency of this postulated source, but in an embryonic manner this may be the type of phenomenon that Streeter was trying to describe.

The estimate of the size of the M source at over 230 verses resulted in this hypothetical source being only approximately 15 percent shorter than the postulated length of Q—which was estimated by Streeter to be around 270+ verses. However, unlike in his work on Q, Streeter did not specifically identify which material he considered to constitute these 230+ verses. Yet in more general terms, Streeter described M traditions as discourse or parable material unique to the first Gospel, excluding, however, "any *narrative* peculiar to Matthew."[72] Thus, without specifically listing the contents of the M source, Streeter gives the following description that provides some indication of his perception of the contents.

> There are eight parables (=59 verses) peculiar to Matthew—not including the Lost Sheep, The Marriage Feast, and the Talents (=34 verses)—to which must be added approximately 140 verses of discourse of the same character as the bulk of Q... Thus, if we assign the bulk of the discourse and parables peculiar to Matthew to M, we have a document quite as considerable in extent as Q. This, however, is merely a matter of arithmetic; the points on which our arguments turn are: (1) the evidence that M and Q to some extent overlapped; (2) the Judaistic character of the M source.[73]

On Streeter's first point, Matthew's Sermon on the Mount is considered to be distinctive enough so as to differentiate it from what Streeter considers the Q version of the sermon preserved in Luke. Similarly, the Matthean "woes" (Matt 23:13–33) are seen as representing another form of the tradition contained in Luke 11:37–52. Hence, these two passages are considered examples of Q-M overlaps, and in these passages the evangelist has conflated the two versions of the tradition before him. So, both in terms of technical consideration of overlapping sources, and based on distinctive theological tendencies, Streeter advanced his theory of a Judaistic source utilized by the first evangelist.

---

70. These points are discussed throughout chapter 9, ibid., 223–70.
71. Ibid., 512.
72. Ibid., 235.
73. Ibid.

The failure of this aspect of Streeter's Four Document hypothesis to achieve lasting acceptance can perhaps be traced to three main factors. First, the development of redaction criticism meant that much of the material unique to Matthew could be attributed to the hand of the evangelist, rather than stemming from a prior source. Second, Streeter's perception that Q was pro-Gentile and hence distinguishable from the pro-Jewish M sources was not seen as persuasive. Thus, scholars such as Robinson,[74] who linked the genre of Q with Jewish wisdom, and Kloppenborg, who situated the social location of the document in Galilee, broke the key element in Streeter's formulation that allowed for the differentiation between Q and M traditions.[75] Finally, once the distinction between Q and M material was removed, the basis for finding coherence for the unparalleled Matthean material became problematic. Instead of basing such claims of unity on a theological outlook, it became necessary to mount arguments in terms of stylistic and verbal affinities. Attempts to do so have proved largely unsuccessful and in fact suggest, to the contrary, that so-called M material actually represents a plurality of traditions. Consequently, with the benefit of hindsight, the theory of an M source appears to come from a period of scholarship that had been impressed by the clarity that the hypothesis of the Q source had brought to analyzing double tradition material, and then overplayed the application of source criticism as a panacea for explaining all the material contained in the Synoptic Gospels.

The Four Document Hypothesis

While Streeter's fundamental solution to the Synoptic problem was the Two Source Hypothesis, his thinking between 1911 and 1924 evolved in such a way as to envisage a more complete source-critical description of the traditions contained in the Synoptic Gospels. Since the perspective of redaction criticism had not been developed, which saw the evangelists as theologians in their own right who shaped, created, and modified Gospel material, the basis for accounting for these traditions was the postulation of pre-existing sources. Streeter's overall theory is without doubt a *tour de force* when appreciated within the conceptual confines of the prevailing scholarly framework of his own period. His elegant, diagrammatic representation was compelling and the arguments adduced in its favor were based on detailed textual analysis both of manuscripts and of individual traditions contained in the Gospels. The ability to integrate so much data into the theory was a particular strength, yet it would also prove to be the primary weakness of the thesis. Streeter's own diagrammatic representation was as follows:[76]

---

74. Robinson, "LOGOI SOPHON."
75. Kloppenborg, *Excavating Q*, 210–11, 214–61.
76. Streeter, *Four Gospels*, 150.

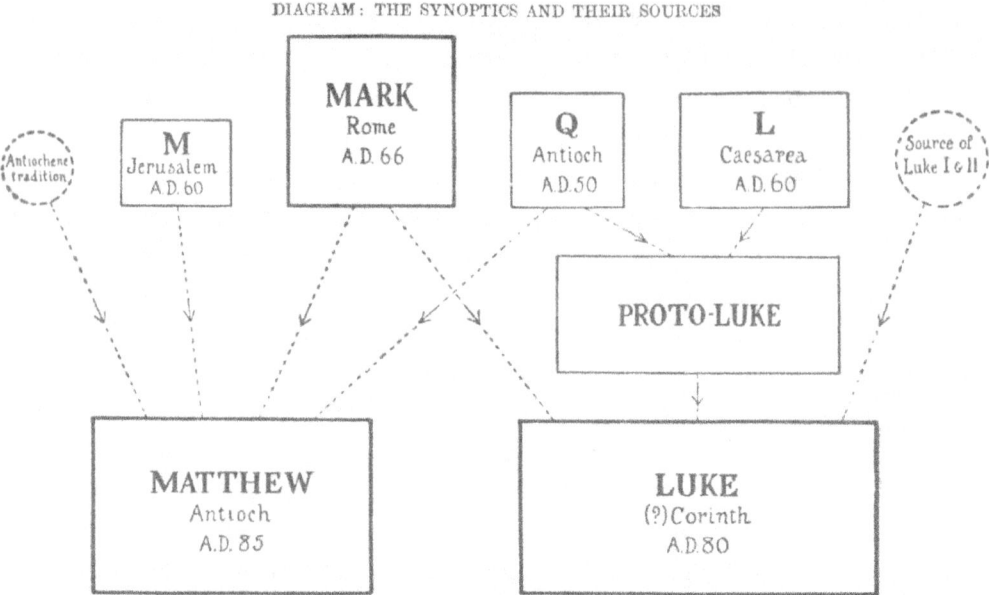

Figure 1: Streeter's representation of the Four Document Hypothesis

Often those who discuss the Four Document Hypothesis present a simplified version of this diagram. Not only are the tentative suggestions of Antochene tradition and putative sources for Luke 1–2 removed, but not infrequently the intermediate step of the Proto-Luke hypothesis is also deleted, so that the Gospel of Luke becomes the editorial product of an evangelist melding together three sources, Mark, Q, and L.[77] In effect, this diagram represented the totality of Streeter's thinking involving four sources linked to each of the great sees of the early church. Moreover, the bulk of material in the Synoptic Gospels is traced to a pre-Gospel source and the evangelists are mere scissors and paste editors who arrange the "pearls" of tradition they receive on the finest of narrative threads.

For all its elegance, Streeter's Four Document Hypothesis has few contemporary followers, and in the intervening period from the publication of his work in 1924 till the present day the majority of Gospel critics have operated with his fundamental solution, the Two Document Hypothesis. If the ideas of M and L material have retained any currency, it is as convenient shorthand ways to represent traditions received by the evangelists in addition to Mark and Q, but without any strong claims for these forming single written sources, or even for these traditions being received in written form. In part, this is due to a greater creativity being attributed to the evangelists by

---

77. See for instance the representation in Stein, *Studying the Synoptic Gospels*, 281. A more helpful discussion is found on Carlson's "Synoptic Problem Website," where he presents two versions of the 4DH—one with Proto-Luke and one without.

biblical scholars writing in the second half of the twentieth century, as well as due to the recognition that oral traditions may well have survived alongside written traditions throughout the first century and maybe beyond.

AN APPLICATION OF STREETER'S FUNDAMENTAL SOLUTION

Source criticism remains a vital tool for scholars engaged in historio-critical exegesis of the Synoptic Gospels. One of Streeter's lasting legacies was in his handling and explanation of the double tradition. While his work on Mark-Q overlaps and the minor agreements remains foundational, it is perhaps most helpful to consider, for the purposes of application and example, a more straightforward treatment of the modern handling of a double tradition passage based on Streeter's ideas concerning the Q source. This will also illustrate the way in which the discussion has advanced.

The story of the centurion's servant (Matt 8:5–13//Luke 7:1–10, cf. John 4:46b–54) is generally agreed to be Q tradition in some form. As an initial observation, it should be noted that Luke preserves a slightly longer form of the story (Luke 186 words, Matthew 170 words), but that there are significant deviations between the two versions. First, the occurrence of the introductory phrase καὶ ἐγένετο ὅτι ἐτέλεσεν ὁ Ἰησοῦς τοὺς λόγους τούτους ("and it happened when Jesus finished these words" Matt 7:28a; cf. Luke 7:1a) was seen by Streeter as being present in Q. In 1911 he stated that this was a formula indicating "the resumption of a narrative, and therefore due to the editor, though the first instance of it, which perhaps suggested to him the others, may have occurred in his source Q, connecting the Great Sermon with the narrative of the healing of the Centurion's Servant."[78] Streeter expresses the same view in 1924: "It would seem likely, then, that Matthew found the formula in Q, and thought it a convenient one to repeat whenever he had occasion to mark a similar transition from a long discourse to narrative."[79] While this position has been debated in recent scholarship, it is interesting to note that Streeter's position is the one adopted by the IQP (International Q Project).[80]

In relation to the rest of the narrative, Streeter adopts a very broad-brush approach. In the more succinct form in 1924, he simply lists "Lk vi.20—vii.10" as one of the passages assigned to Q.[81] Similarly, in his earlier discussion Streeter simply stated what was self-evident to him, that in Q after the Great Sermon followed the "Centurion's Servant, vii.2–10."[82] Compared with Streeter's initial discussion, there has been a much more detailed analysis in scholarship of the precise form of the tradition of the Centurion's Servant as it might have occurred in the Q source. The IQP's reconstruc-

---

78. Streeter, "Original Order of Q," 148.
79. Streeter, *Four Gospels*, 262.
80. Robinson, *Critical Edition of Q*, 102–3. See also Johnson, *Q 7:1–10*.
81. Streeter, *Four Gospels*, 291.
82. Streeter, "Original Extent of Q," 187.

tion lists the Q form of the pericope as "Q 7:1, 2, 3, 4-6a, 6b-9, ?10?"[83] A different analysis of the actual Q material can be found in Fitzmyer's commentary on Luke. He states, "the clear 'Q' material is found in 7:1b–2, 3a, 6e, 7b, 8–9, 10b (=Matt 8:5–6, 8–10, 13b)."[84] Regardless of which reconstruction is viewed as the more convincing, both testify to a significant development in the way in which the practice of source criticism in relation to Q has been advanced since Streeter's day. Scholarship now gives far greater attention to reconstructing the actual words of Q, rather than just identifying the blocks of tradition that belonged to Q and the ordering of the material within that source.

Furthermore, source criticism is not practiced in isolation from the other critical techniques that have been developed since Streeter—most notably redaction criticism. Given that the material in Luke 7:4–6a is generally agreed not to have formed part of the Q source, it may be asked how this, along with other deviations between the Matthean and Lukan versions, are to be explained. Fleddermann summarizes a number of the key issues:

> The Q reconstruction faces formidable difficulties. Although Matthew and Luke agree closely in the second half of the pericope, they offer radically different texts in the first half. The major difference in the first half centers on whether or not the centurion meets Jesus. In Matthew the centurion himself comes to Jesus, but in Luke the centurion has no direct contact with Jesus, sending instead two delegations, first some "elders of the Jews" (Luke 7,3), then some "friends" (Luke 7,6). Should we hold Luke or his sources responsible for this double delegation?[85]

From the perspective of redaction criticism, the material in Luke 7:4–6a appears to reflect a specifically Lukan concern in its portrayal of god-fearing Gentiles, exemplified by Roman centurions. Moreover, the avoidance of a meeting between Jesus and a centurion may be theologically motivated. For Luke, the decisive expansion of the Gospel being proclaimed to Gentiles occurs in Acts 10–11, when Peter, led by a visionary experience, visits the centurion Cornelius. The accompanying outpouring of the Spirit confirms this expansion in the mission. If Luke had allowed the meeting of Jesus with a Roman centurion in Luke 7:1–10 to remain in the narrative, this would have undone much of Luke's carefully orchestrated structure of the geographical and cultural expansion of the proclamation of the gospel.

It is no longer helpful to apply Streeter's source-critical insights in isolation from newer methodologies employed in the historio-critical exegesis of the Gospels. However, neither is it possible to dispense with the work of source criticism. The greater precision that Streeter introduced into the consideration and reconstruction

---

83. Robinson, *Critical Edition of Q*, 102–17.
84. Fitzmyer, *Luke I–IX*, 648.
85. Fleddermann, *Q: A Reconstruction*, 335.

of pre-Gospel sources has allowed subsequent generations of Synoptic Gospel commentators to perceive more clearly the theological motivations of the evangelists in both selecting and modifying the traditions they inherited. This in turn has led to a far greater clarity in appreciating the individual messages of the Gospel writers, and Streeter's contribution through source criticism should be seen as vital in this endeavor.

CONCLUSIONS

Burnett Hillman Streeter was a polymath who was equally competent when writing about contemporary issues facing the church, mounting arguments about the interplay between science and religion, presenting studies on comparative religion, probing fundamental metaphysical questions, or, as he is best known to New Testament scholars, analyzing the sources behind the Synoptic Gospels.[86] While Streeter's impact in many of these areas may be forgotten, his contribution in formulating what is widely perceived as still being the fundamental solution to the Synoptic problem—the Two Document Hypothesis—remains his lasting legacy. Although he was by no means the first to formulate this theory, he gave it its classic articulation for English-speaking readers. It is due to the clarity of presentation of this theory in his monumental work *The Four Gospels*, which remained a standard text for over half a century, that his status and influence are assured. Those who wish to propose other solutions to the Synoptic problem, although they may not be fully aware of the fact, are still engaged in an exercise of attempting to rebut arguments often originally formulated by Streeter. Admittedly, his full solution to the Synoptic problem—the Four Document Hypothesis—commands little widespread following in contemporary scholarship. His ideas relating to the M and L sources and the notion of the intermediate step of a Proto-Luke have indeed largely fallen by the wayside. Nonetheless, these other hypothetical sources (in addition to Q) reflect the heyday of the dominance of source criticism, and understanding the reasons behind the formulation of these aspects of Streeter's theory allows an appreciation of the way in which a previous generation of biblical scholars attempted to claim Gospel materials as stemming from the historical Jesus. Streeter's methods are still vital for Gospel scholarship in combination with other methodologies such as redaction criticism. It is here, in an often unacknowledged way, that the scholarship of B. H. Streeter continues to shape contemporary New Testament studies.

BIBLIOGRAPHY

Burton, E. *Some Principles of Literary Criticism and Their Application to the Synoptic Problem*. Chicago: University of Chicago Press, 1904.

Carlson, Stephen C. "Synoptic Problem Website." http://www.hypotyposeis.org/synoptic-problem/2004/09/overview-of-proposed-solutions.html.

Catchpole, D. R. *The Quest for Q*. Edinburgh: T. & T. Clark, 1993.

---

86. For a further assessment of his life and impact, see Court, "Streeter."

Court, J. M. "Burnett Hillman Streeter (17th November 1874—10th September 1937)." *ExpTim* 118 (2006) 19–25.

Ensor, R. C. K. *England 1870–1914*. The Oxford History of England. Oxford: Oxford University Press, 1936.

Farrer, A. M. "On Dispensing with Q." In *Studies in the Gospels in Memory of R. H. Lightfoot*, edited by D. E. Nineham, 57–88. Oxford: Basil Blackwell, 1955.

Feine, P. *Eine vorkanonische Überlieferung des Lukas in Evangelium und Apostelgeschichte: Eine Untersuchung*. Gotha: Perthes, 1891.

Fitzmyer, J. A. *The Gospel according to Luke I–IX*. AB 28. New York: Doubleday, 1981.

Fleddermann, H. T. "Mark's Use of Q: The Beelzebul Controversy and the Cross Saying." In *Jesus, Mark and Q: The Teaching of Jesus and Its Earliest Records*, edited by M. Labahn and A. Schmidt, 17–33. JSNTSup 214. Sheffield: Sheffield Academic, 2001.

———. *Q: A Reconstruction and Commentary*. Biblical Tools and Studies 1. Leuven: Peeters, 2005.

Foster, P. "The M Source: Its History and Demise in Biblical Scholarship." In *New Studies in the Synoptic Problem*, edited by P. Foster et al., 591–616. Leuven: Peeters, 2011.

Goodacre, M. A. *The Case against Q*. Harrisburg, PA: Trinity International, 2002.

Grensted, L. W. "Streeter, Burnett Hillman." In *The Oxford Dictionary of National Biography*, 53:837. Revised by R. Brown. Oxford: Oxford University Press, 2004.

Hardwick, J. C. "Burnett Hillman Streeter." *ExpTim* 49 (1937/38) 249–54.

Hodgkin, R. H. *Six Centuries of an Oxford College: A History of the Queen's College 1340–1940*. Oxford: Blackwell, 1949.

Johnson, S. R. *Q 7:1–10 the Centurion's Faith in Jesus' Word*. Documenta Q. Leuven: Peeters, 2002.

Kloppenborg, J. S. *Excavating Q: The History and Setting of the Sayings Gospel*. Edinburgh: T. & T. Clark, 2000.

Manson, T. W. *The Sayings of Jesus*. London: SCM, 1949.

Neirynck, F. "Assessment." In *Mark and Q: A Study of the Overlap Texts*, edited by H. T. Fleddermann, 263–307. BETL 122. Louvain: Louvain University Press, 1995.

Owens, N. *The British Left and India: Metropolitan Anti-Imperialism, 1885–1947*. Oxford: Oxford University Press, 2007.

Robinson, J. M. "LOGOI SOPHON on the Gattung of Q." In *Trajectories through Early Christianity*, by J. M. Robinson and H. Koester, 71–113. Philadelphia: Fortress, 1971. Enlargement of German original: "ΛΟΓΟΙ ΣΟΦΩΝ: Zur Gattung der Spruchquelle Q." In *Zeit und Geschichte: Dankesgabe an Rudolf Bultmann zum 80 Gerburstag*, edited by E. Dinkler, 77–96. Tübingen: Mohr Siebeck, 1964.

Robinson, J. M., et al., eds. *The Critical Edition of Q*. Minneapolis: Fortress, 2000.

Sanday, W., ed. *Oxford Studies in the Synoptic Problem*. Oxford: Clarendon, 1911.

Sato, M. *Q und Prophetie: Studien zur Gattungs- und Traditionsgeschichte der Quelle Q*. WUNT 2.29. Tübingen: Mohr Siebeck, 1988.

Stein, R. H. *Studying the Synoptic Gospels: Origin and Interpretation*. 2nd ed. Grand Rapids: Baker, 2001.

Streeter, B. H. *The Buddha and the Christ: An Exploration of the Meaning of the Universe and of the Purpose of Human Life*. London: Macmillan, 1932.

———. *The Chained Library: A Survey of Four Centuries in the Evolution of the English Library*. London: Macmillan, 1931.

———. *Doubts and Difficulties: A Personal Impression of the Conclusion of the Conference of Theological Teachers and the Student Christian Movement Leaders, Swanwick July 4–7, 1911*. London, SCM, 1911

———, ed. *Foundations: A Statement of Christian Thought in Modern Terms by Seven Oxford Men*. London: Macmillan, 1912.

———. *The Four Gospels: A Study in Origins—Treating of the Manuscript Tradition, Sources, Authorship and Dates*. London: Macmillan, 1924.

———. "Fresh Light on the Synoptic Problem." *Hibbert Journal* 20 (1921) 103–12.

———. "God and the World's Pain." In *Concerning Prayer: Its Nature, Its Difficulties, and Its Value*, 1–39. London: Macmillan, 1916.

———. *The God Who Speaks: Warburton Lectures for 1933–35*. London: Macmillan, 1936.

———. "The Historic Christ." In *Foundations: A Statement of Christian Thought in Modern Terms by Seven Oxford Men*, edited by B. H. Streeter, 73–145. London: Macmillan, 1912.

———. *The In-Dwelling of God in Man*. London: Hodder & Stoughton, 1935.

———. "The Literary Evolution of the Gospels." In *Oxford Studies in the Synoptic Problem*, edited by W. Sanday, 209–27. Oxford: Clarendon, 1911.

———. "On the Original Order of Q." In *Oxford Studies in the Synoptic Problem*, edited by W. Sanday, 141–64. Oxford: Clarendon, 1911.

———. "The Original Extent of Q." In *Oxford Studies in the Synoptic Problem*, edited by W. Sanday, 185–208. Oxford: Clarendon, 1911.

———. *The Primitive Church, Studied with Special Reference to the Origins of the Christian Ministry: The Hewett Lectures, 1928*. London: Macmillan, 1929.

———. *Reality: A New Correlation of Science and Religion*. London: Macmillan, 1926.

———. *Restatement and Reunion: A Study in First Principles*. London: Macmillan, 1914.

———. "St Mark's Knowledge and Use of Q." In *Oxford Studies in the Synoptic Problem*, edited by W. Sanday, 165–83. Oxford: Clarendon, 1911.

———. *The Spirit: The Relation of God and Man, Considered from the Standpoint of Recent Philosophy and Science*. London: Macmillan, 1919.

———. "Synoptic Criticism and the Eschatological Problem." In *Oxford Studies in the Synoptic Problem*, edited by W. Sanday, 425–36. Oxford: Clarendon, 1911.

———. "The Trial of our Lord before Herod." In *Oxford Studies in the Synoptic Problem*, edited by W. Sanday, 229–31. Oxford: Clarendon, 1911.

Streeter, B. H., and A. J. Appasamy. *The Sadhu: A Study in Mysticism and Practical Religion*. London: Macmillan, 1921.

Streeter, B. H., et al. *Adventure: The Faith of Science and the Science of Faith*. London: Macmillan, 1927.

———. *God and the Struggle for Existence*. London: Macmillan, 1919.

———. *Immortality: An Essay in Discovery, Co-ordinating Scientific, Psychical and Biblical Research*. London: Macmillan, 1917.

Taylor, V. *Behind the Third Gospel: A Study of the Proto-Luke Hypothesis*. Oxford: Clarendon, 1926.

Thornhill, A. *One Fight More*. London: Frederick Muller, 1943.

Tuckett, C. M. "Mark and Q." In *The Synoptic Gospels: Source Criticism and New Literary Criticism*, edited by C. Focant, 149–75. BETL 110. Louvain: Louvain University Press, 1993.

Verheyden, J. "Unity of Luke–Acts." In *The Unity of Luke–Acts*, edited by J. Verheyden, 3–56. BETL 142. Leuven: Peeters, 1999.

11

William Ramsay and Ernst Haenchen

Daniel So

INTRODUCTION

GERMAN SCHOLARSHIP OF THE nineteenth and twentieth centuries made a tremendous impact on the field of New Testament studies. Tendency, source, form, and redaction criticisms are approaches developed in this tradition, and they continue to exert influence on the field as a whole. Sir William Ramsay and Ernst Haenchen, the two scholars discussed in this chapter, were both heavily influenced by this development in Germany. Interestingly, however, each responded to this development in a radically different way. What fueled much of the German scholarship of the period was the strong historical skepticism with which the New Testament was viewed. Against such skepticism, Ramsay, with his interest and knowledge in archaeology, argued for the historical reliability of the New Testament. The most notable attempt is his work on the book of Acts. Haenchen, on the other hand, took the historical skepticism of the German scholarship to its logical end and developed a brand of redaction criticism also known as composition criticism. The present chapter seeks to summarize and evaluate the approaches of these two divergent scholars.

BIOGRAPHICAL SKETCHES AND MAJOR WORKS

Sir William Ramsay (1851–1939)

As Gasque rightly notes, one finds an exceptional scholar in Ramsay, who had mastered two different fields of study—archaeology and the New Testament.[1] From the vantage point of New Testament studies, this rare combination is what made Ramsay's work original. Being able to bring his first-hand experience in archeology to bear on

---

1. Gasque, *Sir William M. Ramsay*, 13. See chapter 1 of his work for an excellent summary of Ramsay's life and his major works. What is offered here is a brief summary of what is found in Gasque's chapter.

the interpretation of the New Testament, a task that very few New Testament scholars of the day were able to do, Ramsay was able to offer new and pertinent insights into the text.

In 1885, he became the first Professor of Classical Art and Archaeology at Oxford. In the following year, he was appointed Regius Professor of Humanity at the University of Aberdeen where he remained until his retirement in 1911. His well-known published works on the New Testament include *The Bearing of Recent Discovery on the Trustworthiness of the New Testament*, *The Church in the Roman Empire before A.D. 170*, and *St Paul the Traveller and the Roman Citizen*. Ramsay is also well-known for his *Historical Commentary on St Paul's Epistle to the Galatians*, in which he makes a strong argument in support of the South Galatian theory, challenging the dominant view of his day. His work on the Book of Revelation, titled *The Letters to the Seven Churches of Asia and Their Place in the Plan of the Apocalypse* is also worthy of mention. As Gasque writes, "until someone writes a better and more up-to-date book on the subject, *The Letters to the Seven Churches* will remain a basic tool for the student in his study of the Book of Revelation."[2] Many years have passed since this comment was made, but in many ways it still stands true for the study of Revelation.

Ernst Haenchen (1895–1975)

Despite being best known for his work as a New Testament scholar, Haenchen first began his theological studies in contemporary philosophy and systematic theology. Beginning as Karl Heim's assistant in Tübingen, he taught systematic theology in Giessen and Münster. His fragile health forced him into convalescence in Davos, Switzerland from 1944 to 1948. Interestingly, however, it was during this period that much of his intensive exegetical work was done, the result of which became the foundation for his commentaries on Acts, Mark, and John. Among New Testament scholars, Haenchen seems to have been influenced greatly by Dibelius, his *Lehrer*, to whom he dedicates his work, *Der Weg Jesu*. In many ways he built upon Dibelius's work. Also, redaction critics, such as Conzelmann, had a great influence on Haenchen.

Haenchen's major works on the New Testament include his two commentaries, which have both been translated into English, *The Acts of the Apostles: A Commentary* and *John: A Commentary on the Gospel of John*, and other books published in German, such as *Gott und Mensch* and *Der Weg Jesu*.

TENDENCY, SOURCE, FORM, AND REDACTION CRITICISM

As mentioned in the introduction of this chapter, both Ramsay and Haenchen were influenced greatly by the German scholarship of the nineteenth and twentieth centuries. Therefore, before delving into a discussion of their work, a brief overview of these four approaches to biblical criticism will be helpful.

2. Gasque, *Sir William M. Ramsay*, 55.

The first approach that shaped the field of New Testament Studies in Ramsay and Haenchen's days was tendency criticism (*Tendenzkritik*). Developed in the late nineteenth century, the focus of tendency criticism was to draw attention to the "intention of an author or, more pointedly to the particular bias with which the author treats his subject matter."[3] Tendency criticism is especially identified with F. C. Baur and the Tübingen School. Applying the Hegelian dialectic of thesis, antithesis, and synthesis to New Testament history, Baur concluded that early Christianity was divided between two main parties—the law-committed Petrine and the law-free Pauline parties.[4] Following the struggle between the two parties, there came reconciliation and fusion around the middle of the second century, resulting in modifications by each party.[5] Based on this picture, Baur suggested that the four authentic letters of Paul (Romans, 1–2 Corinthians, and Galatians) represented the Pauline party, while the Apocalypse and later pseudo-Clementine writings represented the Petrine party.[6] The other books, such as Acts, which seem to minimize conflicts, represent stages toward compromise and reconciliation.[7]

The second important approach that shaped the field was source criticism. In New Testament studies, source criticism revolves around explaining the similarities found in Matthew, Mark, and Luke. The various ideas are largely grouped into four theories: (1) the Augustinian theory, (2) the Griesbach theory, (3) the two-source theory, and (4) the four-source theory.[8] Besides the Gospels, the question of sources has also played a role in Acts. Among the representative scholars of source criticism is Harnack, who posited Jerusalem A, Jerusalem B, and Antiochene sources as standing behind Acts 1–15.[9] Based on the "we passage," Dibelius also proposed that an "itinerary" source was consulted for Acts 16–28.[10]

The third approach that shaped the field was form criticism. Form criticism came into full fruition after the First World War, mainly through the works of three scholars—Dibelius, Schmidt, and Bultmann.[11] Despite the differences in these writers, there are some common ideas and emphases. Perrin lists three. First, the Gospels are not single creations out of whole cloth, but rather collections of material put together by the evangelists.[12] Second, the material in the Gospels has a history of oral transmission

---

3. Soulen and Soulen, *Handbook*, 187.

4. Riches, *Century*, 3.

5. Neill and Wright, *Interpretation*, 26.

6. Ibid.

7. Ibid.

8. For a brief overview of each of the four, see Carson et al., *Introduction to the New Testament*, 29–32.

9. Harnack, *Acts*, 162–202.

10. Dibelius, "Style Criticism," 4.

11. Dibelius, *Tradition to Gospel*; Schmidt, *Rahmen*; Bultmann, *History*.

12. Perrin, *Redaction Criticism*, 15.

as it circulated in the church in the form of individual units and collections.[13] Third, each of the small units served a definite function in a concrete situation, referred to as the *Sitz im Leben*, in the life of the early church.[14] Underlying these ideas and emphases is the assumption of form criticism, namely that the evangelists were not authors with creativity of their own, but mere collectors of sources (*Sammler*).[15]

The fourth approach was redaction criticism. First developed after the Second World War, redaction criticism's chief proponents were Bornkamm, Conzelmann, and Marxsen.[16] According to Osborne, redaction criticism may be defined as "a historical discipline that seeks to uncover the theology and setting of a writing by studying the ways the redactor or editor changed the tradition he inherited and the seams or traditions that the redactor utilized to link those traditions together."[17] What became important as a result of redaction criticism was the role of each evangelist as a theologian. To borrow Stein's words, form critics believed that the evangelists were mere "scissors and paste men." However, redaction critics now believed that the "'scissors' were manipulated by a theological hand and the 'paste' was impregnated with a particular theology."[18]

THE APPROACHES OF RAMSAY AND HAENCHEN

Ramsay's Approach

Much of Ramsay's contribution to New Testament studies is found in the way he brought his extensive knowledge of the historical and geographical condition of Asia Minor to bear on the interpretation of the New Testament. In doing so, Ramsay came to a very different set of conclusions than those reached by the critical scholars of Germany in his day. Where Ramsay's conclusions are most clearly elucidated is in his work on the book of Acts.

Ramsay and Tendency Criticism

During Ramsay's day, it was tendency criticism that had the most influence on the field of New Testament studies. In fact, Ramsay indicated that, like many other scholars in his day, he was heavily influenced by Baur's theory and had accepted the view that suggested that Acts was written "during the second half of the second century by an author who wished to influence the minds of people in his own time by a highly

---

13. Ibid., 16.
14. Ibid., 15–16.
15. Dibelius, *Tradition to Gospel*, 3.
16. Bornkamm et al., *Tradition and Interpretation*; Conzelmann, *Theology of St. Luke*; Marxsen, *Mark*.
17. Osborne, "Redaction Criticism," 199.
18. Stein, *Synoptic Problem*, 22.

wrought and imaginative description of the early Church."[19] However, studying Acts in search of geographical and antiquarian evidence led Ramsay to doubt such a view. For example, Acts 14:6 says that Paul and Barnabas fled from Iconium "to the Lycaonian cities of Lystra and Derbe and to the surrounding country." According to the dominant view of Ramsay's day, it was believed that in the first century, Iconium was a city of Lycaonia and, based on this, it was argued that the author of Acts was an uninformed second-century author who paid little attention to historical details. However, through his own investigation, Ramsay came to the conclusion that Iconium actually belonged to Phrygia, which then meant that Acts 14:6 was actually accurate in its historical details.[20]

This discovery led Ramsay to a view that if Luke was accurate in one detail, it is likely that he would be accurate in other details. Ramsay wrote, "There is a certain presumption that a writer who proves to be exact and correct in one point will show the same qualities in other matters. No writer is correct by mere chance, or accurate sporadically. He is accurate by virtue of a certain habit of mind."[21] With this in mind, Ramsay then researched further into the historical accuracy of Acts, eventually coming to the following conclusion:

> The more I have studied the narrative of the Acts, and the more I have learned year after year about Graeco-Roman society and thoughts and fashions, and organization in those provinces, the more I admire and the better I understand. I set out to look for truth on the borderland where Greece and Asia meet, and found it here. You may press the words of Luke in a degree far beyond any other historian's, and they stand the keenest scrutiny and the hardest treatment.[22]

According to Ramsay, there are four kinds of work professing to be historical. The first is the historical romance, which "in a framework of history interweaves an invented tale."[23] The second is the legend, in which a small "historical kernel" is discernible.[24] The third is the history of the second or third rate, which is to a certain degree trustworthy but contains errors stemming from the author giving a "narrative of the past with the color of his own time."[25] The fourth is what Ramsay calls the "historical work of the highest order" in which a "writer commands excellent means of knowledge either through personal acquaintance or through access to original authorities, and brings to treatment of his subject genius, literary skill, and sympathetic

---

19. Ramsay, *Bearing of Recent Discovery*, 38.
20. Ibid., 53–78.
21. Ibid., 80.
22. Ibid., 89.
23. Ramsay, *St Paul the Traveller*, 2.
24. Ibid.
25. Ibid.

historical insight into human character and the movement of events."²⁶ Against the dominant view of his day, which placed the author of Acts in the third category, Ramsay concluded that Acts belongs to the fourth category with its author to be seen as a first-rate historian.²⁷ Later, in another work, Ramsay further concluded that this author of Acts was none other than Luke, a personal friend and disciple of Paul.²⁸

Ramsay and Redaction Criticism

Though many date the development of redaction criticism to after the Second World War, there was probably enough material that may be thought of as a primitive version of this approach to merit a response by Ramsay. He interacted with "recent critics [who] take the line that Acts consists of various first-century scraps put together in the book as we have it by a second-century Redactor."²⁹ He divided these redactional critics into two groups: those who attributed considerable additions to the redactor and those who reduced the redactor's action to a minimum.³⁰ Ramsay also noted how this "redaction-theory" differed from the "old tendency theories." The latter "supposed that the second-century author colored the whole narrative and put his own views into every paragraph," while for the former, "the Redactor added nothing of consequence to his first-century materials except some blunders of arrangement."

One "redaction-theory" that Ramsay deals with is the theory of Carl Clemen, which builds on both tendency and source criticism.³¹ Ramsay notes that Clemen identified three sources or "documents" found in Acts: (1) a history of the Hellenistic Jews, (2) a history of Peter, and (3) a history of Paul.³² Clemen conjectures that, at first, these sources were combined into one work by a Judaistic redactor, adding details that gave a favorable picture of Judaizing Christianity. This then was worked again by an anti-Judaistic redactor, giving an unfavorable picture of Judaizing Christianity. Finally, a third redactor of neutral stance incorporated a new document, producing Acts in its final form.

Ramsay acknowledged that Clemen was right to pick up on the many-sidedness of Acts. However, he differed from Clemen in that he believed that this many-sidedness was due to the "many-sided character of a thoughtful and highly educated man" who was responsible for this work.³³ And rather than the parts of Acts with varied tone being due to different redactors (i.e., Judaistic and anti-Judaistic), it is possible that the author of Acts has preserved both types of incidents in the interest of preserv-

26. Ibid., 8–9.
27. Ibid., 4–6.
28. Ibid., 14.
29. Ibid., 11.
30. Ibid.
31. Ibid., 12–14.
32. Ibid.; cf. Clemen, *Chronologie*, 146–62.
33. Ramsay, *St Paul the Traveller*, 13.

ing what actually took place in history. Therefore, rather than treating every instance where Paul is conciliatory towards the Jews as being the work of a Judaistic redactor, and where he is not conciliatory as being the work of an anti-Judaistic redactor, it is possible that the author may have simply recorded the gradual process that actually took place in the life of the historical Paul. As shown in Acts 13:46, Paul believed the Jews had the first claim and always tried to conciliate them; however, once he realized that they rejected him and Christianity, he turned his back on them.

In summary, Ramsay's approach to the New Testament takes what I would call a "text-based historical approach" that proceeds in three steps. First, he begins by taking the text of the New Testament at face value. Second, the text's details are studied in light of the historical and archaeological evidence. Third, based on this analysis, a theory of "what really happened" along with the interpretation of the text is drawn. For the four approaches discussed above, however, this last step in Ramsay's analysis is what comes at the beginning, as each of these approaches begins with a preconceived notion of "what really happened" in history, which then drives the interpretation of the text.

Haenchen's Approach

Among his published works, Haenchen is best known for his commentary on Acts. In this work, he interacts with the four major approaches discussed above. A summary of the points raised in this work will lead us into the details of Haenchen's approach.

Haenchen and Tendency Criticism

In his commentary on Acts, Haenchen notes that the weakening of the traditional view of Acts toward the end of the eighteenth century took place in two forms—tendency criticism and source criticism, with the former explained by the New Testament author's "*unwillingness* to say more" and the latter by the author's "*inability* to say more."[34] According to Haenchen, the strength of Baur's theory lies in the "elevated vantage point from which it was drawn—permitting a broad survey of the development of Christianity as far as the early Catholic Church."[35] At the same time, however, he shows his disapproval of tendency criticism by suggesting that "it makes an unwarranted simplification of history, rigidly differentiating 'Gentile Christianity' from 'Jewish Christianity.'"[36]

Despite his negative assessment, it is, however, interesting to note the traces of tendency criticism found in Haenchen's own approach. In fact, his section "Lucan Theology in Acts" in his commentary on Acts[37] reveals that, insofar as tendency criti-

---

34. Ramsay, *St Paul the Traveller*, 15.
35. Ibid., 17.
36. Ibid.
37. Ibid., 91–98.

cism is defined as the "analysis of the intention of an author or, more pointedly to the particular bias with which the author treats his subject matter," Haenchen may be guilty of employing a tendency criticism of his own, just not the type advocated by Baur. If Baur had the Hegelian dialectic as the paradigm that forced his reading of the New Testament, Haenchen had a paradigm of his own that also forced his reading of the New Testament. This paradigm of Haenchen suggests that the first generation of Christians expected that the end was near. However, as their expectation of the imminent end evaporated, there were only two options available for the early Christians: (1) to "see the last things happening here and now, in the present" or (2) to "expect their realization only in a remote, indefinite future."[38] Faced with this dilemma, John focused on the possibility of resurrection and the life here and now (the former), and Luke took the chronological dimension in another direction (the latter).[39]

In sum, as much as Haenchen tried to part company with tendency criticism, the retrospective view suggests that he was doing something quite similar to what Baur was doing, that is, reading a theory of "what really happened" into the text. The only difference was that Haenchen started with a different theory than Baur's.

Haenchen and Source Criticism

In his interaction with source criticism, Haenchen demonstrates that though he acknowledges the existence of various sources behind the New Testament text, he refrains from making conjectures about any source that is only speculative at best.[40]

In his commentary on Acts, Haenchen distances himself from the source critics by putting less confidence in our ability to extract the sources from texts. He remarks that source research and its preoccupation with "what really happened" has resulted in a failure to "do justice to the aim and intentions of biblical writings."[41] The sources that scholars have suggested as underlying Acts are only "hypothetical."[42] Besides, unlike the Gospel of Luke, for which there is one clear source (the Gospel of Mark), such evidence is not available for the book of Acts, which makes the ascertaining of sources much more difficult.[43]

On the source of John, Haenchen took a similar approach to the one he took regarding Acts. It is best summed up in his own statement: "A gospel as extensive as the Gospel of John cannot have been written without the use of some sources. But what

---

38. Ibid., 95.

39. Ibid., 95–96. Here, Haenchen follows the well-known position of Conzelmann.

40. Ibid., 81. This is noted in his statement that begins his discussion on the sources behind Acts. He writes, "Scholars have long been in suspense over the question of sources in Acts. Even today it has not been finally answered."

41. Ibid.

42. Ibid., 84.

43. Ibid., 81. He also writes, "there just were no 'histories of the Apostles' which Luke could have woven together as, in the case of the third gospel, he wove together Mark, Q, and that other gospel from which he derived his special material" (ibid., 82).

sorts of sources are involved has not yet been determined."[44] Nevertheless, he did entertain source theories, such as that of Wendt, who suggested that John is composed from a narrative source and a discourse source.[45] Still, Haenchen's main interest was in the later stage of source-development, especially how the sources were put together by the evangelist to form a story.

In short, Haenchen seems to have considered source criticism to be speculative and hypothetical, at least for the Book of Acts and the Gospel of John. In doing so, he joined forces with other redaction critics in mounting an attack against source criticism. As a matter of fact, it may be suggested that Haenchen went even a step further than the other redaction critics in his disregard of sources. The redaction critics, whose main focus was on the editor's alterations of sources, needed first to determine what the sources were. In this light, it would be correct to say that redaction criticism builds on the results of source criticism work.[46] However, as will be discussed below, Haenchen shifted the focus to the author's work as a whole, and as a result, the question of sources became less important in his approach. Thus, one begins to see in Haenchen an approach that has certain similarities to more recent synchronic approaches, such as narrative criticism.

It seems that among the four approaches (tendency, source, form, and redaction criticism), it was source criticism against which Haenchen leveled his strongest attack. Perhaps he felt that tendency criticism had already been refuted adequately, and he was now trying to debilitate some of the negative impact that source criticism had had, especially on the study of Acts. Of course, here we need to be careful not to see Haenchen as ruling out the source question in its entirety. When it comes to the other New Testament books such as the Synoptic Gospels, he treated the issue of sources rather carefully. He saw a problem when source questions lead the interpreter astray from the final form of the text and immerse him or her in the world behind the text. To a certain extent, Haenchen seems to have raised a valid point.

Haenchen and Form Criticism

Unlike his attitude towards tendency and source criticisms, Haenchen was rather positive about form criticism. He saw two stages in the development of form criticism: (1) the period leading up to 1945 and (2) the period after 1945.[47] For Haenchen, what many call redaction criticism simply represents the second of the two stages of form criticism. He saw more continuity between the two approaches than many other redaction critics did and do.

Haenchen's putting together of form and redaction criticism stands in stark contrast to Marxsen's method. According to Marxsen, the form critics divide *Sitze im*

---

44. Haenchen, *John*, 74.
45. Ibid., 76.
46. Osborne, "Redaction Criticism," 200.
47. Haenchen, *Acts*, 34–49.

Leben into two: the first situation-in-life of Jesus' setting, and the second situation-in-life of the primitive church.[48] To this, he adds a third *Sitz im Leben*, the situation-in-life in the purpose of theology of the evangelist; he calls this *Redaktionsgeschichte*.[49] Haenchen, however, did not agree with Marxsen's three-fold division since he saw less distinction between the theology of the early church and that of the evangelist than Marxsen did.[50]

Haenchen also spoke favorably of Dibelius's form-critical work on Acts. He viewed Dibelius's work as having a three-fold impact. First, Dibelius's essay applying his form-critical method to Acts[51] brought an end to the "one-sided attention to the source-question."[52] Second, through a collection of essays published after his death in 1951 by H. Greeven under the title, *Aufsätze zur Apostelgeschichte*,[53] Dibelius also gave due prominence to the New Testament author, successfully showing that Luke was not a "'compiler or transmitter,' but a writer with his own positive characteristics—and a theologian."[54] Third, with Dibelius's view of Luke as a theologian, other scholars such as Vielhauer, Conzelmann, and Haenchen himself, followed Dibelius in further expanding his line of thinking.[55]

Despite the confusion caused by Haenchen's effort to maintain redaction criticism within the domain of form criticism, there is much to be gained in his categorization. Most notably, it readily acknowledges the fact that redaction criticism presupposes and continues the procedure set by form criticism.[56] As Haenchen rightly observes, we see this gradual movement in Dibelius, who in his later works begins to move closer towards redaction criticism. Also, Haenchen seems to be on target when he suggests that it is not always easy to separate the theology of the community and that of the New Testament individual author.[57] Thus, it provides a fitting critique of those redaction critics such as Marxsen who put a harsh demarcation between the two.

Haenchen and Redaction Criticism

Among the four approaches of interpretation, Haenchen's approach most resembles redaction criticism. Stein makes note of this when he says, "It would be a mistake to think that Haenchen minimizes the importance of *Redaktionsgeschichte* by placing it

48. Marxsen, *Mark*, 23.
49. Ibid., 24.
50. Haenchen, *Der Weg Jesu*, 23.
51. Dibelius, "Zur Formgeschichte."
52. Here, Haenchen is quoting Dibelius (Haenchen, *Acts*, 35; cf. Dibelius, "Zur Formgeschichte," 211).
53. The English translation, *Studies in the Acts of the Apostles*, was published in 1956.
54. Ibid., 41.
55. Ibid., 48–49.
56. Perrin, *Redaction Criticism*, vi.
57. Haenchen, *Acts*, 91.

under form criticism."⁵⁸ Regardless of how Haenchen defined form criticism and how he situated his approach within it, his approach corresponds rather well to redaction criticism. He was deeply interested in the theology of the New Testament writers—a point shared by all redaction critics. With redaction criticism, the creative force behind the New Testament shifted from Jesus (the traditional view) and the early church (form criticism) to the authors (redaction criticism).⁵⁹ While Haenchen is careful not to make too harsh a distinction between the theology of the early church and that of each New Testament author, the fact that he gives more weight to the author makes Haenchen a redaction critic.

Haenchen is often credited for further expanding redaction criticism, moving from "the editorial alterations of the traditions" (envisioned by the earlier redaction critics) and by adding into his analysis "the process by which the authors combined the traditions into a holistic work" (like the later redaction critics), as Osborne suggests.⁶⁰ Although Osborne does not mention any scholar by name, the evidence found in Haenchen's works indicates that he may well be one of the major figures of the "later redaction critics" to whom Osborne refers.

Suggesting that Marxsen's term *Redaktionsgeschichte*, which implies "editorship," does not fully describe the unique contribution of the author, Haenchen proposes another term, *Kompositionsgeschichte* or "composition-history" as a more fitting term to take into account the author's ability,⁶¹ implying that it is not enough to simply examine the editorial alterations of the traditions made by the author. Rather, the interpreter needs to go a step further by examining the process by which the author has combined the traditions into a holistic work. This, Haenchen remarks, is how he distinguishes his own approach from the approach of the other redaction critics such as Marxsen, Conzelmann, or Käsemann.

Haenchen revealed that the process by which he came to have an interest in composition was through the time of forced convalescence in Switzerland. Due to a law that forbade him to take books across the border, the only book he managed to take with him was the "thin-paper edition" of Nestle's *Novum Testamentum Graece*.⁶² According to Haenchen, however, this turned out to be a great blessing in disguise because it kept him from being "led astray by any secondary literature" and the obsession with Luke's sources.⁶³ Instead, he was able to ask questions that the source critics did not ask—"what the author of Acts had wanted to say to his readers through the varied scenes of his book."⁶⁴ In this light, his time of convalescence that impelled

58. Stein, *Gospels and Tradition*, 27 n. 32.
59. Osborne, "Redaction Criticism," 199.
60. Ibid., 199–200.
61. Haenchen, *Der Weg Jesu*, 24.
62. Haenchen, *Acts*, vii.
63. Ibid.
64. Ibid.

him to devote his attention to the Greek text may have been one of the major factors contributing to his composition approach.

His interest in the author's composition led him to consider not only history and theology, but also the artistry of the New Testament author as a writer. This feature is somewhat unique to his work and is not found in the works of the other redaction critics. In his commentary on Acts, Haenchen remarks that, while the scholars of the past generations regarded Luke as above all a historian, and the scholars of recent years consider Luke as a theologian, what is needed is to consider him as a writer.[65] His discussion of Acts 1:1–8, titled "Retrospect and a Farewell Speech," captures lucidly what it means to give full attention to Luke as a writer.[66] He refers to some, such as Beyer and Bauernfeind, who have noticed the way in which this proem of Acts comes short in comparison to the ways in which the proems of classical times were usually constructed.[67] Others, such as Michaelis, by noting the discrepancies between the two ascension accounts in Luke 24:51 and Acts 1:9 have argued that Jesus came down from heaven for each of the appearances.[68] However, Haenchen warns his readers: "Here we must remind ourselves that Luke does not set as much store as we upon consistency in the story."[69] Just as Luke recounts the three differing stories of Paul's conversion, each answering the needs of the moment, he is doing a similar thing with the proem: "To Luke it is of the utmost importance that Acts should begin not with the disciples left to their own devices, but with the Lord, who visits and instructs them for forty days more. In this way the Christian mission on which they then embark becomes not a merely human enterprise but a process which the Lord himself has guided on its way."[70] From examples such as this, it is clear that Haenchen gives much credit to the author as an able writer, although he seems to give very little credit to him as an able historian.

Haenchen suggests that Luke's purpose in writing Acts was for edification.[71] To accomplish this task, however, Luke had to "employ a special technique and offer his readers history in the guise of stories," in the language of vivid and dramatic scenes.[72] To illustrate this point, Haenchen mentions the choosing of Matthias told in the early part of Acts. Rather than giving a mere straightforward report of what happened, Luke goes about creating a "living scene to rise before [the readers'] eyes" involving Peter's rising and giving of his speech, the casting of lots and so on.[73] Such

65. Ibid., 91.
66. Ibid., 135–47.
67. Ibid., 144.
68. Ibid., 145.
69. Ibid., 146.
70. Ibid.
71. Ibid., 103.
72. Ibid.
73. Ibid., 104.

story-telling demonstrates Luke's ability to transform a simple report into a dramatic scene.[74] Haenchen also points to Luke's ability to condense events of long periods into a single scene, which he calls the "device of condensation."[75] The example of this is seen in Luke's telling of the two disciples' encounter with Jesus at the end of his Gospel. In this scene, the scriptural proofs for the passion and resurrection of the Messiah from Moses and the prophets are painted as though they were given to the disciples in their entirety by Jesus, even though in reality they represent the knowledge of the church developed and accumulated over a long period of time.[76] In reading this, it is clear that historicity is the least of Haenchen's concerns. He further comments:

> That a writer should thus make free with tradition must at first strike us as irresponsible, as an unwarranted license. But evidently Luke has a conception of the narrator's calling that is different from ours. For him, a narration should not describe an event with the precision of a police report, but must make the listener or reader aware of the inner significance of what happened, and impress upon him, unforgettably, the truth of the power of God made manifest in it. The writer's obedience is indeed fulfilled in the very freedom of his rendering.[77]

Herein lies Haenchen's approach at its core—theology through composition. Just because Haenchen undermines history in Acts does not mean that he is not interested in it. He just does not see Acts as providing accurate historical information of the events that it describes. According to Haenchen, what one should focus on when reading Acts is the way in which the author has re-shaped the first-century events to tell a theological story that addresses the historical issues of his own time. In fact, what is foundational to Haenchen's approach is his pre-established understanding of "what really happened" in history, which ultimately drives how he views and interprets the text. This is where Haenchen's approach differs from Ramsay's; the former begins with a predetermined certain historical reconstruction that is used as a framework to read the text, while for the latter, the historical reconstruction comes at the end of analysis, once all the evidence at the analyst's hand, including the text, is studied.

APPLICATION: MATTHEW 1–2

Based on the previous discussion, the present section will take Haenchen's approach and apply it to Matthew 1–2. The application will follow the three areas of interest for interpretation as laid out in Haenchen's commentary on Acts—history, theology, and composition.

---

74. Ibid.
75. Ibid., 105.
76. Ibid.
77. Ibid., 110.

History

While Haenchen downplays the issue of sources for Acts, he nevertheless acknowledges its importance, especially when it comes to the Synoptic Gospels.[78] With that said, Haenchen's historical interest would not so much be in the source of the information, but in the historical situation that prompted the writing of the Gospel. Today, it is widely acknowledged that the Gospel of Matthew was written during a period when tension between Jews and Christians was high.[79] If Haenchen were to accept this view, this historical situation would probably act as the framework through which he would interpret the text. Accordingly, one of Haenchen's main goals would be to determine the theological issues that the author was trying to address, given the tension in which his community found itself.

With his skepticism about the historical accuracy of New Testament accounts, Haenchen might point out how the events reported in Matthew 1–2 are historically improbable. He might also turn to the Old Testament quotations found in these chapters such as Matt 1:23, and point out how the author of Matthew "twists the Scriptures," to use McCasland's expression,[80] or how he offers something as a scriptural quotation when it in fact is not, as noted in Matt 2:23. But at the end of the day, these things would matter little for Haenchen because, in line with other form and redaction critics, what Haenchen is ultimately after is theology, not history.

Theology

For Haenchen Matthew 1–2 would likely provide much ground for understanding the theology of Matthew's Gospel. Given the historical situation of the Jewish opposition faced by the church, Haenchen might point out the various ways in which these chapters reflect the church's theological reaction to this opposition. For instance, Jesus is the long-awaited Messiah, the son of David, son of Abraham (Matt 1:1), as confirmed by his genealogy. And this genealogy also places Matthew's story of Jesus within Israel's story.[81] What is more, Jesus is the one who fulfills the messianic promise of the Old Testament (Matt 1:23; 2:6, 18, 23). And not only is he the Davidic Messiah, but he is also the true heir of the promise made to Abraham.

Composition

How, then, does the author of Matthew shape his narrative to make these theological points? Here, what Haenchen is after is to determine ways in which Matthew "employ[s] a special technique and offer[s] his readers history in the guise of stories"

---

78. This is confirmed by his work on Mark, in which he deals with issues of source (Haenchen, *Der Weg Jesu*).

79. Carson et al., *Introduction*, 77; Gundry, *Matthew*, 5–6.

80. McCasland, "Matthew Twists the Scriptures."

81. Wright, *New Testament and the People of God*, 385.

in the language of vivid and dramatic scenes.[82] Matthew 1–2 lends itself well to the kind of analysis Haenchen advocates. Take, for example, the genealogy of Matthew 1, which begins with Jesus as the son of David, the son of Abraham, placing Jesus within the story of Israel. In addition to this, however, the author of Matthew also inserts the names of certain Gentiles such as Rahab, Ruth, and Tamar. With his community being composed of both Jews and Gentiles, such a genealogy would serve the author's purpose well by showing that it is the members of the church, now made up of both Jews and Gentiles, who have become the true heirs of the promises made to Abraham and David.[83]

EVALUATION OF RAMSAY'S AND HAENCHEN'S APPROACHES

Ramsay

As a scholar, Ramsay was an established historian of Asia Minor who had extensive historical and archaeological knowledge. This was something very few scholars of the day were able to claim for themselves, which made it possible for Ramsay to produce work that was truly original in its time. In fact, reading through Ramsay's works, it is hard to deny the significance of studying the background information, whether historical, archaeological, or geographical when interpreting the New Testament.

Without a doubt, Ramsay's greatest contribution is found in the work he did on the Book of Acts. While certain details of his points may be questioned, he nevertheless made a very strong argument for the book as being a good work of historiography, a point that is supported also by many New Testament scholars today.[84]

Ramsay was one who always sought to think for himself based on his own extensive research, rather than just accepting the opinions of the day. In fact, in his preface to *The Bearing of Recent Discovery on the Trustworthiness of the New Testament*, Ramsay criticized many scholars of his time who seemed to readily accept the research of others as long as it was German. Ramsay wrote: "In the preface to several books, I have referred to the charge brought against me of having slighted the opinions of the Germans. I have learned much from the great German scholars in my own subject; but their teaching was to judge for myself and to accept no man's dictum on the credit of his name and fame."[85]

Also noteworthy is the way Ramsay's approach takes the text of the New Testament at face value. The four approaches developed in Germany discussed above begin with a predetermined theory of "what really happened" in history that then is read into the text of the New Testament. Ramsay formulates his own theories too, except

---

82. Haenchen, *Acts*, 103.
83. Davies and Allison, *Matthew*, 1:188.
84. Neill also makes this point in Neill and Wright, *Interpretation*, 153.
85. Ramsay, *Bearing of Recent Discovery*, viii.

that for him, they come only at the end once all the evidence set before him—historical, archaeological, geographical, and textual—is analyzed. This is not to say that Ramsay was completely free of bias, but he was always willing to be led by the historical evidence before him and to change his views because of it. Gasque notes how it was significant that Ramsay was a historian, not a theologian, who did not come to prove a certain point of view, but simply "aimed at an examination of the facts."[86] And it was this willingness to examine the facts that led Ramsay to discover new insights and offer them to the field of New Testament Studies.

Haenchen

In New Testament Studies, Haenchen will always be known for the historical skepticism with which he approached the New Testament, especially the Book of Acts. In fact, the level of skepticism in Haenchen was even greater than in many New Testament scholars of his period. Marshall, in his commentary on Acts, suggests that Haenchen's suspicion of the historicity of New Testament accounts goes even further than that of Bultmann, a figure often seen by many as representing the ultimate in historical skepticism.[87]

In some way, there were factors that naturally led Haenchen to his position on history. As he states in his commentaries, many scholars of his day, in his opinion, were too preoccupied with history—whether it was the source critics who devoted all their attention to hypothesizing about possible sources or the traditional scholars who refused to give up their dogmatic position on the accuracy of Acts as history. As far as Haenchen was concerned, he was only trying to counter this negative trend. However, the difficulty with his approach was that, in doing so, Haenchen may have gone too far in the other direction. According to his understanding, Luke became a mere "historical novelist with little or no concern for such tiresome things as facts."[88] There is, however, one major problem: Luke's own statement in his prologue (Luke 1:1–4).[89] How would Haenchen's disregard for history account for Luke's assertion that he "carefully investigated everything from the beginning" (1:3) before he wrote his account? While Haenchen tried to get around this issue by suggesting that Luke 1:1–4 applied only to the Gospel,[90] this seems to be just a convenient means of avoiding the issue on Haenchen's part.

Related to the first point, there seems to be, in Haenchen's approach, a lack of connection among what he calls theology, historiography, and literary prowess.[91]

---

86. Gasque, *Sir William M. Ramsay*, 28.

87. Marshall, *Acts*, 35.

88. Ibid.

89. In recent years, the prologues of Luke and Acts have become an intense topic of scholarly debates (Moessner, *Jesus*).

90. Haenchen, *Acts*, 136 n. 3.

91. Ibid., 91.

Granted, he suggests that there is an uncommonly close tie in Luke among all three.[92] Nonetheless, Haenchen does not quite succeed in showing how the three are actually connected, especially the relationship that history has to the other two. In fact, he seems to be suggesting that Luke's concern for theology and composition led him to write a bad work of history.[93] If this were the case, why bother mentioning history in the first place? Did Haenchen really think that history is important, or was he merely giving lip service to it? The evidence of his own works seems to suggest that the latter is the case.

Despite these points of criticism, Haenchen also made significant contributions to New Testament studies. The first contribution is a general one that applies to redaction criticism. With the work of Haenchen and other redactional critics, what took place was a definite change towards the appreciation of the evangelists and their theology. Subsequently, such change of focus led to the end of the trend in which the Epistles were seen as the only appropriate ground for theology.[94] Now the Gospels and the Acts also have to be included in the mix.

At the same time, however, Haenchen's approach is superior to the approaches of many other redaction critics in that it avoids what McKnight calls the "problem of interpretive priority,"[95] in which redaction critics find meaning only in the redaction and not in the tradition. Haenchen puts emphasis on the author's composition as a whole and as a result avoids such a shortcoming. He has successfully shown that theology is gleaned from the pericope as a whole and not just from the modifications of the source as some redaction critics have thought. Similarly, Haenchen's composition approach also avoids the mistake of reading theological emphases into every individual change. Instead, it strives to find theological emphases that are part of a larger pattern, a much sounder approach to theology than that of certain other redaction critics. This aspect of Haenchen's approach may be seen as his most notable contribution.

CONCLUSION

Considering that Ramsay and Haenchen lived and worked in a similar time period, it is interesting to compare the two, especially the way each scholar approached the New Testament. For Ramsay, the high level of historical skepticism with which much of the German scholarship of the day approached the New Testament was a position that lacked support, and he did much to argue against it based on historical evidence. In this light, Ramsay was certainly original in his work. As for Haenchen, the high level of historical skepticism was something that he took for granted based on the work of predecessors who had gone before him. While this was unfortunate, it led Haenchen to focus more on the composition of the final text and further develop the strengths

92. Ibid., 91.
93. Ibid., 98–103.
94. Osborne, "Redaction Criticism," 216.
95. McKnight, *Interpreting the Synoptic Gospels*, 90.

of redaction criticism. For this reason, if Ramsay's success came in being original in his work, Haenchen's success came in synthesizing the work of others and taking it a step further.

BIBLIOGRAPHY

Bornkamm, G., et al. *Tradition and Interpretation in Matthew*. Translated by P. Scott. Philadelphia: Westminster, 1963.

Bultmann, R. *The History of the Synoptic Tradition*. Translated by J. Marsh. 2nd ed. New York: Harper & Row, 1968.

Carson, D. A., et al. *An Introduction to the New Testament*. Grand Rapids: Zondervan, 1992.

Clemen, Carl. *Chronologie der Paulinischen Briefe: Aufs neue Untersucht*. Halle: Max Niemeyer, 1893.

Conzelmann, H. *The Theology of St. Luke*. Translated by G. Buswell. New York: Harper & Brothers, 1960.

Davies, W. D., and D. C. Allison. *A Critical and Exegetical Commentary on the Gospel according to Saint Matthew*. 3 vols. Edinburgh: T. & T. Clark, 1988–97.

Dibelius, M. *From Tradition to Gospel*. Translated by B. L. Woolf. London: Ivor Nicholson and Watson, 1934.

———. "Style Criticism." In *Studies in the Acts of the Apostles*, 1–13. London: SCM, 1956.

———. *Studies in the Acts of the Apostles*. Translated by M. Ling. London: SCM, 1956. A translation of *Aufsätze zur Apostelgeschichte*, edited by H. Greeven. FRLANT. Göttingen: Vandenhoeck & Ruprecht, 1951.

———. "Zur Formgeschichte des Neuen Testaments." *ThR* New Series 3 (1931) 207–42.

Gasque, W. Ward. *Sir William M. Ramsay: Archaeologist and New Testament Scholar*. Grand Rapids: Baker, 1966.

Gundry, R. H. *Matthew: A Commentary on His Handbook for a Mixed Church under Persecution*. Grand Rapids: Eerdmans, 1994.

Haenchen, E. *The Acts of the Apostles: A Commentary*. Philadelphia: Westminster, 1971. A translation of *Die Apostelgeschichte*. KEK 3. Göttingen: Vanderhoeck & Ruprecht, 1961.

———. *Der Weg Jesu: Eine Erklärung des Markus-Evangeliums und der kanonischen Parallelen*. Berlin: Töpelmann, 1966.

———. *Gott und Mensch: Gesammelte Aufsätze*. Tübingen: Mohr, 1965.

———. *John: A Commentary on the Gospel of John*. Translated by W. Funk. 2 vols. Philadelphia: Fortress, 1984. A translation of *Das Johannesevangelium: Ein Kommentar*. Tübingen: Mohr, 1980.

Harnack, A. *The Acts of the Apostles*. London: Williams & Norgate, 1909.

McCasland, S. V. "Matthew Twists the Scriptures." *JBL* 80 (1961) 143–48.

Marshall, I. H. *The Acts of the Apostles*. Grand Rapids: Eerdmans, 1980.

Marxsen, W. *Mark the Evangelist*. Translated by J. Boyce et al. Nashville: Abingdon, 1969.

McKnight, S. *Interpreting the Synoptic Gospels*. Grand Rapids: Baker, 1988.

Moessner, D. P., ed. *Jesus and the Heritage of Israel: Luke's Narrative Claim upon Israel's Legacy*. Harrisburg, PA: Trinity International, 1999.

Neill, S., and T. Wright. *Interpretation of the New Testament 1861–1986*. 2nd ed. Oxford: Oxford University Press, 1988.

Osborne, G. R. "Redaction Criticism." In *New Testament Criticism and Interpretation*, edited by D. A. Black and D. S. Dockery, 199–224. Grand Rapids: Zondervan, 1991.

Perrin, N. *What Is Redaction Criticism?* Philadelphia: Fortress, 1971.
Ramsay, W. M. *The Bearing of Recent Discovery on the Trustworthiness of the New Testament.* London: Hodder & Stoughton, 1915.
———. *The Church in the Roman Empire before A.D. 170.* London: Hodder & Stoughton, 1897.
———. *A Historical Commentary on St Paul's Epistle to the Galatians.* London: Hodder & Stoughton, 1899.
———. *The Letters to the Seven Churches of Asia and Their Place in the Plan of the Apocalypse.* London: Hodder & Stoughton, 1904.
———. *St Paul the Traveller and Roman Citizen.* London: Hodder & Stoughton, 1897.
Riches, J. K. *A Century of New Testament Study.* Valley Forge, PA: Trinity International, 1993.
Schmidt, K. L. *Der Rahmen der Geschichte Jesu.* Berlin: Trowitzsch, 1919.
Soulen, R. N., and R. K. Soulen, eds. *Handbook of Biblical Criticism.* 3rd ed. Louisville, KY: Westminster John Knox, 2001.
Stein, R. H. *Gospels and Tradition: Studies on Redaction Criticism of the Synoptic Gospels.* Grand Rapids: Baker, 1991.
———. *The Synoptic Problem: An Introduction.* Grand Rapids: Baker, 1987.
Wright, N. T. *The New Testament and the People of God.* Minneapolis: Fortress, 1992.

12

Günther Bornkamm and Redaction Criticism

JAE HYUN LEE

WHAT IS REDACTION CRITICISM?

AFTER THE SECOND WORLD War, fresh approaches to the Synoptic Gospels began to appear in the field of New Testament interpretation. Among the pioneers was Günther Bornkamm, a student of Rudolf Bultmann, who opened a new door with the article, "The Stilling of the Storm in Matthew" in 1948.[1] His approach changed the direction of the study, and was followed by the work of Hans Conzelmann[2] and Willi Marxsen[3] in the areas of Luke and Mark respectively. This new approach was called redaction criticism (*Redaktiongeschichte*).

Norman Perrin defines redaction criticism as the determination of "the theological motivation of an author as is revealed in the collection, arrangement, editing and modification of traditional material, and in the composition of new material or the creation of new forms within the traditions of early Christianity."[4] Thus, redaction criticism focuses on the "editorial work carried out by the evangelists on their sources when they composed the Gospels."[5]

Redaction criticism is established upon a twofold foundation. The first is form criticism. Basically, the beginning of redaction criticism is connected with the ending of form criticism, in the sense that Bornkamm's approach was developed from the last section of Bultmann's *History of the Synoptic Tradition*, titled "The Editing (*Redaktion*)

---

1. Originally, it appeared in 1948 as "Die Sturmstillung im Matthäusevangelium" in *Wort und Dienst*.
2. Conzelmann, *Die Mitte der Zeit* (ET: *Theology of St. Luke*).
3. Marxsen, *Der Evangelist Markus* (ET: *Mark the Evangelist*).
4. Perrin, *What Is Redaction Criticism*, 1.
5. Smalley, "Redaction Criticism," 181.

of the Narrative Material and the Composition of the Gospel."[6] However, redaction criticism is different from form criticism in many respects.

First, the directions of the investigations are different. While form criticism has a tendency to move from the text to its sources or traditions, redaction criticism moves from traditions to the text. Based upon the assumption that "the pericopes can be separated from the narrative framework which introduces and often concludes them," form criticism views a Gospel as just the collection of various forms of tradition, such as miracles, tales, parables, and so on. Also it focuses on the origin, history, and situation (*Sitz im Leben*: "setting in the life") of each tradition in the Gospels.[7] However, redaction criticism does not focus on the individual traditions or sources per se, but on how the traditions are linked, ordered, and organized to make the final form of a Gospel.

The second difference between form and redaction criticism is that even though both are concerned with the history of the text, the final goal of historical reconstruction is different. While form criticism concentrates on the historical context of each form of a tradition, redaction criticism pays attention to the context of the community that made the final form of a Gospel. Thus, in light of redaction criticism, there are three kinds of historical contexts in a Gospel. One is the historical context of Jesus' earthly ministry, the second is that of the early Christian community that passed on each form of tradition, and the third is the historical situation of the evangelist or his community.[8]

The third difference is relevant to the perspective of the final editor. In form criticism the role of the final editor is passive, collecting various forms of tradition and putting them together with a method of "scissors and paste." However, the final editor in redaction criticism is not a simple collector or transmitter, but a theologian in the sense that through the work of *Redaktion*, he provides theological advice about the problem(s) that his community faces, thus revealing to us, the later readers, what those problems were. Bornkamm describes this concept thus:

> The particular theology and theme of the first three Gospels goes deeper into the substance of them than is generally recognized, and modifies their message not insignificantly, even though over a large area their traditions are the same ... At the same time the Synoptic writers show—all three and each in his own special way—by their editing and construction, by their selection, inclusion and omission, and not least by what at first sight appears an insignificant, but on closer examination is seen to be a characteristic treatment of the traditional

---

6. Bultmann, *History of the Synoptic Tradition*, 337–67.

7. Sanders and Davies, *Studying the Synoptic Gospels*, 123. In addition to this assumption, they state two more principles of form criticism: (1) each form grew out of a specific activity of the early church, and it reflects its *Sitz im Leben*; and (2) the history of each pericope can be traced by analyzing how close it is to the "pure form" (ibid., 124–25).

8. Smalley, "Redaction Criticism," 184.

material, that they are by no means mere collectors and handers-on of the tradition, but are also interpreters of it.[9]

The second foundation on which redaction criticism relies, in order to understand the theology or concerns of the final editor, is source criticism. Source criticism is "the process of bringing to light the earlier resources available to an author."[10] In the analysis of the Gospels, redaction criticism typically follows the two-source hypothesis, whose core is the combination of two prior sources (Mark and the hypothetically reconstructed Q) as sources for Matthew and Luke. Through comparison of how Matthew and Luke use these sources, and how Mark's treatment differs from either, redaction criticism tries to find differences or peculiar features of each Gospel. From the outcome of such observations, redaction criticism attempts to distinguish the final editor's or evangelist's theology and his historical context.

We will now examine the work of Günther Borkamm and his method. After giving a brief biographical sketch, I will apply his method to Matt 17:14–20 and evaluate this model of interpretation.

GÜNTHER BORNKAMM AND HIS METHOD
Biography

Günther Bornkamm was born in 1905 at Görlitz, and studied at Marburg under Bultmann. His doctoral thesis was about the myth and legend of the Acts of Thomas, which was related to the history of Gnosticism and reflected his teacher's major concern at that time. His career as a teacher began at the University of Königsberg in 1934. However, because of his activities in the Confessing Church, he had difficulties in continuing his teaching until the end of the Second World War. After the war was over, his full-time activity as a New Testament scholar began at the universities of Göttingen (1946–49) and Heidelberg (1949–90).

His major concerns can be seen in his three most influential books. The first was *Tradition and Interpretation in Matthew* published in 1960. As a collection of the results of his new approach to Matthew, this book contained an article that launched the movement of redaction criticism, "The Stilling of the Storm in Matthew."

The second book was *Jesus of Nazareth*, and it reflected his interest in the historical Jesus. Refuting his teacher's claim that it was not a historical person but the kerygma of the earliest Christian community that was significant to the Christian faith, Bornkamm followed E. Käsemann's argument[11] and contended that Christian faith and theology are related to the historical reality of Jesus. His perspective was well reflected in his remark,

---

9. Bornkamm, *Tradition and Interpretation in Matthew*, 11.
10. Catchpole, "Source, Form and Redaction Criticism," 168.
11. Käsemann, "Problem of the Historical Jesus."

In every layer, therefore, and in each individual part, the tradition is witness of the reality of his [Jesus'] history and the reality of his resurrection. Our task, then, is to seek the history *in* the Kerygma of the Gospels, and in this history to seek the Kerygma of the Gospel.[12]

Bornkamm's third major book was *Paul*. Challenging the motto "Jesus, not Paul," which had been popular, and which implies a big chasm between the teachings of the historical Jesus and those of Paul, he strongly defended the connection between the two in his book.[13] However, while Bornkamm showed much affinity for the views of Käsemann in the area of historical Jesus research, he stood against him in the area of Paul's theology. He rejected Käsemann's emphasis on the apocalyptic aspects,[14] and claimed to consider Christology and community as the important factors in approaching Paul's thought.

Bornkamm died on February 18, 1990, in Heidelberg.

Günther Bornkamm's Redaction Criticism

The method of Bornkamm's redaction criticism is well demonstrated in his early article on the stilling of the storm. The fundamental principle is that the final editor of each Gospel is not only a collector, but in some sense, a maker of "Kerygma."[15] Believing that the traditions of Jesus were preserved faithfully, on the one hand, and presented with some freedom to alter, on the other hand, Borkamm regards the final editor of a Gospel as a fresh interpreter of the Jesus tradition in his (the author's) own historical context (*Sitz im Leben*). Based upon this principle, Bornkamm tries to figure out the theological concerns of the evangelist through the following procedure.

First, he compares the contextual differences among the first three Gospels, especially the discrepancies between Mark 4:35-41 and Matt 8:23-27. Unlike Mark and Luke, Matthew's story is located in a cluster of messianic miracle stories (Matt 8–9) that occur after a long messianic teaching (Matt 5–7). Bornkamm explains the significance of this contextual difference thus: "By inserting it [Matt 8:23-27] into a definite context and by his own presentation of it, he [the evangelist] gives it a new meaning which it does not yet have with the other evangelists."[16]

Second, after considering the contextual differences, Bornkamm examines the detailed characteristics of Matthew's version by comparing it with Mark's version:[17]

---

12. Bornkamm, *Jesus of Nazareth*, 21. Emphasis his.
13. Bornkamm, *Paul*, 228-39.
14. E.g. Käsemann, "Primitive Christian Apocalyptic."
15. Bornkamm, "Stilling of the Storm," 52.
16. Ibid., 53.
17. Here, the English version is from the NRSV.

Matt 8:23–27	Mark 4:35–41
²³ Καὶ ἐμβάντι αὐτῷ εἰς τὸ πλοῖον ἠκολούθησαν αὐτῷ οἱ μαθηταὶ αὐτοῦ.	³⁵ Καὶ λέγει αὐτοῖς ἐν ἐκείνῃ τῇ ἡμέρᾳ ὀψίας γενομένης· διέλθωμεν εἰς τὸ πέραν.
	³⁶ καὶ ἀφέντες τὸν ὄχλον παραλαμβάνουσιν αὐτὸν ὡς ἦν ἐν τῷ πλοίῳ, καὶ ἄλλα πλοῖα ἦν μετ' αὐτοῦ.
²⁴ καὶ ἰδοὺ σεισμὸς μέγας ἐγένετο ἐν τῇ θαλάσσῃ, ὥστε τὸ πλοῖον καλύπτεσθαι ὑπὸ τῶν κυμάτων,	³⁷ καὶ γίνεται λαῖλαψ μεγάλη ἀνέμου καὶ τὰ κύματα ἐπέβαλλεν εἰς τὸ πλοῖον, ὥστε ἤδη γεμίζεσθαι τὸ πλοῖον.
αὐτὸς δὲ ἐκάθευδεν. ²⁵καὶ προσελθόντες ἤγειραν αὐτὸν λέγοντες· κύριε, σῶσον, ἀπολλύμεθα.	³⁸ καὶ αὐτὸς ἦν ἐν τῇ πρύμνῃ ἐπὶ τὸ προσκεφάλαιον καθεύδων. καὶ ἐγείρουσιν αὐτὸν καὶ λέγουσιν αὐτῷ· διδάσκαλε, οὐ μέλει σοι ὅτι ἀπολλύμεθα;
²⁶ καὶ λέγει αὐτοῖς· τί δειλοί ἐστε, ὀλιγόπιστοι; τότε ἐγερθεὶς ἐπετίμησεν τοῖς ἀνέμοις καὶ τῇ θαλάσσῃ, καὶ ἐγένετο γαλήνη μεγάλη.	³⁹ καὶ διεγερθεὶς ἐπετίμησεν τῷ ἀνέμῳ καὶ εἶπεν τῇ θαλάσσῃ· σιώπα, πεφίμωσο. καὶ ἐκόπασεν ὁ ἄνεμος καὶ ἐγένετο γαλήνη μεγάλη.
	⁴⁰ καὶ εἶπεν αὐτοῖς· τί δειλοί ἐστε; οὔπω ἔχετε πίστιν;
²⁷ οἱ δὲ ἄνθρωποι ἐθαύμασαν λέγοντες ποταπός ἐστιν οὗτος ὅτι καὶ οἱ ἄνεμοι καὶ ἡ θάλασσα αὐτῷ ὑπακούουσιν;	⁴¹ καὶ ἐφοβήθησαν φόβον μέγαν καὶ ἔλεγον πρὸς ἀλλήλους· τίς ἄρα οὗτός ἐστιν ὅτι καὶ ὁ ἄνεμος καὶ ἡ θάλασσα ὑπακούει αὐτῷ;
²³ And when he got into the boat, his disciples followed him.	³⁵ On that day, when evening had come, he said to them, "Let us go across to the other side." ³⁶ And leaving the crowd behind, they took him with them in the boat, just as he was. Other boats were with him.
²⁴ A windstorm arose on the sea, so great that the boat was being swamped by the waves; but he was asleep.	³⁷ A great windstorm arose, and the waves beat into the boat, so that the boat was already being swamped.
²⁵ And they went and woke him up, saying, "Lord, save us! We are perishing!"	³⁸ But he was in the stern, asleep on the cushion; and they woke him up and said to him, "Teacher, do you not care that we are perishing?"
²⁶ And he said to them, "Why are you afraid, you of little faith?" Then he got up and rebuked the winds and the sea; and there was a dead calm.	³⁹ He woke up and rebuked the wind, and said to the sea, "Peace! Be still!" Then the wind ceased, and there was a dead calm.
	⁴⁰ He said to them, "Why are you afraid? Have you still no faith?"
²⁷ They were amazed, saying, "What sort of man is this, that even the winds and the sea obey him?"	⁴¹ And they were filled with great awe and said to one another, "Who then is this, that even the wind and the sea obey him?

According to Bornkamm, the Markan version describes the miraculous features of the story more strongly. The stormy sea and the perilous situation of the disciples are depicted vividly and they are contrasted to the peaceful sleep of Jesus. The direct speech of Jesus' command to the raging wind and sea[18] and its amazing result show Jesus as a great miracle worker.[19] Yet, he insists that the Matthean story has several different aspects and focuses from Mark's, and that they can be detected through Matthean insertion, omission, alterations, etc. In the first place, he notices an insertion of ἠκολούθησαν in Matt 8:23 and its semantic links to the preceding pericope.[20] He believes that this insertion reflects the intention of the evangelist, who does not want to put this story into a new context of discipleship.[21] He also points out the different order of Jesus' response to his disciples. In Mark, Jesus calms the storm first and then rebukes his disciples for not having faith (Mark 4:39–40). However, the order is reversed in Matt 8:26, where Jesus rebukes his disciples before his miracle. Moreover, Bornkamm takes note of Matthew's special expression, ὀλιγόπιστος ("of little faith") in Matt 8:26. While it never appears in Mark, Matthew uses the root of this word five times indicating the weakness of the disciples' faith.[22]

Lastly, from the above differences, Bornkamm develops some of the theological interests and historical situation of Matthew and his community. He believes that the "little ship" (πλοῖον) in Matthew's story denotes the risky situation of the evangelist's community, and the entreaty of the disciples for help in Matt 8:25 reflects the urgency of its condition: κύριε, σῶσον, ἀπολλύμεθα ("Lord, save us! We are perishing!" [NRSV]). For him, Matthew's change and insertion, especially the term κύριε, reflect the confession of discipleship. In the same sense, he thinks that ἄνθρωποι in Matt 8:27 does not indicate Jesus' disciples, but the disciples in the evangelist's community. He notes that:

> The ἄνθρωποι in our passage, however, are obviously intended to represent *the men who are encountered by the story through preaching* . . . The *setting of the pericope* is thus extended, its horizon is widened and from being a description of discipleship in which the disciples of Jesus experience trial and rescue, storm and security, it becomes a call to imitation and discipleship.[23]

Thus, in the evangelist's mind, the story of Jesus stilling the storm is not a biographical episode in the life of Jesus, but a reinterpreted "kerygmatic paradigm of the danger and glory of discipleship."[24]

---

18. καὶ διεγερθεὶς ἐπετίμησεν τῷ ἀνέμῳ καὶ εἶπεν τῇ θαλάσσῃ· σιώπα, πεφίμωσο (Mark 4:39)
19. Bornkamm, "Stilling of the Storm," 54.
20. Cf. Matt 8:1, 10, 19, and 22.
21. Bornkamm, "Stilling of the Storm," 54–55.
22. Matt 6:30; 8:26; 14:31; 16:8; 17:20. Ibid., 56.
23. Ibid.; italics mine.
24. Ibid., 57.

In conclusion, Bornkamm's method of redaction criticism consists of three steps:

1. Compare Matthew with the other Gospels in regard to the location or context of each pericope.

2. Determine the differences between Matthew and the other Gospels.

3. Synthesize the differences and develop Matthew's theological or historical interests from them.

AN APPLICATION OF GÜNTHER BORNKAMM'S METHOD TO MATTHEW 17:14–20

Contextual Analysis

Regarding the context of the miracle story of Jesus in Matt 17:14–20 (healing of the epileptic boy), all three Synoptic Gospels have the same immediate context, in that the incident appears after the episode of Jesus' transfiguration (Matt 17:1–13; Mark 9:2–7; Luke 9:28–36). As most scholars agree, Matthew follows the Markan story and order.

Comparisons among the Synoptic Gospels

Comparison between Matthew and Mark

Compared with Mark, Matthew's version is relatively short and has some traces of his redactional work. First, with regard to omission, it lacks the scene of the dispute between the disciples and the scribes including the inquiry of Jesus in Mark 9:14–17. The detailed depiction of the symptoms of the boy in Mark 9:19 is also omitted. The Matthean version does not include the conversation between Jesus and the father of the boy in Mark 9:20–24 and the coming of the crowd in Mark 9:25. Finally, there is no utterance of the content of Jesus' command and the convulsion of the boy as in Mark 9:26. There seem to be two reasons for such differences: one is christological, to increase the dignity of Jesus, and the other is to depict this episode not as a pure exorcism but as a healing story mixed with exorcism.

Second, in relation to alteration, Matthew changes some of the Markan wordings to show his intention; these changes can be placed into three categories. The first category is about the dignity of Jesus. Using προσῆλθεν ("come") and γονυπετῶν ("kneeling down") in Matt 17:14, Matthew describes the father of the epileptic boy as a worshiper. Also, he changes "teacher" in Mark 9:17 into "Lord" in Matt 17:15 and the disciples' questioning in Mark 9:28 into their "coming (προσελθόντες)" in Matt 17:19. In Matt 17:18, moreover, the writer stresses Jesus' healing power by the expression that the boy was cured instantly (ἀπὸ τῆς ὥρας ἐκείνης). The second category is his interest in healing. Unlike Mark, Matthew seems to refrain from using the terms related to exorcism. He does not describe the boy as demon possessed as in Mark. Rather, the boy is depicted as a sick one: "for he is an epileptic and he suffers terribly" (Matt 17:15 [NRSV]). When the father of the boy speaks of the failure of the disciples,

Matthew connects it with healing (θεραπεῦσαι: Matt 17:16), while Mark with exorcism (ἐκβάλωσιν: Mark 9:18). Moreover, Matthew uses an expression "Jesus rebuked him" in Matt 17:18 instead of "he rebuked the unclean spirit" in Mark 9:25. Finally, Matthew mentions the result of Jesus' miracle as "the boy was cured instantly" (Matt 17:18). The third category is related to faith. Instead of Jesus' teaching on prayer in Mark 9:29, Matthew highlights the teaching about the need for faith in Matt 17:20.

Comparison between Mark and Luke

The Lukan version shows some detailed explanations of the episode in Mark. By inserting "on the next day" in Luke 9:37, the writer informs the reader when this episode happened. Luke emphasizes the seriousness of the demonic action by addition of "[the demon] will hardly leave him" (Luke 9:39). However, he does not speak of what Matthew also omits: a dispute between the disciples and the scribes, the conversation between Jesus and the father of the boy, and the struggle of the demon after Jesus' command. As in Matthew, Luke thus also reveals a developed theme of Jesus' dignity. Unlike Mark, he finishes this episode by reporting the response of the crowd to Jesus' exorcism: "and all were astonished at the majesty of God" (Luke 9:43a). Finally, Luke does not include the private conversation between Jesus and his disciples shown in Mark 9:20.

Comparison between Matthew and Luke

In general, Matthew and Luke share the same omissions, in that both develop the aspect of Jesus' dignity. However, there are some differences between the two. First, while Matthew seems to focus more on the aspect of healing than on exorcism, Luke follows Mark and describes this episode as a typical story of exorcism. As in Mark, Luke reports how the spirit tormented the boy (Luke 9:39; cf. Mark 9:18), and how the demon recognized Jesus (Luke 9:42; cf. Mark 9:20). He retains Mark's term "cast [the demon] out" (Luke 9:40; Mark 9:18), and speaks of Jesus' command with the Markan expression, "Jesus rebuked the unclean spirit" (Luke 9:42; Mark 9:25).

Second, even though both Matthew and Luke have a developed Christology, they demonstrate it in different ways. While Matthew shows it with his typical word, προσέρχομαι, Luke develops it by adding the response of the crowd. In addition, the title of Jesus is different in the two narratives. Unlike Matthew, Luke seems to use the term "Lord" as an interchangeable or inseparable title of Jesus: e.g., "and the Lord said" in Luke 17:6 versus "he said to them" in Matt 17:20. In fact, the frequency of this word is very different in Matthew and Luke. While the meaning of this term as "divine Lord" not "sir" or "master" occurs fifty times in Matthew, Luke uses it seventy-four times in his Gospel and ninety-seven times in Acts. Moreover, Matthew never uses "the Lord" and "Jesus" interchangeably, but Luke does in 7:13, 19; 10:1, 41; 11:39;

12:42; 13:15; 17:5, 6; 18:6; 19:8; and 22:61. Thus, it seems to be natural for Luke to apply "the Lord" to Jesus in this episode.[25]

Lastly, Luke does not include the private teaching about faith in this episode (cf. Matt 17:19–20), but relocates it to a different context (Luke 17:6). Even in the teaching of Jesus about faith, the example that Jesus uses is different. While the mountain is used in Matthew, a sycamore tree is used in Luke.

Summary of the Comparisons

From the observations above, some conclusions can be drawn: (1) Since the Markan version has a less developed Christology, Mark could be regarded as the earliest Gospel, with Matthew and Luke being written later; (2) Matthew performs redactional work for his own emphasis, such as Jesus' dignity, the healing ministry of Jesus, discipleship, and the emphasis on faith; and (3) Matthew and Luke share some modifications of the Markan version.[26] Since they also have differences, however, they appear to carry out their own redactional work in line with their individual theological interests.

Exegetical Comments on Matthew 17:14–20

Entreaty for the Healing of the Epileptic Boy (Matt 17:14–16)

SETTING THE SCENE (MATT 17:14)

After the event of Jesus' transfiguration on the mountain, Jesus and his three disciples came down to the crowd, and a man came to Jesus. Here, Matthew omits several things, such as the dispute between the disciples and the scribes, the amazement of the crowds, and the inquiry of Jesus, "why are you arguing with them?" (cf. Mark 9:14–16). Why does Matthew do this? Some scholars think that Matthew omits the dispute because the subject matter of the dispute lacks clarity.[27] However, there seems to be another reason for this omission. Probably it is related to Matthew's intention to defend Jesus' omniscient power, because the Markan version could give an unnecessary impression that there are some things that Jesus does not know.[28] Interestingly, the major omissions in Matthew of words in the Markan version (Mark 9:14–16,

---

25. However, this observation could not lead one to the conclusion that the Matthean version is earlier than the Lukan one, because the Matthean version also depicts Jesus as the "Lord" through the confession of the father of the boy (Matt 17:15). Moreover, even though we do not know the exact date of the writing of Matthew and Luke, it is sure that to call Jesus "the Lord" was common in the mid first century. Thus, the use of "Lord" itself cannot be a decisive factor in determining the chronological order of the compositions of Matthew and Luke.

26. It includes the so-called minor agreements: e.g., ἄπιστος καὶ διεστραμμένη ("faithless and perverse generation") in Matt 17:17 and Luke 9:41 vs. ἄπιστος ("faithless") in Mark 9:19; cf. ἐθεραπεύθη ὁ παῖς ("the boy was cured") in Matt 17:18 and ἰάσατο τὸν παῖδα ("[Jesus] healed the boy") in Luke 9:42 vs. ὁ δὲ Ἰησοῦς κρατήσας τῆς χειρὸς αὐτοῦ ἤγειρεν αὐτόν, καὶ ἀνέστη ("But Jesus took him by the hand and lifted him up, and he was able to stand") in Mark 9:27.

27. Gundry, *Matthew*, 349; Allen, *St Matthew*, 188.

28. Davies and Allison, *Matthew*, 2:721.

20–25a, and 25c–26) are relevant to Christology. The first two (Mark 9:16 and 21) are about Jesus' inquiry.[29] Thus, Matthew's omission seems to be not only because the matter of the dispute is unclear, but also because of Matthew's interest in depicting a high Christology.

This kind of christological intention is also reflected in his depiction of the approach of the man: "a man came to (προσῆλθεν) him, knelt before (γονυπετῶν) him" (NRSV). In many cases, Matthew uses προσέρχομαι in relation to a reverential approach to Jesus and the recognition of his authority.[30] Also, even though γονυπετέω itself does not have a meaning of worship, the combination of this word with προσέρχομαι and the address "Lord" (Matt 17:15) may imply a worship situation (cf. Matt 2:11; 8:2; 9:18; 14:33; 15:25; 27:29).[31]

Request of the father for healing of his son (Matt 17:15–16)

The father of the sick boy implores Jesus to cure his son in Matt 17:15. Here, this man does not call Jesus a teacher but "Lord." Before outlining the problem of his son, he shows total dependence on Jesus by stating "have mercy on my son!"[32] Thus, Matthew seems to describe this man as one who has faith. This is also supported by the evidence that Matthew omits the conversation between Jesus and this man given in Mark 9:22 and 24, where the man reveals his unbelief.

When the father of the boy speaks of the symptoms of his son, he does not mention the demon as their cause. Instead, he depicts the problem as σεληνιάζεται (literally "he is moonstuck"), a word that appears only here and in Matt 4:24 in the entire New Testament. It may imply that Matthew probably intends to describe this miracle not as a pure exorcism but as a healing, although the symptoms of the boy are not totally unlike those of one who is demon possessed (cf. Matt 17:18).[33]

---

29. When providing a list of Matthew's redactional work promoting his christological interest, Allen (*St Matthew*, xxxii) includes the questions that Matthew omits, which Mark puts in the mouth of Jesus: e.g., Mark 5:9, 30; 6:38; 8:12, 23; 9:12, 16, 21, 33; 10:3; 14:14.

30. Matt 4:3, 11; 5:1; 8:2, 5, 19, 25; 9:14, 18, 20, 28; 13:10, 27, 36; 14:12, 15, 33; 15:1, 12, 23, 30; 16:1; 28:9. Gundry, *Matthew*, 349; Hagner, *Matthew 14–28*, 503; Carter, *Matthew and the Margins*, 353.

31. The word, γονυπετέω appears in Matt 27:29 as an action of mocking soldiers, but ironically it can function to show Jesus' true kingship to the reader (Gundry, *Matthew*, 349; Hagner, *Matthew 14–28*, 503; Schnackenburg, *Gospel of Matthew*, 168; contra Carson, *Matthew*, 390; Morris, *Matthew*, 490). France, *Matthew*, 659, comments that "the term [γονυπετῶν] probably does not significantly differ in connotation from the 'low bow (*proskyneō*)' which is Matthew's usual term for the posture of a suppliant."

32. The same expression appears in Matt 9:27; 15:22; 20:30–31. Of the three, only the last one has a parallel in the other Gospels (cf. Mark 10:47; Luke 18:38).

33. Keener, *Matthew*, 441; cf. Gundry, *Matthew*, 349; Morris, *Matthew*, 446; contra Hagner, *Matthew 14–28*, 503. Hagner thinks that the subject of πίπτει ("he falls") is the demon. However, his view is not convincing because certainly Matthew changes the subject from the unclean spirit in Mark 9:18 to the boy.

In Matt 17:16, the man informs Jesus that his afflicted son was brought to the disciples, but they could not heal him. Like Mark, Matthew mentions the inability of the disciples, but his modification reveals his twofold interest. One is that Matthew still depicts this man as the one who has faith. Instead of φέρω in Mark 9:17, he uses προσφέρω ("bring"), which is Matthew's preferred term to describe a scene in which a sick person is brought for healing (Matt 4:24; 8:16; 9:2, 32; 12:22; 14:35 [all unparalleled]). Moreover, the faith of this man is contrasted to the little faith of the disciples, which results in their failure to heal the boy. Even though the disciples received authority to cast out demons and heal the sick in Matt 10:1, they could not (ἠδυνήθησαν) cure this boy. This inability of the disciples is linked with their inquiry (ἠδυνήθησαν, v. 19) and Jesus' teaching of faith (ἀδυνατήσει, v. 20) in Matt 17:19–20. Thus, as D. A. Hagner rightly comments, Matthew seems to depict the faith of this man as a foil to the lack of faith in the disciples.[34]

The other interest that Matthew wants to reveal through his redactional work in v. 16 is to show the miracle of Jesus as a healing. He omits "to cast it out (ἐκβαλεῖν αὐτό)," which is a typical phrase of exorcism, and adds healing (αὐτὸν θεραπεῦσαι). Together with σεληνιάζεται in v. 15, this term reflects the evangelist's interest in Jesus' healing. It is only Matthew that inserts healing in the summary of Jesus' Galilean ministry in Matt 4:23 and 9:35. In chapter 10, when Jesus calls the twelve and gives authority to them, Matthew adds the authority to cure every disease and sickness to Mark's version (cf. Mark 3:13–14). In addition, while Mark mentions an exorcism as the first miracle of Jesus (Mark 1:21–28), in Matthew it is the healing of a leper (Matt 8:1–4). When Matthew tells of Jesus' entry into the region of Judea, he replaces Mark's "teaching" (Mark 10:1) with "healing" (Matt 19:1). Moreover, only Matthew reports Jesus' healing in the temple in Jerusalem (Matt 21:14). Finally, only Matthew explains Jesus' healing miracles as the fulfillment of Old Testament prophecy, especially of Isaiah (Matt 8:17). Thus, the healing ministry of Jesus can be regarded as one of Matthew's interests, and that may explain why he changes the Markan version in this verse.[35]

---

34. Hagner, *Matthew 14–28*, 503.

35. Interestingly, Witmer ascribes the different focus on the nature of Jesus' miracle between Matthew and Mark to their geographical difference. She explains, "The fact that Matthew alone has made this connection [to see the situation of the boy as a clinical illness] explicitly may be a result of his location or cosmopolitan perspective. Similarly, Mark's failure to do so may reflect his reception of an early exorcism story rooted in local Palestinian tradition, where epilepsy was not recognized as distinct from spirit possession" (Witmer, *Jesus, the Galilean Exorcist*, 188). However, she does not seem to consider that the depiction of Jesus in this story is closely related to the overall purpose of each evangelist in introducing who Jesus is.

Jesus' Healing (Matt 17:17–18)

Jesus' response (Matt 17:17)

In response to the request of the man, Jesus laments over the unbelieving generation and orders them to bring the boy to him. In his lament, Jesus says, "You faithless and perverse generation, how much longer must I be with you? How much longer must I put up with you?" To whom, then, does Jesus speak? Certainly not to the father of the boy, because Matthew depicts him as having faith.[36] In Matthew, "generation" sometimes indicates Israel (Matt 11:16; 12:39, 41, 42, 45; 16:4; 23:6). He adds "perverse" to the Markan version, which appears in Deut 32:5, 20 as indicating corrupted Israel who did not respond to God. Thus, this insertion may imply that Matthew emphasizes the unbelief of Jesus' contemporaries who are analogous to the contemporaries of Moses.[37] However, the disciples are not exonerated from this blame because they have "little faith" (Matt 17:20) and cannot heal the boy. Therefore, it is more reasonable to think that Jesus reproves not only his contemporaries but also his disciples.[38]

Jesus' healing (Matt 17:18)

Matthew omits eight verses of Mark, whose contents are (1) the manner by which the boy is brought to Jesus, (2) the encounter between Jesus and the demon, and (3) the conversation between Jesus and the father of the boy. These omissions are in line with Matthew's intention mentioned above. First, in relation to Christology, Matthew omits Jesus' question, "How long has he had this?" (cf. Mark 9:21). Nor does he mention the doubting expression of the father of the boy, "If you can do anything" (cf. Mark 9:21), which may indicate a questioning of Jesus' ability.[39] Second, with regard to the focus on the healing ministry of Jesus, Matthew does not mention that the demon recognizes Jesus' authority and shows a negative response to him, which is one of the elements of the exorcism story.[40] Lastly, concerning the faith of the man, Matthew seeks to show him as a believer through the omission of his entreaties "if you can do anything" and "help my unbelief" (cf. Mark 9:22–24).

---

36. However, Luke seems to imply that the father of the boy is included in the unbelieving generation, in the sense that Luke changes "him (a boy)" to "*your* son" (Luke 9:41) (Davies and Allison, *Matthew*, 2:724).

37. Gundry, *Matthew*, 350; Hagner, *Matthew 14–28*, 504; contra Keener, *Matthew*, 441.

38. Carson, *Matthew*, 391; Carter, *Matthew and the Margins*, 354; Davies and Allison, *Matthew*, 2:724; Osborne, *Matthew*, 656. However, Luke omits the disciples' question, so that he seems to exclude the disciples from this blame.

39. Gundry, *Matthew*, 351; Davies and Allison, *Matthew*, 2:725.

40. Fitzmyer lists some patterns in exorcism stories: (1) the encounter between Jesus and the demoniac; (2) the description of the demoniac's condition and symptoms; (3) the demoniac's recognition of Jesus the exorcist; (4) exorcism; (5) the proof of the exit of the demons; (6) the reaction of spectators and others; and (7) the missionary conclusion (Fitzmyer, *Luke*, 1:733–34).

In the scene of Jesus' healing, Matthew's redaction also appears. Although the expression, "the demon came out of him," shows the connection of the cause of the disease to the demon, Matthew still preserves his intention of depicting this story as healing. In Matt 17:18, Matthew mentions that Jesus rebuked him (αὐτῷ), which is dissimilar to Mark and Luke. Some scholars insist that αὐτῷ indicates the boy,[41] and others think that it refers to the demon.[42] Whether it refers to the boy or the demon, however, it is certain that Matthew changes the apparent reference to the demon in Mark 9:25 ("the unclean spirit" [τῷ πνεύματι τῷ ἀκαθάρτῳ]: cf. Luke 9:42) into the third person pronoun. This change could work to obscure the exorcistic nature of this story. Two other redactions also support this view: one is the omission of the detailed depiction of Jesus' command and the response of the demon (cf. Mark 9:25–26), and the other is the depiction of Jesus' work as a cure (ἐθεραπεύθη). All these things work to emphasize the theme of Jesus' healing.

Similarly, the theme of Jesus' authority is also evident in this verse. Matthew does not mention that the boy was like a corpse when the demon was cast out (cf. Mark 9:26). Rather, he emphasizes Jesus' power by stating that the boy was cured instantly.

Jesus' Teaching on Faith to His Disciples (Matt 17:19–20)

THE DISCIPLES' QUESTION (MATT 17:19)

From this verse on, Matthew goes his own way to deal with the disciples, especially with regard to their faith. The disciples open the conversation with the question about the reason for their failure. Even though this verse follows the Markan version in general, Matthew does not forget to alter this scene with his redactional hand. At the outset, the use of τότε ("then") informs that the story is turning to an important phase, since this term is used in Matthew for either "marking paragraphs within an episode" or "marking the use of a theologically significant lexical form or a climactic point within a pericope."[43] In addition, the conversation and teaching of Jesus could signify the positional function of Matt 17:19–20 in this episode. Among the elements of the healing story,[44] Matthew often puts an emphasis on the conversation between

---

41. Gundry, *Matthew*, 351; France, *Matthew*, 661; RSV; NEB.

42. Hagner, *Matthew 14–28*, 504; Carter, *Matthew and the Margins*, 354; Morris, *Matthew*, 447; Osborne, *Matthew*, 654; NRSV; TNIV.

43. Black, *Sentence Conjunctions*, 253.

44. Held, "Matthew as Interpreter," 241, lists several elements of the healing miracles: (1) formal introduction in which the suppliant is quite briefly introduced and an attitude of supplication is expressed; (2) the request in direct speech in which faith is expressed; (3) the reply of Jesus corresponding to the request, healing saying or action; and (4) a brief formalistic notice that the miracle has taken place. He also adds three patterns of conversation in the healing miracle here: (1) formalistic introduction in which the question is briefly introduced (cf. Matt 18:1a); (2) the question in direct speech for which an answer is sought (cf. Matt 18:1b); and (3) the answer of Jesus in clear correspondence to the question, together with an instructive action (cf. Matt 18:2–4).

Jesus and his disciples, especially in the teaching of Jesus.[45] Interestingly, most of these sayings of Jesus in the context of a healing miracle are relevant to faith (cf. Matt 8:13; 9:22, 29; 15:28). Therefore, this verse also contains the redactional work of Matthew, and it contributes to reveal the importance of faith in discipleship.

Although Matthew deals with discipleship here, this verse also has a christological theme. The word προσέρχομαι in this verse could give an impression that the disciples come to Jesus with adoration. Jesus' power is emphasized by the reiteration of the failure of the disciples with ἠδυνήθημεν, which is used to describe their inability in Matt 17:16. Thus, Matthew's redactional work to emphasize Christology seems to be a frame of reference for all other themes.

Jesus' Answer and Teaching (Matt 17:20)

In response to the question of the disciples, Jesus teaches the importance of faith. To begin with, he diagnoses that the failure of the disciples results from their little faith (ὀλιγοπιστία), a term that appears only here in the New Testament. However, Matthew uses the cognate adjective (ὀλιγόπιστος) several times (Matt 6:30; 8:26; 16:8), and all are applied only to the disciples. After examining the parallel between Matthew and Mark, H. J. Held concludes that as Matthew's redactional term, ὀλιγοπιστία describes "on the one hand a broken form of faith—in that it means a failure in discipleship—but on the other hand, a broken form of unbelief—in that it does not mean a fundamental rejection of Jesus."[46] Thus, the little faith of the disciples does not refer to their total distrust in God, but the partial nature of their faith, since it is applied only to the cognitive area. It is because of this type of faith that they could not cure the boy.

After pointing out the inability of the disciples, Jesus teaches the significance of faith with his typical phrase "for truly I tell you" (ἀμὴν γὰρ λέγω ὑμῖν) and the contrast between a mustard seed and moving a mountain. A mustard seed is thought to be the smallest of all the seeds, and moving a mountain is regarded as an impossible thing.[47] Thus, Jesus not only teaches the importance of faith, but is also critical of the little faith of his disciples, who do not have even the smallest bit of the mountain-moving type of faith.

As in the case of the preceding verses, Matt 17:20 also demonstrates the redactional work of the evangelist, in that he changes the reason for failure from a lack of prayer in the Markan story to a lack of faith.

---

45. Ibid., 242.
46. Ibid., 295.
47. Keener, *Matthew*, 442.

Conclusion of the Exegetical Example

According to the exegetical observations above, several considerations can be drawn. First, the comparison between Mark and Matthew shows that the Matthean story contains many traces of the evangelist's redactional work, such as omission, alteration, and insertion.

Second, there are several consistent tendencies in Matthew's redactional changes, and they can be placed into three categories. The first category is the emphasis on Jesus' dignity. From the beginning to the end, this topical interest appears as the backbone of the story. It is identified by the modified or developed portrayal of Jesus and the attitude of the people to him. The second category is to depict this story as a part of Jesus' healing ministry. The editorial work in this category is performed mainly in relation to the lexical-semantic aspects. The last one is the significance of faith. As one of the issues of discipleship in Matthew, this topic is demonstrated through the contrast between the faith of the disciples and that of the father, on the one hand, and between the failure of the disciples and the power of Jesus, on the other hand.

The last consideration from the above observation is that all these categories are relevant to the evangelist's overall interests. For example, healing by Jesus is not merely miraculous in Matthew. Rather, it is regarded as the fulfillment of Old Testament prophecy (Matt 8:17), and as one of the powerful pieces of evidence of Jesus' messianic identity (Matt 11:5). Consequently, the editorial work showing this episode as a healing story seems to reflect the evangelist's intention to portray Jesus as the promised Messiah.

EVALUATION OF GÜNTHER BORNKAMM'S REDACTION CRITICISM

From the examination of redaction criticism and its application above, we can discuss some of the strengths and weaknesses of this theory. First, regarding weaknesses, since redaction criticism was developed from form criticism and the two-source hypothesis, it also contains some of the weaknesses inherent within these two theories. Redaction criticism presupposes Markan priority, and, as a result, it assumes that Matthew was written later than Mark. It is true that most scholars adhere to the theory of Markan priority, but not all are convinced. The followers of the Griesbach hypothesis, who insist on Matthean priority, cannot accept the method and the result of Bornkamm's redaction criticism.[48] If one approaches Matt 17:17–20 with the Griesbach hypothesis, the above construction of Matthew's theology will not be sustained. Moreover, Markan theology would also be viewed very differently.

In relation to the problems of form criticism, redaction criticism has a tendency to think lightly of the historicity of Jesus portrayed in the Gospels, just as form criticism did. In fact, though Bornkamm does not totally neglect the historicity of Jesus

---

48. A defense of the Griesbach hypothesis is found in Peabody, *One Gospel from Two*.

in his study of redaction criticism, his main focus is on the theology and historical situation of the evangelist. Moreover, just as the historical reconstruction of the early church by form criticism has been criticized, the historical conjecture of the situation of the evangelist's community obtained by redaction criticism is also problematic. Can we know the historical situation from the differences among the Gospels? If we can, what degree of correct historical information can we get from redaction criticism? According to the application of Bornkamm's method to Matt 17:20, for example, I have observed that Matthew's redactional work is related to three theological themes: Jesus' dignity, the portrayal of this story as a healing miracle, and the importance of faith. However, it is not certain that these three themes reflect problematic situations in the evangelist's community. Actually, there is no textual clue in Matt 17:14–20 with which to reconstruct the historical situation of the evangelist or his community. Therefore, one should be very cautious in trying to come to historical conclusions about the final editor's community by way of redaction criticism.[49]

Another weakness of redaction criticism is its method in finding the final editor's theology. Redaction criticism mainly focuses and relies on the differences among Gospels. However, there are some problems with this method. How can one handle the information of differences among Gospels? Does every omission or insertion have significant theological meaning? If not, how can one determine the degree of importance from such information? Bornkamm does not seem to consider the possibility that the differences are just stylistic changes or accidental ones. Furthermore, it is not at all clear that every difference was made by the evangelist. It is possible that the evangelist just used the already-changed story when he wrote his Gospel. Thus, it seems to be more reasonable to believe that in order to understand the theology of the evangelist, one should examine both the differences among Gospels and what they have in common, that is, the preserved traditions. Moreover, it is also important to apply redaction criticism not only to find individual differences in isolated pericopes, but also to see how the author uses his sources throughout his whole book. In this sense, the compositional aspect of redaction criticism seems to be more useful in understanding the theology of the evangelist.[50]

In spite of such weaknesses, redaction criticism has some interpretive benefits. First, redaction criticism gives a proper emphasis to the creative role of the author. Thus, it is possible to some extent to outline the emphases and theologies of the author of each Gospel. Redaction criticism also implies that a Gospel account is not just a collection of independent or fragmented sources. Rather each Gospel is unified according to the final editor's concerns and theologies. In this sense, redaction criticism

---

49. Actually, since the publication of Bauckham's *Gospels for All Christians*, scholars have become more cautious in reconstructing the historical situation of an evangelist's community. For more recent study on the Gospel community, see Klink, "Gospel Community Debate"; Klink, *Audience of the Gospels*.

50. Goodacre, *Case against Q*, applies this compositional aspect of redaction criticism to Luke in order to oppose the Q hypothesis.

contributes to New Testament interpretation by paving the way for regarding each Gospel as a compositional whole.

If one uses redaction criticism properly to trace the theology of the evangelist and does not adopt an extreme skepticism regarding the historical Jesus, redaction criticism can be a useful tool in examining both the context of the historical Jesus and the theological reinterpretations of the early church. Moreover, if we admit that the redactional work of the evangelist is not for academic but for pastoral purposes, this redactional work can shed some light on how we build a bridge between Jesus and our contemporary situation. This is not to say that we can add to or omit from the story of Jesus, but that we can apply and reword the story of Jesus and his teaching creatively. As Osborne says:

> [R]edaction criticism is a preaching and not just an academic tool. The Gospels were originally contextualizations of the life and teaching of Jesus for the reading and listening audiences of the Evangelists' time. They were biographical sermons (one aspect of the meaning of the term "Gospel") applying Jesus' impact on his disciples, the crowds and the Jewish leaders to first-century readers and listeners. This is perhaps the best use of life-situation approaches, for they show how Matthew or Luke addressed problems in their communities and demonstrate how they can address similar problems in our churches.[51]

CONCLUSION

In the history of biblical interpretation, various people and methods have emerged. Some people are still remembered as influential figures, and their methods are considered useful tools in interpreting the Scripture, and are still used in actual interpretation. It is probably true that Bornkamm was not the most influential New Testament scholar in the history of biblical interpretation, and that redaction criticism on its own is not enough for completely understanding the Gospels. Nevertheless, it is hard to deny the fact that Bornkamm provided a very important contribution in the history of biblical interpretation. This is because redaction criticism not only makes interpreters pay attention to the role and theology of the final editor in understanding the Gospels, but also paves the way for acknowledging each Gospel as a holistic unit. Thus, in the area of Gospel study, redaction criticism was, is, and will be an important method to use for understanding the biblical text.

---

51. Osborne, "Redaction Criticism," 668.

APPENDIX: SYNOPSIS OF JESUS' HEALING/EXORCISM OF THE BOY WITH AN UNCLEAN SPIRIT

Matt 17:14–21	Mark 9:14–29	Luke 9:37–43; 17:6
¹⁴ Καὶ ἐλθόντων πρὸς τὸν ὄχλον προσῆλθεν αὐτῷ ἄνθρωπος γονυπετῶν αὐτὸν ¹⁵καὶ λέγων· κύριε, ἐλέησόν μου τὸν υἱόν, ὅτι σεληνιάζεται καὶ κακῶς πάσχει· πολλάκις γὰρ πίπτει εἰς τὸ πῦρ καὶ πολλάκις εἰς τὸ ὕδωρ. ¹⁶ καὶ προσήνεγκα αὐτὸν τοῖς μαθηταῖς σου, καὶ οὐκ ἠδυνήθησαν αὐτὸν θεραπεῦσαι.	¹⁴ Καὶ ἐλθόντες πρὸς τοὺς μαθητὰς εἶδον ὄχλον πολὺν περὶ αὐτοὺς καὶ γραμματεῖς συζητοῦντας πρὸς αὐτούς. ¹⁵ καὶ εὐθὺς πᾶς ὁ ὄχλος ἰδόντες αὐτὸν ἐξεθαμβήθησαν καὶ προστρέχοντες ἠσπάζοντο αὐτόν. ¹⁶ καὶ ἐπηρώτησεν αὐτούς· τί συζητεῖτε πρὸς αὐτούς; ¹⁷ καὶ ἀπεκρίθη αὐτῷ εἷς ἐκ τοῦ ὄχλου· διδάσκαλε, ἤνεγκα τὸν υἱόν μου πρὸς σέ, ἔχοντα πνεῦμα ἄλαλον· ¹⁸ καὶ ὅπου ἐὰν αὐτὸν καταλάβῃ ῥήσσει αὐτόν, καὶ ἀφρίζει καὶ τρίζει τοὺς ὀδόντας καὶ ξηραίνεται· καὶ εἶπα τοῖς μαθηταῖς σου ἵνα αὐτὸ ἐκβάλωσιν, καὶ οὐκ ἴσχυσαν.	³⁷Ἐγένετο δὲ τῇ ἑξῆς ἡμέρᾳ κατελθόντων αὐτῶν ἀπὸ τοῦ ὄρους συνήντησεν αὐτῷ ὄχλος πολύς. ³⁸ καὶ ἰδοὺ ἀνὴρ ἀπὸ τοῦ ὄχλου ἐβόησεν λέγων· διδάσκαλε, δέομαί σου ἐπιβλέψαι ἐπὶ τὸν υἱόν μου, ὅτι μονογενής μοί ἐστιν, ³⁹ καὶ ἰδοὺ πνεῦμα λαμβάνει αὐτὸν καὶ ἐξαίφνης κράζει καὶ σπαράσσει αὐτὸν μετὰ ἀφροῦ καὶ μόγις ἀποχωρεῖ ἀπ' αὐτοῦ συντρῖβον αὐτόν· ⁴⁰ καὶ ἐδεήθην τῶν μαθητῶν σου ἵνα ἐκβάλωσιν αὐτό, καὶ οὐκ ἠδυνήθησαν.
¹⁷ ἀποκριθεὶς δὲ ὁ Ἰησοῦς εἶπεν· ὦ γενεὰ ἄπιστος καὶ διεστραμμένη, ἕως πότε μεθ' ὑμῶν ἔσομαι; ἕως πότε ἀνέξομαι ὑμῶν; φέρετέ μοι αὐτὸν ὧδε.	¹⁹ ὁ δὲ ἀποκριθεὶς αὐτοῖς λέγει· ὦ γενεὰ ἄπιστος, ἕως πότε πρὸς ὑμᾶς ἔσομαι; ἕως πότε ἀνέξομαι ὑμῶν; φέρετε αὐτὸν πρός με. ²⁰ καὶ ἤνεγκαν αὐτὸν πρὸς αὐτόν. καὶ ἰδὼν αὐτὸν τὸ πνεῦμα εὐθὺς συνεσπάραξεν αὐτόν, καὶ πεσὼν ἐπὶ τῆς γῆς ἐκυλίετο ἀφρίζων. ²¹ καὶ ἐπηρώτησεν τὸν πατέρα αὐτοῦ· πόσος χρόνος ἐστὶν ὡς τοῦτο γέγονεν αὐτῷ; ὁ δὲ εἶπεν· ἐκ παιδιόθεν· ²² καὶ πολλάκις καὶ εἰς πῦρ αὐτὸν ἔβαλεν καὶ εἰς ὕδατα ἵνα ἀπολέσῃ αὐτόν· ἀλλ' εἴ τι δύνῃ, βοήθησον ἡμῖν σπλαγχνισθεὶς ἐφ' ἡμᾶς.	⁴¹ ἀποκριθεὶς δὲ ὁ Ἰησοῦς εἶπεν· ὦ γενεὰ ἄπιστος καὶ διεστραμμένη, ἕως πότε ἔσομαι πρὸς ὑμᾶς καὶ ἀνέξομαι ὑμῶν; προσάγαγε ὧδε τὸν υἱόν σου.

Matt 17:14–21	Mark 9:14–29	Luke 9:37–43; 17:6
	²³ ὁ δὲ Ἰησοῦς εἶπεν αὐτῷ τὸ εἰ δύνῃ, πάντα δυνατὰ τῷ πιστεύοντι.	
	²⁴ εὐθὺς κράξας ὁ πατὴρ τοῦ παιδίου ἔλεγεν πιστεύω βοήθει μου τῇ ἀπιστίᾳ.	
¹⁸ καὶ ἐπετίμησεν αὐτῷ ὁ Ἰησοῦς καὶ ἐξῆλθεν ἀπ' αὐτοῦ τὸ δαιμόνιον καὶ ἐθεραπεύθη ὁ παῖς ἀπὸ τῆς ὥρας ἐκείνης.	²⁵ ἰδὼν δὲ ὁ Ἰησοῦς ὅτι ἐπισυντρέχει ὄχλος, ἐπετίμησεν τῷ πνεύματι τῷ ἀκαθάρτῳ λέγων αὐτῷ· τὸ ἄλαλον καὶ κωφὸν πνεῦμα, ἐγὼ ἐπιτάσσω σοι, ἔξελθε ἐξ αὐτοῦ καὶ μηκέτι εἰσέλθῃς εἰς αὐτόν.	⁴² ἔτι δὲ προσερχομένου αὐτοῦ ἔρρηξεν αὐτὸν τὸ δαιμόνιον καὶ συνεσπάραξεν· ἐπετίμησεν δὲ ὁ Ἰησοῦς τῷ πνεύματι τῷ ἀκαθάρτῳ καὶ ἰάσατο τὸν παῖδα καὶ ἀπέδωκεν αὐτὸν τῷ πατρὶ αὐτοῦ.
	²⁶ καὶ κράξας καὶ πολλὰ σπαράξας ἐξῆλθεν καὶ ἐγένετο ὡσεὶ νεκρός, ὥστε τοὺς πολλοὺς λέγειν ὅτι ἀπέθανεν.	⁴³ ἐξεπλήσσοντο δὲ πάντες ἐπὶ τῇ μεγαλειότητι τοῦ θεοῦ.
	²⁷ ὁ δὲ Ἰησοῦς κρατήσας τῆς χειρὸς αὐτοῦ ἤγειρεν αὐτόν, καὶ ἀνέστη.	
¹⁹ Τότε προσελθόντες οἱ μαθηταὶ τῷ Ἰησοῦ κατ' ἰδίαν εἶπον· διὰ τί ἡμεῖς οὐκ ἠδυνήθημεν ἐκβαλεῖν αὐτό;	²⁸ Καὶ εἰσελθόντος αὐτοῦ εἰς οἶκον οἱ μαθηταὶ αὐτοῦ κατ' ἰδίαν ἐπηρώτων αὐτόν· ὅτι ἡμεῖς οὐκ ἠδυνήθημεν ἐκβαλεῖν αὐτό;	
²⁰ ὁ δὲ λέγει αὐτοῖς διὰ τὴν ὀλιγοπιστίαν ὑμῶν· ἀμὴν γὰρ λέγω ὑμῖν, ἐὰν ἔχητε πίστιν ὡς κόκκον σινάπεως, ἐρεῖτε τῷ ὄρει τούτῳ· μετάβα ἔνθεν ἐκεῖ, καὶ μεταβήσεται καὶ οὐδὲν ἀδυνατήσει ὑμῖν	²⁹ καὶ εἶπεν αὐτοῖς· τοῦτο τὸ γένος ἐν οὐδενὶ δύναται ἐξελθεῖν εἰ μὴ ἐν προσευχῇ.	¹⁷:⁶ εἶπεν δὲ ὁ κύριος· εἰ ἔχετε πίστιν ὡς κόκκον σινάπεως, ἐλέγετε ἂν τῇ συκαμίνῳ [ταύτῃ] ἐκριζώθητι καὶ φυτεύθητι ἐν τῇ θαλάσσῃ· καὶ ὑπήκουσεν ἂν ὑμῖν

BIBLIOGRAPHY

Allen, W. C. *St Matthew*. ICC. Edinburgh: T. & T. Clark, 1972.

Bauckham, R., ed. *The Gospels for All Christians: Rethinking the Gospel Audiences*. Grand Rapids: Eerdmans, 1998.

Black, Stephanie L. *Sentence Conjunctions in the Gospel of Matthew: καὶ, δὲ, τότε, οὖν and Asyndeton in Narrative Discourse*. JSNTSup 216. Sheffield: Sheffield Academic, 2002.

Bornkamm, Günther. *Jesus of Nazareth*. New York: Harper & Row, 1960.

———. *Paul*. New York: Harper & Row, 1971.

———. "The Stilling of the Storm in Matthew." In *Traditional and Interpretation in Matthew*, by Günther Bornkamm, Gerhard Barth, and Heinz Joachim Held, 52–57. London:

SCM, 1963. Originally published as "Die Sturmstillung im Matthäusevangelium." *Wort und Dienst* 2 (1948) 49–54.

Bornkamm, Günther, Gerhard Barth, and Heinz Joachim Held. *Tradition and Interpretation in Matthew*. London: SCM, 1963.

Bultmann, R. *History of the Synoptic Tradition*. New York: Harper & Row, 1976.

Carson, D. A. *Matthew*. EBC. Grand Rapids: Zondervan, 1984.

Carter, W. *Matthew and the Margins*. JSNTSup 204. Sheffield: Sheffield Academic, 2000.

Catchpole, D. R. "Source, Form and Redaction Criticism of the New Testament." In *A Handbook to the Exegesis of the New Testament*, edited by Stanley E. Porter, 167–88. Leiden: Brill, 1997.

Conzelmann, H. *Die Mitte der Zeit*. Tübingen: Mohr Siebeck, 1953.

———. *The Theology of St. Luke*. New York: Harper & Row, 1960.

Davies, W. D., and D. C. Allison. *A Critical and Exegetical Commentary on the Gospel according to St Matthew*. 3 vols. ICC. Edinburgh: T. & T. Clark, 1988–97.

Fitzmyer, J. A. *The Gospel according to Luke*. 2 vols. AB. New York: Doubleday, 1981, 1985.

France, R. T. *Matthew: Evangelist and Teacher*. Downers Grove, IL: InterVarsity, 1988.

Goodacre, Mark S. *The Case against Q*. Harrisburg, PA: Trinity International, 2002.

Gundry, R. H. *Matthew: A Commentary on His Literary and Theological Art*. Grand Rapids: Eerdmans, 1982.

Hagner, D. A. *Matthew 14–28*. WBC 33B. Dallas: Word, 1995.

Held, H. J. "Matthew as Interpreter of the Miracle Stories." In *Tradition and Interpretation in Matthew*, by Günther Bornkamm, Gerhard Barth, and Heinz Joachim Held, 165–299. London: SCM, 1963.

Käsemann, E. "The Problem of the Historical Jesus." In *Essays on New Testament Themes*, 15–47. London: SCM, 1964.

———. "On the Subject of Primitive Christian Apocalyptic." In *New Testament Questions of Today*, 108–37. Philadelphia: Fortress, 1969.

Keener, Craig S. *A Commentary on the Gospel of Matthew*. Grand Rapids: Eerdmans, 1999.

Klink, Edward W., III, ed. *The Audience of the Gospels*. LNTS 353. London: T. & T. Clark, 2010.

———. "The Gospel Community Debate: State of the Question." *CurRBS* 3 (2004) 60–85.

Marxsen, W. *Der Evangelist Markus*. Göttingen: Vandenhoeck & Ruprecht, 1959.

———. *Mark the Evangelist: Studies on the Redaction History of the Gospel*. New York: Abingdon, 1969.

Morris, L. *The Gospel according to Matthew*. PNTC. Grand Rapids: Eerdmans, 1992.

Osborne, G. R. *Matthew*. ZECNT. Grand Rapids: Zondervan, 2010.

———. "Redaction Criticism." In *Dictionary of Jesus and the Gospels*, edited by J. G. Green et al., 662–69. Downers Grove, IL: InterVarsity, 1992.

Peabody, David, et al. *One Gospel from Two: Mark's Use of Matthew and Luke*. Valley Forge, PA: Trinity International, 2002.

Perrin, Norman. *What Is Redaction Criticism?* Philadelphia: Fortress, 1969.

Sanders, E. P., and M. Davies. *Studying the Synoptic Gospels*. London: SCM, 1989.

Schnackenburg, R. *The Gospel of Matthew*. Grand Rapids: Eerdmans, 2002.

Smalley, S. S. "Redaction Criticism." In *New Testament Interpretation*, edited by I. H. Marshall, 181–95. Grand Rapids: Eerdmans, 1977.

Witmer, Amanda. *Jesus, the Galilean Exorcist*. LNTS 459. London: T. & T. Clark, 2012.

13

C. H. Dodd as New Testament Interpreter and Theologian

Beth M. Stovell

In the field of New Testament studies, many scholars are renowned for originating criticisms. We recognize their names readily: Bultmann, Dibelius, and Schmidt, for example, in the field of form criticism. There are also scholars who use these already-developed models and provide new and enlightening interpretations of the biblical text. C. H. Dodd is a striking example of this second type of scholar. While Dodd did not originate a type of biblical criticism, he is well remembered for his unique adaptations of various methods of interpretation, for the theological insights that he gained from his interpretations, and for the way he shared these insights with academia, the church, and the world.

In this chapter, we will examine Dodd's use of form criticism specifically, while considering the overall impact of Dodd's scholarship as a whole. We will begin by examining the life and works of Dodd in order to understand the context of his scholarship and his contribution. We will then look at Dodd's relationship to form criticism, analyzing in what ways he adhered to its basic tenets while rejecting some elements put forward by its proponents.

Examining Dodd's method of form-critical analysis, I will use his work *According to the Scriptures* as the primary source because this work reflects many of Dodd's key principles. I will then use Dodd's method to interpret John 12:12–15 and its use of Ps 118:26 and Zech 9:9. Finally, I will analyze critically Dodd's method, work, and contribution to modern scholarship.

DODD'S LIFE AND WORKS
Dodd's Life

Charles Harold Dodd was born on April 7, 1884, in Wrexham, Wales. Dodd's family were Welsh Dissenters.[1] This group consisted of the socially lower class, and there was a sharp division between them and members of the Established Church (i.e., the Church of England), who were the "gentry and superior professional class."[2] In Dodd's description of his upbringing, he explains that his Congregationalist background instilled in him a belief in the authority of the Scriptures, which remained with him for the rest of his life.[3]

In 1902, Dodd began his academic career at University College, Oxford. Dodd studied classical languages and history as well as philosophy, and received a highly coveted "double first" upon examination. Upon completion of this initial program, he taught briefly at Leeds University as a lecturer and then shortly after spent a term in Berlin. Though Dodd was only in Berlin for a short time, the impact of this trip on his future academic work was immense. There he studied with Adolf Harnack, the encounter with whom was seminal for the formulation of Dodd's views of history and theology.[4] Dodd also encountered the views of Albert Schweitzer while in Germany. Some have suggested that Dodd's works throughout his life "fought against Schweitzer."[5] Against Schweitzer's view of eschatology, Dodd developed his own view of realized eschatology, and against Schweitzer's doubts about the possibility of historical reconstruction of Jesus' life and ministry, Dodd consistently sought the historical Jesus in his work.[6] Dodd's experience in Berlin also made him continually aware of German scholarship as it developed, and gave him the opportunity to share its methods with British academia. Dodd's interest in the backgrounds of the New Testament, evident throughout his work, was greatly impacted by German scholarship.[7]

Upon returning from Berlin, Dodd was elected to a senior demyship (a half-fellowship) which paid for four more years of education and an opportunity for research. During this time, Dodd studied Hebrew and the Old Testament as well as Aramaic and Syriac. In 1909, he became a student minister to a small congregation ten miles from Oxford. This experience would have a great impact on Dodd's future.[8] In 1912,

---

1. Dillistone, *C. H. Dodd*, 29.
2. Dillistone quotes Dodd here (ibid., 28–29).
3. Ibid., 34–35.
4. Ibid., 54.
5. Ibid., 56–57.
6. Dodd contended against the views that Schweitzer presented in his *Quest of the Historical Jesus*. See also Koester, "Progress and Paradox," 55–56.
7. Dillistone, *C. H. Dodd*, 117.
8. Dodd attributed his decision to join the ministry of the Congregational Church in part to "the satisfaction [he had] already found in the work . . . during a year as student pastor in the village of Benson." Dillistone quotes Dodd's ordination speech (ibid., 60).

after his demyship had come to an end, he decided to enter pastoral ministry. For the next three years, he was an ordained pastor for the Brook Street Congregational Church in Warwick. Dillistone notes that Dodd's experience in pastoral ministry both demonstrated his continued loyalty to the Congregational Church and led Dodd to develop methods for sharing the theology of the New Testament in approachable ways for people of all educational and class backgrounds.[9] Dillistone notes that Dodd's "Welsh 'timbre,' the Oxford scholarly discipline, the Warwick pastorate experience . . . had given him a combination of qualities which together constituted a firm foundation for all his future work."[10]

In 1915, Dodd made the difficult decision to leave the pastorate to take the position of Yates Professor at Mansfield College. Part of the reason for his decision was his sense of loyalty to his Church. Dodd felt that the Congregational Church needed to be more widely represented at Oxford.[11] This was a time of change for biblical studies and Britain. The First World War had devastated the British psyche, overturning many presuppositions about the nature of progress, the goodness of humanity, and the goodness of God. Shortly after the war, Continental scholarship began to circulate in Britain, further influencing religious thought in biblical and theological studies.[12] In this intellectual and spiritual climate, Dodd wrote his first books and began his teaching career.

In 1930, Dodd left Mansfield to succeed A. S. Peake in the Rylands Chair of Biblical Criticism and Exegesis at Manchester University.[13] The Rylands Chair was a position of great prestige, providing ample time for research and writing. Dodd was particularly prolific during this period of his career.[14] In 1939, he was offered the Norris-Hulse Chair of Divinity in the University of Cambridge. This was the first time a non-Anglican was given full status as a divinity professor at any of the English universities.[15] During Dodd's time at Cambridge, the Second World War began and the war brought with it a strain on resources for the nation and on Dodd's family personally. Dodd's health wavered and he struggled between the pacifist views he had held all his life and his loyalty to his country. This was further complicated by Dodd's

9. Ibid., 69–83.

10. Ibid., 76.

11. Both students and professors at Oxford and Cambridge were usually affiliated with the Church of England (ibid., 74). In fact, other affiliations were forbidden until the twentieth century.

12. Ibid., 133.

13. The Rylands Chair is usually held by scholars who master both New Testament and Old Testament studies.

14. At the end of this chapter is a chronological chart of Dodd's life and works.

15. Dillistone, *C. H. Dodd*, 145. In this position, Dodd lectured, began his work on the problem of the place of the Fourth Gospel in early Christianity, supervised advanced students, and, in his most distinctive contribution, encouraged a seminar among the faculty on the problems of the New Testament's background, literary structure, and interpretation.

long-standing friendships with German scholars.[16] One can more easily understand Dodd's struggle with a politicized Kingdom of God amidst this context, and his shift to realized eschatology.[17]

In 1949, Dodd was required to retire from his position at Cambridge, but retirement was by no means the end of his academic career. In the years following his retirement he wrote two of his most important tomes on the Fourth Gospel (as well as a wealth of other books) and he was asked to become general director (and translator) for the New English Bible translation project, which began in 1949 and was completed in 1970.

Dodd also contributed to the wider world through his talks on biblical studies and theology for the BBC from 1931 until 1968.[18] His talks even included a children's show. Dodd also had a role in encouraging ecumenism with his participation in two ecumenical associations, Friends of Reunion and the Faith and Order Commission.[19]

Dodd's Works

In a prolific, fifty-year writing career (1920–70), Dodd wrote an abundance of small books on a wide variety of topics as well as several longer works. His contribution to biblical studies was predominantly in the study of the background of the New Testament and in the area of eschatology.[20] Our discussion will focus on several of his major works and their implications for scholarship as they relate to the two areas listed above.

Writings on Paul

Several of Dodd's earliest works explore the background of Paul's writings. His first book, *The Meaning of Paul for To-day* (1920), was written soon after the First World War. This book offered insights from ancient history and the new field of psychology in Dodd's reading of Paul's writing and its impact for his day. In "The Mind of Paul: A Psychological Approach" (1933), Dodd approaches Paul's writings again with the tool of psychology, exploring the background of Paul's writings. Dodd also wrote an

---

16. During this time, Dodd wrote a document titled "The Theology of Christian Pacifism" that was included with two addresses by other scholars delivered to the Council of Christian Pacifist Groups, which met in London in 1938.

17. Though we must be careful not to attribute Dodd's eschatology only to these causes, they no doubt played a part in his overall thinking.

18. Dillistone describes the long-term relationship Dodd developed with the BBC and his impact on adults and children alike by presenting biblical and theological interpretation in a way that reached the masses (Dillistone, *C. H. Dodd*, 183–92).

19. For further discussion on Dodd's impact, see ibid., 193–201.

20. The Festschrift for Dodd notes his contribution in these two fields by its two main divisions. See the introduction of Davies and Daube, *Background of the New Testament and Its Eschatology*.

influential commentary on Romans that delineates the foundational message of the prophets in contrast to the legalism of the Judaism of Paul's day.[21]

Theological Writings

Dodd's theological writings are among his greatest contributions. Many of these works are still a source of encouragement and controversy today. While Dodd's theology is quite diverse, most of his scholarship focuses on two major areas of his theology: his view of the authority of Scripture and his eschatology.

In Dodd's first major work of theology, *The Authority of the Bible* (1928), he establishes four areas of biblical authority: (1) authority of individual inspiration, giving the prophets as examples; (2) authority of corporate experience, describing the relationship between the Bible and the community; (3) authority of the incarnation, describing the role of Christ coming at a particular time and space and the Hellenistic context of the Gospel; (4) authority of history, explaining the necessity of historical grounding for our faith in the biblical message. These same four themes are present in Dodd's *The Bible To-day* (1943), but with a greater emphasis on history. This focus on the relationship between history and the biblical message is also a theme in *History and the Gospel* (1938), *The Study of Theology* (1939), and *The Founder of Christianity* (1970). This view of Scripture, in turn, influences Dodd's use of form criticism.

Parables of the Kingdom (1935) introduces another continuing theological theme in Dodd's later work: realized eschatology. In *Parables of the Kingdom*, Dodd uses form-critical analysis with a central focus on the place of the parables in the context of the whole gospel story and Jesus' original intent within history in telling the parables.[22] Dodd surmises that the Kingdom of God referenced throughout the Synoptic Gospels was realized in the ministry of Jesus:

> The absolute, the "wholly other," has entered into time and space. And so the Kingdom of God has come and the Son of Man has come, so also judgment

---

21. Dodd argues that Paul "appeal[s] to the prophetic strain in biblical religion against the legal strain which prevailed in the Judaism of his own time" (Dodd, *Epistle of Paul to the Romans*, 74). Dodd is also known for his minimization of the wrath of God in Romans. Regarding Rom 1:18, for example, Dodd argues that God's wrath is impersonal, pointing to God's numinous quality (ibid., 21–23). As Dodd explains, "in the long run we cannot think with full consistency of God in terms of the highest human ideals of personality and yet attribute to Him the irrational passion of anger" (ibid., 24). Dodd argues further that we must translate ἱλαστήριον as expiation rather than propitiation. "The rendering of propitiation is therefore misleading, for it suggests the placating of an angry God" (ibid., 55). Dodd repeats this idea in his later work, *The Bible and the Greeks*, 82–95. Several scholars have examined and refuted Dodd's interpretation of ἱλαστήριον, including: Morris, *Apostolic Preaching of the Cross*, 125–85; Morris, "Meaning of Hilasterion"; Morris, "Use of *Hilaskesthai*"; and Nicole, "C. H. Dodd and the Doctrine of Propitiation." For brief and succinct overviews on the issue, see Fitzmyer, *Romans*, 349–50, and Ladd, *Theology of the New Testament*, 429–33. I am indebted to Jacqueline C. R. De Roo for this list of scholars. See De Roo, "Goat for Azazel," 242 n. 35.

22. On Dodd's use of form-critical analysis in his book *Parables of the Kingdom*, see McKnight, *What Is Form Criticism*, 51–56.

and blessedness have come into human experience. The ancient images of the heavenly feast, of Doomsday, of the Son of Man at the right hand of power, are not only symbols of supra-sensible, supra-historical realities; they have also their corresponding actuality in history. Thus both the facts of the life of Jesus and the events which He foretells within the historical order, are "eschatological" events, for they fall within the coming of the Kingdom of God.[23]

This work marked a crucial turning point in the study of eschatology and the parables during his time and still has effects on modern scholarship in these areas.[24] After this work, Dodd's concept of realized eschatology became a hallmark of his theological interpretation.[25]

Johannine Writings[26]

In his inaugural lecture as Professor of Divinity at Cambridge, Dodd pointed to the importance of the Fourth Gospel for our understanding of early Christianity. Dodd stated that "the Fourth Gospel may well prove to be the keystone of an arch" that allows us to address "the problem of the New Testament as a whole."[27] Thus the two largest and most in-depth works of Dodd center on the interpretation of the Fourth Gospel (*Interpretation of the Fourth Gospel*, 1953) and its historical tradition (*Historical Tradition in the Fourth Gospel*, 1963). Dodd relies heavily on form criticism in these two works to interpret the Gospel's message and to validate its historicity. *Interpretation of the Fourth Gospel* is often considered Dodd's *magnum opus* and both books are still frequently cited today in scholarly debate.[28]

---

23. Dodd, *Parables of the Kingdom*, 82.

24. I discuss this impact in greater detail in the last section of this chapter.

25. A key part of Dodd's position on realized eschatology centers on his translation of the verb φθάνω. Dodd argued that this verb means "to arrive" in the same way as ἤγγικεν. Dodd argued this based on how the Greek verbs are used in the LXX to translate the Hebrew. See Dodd, *Parables of the Kingdom*, 43–46. Campbell argued against Dodd's translation of φθάνω as ἤγγικεν, and Dodd's subsequent conclusions based on his translation. Campbell, "Contributions and Comments," noted that Dodd's conclusions are not grammatically consistent across other accounts of usage and contain some logical errors when viewed in this light. Dodd replied to Campbell's critique the following month in the same journal (again under "Contributions and Comments") defending his position. It is interesting to note that Dodd based a portion of his case on the Greek perfect as "durative-punctiliar" in its *Aktionsart*, citing the grammar of Robertson (Robertson, *Grammar of the Greek New Testament*, 895). Dodd used this grammatical construct to argue that the meaning of ἤγγικεν could move developmentally from "approach" to "arrive." This theory is certainly unstable, particularly in light of current arguments of verbal aspect theory. For discussion of verbal aspect theory, see Porter, *Verbal Aspect*.

26. For an extensive recent study of Dodd's impact on the study of Johannine literature, see Tom Thatcher and Catrin Williams, *Engaging with C. H. Dodd on the Gospel of John*.

27. Dodd, *Present Task*, 29.

28. Examples include Thompson, "Eternal Life"; Skinner, "Another Look"; Koester, *Symbolism in the Fourth Gospel*. All of these scholars deal with Dodd's discussion of symbolism specifically.

Use of the Old Testament in the New Testament

Dodd also contributed to the study of the use of the Old Testament in the New Testament. In *The Apostolic Preaching and Its Development* (1936), Dodd argues that underlying the New Testament are two oral sources: the *kerygma* and the *didache*. The *kerygma* is the proclamation of the gospel, "not the action of the preacher, but that which he preaches, his message."[29] The *kerygma* "is the public proclamation of Christianity to the non-Christian world."[30] The *didache*, on the other hand, is the teaching of ethical instruction.[31]

As Dodd explains the *kerygma* further, we see the influence of his realized eschatology on his description:

> *Kerygma* is a proclamation of the facts of the death and resurrection of Christ in an eschatological setting which gives significance to the facts. They mark the transition from "this evil Age" to the "Age to Come." The "Age to Come" is the age of fulfilment. Hence the importance of the statement that Christ died and rose "according to the Scriptures." Whatever events the Old Testament prophets may indicate as impending, these events are for them significant as elements in the coming of "the Day of the Lord." Thus the fulfilment of prophecy means that the Day of the Lord has dawned: the Age to Come has begun.[32]

Dodd arrives at an outline for this *kerygma*:

> The prophecies are fulfilled, and the new Age is inaugurated by the coming of Christ. He was born of the seed of David. He died according to the Scriptures, to deliver us out of the present evil age. He was buried. He rose on the third day according to the Scriptures. He is exalted at the right hand of God, as Son of God and Lord of quick and dead. He will come again as Judge and Saviour of men.[33]

Dodd's discussion of *kerygma* is similar to that of Martin Dibelius.[34] Dodd, however, differs from Dibelius on several key points to be discussed in the next section of this chapter.

---

29. Dodd, *Apostolic Preaching*, 7.

30. Ibid.

31. Kevane, *Jesus the Divine Teacher*, uses the categories of *didache* and *kergyma* to discuss the role of catechetical teaching (*didache*) in relation to the message of Jesus (*kerygma*), which were a set of truths coming directly from God. This sets Dodd's two categories in a Catholic context. This is particularly interesting considering Pope Benedict XVI's comments in his book *Jesus of Nazareth*, 188, praising Dodd's realized eschatology.

32. Dodd, *Apostolic Preaching*, 8.

33. Ibid., 17.

34. As noted below, Dibelius and Dodd were friends, and Dodd refers to his agreement with Dibelius's work in "Framework," 7–9.

The differentiation between *kerygma* and *didache* influences Dodd's attribution of influential biblical texts to each category in his book. In *According to the Scriptures* (1952), Dodd seeks not only the form of the *kerygma*, but the form behind the form of the *kerygma*.[35] He argues that behind the New Testament is the oral tradition of the *kerygma* and behind the *kerygma* are the Old Testament prophecies fulfilled by Jesus in his life, death, and resurrection, memorized as oral tradition. Further, Dodd argues against the theory prevailing at the time that these quotations were part of *testimonia*, which were collections of Old Testament proof-texts. Instead, Dodd argues that entire passages were in mind.[36] These Old Testament prophecies form the "substructure of New Testament theology."[37]

In sum, Dodd's life and works contributed to the academic world, the church, and the public. His study of the background of the New Testament and his theological explorations of biblical authority and eschatology have remained a powerful force in modern scholarship. We now turn to Dodd's use of and contribution in the area of form criticism.

DODD AND FORM CRITICISM

It is likely that Dodd's relationship to form criticism began on his trip to Germany, although he continued his studies of German scholarship over the years. In the years following the First World War, Dodd befriended Martin Dibelius during Dibelius's visit to England, and learned about the new critical method called *Formgeschichte*.[38] Dodd became a pioneer in the study of form criticism in Britain, giving lectures on form-critical analysis in 1928 to his students at Mansfield College before any of the works of German form critics were translated into English.[39] Dodd appreciated the focus on forms of speech rather than on written texts, primarily because it acknowledged the connection between the biblical texts and the needs of the life of the early church. As Dodd explains:

---

35. Dillistone discusses in detail this care for the background of the New Testament in Dodd's work, describing it as the "form behind the forms" (Dillistone, *C. H. Dodd*, 117).

36. Dodd, *According to the Scriptures*, 59–60.

37. This phrase is the subtitle of *According to the Scriptures*.

38. Dodd, "Thirty Years of New Testament Study," 323–33.

39. Dillistone, *C. H. Dodd*, 100. Most British scholars were introduced to the discipline of form criticism in 1933 with the publication of the important work, *The Formation of the Gospel Tradition*, by Vincent Taylor. Like Dodd, Taylor is known for his "discriminating use of the positive results of Form-Critical study of the Gospel tradition" (Evans, "Theologians of Our Time," 166), put to good use in his commentary *Mark* in 1952. As *Interpretation of the Fourth Gospel* serves as Dodd's *magnum opus*, Taylor's commentary on Mark holds a similar place for him. Taylor (*Romans*), like Dodd (*Epistle of Paul to the Romans*), wrote a commentary on Romans; further, like Dodd, Taylor is known for his role as an exegete and a theologian, becoming known for his theories of the Atonement. For a fuller picture of Taylor's life, see Evans, "Theologians of Our Time."

> We are beginning to discern the lineaments of the living tradition, nurtured on the prophetic faith of Israel, witnessed by the preaching, teaching and worship of the primitive Church, and handed down as a heritage to the Church of succeeding ages.[40]

Dillistone argues that Dodd's approach to scholarly inquiry made him especially able to find the strengths in a method like form criticism and adapt them to his particular uses. When Dodd found himself between "two alternative possibilities of cultural and religious life, his constant aim was not to decide between the two but to embrace the two and bring them into a potentially harmonious and fruitful relationship."[41] Appreciating the good in other approaches, and integrating these approaches into his own, Dodd would then apply his interpretations to the issues of his day.[42] This in part explains Dodd's use of various kinds of criticism together and his multi-focal approach to New Testament backgrounds (Greek, Jewish, Gnostic, etc.). We should keep this in mind as we approach Dodd's use of form criticism. Dodd's tendency was to use the insight of German scholars as "a particular *instrument* of interpretation," but he would then "adopt and adapt that instrument in his own distinctive way in accordance with his own distinctive tradition."[43]

To see more clearly Dodd's "adoption and adaptation" of form criticism, we will first lay out the basic tenets of form criticism, identify its primary proponents, and then discuss Dodd's rejection or acceptance of their various positions.

The Essentials of Form Criticism

Scholars trace the beginnings of form criticism to the life-of-Jesus studies in the eighteenth century and the development of source criticism of the nineteenth century.[44] Arriving in the twentieth century, form criticism posited that the differences in sources, witnessed in source criticism, were due to the *Sitz im Leben* of the early church, and behind these sources lay an oral tradition. In Old Testament study, Hermann Gunkel was the originator of form criticism. In New Testament study, Karl Ludwig Schmidt, Martin Dibelius, and Rudolf Bultmann were the major figures. Schmidt began by taking apart the Markan framework, Dibelius then applied form criticism to the Synoptics, and Bultmann pushed the theory further to the whole Synoptic tradition.[45]

One of the basic tenets of form criticism is that the New Testament tradition was based on individual sayings and narratives that were part of an oral tradition, joined together in the Gospels by the work of editors. There are varying positions on

---

40. Dodd, "Thirty Years of New Testament Study," 323.
41. Dillistone, *C. H. Dodd*, 219.
42. Ibid.
43. Ibid., 223.
44. McKnight, *What Is Form Criticism*, 3.
45. Ibid., 15–16.

whether these oral traditions were in the form of collections, but most form critics agree that the Passion narrative is an example of one connected narrative.[46] Form critics further argue that the *Sitz im Leben* of the primitive church community behind each Gospel determines how the material was shaped to meet each church's needs and purposes.[47] In order to identify the oral tradition behind the Gospels, form critics identify the different forms of materials in the Gospels. These forms or units served a specific function in the life of the early church. "Every literary category then will have its own 'life situation' [*Sitz im Leben*] which is a typical situation in the life of the early Christian community."[48] For Dibelius, these forms were paradigms, tales, legends, and myths.[49] Bultmann had two main divisions: narrative material and discourses of Jesus. Discourses included apophthegms and dominical sayings, while narrative material included miracle stories, historical narrative, and legends.[50] Most form critics also assumed certain presuppositions about the historicity of each of the various forms and their relationship to the life of Jesus. Some of the forms were considered historical or quasi-historical, while others were considered fabricated. Moreover, according to many of these proponents, these forms did not lead us back to the life of the actual historical Jesus.[51]

Dodd's Type of Form Criticism

While in many ways Dodd was a pioneer for form criticism within Britain, he also challenged many of the presuppositions of form criticism, challenging particular ideas in the work of Schmidt, Dibelius, and Bultmann.[52]

In 1932, Dodd challenged Schmidt's thesis that the Markan Gospel was compiled out of separate pericopes, which were independent units, and that the evangelist compiled this material with no care for chronology or topography. Dodd dismissed Schmidt's subsequent idea that there was no secure basis for a chronology of Jesus' ministry.[53] Dodd argued that both topical and chronological concerns were present in the ordering, and this ordering was intentional. As Dodd put it, "it seems likely that in addition to materials in *pericope* form, Mark had an outline, itself also tra-

---

46. This idea of a connected narrative was by no means common to other narratives. Schmidt and Bultmann both argued in various ways for the independent nature of the individual pericopes and a lack of cohesion between the various forms represented in the Gospels. For the positions of Schmidt, Dibelius, and Bultmann, see McKnight, *What Is Form Criticism*, 18–19 and 25–33; Mournet, *Oral Tradition*, 55–62.

47. McKnight, *What Is Form Criticism*, 18–19.

48. Ibid., 20.

49. For a full description of each of Dibelius's forms, see ibid., 21–25.

50. For a full description of Bultmann's forms, see ibid., 25–33.

51. Yet one should note that Dibelius and Bultmann both wrote "life of Jesus" books (ibid., 33–37).

52. Ibid., 51–56; Dillistone, *C. H. Dodd*, 224; Koester, "Progress and Paradox," 49–65.

53. Dodd, "Framework," 9–11.

ditional, to which he attempted to work, with incomplete success."[54] Further, this outline "does represent a genuine succession of events, within which movement and development can be traced."[55]

Dodd followed Dibelius in his belief that a traditional outline can be found beneath the Gospels. Dodd devoted much of his scholarship to excavating the foundational *kerygma* in such works as his *Apostolic Preaching and Its Development*, *Interpretation of the Fourth Gospel,* and *According to the Scriptures*. Unlike Dibelius, Dodd did not judge the various forms within the Gospels to contain varying degrees of historical material nor did he see disunity in the text because of its various forms.[56]

Bultmann and Dodd stood at either end of the spectrum of form critics. While Dodd was more conservative than the conservative Dibelius, Bultmann was the most radical of the three originators in his approach. Whereas Bultmann had little or no confidence in our ability to get back to Jesus' career and person, Dodd believed that we can get back to the historical Jesus.[57]

Dodd's critiques of the form critics show his continuities and his discontinuities with the presuppositions of form criticism. Dodd maintained the form-critical method of seeking the oral tradition behind the texts and of designating various types of forms in this endeavor. Yet there are key differences in Dodd's approach. Dodd believed in recovering history behind the text; he focused on forms with the goal of reading the biblical text as unified rather than disparate, and he believed that this history is essential to a life-giving faith in Jesus Christ.[58] Dillistone summarizes the difference of Dodd's approach nicely:

---

54. Ibid., 9.

55. Ibid., 11.

56. McKnight, *What Is Form Criticism*, 33–37. This is a debatable point. D. A. Carson and J. S. King have argued over this specific point in Dodd's *Historical Tradition*. Carson maintains that Dodd's use of form criticism moves him further away from establishing a historical background to the Fourth Gospel, because Dodd uses the language of form critics to discuss certain passages within the Johannine account as "coloured" and "shaped" by the needs of the early church. Carson argues that Dodd is undercutting his argument towards historicity here and that while Dodd argues for the essential need for history, his use of form criticism is inconsistent with this view. King believes Carson has "been unfair to Dodd" in this and many other respects. For the debate, see Carson, "Historical Tradition in the Fourth Gospel"; King, "Has D. A. Carson Been Fair to C. H. Dodd"; Carson, "Historical Tradition in the Fourth Gospel."

57. Both Dillistone and McKnight note this key difference between Dodd and Bultmann (McKnight, *What Is Form Criticism*, 57; Dillistone, *C. H. Dodd*, 223). Dodd takes aim at Bultmann's form-critical analysis of the Gospel of John, pointing to the critical issue of proving historical relationship (Dodd, *Interpretation of the Fourth Gospel*, 122–24). Dodd's belief in the possibility of retrieving the original story of Jesus seems to have intensified over the course of his life, eventually leading him to write a book reconstructing the life and personality of Jesus, which has taken a good deal of critique for its conservative beliefs (*Founder of Christianity*, 1970). For the critiques of *Founder of Christianity*, Dillistone provides a helpful list (*C. H. Dodd*, 178–79).

58. Dodd makes clear the importance of history for faith in several of his books including *History and the Gospel* (1938), *Study of Theology* (1939), and *Founder of Christianity* (1970).

Behind all traditions and testimonies Dodd looked for the lineaments of a *Person*, a Person who was himself the image of the invisible God, a Person who brought to fulfilment all that could otherwise be known of the activity of God in the whole process of history. The concern for *forms* he shared to the full. But whereas Bultmann wished to operate dialectically, separating the authentic form from the inauthentic by a continuous exclusion of alternatives, Dodd wished to proceed organically, detecting the life-substance in each tradition and pointing to the way in which each element contributed to the process of integration into a living whole.[59]

This difference is most likely connected to the general difference between British scholarship and German scholarship. Dodd represented the British emphasis on historicity over and against the German idealism.[60] Both N. T. Wright and Dillistone point to this difference as key to understanding Dodd's approach.[61]

ANALYZING DODD'S METHOD

This section will analyze Dodd's method of form criticism using *According to the Scriptures*, chosen because it combines many of Dodd's recurring themes found in his other form-critical works and it is among the most methodologically focused of Dodd's writings. The goal of *According to the Scriptures* is to find the substructure of New Testament theology by examining the use of Old Testament quotations in the New Testament and their place in testimonies foundational to the *kerygma* of the early church. Dodd argued that the *kerygma* represents the core of the "common and central tradition" of the New Testament. "In its most summary form the *kerygma* consists of the announcement of certain historical events in a setting which displays the significance of those events . . . the significance attached to these events is mainly indicated by reference to the Old Testament."[62]

Using Dodd's own analogy, we might look at the New Testament texts as a series of buildings. The outer face "may show various characteristics of Romanesque, Gothic, or Baroque, so each of these theologians builds after his own style." Yet Dodd argues that these buildings are based on the same "ground-plan" (i.e., the *kerygma*) and beneath their exterior styles, their "substructure—a part of the actual edifice" is the same (i.e., the prophecies of the Old Testament fulfilled).[63]

---

59. Dillistone, *C. H. Dodd*, 224.

60. One such example is the Bultmannian division between the historical Jesus and the Christ of faith.

61. This is well demonstrated by Dodd's debate with Tillich described in Appendix 1 of Dillistone, *C. H. Dodd*, 241–43. Wright emphasizes this distinction in his writings as well, using Dodd as characteristic of a line of scholarship. See Wright, *New Testament and the People of God*, 12, 22, 39.

62. Dodd, *According to the Scriptures*, 11–12.

63. Ibid., 13.

Thus, in Dodd's method, we must first identify the type of form within the Gospel that we have before us before we can analyze its use of Old Testament quotation. Dodd describes two major groups of forms following Bultmann's categories of narrative and discourse. These two larger categories have smaller forms within them, defined by which Gospel is at hand.[64]

Next, we must access the quotation of the Old Testament in the New Testament by comparing the source with the other Gospels and analyzing how they are using the quoted material. Is it a text that is common to other sources? If the quotation is common to more than one Gospel, how is it used in each Gospel as compared to the MT and LXX? Which version is the New Testament writer using? How does this differ from other Gospels or overlap with them? If this Old Testament quotation exists in more than one place in the New Testament and the chapter of this particular quotation is frequently used in other parts of Scripture, we can deduce that this passage is part of the *kerygma*.[65] If this Old Testament quotation is part of the *kerygma*, we must identify what type of quotation it is. Dodd suggests two main types of quotations: primary sources of *testimonia* and subordinate and supplementary sources. Dodd arranges these types of quotation into four sub-groups: Group I—Apocalyptic-eschatological Scriptures; Group II—Scriptures of the New Israel; Group III—Scriptures of the Servant of the Lord and the Righteous Sufferer; Group IV—Unclassified Scriptures.[66]

---

64. Dodd identifies three forms in his work on the "framework" in Mark's Gospel: independent units, larger complexes of materials, and an outline of the ministry of Jesus (Dodd, "Framework," 9–11). In *Parables of the Kingdom*, Dodd works specifically with parables as a sub-form of narrative, and uses form-critical principles to access which parables apply directly to Jesus' ministry and have been reapplied to the early church's situation. Dodd identifies Bultmann's three forms of parables and argues against him that the lines between the three are indistinct. See Dodd, *Parables of the Kingdom*, 6–8; McKnight, *What Is Form Criticism*, 54–56. Dodd suggests different forms again in his discussion of the Fourth Gospel. Again Dodd maintains the discourse/narrative division, but also notes the sub-form of signs as similar to parables, but with a closer affinity to "sign-acts" in the Old Testament. The term "sign-acts," however, is a nomenclature developed after Dodd's time (Dodd, *Interpretation of the Fourth Gospel* and *Historical Tradition in the Fourth Gospel*).

65. Dodd draws out this line of reasoning in his "Testimonies" chapter (Dodd, *According to the Scriptures*, 28–60). Boda and Porter have critiqued Dodd's presentation of *testimonia* in their article "Literature to the Third Degree." They argue that "Dodd's hypothesis was less useful in indicating what had been selected, or what it invoked, than it was in suggesting a method of biblical interpretation." Here Boda and Porter cite E. E. Ellis, "How the New Testament Uses the Old" (in *New Testament Interpretation: Essays on Principles and Methods*, edited by I. H. Marshall, 199–219. Grand Rapids: Eerdmans, 1977), 201, which equates what Dodd is describing to *midrash*. See Boda and Porter, "Literature to the Third Degree," 240. Further, Boda and Porter point out that, unlike Qumran *testimonia*, Dodd's examples do not invoke a lead line of the Old Testament passage, but rather seem to point to the importance of the specific quotations themselves. Boda and Porter then demonstrate through several examples in the Gospels that Dodd's broader hypothesis appears less likely than the more narrow definition of *testimonia*. They also argue against Dodd's contention that the *entire* New Testament contains these underlying *testimonia*. Instead of the language of "allusion" or "echo," Boda and Porter suggest that "one must restrict oneself to quotation" (ibid., 245).

66. Dodd, *According to the Scriptures*, Group I, 62–74; Group II, 74–88; Group III, 88–103; Group IV, 104–10.

Based on findings from above, we analyze the entire passage regarding whether this particular Old Testament quotation comes from Group I, II, III, or IV. We then interpret our New Testament passage based on the inclusion of the entire passage of the Old Testament in question. If there are two Old Testament passages in close proximity, Dodd argues that one passage "can be adduced to illustrate or elucidate the meaning of the main section under consideration. But in the fundamental passages it is the *total context* that is in view, and is the basis of the argument."[67] Understanding the essential argument presented in our passage and its role in the *kerygma*, our final step is to examine the theology behind the passage and its implications for today. Dodd reads this theology in light of his views on realized eschatology.[68]

These steps can be summarized thus:

1. Determine what form is being examined: narrative or discourse, with subforms based on the particular Gospel.

2. Assess the quotation of the Old Testament in the New Testament

    a. Compare the quotations in the four Gospels.

    b. Determine the sources of the Old Testament quotation (LXX/MT).

    c. Determine the type of quotation in the *testimonia*, whether primary or subordinate and part of which of the four groups.

    d. If the quotation is part of the principal testimonies of the *kerygma*, read the entire passage of the Old Testament as part of the New Testament passage at hand.

    e. If several Old Testament quotations exist in close proximity, determine which quotation is fundamental and which is secondary. Use the entire context of the fundamental quotation to proceed and explain how the secondary quotation elucidates or illustrates the fundamental quotation.

3. Based on this assessment, access the contribution of this Old Testament passage within the New Testament for theology in its original context in early Christianity and its implications for today.

USING DODD'S METHOD: THE USE OF PSALM 118:26 AND ZECHARIAH 9:9 IN JOHN 12:12–15

As we apply Dodd's method to John 12:12–15 and its use of Ps 118:26 and Zech 9:9, we will primarily follow the method as it is described above, but will as necessary note

---

67. Ibid., 126.

68. This paradigm of realized eschatology as the eschatological understanding of the text begins in *Parables of the Kingdom* and continues into Dodd's final works. In *According to the Scriptures*, Dodd articulates the implications of testimonies for the *kerygma* and for New Testament theology in his chapter titled "Fundamentals of Christian Theology" (ibid., 111–25).

comparisons with Dodd's interpretations of the passage in *Interpretation of the Fourth Gospel* and *Historical Tradition in the Fourth Gospel*.[69]

Determine What Form Is Being Examined: Narrative or Discourse, with Sub-forms Based on the Particular Gospel

According to Dodd, the Fourth Gospel has two books: The Book of Signs (John 2–12)[70] and The Book of the Passion (John 13–21).[71] Dodd identifies within these books narratives of Jesus' acts and discourses that explain the significance of these acts. In the Book of Signs, narratives precede discourses; in the Book of the Passion, discourses precede narratives.[72] Dodd believes that the Book of Signs is the dynamic story that builds to the ultimate metonymic sign: The Passion of Christ.

With this in mind, we approach John 12:12–15 as part of the final chapter in the Book of Signs and the final section on Jesus' ministry before his Passion narrative begins. Dodd designates John 12:12–15, the Triumphal Entry, as a narrative functioning closely with its preceding narrative in John 12:1–8, the Anointing at Bethany, and also closely related to its following discourse in John 12:20–22. The narrative in John 12:12–15 is framed on either side with discussions of Lazarus's resurrection from the dead (John 12:9–11, 16–18).[73]

Assess the Quotation of the Old Testament in the New Testament

Compare the Quotations in the Four Gospels

John 12:12–15 contains two quotations from the Old Testament: Ps 118:26 and Zech 9:9. When compared to the Synoptics, Matthew's account of the Triumphal Entry bears the closest resemblance in his common usage of the same two quotations (Matt 21:5). Yet Dodd points out that despite this similarity, the quotations are used "in a different translation and at a different point in the story."[74] The Markan and Lukan accounts both clearly use Ps 118:26, but do not identify their usage of Zech 9.[75]

---

69. As *According to the Scriptures* has a slightly different focus than both of these other works, our conclusions using our developed description of Dodd's method from *According to the Scriptures* may differ at times from those of *Interpretation of the Fourth Gospel* and/or *Historical Tradition in the Fourth Gospel*, but should remain consistent in the essentials.

70. Chapter 1 is properly "The Proem" rather than part of the "Book of Signs" (Dodd, *Interpretation of the Fourth Gospel*, 289).

71. Dodd follows the traditional form-critical view that the Passion narrative is one connected narrative (ibid.).

72. Ibid., 290.

73. Ibid., 368–69.

74. Dodd, *Historical Tradition in the Fourth Gospel*, 155.

75. One might argue that the symbolism of Zech 9:9 is assumed in both Mark and Luke, especially as both add a reference to king in their adaptations of Ps 118:26. Mark adds ἡ ἐρχομένη βασιλεία τοῦ πατρὸς ἡμῶν Δαυίδ (the coming kingdom of our father David) while Luke adds ὁ βασιλεὺς (the king).

Determine the Sources of the Old Testament Quotation (LXX/MT)

Dodd argues that in their quotation of Zech 9:9, neither Matthew nor John is using the LXX directly. Each uses different formulaic phrases to introduce Zech 9:9 as Scripture fulfilled.[76] Since there is no direct Markan equivalent and the quotations in Matthew's and John's Gospels are so divergent, Dodd points to this passage as "a true case of independent citation, surely on a basis of a common tradition of *testimonia* rather than of any written source."[77]

Dodd describes Ps 118:26 as the "irreducible nucleus of the *pericope* itself" in both the Markan and Johannine accounts.[78] Both follow the LXX, except for the Markan addition of ἡ ἐρχομένη βασιλεία τοῦ πατρὸς ἡμῶν Δαυίδ (the coming kingdom of our father David) and the Johannine addition of ὁ βασιλεὺς τοῦ Ἰσραήλ (the king of Israel) to describe "he who comes." The Lukan addition of ὁ βασιλεύς (the king) and the Matthean τῷ υἱῷ Δαυίδ (the son of David) also represent similar additions of kingship imagery while following relatively closely to the LXX. But Dodd argues that there is "nothing to suggest a literary dependence of our Gospel on either of the others"[79] and there is nothing to suggest dependence on the Markan account.[80]

Thus here we have two quotations from the Old Testament with multiple attestations, but enough variance between the evangelists' usage to suggest a separate oral tradition of *testimonia* foundational to the Gospel usage.[81]

Determine the Type of Quotation in the Testimonia, whether Primary or Subordinate and to Which of the Four Groups It Belongs

Not only are these two quotations part of the *testimonia*, but Dodd classifies them both among the primary *testimonia*. Zechariah 9:9 is part of the larger section in Zech 9–14, which Dodd places in Group I as apocalyptic-eschatological Scriptures.

---

76. Dodd, *According to the Scriptures*, 48–49. Matthew uses "that which was spoken through the prophet" and John uses "as it was written."

77. Ibid., 49.

78. Dodd, *Historical Tradition in the Fourth Gospel*, 154. Dodd notes of course that both accounts are following Ps 117:26 in the LXX.

79. Ibid., 155.

80. Ibid., 154.

81. Dodd is known for his contribution to the criteria for authenticity, specifically in the criterion of multiple forms. As Stein explains, "Dodd lists six gospel motifs as authentic because they appeared in multiple forms, i.e., in different form-critical categories . . . the assumption of this criterion is that the various forms of the gospel stories about Jesus, parables, sayings, etc., centered in different contexts and spheres of interest in the early church and were therefore preserved and passed down through different channels. As a result if a motif is found in multiple literary forms, that motif came from a broad section of the early church and was deeply embedded in the earliest church tradition." Stein argues that this does not, however, prove authenticity conclusively, but does help in suggesting an early date for the material (Stein, "The 'Criteria' for Authenticity," 232–33). For Dodd's uses of this criterion, see Dodd, *History and the Gospel*, 91–103; and Dodd, *Parables of the Kingdom*, 26–27. For further discussion on criteria for authenticity, see Porter, *Criteria for Authenticity*.

Psalm 118 is among the Psalms listed in Group III as Scriptures of the Servant of the Lord and the righteous sufferer. Psalm 118 also refers to the "prophetic 'Day of the Lord'" (Ps 118:23), thus, according to Dodd, Ps 118 has a place alongside Zech 9 in the apocalyptic-eschatological category.[82]

If Part of Primary Testimonies of the Kerygma, Read the Entire Passage of the Old Testament as Part of the New Testament. If Several Old Testament Quotations Exist in Close Proximity, Determine Which Quotation Is Fundamental and Which Is Secondary. Use the Entire Context of the Fundamental Quotation to Proceed and Explain How the Secondary Quotation Elucidates or Illustrates the Fundamental Quotation

The quotation of two primary sources of *testimonia* in John 12:12–15 makes discerning which quotation is considered fundamental and which is secondary particularly difficult. It is also difficult to discern Dodd's position.[83] For our purposes, we will focus on particular aspects of the wider context of both of these passages that Dodd would have found especially applicable to his interpretation of John 12:12–15.

First, both Ps 118 and Zech 9 should be viewed in their wider apocalyptic-eschatological setting. Zechariah 9–14 "has the character of an apocalypse" and "it can be understood as setting forth a whole eschatological programme."[84] This eschatological program begins with Zech 9:9, the picture of the King, riding into Zion on a donkey, destroying Israel's enemies, bringing peace to the nations, and freeing the captives through the "blood of the covenant" (Zech 9:11). A trumpet call announces the Lord's arrival (Zech 9:14) as he saves his flock (Zech 9:16).

Psalm 118 also presents an eschatological event: the Day that the Lord has made. The psalm is mainly a psalm of praise that recalls the suffering of the psalmist and his deliverance. It moves from the praise of all of Israel to the praise of the individual sufferer.[85] Dodd explains that the "importance of this psalm as a source of *testimonia* is manifest."[86] Dodd argues that "the Stone rejected, the Stone of stumbling, the Foundation-stone of Zion" became associated at a very early stage as "symbolic of the coming of Christ and its effects . . . the whole psalm was evidently interpreted with reference to the sufferings and rejections of Christ, succeeded by His glorious resurrection and exaltation."[87] As Dodd explains, the Day of the Lord's making would

---

82. Dodd, *According to the Scriptures*, 65–67, 99–100.

83. In *Interpretation of the Fourth Gospel*, 370, Dodd focuses on the passage in Zechariah without mentioning the quotation of Ps 118, whereas in *Historical Tradition in the Fourth Gospel*, 154 (written ten years later), Dodd describes Ps 118 as the "irreducible nucleus of this *pericope*."

84. Dodd, *According to the Scriptures*, 64.

85. Ibid., 99.

86. Ibid., 100.

87. Ibid.

"naturally be understood as indicating that the day of Christ's coming is the prophetic 'Day of the Lord.'"[88]

Thus, in John 12:12–15 the evangelist is not only describing the shouts from a crowd declaring Jesus' kingship and describing his location upon a donkey, but by using these important sources of *testimonia*, the evangelist is pointing back to the original substructure of New Testament theology and the foundations behind this passage. In Jesus' arrival, both Ps 118 and Zech 9 tell us that the eschatological Day of the Lord has now come; with this Day of the Lord comes peace to the nations and freedom for captives through "the blood of the covenant" and through the stumbling Stone who becomes the Foundation-stone of Zion. Further, the framework surrounding this passage points us to the resurrection of Lazarus and thereby gives us further insight into reading this text theologically.

Based on This Assessment, Access the Contribution of This Old Testament Passage within the New Testament in Its Original Context in Early Christianity and Its Implications for Theology Today

Thus we naturally move from interpretation of the passage to the theology behind the passage and its implications for today. Dodd believes that the editorial framework of John 12:16 gives us an important clue for reading the theological truth behind this passage.

> The disciples, we are told, did not understand the purport of the Triumphal Entry until Jesus was "glorified" (xii.16). In Johannine terms, Jesus was glorified in dying and rising again . . . it is Christ dead and risen who is symbolically set forth in the Rider on the ass whom the crowds acclaim king . . . the person thus acclaimed, we are reminded, is He who "called Lazarus out of the tomb and raised him from the dead" (xii.17–18). The King who comes is the Conqueror of death (by dying) . . . the crowd acclaiming the coming King is a πρόληψις of all mankind united under the sovereignty of Christ.[89]

This in turn has implications for our understanding of the theology of early Christianity. Dodd suggests that our study of the primitive *testimonia* tells us "that from as early a stage as we can hope to reach . . . the primitive Church were aware that they belonged to the new 'Israel of God' . . . the universality of the ultimate people of God is an integral feature of the final *dénouement* in various prophetic passages," most notably in Zechariah, Joel, and 2 Isaiah.[90]

Further, this passage demonstrates christological principles in the early church, if we follow Dodd's interpretation of the *testimonium* of Zech 9:9. Here we see the "conception of the Messiah as the 'inclusive representative' of the people of God combined

---

88. Ibid.
89. Dodd, *Interpretation of the Fourth Gospel*, 371.
90. Dodd, *According to the Scriptures*, 112.

with another view which sets him over against God's people as its Lord or anointed King."[91] Dodd emphatically states that "the kingship of Christ . . . is disassociated from the messianic kingship as understood in popular Judaism of the time."[92] The Jewish political expectations become spiritual realities instead. Christ becomes king of our hearts, not the earthly realm.

Finally, the joining of Ps 118 to Zech 9 links the Servant of the Lord to the King "who comes in humility to liberate prisoners and to speak peace to the nations" in association with a blood-sacrifice, and thus "it was almost inevitable that the death of the Servant should be thought of as covenant-sacrifice."[93] In this way, our passage demonstrates the undergirding beliefs of the *kerygma* in its ecclesiology, its Christology, and its soteriology.

ANALYSIS OF THE STRENGTHS AND WEAKNESSES OF DODD'S APPROACH

There is much to be gained from Dodd's form-critical approach. First, Dodd demonstrates the continuity between the Old Testament and the New Testament in terms of its prophetic message. In our time when we are separating Old Testament and New Testament theology and further separating the "theologies" of the New Testament towards an ever-increasing spiral into minutiae, Dodd suggests that beneath the New Testament lies the Old Testament. His theories of Old Testament and New Testament relationship continue to influence scholarship today.[94] Second, Dodd's approach to the biblical text consistently moves from textual interpretation to theological meaning for his times. This is a valuable skill for the practitioner of New Testament studies. Dodd spoke in ways that were comprehensible not only to academia, but to the church and the world. Third, Dodd's discussion of the backgrounds of the New Testament included comprehensive study in the Hermetic, Greco-Roman, and rabbinic Jewish literature.[95] Dodd's ability to find usefulness in various methods and backgrounds allowed him to approach the backgrounds of the New Testament with depth and breadth, and his grasp of methodological diversity continues to provide challenges for us in the methodologically diverse world of biblical studies today.

91. Ibid., 119.

92. Ibid., 120.

93. Ibid., 124.

94. Scholars like Rikki Watts and Kenneth Bailey attribute aspects of their methods to Dodd. See Watts, *Isaiah's New Exodus in Mark*, 3, 26; Bailey, "Informed Controlled Oral Tradition and the Synoptic Gospels," esp. 40. Wright follows some of Dodd's argument regarding the underlying foundation of New Testament belief coming from Old Testament prophecy (*Jesus and the Victory of God*, 175).

95. Yet many questions have been raised regarding the dating of the various sources that Dodd references. For example, in their chapter, "Salvation Is of the Jews," Neill and Wright point to the complications in dating and influence that have arisen in the areas of rabbinic and Hermetic studies, specifically in Dodd's work. See ch. 8 in Neill and Wright, *Interpretation of the New Testament*, esp. 316–28, 346–47.

Yet with Dodd's strengths come a number of weaknesses. In fact, Dodd's diverse writings have led to an equally diverse number of negative critiques of his works. We might divide these criticisms into two categories: issues of methodological imprecision and issues concerning Dodd's eschatology. First, Dodd's interpretation of our passage indicates areas of imprecision in his work. For example, in comparing the Matthean Old Testament quotation to the Johannine quotation, Dodd argues that their use of the LXX is "a true case of independent citation," proving his theory of *testimonia*, yet Dodd does not justify why he believes this. There are other possibilities for the differences between Matthew's and John's usage of the LXX, and revision could certainly be among them.[96]

A similar point of imprecision becomes apparent when we actually apply the *entire* context of either Zech 9 or Ps 118 to John 12:12–15. Dodd's method does not account for differences in the original intent or perspective within the Old Testament context. While many scholars maintain Dodd's position that the entire context should be understood in the New Testament usage, these scholars give explanations for the changes rendered to the passages' meaning due to the difference in historical setting. Other scholars question whether the entire context of the Old Testament should be read into any New Testament passage.[97] Dodd is also inconsistent in describing the Johannine view of messianic kingship, proclaiming the intentional lack of Davidic reference in one of his works and then describing John's focus on messianic kingship in another.[98]

---

96. One could carefully note the possibility of correcting the LXX's Greek by both parties, but in different ways. For example, both use the form ὄνος, but this could easily be because of an update in the usage of the Greek. John seems to be actively choosing in his use of the word καθήμενος over ἐπιβεβηκώς to point out something else with his use of a different word for sitting. Whereas Matthew's verb implies, with the LXX, a moving/coming notion in his word "sit" (Domain 15 of Louw and Nida), John uses a verb that conveys a semantic notion of stance as in "to sit in a particular position" (Domain 17). Dodd asserts that "neither of [the wide differences between the two forms of quotation] could be accounted for by the hypothesis of a revision on the basis of the LXX" yet he does not explain why he believes this (Dodd, *According to the Scriptures*, 49). It is possible that John was either updating the Greek or moving the attention away from Jesus' position (changing the LXX's perfect active participle to a present middle participle). Thus, if we follow Porter's verbal aspect theory, John moves this verb from the foreground to the middle, thus making the announcement of the king of equal standing to his location (rather than placing greater emphasis on his location upon a colt). This may be consistent with John's emphasis on Jesus' kingship in the passage.

97. For a more detailed discussion of this issue, see Beale, *Right Doctrine from the Wrong Texts*.

98. Dodd suggests in *Interpretation of the Fourth Gospel*, 83–89, that John's Gospel carefully downplays the element of Jesus' Davidic kingship, yet in the considered passage Dodd's own method seems to suggest otherwise. Our careful reading using Dodd's method points to John's addition of the phrase "king of Israel," and Dodd's own analysis of the passage focuses on the kingdom of God and its eschatological character being very present in this section of Old Testament Scripture. This seems inconsistent with Dodd's assertions in *Interpretation of the Fourth Gospel*. Further, Dodd seems to change his position in his discussion of the same passage in *Historical Tradition in the Fourth Gospel*, 155, stating that "it is probable that the Fourth Evangelist, who shows himself more sensitive than the others to the idea of the messianic kingship, has preserved" the title "King of Israel." For a more extensive study of Jesus as king in John's Gospel in relation to Old Testament metaphors, see Stovell,

This problem in Dodd's work is closely connected to the problems associated with realized eschatology. Dodd's method strips the Old Testament entirely of its political and social meaning and moves all theological meaning to an eternal "now" realized in Christ's coming. This creates problems on several fronts. First, it limits the meaning of the Old Testament text and its possible impact on our understanding of the New Testament.[99] Second, it limits the implications of Jesus' mission on one side and downplays the future hope of Christianity on the other.[100] Third, the presuppositions of form-critical analysis have caused scholars to dismantle much of Dodd's realized eschatology by questioning its basis in the Two-Document Hypothesis and pointing to Dodd's inconsistent use of the term *basileia*.[101] These issues have also called into question Dodd's divide of *kerygma* and *didache* and its implications.[102]

Mapping Metaphorical Discourse in the Fourth Gospel.

99. By ignoring the historical issues of both the Zech 9 and the Ps 118 passages (in *Interpretation of the Fourth Gospel*, he does not even mention the usage of Ps 118), Dodd loses a chance to explore the shift in political and social significance from the situation of the Zechariah passage in particular to John 12. Zechariah 9 is a promise to Israel in the midst of their experience in exile of God's presence as a warrior against their enemies. As Boda points out, this passage is a reference to Davidic Kingship (made more apparent in John 12's inclusion of "King of Israel"). Zechariah 9 promises that a king shall come like David to the people of Israel as they struggle in the midst of political and social oppression. Could this be the reason that John changes the phrase "Rejoice" to "Do not be afraid"? Indeed, Dodd may be right that John is referencing the whole passage; if this is the case, John's usage change here would make sense. In being called to rejoice, Israel is being told that instead of fear because of the opposing forces, they instead can have joy, because their king, YHWH, has come! As LaRondelle points out (see Boda, *Haggai–Zechariah*, 424–25), Christ is not "'spiritualizing' the kingdom, but extend[ing] the boundaries of the Davidic Kingdom globally." Though this may in some ways connect to Dodd's concept of the prolepsis of the final vision of all the nations bowing, yet he does not fully develop the concept to this point, and his vision of realized eschatology tends to lose the future aspect of the eschaton in its repeated focus on the present. For more on the Old Testament background of Zech 9 and its possible implications for New Testament scholarship and today, see Boda, *Haggai–Zechariah*, 408–34. Further, Boda and Porter have called Dodd's theories of *testimonia* into question with a specific focus on his use of Zechariah as an example of Dodd's overall theory. For example, they point to Dodd's argument that Zechariah should be read as a whole in light of its usage in John. As they explain contra Dodd, "even for these Gospel writers it is far from obvious that there are no lengthy passages without quotation or allusion . . . John [does] not know Zech 11 and 13." See Boda and Porter, "Literature to the Third Degree," 235–54, quotation from 245.

100. In recent scholarship, there has been a greater awareness of the political and social implications of Jesus' message, which Dodd's method misses entirely, since he brackets out political and social implications from the Gospel message. On the other side, Dodd downplays the future hope of the kingdom, causing many scholars to state that Dodd moved too far to one side in reaction to Schweitzer. For the second position, see Sullivan, *Rethinking Realized Eschatology*.

101. Sullivan, *Rethinking Realized Eschatology*, devotes a chapter to each problem. One should perhaps note that his second critique of Dodd's use of *basileia* is not an issue of form criticism specifically, but of its application by Dodd.

102. For a detailed explanation of the implications of recent scholarship on the *kerygma* and *didache* divide, see Worley, *Preaching and Teaching*.

CONCLUSION

Dodd's life as a professor, scholar, and speaker has had a profound impact on the field of biblical studies and on related fields of theology. His adaptations of form criticism made form criticism an amenable method to scholars who may have been hesitant to follow its more extreme versions, and his introduction of form criticism to British scholarship provided a way forward for new interpretations. Despite the controversy surrounding some of Dodd's ideas and the weaknesses of elements of his methodology, his contribution through his writings and his life will likely continue to impact the field of New Testament studies and the Christian church as they have done since his own time.

TIMELINE OF DODD'S LIFE AND PUBLISHED WORK

1884—Born 7 April, in Wrexham, Wales, UK

1902–6—Early Oxford Years, "double first" in philosophy and classical literature and history.

1906—Brief position as lecturer at Leeds University

1907—Term in Berlin, studying with Harnack

1908–12—Continued study at Mansfield College, Oxford, proficiency in Hebrew and Old Testament studies

1912–15—Ordained, pastor of Brook Street Congregational Church in Warwick

1916–30—Yates Professor at Mansfield College, Oxford

1920—Publishes *The Meaning of Paul for To-day*

1925—Marriage to Phyllis Terry

1927—Offered and rejected Yale chair

1928—Publishes *The Authority of the Bible*

1930–38—Succeeds A. S. Peake in Rylands Chair at Manchester

1932—Publishes *Epistle of Paul to the Romans*, Moffatt Commentary Series; "The Framework of the Gospel Narrative"

1933—Publishes "The Mind of Paul: A Psychological Approach"

1935—Publishes *The Bible and Its Background*; *The Bible and the Greeks*; *The Parables of the Kingdom*

1936—Publishes *The Apostolic Preaching and Its Developments*

1937—Publishes *The First Epistle of John and the Fourth Gospel*

1938—Publishes *History and the Gospel*

1939–49—Holds Norris-Hulse Chair of Divinity at Cambridge

1946—Publishes *The Bible Today*; *The Johannine Epistles*, Moffatt Commentary Series

1949–70—General Director of New English Bible translation project

1950—Publishes *About the Gospels*

1951—Publishes *The Coming of Christ: Four Broadcast Addresses for the Season of Advent*; *Gospel and Law: The Relation of Faith and Ethics in Early Christianity* (Bampton Lectures at Columbia University)

1952—Publishes *According to the Scriptures: The Sub-structure of New Testament Theology*; *Christianity and the Reconciliation of the Nations*

1953—Publishes *Man in God's Design according to the New Testament* with Panagiotis Bratsiotis, R. Bultmann, and Henri Clavier; *The Interpretation of the Fourth Gospel*; *New Testament Studies*

1955—Publishes *The Dialogue Form in the Gospels*

1955—Publishes *A New Testament Triptych on Christ's Coming, His Gospel, His Passion*

1956—Publishes *Benefits of His Passion*; *How to Read the Gospels*

1963—Publishes *Historical Tradition in the Fourth Gospel*

1968—Publishes *More New Testament Studies*

1970—Publishes *The Founder of Christianity*

1973—Dies 22 September

BIBLIOGRAPHY

Bailey, Kenneth E. "Informed Controlled Oral Tradition and the Synoptic Gospels." *Asia Journal of Theology* 5 (1991) 34–54.

Beale, G. K. *The Right Doctrine from the Wrong Texts: Essays on the Use of the Old Testament in the New*. Grand Rapids: Baker, 1994.

Benedict XVI. *Jesus of Nazareth*. New York: Doubleday, 2007.

Boda, Mark J. *Haggai–Zechariah*. NIVAC. Grand Rapids: Zondervan, 2004.

Boda, Mark J., and Stanley E. Porter. "Literature to the Third Degree: Prophecy in Zechariah 9–14 and the Passion of Christ." In *Traduire la Bible hébraïque: De la Septante à la Nouvelle Bible Segond / Translating the Hebrew Bible: From the Septuagint to the Nouvelle Bible Segond*, edited by Robert David and Manuel Jinbachian, 215–54. Montreal: Médiaspaul, 2006.

Campbell, J. Y. "Contributions and Comments." *ExpTim* 48 (1936) 91–94.

Carson, D. A. "Historical Tradition in the Fourth Gospel: After Dodd, What?" In *Gospel Perspectives II*, edited by R. T. France and David Wenham, 83–145. Sheffield: JSOT, 1981.

———. "Historical Tradition in the Fourth Gospel: A Response to J. S. King." *JSNT* 23 (1985) 73–81.

Davies, W. D., and D. Daube, eds. *Background of the New Testament and Its Eschatology.* Cambridge: Cambridge University Press, 1956.

De Roo, Jacqueline C. R. "Was the Goat for Azazel Destined for the Wrath of God?" *Biblica* 81 (2000) 233–42.

Dillistone, Frederick William. *C. H. Dodd: Interpreter of the New Testament.* London: Hodder & Stoughton, 1977.

Dodd, C. H. *About the Gospels.* Cambridge: Cambridge University Press, 1950.

———. *According to the Scriptures: The Sub-structure of New Testament Theology.* London: Nisbet, 1952.

———. *The Apostolic Preaching and Its Developments: With an Appendix on Eschatology and History.* London: Hodder & Stoughton, 1936.

———. *The Authority of the Bible.* London: Nisbet, 1955.

———. *The Bible and Its Background.* London: Unwin, 1931.

———. *The Bible and the Greeks.* London: Hodder & Stoughton, 1935.

———. *The Bible To-day.* Cambridge: Cambridge University Press, 1962.

———. *Christianity and the Reconciliation of the Nations.* London: SCM, 1952.

———. *The Coming of Christ: Four Broadcast Addresses for the Season of Advent.* Cambridge: Cambridge University Press, 1951.

———. "Contributions and Comments." *ExpTim* 48 (1936) 138–42.

———. "The Dialogue Form in the Gospels." *BJRL* 37 (1954–55) 54–67.

———. *The Epistle of Paul to the Romans.* London: Hodder & Stoughton, 1932.

———. "The First Epistle of John and the Fourth Gospel." *BJRL* 21 (1937) 129–56.

———. *The Founder of Christianity.* New York: Macmillan, 1970.

———. "The Framework of the Gospel Narrative." *ExpTim* 43 (1932) 396–400.

———. *Gospel and Law: The Relation of Faith and Ethics in Early Christianity.* New York: Columbia University Press, 1951.

———. *Historical Tradition in the Fourth Gospel.* Cambridge: Cambridge University Press, 1963.

———. *History and the Gospel.* London: Nisbet, 1938.

———. *How to Read the Gospels.* Cambridge: Cambridge University Press, 1956.

———. *The Interpretation of the Fourth Gospel.* Cambridge: Cambridge University Press, 1953.

———. *The Johannine Epistles.* New York: Harper, 1946.

———. *The Meaning of Paul for To-day.* London: Collins, Fontana, 1958.

———. "The Mind of Paul: A Psychological Approach." *BJRL* 17 (1933) 91–105.

———. *More New Testament Studies.* Manchester: Manchester University Press, 1968.

———. *New Testament Studies.* Manchester: Manchester University Press, 1953.

———. *The Parables of the Kingdom.* New York: Scribner, 1961.

———. *The Present Task in New Testament Studies.* Cambridge: Cambridge University Press, 1936.

———. "New Testament." In *The Study of Theology,* edited Kenneth E. Kirk, 217–46. London: Harper & Brothers, 1939.

———. "The Theology of Christian Pacifism." In *The Bases of Christian Pacifism: Addresses to the Congress of Christian Pacifists 1938,* edited by Charles E. Raven, C. H. Dodd, and G. H. C. MacGregor, 5–15. London: Council of Christian Pacifist Groups, 1938.

———. "Thirty Years of New Testament Study." *RL* 19 (1950) 323–33.

———. *A New Testament Triptych on Christ's Coming, His Gospel, His Passion*. Cincinnati: Forward Movement Publications, 1955.

Dodd, C. H., Panagiotis Bratsiotis, R. Bultmann, and Henri Clavier. *Man in God's Design according to the New Testament / L'homme selon le dessein de Dieu d'après le Nouveau Testament / Er Mensch in Gottes Heilsplan nach dem Neuen Testament*. Paper presented at the 6th General Meeting of the Society for New Testament Studies at Bern, 1952. Published as a monograph, Newcastle: SNTS/Imprimeries Réunies, 1953.

Evans, Owen. "Theologians of Our Time: Vincent Taylor." *ExpTim* 75 (1964) 164–68.

Fitzmyer, J. A. *Romans*. AB 33. New York: Doubleday, 1993.

Kevane, E. *Jesus the Divine Teacher*. New York: Vantage, 2003.

King, J. S. "Has D. A. Carson Been Fair to C. H. Dodd?" *JSNT* 17 (1983) 97–102.

Koester, Craig R. "Progress and Paradox: C. H. Dodd and Rudolf Bultmann on History, Jesus Tradition, and the Fourth Gospel." In *Engaging with C. H. Dodd on the Gospel of John: Sixty Years of Tradition and Interpretation*, edited by Tom Thatcher and Catrin H. Williams, 49–65. Cambridge: Cambridge University Press, 2013.

———. *Symbolism in the Fourth Gospel: Meaning, Mystery, Community*. 2nd ed. Minneapolis: Fortress, 2003.

Ladd, George Eldon. *Theology of the New Testament*. Grand Rapids: Eerdmans, 1989.

McKnight, Edgar V. *What Is Form Criticism?* Philadelphia: Fortress, 1969.

Morris, L. L. *The Apostolic Preaching of the Cross*. Grand Rapids: Eerdmans, 1955.

———. "The Meaning of *Hilasterion* in Romans 3:25." *NTS* 2 (1955) 33–43.

———. "The Use of *Hilaskesthai* in Biblical Greek." *ExpTim* 62 (1961) 227–39.

Mournet, T. C. *Oral Tradition and Literary Dependency: Variability and Stability in the Synoptic Tradition and Q*. Tübingen: Mohr Siebeck, 2005.

Neill, Stephen, and N. T. Wright. *The Interpretation of the New Testament 1861–1986*. Oxford: Oxford University Press, 1988.

Nicole, R. "C. H. Dodd and the Doctrine of Propitiation." *WTJ* 17 (1955) 117–57.

Porter, Stanley E. *Verbal Aspect in the Greek of the New Testament: With Reference to Tense and Mood*. SBG 1. New York: Peter Lang, 1993.

———. *The Criteria for Authenticity in Historical-Jesus Research: Previous Discussion and New Proposals*. JSNTSup 191. Sheffield: Sheffield Academic, 2000.

Robertson, A. T. *A Grammar of the Greek New Testament in the Light of Historical Research*. 4th ed. Nashville: Broadman, 1934.

Schweitzer, Albert. *The Quest of the Historical Jesus: A Critical Study of Its Progress from Reimarus to Wrede*. London: A. & C. Black, 1954.

Skinner, Christopher. "Another Look at 'the Lamb of God.'" *BSac* 161 (2004) 89–104.

Stein, Robert. "The 'Criteria' for Authenticity." In *Gospel Perspectives*. Vol 1., *Studies of History and Tradition in the Four Gospels*, edited by R. T. France and David Wenham, 225–63. Sheffield: JSOT, 1980.

Stovell, Beth M. *Mapping Metaphorical Discourse in the Fourth Gospel: John's Eternal King*. LBS 6. Leiden: Brill, 2012.

Sullivan, Clayton. *Rethinking Realized Eschatology*. Macon, GA: Mercer University Press, 1988.

Taylor, Vincent. *The Formation of the Gospel Tradition*. London: Macmillan, 1933.

———. *The Gospel according to St. Mark: The Greek Text with Introduction, Notes, and Indexes*. London: Macmillan, 1952.

———. *The Epistle to the Romans*. London: Epworth, 1955.
Thompson, Marianne Meye. "Eternal Life in the Gospel of John." *ExAud* 5 (1989) 35–55.
Watts, Rikki E. *Isaiah's New Exodus in Mark*. Grand Rapids: Baker Academic, 1997.
Worley, R. C. *Preaching and Teaching in the Earliest Church*. Philadelphia: Westminster, 1967.
Wright, N. T. *Jesus and the Victory of God*. Minneapolis: Fortress, 1997.
———. *The New Testament and the People of God*. Minneapolis: Fortress, 1996.

14

Walther Eichrodt
His Times and His Theology

WILLIAM K. K. KAPAHU

INTRODUCTION

THE POLITICAL AND SOCIAL environment of Europe in the late nineteenth and early twentieth centuries spawned a series of events that would forever change the landscape of the world. Massive world wars and unparalleled human suffering left generations of Europeans, North Americans, and many others forever changed. Never before in the history of the world did something have such far-reaching and global ramifications. It is difficult to think of anything today that has not been affected in some way by the events of those years. What is amazing is that amidst all of the atrocity and chaos came some of the most enduring and monumental achievements in the field of biblical academics and theological studies. It was out of the ashes of those years, in the very heart of the turmoil, that some of the greatest modern biblical and theological scholars have risen.

This chapter is about one such notable scholar. What follows is a summary of the life, times, and contribution of the Old Testament theologian Walther Eichrodt. My aim is to present an overview of his life, describe the social and political environment surrounding the formative years of his life and work, present a cursory view of his contributions to the field, and explore his concept of covenant.

BACKGROUND

Walther Eichrodt was born to August and Mathilde Eichrodt on August 1, 1890, in the southern German state of Baden, in Gernsbach. He was educated in Germany at the Theological School Bethel-Bielefeld and the universities of Greifswald, Heidelberg, and Erlangen.[1] It was at Heidelberg that he completed his dissertation in 1915, titled "Die Priesterschrift in der Genesis" ("The Priestly Writer in Genesis"), under the supervision of Professor George Beer.[2] Eichrodt began teaching Biblical Theology at the University of Erlangen in 1917. One year later, under the watch of Otto Procksch, he completed his *Habilitation* and continued to serve as a *Privatdozent* at Erlangen till 1922. It was during his stay at Erlangen that he completed and published his *Die Hoffnung des ewigen Friedens im alten Israel* (*The Hope of Eternal Peace in Israel*) in 1920. Transitioning to the University of Basel in Switzerland in 1922, he took on the post of Associate Professor of Old Testament and History of Religion. This is where he stayed for the remainder of his career, becoming full professor in 1934 and serving as rector from 1953 to 1955.[3] Prior to his retirement in 1960, Eichrodt was awarded honorary doctorates in theology by the University of Erlangen in 1927 and the University of Glasgow in 1951.[4] It was during his years at Basel that he produced his most significant and enduring contributions to the field of biblical and theological studies. Eichrodt is best known for his massive three-volume work, which he completed between the years of 1933 and 1936, titled *Theologie des Alten Testaments* (*Theology of the Old Testament*). By 1959 this work was in its sixth edition and was translated into English in two volumes by J. A. Baker (1961 and 1967). Walther Eichrodt died in Basel, Switzerland on May 20, 1978.

Growing Pains

It is illuminating to notice the social and political environments during the formative years of Eichrodt's life and research. The landscape of Germany is one not unacquainted with the effects of social upheaval, political unrest, and outright war. In the specific case of Eichrodt, this unrest was evident even prior to his birth. Although the events in 1848–49 have been overshadowed in our minds by the revolutionary events of 1789 (France) and 1917 (Russia), much of Europe was affected by the widespread Revolution of 1848. This consisted of loosely connected, mild to militant protests throughout Europe calling for a variety of political and social changes.[5] The efforts of this revolution were manifested strongly in Baden, Germany, one of only three revolutionary centers throughout all of Europe that had military support.[6] Baden, which encompassed Eichrodt's hometown of Gernsbach, was considered to be the most

---

1. Spampinato, "Rektoren der Universität Basel"; Willi, "Eichrodt"; Jenni, "Zum siebzigsten Geburtstag Walther Eichrodt." See also Gottwald, "W. Eichrodt," 25; Eichrodt, *Theology of the Old Testament*, 1:back cover flap; Stoebe, "Walther Eichrodt," 955–56.

2. It was published in part as Eichrodt, *Die Quellen der Genesis*. See Jenni, "Zum siebzigsten Geburtstag Walther Eichrodt," 630.

3. Spampinato, "Rektoren der Universität Basel."

4. Jenni, "Eichrodt, Walther."

5. For more detailed reading, see Robertson, *Revolutions of 1848*, and Dowe, *Europe in 1848*.

6. Price, "Holy Struggle against Anarchy," 35.

politically liberal of the German states. The call for reform there largely consisted of pleas for overall German unity and freedom. Though the rallying cry "*Einheit und Freiheit*" (unity and freedom) was for all of Germany,[7] the leaders and primary voices of this charge were noted to be the statesmen of Baden.[8] The result of their protests was a declaration of war upon the statesmen and their cohorts by the government of Prussia, which ended in Baden's defeat. While history has identified the European Revolution of 1848 ultimately as a failure, it did succeed in expressing the unsettled European (especially German) mindset and social climate of the day.[9] It was in the wake of these events that Walther Eichrodt was born and raised.

The turmoil in Germany and Europe originating from those events, unfortunately, did not dissipate. The events that took place before Eichrodt's birth, as significant as they may have been, were soon to be eclipsed by something far more devastating. The Great War, or First World War—its inception, expression, and completion—was the world that surrounded Eichrodt's scholastic and theological development (1908–20). Karl Barth, a contemporary to Eichrodt, had this to say about the effects of the First World War on theological teaching of the time:[10]

> One day in early August 1914 stands out in my personal memory as a black day. Ninety-three German intellectuals impressed public opinion by their proclamation in support of the war policy of Wilhelm II and his counselors. Among these intellectuals I discovered to my horror almost all of my theological teachers whom I had venerated. In despair over what this indicated about the signs of the time I suddenly realized that I could not any longer follow either their ethics and dogmatics or their understanding of the Bible and of history.[11]

Over nine million soldiers died over the span of the war (1914–18). Germany lost two million of that number with an additional civilian loss of over three-quarters of a million people.[12] No one in Europe, much less Germany, was left unaffected by this conflict. The aftermath of this tragedy was a present reality for German theologians, academics, and clergymen. In lectures given at Union Theological Seminary in 1926, Gustav Krüger, Professor of Church History in Giessen, Germany, described this new environment:

> Then came the war, and with it a reaction. Students of theology, and those who still looked forward to that vocation, were summoned to the field of battle. They fought and bled for honor, home, and country . . . They had experienced

---

7. Sperber, "Festivals of National Unity."
8. Robertson, *Revolutions of 1848*, 168.
9. Strandmann, "1848–49: A European Revolution," 7–8.
10. Cf. Maxfield, "Effects of World War I."
11. Barth, *Humanity of God*, 14.
12. Gilbert, *First World War*, xv; Meyer, *World Undone*, 705.

the infinite, the unspeakable . . . things to confirm their faith and things to provoke despair . . . Could one preach war in Christ's name? . . . they longed for revelation. And now, when they returned to the university and sat at the feet of their theological teachers, they were confronted with this historicism . . . Instead of reviving, this historicism repelled them; instead of refreshing, it chilled them . . . it was as dust to souls thirsting for the absolute.[13]

The First World War served as one of the most significant catalysts for the change in trajectory for theological studies. The paradigm shift for Krüger, Barth, and other established theologians and scholars of the day is summed up by Krüger's statement that, "this movement is entirely opposed to what we older men have been taught and have ourselves been teaching."[14] The landscape of German biblical academics, so it seemed, was primed of Eichrodt's imminent contributions.

History has shown that the end of the First World War was not the end of conflict for Germany and for Europe. Germany's defeat bred a spirit of nationalistic defiance that fueled the rise of the National Socialist movement. This presented its own challenges to social order and theological exposition. The dominant position of Nazism and its ideology was forced (or in some cases welcomed) upon the country of Germany. The Nazi "invasion" of the German Protestant church was met with resistance, the results of which produced what is known as the Barmen Declaration.[15] The declaration consisted of six articles that defined the German Christian Evangelical opposition to the new regime's beliefs and practices. One of the leaders selected to help prepare the declaration was none other than Karl Barth, who was now Eichrodt's colleague at the University of Basel.[16]

Although the degree to which Eichrodt and Barth interacted is uncertain, it is evident that Eichrodt was in extremely close proximity to the concerns now permeating Germany. It was also during this new uprising that Eichrodt's major work was produced and published. Jantzen goes as far as saying that, "with the Nazi ideology in the ascendant, Eichrodt was at pains to distinguish the theology of covenant from that of a popular Nature religion based on blood and soil."[17] Jantzen's assessment of Eichrodt, whether completely accurate or not, puts voice to what she sees as a direct influence of his times.[18]

---

13. Krüger, "Theology of Crisis," 231–32.
14. Ibid., 227.
15. For more on the subject, see Mauser, "Barmen Revisited."
16. Ibid., 8; Brueggemann, *Theology of the Old Testament*, 27.
17. Jantzen, *Death and the Displacement of Beauty*, 87.
18. Although not directly opposed to Jantzen's observation, Balentine, *Prayer in the Hebrew Bible*, 253–54, sees a surprising lack of impact of the realities of the 1930s on Eichrodt (and von Rad) in their understanding of the OT.

OLD (SCHOOL) TESTAMENT REVIVAL

The dramatic shifts in power in the political and social world of Europe, especially in the years following the First World War, were in some ways mirrored in the world of biblical and theological studies. The biggest shift, particularly in the area of Old Testament (OT) studies, came against the dominant history-of-religions approach, which long held the position of primacy for the field. As its influence began to weaken, the reemergence of the discipline of OT theology became apparent. The end of the war not only revealed a desire to recapture the revelatory nature of the OT, but also paved the way for this to happen. The extreme historicism of the nineteenth century was found inadequate to address the concerns and questions newly emerging in German theological thought. The complete objectivity claimed by the purely historical method was seen to be unachievable,[19] thus further fueling the desire for theological revelation.

Eichrodt's work filled this gap found in OT theological studies and his *Theologie des Alten Testaments* is seen by many scholars as the finest and most influential representation of OT theology of the twentieth century.[20] Part of what made his work so significant is the fact that it came in the wake of over forty years of *Religionsgeschichte* dominance (even oppression) over OT studies and OT theology in particular. In reflecting on E. König's work, *Theologie des Alten Testaments*, Eichrodt comments that his "venture to publish a Theology of the OT which attempted to take its title seriously . . . was a real act of courage which deserves to be recorded."[21] While for some, the characterization of historicism as "oppressive" may be too strong, for Eichrodt it was much too mild. He further comments that it was "high time that the *tyranny* of historicism in OT studies was broken and the *proper* approach to our task re-discovered."[22]

It is quite evident that for Eichrodt the demise of the idea of the unity of the OT was an unacceptable and even disastrous outcome of previous scholarship. The OT being reduced to simply a collection of documents from separate, loosely connected periods, expressing Israelite reflections of pagan religion, was not, in his understanding, an acceptable view of the OT.[23] He saw that this approach had severely damaging consequences (he used the term "fatal") for OT theology and the understanding of OT thought as a whole. This "appalling" concept also contributed to the weakening of what he thought was the "essential inner coherence" of both the New Testament (NT) and the Old.[24] He sought to preserve the theology of the OT as a historical discipline

---

19. Hasel, *Old Testament Theology*, 26, 48.
20. Gottwald, "W. Eichrodt," 25; Barr, *Concept of Biblical Theology*, 27; Hayes and Prussner, *Old Testament Theology*, 179.
21. Eichrodt, *Theology of the Old Testament*, 1:31; König, *Theologie des Alten Testaments*.
22. Eichrodt, *Theology of the Old Testament*, 1:31; italics mine.
23. Ibid., 1:28.
24. Ibid., 1:30.

that moved beyond simply assessing the development of Israel's religion, to one that addressed its core "essence" instead.²⁵

For Eichrodt, unity was not a precept for the OT alone; it applied to the whole of Christian Scripture. In his theology he desired "to understand the realm of OT belief in its structural unity" *and* "its essential coherence with the NT."²⁶ What binds together the Old and New Testaments, despite their intrinsic differences, is the "irruption of the Kingship of God into this world and its establishment."²⁷ It is in his understanding of a reciprocal relationship between Old and New Testaments that he derives his method to bring to realization the theology of the OT.²⁸

In his opening chapter on the problem and method of OT theology, Eichrodt describes the purpose of OT theology as the construction of a "complete picture" of the realm of OT belief.²⁹ This is to comprehend the entirety of the OT in both its vastness and its variety. He envisions this to be done by way of the constant assessment of two seemingly opposing realities—the world of Ancient Near Eastern (ANE) religion and the realm of NT belief. Although it should be understood that both aspects are to be given equal merit in developing his OT theology, Eichrodt's exercise of it gives more credence to the ANE background than to the NT. One thing he made clear in his method was that it sought to avoid all schemes derived from Christian dogma.³⁰ The abiding structure of analysis was to be derived strictly from the dialectic of the OT itself.

He uses this dialectic, in combination with his complementary synthesis of historical and systematic principles, to present the three main categories of his OT theology: (1) God and the people; (2) God and the world; and (3) God and man.³¹ These categories are undergirded by the central concept of "covenant" (which he often expresses as the Hebrew *bĕrît*), which Eichrodt saw as being both identifiable throughout the variations of the OT and reflective of the relationship between God and Israel since the time of Moses.³² It was his understanding that "Israel's most fundamental conviction, namely its unique relationship with God," was preserved centrally in covenant.³³ Eichrodt's covenant was not to be understood as a "doctrinal concept" but

---

25. Ollenburger, "Covenant," 58.

26. Eichrodt, *Theology of the Old Testament*, 1:31.

27. Ibid., 1:26.

28. Gottwald, "W. Eichrodt"; Hasel, *Old Testament Theology*, 47–51; Eichrodt, *Theology of the Old Testament*, 1:36–69.

29. Ibid., 1:25.

30. Ibid., 1:33.

31. Ibid.

32. Hayes and Prussner, *Old Testament Theology*, 181.

33. Eichrodt, *Theology of the Old Testament*, 1:17. "Covenant" as a central concept could be said to have originated with Johannes Cocceius (1603–69). See Scobie, *Ways of Our God*, 13.

rather the "description of a living process" making known a "divine reality" unparalleled throughout the history of religion.[34]

CROSSING THE LINE

Though there are numerous ways in which Eichrodt's life and work has enriched the landscape of biblical scholarship, three in particular[35] have made the greatest impact. The first is in the area of methodology. Eichrodt established a unique methodological approach to OT theology by bringing to the forefront what has come to be known as the cross-section (*querschnitt*) approach to OT theology.[36] The public pronouncement of his approach came at least as early as his 1929 article titled "Hat die alttestamentliche Theologie noch selbständige Bedeutung innerhalb der alttestamentlichen Wissenschaft?"[37] In this he openly states that current OT theological research could not stay satisfied "with a genetic analysis but has a vast systematic assignment to carry out: It must lay a cross section through the developed whole in order to demonstrate the inner structure of a religion."[38] This comment came during a time when the Theology-Anthropology-Soteriology presentations of OT theology were dominating.[39]

As mentioned above, he was able to actualize a cross-section throughout the OT using the theme of covenant, which, by Eichrodt's measure, was able to bridge (cut across) the entirety of the OT. As such, he was able to begin, and arrive back, at the central theme of covenant. He maintained that a theologian could, at any point throughout the span of the OT, examine a cross-section of it and find a consistent inner structure relating it back to the whole. So groundbreaking was his presentation of this that it even inspired application within the realm of NT theology.[40]

CENTER-FUGUE

Assuredly, his success with this cross-section approach rested largely with what he chose as the "center" (*Mitte*) for his OT theology. It was clear to Eichrodt that covenant was the enduring center of the OT. He believed that the OT overtly expressed

---

34. Eichrodt, *Theology of the Old Testament*, 1:14.

35. All of these three items—OT cross-section methodology, OT center, and OT covenant—are strongly interrelated and have made an impact both individually and collectively.

36. Hayes and Prussner, *Old Testament Theology*, 180.

37. The English translation of this article was published as "Does Old Testament Theology Still Have Independent Significance?"

38. Eichrodt, "Does Old Testament Theology Still Have Independent Significance?" 32. See also Dentan, *Preface to Old Testament Theology*, 36. This essay was in large part a response to Eissfeldt, "Israelitisch-Jüdische Religionsgeschichte." See the English translation of Eissfeldt's essay: "History of Israelite-Jewish Religion."

39. Examples as König, *Theologie des Alten Testaments* (1922), and later Sellin, *Theologie des Alten Testaments* (1933), and Köhler, *Theologie des Alten Testaments* (1936), were to some extent following the God-Man-Salvation paradigm. See Hayes and Prussner, *Old Testament Theology*, 178–89.

40. See Loretz, *Die Wahrheit der Bibel*. Cf. Hasel, *New Testament Theology*, 153–54.

covenant as its "natural" central concept; he simply identified it and put it to use. The validity of his proposal is apparent throughout the OT, as it is clear that large sections of the OT are built upon the premise of covenant. This is especially true with regard to the Pentateuch. The establishment and perpetuation of Israel as a nation is utterly dependent on its expressed covenant with Yahweh. The rest of the OT could be said to move in accordance with this dependency. A quick glance through the arrangement of the chapters of Eichrodt's initial volume (*Theology of the Old Testament*, vol. 1) attests to his belief.

I	Old Testament Theology: The Problem and the Method
II	The Covenant Relationship
	(1) The Meaning of the Covenant Concept
	(2) The History of the Covenant Concept
	i. The Jeopardizing of the Yahweh Covenant
	ii. The Re-Fashioning of the Covenant Concept
III–IV	The Covenant Statutes
V	The Name of the Covenant God
VI–VII	The Nature of the Covenant God
VIII–IX	The Instruments of Covenant
X	Covenant Breaking and Judgment
XI	Fulfilling the Covenant: The Consummation of God's Dominion

Although covenant can be seen as a dominant theme throughout the OT, it is certainly not the only theme that can be found. Eichrodt's work in this area has been the catalyst for debate among scholars on the appropriate selection, even the genuine existence, of a center for OT theology. The question of whether or not the OT has something that can be looked upon as a center is of considerable importance for the understanding and application of OT theology.

Eichrodt's expression of this center, monumental as it was, was but one of many to have come upon the landscape of OT theology. German contemporaries such as Sellin[41] (who chose "holiness of God") and Köhler[42] (who saw "God as Lord") had other choices as their center for theological exposition. The sheer possibilities of potential OT centers are, as Hayes comments, "almost legion."[43] This is case-in-point for Gerhard von Rad, who was Eichrodt's greatest detractor. Von Rad out-rightly rejects the notion of an OT *Mitte*. As for a theology of the OT, he states that the OT embodies "not one, but quite a number of theologies which are widely divergent both in structure and method of argument."[44] According to von Rad, the OT in its entirety validates his observation and objection. He continues that "on the very basis of the

41. Sellin, *Theologie des Alten Testaments*.
42. Köhler, *Theologie des Alten Testaments*.
43. Hayes and Prussner, *Old Testament Theology*, 257.
44. Von Rad, *Old Testament Theology*, 2:414.

OT itself, it is truly difficult to answer the question of the unity of that Testament, for it has *no* focal-point."[45]

Although the shortcomings of holding to a central theme permeating the whole of the OT are undeniable, they do not diminish the significance of Eichrodt's overall contribution to the field of OT theology. With regard to its center especially, his contribution remains unsurpassed in its methodological thoroughness. Waltke recently commented on Eichrodt in this endeavor and said, "in my thinking Eichrodt came closest to a center when he proposed the irruption . . . of the kingship of God as the center of pan-biblical theology."[46] Further, Brueggemann supports Eichrodt's past endeavor by saying:

> It is unfortunate that Eichrodt's work is too easily and too often understood methodologically simply as presenting the OT under "one idea." Covenant is no accidental "one idea" . . . In this theme, it is evident that Eichrodt has broken new ground within the context of historical criticism. Not only his method but also the substance of his exposition broke decisively with rationalistic developmentalism.[47]

COVENANT SUMMARY

It is fitting to follow Brueggemann's comment with a description of Eichrodt's understanding of the term "covenant" used so much throughout his work and in this chapter. The final "C" in his triplet[48] is, in many ways, the lynchpin factor of his theology. What follows is a detailed account of Eichrodt's OT theology section titled "The Meaning of the Covenant Concept."[49]

Eichrodt begins with the understanding that this "covenant-union" between Israel and Yahweh, though fragmentary in places, is both an evident and an original element in the history of Israelite religion. He applies this "covenant-union" concept even "to those sections of the OT where the word *bĕrît* has disappeared altogether."[50] Eichrodt validates this proposal by the "sense of solidarity" held in the Sinai tradition and the "relationships of grace" and guardianship apparent in the post-Mosaic era.[51] So where there is no explicit mention of *bĕrît* (he uses this term throughout his explanation) there still can be an implicit covenant relationship between God and a human recipient.

---

45. Ibid., 2:362; italics mine.
46. Waltke and Yu, *Old Testament Theology*, 156.
47. Brueggemann, *Theology of the Old Testament*, 31.
48. Eichrodt's triplet of OT cross-section methodology, OT center, and OT covenant.
49. Eichrodt, *Theology of the Old Testament*, 1:36–45.
50. Ibid., 1:36. He points to Exod 24:9–11; 24:3–8 (E); 34:10, 27 (J2).
51. Judg 5:4, 9, 23; 6:13; 1 Sam 2:27; 4:8; 10:18; 15:6; Exod 15:1, 21; Num 23:22; 24:8.

A basis for *bĕrît*, derived from ANE secular examples, is that it is a bilateral relationship between two consenting parties, usually of unequal status. Eichrodt sees the inequality in this relationship to be the normative experience; this is of course the case between Yahweh and Israel.[52] This inequality, however, does not lessen the responsibility to uphold the terms of the covenant by either participant. He states that in the critical examination of Israel's relationship (*bĕrît*) with God, what prevails is "still the plain impression given by the OT itself"—which is the inference that Moses took the longstanding secular ANE understanding and practice of covenant and applied it to the worship of Yahweh. Because of this, it is all the more important to distinguish its unique theological significance apart from its secular origins.

To accomplish this task Eichrodt separates his explanation into five, vaguely distinct, elements. The first of these he identifies as the "factual *nature of the divine revelation*."[53] The Yahweh-Moses covenant-making event, understood as an actual historical moment in time, underscores the reality of Yahweh's experiential presence in the life of his people. As *bĕrît* is the center (so to speak) of this critical first interaction, so *bĕrît* will be at the center of all other such interactions in the future. Yahweh is immanently real to Israel and his disclosure of himself is not "speculative." It is rather the in-breaking of his presence into the lives of his people. It is in this intimate and intense fashion that his relations with Israel shape them "according to his will."[54] The knowledge and experience of his "being" are not just part of the covenant act, but are largely its purpose.

Eichrodt sees that the culmination of this is the Exodus event and the deliverance of Israel. God's "mighty act" is what secures, or consummates, *bĕrît*. Yahweh's display of power and faithfulness are gifts to his people, "for their permanent enjoyment."[55] Simultaneously, however, their behavior is subjected to his exacting standards. Because Eichrodt views this as a factual moment in history, "as a covenant expressed in the form of actual events," he understands it to represent the expression of life that is to be characteristic of the relationship between Yahweh and his people.[56] The events of this deliverance—the display of power, the intimate rescue, and the celebratory joy—are to be formulated as religious concepts innate to their experience of covenant.[57]

The second element is a clear, discernable "divine will," which can be appealed to and depended on. The covenant now grows to both a promise and a demand. "You shall be my people and I will be your God." Eichrodt sees this element as the means by which covenant provides meaningful goals for the future and a historically significant

---

52. Gen 21:23; 26:29; Josh 9:1; 1 Sam 11:1; 20:1; 1 Kings 20:34; Ezek 17:18; etc.
53. Eichrodt, *Theology of the Old Testament*, 1:37; italics his.
54. Ibid.
55. Ibid., 1:38.
56. Ibid., 1:37.
57. Ibid., 1:38.

past and relevancy.⁵⁸ This, in effect, relieves the fear and uncertainty, even volatility, that plagues pagan life. Covenant participants are assured of their good standing and are greeted with "*an atmosphere of trust and security.*"⁵⁹ Those in covenant are given both the strength and the desire to surrender to the will of God. This in turn grants the ability to engage life's problems with a "joyful courage."⁶⁰ It is obvious at this point that Eichrodt's portrait of covenant as it develops, or as it is to be ultimately understood, progressively becomes a sanctuary and shelter from a world outside of its protected boundaries.

Here is where Eichrodt breaks from his idealized covenantal account and suggests that this proposal can only be fully realized if the foundational elements that undergird the covenant are maintained. The "formal character" of the covenant agreement is derived from the core laws of ancient Israel, "infused with a deep feeling for righteousness," as represented by the "Book of the Covenant" and the Decalogue.⁶¹ According to Eichrodt, these things must form the basis of the actual Mosaic covenant⁶² contract in order to actualize the true benefits of the covenant relationship. That is the only way to move beyond nice suppositions and heavenly ideals to real divine fulfillment.

The third element is the "content," as he calls it, of the will of God enacting its formative power upon the human covenant recipients, making them cognizant of their unique position in relation to God. In other words, it is the divine presence of God in covenant that grants to those within the covenant community special understanding of their unique, and thus unified, status under Yahweh. It is not a national affiliation that gives the people of Israel their identity. Such was true for surrounding pagan nations (e.g., Egypt). Israelite solidarity came only by way of covenantal participation. The loosely connected and widespread tribal units of Israel were united in and through Yahweh by means of their faithfulness to covenant. This supplied a set of commonalities for all the tribes, such as universal law codes, worship practices, and collective historical awareness.⁶³

Eichrodt notes that one of the unique and surprising aspects to this element of covenant is its propensity for inclusion. There are no clear borders drawn excluding the stranger from covenant involvement and absorption.⁶⁴ The only requirement for

58. Ibid.
59. Ibid.; italics his.
60. Ibid.
61. Ibid.
62. Eichrodt himself is uncertain as to the exact nature of this. For a discussion on Mosaic covenant, see Barrick, "Mosaic Covenant."
63. Eichrodt, *Theology of the Old Testament*, 1:39.
64. Ibid. He footnotes: "From the time of the Exodus from Egypt onwards new elements were continually entering the tribal covenant union. Sometimes these were Hebrew—the Joshua covenant of Josh. 24 refers to such a case—sometimes foreign, especially among the southern tribes which had not been into Egypt. This explains why the twelve tribes are enumerated differently in Judg. 5; Gen.

admittance is to take upon oneself the lordship of the Keeper of the covenant. In other words, submission is the price of admission. Eichrodt suggests that one of the key highlights of this type of admissions policy is that growth is not dependent on, or determined by, natural or socialistic factors. He states:

> [The covenant community] does not receive the law of its being from blood and soil. It is a historically determined divine creation, a "psychical totality," which acquires cohesion and character from an inward order and strength. The *foedus iniquum* of the Sinai covenant, therefore, in fact created a domain with an overlord and subjects; henceforward the idea of the *Kingdom of God* is in the air.[65]

I find his choice of words and the argument that he presents here interesting. He further remarks that this concept is formed by a reflection on political life.[66] The question is, however, to whose political life is this analogous? Although Eichrodt does not explicitly share his motivation or inspiration, it is difficult to believe that the national events surrounding his life did not influence, at least in part, his formulation and presentation of this idea. In any case Eichrodt affirms that this element of covenant, although seemingly nationalistic in its focus, is more concerned with religious and spiritual affiliations.

He desires instead to focus more on the "purely religious" identification of the "peculiar" position of Israel as the covenant people.[67] Eichrodt labels the gathering of the people as the "Assembly" and "Congregation."[68] These designations are specific to the covenant people when rallied together in obedient response to God's call. While these are assuredly theologically charged terms, what is interesting is that Eichrodt does not himself name these gatherings. He merely repeats the language of the OT itself.[69] Other labels such as, "People of God" and "People of YHWH," are more general descriptions that show no specific cultic associations. These designations speak to the commonality of a shared God and a unified religious affiliation.

Even the name Israel is to be considered a type of unifying banner, so to speak, to be understood to mean "God rules."[70] Again this title bears more of a religious impetus than a political or national one. This is an extremely important aspect for this particular element of covenant. The nation cannot exist or be maintained outside of, or be independent of, their Divine covenant benefactor. Eichrodt sees that Israel's purpose from their very inception as a people was to be subjugated to a greater divine

---

49; and Deut. 33."

65. Ibid., 1:40.

66. Ibid.

67. Ibid.

68. Ibid.

69. He states that "a complete list of references would be out of the question, but by way of example the following may be cited: Num 23:22; 24:8; Judg 5:4f; 6:13; 1 Sam 4.8; et al." (ibid., 1:42).

70. Ibid., 1:40.

purpose. The concept of covenant was ideally suited to express Israel's new religious affiliation with God. Eichrodt understands the mode of covenant to be organic, allowing for the people to simultaneously engage their new faith "without bringing that faith into a false dependence on the people's own will."[71] The emphasis of this element is on maintaining a religious and spiritual identity through covenant.

The fourth element is largely concerned with the engagement of faith through covenant within history. Eichrodt says that "faith in the covenant God" presumes an "interior attitude toward history."[72] History is the proving ground for Israel's faith and covenant is the means by which it is to be expressed. Just as covenant began with a historical act of faith (see the first element above), it must continue as historical *acts* of faith. History allows for the people of God to experience the "divine will" in the formation of their social life and national prosperity. "In this way history acquires a value which it does not possess in the religions of the ancient civilizations."[73]

Eichrodt points out that while it is true that other ANE religions affirmed the movement of their gods through time in isolated events, they did not see how history as a whole was the purposeful activity of the divine in the world. The religions of the ANE were more limited in their understanding of the divine-historical and divine-human actions of God/gods. They were governed by the "thought-forms" of their Nature mythology.[74] This, however, was not the case for Israel. Their experience of their covenant God as "redeemer" broadened their understanding of the immanent workings of God in their day-to-day life. It is clear that, for Israel, the fundamental events of the Mosaic era, namely their deliverance from Egypt, permanently expanded their understanding of the divine and their relationship to the divine through covenant. The Israelite view of history had been shaped by the motifs of the Holy Land, the Exodus, and the ideas of election and covenant.

The fifth and final element addresses the distinctions between Israelite covenant and pagan religion. This element provides "*safeguards against an identification of religion with the national interest.*"[75] This is largely speaking against the various forms of nature religions.[76] He says that "*any understanding of God's involvement with his people in terms of popular Nature religion was rejected.*"[77] At the same time this element speaks to the importance of the personal and ongoing relationship between Yahweh and Israel. Covenant, in effect, is what makes Israel's relationship with Yahweh different from other contemporary worship practices. Israel's religion is one of election,

---

71. Ibid., 1:41.

72. Ibid.

73. Ibid.

74. Ibid.

75. Ibid., 1:42; italics his.

76. For a comparison of Israelite and Canaanite worship practices, see Cross, *Canaanite Myth*, and, more recently, Miller, *Israelite Religion*.

77. Eichrodt, *Theology of the Old Testament*, 1:42; italics his.

which means that their God is free to de-elect them if the covenant agreement is not maintained—"*he on his side may dissolve [it] at anytime.*"[78] Eichrodt again stresses the massive inequality in the status of the covenant participants. Yahweh, unlike the pagan gods worshiped, is truly independent and needs nothing from his people.

The independence of Israel's God and his highly elevated status above them serves also as a reminder that covenant is not a partnership of mutual interest. God's choice to engage Israel, in Egypt, at Sinai, and through covenant, is a vivid illustration of his sovereignty over their relationship. His presence through these events was "felt so powerfully in human consciousness that it comes naturally to men to bow in fear and trembling before this gracious Being."[79] The display of the obvious disparity of power between the covenant participants should preclude any attempts by the weaker party to assume any measure of control. Covenant, therefore, "lays claim to the whole man and calls him to surrender with no reservations."[80]

BRIEF REVIEW

The above analysis of Eichrodt's main section, titled "The Meaning of the Covenant Concept," follows the organization and presentation of his chapter. The original three-volume German edition of Eichrodt's *Theology of the Old Testament* is presented in two volumes for its English readers. Volumes two and three of the German edition are combined in volume two of the English. One section of Eichrodt's theology of God and the People, God and the World, and God and Man is treated in each of the three volumes. The volume outline given above shows the content and focus for the initial volume. While it is clear that the focus is on covenant, the volume is specifically concerned with developing the covenant concept as it relates to Israelite identity as a tribal nation. The covenant analysis presented above reflects the core elements that are portrayed throughout the entirety of this volume. This first section of his theology is given a disproportionately large amount of attention in comparison to the other two sections. Eichrodt devoted 511 pages to this first section, but approximately half that amount is given to each of the other two.[81] Part of the reason for this disparity is that much of the needed discussion of the last two volumes is absorbed into the first.

The second section of his theology is built around describing God in the World, or more appropriately, God's communicative dealings with the world. Various modes of God's manifest presence are described. The three primary ways God is shown to communicate are by his physical manifestations, by his spirit, and by his word. The remaining portions of this section speak to the details of the cosmos, its creation, and mankind's role and purpose in it. The third and final section of his three-part theology

78. Ibid., 1:44.
79. Ibid.
80. Ibid., 1:45.
81. In the English edition, vol. 2 consists of Part Two of his theology, "God and the World" (228 pages), and Part Three, "God and Man" (301 pages).

discusses God and Man. This largely addresses the individual dimension of a person's life as it relates to community, God, and proper godly living. The last two major parts of Eichrodt's theology (God in the World, God and Man) appear to be a kind of addendum that pertains to questions of existence. They are noticeably more segmented and use covenant more sparingly and in more universal ways. It is evident that the force of his theological presentation is found in his first volume.

SUMMARY OF CONTRIBUTIONS

Although it is correct to identify Eichrodt's importance in relation to his attempt to unify the OT under one theme or idea, the lasting significance of his contribution resides with the specific theme of covenant that he chose. Covenantal identity and the connection between God and nation that it provided were central to the faith of Israel. It was through his utilization of this relational dimension of the covenant concept that he was able to present a structure of argument for his theology that continues to be propagative. From the very outset, his presentation is an aggressive response against the classifications of modernity that were imposed upon the biblical text by the critical scholarship of the day. Eichrodt saw that critical theological study was "miserably inadequate" in its view that the core of OT religion could be seen in the "bloodless abstraction of 'ethical monotheism.'"[82] Its adherence to "the values of rationalistic individualism and the structure-patterns of developmental theories"[83] were in direct opposition to the fundamental nature of covenantal relationship in the OT. Although Eichrodt was not able to completely free himself from the bonds of the modernity to which he was so averse, his work remains a clear challenge to such influences upon biblical interpretation.

It is in the covenantal relationship between the people of Israel and their God that Eichrodt revealed one of the more groundbreaking and controversial aspects of his theology. Against the more conventional views of his time, which largely saw the God-Man interaction as unilateral from God to man, Eichrodt understood the relationship to be "two-sided." Covenant enacted and enabled a bilateral relationship between God and his people. This unique understanding provided the basis for his following work, *Man in the Old Testament*. Unfortunately, however, he did not much further this new-found insight in this book. He instead focused more on man's required obedience to the will of a sovereign God.[84] Although Eichrodt himself did not actually explore the implications of the bilateral relationship afforded by covenant, he was instrumental in bringing this radical, newly-found dimension in the bond between God and man to light.

---

82. Eichrodt, *Theology of the Old Testament*, 1:12.
83. Ibid.
84. For examples, see Eichrodt, *Man in the Old Testament*, 21, 26, 44.

Eichrodt's idea of covenant connectedness extends beyond mankind to creation itself. He clearly ties the natural world to its Creator through the pervasiveness of the covenant concept.[85] The world does not exist as an autonomous entity apart from the God who created it, but rather remains subject to his divine will and purpose. This assertion was a stark departure from the prevalent teachings of the day that preferred the separation of the scientific world from the spiritual. Eichrodt understood that the natural world, its existence and function, could not be divorced from its divine Creator and his intended purposes for it. Instead of being subjugated to the whims of mankind, the world rightfully falls under the dominion of God, and is to be stewarded and treated in a manner befitting God's rule.

Eichrodt's understanding of God and creation in light of the covenant concept, as groundbreaking and insightful as it was for his time, may be even more pertinent for the present climate of the world today. Current global ecological concerns, and the resulting emergence of eco-centered or ecologically focused theologies,[86] can readily benefit from Eichrodt's covenantal view of the world and its relation to God and mankind. As it was for Israel, understanding creation as the work of the covenant God would not only clarify our vision of the world, it would also endue "the will of the Creator from the start with the *characteristics of personal and spiritual activity*, and of moral purpose."[87]

Eichrodt's contributions to OT theology and biblical studies as a whole, as we have seen, were truly innovative for his time and continue to serve as a primer for those who follow in his footsteps.[88] One cannot help but agree with the praises given to Eichrodt by the multitude of influential scholars who see his work as nothing short of monumental. This judgment is confirmed by the creativity, influence, and longevity of his work. Although new contributions that bear the likeness of his own continue to be produced, they have not moved much beyond his initial presentation of a center-themed theology. As Gottwald astutely notes, "with the material and method at his disposal in the thirties Eichrodt executed his task of writing an Old Testament theology so well that there is no point in trying to do a better job on his terms."[89] Gottwald's statement, which was made over 50 years ago, still remains true today.

CONCLUSION

Walther Eichrodt was certainly one of the most influential scholars of the twentieth century. His many notable contributions to the fields of biblical and theological studies are still helping to shape the landscape of the biblical academy today. From

---

85. Eichrodt, *Theology of the Old Testament*, 2:98.

86. See Dalton and Simmons, *Ecotheology*, for a detailed introduction to the topic. See also Maudlin and Baer, *Green Bible*, and Sabin and Ide, *Tending to Eden*.

87. Eichrodt, *Theology of the Old Testament*, 2:98; italics his.

88. Such as Kaiser, *Promise-Plan of God*, and Hamilton, *God's Glory*.

89. Gottwald, "Recent Biblical Theologies: IX," 212.

the tumultuous environment of two World Wars he was able to provide monumental research that both inspired and challenged generations of scholars that followed him. It has been my aim in this chapter to present an overview of who he was, describe the social and political environments surrounding the formative years of his life and work, present a cursory view of his contributions to the field, and explore his concept of covenant. Although the events of early twentieth-century Europe brought misery to many, great good resulted from it as well. Walther Eichrodt and his life and work are a prime example of great good that arose out of much evil.

BIBLIOGRAPHY

Balentine, Samuel E. *Prayer in the Hebrew Bible: The Drama of Divine–Human Dialogue*. Overtures to Biblical Theology. Minneapolis: Fortress, 1993.

Barr, James. *The Concept of Biblical Theology: An Old Testament Perspective*. Minneapolis: Fortress, 1999.

Barrick, William D. "The Mosaic Covenant." *TMSJ* 10, no. 2 (1999) 213–32.

Barth, Karl. *The Humanity of God*. Translated by John Newton Thomas and Thomas Wieser. Richmond: John Knox, 1960.

Brueggemann, Walter. *Theology of the Old Testament: Testimony, Dispute, Advocacy*. Minneapolis: Fortress, 1997.

Cross, Frank Moore. *Canaanite Myth and Hebrew Epic: Essays in the History of the Religion of Israel*. Cambridge, MA: Harvard University Press, 1973.

Dalton, Anne Marie, and Henry C. Simmons. *Ecotheology and the Practice of Hope*. SUNY Series on Religion and the Environment. Albany: State University of New York Press, 2010.

Dentan, Robert C. *Preface to Old Testament Theology*. Yale Studies in Religion. New Haven: Yale University Press, 1950.

Dowe, Dieter, et al. *Europe in 1848: Revolution and Reform*. Translated by David Higgins. New York: Berghahn, 2001.

Eichrodt, Walther. *Die Hoffnung des ewigen Friedens im alten Israel: Ein Beitrag zu der Frage nach der israelitischen Eschatologie*. BFCT 3.25. Gütersloh: Bertelsmann, 1920.

———. *Die Quellen der Genesis von neuem Untersucht*. BZAW. Giessen: A. Töpelmann, 1916.

———. "Does Old Testament Theology Still Have Independent Significance within Old Testament Scholarship?" In *The Flowering of Old Testament Theology: A Reader in Twentieth-Century Old Testament Theology, 1930–1990*, edited by Ben C. Ollenburger et al., 30–39. Winona Lake, IN: Eisenbrauns, 1992.

———. "Hat die alttestamentliche Theologie noch selbständige Bedeutung innerhalb der alttestamentlichen Wissenschaft?" *ZAW* 47 (1929) 83–91.

———. *Man in the Old Testament*. Translated by K. Smith and R. Gregor Smith. SBT 4. London: SCM, 1951.

———. *Theologie des Alten Testaments*. 3 vols. Leipzig: J. C. Hinrichs, 1933–37.

———. *Theology of the Old Testament*. 2 vols. Translated by J. A. Baker. OTL. London: SCM, 1961, 1967.

Eissfeldt, Otto. "The History of Israelite-Jewish Religion and Old Testament Theology." In *The Flowering of Old Testament Theology: A Reader in Twentieth-Century Old Testament*

Theology, 1930–1990, edited by Ben C. Ollenburger et al., 20–29. Winona Lake, IN: Eisenbrauns, 1992.

———. "Israelitisch-Jüdische Religionsgeschichte und alttestamentliche Theologie." *ZAW* 44 (1926) 1–12.

Gilbert, Martin. *The First World War: A Complete History*. 2nd ed. New York: H. Holt, 2004.

Gottwald, Norman K. "Recent Biblical Theologies: IX. Walther Eichrodt's 'Theology of the Old Testament.'" *ExpTim* 74, no. 7 (1963) 209–12.

———. "W. Eichrodt: Theology of the Old Testament." In *Contemporary Old Testament Theologians*, edited by Robert B. Laurin, 23–62. Valley Forge, PA: Judson, 1970.

Hamilton, James M. *God's Glory in Salvation through Judgment: A Biblical Theology*. Wheaton: Crossway, 2010.

Hasel, Gerhard F. *New Testament Theology: Basic Issues in the Current Debate*. Grand Rapids: Eerdmans, 1978.

———. *Old Testament Theology: Basic Issues in the Current Debate*. 4th ed. Grand Rapids: Eerdmans, 1991.

Hayes, John H., and Frederick C. Prussner. *Old Testament Theology: Its History and Development*. Atlanta: John Knox, 1985.

Jantzen, Grace. *Death and the Displacement of Beauty*. New York: Routledge, 2004.

Jenni, Ernst. "Eichrodt, Walther." Brill Online Reference Works. No pages. Online: http://referenceworks.brillonline.com/entries/religion-past-and-present/eichrodt-walther-SIM_04101

———. "Zum siebzigsten Geburtstag Walther Eichrodt." *TLZ* 85 (1960) 629–34.

Kaiser, Walter C. *The Promise-Plan of God: A Biblical Theology of the Old and New Testaments*. Grand Rapids: Zondervan, 2008.

Köhler, Ludwig. *Theologie des Alten Testaments*. Neue Theologische Grundrisse. Tübingen: Mohr, 1936.

König, Eduard. *Theologie des Alten Testaments: Kritisch und vergleichend Dargestellt*. Stuttgart: C. Belser, 1922.

Krüger, Gustav. "The 'Theology of Crisis': Remarks on a Recent Movement in German Theology." *HTR* 19, no. 3 (1926) 227–58.

Loretz, Oswald. *Die Wahrheit der Bibel*. Freiburg: Herder, 1964.

Maudlin, Michael G., and Marlene Baer. *The Green Bible: New Revised Standard Version*. San Francisco: HarperOne, 2008.

Mauser, Ulrich. "The Theological Declaration of Barmen Revisited." *Theology Matters* 6, no. 6 (2000) 1–16.

Maxfield, Charles A. "The Effects of World War I on Christian Thought in Europe." No pages. Online: http://www.maxfieldbooks.com/WorldWar1.html#11

Meyer, G. J. *A World Undone: The Story of the Great War, 1914 to 1918*. New York: Delacorte, 2006.

Miller, Patrick D. *Israelite Religion and Biblical Theology: Collected Essays*. JSOTSup 267. Sheffield: Sheffield Academic, 2000.

Ollenburger, Ben C. "Covenant." In *The Flowering of Old Testament Theology: A Reader in Twentieth-Century Old Testament Theology, 1930–1990*, edited by Ben C. Ollenburger et al., 58–60. Winona Lake, IN: Eisenbrauns, 1992.

Price, Roger. "The Holy Struggle against Anarchy." In *Europe in 1848: Revolution and Reform*, edited by Dieter Dowe, 25–54. New York: Berghahn, 2001.

Robertson, Priscilla. *Revolutions of 1848: A Social History*. Princeton: Princeton University Press, 1952.

Sabin, Scott C., and Kathy Ide. *Tending to Eden: Environmental Stewardship for God's People*. Valley Forge, PA: Judson, 2010.

Scobie, Charles H. H. *The Ways of Our God: An Approach to Biblical Theology*. Grand Rapids: Eerdmans, 2003.

Sellin, Ernst. *Theologie des Alten Testaments*. 2nd ed. Alttestamentliche Theologie auf religionsgeschichtlicher Grundlage. Leipzig: Quelle & Meyer, 1936.

Spampinato, Thierry. "Rektoren der Universität Basel." No pages. 2012. Online: http://www.unigeschichte.unibas.ch/materialien/rektoren/

Sperber, Jonathan. "Festivals of National Unity in the German Revolution of 1848–1849." *Past & Present* 136 (1992) 114–38.

Stoebe, Hans Joachim. "Walther Eichrodt zum achtzigsten Geburtstag." *TLZ* 95 (1970) 955–58.

Strandmann, Hartmut Pogge von. "1848–49: A European Revolution?" In *The Revolutions in Europe 1848–1849: From Reform to Reaction*, edited by Robert John Weston Evans and H. Pogge von Strandmann, 1–8. Oxford: Oxford University Press, 2000.

Von Rad, Gerhard. *Old Testament Theology*. Translated by D. M. G. Stalker. 2 vols. OTL. Louisville, KY: Westminster John Knox, 2001.

Waltke, Bruce K., with Charles Yu. *An Old Testament Theology: An Exegetical, Canonical, and Thematic Approach*. Grand Rapids: Zondervan, 2006.

Willi, Thomas. "Eichrodt, Walther." *Das historische Lexikon der Schweiz*. No pages. 2012. Online: http://www.hls-dhs-dss.ch/textes/d/D10587.php

Index of Modern Authors

Achtemeier, P., 225, 230
Ackerman, J. S., 24
Adams, R. M., 98
Agamben, G., 38
Aland, B., 42, 81, 86
Aland, K., 11, 42, 81, 86
Albright, W. F., 41
Allen, W. C., 279, 330
Allison, D. C., 18, 88, 212, 219, 220, 316, 329, 332
Alter, R., 24, 26
Althusser, L., 46
Amphoux, C.-B., 74
Andersen, F., 47
Andrews, M. E., 118
Anrich, G., 221, 222
Archer, G. L., 16
Arndt, W. F., 42
Arnold, M., 24
Astruc, J., 15
Auerbach, E., 24
Aune, D. E., 24
Austin, J. L., 37
Ayer, A. J., 25

Bach, J. S., 5
Bacon, B. W., 119
Badiou, A., 38
Baer, M., 382
Bailey, K., 359
Baird, J. A., 28
Baird, W., 3-15, 17-24, 30, 31, 37, 40-42, 49-53, 71-75, 79-81, 91, 94, 95, 102-104, 106, 107, 119-24, 166-68, 173, 181, 213, 226
Baker, D. W., 17
Baker, J. A., 368
Bakhtin, M., 43
Bal, M., 45
Balentine, S. E., 370
Bandstra, A. J., 183
Banks, D., 198

Bar-Efrat, S., 26
Barlett, J. H., 279
Barnikolm, E., 198
Barr, J., 22, 23, 371
Barrett, C. K., 212
Barrett, W., 36
Barrick, W. D., 377
Barsky, R. F., 41
Barth, K., 13, 21, 26, 91, 96, 163, 179, 369, 370
Barthes, R., 45
Barton, J., 3, 7, 15, 24, 48, 51, 53
Bauckham, R. J., 18, 23, 102, 229, 336
Bauer, B., 8, 136
Bauer, W., 42
Bauernfeind, O., 313
Baumgarten, M., 135
Baur, F. C., 7, 8, 12, 49-51, 118-36, 168, 201, 221, 304, 305, 308, 309
Beale, G. K., 360
Beardslee, W. A., 24, 26
Beardsley, M. C., 25
Beavis, M. A., 28
Bebbington, D. W., 35
Becker, J., 225, 227
Beer, G., 368
Bell, G. K. A., 241
Bengel, E. G., 120
Bengel, J. A., 4, 9, 74, 86
Benoit, P., 225
Bentley, R., 9
Benveniste, E., 45
Berger, P. L., 49, 54
Berlin, A., 26
Betz, H. D., 30
Beyer, H. W., 313
Black, S. L., 333
Blake, F. R., 46
Blass, F., 41, 47
Blevins, J. L., 195
Blomberg, C. L., 107, 272

387

Index of Modern Authors

Bloom, H., 46
Bloomfield, L., 40, 44
Boas, F., 44, 49
Bockmühl, K., 180
Boda, M. J., 353, 360
Boers, H., 23
Bonhoeffer, D., 36
Booth, W., 25, 29
Bornkamm, G., 19, 305, 321–24, 326, 327, 335–37
Bousset, W., 21, 23, 191, 197, 218
Bowman, J. W., 212
Brandt, R., 96, 97
Bray, G., 2, 3, 6
Bretschneider, K. G., 9
Briggs, C. A., 24, 41
Brinckmann, C. G. von, 93
Brondos, D. A., 250
Brooker, P., 25, 28, 31, 43–45
Brooks, C., 25
Brown, C., 258
Brown, F., 41
Brown, R. E., 14
Bruce, A. B., 119
Bruce, F. F., 22, 75, 81
Brückner, M., 221, 222
Brueggemann, W., 370, 375
Brugmann, K., 40, 47
Brunner, E., 96
Buchman, F., 282, 283
Buck, C. H., 225
Buhl, F., 41
Bühler, K., 43
Bullard, J. M., 240
Bultmann, A., 41
Bultmann, R. K., 14, 15, 18, 19, 36, 171, 177, 179, 180, 206, 213, 218, 257–61, 264–76, 304, 317, 321, 322, 341, 349–53
Burke, K., 35
Burkitt, F. C., 18
Burton, E. D. W., 53, 293
Buss, M. J., 16–18, 24
Butler, B. C., 88

Cadbury, H., 19
Calloud, J., 45
Campbell, A. F., 16
Campbell, J. Y., 345
Carlson, S. C., 296
Carlyle, T., 21
Carson, D. A., 87, 304, 315, 330, 332, 351
Carter, W., 330, 332, 333
Case, S. J., 13, 53
Cassirer, E., 2

Castelli, E. A., 31
Castle, G., 24, 25
Catchpole, D. R., 285, 323
Chalcraft, D. J., 54
Charles, R. H., 51, 225
Chase, M. E., 24
Chatman, S., 27
Childs, B. S., 20, 22
Chomsky, N., 41, 47
Christian, C. W., 6, 91, 93–95, 98, 99
Clark, K., 43
Clemen, C., 221, 222, 307
Clements, K., 6
Cline, D. J. A., 26, 27, 29, 42, 46
Coats, G. W., 24
Collins, A. Y., 31
Comte, A., 48
Conzelmann, H., 19, 105, 257, 305, 309, 311, 312, 321
Cook, J. A., 46
Cook, J. I., 53
Copleston, F., 33, 35, 36
Court, J. M., 17, 18
Crane, R., 25
Cremer, H., 42
Crosman, I., 28
Cross, F. M., 379
Crossan, J. D., 26
Crouter, R. E., 96
Culler, J., 43–45
Cullmann, O., 22, 225, 227
Culpepper, R. A., 27
Cumont, F., 21
Cunningham, V., 32
Curtius, G., 47

Dahl, N. A., 200–202, 205
Dalman, G., 40
Dalton, A. M., 382
Danker, F. W., 42
Darwin, C., 16, 146, 147
Daube, D., 344
Davies, I., 30
Davies, M., 322
Davies, W. D., 52, 88, 212, 225, 227, 316, 329, 333, 344
Davis, C., 38
Dawson, D. A., 47
De Cisneros, C. X., 33
De Condillac, E. B., 39
De Man, P., 46
De Roo, J. C. R., 345
De Saussure, F., 40, 42, 44
De Vaux, R., 53

388

Index of Modern Authors

De Wette, W., 7, 13, 16
Debrunner, A., 41
Deissmann, G. A., 19, 41, 50, 222, 239–51, 253–55
Delbrück, B., 40
Delitzsch, F., 13, 190
Delling, G., 71, 72, 78
Dentan, R. C., 373
Denton, D. L., 220
Derrida, J., 45, 46
Descartes, R., 35
Detweiler, R., 45
DeVries, D., 102
Dibelius, M., 18, 19, 257–68, 273–75, 303, 304, 311, 341, 347–51
Dik, S., 47
Dillistone, F. W., 18, 342–44, 348–52
Dilthey, W., 96, 119
Dodd, C. H., 220, 224–26, 241, 341–62
Donovan, J., 31
Doty, W. G., 19
Douglas, M., 44, 49, 54
Dowe, D., 368
Drews, A., 221, 222
Driver, D., 20
Driver, S. R., 15, 41, 46
Duncan, G. S., 225
Dungan, D., 212
Dunn, J. D. G., 52, 87, 216, 220, 250, 259
Durkheim, E., 48, 50, 54
Dyer, B. R., 18

Eagleton, T., 24, 31
Ebeling, G., 37
Eco, U., 44
Ehrman, B. D., 11, 72–74, 79, 80, 84–86, 144
Eichanbaum, B., 43
Eichhorn, A., 190, 191, 197, 221, 222
Eichhorn, J. G., 16, 102, 107, 114
Eichrodt, W., 22, 367–83
Eissfeldt, O., 16, 17, 373
Eliot, T. S., 25
Elliott, J. H., 54
Elliott, J. K., 11
Elliott, S. S., 28
Ellis, E. E., 353
Ellis, J. M., 45
Empson, W., 25
Endo, Y., 47
Ensor, R. C. K., 279
Epp, E. J., 11
Erasmus, D., 33
Ernesti, J. A., 5, 123
Esler, P., 54

Evang, M., 206
Evans, C. A., 18
Evans, O., 348
Evans, R., 29
Evans, T. V., 47
Ewald, H., 8, 9, 14, 39, 46, 198, 199
Exler, F. X. J., 254
Exum, J. C., 27

Fanning, B., 47
Farmer, W. R., 18, 87
Farrer, A. M., 18, 290
Faw, C. E., 225
Fee, G. D., 23, 75
Feine, P., 291
Filson, F. V., 22
Firth, J. R., 44
Fish, S., 29
Fisk, B., 119
Fitzmyer, J. A., 14, 105, 292, 293, 298, 332, 345
Fleddermann, H. T., 285, 298
Flint, P., 10
Fohrer, G., 15
Fokkelman, J. P., 28
Foss, S. J., 26
Foster, P., 293
Foucault, M., 31, 46
Fowl, S. E., 23
Fowler, R. M., 29
France, R. T., 87, 330, 333
Frazer, J. G., 50
Friedrich, G., 42
Frow, J., 24
Frye, N., 24
Fuchs, E., 37
Fulton, W., 213
Funk, R., 37, 41
Furnish, V., 196, 225

Gabler, J. P., 6, 72, 75
Gadamer, H.-G., 29
Gager, J. G., 54, 213, 214
Gandy, R., 44
Gardiner, A., 16, 44
Gasque, W. W., 51, 135, 136, 302, 303, 317
Gathercole, S. J., 212
Gebhardt, O. von, 182
Gerber, A., 239–41
Gerhardsson, B., 18
Gerrish, B. A., 93
Gesenius, W., 39, 41
Gibson, A., 22
Gieschen, C. A., 23
Gieseler, J. C. L., 9

389

Index of Modern Authors

Gilbert, G. H., 225
Gilbert, M., 369
Giltner, J. H., 5
Gingrich, F. W., 42
Glasson, T. F., 212
Glick, G. W., 170-72
Goethe, J. W. von, 71
Goldthorpe, J. H., 48
Goodacre, M. S., 18, 290, 336
Goodspeed, E. J., 13, 53
Gordon, C. H., 41
Gordon, J. D., 49
Gordon, S., 48
Gottwald, N. K., 54, 368, 371, 372, 382
Goulder, M., 18
Graf, F. W., 191, 258
Graf, K. H., 16
Grant, R. M., 3
Grass, T., 22
Grässer, E., 213
Green, B., 44
Greeven, H., 73, 311
Greimas, A.-J., 45
Grensted, L. W., 279, 281
Greßmann, H., 191
Griesbach, J. J., 9, 11, 17, 71-80, 82, 84-88, 335
Grimm, C. L. W., 42
Grimm, J., 40, 42
Grimm, W., 42
Groos, H., 213
Gros Louis, K. R. R., 24
Grotius, H., 75
Guignon, C. B., 36
Gundry, R. H., 315, 329, 330, 332, 333
Gunkel, H., 16, 18, 21, 24, 40, 44, 191, 192, 202, 203, 205, 221, 222, 349
Gunn, D. M., 26
Guthrie, D., 15
Guthrie, G. H., 47

Habel, N. C., 15
Haenchen, E., 20, 302, 303, 308-19
Hagenbach, K. R., 164
Hagner, D. A., 330-33
Hahn, S. W., 1
Halliday, M. A. K., 43-45
Hamilton, J. M., 382
Hammann, K., 16, 18
Hardwick, J. C., 282
Harink, D., 38
Harmer, J. R., 149
Harnack, A. von, 13, 96, 163, 167-74, 179-86, 190, 198, 221, 222, 342
Harper, W. R., 24, 53

Harris, H., 7, 8, 118, 120-22, 135
Harris, Z., 41
Harrison, R. K., 16, 17, 50
Harrisville, R. A., 3, 5, 6, 12-14, 18, 20, 53
Hartman, G., 46
Hasel, G. F., 19, 22, 371-73
Hatch, E., 51
Hauck, F., 182, 183
Hawkins, J. C., 279
Hayes, D. A., 225
Hayes, J. H., 371-74
Hegel, G. W. F., 7, 33, 34, 96, 121, 123, 124, 126-29, 131, 132, 136
Heidegger, M., 36
Heim, K., 303
Heimerdinger, J.-M., 47
Heitmüller, W., 191, 197
Held, H. J., 333, 334
Helmer, C., 91, 99, 100, 107
Hengel, M., 23, 200
Hengstenberg, E. W., 8
Henn, T. R., 24
Hens-Piazza, G., 31
Herder, J. G., 6
Hertz, M., 78, 79
Hilgenfeld, A., 8
Hill, D., 22
Hill, D. J., 122, 125-27
Hirsch, E. D., 25
Hodgkin, R. H., 280
Hodgson, P. C., 118, 120, 122, 124-28, 130-35
Hofius, O., 23
Hofmann, J. C. K. von, 13, 22, 164
Holmberg, B., 54
Holmes, M. W., 149
Holmström, F., 191
Holquist, M., 43
Holtzmann, H. J., 13, 17, 194, 218, 222
Holub, R. C., 29
Hordern, W. E., 21
Horrell, D. G., 31, 52
Horsley, G. H. R., 240
Hort, F. J. A., 11, 50, 86, 139-42, 144-46, 148-50
Hoskyns, E., 241
Howard, W. F., 41
Hug, J. L., 8
Humboldt, W. von, 35, 40, 96
Hume, D., 35
Hunt, C., 31
Hunter, A., 225
Hupfeld, H., 16
Hurd, J. C., 224
Hurtado, L. W., 23
Husserl, E., 36

Hymes, D., 49

Ide, K., 382
Irwin, W. A., 200
Iser, W., 29
Ittek, G. W., 191

Jackson, L., 45
Jakobson, R., 44
Jameson, F., 43
Jankowsky, K. R., 40
Jantzen, G., 370
Jaspers, K., 36
Jauss, H. R., 29
Jefferson, A., 43
Jenni, E., 368
Jepsen, A., 199, 202
Jeremias, J., 51
Jewett, R., 224
Jobes, K. H., 10
Johnson, B., 45
Johnson, L. T., 225
Johnson, S. R., 297
Jones, W. T., 7, 25, 33, 35-37, 39
Jongkind, D., 48
Joosten, J., 46
Jöuon, P., 42
Jowett, B., 24
Joy, C. R., 211
Judge, E. A., 52
Jülicher, A., 14, 272

Kähler, M., 16
Kahnis, K. F. A., 190
Kaiser, W. C., 382
Kaltner, J., 31
Kant, I., 7, 33, 34, 36, 93, 120, 122, 211
Kantzenbach, F. W., 183
Käsemann, E., 220, 225, 227, 232, 312, 323, 324
Kautzsch, E., 39
Keener, C. S., 330, 332, 334
Keil, G., 166
Keim, T., 8
Kennedy, G., 30
Kermode, F., 24, 27
Kevane, E., 347
Kierkegaard, S., 36
Kilpatrick, G. D., 11
King, J. S., 351
Kingsbury, J. D., 27
Kittel, G., 22, 42, 241
Klatt, W., 191, 199, 202, 203
Klein, W. W., 266
Klemke, E. D., 37

Klink, E. W., 336
Kloppenborg, J., 18, 285, 290, 295
Knierim, R., 16, 17
Knight, D. A., 39, 198, 199
Knox, J., 223-25
Knox, W. L., 225
Koch, K., 214
Koester, C. R., 342, 345, 350
Koester, H., 15, 218
Köhler, L., 261, 373, 374
König, E., 371, 373
Köstenberger, A. J., 174-79
Köstlin, K. R., 8
Krentz, E., 12
Kristeva, J., 45
Kroeze, J. H., 42, 47
Krüger, G., 369, 370
Kugel, J. L., 26
Kuhn, T., 38
Kümmel, W. G., 3, 5, 6, 9, 15, 18, 21, 72, 79-81, 85-87, 118, 124, 170, 189, 212, 213, 219, 225, 258

Lacan, J., 45, 46
Lachmann, K., 9, 17, 78-88
Ladd, G. E., 345
Lagrange, M.-J., 14
Lane, M., 44
Lang, B., 54
Larondelle, H. K., 361
Law, D. R., 262
Leach, E., 44, 49
Leavis, F. R., 25
Lechler, G. V., 135
Lechte, J., 31, 36, 38, 42-47, 49
Leckbusch, C. E., 135
Lee, J. A. L., 42, 43
Leibniz, G. W., 35, 93
Leitch, V. B., 31, 32, 45
Lemcio, E. E., 20
Lemon, L. T., 43
Lentricchia, F., 27
Lepschy, G. C., 43
Leslie, R. C., 48
Lessing, G. E., 6, 17, 124
Lévi-Strauss, C., 44, 49, 54
Levinsohn, S. H., 47, 48
Levinson, S. C., 37
Lightfoot, J. B., 49, 50, 139-42, 144, 145, 147-50, 225
Lightfoot, R. H., 19
Loader, J. A., 258
Locke, J., 35
Lohmeyer, E., 18

Index of Modern Authors

Loisy, A., 14, 15
Longacre, R. E., 47
Longenecker, R. N., 23, 226
Longman, T., 24
Loomba, A., 31
Loretz, O., 373
Louw, J. P., 43, 48
Lowrie, W., 214
Lowth, R., 24
Luckman, T., 49
Lüdemann, G., 190, 191, 202–204
Luthardt, C. E., 190
Lyons, J., 44
Lyotard, J.-F., 31

MacIntyre, A., 37
Mack, B. L., 30
Mair, L., 49
Malina, B. J., 54
Malinowski, B., 16, 44, 48, 49
Manson, T. W., 18, 292
Marcel, G., 36
Marcus, G. E., 49
Mariná, J., 91, 93
Marsh, H., 9
Marshall, I. H., 119, 317, 353
Martin, K., 206
Martin, R. P., 18, 258, 259
Martin, T. W., 30
Marx, K., 48, 54
Marxsen, W., 19, 305, 311, 312, 321
Mästricht, G. von, 74
Mateos, J., 43
Mathesius, V., 43, 44
Matheson, G., 225
Mathews, S., 53
Matlock, R. B., 213, 224, 227
Maudlin, M. G., 382
Mauser, U., 370
Maxfield, C. A., 369
McCarter, P. K., 10
McCasland, S. V., 315
McCumber, J., 33, 34, 36, 38
McGinley, L. J., 257–60, 268, 269
McGrath, A. E., 123, 124
McKay, K. L., 47
McKenzie, S. L., 31
McKim, D. K., 4–9, 11, 13–22, 24, 26, 31, 33, 35–37, 41, 46, 49–53
McKnight, E. V., 18, 257–62, 267–73, 345, 349–51, 353
McKnight, S., 318
Mead, G. H., 53
Meeks, W. A., 52

Meijboom, H. U., 9
Mepham, J., 44
Merk, O., 165, 183
Merleau-Ponty, M., 36
Metzger, B. M., 11, 72–74, 79, 80, 84–86, 144
Meyer, E., 49
Meyer, G. J., 369
Meyer, H. A. W., 135
Michaelis, J. D., 5, 123, 163, 313
Michie, D., 27
Milbank, J., 38
Mill, J. S., 9, 48
Miller, C., 47
Miller, J. H., 46
Milne, P. J., 43
Minear, P. S., 22, 224
Mitchell, W. J. T., 32
Moessner, D. P., 317
Moffatt, J., 15
Möller, K., 30
Montgomery, J., 41
Moo, D. J., 87
Moore, G. F., 51
Moore, S. D., 19, 27, 31, 32, 45, 46, 52
Morgan, R., 3, 7, 15, 24, 48, 51, 53, 119, 121, 132, 133, 174, 190, 192, 212
Morris, L. L., 330, 333, 345
Moulton, J. H., 24, 41, 47, 241
Moulton, R. G., 24
Mournet, T. C., 350
Mowinckel, S., 17
Mozley, E. N., 213
Muilenburg, J., 22, 25, 26
Mukarovsky, J., 43
Müller, K., 191
Munck, J., 227
Muraoka, T., 42
Murphy-O'Connor, J., 14, 254
Myers, C., 31

Naudé, J. A., 42, 47
Neander, J. A. W., 135
Neill, S., 3, 7, 17, 18, 21, 49, 52, 72–74, 85, 130, 140, 163, 205, 212–14, 257–59, 261, 304, 316, 359
Neirynck, F., 285
Nestle, E., 11
Neuenschwander, U., 228
Neuer, W., 14, 175, 181
Nicol, I. G., 212
Nicole, R., 345
Nida, E. A., 43
Niebuhr, H. R., 21
Niebuhr, R. R., 21, 97

Nietzsche, F., 36
Nineham, D. E., 212, 219
Nock, A. D., 51
Nolland, J., 263
Norden, E., 18, 21
Norris, C., 45
Noth, M., 17

O'Connor, M., 39, 41
O'Neill, J. C., 3, 5–8, 13, 16, 33, 46
Olbrechts-Tyteca, L., 35
Olbricht, T. H., 30
Ollenburger, B. C., 372
Olsson, B., 47
Olyan, S. M., 31
Osborne, G. R., 305, 310, 312, 318, 332, 333, 337
Otto, R., 21
Overbeck, F., 14, 136
Owens, N., 281

Palmer, D. J., 24
Palmer, N. H., 81, 87
Pardee, D., 42
Parker, D., 11
Parris, D. P., 29
Patte, D., 45
Pauck, W., 169, 170
Paulus, H. E. G., 72, 103
Peabody, D. B., 18, 257, 335
Peake, A. S., 343
Pearson, B. W. R., 255
Pedersen, J., 53
Peláez, J., 43
Perelman, C., 35
Perlitt, L., 200
Perrin, N., 19, 304, 311, 321
Petersen, N. R., 26, 27
Pfleiderer, O., 51, 198
Phillips, G. A., 31
Phillips, P. M., 29
Pike, K., 47
Pitts, A. W., 10, 47, 213
Planck, K. C., 8
Pleitner, H., 212
Poloma, M. M., 49
Polzin, R. M., 45
Popkin, R., 33
Porter, F. C., 225
Porter, S. E., 3, 6–10, 11, 14, 18, 21, 24, 28, 29, 30, 33, 35–37, 41–48, 120, 125, 134, 144, 157, 220, 226, 255, 345, 353, 356, 360
Powell, M. A., 28
Preuschen, E., 42
Price, R., 368

Procksch, O., 368
Propp, V., 43, 45
Prussner, F. C., 371–74

Räisänen, H., 52, 192, 195, 196
Raison, T., 48
Ramsay, W., 51, 302–308, 314, 316–19
Ransom, J. C., 25
Rast, W. E., 19
Rauser, R. D., 122, 125–27
Reed, J. T., 47
Rehkopf, F., 41
Reicke, B., 72, 75, 78, 86
Reimarus, H. S., 216
Reis, M. J., 43
Reist, J. S., 119–22, 128, 131, 132
Reitzenstein, R., 21
Renan, E., 8, 103
Resseguie, J. L., 28
Reumann, J., 211, 212, 225
Reuss, E., 12
Reventlow, H. G., 1, 2, 4–9, 13, 14, 35, 40
Rex, J., 48
Rhoads, D., 27, 28
Richards, A., 49
Richards, I. A., 25, 35
Richards, J., 29
Riches, J. K., 6, 304
Ridderbos, H., 227
Riesner, R., 18
Ritschl, A., 8, 12, 135, 168, 190, 198
Ritzer, G., 49, 53
Robbins, V., 30, 35
Robertson, A. T., 41, 47, 345
Robertson, D., 26
Robertson, P., 368
Robey, D., 25, 43, 44
Robins, R. H., 39, 42
Robinson, H. W., 53
Robinson, J. A. T., 6, 18, 21, 29, 35–37, 42–46, 225
Robinson, J. C., 120, 125
Robinson, J. M., 212, 295, 297, 298
Rockefeller, J. D., 53
Rödiger, E., 39
Rogerson, J. W., 7, 8, 13, 14, 16, 24, 50, 53, 54
Rollins, W. G., 214
Rollman, H. J., 135, 190, 191, 195, 196, 198, 204
Rorty, R., 38
Rowley, H. H., 22
Rudolph, K., 199
Rumscheidt, H. M., 172
Runge, S. E., 47
Russell, L. M., 31

Index of Modern Authors

Ruthven, K. K., 31
Ryken, L., 24
Rylaarsdam, J. C., 53

Sabin, S. C., 382
Sanday, W., 17, 279, 280, 284
Sanders, E. P., 52, 213, 221, 224, 226, 227, 322
Sanders, J. A., 20
Sandys-Wunsch, J., 3
Sapir, E., 44
Sartre, J.-P., 36
Sato, M., 285
Sawyer, J. F. A., 42
Schlatter, A., 14, 22, 163, 174–86
Schlatter, T., 175
Schlegel, F., 95
Schleiermacher, F., 3, 6–8, 12, 32, 35, 82, 87, 91–116, 120, 124–26, 136, 164, 216
Schmid, J. H., 179
Schmidt, D. D., 19, 48, 212
Schmidt, K. L., 18, 257, 260, 263, 304, 341, 349, 350
Schmiedel, P. W., 136
Schnabel, E., 174
Schnackenburg, R., 330
Schneckenburger, M., 135
Schnelle, U., 225
Schoeps, H.-J., 225, 227
Scholder, K., 131
Scholes, R., 43
Schreiber, J., 203–205
Schröder, M., 190, 202–204
Schultz, H., 190
Schürer, E., 51
Schüssler Fiorenza, E., 30, 31
Schwartz, E., 198, 199
Schwartz, R. M., 31
Schwegler, A., 8
Schweitzer, A., 102, 103, 204, 211–33, 280, 342, 361
Scobie, C. H. H., 372
Scott, W., 25
Searle, J., 37
Selby, D., 225
Selden, R., 25, 28, 31, 43–45
Sellin, E., 15, 373, 374
Semler, J. S., 5, 71, 74, 86, 123, 163
Seymour, C., 45
Sherwood, Y., 32
Shklovsky, V., 43
Silva, M., 10, 42, 43
Sim, M., 48
Simmons, H. C., 382
Skinner, C., 345

Smalley, S. S., 225, 321, 322
Smart, N., 118
Smend, R., 198–200, 202, 203, 206
Smith, N., 47
Smith, W. B., 221, 222
Smith, W. R., 14, 50
Soden, H. von, 11
Sohm, R., 48
Sollors, W., 31
Soulen, R. K., 304
Southgate, C., 31
Spampinato, T., 368
Sparks, K. L., 258
Spencer, H., 48
Spener, P. J., 4
Sperber, J., 369
Spinoza, B., 6, 15, 33, 35, 94
Stavrakopoulou, F., 31
Stein, R. H., 107, 290, 296, 305, 311, 312, 356
Stendahl, K., 52
Sternberg, M., 26
Stibbe, M. W. G., 28
Still, T. D., 52
Stoebe, H. J., 368
Storr, G. C., 75
Stovell, B. M., 360, 361
Stowers, S. K., 254, 255
Strandmann, H. P. von, 369
Strauss, D. F., 7, 103, 120, 124, 127, 217, 218
Strecker, G., 190, 192, 206
Streeter, B. H., 11, 17, 278–99
Strimple, R. B., 136
Stuart, M., 5
Stuhlmacher, P., 23, 175–77
Styler, G. M., 17
Suggs, M. J., 224
Sugirtharajah, R. S., 31
Suleiman, S. R., 28
Sullivan, C., 361
Sundberg, W., 3, 6, 7, 13, 14, 18, 20
Swarat, U., 166, 167, 183

Tabachovitz, D., 41
Talbert, C. H., 27
Tannehill, R. C., 27
Tayler, J. J., 9
Taylor, G., 225
Taylor, J., 14
Taylor, V., 18, 292, 348
Telford, W. R., 259
Temple, W., 280
Thackeray, H. S. J., 41, 225
Thatcher, T., 27, 345
Thayer, J. H., 42

Theissen, G., 54
Thirlwall, C., 96
Thiselton, A. C., 37, 106, 122, 125, 213, 222, 223, 226, 258
Tholuck, A., 8
Thomas, M., 35, 37, 40, 44, 47
Thompson, M. M., 42, 345
Thornhill, A., 282, 283
Tice, T., 6, 92–97, 100, 102, 105
Tillich, P., 21, 352
Tilling, C., 23
Timmer, J., 198–200, 202, 204
Tischendorf, C. von, 9, 10, 84
Todorov, T., 44, 45
Tomashevsky, B., 43
Tompkins, J. P., 28
Tov, E., 10
Tracy, D., 3
Travis, S. H., 263, 265, 267, 269
Trible, P., 31
Troeltsch, E., 21, 96, 191
Trubetzkoy, N., 44
Tucker, G. M., 16, 39
Tuckett, C. M., 87, 285
Turner, N., 41
Turretin, F., 123
Tzamalikos, P., 183

Ulrich, E., 10
Usener, H., 221, 222

Vachek, J., 43
Vaganay, L., 74
Van der Merwe, C. H. J., 42, 47
VanderKam, J., 10
Vatke, J. K. W., 7, 8
Verheule, A. F., 191
Verheyden, J., 291
Vermes, G., 51
Vielhauer, P., 311
Vines, M. E., 44
Volkmar, G., 8
Von Rad, G., 19, 22, 370, 374

Waetjen, H. C., 38
Wall, R. W., 20
Waltke, B. K., 39, 41, 375
Warren, A., 25
Warshaw, T. S., 24
Watson, F., 23
Watt, J., 41
Watts, R., 359
Weaver, W. P., 212, 213, 216, 220
Weber, M., 48, 54

Weingreen, J., 10
Weiss, B., 11, 13, 21
Weiß, J., 21, 191, 216–18
Weisse, C. H., 17
Weizsäcker, C., 12
Wellek, R., 25, 44
Wellhausen, J., 14, 16, 21, 40, 189, 198–206, 259, 275
Wendland, P., 18, 51, 221, 222
Wendt, H. H., 310
Wernle, P., 221, 222
Wesley, J., 92
Westby, D. L., 48
Westcott, B. F., 11, 18, 86, 139–48, 150–55, 161
Westerholm, S., 52, 194, 213
Wettstein, J. J., 5, 9, 123
White, J. L., 255
Whorf, B. L., 44
Widdowson, P., 25, 28, 31, 41–45
Wiefel, W., 196
Wiker, B., 1
Wikgren, A., 200, 201, 205
Wilamowitz-Moellendorf, U. von, 21
Wilckens, U., 213
Wilder, A., 26, 212
Wilke, C. G., 17, 42
Willi, T., 368
Williams, C., 345
Williams, J., 45
Williamson, H. G. M., 17
Willis, W., 212
Wilson, D., 47
Wilson, R. R., 48
Wimsatt, W. K., 25
Wind, J. P., 53
Winer, G. B., 24, 39, 40, 42
Wischmeyer, O., 258
Witmer, A., 331
Wittgenstein, L., 31, 37
Wolde, E. van, 47
Wolf, C., 93
Wolfreys, J., 7, 25, 28, 29, 31, 32, 35–38, 42–46, 49
Wood, I. F., 225
Worley, R. C., 361
Wrede, W., 14, 189–98, 200, 202–206, 214, 216, 218, 258–60
Wright, G. E., 22
Wright, N. T., 3, 7, 17, 18, 21, 49, 52, 72–74, 85, 163, 205, 212–14, 257–59, 261, 304, 315, 316, 352, 359
Wuellner, W. H., 30, 48
Würthwein, E., 10

Index of Modern Authors

Yarbrough, R. W., 22, 175, 176, 178, 179
Yoon, D. I., 6
Yu, C., 375

Zachhuber, J., 6, 8, 12
Zahn, T., 13, 163–67, 176, 179–86
Zeller, E., 8, 122
Žižek, S., 38

Index of Ancient Sources

OLD TESTAMENT

Genesis

21:23	376
26:29	376
49	377, 378

Exodus

15:1	375
15:21	375
24:3–8	375
24:9–11	375
34:10	375
34:27	375

Numbers

23:22	375, 378
24:8	375, 378

Deuteronomy

32:5	332
32:20	332
33	378

Joshua

9:1	376
24	377

Judges

5	377
5:4	375, 378
5:9	375
5:23	375
6:13	375, 378

1 Samuel

2:27	375
4:8	375, 378
10:18	375
11:1	376
15:6	375
20:1	376

1 Kings

20:34	376

Psalms

118	357–61
118:12	184
118:23	357
118:26	341, 354–56

Isaiah

7:14	173, 181

Ezekiel

17:18	376

Daniel

7:13	219
7:14	219

Zechariah

9–14	356, 357
9	355, 357–61
9:9	341, 354–56, 358
9:11	357
9:14	357

Index of Ancient Sources

Zechariah (continued)

9:16	357
11	361
13	361

NEW TESTAMENT

Matthew

1–2	314–16
1	316
1:1	315
1:18–24	266
1:18	110
1:20–21	110
1:23	315
2:1	110
2:4–6	110
2:6	315
2:7	110
2:8–9	111
2:8	111
2:11	330
2:16b	111
2:18	315
2:23	111, 315
2:23b	111
4:1–11	266
4:3	330
4:11	330
4:24—13:58	81
4:24	330, 331
4:25	331
5–7	324
5:1	330
5:3–12	267
5:17–19	271
5:17	271, 272
5:34–37	267
5:39	267
5:44	267
6:20—7:10	297
6:24	267
6:27	270
6:30	326, 334
6:34b	270
6:57b	160
7:1a	297
7:2–10	297
7:28a	297
8–9	324
8:1–4	331
8:1	326
8:2	330
8:5–13	297
8:5–6	298
8:5	330
8:8–10	298
8:10	326
8:13	334
8:13b	298
8:16	331
8:17	331, 335
8:18–22	83
8:18	85
8:19–22	269
8:19	326, 330
8:20	219
8:22	84, 326
8:23–27	83, 324, 325
8:23	326
8:25	326, 330
8:26	326, 334
8:27	326
9:2	331
9:14	330
9:18–31	82
9:18	330
9:20	330
9:22	334
9:27	330
9:28	330
9:29	334
9:32	331
9:35	331
10:1	331
10:16b	270
10:19	331
11:5–6	271
11:5	82, 335
11:16	332
11:19	219
11:21–24	271
12:22	331
12:32	219
12:39	332
12:41	332
12:42	332
12:45	332
13	272
13:10	330
13:27	330
13:36	330
13:53–58	154
13:54	157, 159
13:55	158
13:56	158
13:57	159

13:57a	159		
13:57c	160		**Mark**
13:58	159	1:9–11	266
14:12	330	1:16–20	269
14:15	330	1:21—6:13	81
14:31	326	1:21–28	331
14:33	330	1:23–27	264
14:35	331	1:40–45	265, 273
15:1	330	2:1–12	264, 269, 273
15:12	330	2:13–20	264
15:22	330	2:14	269
15:23	330	2:18–22	264
15:24	272	2:19	270
15:25	330	2:23–28	264
15:28	334	3:1–6	264
15:30	330	3:4	271
16:1	330	3:13–14	331
16:4	332	4	272
16:8	326, 334	4:30–32	267
16:18–19	271	4:35–41	265, 273, 323, 325
17:14–21	338	4:35	83, 85
17:14–20	323, 327, 329, 336	4:37–41	273
17:14–16	329	4:39–40	329
17:14	327, 329	4:39	329
17:15–16	330	5:1–20	265
17:15	327, 329–31	5:9	330
17:16	328, 331, 334	5:30	330
17:17–20	335	6:1–6	154, 264
17:17–18	332	6:2	159
17:17	329, 332	6:3	158, 159
17:18	327–30, 332, 333	6:4a	160
17:19–20	329, 331, 333	6:4b	160
17:19	327, 333	6:4c	160
17:20	326, 328, 332, 334, 336	6:5–6	159
17:22–23	271	6:34–44	273
17:27	266	6:35–44	265
18:1a	333	6:38	330
18:1b	333	7:15	271
18:2–4	333	8:1–9	273
18:15–17	271	8:12	330
18:21–22	271	8:22–27a	273
19:1	331	8:23	330
20:30–31	330	9:2–8	266, 274
21:5	355	9:2–7	327
21:14	331	9:12	330
21:28–31	272	9:14–29	338
23:6	332	9:14–17	327
23:13–33	294	9:14–16	329
23:16–19	271	9:16	330
23:23–24	271	9:17	327, 331
23:25–26	271	9:18	328, 330
24	112	9:19	327, 329
27:29	330	9:20–25a	330
28:9	330	9:20–24	327

Mark (continued)

9:20	328
9:21	330, 332
9:22–24	332
9:22	330
9:24	330
9:25–26	333
9:25	327, 328, 333
9:25c–26	330
9:26	327, 333
9:27	275, 329
9:28	327
9:29	328
9:33	330
10:3	330
10:9	270
10:17–31	264, 269
10:29–30	271
10:45	271
10:47	330
12:28–34	269
13	112
13:5–27	270
13:24–25	77
13:26	77
13:27–32	77
14:14	330
14:61	204
16:9–20	86

Luke

1–2	107, 111, 112, 296
1	108
1:1–4	317
1:1–3	263
1:3	317
1:64	108
1:67	108
2	109, 125
2:1–20	109
2:8–20	266
2:22–40	109
2:22–38	110
2:39	111
2:41–42	266
3:1—9:49	107
3:1—4:30	292
3:2a–9	287
3:10–14	287
3:16–17	287
3:21–22	187
4:1–16a	287
4:16–30	154
4:23	270
4:29–30	266
5:1–11	292
6:1–2	158
6:1	157
6:14–16	292
6:20—8:3	292
6:20—7:10	287
6:24–26	271
6:28	267
7:1–10	297, 298
7:1a	297
7:1b–2	298
7:3	298
7:3a	298
7:4–6a	298
7:6	298
7:6e	298
7:7b	298
7:8–9	298
7:10b	298
7:13	328
7:18–35	287
7:19	328
7:22–23	271
7:41–43	272
8	272
8:22–25	83
9:28–36	327
9:31	275
9:37–43	338
9:37	328
9:39	328
9:40	328
9:41	329, 332
9:42	328, 329, 333
9:43a	328
9:50—18:14	107
9:51—18:14	291, 292
9:51–56	287
9:57–62	83, 269
9:57–60	287
9:61–62	287
10:1	328
10:2–16	287
10:13–15	271
10:17–20	287
10:21–24	287
10:41	328
11:9–52	287
11:37–52	294
11:39	328
12:1b–12	287

12:22–59	287	13–21	355
12:35–58	271	14:5–6	185
12:42	329	14:6	183–85
13:15	329		
13:18–35	287	## Acts	
14:1–6	269		
14:11	287	1–15	304
14:26–27	287	1:1–8	313
14:34–35	287	1:9	313
16:13	287	4:10–11	184
16:16–18	287	4:12	184
17:1–6	287	6	133
17:3–4	271	10–11	298
17:5	329	12:12	77
17:6	328, 329, 337	12:25	77
17:14	273	13	133
17:20–37	287	13:5	77
17:20–21	287	13:46	307
18:6	329	14:6	306
18:15—24:53	107	15:29	173
18:38	330		
19:1–27	292	## Romans	
19:8	329		
19:11–27	287	1:18	345
19:37–44	292	8:3	134
20:1—24:53	112	12:14	266
21	112	13:11–14	226
21:18	292		
21:34–36	271, 292	## 1 Corinthians	
22:1—23:49	112		
22:7–24	112	11	261
22:14	292	15	261
22:20	113	15:3–8	173
22:21	113		
22:23–24	113	## 2 Corinthians	
22:55–62	113		
22:61	113, 329	3:3	247
23:8–12	280	5:1–10	226
24:44	114		
24:51	313	## Galatians	
		1:1—2:21	251
## John		1:1–14	251
		1:2	251
2–12	355	1:18	252
4:46b–54	297	2:1–21	251
12	361	2:3	252
12:1–8	355	2:8	252
12:9–11	355	2:9	252
12:12–15	341, 354, 355, 357, 358, 360	2:11	252
		2:12	252
12:16–18	355	2:13	252
12:16	358	2:14	252
12:17–18	358	3:1–5	252
12:20–22	355		

Galatians (continued)

3:1	251
4:1	251
4:11	251
4:12	251
4:20	252
5:2	251
6:11	251

Philippians

2:7	134

Colossians

4:10	77

Philemon

24	77

Hebrews

1:1–14	253
2:1–4	253
2:3	252
2:5—3:11	253
3:1	230
3:6	230
3:12—4:16	253
3:14	230
4:1–11	230
5:1–14	253
6:1–20	253
6:4	230
6:11–12	230
6:18–19	230
7:1—10:18	253
9:27–28	230
10:2	230
10:19–39	253
10:19–20	114
10:32–34	252
10:35	230
11:32	173, 252
12:1–29	253
12:1–2	230
12:12–14	230
13:19	252
13:22	252
13:23	252

James

2:12	231
5:7–11	231
5:7	231
5:12	267

1 Peter

2:8–10	230
2:12	230
3:18–22	230
4:7	230
4:13	230
5:13	77

1 John

1:7	231
2:6	231
2:8	231
2:9	231
2:10	231
2:13	232
2:14	232
2:18	232
2:28	232
3:6	231
3:9	231, 232
3:14	231
3:24	231
3:28	232
4:15–16	231
4:16	232

Jude

14–15	229

Revelation

12	189, 203–205
12:1–6	204
12:6	204
12:7–14	204
12:11	204
12:14	204
12:15	204
12:17	204

Q

7:1	298
7:2	298

7:3	298	\multicolumn{2}{c}{NEW TESTAMENT}
7:4–6a	298	\multicolumn{2}{c}{APOCRYPHA}
7:6b–9	298		
7:10	298		

NEW TESTAMENT APOCRYPHA

Gospel of Peter

29	266
35–44	266
37	266

www.ingramcontent.com/pod-product-compliance
Lightning Source LLC
Chambersburg PA
CBHW081147290426
44108CB00018B/2462